MARTIN LUTHER

MARTIN LUTHER

THE CHRISTIAN BETWEEN
GOD AND DEATH

Richard Marius

THE BELKNAP PRESS *of*
HARVARD UNIVERSITY PRESS
Cambridge, Massachusetts
London, England

Copyright © 1999 by the President and Fellows of Harvard College
Printed in the United States of America

Third printing, 2000

First Harvard University Press paperback edition, 2000

Library of Congress Cataloging-in-Publication Data
Marius, Richard.
Martin Luther : the Christian between God and death / Richard Curry Marius.
p.   cm.
Includes bibliographical references and index.
ISBN 0-674-55090-0 (cloth)
ISBN 0-674-00387-X (paper)
1. Luther, Martin, 1483–1546.   2. Reformation—Germany—Biography.
I. Title.
BR325.M2955   1999
284.1′092—dc21
[B]   98-36856

For my dear and faithful friend
Paloma Castillo Martinez de Aznar
Asturias, Spain

CONTENTS

ILLUSTRATIONS

Following page 78

Martin Luther, 1520, by Lucas Cranach the Elder, copper engraving, Lutherhalle, Reformationsgeschichtliches Museum, Wittenberg (courtesy of Bilderdienst Süddeutscher Verlag GmbH)

Hans Luther, wood engraving after a 1527 painting by Lucas Cranach the Elder (courtesy of The Granger Collection)

Margarethe Luther, wood engraving after a 1527 painting by Lucas Cranach the Elder (courtesy of The Granger Collection)

Frederick the Wise, oil, 1496, by Albrecht Dürer (courtesy of The Granger Collection)

Duke George of Saxony, 1537, silver medal (courtesy of the Trustees of the British Museum)

A public burning of witches at Derneburg, October 1555, broadside (courtesy of The Granger Collection)

Death and the Maiden, 1517, by Hans Baldung, Künstmuseum, Basel (courtesy of Giraudon/Art Resource, New York City)

Johannnes von Staupitz, engraving from a sixteenth-century painting in St. Peter's Abbey, Salzburg (courtesy of Bilderdienst Süddeutscher Verlag GmbH)

Pope Leo X, 1520–21, by Giulio Romano, black-and-white chalk, Chatsworth Collection, Great Britain (courtesy of Erich Lessing/Art Resource)

Johann Eck, German copper engraving, eighteenth century (courtesy of The Granger Collection)

Desiderius Erasmus, oil on panel, 1523, by Hans Holbein the Younger (courtesy of The Granger Collection)

Martin Luther as "Junker George," oil on panel, 1537, by Lucas Cranach the Elder (courtesy of The Granger Collection)

Thomas Müntzer, Dutch etching, seventeeth century (courtesy of The Granger Collection)

The beast in the book of Revelation in Luther's New Testament, September and December 1522 (courtesy of The British Library)

Katherine von Bora Luther, oil on panel, c. 1526, by Lucas Cranach the Elder (courtesy of The Granger Collection)

Martin Luther, 1529, drawing attributed to Lucas Cranach the Elder (courtesy of The Granger Collection)

PREFACE

MARTIN Luther is a difficult and inexhaustible subject, and this book is my second effort to wrestle his gigantic stature into print. He remains daunting. Luther wrote and talked with almost the regularity of breath, and anyone who sets out to know him well must climb a mountain of his literary output. In the great Weimar edition of his work, in progress for more than a century, we now have some sixty volumes of theological and devotional treatises in Latin and German, fourteen volumes of correspondence, and twelve volumes that include his German translations of and prefaces to the Bible. In addition we have six volumes of his table talk, recorded by students who boarded in the Luther household and wrote down the great man's rambling monologues to sell to printers eager for anything that bore Luther's name. One could easily spend one's own life reading and reading again all that Luther wrote, and all scholars of the man realize soon enough that they cannot read all his work if they are to have any life left to write anything of their own. I am no exception. Perhaps the only person who could claim to have read all of Luther is Martin Brecht, whose monumental three-volume biography represents the most comprehensive study ever written of the man.

Another major and obvious difficulty arises in writing about Luther. For centuries devout scholars, evangelical and Catholic, studied Luther to extol or condemn him. Evangelicals made him a colossus and hero who cleansed the gospel and gave light and freedom to the soul. Catholics portrayed him as demon-possessed, a sex-crazed monk of furious temper, a liar and fraud willing to tumble down the great and beautiful edifice of Catholic Christianity for no better motives than lust and pride. The religious indifference of modern secular culture has cooled these passions, and an ecumenical spirit now prevails in studies of Luther and the sixteenth century. Even so Luther studies remain largely the purview of churchly scholars who have a religious stake in those events of almost half a millennium ago. Consequently the person like myself whose approach to Luther is essentially nonreligious may evoke criticisms on those counts. I have written this book, as I wrote my biography of Thomas More some years ago, in the belief that it is possible to write about an important man whose views I do not share and to write about him both sympathetically and critically without distorting the evidence and with neither malice nor partisanship toward any religious confession.

My estimation of Luther's Reformation is much akin to Simon Schama's of the French Revolution or Richard Pipes's of the Bolshevik Revolution. They believe that these great upheavals were disasters for the peoples involved, and I believe that Luther represents a catastrophe in the history of Western civilization. This is not to say that the catastrophe was all his fault. All sides have a share of blame in the boiling hatreds and carnage that consumed Europe for well over a century after Luther died. But in my view, whatever good Luther did is not matched by the calamities that came because of him.

Our own bloody century has destroyed for the time being the easy vision of progress that prevailed in the West after the Enlightenment and continued through the nineteenth century. In that vision great historical events represented a forward march across time. Revolutions were part of progress, and although people got hurt in them, occasionally even beheaded or shot, they still marked a moral leap forward in a human crusade toward ever-expanding moral consciousness and virtue. It is impossible for a historian today to hold such a rosy view of the past. We know now that things can go terribly and catastrophically wrong and that all the good that comes from great events does not necessarily or even usually overbalance the evil. Some good came from the Reformation as Luther shaped it, but I remain convinced that our world would have been far better off had events taken a different course.

Some readers will object to my ending the book with a brief chapter summarizing Luther's life after 1527 until his death in February 1546. Brecht's exhaustive work is testimony in itself to the many issues Luther addressed in the years after 1527, and Mark U. Edwards has written a smaller book that chronicles Luther's last battles. I can say only that to me the later Luther is not as interesting as the man who broke away from the pope, expecting to be followed by true Christians, only to discover that the number of true Christians as he defined them was disappointingly small. From re-forming the church he was forced by events to create an institution, a task that he undertook with growing frustration, furious distaste, and ultimate bitterness. From time to time I reach forward to Luther's works after 1527 to illuminate some of the subjects addressed in these pages. But I shall leave to others the details of the latter decades.

Insofar as possible in writing about a man whose complications and contradictions were numerous and often baffling, I have tried to write a narrative history about both events and ideas. Others are writing now about the German and broader European societies that either accepted or rejected Luther's doctrines. But my interest remains fixed on the man himself, his acts, his character, and his temperament. The temperament is all-important.

Everyone who knows anything about Luther knows that he had doubts all his life. The traditional understanding is that he doubted that God could save a sinner such as himself. This reading long ago appeared simplistic to me, even when I found it eloquently stated in Roland H. Bainton's seminars at Yale and in his great biography, *Here I Stand*, the most popular book about Luther in the English-speaking world.

My own view is that Luther's doubts were far deeper, swept along by one of the great recurring waves of skepticism in human history, doubts that God exists at all and that he can or will raise the dead. Luther was situated in the Renaissance, where chaos and order, justice and injustice, appearance and reality, darkness and light contended with each other to an uncertain end. For him faith and the most radical kind of doubt dwelt entwined together until the end of his days. His tragic meaning for Western civilization is that to him radical doubt was akin to blasphemy, a sin to be purged from the human heart by vehement assertion and hateful insult.

He grounded his claims to certainty on scripture, and even in his own time scripture proved to be a frail reed. Many of the problems illuminated by later biblical scholarship were known in outline in Luther's time, and he skinned his knees on lots of them. He extracted dogmas from the Bible according to profound needs in his own psyche. He raged against those who disagreed with him, although such disagreements were inevitable. How he read the Bible is an essential part of his biography, and we cannot talk about his doctrines and his furious defense of them unless we can see, by examining the Bible, how tenuous these dogmas were on all sides.

Why did he not face the difficulties of scripture squarely and arrive at the irenic balance between faith and skepticism that characterized Erasmus? The ultimate answer, of course, is temperament, the mysterious and perplexing force that makes all of us unique and gives us our own niche in history. As Luther confessed time and again, his was a temperament driven by fear and by the need to conquer it so he could live day by day. His greatest terror, one that came on him periodically as a horror of darkness, was the fear of death—death in itself, not the terror of a burning and eternal hell awaiting the sinner in an afterlife. It is startling to see how seldom he speaks of hell as a place of eternal torment, and indeed he finally rejected the notion of hell as any sort of place. When he spoke of *inferno* in Latin or *Hölle* in German, he usually meant the Hebrew *sheol*, which he correctly said meant simply the grave. When locked in combat with an especially galling foe, Luther could consign such a person to everlasting flames, but the more reflective Luther scarcely mentions hell. His ultimate question was this: Can I believe that God has the power to raise us from the dead? The corollary to this unanswerable, existential puzzle is another question: How does the Christian deal with the terror that death evokes while reaching for a faith that the triumph over death is possible? It seems to me that Luther's theology arose from these two elemental queries. He would shake the world to its foundations so he could believe in the resurrection of the dead.

Luther, who hated skepticism, was a skeptic in spite of himself, and his titanic wrestling with the dilemma of the desire for faith and the omnipresence of doubt and fear became an augury for the development of the religious consciousness of the West in modern times. Although few scholars seem to have contemplated the idea or studied Luther's works with that possibility in mind, this thesis, I believe, brings Luther closer to us, makes him more human, and explains if it does not excuse some of the more terrible words and deeds in his career.

While writing this book I have profited much from conversations with learned and dear friends. I mention them here not to suggest that they agree with me in all things or even in most things but to say simply that any serious scholarly endeavor gains its joy from the happy meeting of information and argument in talk with friends whose minds are diverse and whose hearts are true. I want especially to thank Mark Edwards, Lilian Handlin, James Hankins, Hans J. Hillerbrand, Gabor Itzzès, Ralph Keen, Ralph Norman, Steven Ozment, Krister Stendahl, Scott Weston, and my faithful research assistants Charles Savage and Rob Mahnke.

In dealing with the manuscript of this book, my editor at Harvard University Press, Ann Hawthorne, demonstrated a combination of talents that leave a writer awash in humility and gratitude. Her patience, tact, lucidity, discipline, and love of language glowed in every mark she made on the manuscript, and whatever its defects, this book is far better for her labors than it would have been without them. Nor can I fail to thank Nancy Hale and Elizabeth Suttell, who provided priceless service in managing the innumerable details of getting a book into production. I must also thank Maud

Wilcox, former editor-in-chief of Harvard University Press, for commissioning this book, and Aida Donald, the present editor-in-chief, for her patience in waiting the years it took to finish it and her generous support once it was done.

My gratitude to the Harvard Library system combines with a ceaseless awe at the immense holdings that have been available to me from my tiny study on the top floor of Widener, with the Houghton Library nearby in the Harvard Yard and the Andover-Harvard Theological Library only a short walk away. Here is all the paradise that a scholar can desire.

As always I must acknowledge the loving support of friends and family without whom life would lose its meaning. Here I mention only my brother John, my three sons Richard, Fred, and John together with Susan and Ellen Marius, and, above all, my best of friends, my wife of nearly thirty years, Lanier Smythe.

Belmont, Massachusetts
July 1998

MARTIN LUTHER

I

LUTHER'S EUROPE

MARTIN Luther was born on November 10, 1483, in the small Saxon town of Eisleben, in east-central Germany. By chance he would die there on a visit in the winter of his sixty-third year, in the wee hours of February 18, 1546, full of tribulations and ailments, leaving his world changed forever because he had lived. He was a German, living in a land formally called the Holy Roman Empire of the German Nation, a vast and scattered collection of territories in central Europe, presided over by an emperor whose authority was an alchemy of shadows, evoking in foes the terror that the shadows might become substance. Real power belonged to princes and princelings, great nobles and petty lords, and the councils of burgeoning cities. The great princes had pride of place and tradition. The lesser nobility sometimes struggled with poverty, gathering about themselves vain recollections of chivalric status. Meanwhile the cities were creating an ethos radically different from the habits and prejudices of the rural and feudal world left over from the dissolving Middle Ages, and the merchant classes that controlled most cities were to find much to like in the movement that Luther would summon into being.

A peculiar feature of German political life was that many bishops and archbishops held political power as princes over vast territories. They were appointed by the pope, who usually took the German political situation into account when he made his choices. In particular the archbishops played a role in German history that we can scarcely imagine today.

By far the majority of Germans in Luther's time were peasants, and their situation was complex. The peasants were restless throughout the fifteenth century, and after 1500 their restlessness swelled into outbreaks that culminated in the great, bloody rebellion of 1525. In the late Middle Ages they adopted as their symbol the *Bundschuh,* the laced peasant work boot made for toil in the fields, heavy and strikingly different from the high boots with pointed toes the landed aristocracy slipped into the stirrups of their saddles.

The lesser nobility, called knights, made up still another, smaller group that posed a danger to the public peace in Germany. Many knights had too little land to support their claims to status. Some became outlaws. Bands of robber knights sometimes fell on villages and small towns for plunder and rapine, and successive meetings of the imperial Diet representing princes, cities, and church frequently dealt with problems of order.

At the apex of society stood the emperor, looked upon with mixed emotions by the people over whom he nominally presided. When Luther's name became a household word, the Emperor Maximilian would have been happy to see him burn. A blazing pyre reducing Luther to ashes would have pleased the Bishop of Rome, Pontifex Maximus of the Roman Catholic Church, pope (or father) of all the faithful. As it turned out, neither a succession of popes nor Kaiser Maximilian nor his grandson and successor Kaiser Charles V could touch him. The divisions of Germany and the tangled jurisdictions of German laws protected Luther and the movement he founded.

The movement endured, but it did not prevail in Germany, and even where it took root, it failed to live up to his hopes, leaving him bitter and angry. He became one of the tragic figures of our history, and the religious hatreds and divisions he left were to ruin hope for real German unity until the Prussians bound most of the German lands together in a new empire in 1871.

In 1483, when Luther was born, the emperor was Frederick III. He was a powerfully built man, the proper son of a mother who according to legend had been able to drive nails with her hands. He ruled as king and emperor for fifty-three years (1440–1493), living into his seventies and becoming for his time a paragon of longevity. His was the longest reign in German imperial history. In office he was weak and ineffectual, unable to stop the consolidation of power by the great princes in their domains or to prevent feuds and wars among lesser lords. He tried to enlarge the Hapsburg domains owned by his family so that, with a sound economic base, he could exercise real authority over the German nobility. It was a good idea, but even his long life was not sufficient to realize his plans. While monarchs in France and England were reining in their feudal nobles, the German emperor steadily lost power to his princes.

Frederick was succeeded in 1493 by his forty-four-year-old son. Maximilian, in the tradition of crown princes in the shadow of a long-lived father, burned with impatience to do great deeds on his own. He became one of the most hyperactive monarchs in history, a restless and complex man nurtured on chivalric values, a sort of Don Quixote of empire. He loved to hunt and to make war, and he aimed at making his family and his nation supreme in Europe. At various times he fought the French, the Turks, the Swiss, and the Italian cities. In 1511, when he happened to be a widower, he considered accepting the invitation of the renegade Council of Pisa to become pope and oppose the military designs of Pope Julius II. But he also worked hard at the more mundane tasks of reforming the empire to halt internecine warfare among German princes.

Through his first marriage in 1476, to Mary of Burgundy, Maximilian acquired the Duchy of Burgundy—not only most of the territory of today's Belgium and the Netherlands but also the French-speaking lands around the city of Dijon to the east of France. He thought of going on crusade and made futile plans to reconquer Constantinople from the Turks. Before Machiavelli wrote, he understood the Florentine's political philosophy, that a prince's power rests on his people and that monarchy offers a stage whereby the ruler moves in a ceaseless drama of state to beguile his subjects to fear, love, and obedience by theatrical gestures. He made a self-conscious effort to become popular, even legendary. He supported at his wandering court a small college of writers who exaggerated his feats and his character in various languages. From them he received the honorific title the "German Hercules."

He tried to strengthen the imperial court system so that Germany might have a uniform system of justice of the sort growing in France and England. The division of Germany made jurisdictions hazy and contradictory. Both capitalism and imperial ambition demanded a national legal system like that signified by the French motto "One King, One Faith, One Law." Reformers also wanted to strengthen the German Diet, the representative assembly of the German people, which met at irregular intervals. A stronger Diet might have the power to tax, to provide money to realize an ambitious emperor's dreams. But Luther's movement finally proved fatal to the Diet's authority.

Maximilian's military adventures and his consequent demands for more money to support his wars inspired more anxiety than pride, and in 1500 a Diet at Augsburg put further limits on his authority. From that time on he could not collect enough taxes to pursue his grandiose projects. He could submit proposals to the Diet. The Diet had no legal obligation to grant his requests, and he had to live within limits enforced on him.[1] Until his death on January 12, 1519, Maximilian's struggles against penury became less and less successful, and imperial power more threadbare in comparison with that of territorial princes, the lesser nobility, and the cities.

Outside Germany, monarchy was increasingly accepted as the guardian of public good. Rulers, nobles, and middle class all feared the poor. Cities might operate tentatively on a republican model, the right to vote carefully limited to the wealthy. But no one supposed that any extended republic could preserve peace, order, and prosperity for very long, and even the republican cities could easily fall into one form or another of tyranny. For larger units, kings, dukes, or princes of some other sort were considered indispensable.

Luther's contemporary Niccolò Machiavelli understood that the practice of monarchy was not as simple as its theory. Fear of rebellion ran through the ruling classes like a chronic fever. Everywhere the poor in their overwhelming numbers were ready to be roused to violence by fanatical preachers who took literally the declaration of Christ that the meek should inherit the earth. Like Luther, Machiavelli took a dim view of human nature. Men were greedy, unreliable, fickle, subject to illusion, and ready to seize the main chance when they thought it profitable to do so. Machiavelli had no time for abstract theological doctrines such as the divine right of kings, and good evidence exists that he scarcely took the doctrines of Christianity literally. For him Christianity seemed to be one more religion of human origin, condemned to rise and fall in the everlasting cycles of history. In his work *The Prince,* written before Luther became notorious and not printed until a decade afterward, Machiavelli set down his observations of how rulers might keep power over the raw human stuff under authority. He asked an essential question: Was it better for a prince to be loved or feared? It was an excellent thing to be both feared and loved, said the Florentine. But if the prince must choose, it was better to be feared. It was, however, dangerous to be hated. Princes who were hated might find themselves cut down by the passionate assassin.

Treason, a concept more abstract than rebellion, became a clearly defined idea in Luther's time. The fear of treason, rebellion, and the chaos that would follow on both stirred the authorities to create ever more horrifying spectacles of torture and execution designed to foster obedience. The executioner loomed over traitors as the last grim enforcer of order. Public executions were common spectacles, intended to impress audiences with swift and hideous punishments of the disobedient. They were part of the almost casual savagery of the times, illustrating Johann Huizinga's comment that the later Middle Ages alternated between extremes of violence and sentimentality, cruelty and compassion.

By the mid-fifteenth century crimes subject to the death penalty in the empire included the following: rebellion, fraud, bigamy, incest, arson, theft, adultery, carrying off a woman against her will, blasphemy, moving signs of property boundaries, attacking someone, high treason, heresy, child murder, using dishonest weights and measures, murder, counterfeiting, rape, attempted suicide, striking someone to death, converting to Judaism, treason, having sex with animals, and sorcery.[2] Executioners had at their command numerous variations. Beheading was common, of course, and so was hanging. Beheading was usually reserved for nobles, with commoners left to more exquisite forms of public death. Women were more often drowned, buried alive, or broken on the wheel. Jews were sometimes hanged with dogs to compound the disgrace of their deaths.

The wheel—vividly depicted by many artists of the time—remained an important mode of capital punishment in Germany until the eighteenth century. With arms and legs bound to a new wheel, the naked victim was beaten with iron rods, the executioner carefully avoiding fatal blows, until bones and muscles were shattered. Finally the wheel was raised into the air on a pole, and the condemned was left to a slow and agonizing death, with bleeding flesh picked by crows. Sometimes the executioner would tear off chunks of flesh with red-hot tongs before this last elevation. The executioner might show mercy by killing his victim before lofting the wheel, but the corpse was left to rot between heaven and earth as an example.

In many countries some felons were boiled to death in oil or water. Witches, heretics, and sometimes criminal priests were burned at the stake. Executions attracted crowds, and it was not unknown for one city to buy another's criminal to provide edifying entertainment for its own citizens. Luther thought capital punishment was ordained by divine law. Prudence, he said, required that punishment be administered with "equity and moderation." But he would leave the art of execution to "Master Hans," the executioner.[3] He never wavered in his conviction that the hangman did the work of government and God. It is worth remembering that once he became notorious, he faced the possibility of suffering some version of these barbarous penalties if he fell into the hands of his enemies.

Much of public life revolved around spectacle intended to form bonds to hold society together. Yet uneasiness swelled underneath both ceremony and elaborate efforts of political thinkers to develop theories of government. The more ceremony flourished, the more doubts arose about the reality behind it. Late in Luther's century, Shakespeare would have King Henry V say of any king, "His ceremonies laid by, in his nakedness he appears but a man . . . And what have kings, that privates have not too,/Save ceremony, save general ceremony?"[4]

As monarchs came to appreciate the fragility of their station, they turned to public relations. Like Maximilian, they brought humanist scholars to court to praise them, to write their documents, to conduct oratory and correspondence in good Latin. They hired architects to build palaces and painters and sculptors to decorate their houses and their capitals. After 1494, many of these artists came from Italy or worked under Italian inspiration. The royal courts of the Renaissance became patrons of culture and spread classical ideas among educated people.

Many of those ideas were dangerous to the religious orthodoxies of the Middle Ages. Luther's life began during the Renaissance, and he was to rebel against many of its impulses and excesses, especially against the way the popes adapted culture to their political needs. Like secular monarchs, popes became obsessed with ceremony, with artistic and architectural display, living beyond their means and always in need of cash. To meet those needs, popes exacted payments from bishops, in effect imposing taxes on ordinary Christians since the bishops took the money from their dioceses. Popes also imposed taxes on Christians for special services, such as hearings in the papal courts that controlled disputes between clergy and laity and dealt with matters such as marriage and wills. Money poured into Rome—enough to rouse the ire of Christians who footed the bills but never enough to satisfy papal needs or desires.

In a country with a strong centralized government like France, kings could negotiate with popes to limit the flow of precious metals out of the country to Rome. In the Holy Roman Empire no central government protected the German people, and complaints against papal exactions rumbled out of Germany throughout the fifteenth century to Luther's time. Germans involved in legal problems concerning clerics or church lands found them remanded to Rome and faced an arduous journey across the Alps to have the case heard before clerical judges whose fairness to foreigners was doubted.

The pope, so the Germans said, appointed unworthy Italians—"gunners, falconers, bakers, donkey drivers, stable grooms, and so on," one famous complaint declared—to hold offices in German churches and to be paid out of German coffers. Many of these appointees remained in Italy and sent poorly paid vicars to perform their duties. "Thus the German laity receives neither spiritual care nor worldly counsel from the Church, while a hoard of money flows yearly to Italy with no return to us, least of all gratitude. We think that German benefices should be awarded to native Germans only and that beneficed persons ought to be required to reside in the place where they are assigned." The pope, said the protest, had increased annates—the tax imposed on new bishops and amounting to one year's worth of their revenues. He had also increased the sale of indulgences in the German lands, "a practice through which simple-minded folk are misled and cheated of their savings."[5] Confronted by German complaints in 1457, Enea Silvio Piccolomini, a papal diplomat who shortly afterward became Pope Pius II, wrote:

> If you observe the conduct of secular rulers, Rome will come out well in the comparison. Take law courts, for example. Everyone knows that common people find no justice before German judges; Roman courts are their only recourse. As for indulgences, their purchase is voluntary; why should this be condemned? You are jealous of the money going to Rome; there you have the root of your accusation. All your lamenting is about money![6]

It was a poor defense that could do no better than impugn the motives of those who objected to manifest abuses by ecclesiastics. So it is no surprise that the German people—especially citizens of towns where public opinion was made and fed by the printing press—chafed at Roman pomp and pride and were ready to listen to a strong voice raised in protest. Protests against the evils of the church were common in Christian Europe when Luther came into the world. In many eyes the church seemed corrupt to the core. The moral degradation of the church at this time has become a commonplace of history. Writers of textbooks delight in detailing spectacular affronts to morality and good order by Renaissance popes, showing that corruption in the church prepared the way for Luther. They usually neglect to mention that when his Reformation had run on for many years, Luther himself acknowledged that it had had no effect on morals, and his old age was embittered by the moral indifference of the people of Wittenberg, where he made his career.

Here is an important question: Was the church any more corrupt in the sixteenth century than it had ever been? Or was it for reasons as yet insufficiently explored that protests against the long-standing corruptions of the church became in the Renaissance more intense, more vehement, more widespread, more tinged with fear than they had been before? From the record it seems clear enough that the institutional church has been deeply flawed in every age. Complaints about evils go back to the New Testament, where we find condemnations of unbelievers, hypocrites, false brothers, quarrels, and errant belief. Only the most romantic of historians can locate a time when a Christian consensus held that the church was in good shape. Was a majority of Christians devout in any orthodox definition of the term despite the corruptions in the institution? Superstitious, yes, but the depth of Christian understanding and practice in the Middle Ages may be questioned.

The Fourth Lateran Council of 1215 decreed that all Christians must confess their sins and partake of the Eucharist at least once a year—scarcely an indication that this was an "age of faith." Diatribes against the morality of clergy and the low conduct of society at large form one of the most enduring patterns in the history of Christianity. The dream of Pope Innocent III in which he saw St. Francis holding up the church is legendary. The church desperately needed to win back the disaffected of society even while the papacy was at what modern historians call the apogee of its power.

Renaissance popes deserved their reputation for immorality. The modern Catholic historian Joseph Lortz blamed them for the Protestant Reformation. But denunciations of the papacy were commonplace for two centuries before Luther came on the scene. Kings supported by their people could withstand papal decrees. The Council of Constance—called by the Emperor Sigismund to end the Great Schism—labored four years to reform the church. It summoned the Bohemian reformer John Hus to appear at what he thought would be a fair hearing of his views. Instead, he was burned at the stake. Despite this offering to orthodoxy, Constance represented a major defeat of papal power. By the time it ended, in 1418, it had produced two major decrees limiting the pope's authority. The first, called *Sacrosancta,* held that councils were superior to popes. The second, called *Frequens,* held that councils should meet at regular intervals to review papal conduct during the period since the last meeting. Constance in effect made the church a constitutional monarchy with the pope as the chief executive.

The lesson drawn by successive popes was that they should be careful. They had to use their wits, to calculate, to negotiate, to make policies fit reality. If anything, this spirit of calculation and diplomacy worked through the fourteenth and fifteenth centuries to deepen the corruption of the papacy and many lesser bishops. Successive popes became absorbed by schemes to increase their power and their revenues to the limits imposed on them by strong monarchs. Popes became expert in political manipulation to the neglect of spiritual reform and the spiritual life. All this is enough to make the standard treatments of the Reformation agree that weariness with ecclesiastical corruption prepared the way for Luther. But was the condition of the church really worse in the sixteenth century than in the time of Charlemagne or the tenth century or at the death of Innocent III in 1215? I doubt it.

A better question, I think, is this: Why did ecclesiastical corruption in Luther's time incite so much protest? In this respect, a biography of Luther becomes in part an inquiry into the larger mentality of a troubled epoch in the history of the West.

The mood of the times indeed favored Luther. His world was swept up in change, much of it fearsome. The French scholar Jean Delumeau has chronicled the terrors of the age.[7] One source of terror was plague, striking in sudden and virulent epidemics, attacking vigorous and healthy-looking people, usually killing within a couple of days of onset. Luther's life was spent amid recurring onslaughts of the disease later to be called the Black Death because of dark splotches it caused on the skin of its victims shortly before they collapsed and died. They usually also suffered huge and painful swellings of the lymph glands in their groins and their armpits, swellings called buboes and giving the disease the still later name bubonic plague.

From 1347, when the plague first struck Europe, and continuing through Luther's time, it was called simply "the death" or "the pestilence." Luther lived through three outbreaks in Wittenberg—in 1527, 1535, and 1539. In its first outbreak of 1347–1350, plague killed anywhere from a third to half of the population of Europe. The disease traveled in the fleas that infested medieval life, the fleas having originally absorbed the bacilli of infection from rats that seem to have brought it in Genoese ships from the Black Sea. No one at the time made the connection between fleas and the sickness that pounded the continent like a flail. When the plague struck, many feared that it meant the end of the world. Later outbreaks were less devastating, perhaps because survivors built up some immunity to the disease.[8]

Many thought the disease was a consequence of the wrath of God. One scholar has suggested that the pestilence introduced another God to the "Christian pantheon" of popular piety that included the Trinity, a mother goddess, her mother, and a multitude of demigods in the saints. This new deity was the "murdering god," death itself personified as a skeletal figure, sometimes on horseback cutting down the living. The image was older than the Black Death, but the pestilence made it common everywhere. A French poet spoke of death "released by God from its cage, filled with force and with rage, unbridled and unrestrained . . . without faith, without love . . . racing through all the world." Theologians made much of two sides of God, the kind and merciful deity and the God of wrath and vengeance, emphasizing especially the angry threats of the Old Testament such as Deuteronomy 32:23: "I shall hurl disasters upon them, on them I shall use up all my arrows." The arrow became the symbol of the plague, and St. Sebastian—supposedly martyred in Roman times by arrows and clubs—became the great patron saint, protecting his own from the plague, usually in paintings by shielding them with his cloak. Devotion to the Virgin Mary became, it seems, more intense as supplicants sought her aid against the wrathful deity—even the wrathful Christ—often portrayed in the iconography of the later Middle Ages.[9]

Some supposed that if they could punish themselves, the wrath of God might be assuaged. In the wake of the Black Death, penitents with bare and bloody torsos marched in parade through European cities beating themselves with whips. It was grimly noted that these processions by flagellants did not mitigate the disease. They may indeed have spread it.[10]

The effort to please God and thus avoid the sudden and horrible death from plague led to a proliferation of lists of sins catalogued in handbooks of confession intended to instruct priests. A surviving example from the catastrophic onslaught of the mid-fourteenth century listed sins of thought, sins of words, sins of action, including acts against God and the neighbor and the seven deadly sins, sins with the senses of the various parts of the body—including sins of the head, the neck, the ears, the eyes, the nose, the mouth, the tongue, the gullet, the hands, stomach, genitals, heart, knees, and feet. Then there were sins of omission, sins against the twelve articles of faith, sins against the seven sacraments, sins against the seven virtues, sins against the seven gifts of the Holy Spirit, sins against the fruits of the Holy Spirit, and sins against the eight beatitudes of the Gospels.[11] This complicating of confession increased through the next centuries, making a satisfactory confession difficult to define and making the serious penitent aware that every part of himself was capable of sin. It naturally gave to priests commanding influence over the lives of ordinary Christians since only priests had the authority to absolve sins—an influence Luther was to smite hip and thigh in his *Babylonian Captivity of the Church* in 1520.

Icons of death, often with no consoling Christian symbolism, called to mind the fragility of life at every turn.[12] When plague struck, cemeteries were often unable to absorb the masses of corpses, and the stench of corruption became a descant on death itself. In his later years Luther counseled against the panic that caused some to flee at rumors of the approach of plague. He denounced rumor mongers and encouraged his people. Plague was a purgation of the world. It was to be endured with trust in the Christ who sat on the right hand of God interceding for us.[13] His encouragement reminds us of the terror that could overcome populations at the onset of plague. The sudden death of multitudes in his age was a fact of life. The young Luther entered the monastery at a moment in 1505 when plague raged in Erfurt, where he had begun to study law.[14] Even without plague, death struck early and unexpectedly in all classes of society. Luther regarded age forty as the gateway to old age. Later in his century Cervantes would describe Don Quixote as an old man—at age fifty.

Recurring plague seems to have been only the most intense of many terrors in an age that felt change and uncertainty everywhere. It is a tendency in human life that when we feel the tectonic plates of history shifting beneath our feet, we cling to such certainties as we may find, making them up when they are not otherwise available. It seems plausible that people in the sixteenth century demanded reformation in the church because they wanted some certain antidote to the terrors that stalked their lives. They sought a pure church because they wanted a true church, one to give them confidence in the meaning of life and in the promise of victory over death. In this regard Luther stands not as a solitary soul fighting a lonely battle for assurance about his place with God but rather as a type of the age, a troubled pilgrim whose quest for God plunged Europe into greater uncertainty than ever and led without Luther's willing it into a modern age radically different from that of his hopes.

Young Luther's Germany was going through a revolution that made money the measure of value and that created strife and in the absence of outright violence, a smoldering fear that society might explode in disorder.[15] Capitalists were not antireligious. Indeed, the precarious nature of business made them eager to seek the assurance of religion in risky affairs. But they were often unwilling to take at face value the claims of prelates to represent the God whose blessing the capitalists sought.

Luther's first notoriety came in 1517 when he protested a papal sale of indulgences that took hard cash out of Germany and sent it off to Italy, where, in the German view, corrupt Italians used it to finance idle luxury and sexual perversion. The combination of ecclesiastical corruption with an outflow of cash in an age of expanding capitalism made for a volatile mix. Flourishing capitalism brought rich and poor close together in cities, the classes made daily dependent upon one another, and thrown into inevitable conflicts. Statutes laying penalties on "sturdy beggars" became common in the sixteenth century, as were sumptuary laws that tried to limit conspicuous consumption by the wealthy and the consequent envy by the lower classes. None succeeded.

In his *Utopia,* published in 1516, the year before Luther's Ninety-five Theses, Thomas More pondered the fortunes of the poor. His wise traveler Raphael Hythlodaeus argued that men might be unemployed by no fault of their own and that workers depended on an economy that no individual could control. In More's mythical state, private property did not exist, and citizens lived happily in patriarchal socialism and accepted the stringent Utopian laws and the near elimination of private life that made it all possible. More did not take his own dreams literally enough to give up any significant part of the substantial fortune he amassed during his government service. Yet pity for the poor was there—along with fear—and reflecting one of the anxieties of the age.

On October 12, 1492, at about two o'clock in the morning, a Spanish sailor named Rodrigo de Triana, standing watch on the *Pinta,* one of the three tiny ships commanded by Christopher Columbus, saw the white cliffs of a minute island gleaming in the moonlight of an uncharted sea. It was the first datable sight of land in the New World made by a European. Luther was not yet ten years old. In 1504, on the eve of Luther's sudden decision to become a monk, another Italian, a Florentine named Amerigo Vespucci, had popularized the amazing fact that this was indeed a New World, and by the time Thomas More wrote his *Utopia* other intrepid explorers had made Europeans aware of a teeming population on continents whose vastness could not yet be imagined.

We should dwell a moment on the revolution in thought stirred by his unexpected discovery of a new world out beyond the vast "green sea of darkness."[16] Even before the voyages of the great Admiral of the Ocean Sea, the explorations of Bartholomeu Diaz (1450?–1500) and Vasco da Gama (1460?–1524) opened an ocean route around the Cape of Good Hope to India. These voyages presented problems to Christian orthodoxy. The continents eventually called the Americas had not been known to the wise ancients. How could that be? If Columbus proved Ptolemy wrong in his estimate of geography and the circumference of the earth, why should Copernicus within a generation not argue that Ptolemy had erred in his judgment of the nature of the universe? And why should seekers of all sorts into the nature of Nature not find other truths that had evaded the ancients altogether?

These matters individually were scarcely troubling to many Europeans in the century after Columbus. Neither was there much concern that many of the adored Christian fathers had been wrong because they accepted scientific notions of their times. Lactantius (240?–320) and Augustine (354–430) after him alike had scorned the idea of "antipodeans," people who lived on the other side of the earth so that they might be opposite our feet. Lactantius and Augustine believed not in a flat earth, but in a globe, so constituted that things fell off the bottom half. Even before Columbus, sailors who voyaged below the Equator proved their views wrong. Simple geography could be absorbed by the theology of the fifteenth and sixteenth centuries—although Luther scoffed at the Copernican theory that the earth moved around the sun. Joshua, said Luther, had commanded the sun, not the earth, to stand still in the great miracle during Israel's battle with the Amorites during the conquest of Caanan.[17]

A far greater problem was the discovery of multitudes of non-Europeans who worshiped strange gods. What did one do with them? Christian Europeans were confronted with the reality that they were a minority in a world swarming with populations who knew nothing of Christ. Europeans knew of Asians and of Africans before they knew of the Americas, but Vasco da Gama's men, looking at the images of Shiva in India, assumed that these were bizarre images of Christian saints, and they took Hindu religion to be a version of Christianity. Their mistake was born of legends of Prester John, whose mythological Christian kingdom was said to be located first in distant Asia and then in Africa. That tale was the legacy of the legendary travels of St. Thomas, the doubting apostle, who supposedly went to India and converted the people he found. When Vasco da Gama's men were asked what brought them to India, they replied, "Christians and spices."[18]

Now with the excitement created by the age of reconnaissance, these pleasant inventions broke on the anvil of reality, the irreducible observations of seamen who knew to navigate the seven seas and to sail before and against the wind but who had no more imagination than to say what they had seen with their own eyes. More made his Utopians, located on an island off the coast of the New World, eager for Christianity once they heard about it. He envisioned peaceful conversion in his fiction. His optimism was not borne out in the real world. In time, the Catholic Church subjected these unchristian multitudes to the tender mercies of missionaries under the delusion that sincere and right-thinking pagans would be converted when offered the gospel. When pagans persisted in their own religions, the natives of some lands—Africa in particular but also the American Indians—were viewed by some as irrational and then as subhuman, a convenient justification for enslaving them.

The printing press gave a thousand tongues to the protests of the age. It seems to have been a German invention, and Johann Gutenberg (1400–1468?) has been traditionally claimed as the creator of movable type that could be set up in frames, inked, and pressed down on paper, bound up, and sold to anybody who had the price. His first important job was a great Latin Bible. Forty-seven copies survive, thirteen in the United States.[19] Printing ignited one of the great revolutions in history. Its advent indicated that literacy was no longer a monopoly of the clergy but rather belonged to a much larger and more diverse audience. Although religious works—such as the Gutenberg Bible and miraculous tales of the saints—became staples in trade, more secular texts became quickly available to satisfy the tastes of lay people more interested in this world than the next. Classical literature—philosophy, drama, epics, satire, and history—rushed out of the printing press into eager hands, clerical and lay alike.

A barrage of books could create a barrage of talk, and those with anything to lose could imagine a popular flood about to wash away their place in the world. From the same evidence a modern specialist in demography and statistics might see only a bubble on the surface of a calm sea of public acceptance. Printing with its propensity for the sensational could create its own crises, and that was in part the story of the Reformation. A seditious broadside spread through a town at night might make the authorities quake, vastly overestimating the force behind it and reacting with paranoid terror to suppress opposition. On the other side, the existence of print in book or broadside might serve to encourage secret minorities who without it might suppose that they were too few and too weak to be of any consequence. Luther's Bible in Germany and Tyndale's Bible in England had this effect on both sides—the Catholics fearing it enough to seek it out and burn it, often killing or imprisoning the owners, and the Protestants finding the solid presence of the sacred book an assurance that they possessed in one volume all they needed for spiritual sustenance on earth and in hope of heaven and the confidence that everyone who read it would find the same powerful truth radiating from its pages.

Printing made possible corrected editions in which the ancient texts were diligently compared and mistakes by copyists weeded out. Many people could work on one edition of a printed work, and although printers made typographic errors and were cursed by writers (including Luther) for stupidity, drunkenness, and carelessness, their labors commanded authority.

The editing of old texts generates a unique psychology. Editors become addicts, wrestling with every line to get it right, and as they work, the text stands out of its context and out of the history that has carried it along on its stream since its origin. Lorenzo Valla (1406–1457), studying the text of the so-called Donation of Constantine preserved in the Vatican Library, determined that it was a forgery because of its many anachronisms. Valla has been criticized by modern scholars for arriving at the right conclusions by sloppy methods. Still, he undermined papal claim to temporal authority over Christian rulers in the West. Perhaps more important, other scholars began to use printing to locate what Elizabeth L. Eisenstein has called "a permanent temporal location . . . for antique objects, place names, personages, and events" in the classical past, allowing readers to feel themselves at a "fixed distance" from antiquity. They were therefore not only able to locate anachronism but also to discover chronology and to perceive how far into the past the glory of Greece and the grandeur of Rome had receded.[20]

The printing of editions and translations created an interest in books as *books* rather than as disjointed proof texts. Humanist editors fixed their attention on the histories of books and in their philological commentaries studied the relations of the parts of a book to the whole, not primarily for moral amplification or preachments but for the establishment of the text itself and for interpreting it by its historical context.

The printing of Greek and Latin classics seemed to be a means of expanding a treasury of ethics and philosophy. One of the early celebrated works of Erasmus of Rotterdam (1466?–1536) was his collection of "adages" from classical sources, short quotations to which he attached moralizing commentaries. In his view the moral precepts of the classical world were one with the ethics of Christianity—a natural assumption for a monotheist. But it could also be the view of one who believed that the fundamentals of ethics were the same in every good society and that ethics should be more important and more satisfying than dogma founded on a quest for certainty of one's salvation in a life after death.

Many of these *Adagia* came from Lucian's cynical epigrams—some to be translated later by Erasmus from Greek into Latin in collaboration with Thomas More in England. Lucian was one of the great skeptics of the classical world. He mocked the superstitions of his time, false miracles, and the credulity of the masses. Interest in his work demonstrated what Henri Busson has called the tendency of humanists "to seek in the ancients the rules and examples for life that had been previously sought only in the gospel, among Christian moralists, and in the lives of the saints."[21] A devotee of Lucian might, in his spirit, also mock some crass Christian superstitions of the sixteenth century, as Erasmus did. But were the superstitions the essence of the faith? Luther attacked superstitions, too, but he was repelled by Lucian and thought him an atheist.

Whatever Erasmus's intention, the *Adagia* gave educated Europeans not merely a complementary ethical system but an alternative, based not on divine command with the fear of punishment but on human nature and considerations of good and evil based on social utility and an intuitive understanding of good and bad. Here was a vision of the classical world seen on its own terms, a society romanticized by devotees of the classics—including Erasmus—who tended to overlook or remain silent about its brutality, its cruelty, its debauchery, and its exploitation of the poor by the rich. Many humanists conjured up a myth of a golden age and set it down on the ruins of antiquity and believed they had found the ideal. Printing put classical wisdom into the hands of any educated person who could afford a book, and enthusiasm abounded for lectures that explained what people read and talked about.

How safe for Christianity was classical wisdom? The answer is "not very," but to many Europeans classical studies were invincibly appealing. The introduction of Aristotle into the Christian culture of the high Middle Ages endangered Catholic orthodoxy in the eleventh and twelfth centuries. Aristotle's logic became the subject of intense debate among theologians, and it was never entirely absorbed into Christian faith despite the monumental efforts of Aquinas. No logic could prove the doctrine of the Trinity or the resurrection of the dead. Because theological works were almost the exclusive property of university-educated people and because the universities were tightly controlled by the church, the dangers of Aristotle could be contained.

But humanism operated largely outside the universities, and printing made the classics the common property of cultivated laypeople able to afford books. Here were much greater dangers than the cold, analytical spirit of Aristotle. Pagan writers such as Cicero, Lucian, Seneca the Younger, Lucretius, and many others noted for wisdom and eloquence assumed that death was the end of life and that the truest wisdom was to live as if death did not matter. Cicero's dialogue *On the Nature of the Gods* represents a valiant effort following the death of his only daughter to find some hope of immortality—and ends in skepticism. The warmth of his sincere quest and its sad failure seem much more affecting than Aristotle's syllogisms. As Jacob Burckhardt pointed out, one effect of the revival of classicism was to create widespread skepticism about the authority of Christian doctrine. In Italy, he says, pagan attitudes toward life after death "partly presuppose and largely promote the dissolution of the most essential dogmas of Christianity."[22]

A consequence was widespread skepticism that the human mind could comprehend anything about ultimate purpose for either the human race as a whole or the individuals who made it up. If humankind could not understand the mysteries of life, it might be that we are all puppets, manipulated on a stage by fortune.[23] No wonder that a foreboding about destiny or fate marked much of the iconography and literature of the age and that belief in astrology was popular among educated and uneducated alike. These notions were fed by the tragic ironies of destiny depicted in much of the classical literature that some Europeans read so avidly. One might hold that fate was ordained by God and that it therefore had some eternal purpose and meaning. But one might also drift into the somber fear that nothing had meaning and that it did no good to seek any ultimate purpose and that the essence of life was tragedy, chaos intruding into the ordered patterns that people sketch for their own lives.

Luther was thus born into an age when fear and uncertainty seemed unusually intense. To many thoughtful people, an old order seemed to be dissolving, and whatever might replace it filled many hearts with melancholy and dread. Amid such uncertainties, waves of fear and religious remorse swept over many regions of Europe as preachers arose to tell them that if the old faith was truly practiced, it would prove itself.

Burckhardt pointed out that fervent preachers during the Renaissance sent crowds into paroxysms of confession and repentance. Of these preachers, the most significant was Girolamo Savonarola, whose fiery sermons created a religious revolution in the wake of the French invasion of Italy of 1494. He became tyrannical and, perhaps worse, boring, and the Florentines hanged him and incinerated his body on a pyre in 1498. Other prophets of asceticism and doom were less notorious and less successful, and usually suffered less atrocious deaths. Most did not have Savonarola's success in attracting converts above the lower classes, and, as we shall see, the revolts these prophets inspired represented class war in religious trappings and were quickly crushed. The enthusiasm they kindled died quickly when the populace discovered that God remained silent even when they risked their lives to demonstrate their faith that he could come down in mighty power to help them.

Most Europeans persisted nominally in the old faith because its ancient ceremonies and its traditional usages were so indissolubly intertwined with daily life, its mystic comforts at least temporarily real in the holy sacraments that measured out the voyage of the earthly pilgrim through life to death. But multitudes were caught in a dilemma. They felt rational belief in an old religious order eroding, and they could not imagine what life and death might be if the cold sea of skepticism continued pounding at their unstable patch of sand. Because they felt the encroachments of unbelief from so many directions, many sought all the more to confirm the faith that they felt slipping away. They wanted a prophet not merely to reform the church but to assure them that God still acted in the world and that Christians could find some sure proof as a bulwark against this tide of meaninglessness. Many frantic religious practices of the time look like bets placed on the chance that God might be present in the world just as the church proclaimed.

Lucien Febvre, a great modern French historian of the later Middle Ages, attacked the idea that the philosophical tradition of the Greeks and the Romans could have made Christians of the sixteenth century doubt their own faith. He thought it impossible for radical doubt to emerge in a society permeated by religious symbols and usages. Atheism was an epithet hurled at foes, but it was not a philosophy that anyone could willingly adopt. Having declared that unbelief is impossible, Febvre was relieved of the necessity of looking closely at texts that might have provided an opposite point of view.[24] Febvre believed that to find radical religious skepticism in the fifteenth and sixteenth centuries is to read our own skepticism back into the past. It would seem more plausible to suggest that religious skepticism is part of all the ages and that to deny it is to assume that our ancestors were unusually dull, removed from the common human concerns that bind generations together and make history possible. Of these forces and counterforces, we shall have more to say.

2

THE EARLY YEARS

LUTHER came from peasant stock. His father, Hans, had been born on the land but by the custom of his region in Germany could not inherit because he was an older son where the youngest son inherited—a favoritism reflected in tales collected by the brothers Grimm where the good child is always the youngest. A portrait of Hans done from life in 1527 by Lucas Cranach shows a hard mouth in a face with hard eyes, not a man who seems at peace with himself or the world. He went to work in the copper mines as a young man and proved himself industrious and capable. Young Hans evidently seemed like a man with prospects, for he made a good marriage to Margarethe Lindemann, daughter to one of the old families of the region.[1] Martin was their second son. Two other sons died of plague about the time Martin entered the monastery in 1505. We know little of them. A brother James survived and visited Martin in Wittenberg in the 1530s.

Martin's relations with his mother and father have been subjected to close scrutiny or at least as close as a distance of half a millennium will allow. Erik Erikson thought that Luther was repressed by his harsh father and then, in the Reformation, burst out in a torrent of words and rebellion against the artificial fathers men construct for themselves in a tempestuous world. Wrote Erikson:

> Hans Luder [Erikson used the spelling that Martin used for his own name until he had become well known] in all his more basic charac-teristics belonged to the narrow, suspicious, primitive-religious, catas-trophe-minded people . . . Hans beat into Martin what was charac-

teristic of his own past, even while he meant to prepare him for a future better than his own present. This conflictedness of Martin's early education, which was *in* and *behind* him when he entered the world of school and college, corresponded to the conflicts inherent in the ideological-historical universe which lay *around* him. The theological problems which he tackled as a young adult of course reflected the peculiarly tenacious problem of the domestic relationship to his own father; but this was true to a large extent because both problems, the domestic and the universal, were part of one ideological crisis: a crisis about the theory and practice, the power and responsibility, of the moral authority invested in fathers; on earth and in heaven; at home in the market-place, and in politics; in the castles, the capitals, and in Rome. But it undoubtedly took a father and a son of tenacious sincerity and almost criminal egotism to make the most of this crisis, and to initiate a struggle in which were combined elements of the drama of King Oedipus and the passion of Golgotha, with an admixture of cussedness made in Saxony.[2]

Erikson was a psychiatrist with a Freudian bent. He has been pummeled by Luther scholars, perhaps in part because he wrote so well and was read by so many. He was not a "professional historian," says Heiko A. Oberman, who claims Erikson misread the evidence. Erikson made much of Luther's gutter language, his "anality," as the psychiatrist called it. It was, says Erikson, a revolt against the excessive discipline forced on him by his father at home and by teachers at school.[3] Oberman holds that obscenity was common even in theological treatises, and he dredges up a delicious example or two from Jean Gerson a century before Luther to show, it seems, that obscenity meant nothing at all in the time.[4] Mikhail Bakhtin may be more to the point. In considering Luther's contemporary François Rabelais, Bakhtin says, "Excrement was conceived as an essential element in the life of the body and of the earth in the struggle against death. It was part of man's vivid awareness of his materiality, of his bodily nature, closely related to the life of the earth."[5] Luther frequently called himself a piece of shit, and in a part of his table talk of 1542–43 that fascinated Erikson he said, "I am the ripe shit; so also is the world a wide asshole; then shall we soon part."[6]

Freudians such as Erikson make much of our casual remarks, our dreams, our slips of tongue, our nether parts, including our obscenities, and Erikson doubtless goes too far. For many of us, Freudianism has been discredited as a sort of arcane astrology, adept at giving explanations after the fact but almost useless in predicting behavior. Yet even accepting cautions against the extremes of psychological interpretation, we stumble into curious paradox when we assume that any style of writing represents only a topos, that the writer did not truly mean it. Erikson manages to haul a pile of obscenity from Luther's works; anyone who peruses the table talk will find much more. Somehow the few examples that Oberman finds in Gerson seem not to balance the account.

Writers fall into the habits of their times, but no single rhetorical habit in any time is universal, and writers have reasons for the choices they make. Not all theologians in the later Middle Ages were obscene. Luther was attacked for his own obscenity by members of the evangelical camp. Why did obscenity come readily to Luther's pen? The reasons may be subconscious as Erikson suggests or unconscious as Oberman holds—the acceptance of one style among many.

Perhaps Luther's scatological usages come from the communal nature of monastic latrines. The monastery of St. Gall in Switzerland had a latrine with nine holes side by side and a bench nearby for monks to wait until one of the holes was free.[7] In such circumstances, in a world isolated from polite company and women and children, a world of monks chatting and joking as they defecated together, language might be commonplace and not be judged obscene.

But it may be, too, that writers make deliberate choices according to their own personalities, background, experience, character, and that as Dionysius of Halicarnassus said, "the words are the soul," a sentiment not unjustly translated as "The style is the man."[8] It would seem to be as false to dismiss Luther's scatological language as it would be to read into it some final scientific understanding of the man. My view is that Bakhtin's words apply to Luther as well as to Rabelais, and Erikson is to be praised because he takes into account an essential matter—Luther's temperament, the quality that drove him to make his reformation. The "professional historian" at times writes as though Luther may be reduced to his textual sources, as though Luther's insights came chiefly from the intellect and not from the gut—an attitude as wrongheaded as any effort to define Luther by psychology alone.

So what influence did his parents have on him? The least that can be said is that Luther's recollections of both mother and father but particularly of his father are ambivalent. On several occasions in his table talk, Luther recalled that his parents were severe with him—too severe, he thought. "One shouldn't whip children too hard. My father once whipped me so severely that I ran away from him, and he was anxious until he won me to him again. I never wanted to beat my own little Hans lest he become weak-willed and my enemy; I know no greater hurt."[9] The words sound heartfelt. Did they mean that Luther felt alienated from his own father?

Many felt such alienation and responded to it violently in the German lands. Society was patriarchal, sometimes brutally so. The chateau of the counts of Flanders in Ghent preserves various instruments of torture and executions, including an intricate device used to cut off the hand of a son who had killed his father. After the amputation of the hand, the parricide was beheaded. The law and the device indicate that enough sons murdered their fathers to require savage laws to deter them. Luther's feelings were not murderous, and it seems that his ability to talk about his father's anger is proof enough of his having come to terms with it.

He also recalled that "for the sake of a nut my mother beat me until the blood flowed."[10] It is one of his few recollections of his mother to appear in his work. Her portrait, like that of his father, was done by Luther's friend Cranach in 1527. She appears with a kerchief wrapped about her head and neck, a lean, strong-featured, stern-looking woman. Luther records a little ditty she used to sing:

> Mir und dir is keiner hold;
> das is unser beider Schuld.
>
> For me and you, no one cares;
> For that we are both guilty.[11]

Some have said that she sang this little song out of a cheerful disposition and that Luther remembered her singing happily. Perhaps so, but the words sound grim. Luther remembered harsh things about her, and one was the beating she gave him because he stole a nut. He seldom mentioned her otherwise. Too much whipping broke a child's spirit, he said. He implied that his parents had almost broken his. The German attitude was that children were beasts to be tamed, an attitude common both at home and at school. "Some teachers are as cruel as hangmen," he said. "I was once beaten fifteen times before noon, without any fault of mine, because I was expected to decline and conjugate although I had not yet been taught this."[12] Yet late in life when a child relative of his stole a trifle, Luther recommended that she be beaten until the blood came.[13]

It was an authoritarian world. Fathers ruled at home, teachers in the classroom. The stick was applied to the backs of children with the alacrity with which it was used on cattle, horses, and dogs. The worst crime parents could commit against children was to indulge them. Steven Ozment has pointed out that medieval theologians considered children capable of committing mortal sin at the age of six or seven. At that age, manuals on childrearing recommended that the father take over discipline of the child from the softer mother. The severe disciplinarian was considered much better than the lax. Spanking was always acceptable and always common. Fathers were not to be brutal; neither were teachers. Even so, says Ozment, "There are horror stories."[14]

Did German youngsters take such treatment in stride? Luther's recollections seem to mean that he at least did not. Did he then transfer fears instilled into him by his parents to God? Who can tell? He seems not to have brooded explicitly about his parents. In the great Weimar edition of Luther's works, the complete table talk takes up six hefty volumes and includes 7,075 entries. In these he mentions his father only twenty-seven times. He recalls his father now and then in letters and theological works. But he hardly seemed as obsessed with Hans as Erikson supposed.

Hans made plans for young Martin—and angrily resented his decision to enter the monastery. When Martin broke with Rome, the elder Luther came over to his son's faith and died in it. Martin reported that someone had asked old Hans on his deathbed, "Do you believe?" The dying man replied, "If I did not believe, I would be a clown."[15] Yet Martin did not visit his father when Hans lay dying in February 1530 in Mansfeld. He wrote to him instead: travel was dangerous, he said. Protestant and Catholic princes were squaring off to fight the religious wars of the 1530s. Martin told his father that the peasants hated him and might well do him harm if they caught him on a journey—even, it seems, the short one to Mansfeld. Martin's letter, written February 15, 1530, is regarded as one of his finest epistles. In it he expresses a wish that his father and mother come to Wittenberg. "I hope we would be able to take care of you in the best way," he says.[16] But he quickly lapses into a sermon, urging on Hans the comforts of Christ in the hour of death. It is devoid of personal reminiscence. To me it sounds formal, dutiful. Nothing in the record shows Martin as the devoted, loving son that Thomas More was to his father, Judge John More, and nothing in this letter matches the personal touches in More's last letter to his daughter Margaret on the eve of his execution.

On June 5, 1530, Luther wrote from Coburg to his friend and righthand man, Philipp Melanchthon, giving him a gossipy rundown of the political situation. Despite the fear of danger that had kept him from making the rather short trip to Mansfeld in February, Luther had no trouble making the much longer journey south to Coburg where he could keep in touch with the Diet that was to meet in Augsburg. The Diet would consider the religious situation in Germany, and he might be expected to take more risks in so important and public a cause than one might take in a private matter such as the death of a father. Toward the end of his letter to Melanchthon he turns to the news that his father had died on May 29. "This death has certainly thrown me into sadness, thinking not only of nature, but also of the very kind love, for through him my Creator has given me all that I am and have." He contemplates death. "We die many times before we die once for all," he says. "I am almost the oldest Luther in my family." A friend noted that on hearing the news Luther withdrew into a room apart and wept so hard that his head hurt. Afterward his calm was restored, and he gave no further hint of suffering.[17]

It may have been grief for a father, but his comments let us surmise that his feelings involved the natural meditation and sorrow for the self that come to any son whose father dies after a long life, leaving a middle-aged son sharply confronted by his own mortality. One may read the text and find Luther sorrowing for time and death implicit in the human condition and made more vivid by the demise of old Hans. He did name a son for his father, and we might make something of that. It is hard to say what.

A whiff of hardship hangs over the family history as Luther told it—though like many successful men recounting their autobiography to adoring disciples, he may have exaggerated his youthful rigors. Part of the implied author in his autobiographical statements is that of a pious and simple man of the people driven into revolt by wickedness in the Catholic Church. His stories of his life favor extremes—a swinging from one pole to another, an either/or disposition. There was something heroic in the climb of an earnest young man from penury to fame—a tale with literary appeal told in various guises far back in the mists of our tradition.

Luther was not brought up in grinding poverty. But Hans's position in the world carried unending economic anxiety and risk. By Martin's account Hans had gone into the silver and copper mines as a laborer and had been poor when he married. "My mother carried all her wood home on her back," Martin said.[18] The image of carrying wood on one's back seems almost a trope betokening misery and servitude, and Shakespeare used it in *The Tempest*.[19] If Ian Siggens is correct, Luther's mother came from a well-established burgher family. When the family moved to Eisleben not long before Luther was born, it may have been to be closer to Margarethe Luther's father. Her family may have helped Hans get started in the smelting business. Margarethe might also have helped her son learn to read because she was the more educated of the parents, and her family may have helped young Martin get on in school.[20] By this reckoning Margarethe Lindemann came from a slightly higher social class than Hans Luther, and her relatives helped Hans rise in the world.

Whatever the propulsion, rise in the world he did. By the time Martin was born, Hans owned several small foundries. Even then life was not easy. Such enterprises responded quickly to capitalist cycles of boom and bust, and miners were considered only a step or two above the peasantry in the hierarchy of status in Germany. Not surprisingly, miners were often political and social radicals.[21] They were also anticlerical and rebellious. Luther's earliest disaffection from the Catholic Church may have been cultivated at his father's table so that the son followed the father in a resentment that led to revolution. And there may have been a more personal reason for a father's animosity.

Since Martin was born on November 10, the eve of St. Martin's Day, it has seemed natural that he received the name he made famous. Allen Temko has observed of St. Martin that he

> was, in a sense, the first Christian bigot in France. He was a remarkable personality, split by an incompatible mixture of force and mildness. He was a creature of brutal exterior environment and gentle inner faith . . . The saint invaded oak groves and cut down the sacred trees. He smashed images. It is no accident that his feast day is November eleventh, which apparently was the date of pagan autumnal sacrifices. St. Martin stepped in and conquered a living religion as green and vigorous and with roots as deep as the consecrated oaks. Ancient miraculous wells became baptismal fonts, and where a Druid tree had stood, he built a church with its wood.[22]

This description of Luther's name saint seems almost a prophecy of Luther himself. Yet we should recall that in the iconography of the time, St. Martin cut his cloak in two to share with a beggar. He was popular, the first major saint not a martyr, the patron of corporations and societies, and beloved because he cared for the poor. It may be that Hans Luther named his son for the saint whose care Hans thought he might need for himself.[23] Luther later recalled going about as a young student in Eisenach, begging for food from house to house.[24] Did he beg because he had to, or was begging merely the custom of students? Siggins and most others say that begging was customary, a bow to the humility supposed to be inculcated in all clergy—and students were assumed to belong to the clerical caste. Luther's mother's relatives in Eisenach may have been willing to support her gifted son in school but unwilling to supply luxury. Luther himself declared that his father paid "bitter sweat and toil" to put him through the university.[25]

A recent discovery offers another possibility for Luther's name and opens a window onto a mystery that is being avidly explored. An entry in a register in the papal archives dated October 10, 1487, requests a dispensation for one "Martinus Luther, a student in the diocese of Mainz," whose father and mother were not married when he was born. The canon law of the church forbade those of illegitimate birth to become priests, but such a prohibition could be set aside by a canonical dispensation. According to the records, this Martin Luther appealed to Rome for help. He seems to have made the trip to Rome in person to get the dispensation, indicating perhaps some difficulty that prevented it being granted within the archdiocese of Mainz, where it might have been routinely handled. Whatever the reason, the dispensation was granted, and it seems that this Martin Luther was ordained to the priesthood some days later and assumed duties in the church of St. Cecilia in the town of Rasdorf in the diocese of Würzburg. The position carried an income that could be paid to the holder only after the dispensation granted the right for this Martin Luther's ordination.[26]

The entire business is tantalizingly mysterious. Hans Luther came from the village of Möhra, in the diocese of Mainz, and it may be that the Martin Luther who requested the papal dispensation for illegitimacy was a relative, perhaps Hans's brother. Martin Luther the reformer may thus have been named for his uncle as well as for the saint, and Hans, too, may have been born out of wedlock. Exactly what constituted a formal marriage ceremony in this time was ambiguous, and it may be that this startlingly named Martin Luther felt obliged and annoyed to journey to Rome to seek a dispensation because some ecclesiastical technicality had not been observed. We cannot know. Certain it is that our Martin Luther encountered no opposition from his father or mother when he broke with the old church—some indication, I think, that Hans might have soured on the papal allegiance even before his son strode onto the stage of history.

Luther seems to have been much attached in childhood to his younger brother, James, who visited him in Wittenberg. Yet Luther spoke seldom of him in his table talk—as he spoke rarely of his mother. Luther's later associate at Wittenberg, Philipp Melanchthon, venerated her because of her piety.[27] She believed in witches and enchantments, and so did her famous son. In his table talk Luther declared that a neighbor in his childhood had been a witch. He said his mother had been wary around her, for the witch had power to cause asthma and nightmares and to make children cry themselves to death. A priest punished the witch, said Luther, but she cast a spell on him, and he died. Luther opined that his own many illnesses were not natural but were caused by malign enchantments.[28]

Witches could, he thought, keep butter from forming in the churn. He told of the witch who changed herself into a mouse to steal her neighbor's milk, but the neighbor caught the mouse and wounded it in the feet. The next day the witch, changed again to the form of a woman, came seeking oil to put on her injured hands and feet. In keeping with superstitions of his time, he thought Satan had power to delude our senses. He told of the "man" near the town of Nordhausen who ate a peasant and the peasant's horse and wagon—and the peasant woke up in the mud some distance away.[29] His world swarmed with devils and poltergeists. Apes, he said, were "idle devils," and sometimes the devil appeared in the form of a goat.[30]

Luther's mother was hardly alone in her superstitions about witches. The witchcraft delusion was swelling and would continue during Luther's lifetime, much stronger than it had been in the Middle Ages without yet reaching the crescendo of later decades. It became widespread through all ranks of society. Luther's vehemence on the subject was constant. Witches, he thought, sometimes turned butter into dung. He said that one should have no mercy on witches. He would burn them, he said, although according to the law of Moses they were to be stoned by the priests.[31] Other educated men accepted the delusion. Still, we can scarcely imagine such comments about witches and demons from the urbane Thomas More in England or from Luther's great rival, Erasmus. His capacity for vehement, unrestrained anger was part of his temperament. Anger is only another side of fear, and it seems plausible to find roots of his fear in his childhood with its frequent reminders of supernatural terror.

An unresolved contradiction within Christianity lies here. God remained sovereign over all the powers of darkness. God's almighty power became the major theme of Luther's theology. Yet his experience located him and multitudes of others in a world where supernatural minions raged in warfare against divine goodness and purpose. Strange noises in the night, the wind in the forest, the odd behavior of a neighbor—especially an older woman living alone who might be mad with poverty, hunger, and solitude—all provoked the conviction that demonic force went about the world like a roaring lion, seeking whom it might devour. The witchcraft delusion represented a terror of the familiar, a sort of *jamais vu* that may suddenly make us see the familiar in a different and baleful light. Jean Delumeau points out that those most frequently denounced as witches or sorcerers were well known to their accusers. The sorcerers might be those who had put a hex on neighbors by bumping into them or breathing poisonous breath on them or perhaps flinging only a diabolical look—the evil eye. A thousand terrors stalked the late-medieval night.[32]

Luther's superstitions and fears were in part born of his time and place.

Much of Germany was covered with forests, especially conifers, and it is easy to suppose that the darkly wooded east German landscape affected Luther's religious views. The celebrated *Maleus Malificarum,* the semiofficial priestly handbook intended to identify and guide judges in rooting out witchcraft, originated in Germany in 1486 and went through fourteen editions by 1520. Witches were said to hold their sabbaths in the forests; the dense woodlands of Germany inspired fears of malign spirits. The folk tales collected by the brothers Grimm depict the forest as a frightening place where evil and mystery lurk and the ordinary rules of life do not apply, and witches in these stories are common. German and Flemish artists painted the wilderness as a dangerous and spooky place. Max J. Friedländer says of Luther's older contemporary Hieronymus Bosch's painting, *St. Jerome Praying,* "the wilderness . . . stretches out, so weird and creepy that nothing that looms up in the way of beasts and monsters or preposterous edifices can possibly astonish us."[33] Lucas Cranach the Elder, Luther's good friend, and Albrecht Dürer also made the forest mysterious and threatening in their works. Was the witch craze more virulent in Germany than in other places of Europe? Perhaps not. Still, the German landscape gave to the witchcraft delusion its own cast, and witches were still being burned in the German lands long after the delusion had dissolved in England.

Luther's fear of witchcraft fits into a larger feature of his mind. For him the world was a combat zone where the forces of darkness and light battled each other for creation, including the souls of human beings. Luther's lifelong declarations of the almighty power of God have the look sometimes of confidence building, assertions of faith that served as an anodyne to a deeper fear that the powers of darkness were stronger than he could overtly admit, strong enough perhaps to defeat God in the end by bringing all the world to death. However that may be, the satanic powers were mysterious and immeasurable. He saw scarcely anything as a "natural" phenomenon. He was always afraid of storms. In 1533 a violent winter storm tore through Nuremberg, knocking down thousands of trees and tearing the roofs off houses. Luther said such tempests came from the devil while good winds were sent by angels. The winds, he said, are nothing but spirits, whether good or bad.[34] Once while he was still in the monastery, he said, he neglected to say his canonical prayers, and a terrible storm broke out in the night. He got out of bed and fell on his knees to pray, for he was sure the storm had come on account of his oversight.[35] He was able later in life to shake off the fear that storms came because he did not strictly follow the rules of prayer, but his notion that storms were supernatural events endured.

The ravages of plague after the first epidemic of the Black Death evidently added to the sense of the presence of death in the midst of life. As Ian Siggins has shown, the young Luther would have heard sermons in church intended to heighten fear of death. Judging from the surviving sermonic literature from the period, we may say that these sermons were blunt. The priest wanted his people to be good and to observe the sacraments. He hurled biblical texts at them to prove that those who were not good—including those who neglected the proper church practices—suffered punishment for sins and that no matter how the worldly-wise might hate the idea, death was inevitable and that for the wicked, it came soon and often horribly.[36] If people did not repent of their sins, they would die and go to hell. Such preaching may bounce off most people like rain off stone. But for some, especially impressionable children, continual declarations of terror may flood the soul with anxiety. It may not be a focused terror so much as a general terror of all the unknown and the fragility of life.

Luther spoke all his life of recurrent fears and bouts of *tristitia* when he was sunk in almost unbearable melancholy. His fears early in life focused on death. In traditional Christian teaching, death is to be feared not for itself but because it ends the opportunity mortals have to prepare themselves for the judgment of God. By Luther's time, as we have seen, a terror of death and decay permeated much of Christian Europe. Representations of rotting corpses and skeletons were commonplace in painting, drawing, sculpture, and in literature. Decades ago Johan Huizinga turned general attention on this morbid imagery. "No other epoch has laid so much stress as the expiring Middle Ages on the thought of death," wrote Huizinga in *The Waning of the Middle Ages*. "Ascetic meditation had, in all ages, dwelt on dust and worms. The treatises on the contempt of the world had, long since, evoked all the horrors of decomposition, but it is only towards the end of the fourteenth century that pictorial art, in its turn, seizes upon this motif."[37]

Some version of the dance of death was painted on the walls of many churches large and small. Skeletal, malign-looking corpses cavorted around startled figures of men and women from all levels of society—including bishops, priests, and nuns—seizing them in bony hands, snatching them away to corruption. The German painter Hans Baldung, one of Luther's contemporaries, painted vivid images of naked or nearly naked women gripped by a leering and rotting skeleton, preserving, in a more striking form than the egg and the arrow, the ancient antagonism between love and death. An especially horrifying painting of Baldung's now in the Prado in Madrid, shows the three ages of life—a baby, a voluptuous naked woman in youth, a withered old crone—and death as a skeletal figure with hourglass and clock in the background. As Philippe Ariès has shown, the corpse and the cemetery became prominent features of art in the later Middle Ages, and the half-decomposed body was frequently represented on tombs and in churches and even more frequently in books of hours meant for wealthy laymen. And I have mentioned already the "murdering God" of the Black Death. One of the most horrific paintings of the fifteenth century is a *Triumph of Death* by an unknown artist in Florence. Here death stands leering above the earth, holding his scythe in his hand and grinning down at the humanity that he is cutting like grain. "The moral purpose," says Ariès. "was to remind the viewer of the uncertainty of the hour of death and of the equality of all people in the face of death."[38]

But to what end? Burckhardt, as we have noticed, held that in Italy many scholars influenced by classical literature became skeptical about life after death and implicitly rejected the resurrection of the body and the immortality of the soul. More recent commentators have been reluctant to find such final skepticism in the later Middle Ages. Their interpretation has been the simplest, that these stark representations of death were intended only to remind unthinking people that they should recall the last things—death, judgment, heaven, and hell—and prepare to meet them. In this view, death does not stand as *the* last thing but only as a prelude to what comes after death, and so the iconography remains Christian. Its aim is to make us despise the body so that we may attend all the more to the cure of the soul. "We must repeat it," says Delumeau. "The *danse macabre* was a sermon."[39] It could be said that repeated and horrifying images of corruption played an iconographic role not unlike the notion of the absolute power of God, the view that God could do anything—a concept much discussed among the scholastic theologians of the fifteenth and early sixteenth centuries. The putrefying corpse might seem to be beyond the power of resurrection, but God's power was infinite, and the more horrid the image of death, the more Christians might exalt the power of God, which, in Christ, might overcome death.

As will be clear throughout this book, my sympathies and, I think, the evidence lie with Burckhardt's view, and I find it plausible to assume that beneath the sense of the macabre lay a frightened and unwilling skepticism about the destiny of humankind. My opinion is much confirmed by the long and substantial labors of Henri Busson, whose *Le rationalisme dans la littérature française* represents a major blow to the notion that religious skepticism did not exist in the sixteenth century.[40] According to abundant testimony, the hold of Christian doctrine on the masses now appears to have been less strong than is usually assumed. Such sermons about mortality and the strong medicine of stark images of death and corruption indicate a populace requiring remorseless rhetorical whipping to be reminded to forsake its addiction to the charms of this life and heed the call of the life to come. Rather than prepare piously for death throughout life, many chose the way of the Hostess who describes the death of Falstaff in Shakespeare's *Henry V.* Falstaff cried out, "God, God, God!" three or four times. Says the Hostess in telling the story, "Now I, to comfort him, bid him he should not think of God; I hoped there was no need to trouble himself with any such thoughts yet."[41] The view of the Hostess was that one did not think of God until death was nigh, and in the meantime, one tried not to think about death at all.

Some presume that horror before death included the prospect of divine judgment afterward—although Philippe Ariès and Pierre Chaunu have argued that the emphasis on the rotting corpse pushed into the distance the idea of judgment and in effect separated death in the popular mind from the notion of resurrection and the judgment to follow.[42] Ariès and Chaunu have, in my view, the better arguments here—*pace* Delumeau.[43] Despite the proliferation of paintings of the Last Judgment, the literary culture of the educated seems to have pushed the day of doom away to such a distance that it scarcely intrudes. Further, it seems incomprehensible that people in the fifteenth and sixteenth centuries might have been assaulted by such images of death and not pondered the possibility that death might be the end, that nothing lay beyond, and that life itself might be considered, as Macbeth described it a little more than a half century after Luther died, "full of sound and fury, signifying nothing," or that it was "endless night," as others of Shakespeare's characters called it.[44] Much poetry of the age takes a melancholy path, reflecting on time and death in the gloomy resignation that marks much of the classical literature of Greece and Rome being resurrected by humanist scholars.

Baldung went over to some variety of the Reformation, drifting eventually to Protestant Strasbourg, where he lived in comfort, his work much in demand both by religious authorities and by the wealthy who wanted their portraits painted. It is difficult to be sure of his beliefs. He did not set them down in writing. Pictorial art is more difficult to analyze for precise ideas about religion or anything else, but Baldung has been suspected of belonging to the nebulous group called "Epicureans" in Strasbourg, a group that included some of the "libertines" forced to flee Calvin's Geneva.[45] No one, at least, can deny his lifelong preoccupation with representing death as horror, usually unrelieved by Christian symbols of hope.

The Italian scholar Alberto Tenenti followed Burckhardt when he argued that the fearsome attention to death meant that people of the late Middle Ages had given up on hope of a life to come and had focused their attention deliberately on enjoying this life. The more people drank in the joy of life, the more death became a dread antagonist, and yet in time it was gloomily accepted, put in a compartment, and kept aside so as not to cause people to live in panic every day.[46]

As we shall see, such a view of the masses may easily be inferred from Luther's own lectures and sermons. Ariès disagrees only to the extent that Tenenti limited this passionate love of life to the Renaissance (which is best understood as the end of the Middle Ages rather than a distinct period). "The truth is," says Ariès, "that probably at no time has man so loved life as he did at the end of the Middle Ages."[47] He links this delight in life and the consequent fear of death to individualism, to a passionate desire to make as much as one could out of one's own life and to the sober, melancholy awareness that all one would do would inevitably be cut off by death. Luther seemed to reflect this sense of finality later on when he reflected, "Reason sees death before it; that it cannot be terrified by that experience cannot be."[48] It would seem that Luther meant that the most profound sentiment of human reason—perhaps here understood as common sense—is that death is the end.

But we are speaking of birth—birth of a high-strung and brilliant man into an age of fear and trembling. Six months after Martin was born, the family moved from Eisenach to the larger town of Mansfeld. Here Martin went to school until he was fourteen. It was a town he always loved.[49] Then he was sent off to Magdeburg on the Elbe to another school for a year and after that for yet another year at Eisenach. At Magdeburg he was taught by the Brethren of the Common Life, dedicated to heartfelt piety and humble devotion. Three years later he went to the university at Erfurt, first as a student in the faculty of arts and later in the faculty of law.

He had obviously been marked as a bright lad, and his father could have high hopes for him. Then as now the university offered able men of low birth a chance to rise in the world. So it was with Thomas Wolsey in England, Luther's older contemporary and the son of a butcher from Ipswich. So it was with Luther—who unlike Wolsey chose law as a profession. Lawyers had prospects. Governments—including government in the church—were becoming more bureaucratic, and those in authority needed all the help they could get. A clever young lawyer could look forward to lucrative employment and the company of powerful men.

Erfurt was a large city as German cities went, with a population of about 20,000 souls, and its authority extended to surrounding villages.[50] We would have found it cramped and small within its walls. But one walked easily in a few minutes from the center of town to the outskirts—if the streets were not too crowded—and in a few minutes more into open country beyond the city walls. Erfurt was wealthy, with a flourishing trade in dyes. Within the city were twenty-two monasteries, twenty-three churches, thirty-six chapels, and six hospitals.[51] Ultimately the money to support them came from the pockets of the middle class. It was not always gracefully given. Erfurt knew frequent conflict, both between the upper and lower classes in the city and with the competing authorities of Saxony and the archdiocese of Mainz from without.[52]

Young Luther enrolled in the faculty of arts to prepare for legal studies. The curriculum was still largely the scholastic regimen of the Middle Ages. Scholasticism depended on the classification of data so that contradictions might be exposed and reconciled by ceaseless debate. Students learned to debate, to define their terms, to identify their premises, to build logical arguments, and to locate fallacies in the arguments of their foes. Such stuff was supposed to quicken the mind. The art of disputation had for centuries been seen as a means of confirming Christian faith by showing that all its doctrines fitted together in a coherent whole.

It is worthwhile to linger a moment over the scholastic ideal that permeated Luther's education. The scholastic method had been promulgated by Abelard in the twelfth century to sort out Christian doctrine to demonstrate it as a unified system, free of contradictions, thus deepening understanding of Christian faith. Contradictions in Christian doctrine posed a danger to belief, for how could God contradict himself? The implicit aim of scholastic theology was to make doctrines as coherent as God himself was thought to be. By the early sixteenth century the ideal had collapsed into the reality that not everything could be neatly sorted out, that the proliferation of logical arguments did little to uncover new truths. Scholastic books became more and more intricate, less and less convincing, multiplying logic to prove the impossible—that the very coherence of the faith testified to its validity.

In 1501, the year Luther enrolled at Erfurt, Erasmus published his *Enchiridion,* a manual of Christian piety—starting the great Dutch humanist in a direction ultimately more radical than the one Luther was later to take. Already in the *Enchiridion* Erasmus extolled a piety that accepts the inability of the human mind to understand God, and that has no room for the logic chopping of the scholastics. Some teachers at Erfurt rebelled against scholastic forms and advocated the study of Greek and classical literature.

In the *Praise of Folly,* published first in 1511 under the guise of a joke on the world, Erasmus made a devastating critique of the capacity of linear, syllogistic reasoning to encompass divine truth. Erasmus was a precursor of Hegel's later great insight, that one cannot produce a chain of syllogistic reasoning from a beginning theorem without eventually having some of the conclusions contradict one another. Aristotelian scholasticism in the Middle Ages strained to be like Euclidian geometry. It inevitably failed because the varieties of human experience surpass the ability of syllogisms to make them cohere.

Some humanists admired scholasticism. Giovanni Pico della Mirandola (1463–1494) is an example. But the spirit of humanism nourished the conviction that one learned about life not by scholastic logic with its linear march from conclusion to conclusion but by the study of the great thoughts of human beings from the past, men engaged with civil society and with the fundamental issues of life and death. Humanism was obdurately exemplary. One read the wisdom of the past and absorbed it and applied it to the present. The Christian humanist hoped to build character and intuitions and to learn lessons from the virtues and the errors of great men of Greece and Rome, especially men who had served their societies. The underlying theory held that good men of all ages came to the same general ideal of the virtuous life—a sense of duty to the civic order, the cultivation of honesty, honor, self-sacrifice, simplicity, and restraint. With this view that virtue gave meaning to life went a corresponding reluctance to seek too many answers from theology. God was beyond the capacity of the human mind to understand. Far better to be pious, loving, and good rather than to seek to satisfy vain curiosity about divine mysteries.

Burckhardt believed that the Renaissance witnessed the discovery of the individual in Western civilization, and to a large degree that is so. Burckhardt's "individuals" were often tyrants, men like Gian Galeazzo Visconti of Milan, ruthless and devout and fiercely ambitious. Or they were lecherous sadists like Sigismondo Malatesta of Rimini, whose portrait in profile by Piero della Francesco preserves his ruthlessness for us today in the grand gallery of the Louvre. These were men who did as they pleased, existential heroes of a sort, indulging themselves in vice and cruelty in flamboyant scorn for moral precepts of church and society. They lived for power and experience, and many of them paid the penalty for their individualism by being assassinated. Shakespeare captured their essence in the words of the young man who would become Edward IV of England: "But for a kingdom any oath may be broken:/I would break a thousand oaths to reign one year."[53] They knew they ruled not by divine right but by the consent of their people, a consent bought partly by courtship and partly by their ruthless ability to inspire terror in those tempted to oppose them. They knew that they would die, and they tried to wrench as much as they could from life before death took them to oblivion.

Christian humanists sought to tame this wild individualism and to define the moral man as servant to Christian society. Peter Brown has described the individualism of the second-century world, when people "watched individuals in their public *personae,* their masks seen by the population at large, speaking, standing, at the table, reacting, usually in public, to grief, fear, and anger."[54] Humanism in the Renaissance partook of this public quality. Those influenced by humanists built public personae for themselves, images cultivated so that their renown might spread and their names remain imperishable on earth. Humanism might also mean that men defined themselves as part of the community to which they belonged—as the great Romans of antiquity delighted in the proud assertion *Civis romanus sum.*

Greek was studied in Erfurt when Luther was a student there, and music was much prized.[55] But much of his study would have been in the scholastic disciplines of philosophy that supposedly taught young men how to think. Luther would have encountered the nominalist thought that stemmed from the complicated views of William of Occam (c. 1285–c. 1349). Since it is widely assumed that Luther was deeply influenced by nominalism in his formulation of his own theology, we must ponder what this influence meant.

It is much better to describe nominalism as a school of related but not necessarily coherent beliefs than it is to suggest that it occupied a place in medieval philosophy and theology that might have even the unity of "transcendentalism" or "phenomenology" or even "existentialism" in more modern intellectual history.[56] The debate over nominalism and its rival, realism, was an argument about epistemology—how we know things and how the words we use to express knowledge are related to what we know. People we call nominalists held all sorts of theologies, many in conflict with one another.[57] Nominalism was the deconstructionism of its day. In its various forms, it cast doubts on the old certainties of language, and to those intoxicated by it, its critique seemed almost invincible. In Luther's time it was called the "modern way"—though in fact the *via moderna* comprised many other qualities and influences besides a debate on epistemology.

The "old way" had been "realism," and the debate between nominalists and realists had roots in classical philosophy. The great question of nominalism is this: What is the relation of words to what they signify? The realists believed that the general concepts we use to describe, classify, or define things have an objective existence apart from the objects to which they refer. If I employ words like "man," "table," "food," or "beauty," I use concepts that may be applied to many men or tables or foods and to beautiful objects as diverse as starry skies and curly-haired dogs. To confirm our understanding of the world, we would like to believe that our concepts have a necessary relation to what we perceive with our five senses. Many medieval theologians wanted to believe in the reality of universals, as these general terms were called, because this belief made the world more comprehensible and made the affirmations we make about the world more trustworthy. We might say that realists believed in a sort of sixth sense, a further attribute of the mind that helps comprehend the data the senses convey to us.

Realist theologians assumed that when they spoke of God, truth, justice, righteousness, or whatever, their words reflected reality like mirrors gathering and reflecting objects outside themselves. In the fourteenth century, William of Occam contested the reasoning that informed realism. He was first of all a theologian with one major premise: God is all-powerful. If God is all-powerful, he is free to do anything he wants. Human standards of morality or human ideas of what God should or should not do cannot then flow out of God's essence like heat blowing off a fire. God created human morality as we know it, and if he had wanted to do so, he might have created a different morality altogether.

Occam therefore set out to argue against the notion that God is bound by a set of universal ideas that are part of his essence. The perceptions or concepts signified by words may communicate *something* from person to person. But they are not universal, they have no reality beyond their use by mortals, and we understand them according to our own experience. The most certain knowledge we have is by our direct intuition of objects, and at the heart of this intuition is sensory experience.

Whenever we make generalizations, Occam held, we can say only: "This fact is true of all the specific instances I know." The generalizations are valid only insofar as I have known various specific instances. Once we know something by experience, we can describe its properties. When we move this mode of thinking to theological matters, we find ourselves in difficulties. If we assume that Luther lived in a world of increasing doubt that traditional Christian teachings could account for reality, especially the most important reality of Christian life, the status of our souls after death, the difficulties may be acute. Christianity is a historical religion, based on the faith that God appeared incarnate in Jesus Christ, who lived and died at a given historical time and who was resurrected from the dead and after that ascended into heaven. We cannot know the life of Jesus directly; it is mediated to us by history, and history is ultimately a matter of words about the past, not the past itself. To believe in Jesus, we must believe that the stories told about him are true; but these stories are a far different category of reality from the historical life of Jesus himself. If the story has been told the wrong way, all our beliefs about Jesus are endangered.

The intellectual turmoil of the sixteenth century rises not merely out of debates about the true nature of religious belief and practice; it represents a seeking for meaning and certainty about religious beliefs that were more and more uncertain. A tension of uncertainty had accompanied Christian teachings throughout the medieval centuries. In the sixteenth century this tension had reached the breaking point for some.

By the time Martin Luther entered the university, Europe had passed through anxiety-ridden economic and social changes, through one of the greatest plague cycles in the history of humankind, and through more than a hundred years of raging violence. Philosophy, theology, and humanist scholarship did not live in a sealed train passing through history. They were reflections of anxieties that racked the family, the marketplace, the high road, the deathbed, and the endless tangles of class struggle. In the poetry, drama, and literary prose of the period, fear, anxiety, and melancholy abounded.

Aquinas believed that we can infer all sorts of things about God by reason alone. Like Aristotle, he assumed that we can reason from God's effects, the world itself, back to their cause, to God the creator. But what kind of God does creation imply? Aquinas never held that reason alone could bring us to the Christian God, the God revealed in Jesus Christ, the personal God whose nature and meaning came to us in the Bible. Only revelation from God himself could show us so much. Yet Aquinas also said that we can know God by his effects, including creation itself. Creation implies a creator; the continuation of the world implies a God who preserves it. The idea of God implies that he is the ultimate good, that he is all-powerful, and that he knows all things. The order of the world is another proof of God's perfection, for Aquinas—like his mentor Aristotle—saw all things existing in a relation to each other that represents a divinely ordained symmetry. In this and in other ways, Aquinas sought to prove that what we see when we observe the world is compatible with belief in a benevolent creator God who made the world and rules over it, despite the presence of evil.

Yet whatever reason may tell us, Christianity is a historical religion, and we do not discover historical facts by abstract philosophy, by reasoning about what is logical. We determine the "authentic stories," as William Tyndale would call them, of history by deciding on what evidence of the concrete we will believe, and the highest evidence for Christianity, Aquinas believed, was Bible and church—which he saw as one. The tradition of the church—which included the correct interpretation of the Bible—was part of revelation, God's special act of witnessing to himself; it was not something inferred from reason.

But what does the evidence mean? Aquinas believed that having firmly accepted Christian revelation, we can work out many of its implications by logic. We can fit revelation into a system in which no one part contradicts another. It is this systematic impulse that makes reason and faith compatible in Aquinas, not some notion that the Trinity or the Incarnation might be proved by reason alone. If one could prove the consistency of Christian belief, in Aquinas's view that in itself was enough to establish its divine origin, for other religions lacked that consistency. In this principle Aquinas was following Abelard, though from afar.

Occam held, on the contrary, that we know of God's existence and his qualities only by faith in the revelation that he has made to us—supremely in Christ but also in the church permeated by the spirit of Christ. He questioned the enterprise by which Aquinas sought to make sense of revelation by assuming that Aristotelian logic corresponded to reality. Occam was by no means heretical. He was a loyal churchman—though not a believer in papal sovereignty over the church. The relation between reason and faith was not spelled out in the Bible or in the received doctrines of the church. Jesus was not a philosopher, and throughout the Bible those who believed the divine message did so not by logic but by seeing God in action—through miracles that certified the prophets and by the greatest of all miracles, the Resurrection, which certified the person and work of Jesus himself. The New Testament faith was to believe both that the stories people told about Jesus were true and that the miracles Jesus did were done by God's power. Occam's position had a biblical bent to it. Aquinas found similar views mistaken in his time, but he acknowledged their existence.[58] Faith to Occam meant that we must believe the stories of revelation recounted by others, that is, the writers of the Bible and those who had observed miracles and other manifestations of the power of God. But we cannot, in his view, look at creation and deduce much of anything worthwhile about the creator. Occam doubted that reason could do more than suggest that God exists, and he was not always sure that reason proved even that. This was a view that Luther himself was to espouse in later life.[59]

The consequences of this line of argument are to shift attention to the authority of revelation. If God speaks to us out of a burning bush or raises the dead or turns water into wine before our eyes, we believe intuitively—just as we recognize the colors green or red when we see them. But if I do not experience these wonders directly, but only as stories told by others, how can I tell that the stories are true? Only by faith in the stories. Occam's philosophical assumptions resemble those that made David Hume deny miracles centuries later—except that Occam thought Christians should believe the stories, and Hume said we should not.

The church had claimed for centuries that its teachings were infallible. Occam agreed. The church was the vehicle by which God showed himself in the world, and even with the freedom granted to God by nominalist theology, there was a strong conviction that the church had to exist in an unbroken line from Christ if God's presence in the world were to be confirmed. There had to be a succession of the faithful. Occam held that at the time of the Crucifixion, when Peter himself denied Christ, everybody around Jesus lost faith except the Virgin Mary. In her alone was the faith and therefore the church preserved. For Occam, an antipapalist, it was a way of saying that even popes had gone back on the faith now and then as Peter, the first pope, had done when he denied Christ. Faith was preserved not in a hierarchical institution but in a community of the faithful dwelling in the institution but sometimes not occupying its high and visible offices.

But what was the true church? This was the great, devouring question of the later Middle Ages, and many people before Luther answered that the true church was not the Church of Rome. Rome—with its pope at the head, its grand institutional paraphernalia, its bureaucracy, its ceremonies, its bishops, its clergy in every part of the Western world, its panoply of beliefs—claimed an unbroken tradition from Christ himself and believed itself to be infallible. But not everyone agreed, not even in the Middle Ages, not even in the age of faith.

The Middle Ages abounded in heretics, many of them serious threats to the church. The Cathars, the Spiritual Franciscans, the brothers of the "free spirits," John Wycliffe in England, John Hus in Bohemia, and multitudes of other dissidents left the Catholic Church. Their departure, at risk of their lives, testifies that the Church of Rome was to them not only inadequate but possibly the Antichrist, the great demonic force to rise on earth shortly before the final, cataclysmic last judgment of God. When we look into the Middle Ages with romantic ideas about the "age of faith," we miss the smoldering uncertainties that lay beneath what one medieval historian has called the "crust of repression" that secular and religious authorities alike thrust down on the religious striving of common people.[60] A question to be asked in any society is this: Who has the power to make it seem that all good people accept the same ideology? Our experience in the twentieth century with authoritarian governments should make us draw up short before the easy assumption that everybody in the Middle Ages felt the certainty that romanesque and gothic architecture was erected to convey.

Nominalism, with its emphasis on revelation from a God utterly mysterious except for what he chose to tell us about himself, was a defensive philosophy. Luther's world was filled with plague and painted and sculpted with the horrifying iconography of death. It buzzed with pagan alternatives to Christianity and teemed with superstitions that contradicted Christian monotheism. It was a world where the muslim Turks seemed invincible and the Jews steadfastly refused to be converted, a world where capitalism swelled and the church continued to denounce usury as mortal sin, a world where poets soaked their lines in melancholy, and perhaps above all a world where the institutional church, which claimed to be the custodian of revelation, seemed rotten with corruption. Where in all this could reason find God? By renouncing logic as a means of penetrating the divine mystery, nominalism offered a justification for faith against all the appearances. "No matter what may seem true from looking at the world," the nominalists seemed to be saying, "everything has a purpose, and God is in charge. Indeed the very mystery of the world proves that God is all-powerful, for only such a God could create such a world." As Galileo was to do a century later with the heavens, nominalism—and Luther—were striving to do with theology. They were to adjust their theories to the appearances, seeking a believable faith. In that sense Luther the medieval man can be seen as part of the modern age.

The effect of nominalism was to increase reliance on the infallibility of the Catholic Church, and in the queer, paradoxical way that history works, this reliance was to prepare the way for the decline of Christianity in the West on account of Luther's Reformation. To increase the reliance on infallibility was to increase the certainty of collapse and eclipse once infallibility appeared to be broken. In a world where the appearances were increasingly against traditional faith, Catholic Christians gained such religious confidence as they had from the church and its sacraments. The church had survived in an unbroken institutional succession from Christ himself. Christ's promise had confirmed it, for he had said he would be with his church until the end of the earth. If the church that ran directly back to him had erred in any way, Christ had broken his promise, and nothing was to be believed. The institutional leaders who defended the church could not accept the subtle and devastating notion implicit in Occam that the true church was not necessarily the same as the visible institution that comprised its high officers, including the pope.

Attacked by generations of dissidents, the institutional church summoned theologians to defend it. Popes, bishops, and their clerks could not assume that the Catholic Church was a ruined house where a few true Christians crouched, hidden in corners. The hierarchy stood for grandeur, the notion that the glory of the earthly church reflected the eternal glory of God. Those who protested its rule could be accused of heresy, and protest itself could lead to heresy whether its progenitors wanted to be heretics or not. That was the box where the Catholic Church had trapped itself by the time Luther went through his university career at Erfurt: All or nothing . . . It would prove to be the undoing of Christian unity in the West.

But the power of the Church in the late Middle Ages did not rest on reasoned argument. The Catholic Church of Luther's time was an experience. Its sheer physical presence surrounded life from birth to death. Its bells sounded the hours. Its sanctuaries—especially its great cathedrals—sent spires and domes heavenward on almost every street in large cities, and the parish church threw its protective shadow over tiny villages in remote places. Its chapels dotted the wilderness. The familiar old rituals of its liturgies channeled people along the difficult pathway of life from birth, through happiness, suffering, and death, providing ceremonial enrichment to daily existence. Its music—its chants, its choirs, its organs, its trumpets, and its developing harmonies in the sixteenth century—could wrap worshipers in a mystical bond that united them with each other and with the invisible God. The church was in itself the grandest of the sacraments, a divine power animating the physical reality of the institution. Its connections with government were close and ubiquitous, even when individual secular leaders and individual popes or lesser clergy might fall out with one another. Scarcely anyone alive in the later Middle Ages could imagine an orderly society without the restraints imposed by religion.

To admit to irreligion or to skepticism was to confess oneself scornful of the common human bonds that defended morality and held chaos at bay. To some extent it was also to scorn one's fellow human beings, for if nearly everyone in a society professes a religion, those who do not profess faith contemn the collective wisdom of the community and inevitably seem a threat—the threat that God or the gods may punish the entire society for the neglect of a few. Even in our own times to announce oneself as irreligious is in the eyes of multitudes to disqualify oneself for high public office.

It is this impulse that Lucien Febvre missed in his great but wrongheaded book that aimed to prove that atheism was impossible in the sixteenth century. Certainly no one could *profess* atheism in a blatant and public declaration. But in his very long recitation of all the ways that religion influenced the society of the sixteenth century, Febvre seemed to believe that no one could rebel against such an overwhelming presence or that those who do not rebel might still be eaten by doubts that their professions represent truth.

Yet the doubts exist. They exist because the community ardently presses a conformity of faith on everyone; the community does become aware of them; and the religious orders of society in reacting against those doubts push all the harder to make their faith normative and unassailable. The very intensity of this effort to make faith and the culture identical creates in some quarters all the more reaction. And it is one reason why even the doubters often do not want to doubt but rather do everything they can to reconcile themselves with the culture their minds compel them unwillingly to reject.

The late medieval church's response to philosophical skepticism about theology seemed to be an almost subconscious drive to multiply cultic practices that submerged doubt, that made piety so physical, so demanding, that one had no time for reflection and brooding on doubts that reflection might induce. Relics and pilgrimages proliferated. Scarcely any literature was more popular than stories of the saints, their pious adventures, their serene martyrdoms amid sadistic punishments by pagan persecutors, and their miracles for those who venerated them. By Luther's time these practices had become top-heavy and ramshackle and were waiting for the push that would make them collapse.

Luther arrived at Erfurt in the spring of 1501. By the early fall of 1502 he had passed the examinations for his baccalaureate degree and could teach the trivium of the liberal arts—grammar, rhetoric, and simple logic. He received his master's degree by examination in January 1505.[61] In the spring he began the study of law.

But then a storm intervened.

3

THE FLIGHT TO
THE MONASTERY

E VERYONE who knows anything about Luther knows the story of how he entered the monastery. It is found in his table talk of July 16, 1539, thirty-four years after the event.[1] He remarked almost casually that fourteen days earlier had been the anniversary of the day he had been caught in a storm near Stotternheim, a village near Erfurt. In his terror before lightning, he cried out, "Help, St. Anne, I will become a monk." A rough-hewn granite column raised in 1917 to mark the approximate spot stands beside a country road in rolling country not far from Erfurt. "Consecrated Ground," says the topmost inscription. It is a quiet place, the monument raised during a horrible war, to recall a momentous event and to mark Luther as a hero of the German nation in the hour of its peril.

Such a vow carried awful weight. It was a promise made through St. Anne to God himself. To break a vow was to commit a mortal sin, for it was to admit that one did not truly believe in the God to whom the vow was made. God, Luther said these many years later, understood his vow in the Hebrew because Anna (or Hannah) meant "under grace" and not "legally"—a reference to Luther's conviction by 1539 that vows made in fear should not be binding. That was long after he had irrevocably renounced his youthful oath.

Shortly after making his vow, he regretted it, and friends tried to talk him out of it. By then he had begun the study of law, and his intelligence betokened a promising career. To enter the monastery was to become a nobody, even if one was to become a monk-theologian. Long afterward Luther recalled the contempt the law professors at Erfurt had for theologians.

No matter how high ranking the theologians were, the law professors called them asses.[2] He persevered, under superstitious dread, and in a few days gave a valedictory dinner for his friends, who, on the morrow, accompanied him to the monastery. He told them, "Today you see me but nevermore." He expected to disappear into obscurity. His friends wept as they walked with him to the great wooden door where he knocked and entered, leaving them grieving in the street. His father was furious, but Luther followed his own star. "I never thought of leaving the monastery," he said, recalling the event. "I was dead to the world until God's time when Junker Tetzel and Doctor Staupitz incited me against the pope."[3]

What fear drove Luther to make his vow? The best interpreters of Luther have always assumed that he feared to meet God in judgment.[4] But that is not what Luther said. In his earliest accounts of the event, he did not say that he feared to meet God in the judgment so horrifyingly depicted in so many sculptures, so many paintings, and so many garish woodcuts of the Middle Ages. He does not say that he was terrified of hell. The immediate object of his fear was death. Years later in his dedicatory letter to his father Hans as a preface to his treatise *On Monastic Vows,* he wrote, "Suddenly surrounded by the terror and the agony of death, I felt constrained to make my vow."[5] He made a rash vow to ward off death, and when he survived, he felt compelled to keep it. Like other storms, this one seems to have been to him a supernatural event, conveying a divine summons.

Innumerable devotees to various gods have made similar vows, and, having survived, many have kept their promise lest they forfeit divine aid in some later emergency. Luther happened to make his vow to a saint—St. Anne, mythical mother of the Virgin Mary. She was the patron of miners and therefore a familiar saint in his family. The Virgin Mary had been a secret treasure, hidden in St. Anne's womb until she was revealed to the world. Metallic treasures found deep within the earth were revealed to miners who dug for them. Leonardo da Vinci, Luther's older contemporary, painted St. Anne with the Virgin Mary seated upon her lap and gave her a serene and mystical smile, as though sharing a secret with the world. St. Anne's cult was popular throughout Europe in Luther's time. Modern Catholic scholars find her completely mythological.

Luther told another story in 1531 of a narrow escape from death. While he was a student at Erfurt, he said, he was walking in a field near the town when he somehow gave himself a deep wound in the leg with a knife or a sword. The wound gushed blood; he was unable to stanch it, and in terror and pain cried out to the Virgin Mary. A surgeon was brought. He stopped the bleeding, but that night the wound broke open again, and again Luther called on the Virgin for help.[6] The older Luther did not connect this incident to his decision to enter the monastery. He was concerned to show his youthful superstitious devotion to the saints, here Mary rather than her mother. Yet as in the story of the storm, the fear of death was the motivating force. Given the melancholy iconography of death and the grim preaching on the subject, we can assume that young Luther was one of those sensitive souls who brood on death, for whom death is the steady companion of life—until his old age when on the point of death he accepted it with more equanimity, perhaps even with relief. Montaigne remarked toward the end of the century that the fear of death is worst when we are healthy but that when we are sick unto death, we greet our imminent end peacefully. That seems to have been Luther's experience—haunted by death until his later years when his terror lessened and in his fatigue he yearned for the end.

The monastery was the traditional refuge for those who labored to save their souls from death and judgment. Monastic life is so bound up in clichés and romance that it is almost impossible for us to penetrate to the consciousness of late medieval monks who lived their communal routines, performing ceremonious duties, praying and meditating in solitary moments while the noisy world beyond the cloister walls faded in their divine silence. Monasteries were communities of men or women living strictly ordered lives, every hour of the day regulated so that the monks or nuns were freed from worldly contaminations. Sin, flesh, and the devil were to be subdued by continual prayers, meditations, and labor. A gift of the monastery to Western civilization was that as the Roman Empire decayed and fell, monks conceived the study of books to be pious toil—asceticism, discipline against the lusts of the flesh—and made the labor of copying manuscripts a work for love of God, and some monasteries became repositories of great libraries. The advent of printing removed that literary reason for monastic existence.

It was considered a pious act to bequeath wealth to monastic orders. Thereby laymen who had lived in the sinful world of hurly-burly might receive posthumous benefit from monks who had chosen rigor and abstinence and isolation from worldly distraction. Consequently, many monasteries were wealthy, their estates cultivated not by monks but by serfs whose obligations were written in records kept by literate churchmen for decades. Because their careful records helped monks enforce obligations due them, monasteries were often pillaged and burned in peasant uprisings.

Monasticism was ideally speaking a heroic vocation. The monk gave up everything to seek his own salvation and God's grace on the world. But Erasmus, himself a monk for a few years in his youth, scorned monks as lax, lazy, and immoral, and he was only one of many writers who in Luther's time made monks the target of endless jokes. (We should always recall that the contempt for monks that has come down to us has been preserved in literature that may not have reflected a majority opinion.) Merchants in the cities of the empire, busy men with little taste for the contemplative life, resented the monasteries because of ecclesiastical taxes necessary to support them. Monks were detested by many businessmen in a world where work and money counted; monks seemed to be parasites. Monkish prayers lost their value in the eyes of worldly men—except at death, when even the most worldly businessmen might leave property to monasteries and be buried in monkish cowls. It is not surprising that in a hurrying society where everything had a price and time was something to be spent, lost, or wasted, monasticism was in decline.

And there was something more. In a world of exploding knowledge and excitement, the routines of the monastery seemed dull and monotonous to some. Erasmus is an example. His experience in the monastery persuaded him that most monks rotted their brains with mindless ritual that did nothing to improve virtue or help the world. When Henry VIII began confiscating English monasteries in 1536, many were almost empty. Although German monasticism was in better health, Luther's decision to become a monk represented swimming against the tide.

Luther chose to become an Augustinian monk. It seems a strange choice in retrospect, one of those moments pregnant with destiny that we take for granted because its consequences were so monumental. He had another choice. Among the twenty-two cloisters in Erfurt was a Carthusian house, and the Carthusians were much stricter than the Augustinians. They could boast—giving the glory to God, of course—that they had never been reformed because they had never fallen from the pure ideals of their founders. They enjoined silence and simplicity on their houses, and they were perhaps the most highly revered of all the monastic orders in Luther's time. During the Reformation, they remained steadfast and contributed at least fifty martyrs to the old church. Given what Luther said later on about his anxiety, his yearning for God, his ascetic practices, it seems that he might have instinctively chosen the Carthusians as the solution to the sickness of his soul. But the Augustinians had a greater reputation as scholars and teachers. Perhaps even at the beginning and subconsciously he was seeking something more attuned to the intellect than the Carthusians offered.

Like the other houses in Erfurt, the black cloister of the Augustinians was located in the city. Monasteries had once been built in remote valleys or on hilltops where monks could pursue salvation in bucolic quiet, isolated from a whirling world, the monks taking turns at manual labor in the surrounding fields in addition to their prayers and sacraments. In the later Middle Ages, popes summoned monastic orders into the cities to minister to folk in danger of forgetting God in the quest for money amid the endless secular drama city streets and city life presented. In the darkest of the dark ages bishops never left the cities, and indeed the word *cité,* from which the word "city" comes, originally meant the site of a bishop's cathedral. As early as the twelfth century with the great enterprise of building great cathedrals, ecclesiastical leaders understood that Christian influence should be stronger in urban centers. The mendicant orders—including the Augustinians—ministered to urban dwellers and were part of that missionary impulse.

There were two large and powerful groups of Augustinians, each following a version of the Augustinian Rule. Augustine (354–430) was one of the most fanatical, superstitious, and ugly-tempered men in the history of Christianity, a barbarous influence on Western civilization, the worthy recipient of Edward Gibbon's ironic scorn. He has always been the hero of those who condemn human nature for its wickedness, extol God as the arbiter of the universe, and find the life of the senses not only wicked but distasteful. His passion for God and the Catholic Church was intense in proportion to his fear of death and meaninglessness. He wrote voluminously to justify Christianity against all foes, and his works had a heated rhetorical authority that few could equal. He had not been a monk, and he was not the author of the rule that carried his name. No matter. In both groups, he was revered and studied with special veneration. Luther's order was called the Order of the Hermits of St. Augustine and had at the top a prior general who resided in Rome. The title Hermits reflects the earlier history of monasticism in the countryside. The Canons Regular of St. Augustine were more loosely organized and included priests who lived together under fewer restrictions than the hermits practiced.

Erasmus was a member of the Canons Regular. His relation to the Reformation remains ambiguous. When Luther entered his monastery in Erfurt, Erasmus had already left his cloister in Deventer, in the Netherlands. He was supposedly on temporary leave, having been allowed to become the secretary to Henry of Bergen, a bishop who required the temporary services of a Latinist. Erasmus kept postponing his return to the cloister, and on the basis of his literary fame he won a papal dispensation that freed him from monastic life for the rest of his days. In books and letters, he expressed loathing for monks and monasticism and sometimes sounded like Luther. Both may have attacked monastic life to justify themselves before the world for having forsaken it. If anything, Luther was more accepting of the ancient monastic institution than Erasmus. When Luther appeared on the scene, many Europeans—including Erasmus—saw him as a somewhat crude Erasmian.[7]

Both groups of Augustinians combined theology with a piety that was mystical without being extreme. In mystical religion one seeks immediate union with God, a union that can come gently through simple prayer or overwhelmingly through exercises that leave the soul naked and alone in ecstasy before the Almighty. Members of Luther's order were moderates. Their devotion to Augustine, cynosure of orthodoxy, kept them from wandering into giddy transports that could topple into heresy. The Augustinians cultivated a quiet personal piety through vigils and prayer and liturgical practices. Luther's best prose throughout his life was about spiritual communion with God.

The Augustinian monastery at Erfurt was surrounded by a high, thick wall with great wooden doors. In 1508, three years after Luther entered, it housed fifty-two monks, down from sixty-seven in 1488.[8] It was not thriving, but it was not in decay either. Luther seems to have had no thought of becoming a theologian; but in a small company, a bright young man would be quickly noticed. Like all monks, young Luther went through a trial period of one year as a novice, following the rituals of monastic life, every hour regulated with prayer, study, vigils, meals, all at precise times so that the routines of piety became life itself. At the end of the year the monk made his final vow to renounce the world forever and to live wholly for Christ in a community of like-minded souls. He vowed poverty, chastity, and obedience.

Chastity meant abstinence from sex. The Christian aversion to sexual intercourse went back at least to the second century, and the purest Christians were virgins—a phenomenon that separated Christians even further from Jews, who always cherished married life and the family.[9] Married people could gain a higher degree of purity by renouncing sex, and many in the early church did so. Having renounced these powerful natural desires, the monk took yet another step in earning his status as hero. Monks were supposed by some to be like angels, their vows like a second baptism because the monastic vow erased the same sins that baptism cleansed from the human soul. To break the monastic vow was to ensure eternity in hell.[10] When a monk took the vow, he was assumed to have been restored to the state of grace that Adam had enjoyed before the fall. Like Adam, the young monk would inevitably fall into sin again, but now he would have monastic life to help him succeed on his earthly pilgrimage to heaven.[11]

Luther proved to be a good monk, advancing rapidly in the esteem of his brother monks and his superiors. He took his final vows on schedule; his future seemed set. His dedication to monastic observances continued and was seen—and remembered. Later enemies such as Thomas More would castigate him as a lecher who began the Reformation because he could not contain his lust. But no evidence exists that Luther violated his vows of chastity in the monastery. In the frank way he talked about himself, he said in 1531 that as a monk he had not felt much libido. He had on occasion had nocturnal emissions. When young women confessed to him, he did not look them in the face, for he did not wish to recognize them. In Erfurt he heard no woman's confession; in Wittenberg, only three.[12]

On April 4, 1507, when he was twenty-three years old, he was ordained to the priesthood. Not all monks became priests. But it would have been astonishing had Luther's superiors not pushed this brilliant young man into ordination. Priests administered the sacraments. The pious fiction of the church held that each sacrament had been instituted by Christ to be observed by the faithful until the end of time—a view confirmed by the Council of Trent called to resolve Luther's schism.[13] It was less certain among theologians whether these sacraments were instituted directly by Christ or by his spirit after the Resurrection.

In fact the sacramental system developed slowly. Only with Peter the Lombard in the twelfth century did the church come to consensus that there were seven sacraments—the traditional sacred number: baptism, confirmation, the Eucharist, penance, ordination, marriage, and extreme unction. These were considered vehicles of divine grace to help the Christian pilgrim, the *viator*, make the journey from earth to heaven. Each sacrament shared the nature of Christ, for each was an incarnation of sorts, an invisible spirit or power, clothed and communicated in physical form, just as Christ had been divinity clothed in flesh. Pope Leo I wrote, "What was visible in Christ has passed over into the Sacraments of the Church."[14]

After baptism, the greatest sacrament was the Eucharist, observed in the elaborate ceremonial called the Mass. Christians taking the Eucharist could believe that they were sharing the flesh and blood of Christ himself and that the world possessed a mystical and spiritual quality beyond the brute impressions of the senses. It was always to be for Luther an essential part of his religious faith and practice. Just what the Christian meal meant began to be debated fiercely in the ninth century. Given the history of cultic meals in the mystery religions of the classical age, we may suppose that participants believed they shared the life and death of the dying and rising god commemorated by the bread and the wine, the body and the blood of Christ. The point has been debated by modern scholars, but it is clear that to the early church the sacrament was the "medicine of immortality."[15]

Exactly how was Christ present in the Eucharist? The Fourth Lateran Council of 1215 confirmed transubstantiation, the doctrine that the substance of the bread and the wine changes by miracle during the Mass. No longer is it bread and wine; it is the actual body and blood of Jesus. It has the taste, smell, feel, and look of bread and wine, but that constancy of appearance is part of the miracle. God, knowing we would be sickened by the taste of raw flesh and blood, stoops to our weakness by keeping the elements in their familiar form. The form is a saving illusion. Christ is present in real flesh and blood, and no bread and no wine remain in the sacrament.

The bishops at Fourth Lateran were determined to affirm the doctrine of creation—that God had created the material as well as the spiritual worlds. When Fourth Lateran met, the Catholic Church was riven by the Cathar heresy, brought home to Europe by returning crusaders who had encountered it in the East. The Cathars, or "Albigensians," so called because of their strength around the city of Albi in the south of France, resolved the problem of evil by holding that there were two gods. One, the dark god, created matter and the physical world; the other, the bright god, created the world of spirit. History was a struggle between the two gods, and salvation meant liberation from the physical. They represented a rebirth of the ancient Manichaean dualism that had attracted St. Augustine in his early life and from which he was never entirely to escape.

These Cathar doctrines contradicted Christian belief, enunciated in the Apostles' Creed: "I believe in God the Father Almighty, Maker of heaven and earth, and in Jesus Christ his only Son our Lord." They did not contradict the experience of superstitious human beings who felt contending forces in life—good and evil, light and darkness, metaphors as old as the human condition. In our own time Peter Brown has convincingly reasserted David Hume's contention that the religion of the common people always tends toward polytheism and that monotheism is an abstraction arrived at only by a few.[16] Christianity has always had a polytheistic bent. It has had its God—a Trinity, no less—and its Satan in opposition to the good God, not to mention its legions of saints in the Middle Ages whose shrines recognized the holiness of hills and springs and groves and places where once pagan gods had been worshiped. Early monasticism was founded on a dualist supposition, that the world was corrupt, the seat of the devil, and that the monk must flee to the perfection of isolation.[17] The Cathars represented an extreme form of dualistic thought explicit in Christianity itself and in the medieval attitude toward monotheism and especially visible in monastic practice. The busy world of the daily life—marriage, childbearing, buying and selling, social class, politics, war, and all the rest—was the world of sin, flesh, and the devil. The monk fled that world into the godly isolation of the cloister.

Yet it was never quite that simple. God created the world; it had a divine purpose. God had a purpose for the Christian republic that comprised all the Catholic Church. Besides, by the thirteenth century the church had a huge economic, social, and political stake in earthly life, and to renounce the world was to renounce the church's claim to lead Christian society. From the investiture controversy of the eleventh century, the papacy claimed sovereignty over all Christendom, asserting a continuing divine purpose for the physical world, God's creation.

To Lotario Conti, member of an Italian noble family who became pope in 1198, taking the name Innocent III, the Cathars represented a demonic adversary to Catholic faith. "To me," said the pope, "applies the word of the prophet declared in his prophecy of the Advent, 'I have established you over peoples and kingdoms so that you may tear out and destroy and also that you build up and that you plant.'"[18] He called for a crusade against the Cathars—a shocking notion given the previous use of crusades only to attack enemies of Christianity outside Europe. He died before the crusade was done, but successive popes urged on the crusaders with bloodthirsty holiness until Montségur, the last great fortress of the Cathars, fell and its garrison and those who had fled to the castle for refuge were burned alive on a great bonfire on March 16, 1244.

To defeat the Cathars militarily was not to end the threat they posed to normative Christian faith. Cathar beliefs remained strong in southern France. The Inquisition went to work to round up suspected heretics and used psychological and physical tortures to reimpose the age of faith on those tempted to throw it off. In this context, the decision to define the doctrine of transubstantiation at Fourth Lateran in 1215—of which Luther was to make so much later on—made good theological sense. The notion that the bread and the wine in the sacrament became the actual body and blood of Christ marked a sharp distinction between Catholics and Cathars. Cathars could never accept this deification of matter, just as they had not accepted a genuine incarnation of Christ. The context of the definition of transubstantiation makes it clear that the doctrine was directed against them.[19]

The Eucharist had long been considered to have miraculous powers. As early as the fourth century, Gregory of Naziansus had exulted over a cure effected by the elements in the Eucharist over his sister Gorgonia. When all else had failed, she applied the bread and the wine of the Eucharist "to her whole body," apparently rubbing them in, and she was healed.[20] The definition of transubstantiation at Fourth Lateran could only increase the wonder with which the sacrament was observed, for in it the most high God was physically present, held in the hands of the priest. The sacrifice of Christ on the cross was repeated on the altar. The sacred body and holy blood of the Savior were there as they had been when Jesus hung in awful grace for the redemption of humankind.

The Eucharist cannot be said, strictly speaking, to have become more important than the Crucifixion in popular belief, for the Eucharist would have had no meaning without the historical sacrifice of Christ. But many late medieval paintings show angels gathered around the cross of Christ, holding out the eucharistic cup so that it might be filled with the gushing blood of the Savior. One could suppose that without the Eucharist, the blood of Jesus could have no effect on sinners centuries after the Crucifixion. It was powerful stuff, and we can see easily enough how the Eucharist became associated with magical practices. Indeed, it was not far from magic for wills to bequeath an endowment to priests to sing perpetual masses to benefit the souls of benefactors, the repetition day after day taken to be a potent force in ensuring the swift and safe progress of the deceased through purgatory.

In one of the normal human paradoxes, the exalted theological view of the Mass raised among some a jocular irreverence as it did in the goliard poets of the twelfth century in France. In Rome in 1511 Luther would hear priests intone, "Bread thou art; bread thou shalt remain." Yet for priests who took the rite seriously, the Eucharist could inspire fear. Luther recalled in 1532 that he had been terrified when he celebrated his first mass—the first act of a priest after his ordination. His father came to witness the ceremony, presenting a handsome gift of twenty gulden to the monastery. He also brought along twenty companions, indication of pride in his son. When Luther stood before the altar, he came to the part of the ceremony where he should say "To the eternal living true God." Years later he said that he was so afraid that he thought of running away and said as much—probably in a whisper—to his prior, who stood beside him to assist. The prior, surely accustomed to stage fright in new priests, snapped at him, "Get on with it," and Luther did. The later Luther represented his fright as terror before holding the living God in his hands.[21]

This explanation seems straightforward enough. From the early patristic period, Catholic faith held that the sacraments were valid even if an unworthy priest administered them. Since no one can know the heart of the priest and since the sacraments are necessary for spiritual life on earth and eternal life in heaven, it would be monstrous to invalidate a sacrament because the priest was a charlatan. Innocent Christians might be deprived of God's grace.

But if the priest was unworthy, the power of the sacrament turned against him, destroying his soul and perhaps his body even as it healed those whom he served at the altar. Again the fear of death might have stalked Luther as he raised the host before the cross and pronounced those transforming words, *Hoc est enim corpus meum,* by which the miracle occurred in his hands. He may have imagined that the transformation of bread and wine might strike him dead on the spot. Later in life Luther said that such terror at the Mass was common among many priests, that they trembled and stuttered in the fear that to falter in one syllable was sin.[22]

Still we must ask the question: What terrified Luther? Erikson puts the finger on Hans, making Luther's fear the consequence of his father's presence in the congregation. We do not have to be Freudians to suppose that Erikson may have something here. It was the first time Martin had seen Hans since Martin's precipitate entry into the monastery. After the mass father and son ate together. Hans was angry. "Don't you know," Hans said, "that it is written, 'Honor thy father and mother?'" Martin told how frightened he had been by the storm that had made him vow to become a monk. Hans grumbled, "Take care that it was not an evil spirit." His father's words stuck in Martin's mind. Much later on, in his treatise denouncing monastic vows, Martin addressed a dedicatory letter to his father, recalling Hans's words, "as though God had spoken in your mouth, penetrated my most secret parts, and stayed there." He recalled with some satisfaction that his father rejoiced when he left the monastery.[23]

At the time, his fears abounded. In his later years, Luther's steadfast representation of himself was that of the devout and yearning Christian seeker, pushed out of the Catholic Church by the perfidy of popes and other malicious foes. He described his assaults of terror as though under attack by God himself. These assaults he called *Anfechtungen.* Karl Holl, one of the greatest Lutheran scholars of the twentieth century, commented that despite the terror in which the *Anfechtungen* plunged him, Luther was in a certain sense proud of them.[26] It was the pride of a veteran who had survived a battle for life and sanity.

Our only witness to this version of his life is Luther himself, his testimony given in fragments of rumination and polemic while enemies vilified him for what he had done. He had to believe that his course was forced upon him, and his feats, told perhaps "with advantages," justified him before the world and his own sensitive conscience. However exaggerated, something in these descriptions of terror commands belief. These nightmare moments fixed on the fear of death. Luther does not confess specific sins that troubled his conscience. It seems more probable that his suffering arose from a disposition, a state of mind, that he was perhaps like many others at the time prone to melancholy—we would say depression, even (as modern psychological jargon has it) "clinical" depression of a sort that might require treatment by a good paternal figure. Again we can praise Erikson for recognizing a temperament that controlled the way Luther interpreted his experience—including the experience of what he read.

Luther found a mentor—and perhaps a father figure—in Johannes von Staupitz. Staupitz became one of the great influences in Luther's life. He was a cultivated man with a wide circle of friends that included the Elector Frederick the Wise of Saxony and Albrecht Dürer, as well as other political and cultural leaders. Frederick would become Luther's prince and protector. Staupitz seems to have combined warm piety with a zest for administrative efficiency and the good administrator's eye for promising young men. He and Luther probably met shortly before Luther was ordained. As vicar general of the Augustinian order in the German lands, Staupitz had to approve the ordination, and we know that he was in Erfurt a year before Luther became a priest.[27] But only later did the older man become Luther's most important counselor. Whatever good Staupitz did worked slowly, and Luther seems to have absorbed most of it only after his discovery of justification by faith and his break with Rome. By then he had left Staupitz far behind.

4

YEARS OF SILENCE

THE period between Luther's ordination in 1507 and the outbreak of his revolt against Rome in 1517 has been called his years of silence. If the Luther of these years can be called "silent," the term means only that he was not notorious. Within his monastic community he was noticed and marked for leadership. Indeed his life became so active that some modern historians have said that the Luther of these years looks less like a monk in agony over his salvation than like a young man worked to the breaking point.[1]

He said in the table talk that he was a good monk, and we have no reason to disbelieve him. "I was a good monk, and I kept the rule of my order so strictly that I may say that if ever a monk got to heaven by his monkery, it was I. All my brothers in the monastery who knew me will bear me out. If I had kept on any longer, I should have killed myself with vigils, prayers, reading, and other work."[2] A letter he wrote to Staupitz on May 30, 1518, conveyed gratitude for the older man's wise counsel.

I remember, reverend Father, among those happy and wholesome stories of yours, by which the Lord used wonderfully to console me, that you often mentioned the word *poenitentia,* whereupon distressed by our consciences and by those torturers who with endless and intolerable precept taught nothing but what they called a method of confession, we received you as a messenger from Heaven, for penitence is not genuine save when it begins from the love of justice and of God, and this which they consider the end and consummation of repentance is rather its commencement.

Your words on this subject pierced me like the sharp arrows of the mighty, so that I began to see what the Scriptures had to say about penitence, and behold the happy result: the texts all supported and favored your doctrine, in so much that, while there had formerly been no word in the bible more bitter to me than *poenitentia* (although I zealously simulated it before God and tried to express an assumed and forced love), now no word sounds sweeter or more pleasant to me than that. For thus do the commands of God become sweet when we understand that they are not to be read in books only, but in the wounds of the sweetest Savior.[3]

This letter tells us that Luther feared the word *poenitentia,* penance, and we must ask why. On one level, we can find the answer in the theology of the *via moderna,* intended to reconcile the Augustinian teaching of human depravity with the moral requirement that human beings take some responsibility, however weak, for their own salvation. Only the rare theologian taught that anyone could do good works sufficient to deserve salvation. The prevailing theological consensus was that no human being could achieve what theologians called "condign merit"—works so good in themselves that they put God under obligation to reward them. Salvation was by grace alone. In "liberal" interpretations of free will, the most anyone could do on his own was to incline the soul toward God, and only then did God surround the desiring soul with his grace. Through the centuries most theologians, when pressed, taught that even this first inclination to repent came by God's grace.

But why did God incline some and not others? Augustine's doctrine of predestination was one answer. God does what he pleases. The human race is a mass of perdition. Everyone deserves hell. If God chooses to save some, that is his business. The damned have no just complaint; they get what they deserve. The redeemed should rejoice and be thankful; to them God is merciful.[4]

A cold logic combined with a sense of human impotence pervades this means of dealing with the omnipotent holiness of God and the depravity of the human race. It is an uncomfortable doctrine to those who want to preserve some sense of God's justice and love alongside his omnipotence. The doctrine of predestination comes and goes in the history of Christian theology like a fire rising and falling according to the vagaries of the wind. The theologians of the *via moderna* worked out a solution that mitigated the starkness of predestination. They affirmed God's omnipotence with exuberant vigor. It was the centerpiece of their system. God could do anything he willed to do. But they distinguished two powers in God. On the one hand is his absolute power, by which he can do anything he chooses. This notion of absolute power led to debates that struck some as frivolous and irreverent. Can God become incarnate in a stone or an ass? Could God command us to hate him? Sometimes these questions have the smack of a childhood conundrum: Can God make a load so heavy he cannot lift it? But they were serious questions meant to test out both the definition of omnipotence and the limits of reason. When we ask the questions, we should be brought to reverence and humility as we ponder God's mystery. Erasmus, Thomas More, and many others found them trivial and even sacrilegious.[5]

God's other power was his ordained power, the power he used to define his relations with humankind. If God could do anything he wanted, he could make an arrangement with human beings that preserved his holiness and yet gave them choice. He could make a contract with the human race, a covenant like those he made with the biblical patriarchs in the Old Testament. Under this covenant as theologians of the *via moderna* imagined it, we are supposed to do the best we can. They called it *facere quod in se est.* Our best cannot be good enough in itself to merit salvation. But it can be an inclination toward God, a desire for grace; and that desire, however faltering and weak, may be our best, to which God responds with the fullness of his power.

This idea of covenant preserved the omnipotence, mystery, and holiness of God and allowed human beings to take some responsibility for their salvation. We are weak and miserable. But if we do our best to please God, we find him gracious, and he will add to our effort the overwhelming and sufficient gift of mercy, and his grace will make our feeble effort enough. This teaching can embrace various practices and beliefs, even those beyond the limits of Christianity. Gabriel Biel (d. 1495), one of the great German theologians of the *via moderna,* held that infidels or pagans did their best when they conformed their will to reason and sought with all their hearts to be illuminated by truth, justice, and the good.[6] Such a view opened the gates of heaven to the virtuous pagans, just as it allowed Thomas More's fictional Utopians to hope for a life in paradise after death. It provided a solution to problems posed to Christian theology by the growing knowledge of Europeans about multitudes of non-Christians beyond the boundaries of Catholic Europe.

But how do we know when we have done our best? Having been drawn to confess our sins, we are supposed to be sorry for them, to experience contrition, a fervent regret that we have sinned against a holy and loving God. And we are to resolve not to commit that sin again. True contrition may be one sign that we have done our best because it involves a revulsion against ourselves for our sin. But suppose "contrition" is merely a fear of punishment? Fear of punishment and loathing for sin are not especially compatible feelings. But how can we separate the two? And is it not true that we must be sorry for the sin and not its punishment if we are to do our best? How can we ever know when we have done our best?

Here was the unanswerable question that coiled like a viper in the comfortable shoe of this agreeable theology. The expression "I did my best" is a proverbial rationale for failure. It is the torment of modern life that we have no way of knowing if we have done our best, though we may declare that we have and thus justify a mood of complacency. That uncertainty could be agony to the seeking souls of late-medieval men and women.

Theologians with an answer for everything saw uncertainty as a virtue, for it kept Christians within the extremes of presumption and despair. Either extreme could lead to the moral collapse of the individual and society. If I feel certain that I will be redeemed, I may eat, drink, and be merry and live like the devil. This is the sin of presumption. Despair also leads to licentiousness, for if I know that I will be damned, I am foolish if I do not eat, drink, and be merry while I have the opportunity. We recognize this grim view as a traditional Christian pessimism about human nature. Original sin destroys the pleasure of doing good; it makes fallen humankind equate pleasure with sin.[7] If we are not deterred by the fear of punishment, we will live like demons. Society will collapse, and anarchy will rush in. This was Thomas More's view in *Utopia,* and even Voltaire in the age of Enlightenment believed that the fears of religion helped keep the masses in line.[8]

The tension between good and evil, presumption and despair, lasted until the moment of death. Woodcuts and paintings from the late Middle Ages show the dying man, his bed surrounded by angels urging him to hope and demons tempting him to despair. In his painting *Death and the Miser,* Hieronymus Bosch shows a man sitting horror-stricken in bed as a shrouded corpse, representing death and carrying an arrow (his ancient symbol), slips through the doorway into the room. At the dying man's right side stands an angel, one hand on the man's shoulder, the other exhorting him to look up to a high window, where divine light shines from a crucifix.[9] Here on the deathbed was played out the final act in this cosmic drama, for the state of a person's soul at the moment of death determined its eternal destiny. We may die in sin or in grace through penance, Thomas More wrote:

And in whych so euer of these two states a man fynally dyeth in / in that he perpetually dwelleth, and is therby for euer eyther the chylde of god in hys chyrche of the fynall electes in heuen, or ellys the chyld of the deuyll in the chyrche of the fynall reprobatys in hell / accordyng to the word of holy wryte, yf a tre fall south or north, in what place so euer it fall there shall it remayne.[10]

The doctrine of purgatory helps, for if we have tried to do our best but not succeeded, God may punish us in purgatory during a sentence limited by time. When we have been punished enough, he will allow us into paradise. But the punishments of purgatory are severe and not certain. It is a striking fact that Luther never made much of purgatory, even in the years when he professed a formal belief in it. Something else troubled him, a punishment that was more final, more enduring than the purgative suffering of the intermediate state.

Judging from Luther's later remarks about himself in this period, we may picture a zealous young monk, caught up in the implacable routines of the monastery, following them scrupulously, trying to prove to himself that he was doing his best to please God. He said later on that he drove his confessors nearly crazy when he took the sacrament of penance and babbled out every sin he could imagine. When he left the confessional at last, the thought would strike him, "What a fine confession you just made," and he could recognize the deadly sin of pride—which had to be confessed. Back he would go to the confessional. This extreme form of scrupulosity was well known at the time, and an experienced older priest such as Staupitz would have dealt with it in the gently reassuring way that Luther recalled later with such gratitude.[11]

Again the harder question asserts itself: What exactly did Luther fear? He said he feared the judgment of God. Suddenly, says Karl Holl, in the middle of the night the *Ungeheure,* the ultimate horror, stood before him. Holl, apparently taken aback by the intensity of Luther's report of his suffering, comments that these attacks were sometimes clearly related to Luther's physical disorders. But what was the content of this fear? Holl says that it is "surprisingly simple," that Luther's fear was the First Commandment, "I am the Lord thy God; thou shalt have no other gods before me." Holl compiles impressive confirmation from Luther himself as to the importance of this mighty command to his own fear and spirituality. But Holl passes into a conventional exposition of Luther's fear, that he was so unworthy that his sins kept him from standing before God, that his sins separated him from God and made God angry with him. Luther could accept this separation neither in this life nor in hell itself. "Faith by Luther," says Holl, "peaks in the consciousness of a complete unity with God."[12]

Holl's rhetoric, almost as powerful as Luther's own, has carried the day. Yet the question remains: What exactly happens to the soul that faces this holy God and is found wanting? What is the effect, the content, of God's judgment? Holl and generations of scholars who have marched gratefully after him have failed to add another significant word that boils on Luther's lips, to his mind the definition and substance of God's wrath—death.

Luther's horror before death is a continual presence in his work—a presence seldom noticed by modern scholars, almost ignored by biographers, even by those who have seen the melancholy in him that was so common to the age. One exception is Werner Elert, who wrote of a "melody of death" resounding through Luther's work.[13] Another is Carl Stange, who in 1932 began a slender but powerful little book on Luther's fear of death with the sentence "In Luther's theology his thought on the fear of death stands at the center."[14] Roland Bainton's great biography of Luther reproduces Albrecht Dürer's *Melancolia,* the engraving of a winged woman seated amid the signs of human genius and spiritual perfection, a dejected face resting against a weary hand, motionless while above her the sands of time run out. But Bainton provides no firm connection between that image and Luther's brooding about death.[15] Heiko Oberman in his biographical study *Luther: Man between God and the Devil* does not treat Luther's thoughts about death at all until the last page when he recounts Luther's demise.[16]

Bainton's biography reproduces some images of God's judgment—the vision of Revelation, Christ seated on his throne with the lily of life emerging from his right ear, the sword of judgment from his right, and the woodcut used in Luther's New Testament of 1522 as the frontispiece for the book of Revelation, Christ in radiance with the sword of wrath coming from his mouth. So Bainton places Luther in the stream of medieval Christianity where we might presume linear and progressive connections in his thought about the four last things—first death, then judgment, then heaven or hell. The abundance of last judgments in this period—including that of Michaelangelo on the wall of the Sistine Chapel—might make us presume that imagining hell tormented Luther. But it did not. It never did. Neither in his reminiscences nor in his sermons is there anything to match the extensive descriptions of hell so common in the sermons of the time. Here, for example, is an Italian preacher berating his auditors:

Fire, fire! That is the recompense for your perversity, you hardened sinners. Fire, fire, the fires of hell! Fire in your eyes, fire in your mouth, fire in your guts, fire in your throat, fire in your nostrils, fire inside and fire outside, fire beneath and fire above, fire in every part. Ah, miserable folk! You will be like rags burning in the middle of this fire.[17]

As a man obsessed with fear of God's judgment, Luther might be expected to pass from the stories of his *Anfechtungen,* attacks of horror at his unworthiness before God, to some further account of his terror at the prospect of damnation and the fires of hell, something akin to the sermons on the physical and spiritual torments of hell represented in James Joyce's *Portrait of the Artist as a Young Man* or the occasional references to the agonies of eternal fire that we find in Thomas More or in Jonathan Edwards's famous sermon, *Sinners in the Hands of an Angry God.* But he does not.

His mentions of hell as a place of conscious suffering after death are occasional, incidental, and—given his prodigious output—astonishingly rare. In the last of a series of Latin commentaries on the Psalms published in the years 1519–1521 and dedicated to the Elector Frederick the Wise, Luther takes up the passage in Psalm 20 (Vulgate) announcing that the king, perhaps David, will hurl all his enemies into a blazing furnace and that fire will devour them. Luther applies the psalm to the victory of Christ over his enemies. Luther comments that he cannot recall any other place in the Old Testament where the damnation of the wicked is more clearly set forth—and indeed, nowhere else in the Old Testament is there any unambiguous teaching of a life after death, either one of punishment or one of reward, and the language is most probably metaphorical in this psalm. Even so Luther devotes most of his discussion to the internal effects on the wicked of the face of God and at the last in a somewhat perfunctory tone he says that the clause "And fire will devour them" tells of the fire prepared for the devil and his angels where the wicked will suffer the pangs of fire in soul and in body. Then he seems to ask a question almost of himself: "Who said everything so clearly to this prophet? No other person [in the Old Testament?] described hell so clearly."[18] Luther may have been here made to reflect on the absence of any clear teaching about a burning hell in the rest of the Hebrew Bible. But his words seem like an afterthought, and, so far as I can tell, he never returned to this psalm to reflect further on the everlasting torments that he affirms here.

He never flatly denied the existence of hell, but he comes close to doing just that in his German commentary on the book of Jonah published in 1526, where he has this to say: "What hell may be in the last day, I am not altogether sure. I do not believe it is a special place where damned souls now exist like the place painters depict and servants of the belly [evidently the begging friars] preach it." He cites Peter, Paul, and Jesus to argue that Satan is not in hell but that he is in this world and in the air, and this could not be if hell were a particular place. Hell in the Old Testament, he says, is Sheol, which he interprets as the necessity of death and the anguish of each of us before death. "Everyone carries his hell with him wherever he is, as long as he feels and fears the last necessity of death and God's wrath."[19] If hell is not a place, it must be some fearful condition in which the soul carries its terror around with it. But what happens to the soul in that condition?

He was more specific in his Latin lectures on Ecclesiastes. Ecclesiastes is pessimistic, even fatalistic, and death looms over it, the darkest of shadows in a gloomy world. Its most frequently quoted line, "Vanity of vanities, all is vanity," is the Hebrew Bible's version of Macbeth's "tale told by an idiot, full of sound and fury, signifying nothing." Luther believed that King Solomon wrote the little book, and he tried to penetrate the king's meaning in Ecclesiastes 9:10, where "Solomon" says, "Whatever work you find to do, do it with all your might, for there is neither achievement, nor planning, nor science, nor wisdom in Sheol where you are going." Sheol, or *inferno* as the Latin Vulgate has it, is a place, Luther says, where the dead feel nothing. Solomon taught, as Luther understood him, that the innumerable dead sleep all together after this life. It cannot have a physical existence; rather hell is the grave of the soul, and whatever that may be is unknown to us.[20] This seems to be his most common definition of hell—an unconsciousness akin to annihilation, although strictly speaking nothing in God's consciousness can be annihilated.

He was not always consistent. Now and then in rare flights of imagination Luther could veer off into discussions of what the sufferings of hell might be.[21] He could also fervently declare that his foes would go there. These seem to be rhetorical flourishes of the moment. In his table talk when someone brought up the doctrine of hell, he was reluctant to push it very far—never with any thumping conviction such as that expressed by popular evangelists present and past. He seems rather to touch the subject and leap away from it, something this most assertive of men feels no urge to discuss.

For example, in August 1538 he was speaking with what seems to have been extreme depression about the "miseries and calamities" of this present life. It struck him that if such griefs were to be greater and to last forever in a future life, they would be unbearable—unbearable, it seems, in a fundamental and radical sense, for to bear them was to be annihilated. Whatever he intended to say, he broke off his thought and suggested a change in subject. Let us, he said, be among those of whom it is said, "Blessed be those who mourn." There are, he said, different and unequal temptations for different people. Anyone else would have died under the temptations he had sustained, he said. An angel of Satan or even Paul himself could not bear the temptations Christ endured. In sum, he concluded, as though wandering from the subject, the major motive to melancholy is the imminent presence of death. "But this is not for us to argue about but rather to leave the matter to God and to consider those things that are revealed."[22]

On other occasions he followed a similar course, backing away from speculation about what hell might be, choosing to leave it up to God. In what seems to have been a continuation of this conversation about hell, Luther remarked that Erasmus, who had died two years earlier, had lived and died as Epicurus, without ministry and consolation. "He went into hell," Luther said.[23] The remark seems to be almost an asseveration, perhaps a hope. More interesting is his connection of Erasmus with Epicurus, not in the popular sense of the Epicurean as one who lived for carnal pleasure, but as one who denied the interest of the gods in humankind and who believed that it was a comfort, a liberation from fear, to know that nothing waited for the soul after death. Luther saw annihilation not as a promise of peace but as the truest hell, a hopelessness reaching back from the final state of the damned to be present in this world always in the consciousness of the living. Epicurus comes up frequently in Luther's works, always attacked, usually for teaching that death dissolves the soul. A commonplace of Epicurean thought held that we need not fear death because life and death never intersect. When we live, death is not present; when death is present, we are not. At death soul and body dissolve into atoms.

Luther felt surrounded all his life by unbelief in the resurrection of the dead. Preaching in the afternoon of August 11, 1532, he took his text from 1 Corinthians 15 on the resurrection of Christ. There were among the Corinthians, he said, a lot of "rotten spirits" who denied the Resurrection. They made Christian teaching about the Resurrection seem foolish. These people, he said, had their counterparts in his own time, among the peasants and burghers and especially Junker Hans among the nobility who spoke grossly and like heathen on the subject. The Resurrection was recounted in scripture together with the stories of all the witnesses who had seen Jesus afterward. But foolish people deny scripture and see it as dead letters. The spirit must convince us, he said. Without the spirit, scripture is but vain writing. One must not bring reason to such questions, for reason makes scripture foolish, subject to ridicule. In the spirit of Christ, in true faith, we must accept what scripture says and not ask the questions that human reason and wisdom raise.[24] Even scripture does not help if we do not believe it.

His view that unbelief in life after death was common is confirmed by other texts from the times.[25] Luther's older contemporary, the benign and untroubled Pietro Pomponazzi of Mantua, followed Aristotle to the conclusion that reason held that the soul perished with the body. This proposition was condemned by the Fifth Lateran Council in 1513. But in 1516 Pomponazzi published in Bologna his little treatise called *On the Immortality of the Soul,* in which one by one he demolished the rational arguments for the survival of the soul after the death of the body. The book created a scandal. In Venice the clergy pushed the city government into burning it and called

Pomponazzi a heretic.[26] Pomponazzi protected himself by saying that although reason could not prove the immortality of the soul, he nonetheless believed in immortality because the church asserted it. Pope Leo X seemed to enjoy the show; he urged on both sides and considered the matter unthreatening.

Many historians of the Renaissance and the Reformation have taken Pomponazzi literally, arguing that his complex and detailed argument was nothing more than a game and that yes, he truly believed in the immortality of the soul because he said he accepted the teachings of the church. He was a comfortable, witty man, according to records left by his contemporaries, and he knew as well as anyone that to deny the teaching of the church on immortality would have led to his own rapid mortality, most likely at a stake in a burning pyre. But Martin Pine holds that Pomponazzi believed that philosophy was the only truth and that he accepted the "death of the soul pure and simple."[27] I believe Pine has read Pomponazzi correctly.

But whereas Luther was vague on hell and seldom if ever mentioned that he feared it, his meditations on death are frequent and profoundly weighted with melancholy and foreboding. In 1534, in a series of lectures on the Psalms, he dwelled for several days on Psalm 90, with its solemn and sublime evocation of the eternity of God and the brevity of human life. He speaks of "the most serious and horrible" penalty of death Adam and Eve had brought on the world by their sin, scorns the bravado of those who claim not to fear death, and declares that this claim dissolves when confronted by the reality. He condemns those who say that we should spend our lives eating, drinking, and being merry, for there is nothing after death. But he also condemns—and scorns—theologians who speak of death as though it were a haven, a friendly refuge from the cares of this world, a doorway to peace and rest. He notes with distaste the opinion of many pagans of antiquity that we should not grieve for the dead. Death, in Luther's view, is the penalty of the wrath of God. "It often happened to me, when I was a monk," he says, "that when reading this Psalm, I had to lay it aside." He did not understand, he says, that this terror before death is a blessing from God. Those who fear death, learn to trust in God's goodness.[28] Yet we have seen that the early Luther taught the same serenity toward death that he rejects so emphatically here. When he spoke on this psalm in his first series of lectures on Psalms, in 1513–1515, he treated it in a conventional way. If his later testimony is to be believed, he may have been so frightened of death that he could not bear to consider the matter at length in his lectures.

There is more to his long discussion of this psalm, including an attack on Epicurus. But the most pervasive note is that death is the penalty of God's wrath, the judgment of God against sin, and that Christians confronted by God's wrath in death often doubt the efficacy of their prayers and feel that they are sinning by their doubts. Luther sought to calm this fear by an illustration. Adolescents, he says, are tormented by sexual desire and often believe that the desire itself is a sin. But God forgives the desire as long as they do not go from it to fornication. "So also Christians are troubled by agitations of a muttering, blaspheming, and doubting heart; but these agitations must be controlled lest they eventuate, as they do in the case of godless people, either in disdain of God or in despair."[29]

Luther's teaching of death as *penalty* is not the same as his understanding of Aristotle's teaching that the soul dies with the body. Aristotle based his teaching (as Luther understood it at least) on a philosophical understanding of human nature and of Nature itself. To some degree, Aristotle's doctrine of the soul is associated with his teachings about physics—although his thoughts on the matter are scattered through his other works. Intelligible objects in the universe have a "matter," a physical presence, and a "form" that defines them as what they are. We might say that the "matter" of a bicycle is its alloy frame, its wheels, tires, and so on. But what makes it a bicycle is a "form" that, combined with its "matter," makes it what we recognize it to be. In human nature, the soul is the "form," the body is the "matter"; form and matter cannot be separated without destroying the entity they are when combined. So when the body dies, the soul dies, too. That is the nature of human beings.

But in Luther's vision, Adam was created immortal, but God imposed death on Adam for sin, and death is carried on in the original sin that exists in procreation and the concupiscence that inevitably goes with sexual intercourse. The difference in his sense of death and Aristotle's is a personal God who governs the universe versus an impersonal *deus ex machina* that causes everything in nature to conform to rational principles. For Luther the fact that we fear death was evidence that God created us to have eternal life.[30]

Can we can tie these thoughts to Karl Holl's emphasis on Luther's attention to the First Commandment? To be terrified by death may be to doubt that God has power to raise the dead; therefore, that fear may be construed as doubt that God is God. Yet for the stricken soul, depressed and overwhelmed by the fear of death, it can be impossible to believe that anything can prevail against the final dissolution of the body. We may suppose that a young man unusually afflicted by this universal terror might come to God, pray for deliverance and salvation, and yet, with the image of the decaying human body before him, be overcome with doubt and continue to fear even in the midst of his prayers. There was always an intense physicality to Luther's conception of the world and of human being. He could not imagine how human beings could exist as pure spirits, "souls," as Christian Platonists might hold, "liberated" from the body. We can be who we are only if we may express that being in the flesh, and so if we are to exist after death, we must rise as bodies from the grave.

In his disquisitions on Psalm 90, Luther uses the word "despair" to express his own youthful attitude toward his death.[31] Despair in the face of death, as Lucretius, the great Epicurean poet, noted, was such that it often made people take their lives.[32] In these fears as in his hopes, Luther followed his mentor Paul the Apostle. Death for Paul was the mighty judgment of God against sinners. "The wages of sin is death," he wrote to Christians at Rome (Romans 6:23). "But the gift of God is eternal life through Jesus Christ our Lord." He shows no trace of a doctrine of hell or of belief in any continuing consciousness after the judgment day for those who die outside of Christ. Paul writes of Satan now and then, but Satan in his thought is the agent of death, not a Miltonian sovereign over hell, and in the final confrontation, God will destroy him.

The body for Paul was the seat of wickedness because it had fallen into sin. He was not a dualist like a Manichaean or a Cathar; that is, he did not believe that matter itself was evil. God had created the physical world, and Paul did not hold that things were evil merely because they could be apprehended by the senses. Sin, however, put a principle of opposition to God in the body, and therefore in Paul's view the sinful "body of this death" became the object of God's wrath. The corruption of the body at death showed the power of sin and the weakness of the "flesh." Paul writes as if to enter into Christ is to have a changed life, and that the major expectation of the Christian is life in the kingdom of Christ shortly to come on earth, to be inhabited by those resurrected from the dead and by those alive at the return of Christ in glory and who therefore never die.

That view continued into the Middle Ages, although the expectation of the imminent return of Christ faded, to be revived now and then by fanatical preachers and occasional rampaging mobs and kept alive in some quarters by awed speculations about the book of Revelation. Unlike Paul, some parts of the Gospels—written much later than he wrote his epistles—added the doctrine of a burning hell for the damned; it is not at all clear even from the Gospels that the damned shall burn consciously through all eternity. The bizarrely beautiful and terrifying book of Revelation, one of the last books to be accepted into the Christian canon of scripture, added considerably to the imaginative geography of that awful place. But hell did not find a firm place in Christian theology until the third century.[33]

The church developed the doctrine of hell into the familiar and repetitive elaborations of medieval iconography. But for anyone ready to fall back on scripture as the supreme authority, teachings about hell are ambiguous if not frankly uncertain. Luther's struggles in the monastery then would seem to be of a piece with the anxiety about death that led him there. He would share Paul's attitude if he equated sin, death, and damnation so that salvation was not therefore salvation from hell but redemption from the grave, that separation from God was not torment in a blazing furnace but the absence of consciousness of God or anything else. As Luther struggled to believe in God's goodness, his grace, and his power, the terror before death continued—a continuing sign to him of his unbelief. If he had faith in God, why could he not face death with calm? The terror before death became what he called in Psalm 90 a blasphemy against God, for it refused to believe that God was God.[34]

This is not a philosophical skepticism, arrived at by argument and directed by a perverse will to disbelieve. It has none of the calm of Pomponazzi's stoic acceptance of death as the proper end of humankind. Luther willed with all his heart to believe, but kept finding the fatal presence of death in front of him, and his terror before it overcame his earnest desire for faith. Once one succumbs to the terror of death, one is reduced to the assumption that the world is finally meaningless, leading to the Melancolia with her hourglass conceived by Dürer and in other guises imposed on multitudes in the sixteenth century.

But since unbelief is the damnable sin, declared to be so in the New Testament and throughout Christian tradition, the inability to believe brings a double fear—on the one hand the fear of death and, paradoxically but implacably, on the other the fear of God against whom one has unpardonably committed the sin of unbelief. Here is a dilemma of classic proportions, and I think it explains the despair of Luther's quest in the monastery.

Luther was not alone. It is more plausible to suggest that embedded in Christian faith is a double consciousness, that each time I say, "I believe," I know by the nature of the statement that the opposite statement, "I do not believe," is possible. This is not to say that one disbelieves in the supernatural; we cannot thrust the eighteenth century back into the sixteenth, although we can find abundant evidence in the sixteenth century that in some thinkers the sense of the supernatural was muted by an acquaintance with classical skepticism. We can say that in the sixteenth century, belief in a supernatural realm did not make the generality of human beings suppose that Christian doctrine comprised all the unseen world or that belief in the supernatural and belief in immortality amounted to the same thing. Luther should be seen against this perplexing and paradoxical background—which is far from forms of modern atheism that explain everything by scientific law and therefore reject the supernatural. In Luther's world the supernatural abounded. But what sort of supernatural was it? The church's efforts to control the supernatural were never completely successful. One may deconstruct medieval religious rhetoric to lay bare this effort and the never-resolved conflict between ecclesiastical supernaturalism and the superstitions of the masses. The church called on the supernatural to shore up belief in the stories of Christ's mission, his death, his resurrection, and his continuing presence among Christians. As Luther was to say in 1532, Paul brought three witnesses for the Resurrection—the testimony of scripture, the word of those who had seen the resurrected Christ, and his own divinely appointed office as apostle.[35] If, he said, the "rotten spirits" did not accept those witnesses, one could not prove the Resurrection.[36]

The medieval church created other witnesses to the Resurrection—the saints. The typical stories of the saints involved martyrs who among persecutors publicly professed their faith in Christ. The martyrs' testimony provoked fury and a sentence of death among legendary pagans, usually by bloodcurdling tortures. Despite these tortures, the martyrs died amid extravagant miracles, always in great serenity, proving that the faith they had in Christ was true, and at the moment of death having a vision of Christ receiving them into heaven. The martyrs continued to do miracles at their shrines scattered throughout Europe, affirming the miraculous story of Christ, a story that without these continuing divine interventions might descend into the dark shadow land of the myths of antiquity. The cult of martyrs, including miracles done by their relics, was an antidote to the impossibility of reaching the unique moment in history when Christ appeared, died, and rose from the dead. Supernatural events at shrines reaffirmed the authority of the church that sponsored them. These miracle tales doubtless took place within a medieval atmosphere humid with superstition, but they also fulfilled a continuing psychological need on the part of the church and of Christians to have the fundamental story proved once again. If God had done miracles in past times, he had to keep doing them.

This interpretation may explain the proliferation of such stories and the advancing fever for relics, shrines, pilgrimages, as well as an ever more emotional religious art that depicted these tales in the later Middle Ages. Faith in the triumph of Jesus over death required reaffirmation because it was threatened by unbelief of both a conscious and a subconscious sort. This perpetual threat to belief was heightened in the sixteenth century both by the incursion of classical literature among the educated and by the terror before death that seemed to become more extreme during the Renaissance, perhaps because the recovery of ancient skeptical philosophy coincided with the onset of the great plague cycle of the Black Death.

The Catholic Church has traditionally made a distinction between unformed faith, the belief in the historical truth of Christianity, and formed faith, the active faith that makes the believer respond to the historical account of the life of Jesus with love for God and other human beings in the present. In Latin the terms were *fides informis* and *fides formata caritate*—unformed faith and faith formed in love.

To have unformed faith was to accept as true the account the church gave of the life, death, resurrection, and ascent of Christ to heaven. Formed faith meant that the believer would live a virtuous and pious life of Christian love in harmony with these beliefs in an old story.[37]

When Luther developed his concept of justification by faith alone, Thomas More and other Catholic polemicists pushed this distinction between unformed faith and formed faith. They claimed that he was teaching that only belief in the *historical* truth of Christ's life, death, and resurrection could make one a Christian. No, they said. Formed faith—faith that produced works—was also necessary for salvation.[38] In Catholic thought, formed faith followed unformed faith. It may have been that good deeds done in love—or merely the ritual good deeds prescribed by the church—became proofs of faith to those who did them. Or they became a means of cultivating the sentiment of faith in the Christian who did those deeds. The habits of piety may substitute for piety itself, and in time the habits may create the piety they celebrate. If I go on pilgrimage and come to the shrine that is the object of my quest and my devotion, and if I hear the triumphant crash of music around me in the holy gloom of soaring architecture where heaven and earth seem to come together, and if I see the bones of St. James and *know* these very bones were in the presence of the Savior of the world, and if I am in the company of multitudes whose very numbers encourage me to think all this cannot be in vain, I can lift myself to belief, to the assurance that all that I am told by the church is true. The actions of piety thus create the faith that is supposed to come before piety. One could demonstrate formed faith by expressions of love for others. So giving alms—help for the poor—became a prized good work. It involved sacrifice, generosity, and spontaneity, an expression of the love for the neighbor enjoined by Christ, all testifying to a Christian character formed by faith and demonstrating itself through practical good works.

The church also provided ritual possibilities for good works—the sacraments, pilgrimages to shrines, adoration of relics, prayers, and indulgences.

At this point popular piety drifted to a considerable remove from the theology of erudite churchmen careful to preserve the notion of human corruption and incapacity before an almighty God. The late Middle Ages were awash in superstitions, including those that translated sacramental observance into magic. Supposedly one did not age while sharing the Eucharist. Highwaymen might participate in the Mass to ensure success in robbery. Fourteen churches in Europe claimed to have the head of John the Baptist, and Erasmus commented that if all the supposed pieces of the true cross were assembled, one could make a good-sized ship out of them. The shrine of St. Thomas Becket at Canterbury was covered with gold and encrusted with jewels. And if Erasmus is to be believed, preserved also were handkerchiefs on which the saint had blown his nose.[39] Erasmus scorned these superstitions as vile practices of vile multitudes. Luther came to contemn them because none helped in his quest to evade the wrath of God for his weak and sinful flesh condemned to die. For a sensitive soul like his own, the cult of relics and the other forms of cheap piety did nothing to assuage the horrible force of his *Anfechtungen*.

In his suffering before the fear of death, the wrath of God, in the monastery, Luther proved to himself that the distinction between one kind of faith and another was meaningless.[40] A man coming to God for refuge from the fear of death found the fear couching unmoved at the doorway to his heart and recognized that the unvarying presence of this terror meant that he did not sufficiently believe the scriptural accounts of the resurrection of Christ, for if he did believe, the fear would leave him. In his lectures on Romans, Luther declares, "One who believes in Christ . . . fears nothing." Having said that, he turns immediately to Deuteronomy 28:67 and its description of the unrighteous man afraid of death: "In the morning you shall say: Who will grant me evening? and at evening: Who will grant me morning? for the fearfulness of your heart wherewith you shall be terrified?"[41] That sinful man Luther scorned in these early lectures. Yet later in his lectures on Psalm 90, he tells us that he was so terrified of death that he could not read this text. What was happening here? His later lectures on Psalm 90 help us understand his early explicit rejection of his interpretation of the Catholic twofold faith. It also helps us understand his growing emphasis on the feebleness of the will, for throughout this time in the monastery he *willed* with all his might to purge the terror of death away, but to no avail.

Luther's account of his struggle in the monastery has been routinely doubted by Catholic writers. The Augustinians did not practice extreme rigors. They were not nearly as austere as the Cistercians. Henrich Denifle, a German Catholic scholar early in this century, wrote two hefty volumes intended to prove from Luther's own words that as a young monk he had been tormented by sexual desire and that he finally broke his vows out of lust. The stories of his *Anfechtungen,* thought Denifle, were hypocritical nonsense. Like Luther, Denifle was of peasant stock, and he wrote during the *Kulturkampf* Otto von Bismarck launched against the Catholic Church in the German empire cobbled together after the Franco-Prussian War. Denifle's massive attack on Luther represents a counterattack against Protestantism by way of its founder.

Even granting the somewhat fictional quality of all autobiography, we must say that the interior suffering of a melancholy or depressed personality is something that the humane routines of a moderately strict monastery cannot heal or even touch. A drawing by Lucas Cranach in 1520 shows Luther the monk, tonsured, slender if not thin, his face tense and drawn. By then he had endured furious hostility, and he had become a figure of European importance. Cranach's portrait caught from life may reflect these ordeals. But something about that earnest face fits Luther's own later accounts of his tormented soul as a monk. We have no reason to believe that Luther was not depressed. The greater problem is the source or even the object of this depression. The testimony of his own words later on is that he was afflicted with an acute and extreme fear of death that translated into Paul's sense of sin and its punishment, the fatal destiny of the body and the soul without the miraculous intervention of God.

Monastic life imposed order on the monks—if the monastery was well run, and the black cloister at Erfurt (destroyed by bombing in World War II) seemed to be exemplary. Biographers routinely provide some of the details— the day divided into seven parts, each with its ritual prayers, chanting, meditation, study, simple but ample meals, to bed not long after sundown, up at one or two in the morning after eight hours of sleep.[42] These ritual exercises came at precise times; monks were among the first people in Europe who internalized the clocks that most of us carry around with us locked up in our minds and bodies.

A year after his ordination, while he was still studying theology, his monastery received a request for a professor to serve at a new university in Wittenberg, where Staupitz was dean of theology. Wittenberg was a little town with a population of about 2,500 souls crammed together in about 400 houses, located beside the Elbe River at the fringes of nowhere. The name means "white mountain," probably for a sandy hill that by Luther's time had disappeared, leaving the land flat and featureless. It had a castle built in the form of a rectangle with a courtyard within. The castle had its own church. Wittenberg had a Franciscan monastery, an Augustinian monastery, and a city church dedicated to Mary, the mother of Jesus, and smaller churches and chapels were scattered through the town. Within the courtyard of the castle stood a small chapel served by six priests supported by an endowed foundation. These priests, called canons, conducted masses for the princely family living in the castle and for the souls of family members who had died. The city was surrounded by a wall, strengthened in Luther's times. Pictures of Wittenberg from the sixteenth and later centuries make it seem small and cramped. The castle, its church, and much of the rest of Wittenberg were severely damaged by artillery bombardment in 1760 during the Seven Years' War.[43]

Its university was the brainchild of the Elector Frederick the Wise of Saxony (1463–1525), a shy, withdrawn, and finally mysterious man whose personality and motives come down to us as a confusion of shadows.[44] Frederick was religious in a medieval way. He assumed office in 1486 in the vigor of his youth, and in 1493 made a pilgrimage to Palestine that lasted six months. That he could be away so long is tribute to the support of his people, and his part of Saxony remained stable during all his reign. He could read and write Latin, and he spoke French. (Luther's few letters to him are usually in German.) He was interested in theology, history, and law. He corresponded with some of the great figures of the day, including Albrecht Dürer and Erasmus. His court painter, Lucas Cranach the Elder, had a workshop in the town and did a prosperous business. Frederick's chapel choir was renowned throughout Germany. He developed a bureaucracy in line with changes taking place in England and in France leading to the modern bureaucratic state with its proliferating secretaries. He tried to oversee everything in his domains, including the religious life of his people. He collected relics, including a thorn from the crown of thorns that had been thrust onto the head of Christ during the Passion, four pieces of St. Augustine, four hairs of the Virgin Mary, one hair from the beard of Jesus, a piece of the burning bush that Moses saw, and thousands of similar treasures exhibited each year on November 1, the feast of All Saints.[45] The relics were the occasion of indulgences. In his old age he suffered from kidney stones and gout and hated to travel or even to move; he apparently never saw Luther except at the Diet of Worms in 1521 and never conversed with him face to face.

Saxony was divided into two principalities in the late Middle Ages; Frederick's cousin, Duke George (1471–1539), had in his territories the University of Leipzig, founded in 1409. It had been established by German professors expelled from the University of Prague, which had fallen to the heresy of John Hus. Duke George's part of Saxony was more important in every way than electoral Saxony except for the vote the elector cast that made a new emperor on the death of the old. Relations between George and Frederick were often tense, agitated by territorial disputes. Frederick seems to have wanted to put his little town on the map. Usually universities were chartered by the Pope. Frederick turned instead to Maximilian, who approved his university on July 6, 1502, and on October 18 in that year his brainchild opened its doors. He called it the "Leucorea," from the Greek words for "white" and "mountain," an indication that he expected his university to share in the enthusiasm for classical studies that percolated through Europe. Yet the university also had its patron saint—Augustine. Frederick established faculties of theology, law, and medicine and finally a faculty of arts.[46] In 1508 he sent word to the Augustinians at Erfurt that he could use a teacher or two for the liberal arts, and they sent him Luther.

Luther's introduction to university teaching was bitter. Before he took his doctorate, he had to teach Aristotle's ethics. The experience filled him with frustration and later with fury against the Greek philosopher. His later life was deeply colored by this animosity. It became an obsession with him, and later he translated his hatred of Aristotle into a hatred of Thomas Aquinas, the greatest of the scholastic theologians of the Middle Ages—whom he probably did not know well at all. His hatred of Aristotle became hatred of reason itself when reason contradicted Christian views of faith, life, and death.

The explanation of Luther's anger seems simple enough. Aristotle is the master of those who suppose the world to be orderly, no matter how chaotic it seems. Aristotle taught that human reason was the glory of humanity and that reason was adequate in itself to perceive the nature of things. The world we see, hear, taste, feel, and smell is the real world, and the impressions we gain from common sense are true. Everything in the world exists for a purpose defined by nature, and a sensible man can find the purpose by looking for it. We exist to live with others of our kind in society. Truth, virtue, and all the other moral values are open to reason, and when we know what is right, reason helps us do the right thing as long as we keep our passions under control, and virtue is its own reward. In his table talk Luther compared the ethics of Aristotle with the book of Ecclesiastes, saying that Aristotle measured the good life by the dictates of reason whereas Ecclesiastes measured it by observation of the precepts of God.[47]

Aristotle developed proofs for the existence of God that Aquinas adopted. But as we have noted, Aristotle's God was impersonal and abstract. Aristotle would never have thought of speaking to God or calling on him by name or asking him to change something about the world or assuming that God had created the cosmos in time. His naturalist philosophy was in part a rebellion against the idealism of his teacher Plato. It was also in part a rebellion against the irrational impulses of Greek antiquity that found an independent personality in every gushing spring of water and in every breath of wind. Aristotle spoke of God as first mover, the reason behind all things in that God was the intelligible principle of the cosmos. But he spoke with the detachment that one might use today to discuss the age of the moon or the composition of a gas or, as the British theoretical physicist Stephen Hawking uses "God," as a collective noun for all the mysterious forces of the universe that human beings cannot yet understand. Aristotle loved God only as one might love geometry or the orderly shining of the stars in the night sky. Although he and many commentators on his work in the sixteenth century did not believe in the natural immortality of the soul, they believed in the power of the human mind to reach limitless heights by inquiry.

Confronted with the wrath of God in death, Luther considered humankind—and above all himself—to be wretched and helpless, filled with self-destructive pride. He felt contempt for the claims of philosophy to unravel the enigma of the universe and the nature and destiny of humankind. He was awed by the mystery of things. Aristotle with his explanations of everything under the sun was to Luther a charlatan, a huckster of the intellect, offering a worthless tonic to cure a deadly sickness. We can turn this attitude over and look at it from another angle. Luther craved certainty about peace with God and victory over death. Aristotle gave him the wrong answers and showed that reason based on sensory experience led to the collapse of the very certainties Luther wanted to affirm. Luther wanted God to be a person with a name and a will, acting, speaking, giving grace, withholding grace, sustaining the world by his power and directing it till doomsday. This was the living God of the Old Testament, where Luther always felt most at home.

Aristotle's God never spoke, never listened, never comforted, never judged, never interfered with the orderly course of nature. Throughout his life when Luther condemned reason, we may find lurking under the surface of these condemnations the agony that reason created for anyone yearning for the Christian meaning that Luther wished to impose on his universe, the cosmos of the spirit where he floundered around, looking for certainty. Luther was not alone in his dislike of Aristotle. Almost two centuries earlier, the Italian poet Petrarch wrote that he had read all of Aristotle's "moral works," including the ethics. He had admired Aristotle's ability to classify and define, but reading Aristotle had been finally disappointing: "It is one thing to know, another to love; one thing to understand, another to will. He teaches what virtue is; I do not deny that. But his lesson lacks the words that sting and set afire and urge towards love of virtue and hatred of vice or, at any rate, does not have enough of such power."[48]

Luther put the case against philosophy in divine things more bluntly. Philosophy cannot give us a god who cares, he said. Metaphysics in sacred knowledge is "like a cow looking at a new gate."[49]

Luther stayed only a year in Wittenberg before returning to the cloister in Erfurt. His brief teaching experience became the doorway to his true vocation. The time in Wittenberg also brought him into prolonged conversations with Staupitz, not only dean of the faculty of theology but also childhood friend of Frederick the Wise. Luther found Staupitz a comfort in darkest tribulation and the most important influence on his young life. He often said that Staupitz comforted him when he was tempted to despair.[50]

Luther's account of Staupitz makes him look like an older man, at peace with himself, somewhat impatient with the ravenous zeal of his young colleague, often making offhand, dismissive remarks that Luther in his inner turmoil took for profound wisdom. Staupitz's portrait, done by an unknown artist about 1520, shows him looking pleasantly round, calm, wise, and comfortable. His theology was based on acceptance. David Steinmetz comments on sermons Staupitz preached on the book of Job and Job's response to successive calamities he suffered in his tribulations: "The Lord gave, and the Lord has taken away; blessed be the name of the Lord." Steinmetz says of Staupitz's views, "God is to be praised and loved for his own sake and not for the sake of his benefits."[51] He emphasized resignation and made much of the humanity of Christ, and he seems to have suffered no religious traumas of his own, though his surviving work is so small that it is difficult to judge. Like many who stand outside of deep depression, he could perhaps not fathom the depths of melancholy into which Luther sank.

Luther said as much in one of his longer outpourings of table talk. He had often been tempted by Satan's arguments, he recalled—Luther's way of describing the inner voice that tormented him with various kinds of doubt. Often Satan struck him with such force that he did not know whether God existed or not—a not unsurprising notion for one obsessed with death. His solution was to call on the name of Christ. He confessed often to Staupitz, he said, not about women—the temptation Europeans supposed monks had always and to which they yielded often—but about "real knots." Staupitz replied, "I don't understand." He tried other confessors, but they could not understand either. One day when he was sunk in depression Staupitz asked him gently, "Why are you sad?" Luther cried out in despair, "Ah, how shall I escape this?" Staupitz replied, "Ah, but you do not know that this is necessary for you; otherwise nothing good can come of you." We can imagine Staupitz speaking in a wry, genial tone. But his words went straight to Luther's heart. "He himself did not understand," Luther said, "for he supposed me to be so learned that unless I was tempted I might otherwise perish from pride. But I took him as I took Paul. A whip was laid on me lest I vaunt myself; my strength is perfected in weakness."[52]

It sounds like the experience of an acutely depressed young man for whom a casual expression of sympathy from an admired superior became the voice of God. On yet another occasion Luther recalled a conversation when he said to Staupitz, "Dear Herr Doctor, our Lord God does so horribly with people all around. How can we serve him when he smashes people so?" Staupitz replied, "My dear one, you must learn to see God in another way. If he did not do so, how could he put down the stubborn?"[53]

Staupitz also comforted him on predestination. Luther felt tormented by the possibility that he might be predestined to damnation. The later Luther believed passionately that discussion on the matter was to be avoided, for thinking about predestination could lead only to making Christ a tyrant and a devourer rather than the Savior. Staupitz told him, said Luther, that when he was tempted to argue about predestination, he should instead think about the wounds of Christ.[54] To meditate on the wounds of Christ focused attention on the human Jesus, the man of sorrows, not the horrendous judge of creation who presided over the last day. That Man of Sorrows had known death and had been raised; Luther was always to take comfort in the humanity of Jesus, his suffering, his pain, his death. If Christ had died, Luther would share his master's destiny, whatever it was.

In many respects, Staupitz comes down to us as a typical adherent to the *via moderna* that emphasized the almighty power of God amid deepening cultural perceptions of the chaos of the world. God's omnipotence became a canon of faith, something to be believed because the untidy, tragic mess of the cosmos could be explained only by an all-powerful God acting beyond any human comprehension. The righteous suffered; everything was uncertain and unstable; the mystery deepened, but God's power was thereby paradoxically affirmed. Yet how could one serve and love a God who seemed so arbitrary, so beyond the ken of human comprehension?

Staupitz told him that God must reduce the stubborn to obedience, and years later when Luther saw the confusion of some of his adversaries, he made Staupitz's words sound like the conventional wisdom of Job's comforters: God punishes the wicked. Wait long enough, and you will see God's purposes vindicated when the wicked suffer. Yet in other writings, Luther came face to face with the reality that the just suffer and the godless triumph in this life, that the good and the bad alike die. It seems possible to imagine that Staupitz's words—recalled by Luther as a shifting between present and past and a flood of mingled German and Latin—called up a deeper Christian wisdom. That is, we are humbled by our inability to understand the ways of God, and the "hard heads" who might otherwise turn the world upside down are restrained, made to pause before the unpredictability of destiny. The message of Staupitz might then have been that the very mystery of creation acts as a restraint to evil. We do not know why the world is as it is; we should step lightly and trust God, for what else can we do?

Staupitz believed in divine predestination of some to salvation and some to damnation.[55] The doctrine could be a comfort, and Luther eventually found in it a mighty consolation. We should not lose sight of this comforting quality in a hard doctrine. Christians pray the familiar Lord's Prayer, "Thy will be done, on earth as it is in heaven." We cannot explain famine, war, pestilence, and death. We cannot understand calamities that fall on us from nowhere. But God is in charge. He is sovereign. He has purposes that we cannot see. Predestination and monotheism go hand in hand, and the primary use of predestination in pastoral care has always been to comfort the afflicted. That consciousness was to come to Luther later on in great power—but not during these early days in the monastery.

The problem of predestination morally speaking is continually expressed in the Christian tradition, and Luther knew it well. If God predestines some people to "damnation," whatever damnation is, does it not mean that he is malign, that he hates humankind? Luther's habitual response to this question, especially in later life, was that God sent Christ and proved himself to be loving and kind. One should not dwell on what predestination tells us about God's nature, for such mysteries lie beyond human comprehension. We should dwell instead on the gift of Christ and see in Christ the love of God that overwhelms our doubts about God's attitude toward us.[56]

This was not a rational or systematic answer. It left open a huge, dark hole in Luther's religious consciousness. Christ in his love, his suffering, his death, and his resurrection became God's only revelation, and that revelation itself was a mystery, for Luther never presumed to understand a divine economy where the death of Christ was necessary. That death was necessary because it had happened, and God does nothing in vain. Without the revelation we have in Christ, God might seem both unfathomable and malign, and human beings reduced to victims of God's caprice. Again it is an example of how affirmations about religion sometimes summon up the implicit contrary arguments that such affirmations seek to negate. Luther could not speak of God's love without thinking of God's wrath; he could not mention Christ without thinking of the dark side of God that lay behind or beyond Christ, the place in God's being where all darkness is light.

Luther was to make more of Satan as the years went along. Heiko Oberman sees Luther's demonology as the rudder that guided his thought. For the later Luther, this view may be correct. But the preoccupation with Satan seems not to have been so intense, so personal, in the early years of Luther's life. In time Satan became for Luther a personalized expression of the powers of darkness, a brother to death. We are back to the question posed in my earlier comments on witchcraft: How can Satan have such awful power as Luther attributes to him in a world where God is sovereign? The problem is rooted in the contradictory and ambiguous doctrine of Satan as it develops in scripture, Luther's ultimate authority that was to be the source of many of his own contradictions.[57] Luther was to say that Satan was finally God's Satan, doing in a perverse way God's will.[58] It was almost to suggest that "Satan" was the name Luther gave to those powers and actions of God that take place outside of Christ, that God is in himself divided.

AETHERNA IPSE SVAE MENTIS SIMVLACHRA LVTHERVS
EXPRIMIT AT VVLTVS CERA LVCAE OCCIDVOS.

M·D·X·X

Martin Luther, 1520, the year of no return, by his friend Lucas Cranach the Elder.

ANNO 1530 AM 20 TAG IVNII IST HAUS LVTHER
D MARTINVS VATER INN GOTT
VERSCHIE DENN +ᵉ

Hans Luther, after a 1527 painting by Lucas Cranach the Elder.

Margarethe Luther, after a 1527 painting by Lucas Cranach the Elder.

Frederick the Wise, 1496, not long after his return from a pilgrimage to Palestine, by Albrecht Dürer.

Duke George of Saxony, one of Luther's bitterest foes,
from a medal cast in 1537.

A public burning of witches at Derneburg, October 1555.
Four witches were burned in Luther's Wittenberg in 1540.

Death and the Maiden, 1517, one of a number of similar paintings by Hans Baldung. Did the painting mean that one should avoid the voluptuous life because death ended it, or did it mean that one should make the most of sensual pleasures because death ended them?

Johannes von Staupitz, Luther's great father figure, who did not
follow him into the Reformation.

Pope Leo X, 1520-21, a decent human being, utterly unprepared to meet the Lutheran onslaught or to recognize the abuses in the church that made Luther possible.

Johann Eck, one of Luther's earliest and bitterest foes.
Luther called him "a glory-hungry little beast."

Desiderius Erasmus, 1523, one of the greatest scholars of his age and perhaps the man
Luther hated most, by Hans Holbein the Younger.

Martin Luther as "Junker George," December 1521, on a brief trip to Wittenberg from his hiding place in the Wartburg, by Lucas Cranach the Elder.

Thomas Müntzer, the militant prophet who thought God would intervene to give the peasants the victory in their rebellion of 1525.

The beast in the book of Revelation, shown in Luther's "September Testament" of 1522 *(above)* wearing the papal tiara. Duke George objected so vigorously to this depiction that Frederick the Wise seems to have ordered Luther to change it in the December edition *(right)*.

Katherine von Bora Luther, c. 1526, by Lucas Cranach the Elder,
who was one of the few friends invited to the wedding ceremony.

Martin Luther, 1529, attributed to Lucas Cranach the Elder.

5

ROME AND WITTENBERG

THE Augustinian cloister at Erfurt belonged to the Observant wing of the order. The Observants were strict without being as rigorous as the Carthusians. They remained within the walls of their cloister, ate together, gave up all personal property, including books, recited the ritual services together, wore the same habits so that no one could stand out from the group, and could not leave the monastic compound without the abbot's permission—which was seldom given. They were to have no dealings with women, a prohibition that made a difference between them and the Franciscans and the Dominicans, who preached in the streets, heard confessions, and, according to ribald gossip—expressed in the merry tales of Boccaccio's *Decameron*—consorted with women both in public and in private intimacy.[1] The Observants were proud of their rigor and their humility.

Staupitz, an Observant himself, wished to make all the Augustinian monasteries in Saxony Observant, bringing them under one organizational umbrella with himself as head. Seven Observant cloisters, including the one at Erfurt, objected to this amalgamation. They doubtless supposed Staupitz's plan would dilute the purity of the Observant spirit. They had kept their independence, supported by their cities, including Erfurt and Nuremberg, which took pride in them as parts of the civic order.

Staupitz journeyed to Rome twice to argue his point before the prior general of the Augustinian order, Egidius Canisius of Viterbo (1465–1532), an eminent scholar, a Platonist with a reforming spirit eager to see all the Augustinians brought to perfection. Not suprisingly, Staupitz returned from his second trip in the spring of 1510 with full authority over the Saxon cloisters.[2] The Observants objected and sent a delegation to Rome to plead their case. Though not yet thirty, Luther was chosen with a fellow monk to represent their side of the quarrel at the papal curia. He was probably not the chief spokesman but only the *socius itinerarius,* the companion on the journey, required of Augustinian monks when they traveled away from their cloisters.[3] When did they go? Three times later on Luther said that he made the trip in 1510, but it seems likely that he counted January 1511 as part of the year 1510. Churchmen commonly began the new year on March 25, the day the angel Gabriel is supposed to have appeared to the Virgin Mary to announce the birth of Christ.[4]

His later recollections of his longest journey, preserved in the table talk, present his customary self-fashioning—the devout and loyal Catholic yearning to believe what the church taught. His eventual defection seemed then all the more sincere since it was forced upon him. Rome was the holy city of the West, seat of the papacy, gathering place for relics from all the apostles, various other martyrs, the Virgin Mary, and Christ himself. Luther walked to Rome, staying at night in Augustinian monasteries along the way. When he came in sight of the city, he threw himself on the ground, crying, "Salve, sancta Roma!"[5] Here was the holy capital of Christendom whose catacombs sheltered the relics of countless thousands of early Christians, thousands said to be martyrs to their faith, the Rome where Peter and Paul lay buried and where, in the papal church of St. John Lateran, one of the many heads said to be of John the Baptist was enshrined. Luther ran about, according to his own testimony, in a frenzy to see everything he could and to reap the spiritual blessings of these thousands of relics, but his mission was a failure. Apparently he and his companion from Erfurt and perhaps two other monks from Nuremberg made their way to the procurator of the Augustinian order at the Church of S. Augustino, and asked him to open the way for them to make their case before the papal curia. He refused. Did they see Egidius Canisius? It is not certain. The monks remained fruitlessly in Rome for a month and then trudged home across the Alps.[6]

Luther's four weeks in the city gave him a lifetime of reminiscences, although he never wrote a systematic account of his journey. The trip had a quality of miracle about it, he said later, for he had seen for himself that Rome was the head of all crimes and the seat of the devil, the pope worse than the Turk in Constantinople.[7] These were retrospective comments. Nothing survives in what Luther said or wrote before the indulgences controversy of 1517 to reveal such repugnance.

But most literate visitors at the time left the holy city with unfavorable opinions. Rome was hot and malarial in summer, rainy and uncomfortable in winter, dirtier than many other Italian cities, a magnet for people seeking office and favors. Popes fled in summer to take refuge in the coolness of their nearby mountain residences or, as Julius II often did, to spend their time in pleasant surroundings elsewhere in Italy. Michelangelo was working on the ceiling of the Sistine Chapel, and Raphael was painting his great scenes in the Stanza of the Vatican when Luther arrived, but a mere visiting monk would have had no access to such wonders. Beyond the precincts of the Vatican where the foundation of St. Peter's Church was taking shape, the vast and melancholy ruins of antiquity cluttered the landscape and stood in the way of newer construction. Although scholars and artists were beginning to take interest in the recovery of statues and gold work from classical times, ruins for most Romans and others were mere ruins, commonplace and inconvenient, failing to impress visitors with the romantic nostalgia that was two centuries later to enfold the corpulent Gibbon in its beguiling embrace. Most great works of classical art were in private hands and not on display for *hoi polloi.*

Luther took in the sights with an eye to moralizing. He saw the Pantheon, the best preserved of all the Roman pagan temples, long since converted to a church. He said much later that images of all the gods except Christ had been placed there once, that all the world was against Christ and yet that Christ remained. The sentiment is conventional—akin to the typical iconography of monks cloistered among the ruined columns of ancient Rome, sign that Christian humility had triumphed over the grandeur of empire.[8] The great churches of the city—St. John Lateran, S. Croce, S. Maria Maggiore, S. Prassede, and others—stood amid fields, vineyards, ruins, and gardens. Rome had a population of only about 40,000. Pope Julius II had been away for months when Luther arrived. He had taken with him the life of the place, for without the pope Rome had nothing to sustain it. It rained nearly every day Luther was in the city, and the air was unseasonably warm. He slept near an open window, developed splitting headaches, and thought he was cured by eating a pomegranate.[9]

He disliked the Italians, and they returned the favor. He was startled to see how they relieved themselves in the streets without any embarrassment. Some things do not change through the centuries. If one wanted to protect one's house from a flood of urine, one put up a picture of St. Sebastian or St. Anthony on one's walls. Luther mentioned that these saints were especially revered by the Italians but did not say that they were saints called on with special urgency in time of plague. Perhaps the notion was that they sent plague on anyone who urinated in their faces. He noted that the Italians did not drink as much as the Germans and that they scorned the Germans as louts.[10]

The city swarmed with prostitutes, some living in elegant palaces, frequented by members of the high clergy and treated as grandes dames. They came from everywhere in western Europe. Homosexuality among the clergy was common, acknowledged by many Italians, its practice by clergy high and low later condemned by Pope Leo X. Pope Julius II was said to suffer from syphilis, the new disease from the New World, and he was accused by some close to him of homosexuality. The streets were made dangerous by beggars, many of them vagabond monks crowding into the city to live off the tourist traffic.[11]

Luther was most shocked by the irreligion of Rome. Italian priests, he said, scorned those who believed all the scripture, a declaration that seems to indicate the progress of skepticism that may have come from humanistic study of classical texts. Many, he said, did not believe in a life after death.[12] Nor did they take seriously the daily religious rituals that provided most with their living. Luther claimed that he went to mass time and again and was shocked by the irreverence of officiating priests—which made him want to vomit. "Bread thou art, and bread thou shalt remain," they chanted in Latin at the altar, mocking the doctrine of transubstantiation and by extension the tradition of the church and the notion of the unseen world. Roman priests like Christian priests everywhere at the time were paid to say masses for the souls of the dead. They sped along, Luther said, as if doing a trick, and when he took his turn at the altar to say his own mass, slowly in the pious German way, the next priest in line hissed, "Get on with it! Get on!"[13] Rome was, in his later estimate, a whore of a city.[14] He may have picked up in Rome some of the gossip he passed on later—for example, that Pope Alexander VI had committed incest with his daughter, Lucretia Borgia.[15] Luther said he would not take huge sums of money for his journey, because it had brought him face to face with the reality of Rome's wickedness. On his visit, he said in his old age, he looked the pope in the face, caught up in the glory of the pope's town. (He did not actually see the pope.) Now, he said, obviously chortling, he looked the pope in the rectum.[16] It was his ultimate expression of contempt.

Some of his tales have the smack of atrocity stories told from time immemorial about barbarous enemies. What did the command "Touch me not," spoken by Jesus to Mary Magdalene in the Garden after the Resurrection, mean when it was spoken of the pope? Like everything else in the Bible, said Luther, the text was perverted by the church. It now meant that no one could criticize the pope. Luther told of two preachers in Rome whom he dutifully named, Louis the Minorite and Egidius an Augustinian, who preached against the vile morals of the papacy. They were found dead early one morning with their tongues cut out and (in one version of the table talk) stuck into their rectums.[17]

Whatever the pope and his clergy might be, the treasures of Christendom were there, radiating blessings. In the pilgrim mode, Luther toured the relics, seeking indulgences to cleanse away penalties for his past sins and, should he die immediately on adoring them, to make certain that he would rise directly to heaven without enduring the pains of purgatory. Ever afterward even when he had given up his devotion to such things, he commented on the thousands of martyrs buried at Rome, but by the time he recalled them in his later life, Rome was for him an enduring emblem of the ephemeral quality of human achievement, a sign that human history was in flux, that cities such as Athens, Rome, Carthage, and Jerusalem rose, paraded their little while on the human stage, and fell into desolation. The prophets of God declare, said he, that all great cities fall into ashes and sand.[18] It was a familiar Christian theme, repeated over the centuries as testimony that God had his secret purposes, that nothing on a fallen earth endured, and it came enshrouded in melancholy.[19]

He climbed the holy stairway, preserved in the Lateran Palace, that legend said had been attached to Pilate's dwelling in Jerusalem and that, therefore, had been ascended by the scourged and silent Christ while the mobs in the street cried for his death. It had been supposedly miraculously saved from destruction and transported intact from Jerusalem to Rome, and pilgrims dutifully repeated the ascent of Jesus—as indeed they still do. They climbed step by step on their knees, saying a Pater Noster at every step, and at the end they received a plenary indulgence, meaning that they were purged of the necessity of satisfaction for all the sins they had ever committed. He hoped to release the soul of his grandfather from purgatory. At the top Luther stood up and asked himself a question: "Who can know if it is so?"[20]

Luther told this story in a chaotic and rambling sermon of November 1545 only a few months before he died. His question seems to have reverberated in his heart throughout his life. "We are by nature," he said in the same sermon, "inclined to doubt."[21]

He went to Rome hoping to find a sacred place. Once there, he found unbelief abounding even in the clergy and moreover unbelief of the kind that struck him to the heart—a denial of the life after death, full-blown Epicureanism in the heart of Christendom. His early encounter with such manifest unbelief seems to have been shattering—although when he looked back it at from the vantage point of two and three decades afterward, he found much of it and himself amusing as we are likely to find those youthful crises that, when we have them, may threaten to crush us.[22]

As for the legal case that took Luther to Rome, the general of the Augustinians, Egidius Canisius of Viterbo, stood by Staupitz. The controversy dragged on. Egidius tried to patch things up. An agreement was worked out. Luther, back at Erfurt now, went over to Staupitz's side, and the pope gave Staupitz authority to carry out reforms throughout the province.[23] Opposition remained, and Staupitz had to compromise.[24] The continuing quarrel seems to have been one reason Luther left Erfurt yet again. His fellow monks there—holding out against Staupitz—probably resented his defection. Staupitz on the other hand would have welcomed a voluble and intelligent young monk to his side, especially one formerly in opposition who had now seen the light. By the spring of 1512 Luther was back in Wittenberg, under Staupitz's wing, while his journey to Rome and its disappointments were fresh in his mind and heart and just at a moment when Staupitz could use him. That Staupitz used him immediately may be inferred by Luther's journey to Cologne in May to take part in an assembly of the Augustinian leadership.[25]

Small and isolated though it was, Wittenberg would be Luther's stage. He was to dominate the faculty there as he might not have done at Erfurt. Somewhat like Isaac Newton in seventeenth-century Cambridge, Luther lacked colleagues strong enough or even well enough educated to set his agenda for him; he was free to find his own way. At Erfurt as a young "Bachelor of the Bible," he had lectured on the *Sentences* of Peter the Lombard, the comprehensive textbook of medieval theology, the first great synthesis of the scholastic tradition. Luther was to reject it. In Wittenberg he took up the more congenial task of lecturing on the Bible, taking over this duty from Staupitz. The older man was now pressed by so many administrative duties that in 1512 he gave up his professorship altogether.[26] Luther seems to have been his hand-picked successor.[27]

Luther took his doctorate on October 19, 1512, paying a fee of fifty gulden supplied to him by the Elector Frederick the Wise on condition that he continue as professor of biblical studies for the rest of his life. Here was tenure akin to indenture. He acknowledged receipt of the money and the terms by which he accepted it in a note to the prior of the Augustinian cloister, Wenzeslaus Link. It is the first document in German that we have from his hand.[28]

He said much later that he resisted the doctorate. Staupitz, he said, led him out under a tree still standing in 1540 when Luther told the story. He said he gave Staupitz fifteen reasons why he should not take the degree. One was that he was sure he would soon die. Staupitz told him that if that was so, God had plenty of work for doctors to do in heaven. "With a joke he refuted me," Luther said.[29] He was young for the doctorate, although his case was not uncommon. His younger contemporary and later rival Johann Eck of Ingolstadt was born three years before Luther and received his doctorate in 1510.[30]

But it was ordinarily a degree reserved for those who had studied and written for as much as twenty years.[31] Some later Catholic foes, contemporary and modern, have maintained that the doctorate was a quid pro quo, a reward from Staupitz for Luther's adhesion in the matter of administrative reform among the German Augustinians.[32] A grain of truth may lie amid the dirt here, but it was probably not so simple. Staupitz recognized a good man when he saw one. Luther had clearly not done his own cause any harm by coming over to Staupitz's side in the matter of reform. Just as he later represented himself as being pushed against his will into heresy, he spoke of his doctorate as something forced on him by Staupitz.[33]

As a doctor of theology, he not only had to teach classes but was expected to publish on theological matters. His title was "Doctor in Biblia," which might be translated "teacher in the Bible," and it was this biblical aspect of his doctorate that always influenced him most. As Jaroslav Pelikan has said, when Luther took up his polemics it was because polemics were required if biblical teaching was to be done correctly.[34] The lethal assumption here is that there is one correct way of teaching the Bible.

Staupitz also made him official preacher to the Augustinian monks in Wittenberg, a task that required him to preach sometimes several times a week. The job fitted naturally into his role as biblical expositor. One of his perquisites was a little office in the tower that rose over the gate of the monastery.[35] To become a doctor, Luther had to swear to stay true to the teachings of the Catholic Church. The insignia for the doctorate included a symbol of an open and a closed book.[36] The book symbolized was the Bible, and the open book signified the revelation that God had made known to everyone; the closed book signified those secrets that God kept to himself. This was an image that Luther was to hold dear for the rest of his life.

The controversy between the Observants and the Conventuals refused to die. Staupitz never overcame the opposition of the recalcitrant monasteries. Luther's old colleagues at Erfurt bitterly resented his doctorate, in part because by the custom of the time he was supposed to take the degree at the place where he had begun his university studies. Johannes Nathin, Staupitz's bitter foe at Erfurt and one of Luther's teachers, claimed that Luther had violated an oath to Erfurt by taking his doctorate at Wittenberg, and he and others accused Luther of holding Erfurt in contempt. The implication may have been that if Luther had applied to Erfurt for his doctorate, he would not have received it. About February 1514 Luther wrote to Erfurt, denying that he had taken such an oath, calling Nathin a liar and defending himself, and asking his old colleagues at Erfurt to avoid bitterness and to remain silent. His pleas were in vain. The controversy continued. Another more or less conciliatory letter from Luther in August failed to heal the wounds.[37]

In Gotha in early May 1515, a little over two years before Luther wrote his Ninety-five Theses, the chapter of the Augustinians met for a conference, and Luther preached a blistering sermon perhaps directed against those Observants who still resisted Staupitz's decisions and by the bye attacked his doctorate.[38] This unpleasant exercise has not been translated or reprinted so far as I know, and it is seldom mentioned. Yet it serves as a marker for Luther's personality. It came before his notoriety and much before he had occupied the theological positions he was later to defend against the papacy. It is Luther at his vehement and rhetorical worst or best, depending on one's tastes, and it shows the uncompromising soul that in time would go barreling into revolt from Rome.[39]

In the sermon Luther assumes the role of the obedient monk, offended by the self-righteousness of colleagues. He assaults the "detractors" as those who have arrogated to themselves the glories of sainthood. Their pride in their piety is only vanity. He parades before them biblical examples of rebellious persons who resisted the divinely constituted authority and paid the price of their lives. The tongue of the dissident is the tongue of Satan, he says, inspired by demonic impulses and not by the Holy Spirit. The dissidents seek fame among men, but what does that mean? Every dissident, he says, acts like the pig that seeks with its teeth and its nose the stink and the asshole of men—whose shit stinks worse than that of any other animal. Their pride amounts to saying something like this: "Look how much I have shat!" For which the proper reply is, "Then eat it." We are creatures with guts filled with shit whose spots show on the outside. We are destined to die, bound to stink as corpses and to be devoured by worms as though we were to be eaten by dogs in a field. The sinful man is like a corpse already. What is the remedy for this condition? No man can tame his tongue without the help of God. The dissidents can only pray for mercy.

Here are some of Luther's great impulses—a reverence for authority, a vehement spirit, a cutting wit, a special talent for obscenity, and, most important, a contempt for sinful human nature, coupled with a profound and melancholy awareness of the body's fate at death. The most striking element here (for those of us not inclined to elaborate Freudian interpretations) is Luther's low estimate of human nature. That is what his obscenity is all about. He looks around for the most revolting thing he can find as a metaphor for the body and comes up with feces. The prophet Isaiah came up with the metaphor "For all our righteousness is as a menstrual cloth" (64:6). At heart here is a renunciation of any glory from a world made up of such dirty creatures as we humans are. Despite the boldness of his statement, Luther is not far removed from the attitude of the "good" Emperor Marcus Aurelius in the second century, who did the best he could for the part of the human race entrusted to his care but who scorned them nevertheless, hated court life, and felt no pleasure in the glories other human beings heaped upon him. Luther is here radical in a Western tradition of pessimism, and he expresses his pessimism with unusual force, but he is scarcely alone in these sentiments.

We can feel in this sermon the horror of death that I believe to be his ultimate fear. The image of the human body as a stinking corpse is powerful, perhaps more so than the almost stylized images of rotting corpses and half-devoured skeletons so abundant in the visual iconography of the age. Against this fragile, ephemeral quality of human being, Luther holds out the mercy of God. That mercy is humankind's only hope. The sermon is filled with hyperbole. The "detractors" are evidently those who disparage authority, that is, those who have resisted Staupitz and perhaps by extension the doctorate Luther has taken at his urging. Such people, he thunders, are guilty of a "mystical murder" worse than murder of the body. They are guilty of moral sin. They are rapists, devils, infidels. He quotes the Bible so readily that we can imagine the biblical text piled up in his mind like water behind a dike, ready to pour though the slightest opening. Yet it is not a scholarly use of the Bible, with attention to the context of the passages that Luther hurls at his foes. It is rather the Bible as a repository of rhetorical stones to throw at any enemy.

Clearly by 1515 Luther was a firm ally of Staupitz, rising in the restricted world of the Augustinian order, a vigorous young preacher whose charismatic authority and rhetorical power were recognized by men older than he. He was a man with a future. Perhaps more important, he was a man with a firm hand on the wheel of his own theology. He had not yet arrived at his most mature affirmations, but already his was a theology of human helplessness, divine omnipotence, and redemption by grace alone.

6

THE LECTURES ON
THE PSALMS

L
UTHER chose to lecture on the Psalms, beginning on August 16, 1513, working through them over two years. It was natural for a monastic professor, teaching young monks, to choose this book of the Bible, since the devotions spread across the hours of the day in the monastery were guided by readings from Psalms. The Psalms suited Luther's mood, for they run the scale of religious feeling from exuberant faith, hope, and joy through despair, vengeance, and complaints against God that suppose doubt—not atheism but doubt about the God of the covenant, the God who made promises to Israel that he seemed to have broken, God silent to his people, removed from their anguish and indifferent to their fate.

We do not know who wrote most of the Psalms, although the most joyous ones are attributed to King David. We do know that many were written after the Babylonians had conquered and sacked Jerusalem in 587 B.C.E., and bored out the eyes of King Zedekiah after making him watch while they slaughtered his sons. The Babylonians destroyed the temple of Solomon and dispersed many Jews throughout the Babylonian empire. Many Psalms reflect shock and even despair before these events.

Luther followed the scholastic mode of lecturing. He made notes in the margins and between the lines of a 1513 edition of Jerome's Latin Bible, the standard biblical translation of the Middle Ages and of Catholic piety. In a notebook he wrote down clarifications of data contained in the Psalms.[1] This notebook has been preserved, though not without gaps, and it shows Luther's tiny, meticulous hand filling page after page. It has been almost standard for interpreters of Luther to read these commentaries with one question in mind: What do they show about Luther's later understanding of his great motto, "Justification by Faith"? A great debate in recent years has centered upon the exact time that Luther arrived at his doctrine of justification. Scholars have sought in these lectures nuggets of information to help them decide whether he had arrived at his discovery before 1517, when he opened the Reformation with his Ninety-five Theses. His comments in his preface to the 1545 edition of his Latin works indicate that he remembered the "Reformation awareness" as coming afterward.[2]

Throughout these lectures runs a profound and sublime abnegation. Luther almost sings of human depravity and helplessness so that he may magnify the power and holiness of God. His praise of humility may indicate a deeper anxiety, a personal terror that he could not express to students in public lectures. We should expect as much if we take seriously his later comment that he could hardly bear to read Psalm 90 in this period. But it may also be that he had been through anguish in his early days as a monk, that he continued in that condition through his meeting with Staupitz, and that the requirement that he lecture took away the leisure that abject melancholy requires. He later fulminated against leisure and solitude; it appears that lecturing had a medicinal effect on his soul.

He delivered his lectures in Latin—the proper language for instruction throughout Europe. We can imagine young Dr. Martin perched on a chair at six in the morning behind a high lectern, reading slowly from his notes so students could take down his words accurately. Books were expensive. It was traditional for students to copy lectures so that they might have, in effect, a book of their own when the course was done. Luther's lecture room would have been cool in summer but frigid in winter, and he and his students took for granted the necessity of wrapping themselves in layers of wool and to wearing something on their heads. German portraits of the time, including some of Luther, show men wearing caps that covered the ears and otherwise bundled up to an extent that would seem suffocating to us. This abundance of clothing was customary defense against the raw winds blowing down on that part of Germany from the great Eurasian plain.

Luther approached the Psalms with the conventional medieval attitude. Despite clear differences in tone and time of writing of the sixty-six books that make up the Bible (not counting various apocryphal books often included in scripture though not judged canonical), and despite evident contradictions in the text, Christian orthodoxy held that the Bible was a unified document, inspired throughout by God, testifying from first to last to the drama of creation, the Fall, redemption, and the promise of future renovation, every word inspired by the Holy Spirit. Medieval medical practitioners used the classical Greek writer Galen to guide them in dissections of cadavers although Galen had dissected only animals. The medieval surgeons saw in the body what Galen said was there—even when it was not. Medieval exegetes, dissecting scripture, found unity and infallibility because the church said they were there.

A fundamental assumption of the Bible is that a personal creator God is omnipresent in the universe, an intimate and active observer and preserver of the human drama, but that he remains hidden most of the time and shows himself by specific acts of revelation, often accompanied by miracles that confirm the presence of divinity. His eye is on the sparrow, but neither the sparrow nor human beings can see him. No one discovers the God of Christians and Jews by philosophical speculation. God is holy, so elevated above humankind that no one can see him and live. The radical difference between God and humankind lies at the base of Luther's continual practice of setting up dualisms and paradoxes throughout these lectures and in all his theology. Gerhard Ebeling has remarked that Luther continually posed opposites—the spirit and the letter, the visible and the invisible, the intelligible and the sensible, the hidden and the manifest, the higher and the lower, the divine and the human, the celestial and the earthly, the eternal and the temporal, the future and the present. In particular he set in opposition the visible and invisible, the revealed and the hidden.[3] It was to be a lifelong habit, and it indicates a sense of God's "otherness" that had profound meaning to Luther's Reformation. We are here; God is *there*. We are this; God is *that*.

Always these opposites cohered simultaneously in each other. Luther had no Neoplatonic impulse to see the soul as a divine spark imprisoned in a body, striving to work free of the physical to return to its true element. God is not like human beings; we have in us no divinity, and we do not rise to God by a process of purging ourselves from the physical while we fill ourselves with the divine. Throughout these lectures God and humankind appear as opposites, although God is all around us all the time, and only God's grace can lift us to enduring life. Christ is the major actor in the drama of redemption, God incarnate, full of awesome mystery and yet deeply and comfortingly human. Like most Christian commentators in the Middle Ages, Luther saw the Psalms as songs that spoke of Christ, that sometimes spoke the very words of Christ far in advance of his appearance on earth. In this approach he followed the New Testament itself, which often put words from the Psalms into the mouth of Christ or used lines from the Psalms as examples of prophecies that Christ had fulfilled.

Because God often spoke in arcane language, to be understood only by believers, Luther in these early lectures followed the standard medieval heuristic of interpreting scripture under four categories. He read the literal sense of the text, found an allegorical sense, then a moral sense, and finally a prophetic sense expressing the ultimate hopes of Christians for redemption and paradise. These categories offered various approaches to the sacred text so that various messages God had hidden there might be revealed. Unless one is fully committed to scripture as message from a personal God, we may agree with most biblical scholars that these four categories were developed by exegetes to impose a unity on the Bible that does not exist in the texts themselves. Luther could not see it that way.

The literal sense embraced the exact meaning of the words. At its clearest, the literal sense was the historical sense, the record of what was said and done in divine pronouncements recorded in scripture. Yet often the literal sense seemed to contradict Christian teachings in the Gospels. Paul taught in 2 Corinthians 3:6 that scripture had a literal sense and a spiritual sense—allowing him to interpret Old Testament passages as applying to Christ, and to reject many divine commands, such as circumcision and the sabbath, in the old law, commands that by the literal sense of the words seem to apply for eternity. So Christians early began interpreting many difficult or inconvenient texts in both Old and New Testaments allegorically or "spiritually" to take away the literal sting. The allegorical sense thereby became a common device for changing questionable stories into acceptable moral and doctrinal precepts and examples. St. Jerome, one of the most hostile of the early church fathers to women, had been disturbed at the biblical story of how old King David's councillors put a young woman named Abishag in his bed while he lay dying.[4] When David—known for his lustful ways—did not respond, his councillors knew that he was sick unto death and made plans for the succession. Jerome held that the entire incident was an allegory, that Abishag symbolized a wisdom that an old man could clutch to his bosom without fear of committing sin.[5]

Not only did allegory allow commentators to reinterpret morally questionable tales from the Bible; it also allowed them to reinterpret stories that could not be taken literally. That had been one of the purposes of allegory in the ancient world when Greek rationalists could not take literally the stories in the epics of Homer. It allowed Christians not only to "save" the Old Testament for Christianity, but also to interpret all of scripture in keeping with the norms of Greek and Roman philosophy.[6]

Other modes of interpretation performed yet other services. The moral or tropological interpretation was intended to inspire Christians to righteous actions, and the prophetic, the hopeful, or anagogical, interpretation told them how the text illuminated Christian hope—the life after death toward which they as pilgrims marched with toil and pain through this world.

Luther's use of this method can be seen readily enough by his commentary on Psalm 84 in the Vulgate (renumbered Psalm 85 in modern editions). This psalm was written just before or perhaps just after the return of the Israelites from exile in Babylon after the Persians under the tolerant Cyrus overthrew the Babylonian empire and allowed subject peoples—including the Jews—to go home. Luther makes it a cry to God from the true Christian. He provides an expanded reading of the text, giving it a Christian interpretation at every word. *Deus tu conversus vivificabis nos,* says verse 7. "If you turn toward us, God, you will give us life." But Luther inserts after *conversus* the words *per incarnationem,* "by the incarnation." He then provides a Christian sentiment in the text: God in the incarnation turns to humanity and, by that identification with human life, redeems it.[7] Therefore even when Luther provides what seems to him to be a "literal" interpretation, his work is not literal exegesis at all. To him the Psalms speak "literally" the words of Christ. The words inspired his pious imagination to find signs of Christ in every line. The implications of this attitude were profound and far-reaching, although they are usually passed over as if they are so well understood that they need no mention. Scripture became his great authority, but he never approached scripture without bringing to it far more than the text—as we all do when we read any text if modern critical literary theory is to be taken seriously. He interpreted the text according to his intimate experience with God, and therefore he felt less bound by the literal meaning than any modern deconstructionist can imagine. He could scarcely have understood our view of what he was doing, for he and centuries of Christian commentators before him had so internalized his method that they could not see how foreign it was to a truly literal interpretation.

Luther adds a gloss that apparently came out of his expanded reading of the text. The law, he says, operated against the righteousness of the flesh, but grace can stand before the righteousness of God that leaves the law behind. That is, the law given by God in the Old Testament humbles the proud spirit of humankind because no one can obey it. The law is the measure of our inadequacy. God's grace protects us from God's righteousness, which condemns us in our human sinfulness. God's righteousness is so far above ours that without grace we cannot stand at all. We have here the root paradox that we shall find throughout Luther's thought—which he took from the apostle Paul rather than Jesus. God tells us in the law to be good so we may discover how incapable we are of any goodness; God's commands cannot be obeyed; they are not intended to be obeyed.

Following the gloss, we have *scholae,* further lessons to be drawn from the text. These *scholae* make up the bulk of the lectures. They include general and specific observations. As Ebeling has said, they show that Luther found all theology present in every text of scripture.[8] This psalm is attributed to the sons of Kore, and almost always, says Luther, such psalms pertain by the spirit of prophecy to the incarnation of Christ rather than to his passion. The psalms of David speak, on the other hand, of the Passion and the Resurrection. That the sons of Kore are numerous signifies the people of the new faith, spiritually born of a virgin as was Christ, from water and the Holy Spirit. And what does it mean when the psalmist asks God to let glory dwell in *terra nostra,* "our land" (85:9)? "Our land" may mean the Virgin Mary because she received Christ, or it may it may refer to all human beings, or it may simply refer to the land as land. Just as Eve sinned and brought the curse on all humankind and the earth itself, so the Virgin Mary was blessed by God and conveyed that blessing to humankind and, ultimately, to the whole earth.[9]

These lessons go on in the same vein. Luther frequently quotes other parts of the Bible to enlarge a point, persuaded always that the Psalms were words of Christ or words about Christ. Now and then his version of a text is slightly at odds with the text of the Vulgate, an indication that he may have quoted from memory, his ideas and recollections of scriptural texts coming in a flood. He often cites Hebrew words from the Old Testament without demonstrating easy familiarity with the language. He quotes readily from earlier commentators on the Psalms, both the fathers of the church and medieval writers.

He finds in the Psalms themes that became patterns for his life. One is the humility that is the proper attitude of humankind in facing God. We can claim no merit in ourselves, and the true Christian acknowledges worthlessness at every turn. Another is the mystery of God, how far beyond human reason his works are. We can come to God only through Christ, Luther says, but many in New Testament times turned away and refused to be converted because Christ was a man and God was therefore hidden in him.[10] So it is that many are still turned away, scandalized by the truth. Conversion comes to both the mind and the will, but the mind turns away because of ignorance and too much wisdom, and the will turns away because of sensuality or else because of the mind, which in Jews and heretics creates pride. Luther's sense throughout these lectures is that true Christians are a minority, that God is hidden even when he reveals himself, and that things are not what they seem.

He provides a brief moral interpretation, saying that all the consolation and the glory of the saints lies in truth.[11] But he never suggests that truth lies in doing good works to seek consolation and glory. He does not here exhort anyone to be good; he exhorts his students to know themselves, to understand that they can claim no goodness at all.

He is clearer about the definition of truth in his anagogical interpretation, the explanation that draws the mind up to contemplate the hope of heaven and the fear of hell. When the bad shall be damned to hell, their punishments will represent truth, for it has always been promised to them.[12] In this damnation, wrath and truth will meet, just as mercy and truth shall meet in the salvation of the blessed. Truth also means that the Christian cannot expect peace in this world.[13] Peace will come only above, in heaven with Christ. Here Luther passes from a consideration of Christ to his ceaseless and almost monotonous theme, pronounced rather like an incantation—our righteousness comes from Christ and not from ourselves. To say that there is no peace for the Christian in this world seems to run contrary to the Augustinian sense, expressed most powerfully in the *Confessions* that once having encountered God, the Christian knows God's peace forever more—a peace that at times seems less sure than Augustine makes it out, since he, like Luther, was involved in controversy all his life. But at any rate, this comment—which might easily be passed over—by Luther that the Christian never finds peace in this world looks like a foundation stone for his theology of the cross, developed later as part of his Reformation awareness.

To look into these early lectures on the Psalms is much like putting a dipper into a barrel of water. Wherever one dips, the taste is the same. We find Luther's grand themes in most of them. They are not yet fully developed; they are not passionately expressed. But they will be with him in one way or another all his life. He demonstrates throughout a spirit of vociferous humility. The hypocrite says, "Righteousness lifts me from earth up to heaven."[14] But who can dare claim that his righteousness can lift him to merit the blessing of God? Righteousness comes only from God, by his grace, by his mercy, by his truth. Luther does not spell out a doctrine of predestination here, but it is implicit and sometimes close to the surface. God controls our intellect and our will if we have grace.[15] If, as Luther says, all our righteousness comes from God, it follows that we cannot claim even credit for our desire to be among the elect. Luther has not quite arrived at stating the matter so baldly in these lectures, but he never suggests that the Christian deserves credit for anything, not even the faint motion of the will toward God, the inclination to the good that gave to the *via moderna* and to moralists such as Erasmus an opportunity to combine God's grace with some small choice on the part of human beings. In sacred and divine things, he says, we must first hear rather than see, first believe then understand, first be captured rather than capture, first learn rather than teach.[16] No one can come to Christ unless the Father draw him—a sentiment from the Gospel of John but one that Luther uses in these lectures in a predestinarian sense.[17]

One can scarcely avoid comparing the Luther of these pages with the Neoplatonists of the Italian Renaissance, with their confidence in the power of the human soul to climb to God by its own strength. Giovanni Pico della Mirandola, the prodigy of learning who died in 1494 at the age of thirty-one, thought human beings had it in themselves whether to rise or sink in the order of being.

Should you see a man devoted to his appetites crawling along the ground, you see then a plant and not a man. And should you see a man enchanted by the vain forms of imagery, as if by the spells of Calypso, and seduced through these empty wiles into becoming slave to his own senses, you see then a brute and not a man. If, however, you see a philosopher, judging and considering all things according to the rule of reason, you see then a creature worthy of veneration—for he is a creature of heaven and not of earth. And if, finally, you see a pure knower—one who, unmindful of the body, is wholly withdrawn into the inner chambers of the mind—here, indeed, is one who is creature of neither heaven nor earth, but some higher divinity draped about in human flesh.[18]

Pico's goal was to make human beings recognize their natural dignity and the power of their free will. His serenity lay in his conviction that the soul was of a substance akin to God himself and therefore capable of free choice. He lived his convictions, and for many—including Thomas More in England—he was a model of the ascetic Christian whose will triumphed over the flesh and its base desires. Luther was of another persuasion. Already in these lectures on the Psalms the locus of all righteousness is Christ. Even if we are redeemed, the power of sin remains in us in this life, and we can give God only our praise, our thanksgiving, and our confession—all without any expectation that we shall achieve a final peace with God in this world. Christ is the center of all his thought. It is striking in these lectures that Luther's sense of the institutional church seems muted, and that he ignores or passes over with a bare mention various ritual practices of Christian worship.

Neither does he consider the oral tradition, a common feature of Catholic thought in the later Middle Ages. The oral tradition was a device to reconcile the contradictions between orthodox belief and practices on one side and the text of scripture on the other. Christ was said to have passed on orally to his disciples certain doctrines that he did not wish to be written down at the time, and these were preserved in the church as a tradition whose authority equaled that of scripture. Many of these tenets of the oral tradition went beyond scripture, and some of them contradicted scripture altogether. For example, scripture shows little of the veneration accorded to the Virgin Mary by Catholic tradition. Luther mentions her now and then with respect, praising her for her role in bringing Christ into the world. But there is no hint here of the mariolatry by which Christ is seen as the high, commanding judge of heaven and earth while Mary becomes the merciful mother who begs her wrathful son for mercy and welcomes suppliants to her sheltering embrace. Nor does he show any veneration of Mary Queen of Heaven as she became in so much of the Catholic iconography of the later Middle Ages. Nor does he speak of any other saints at any length or with any particular emphasis about their authority with God—this silence on his part at a time when the legends of saints were fulsome staples of popular preaching and reading.

On the contrary, Christ grants grace, mercy, and truth, and God outside Christ is the wrathful judge. It is hard to reconcile these early texts with Luther's later declarations that he had almost ruined his health by trying to please God through extreme asceticism unless we place his ascetic period early in his days as a monk—before these lectures on the Psalms. They show a man already convinced that he can do nothing to please God except humble himself before God's power and his own inadequacy.

Yet it is worth repeating that we find hints that here Luther denied the possibility of complete inner tranquillity for the Christian. He seems to have realized already that monastic asceticism would not calm his fears. Although he may have forsaken tormented vigils and rigorous devotions, he understood that the battle between faith and doubt was to go on all his life. It is striking to read in his lectures on Psalm 90 in 1534 that he was at one time so terrified by death that he could scarcely look at this psalm—when we find Psalm 90 treated dispassionately in these early lectures, with scarcely any equation of the wrath of God with death, an equation that dominates his later interpretation. Rather the wrath of God is here turned on heretics, the Jews, and the "wicked."[19] We find in him at this time an ability to distance himself in lectures from his inner turmoil. He and his text become more mysterious as we reflect on the outer man and the inner soul later revealed.

Luther here gives no sign that he finds the institutional Catholic Church, with its councils, bishops, doctors, and popes, a repository of infallible tradition. Johann Eck, Thomas More, and other, later foes of Luther defined truth as what the institutional church taught. Because Christian truth could not be discovered by philosophy, because it depended on historical events infallibly transmitted by a divinely ordained church, Catholic apologists argued passionately that no one could forsake the institutional church and remain united to Christ. Without an infallible church, no one could tell the difference between truth and error.

These Catholic foes of Luther believed that human beings required infallible Christian teachings—certified by an infallible church—to know how to respond to those divine precepts. This preoccupation did not begin with the Reformation, for in the fierce debate throughout the fifteenth century over the relative authority of popes against councils, the church as repository of final divine truth was continually affirmed by both sides. The great question was the locus of authority within the church. Did one look to the pronouncements of popes or to the decrees of councils? From the Council of Constance a century before, this issue lay beneath the surface of most discussions of church polity and, by extension, of authority within the church. Luther in these lectures bypassed this debate. He did not think of truth in that way. He later commented in the preface to his Latin works that he was once "the most insane papist . . . so drunk, even so submerged in the teachings of popes" that he would have been willing to murder anyone who detracted so much as a syllable from papal teaching.[20] But this declaration would seem to be a hyperbole of late life that finds no glimmer of reflection in these lectures on the Psalms.

He recognizes that the church had foes—Jews and heretics. His attacks on the Jews in these lectures are frequent, sharp, and vicious, although the word "Jews" seems to be an abstraction. There seems to be no evidence that he knew any Jews at this time. The Jews, he says, misread scripture. Their view of the law, as he interprets it, is opposite to his view of human nature, for the Jews believe that we have some capacity to choose to do good and that keeping the law sanctifies us. He thinks the Jews are proud of their ability to keep the law, that pride keeps them from true repentance, and that in consequence God has destroyed their places of worship, scattered them across the world, and made their fall an example of his wrath.[21]

Here again we meet his dichotomy between the spirit and the letter. His conception of truth is not an intellectual matter; it is a divine force, associated intimately in his mind, and in his syntax, with *iustitia* or righteousness. There was, he wrote, truth in the world, that is, the vengeance and the wrath of God. But there was no mercy in such worldly truth. There was, to be sure, a false mercy—that is, a weak and soft attitude toward sin—but there was no truth in such "mercy." Real truth and mercy are possible only in Christ. Christ combined truth, which includes our sinful nature, and the mercy of

God, true mercy. True mercy means that we are whipped in Christ as he was whipped, that we suffer for our sins in the suffering of Christ.[22]

Truth is not merely a collection of true statements about doctrines; it is rather a true understanding of the nature of God and humankind, an understanding that has little to do with assent to complex creeds but that has everything to do with a deep personal awareness of one's miserable and unworthy state in the presence of the Almighty and the power and the mystery of God over against frail humanity. This is a dynamic, living truth and not a static, factual truth, yet the truth implies some factual information, namely the historical life of Christ and his continuing presence as Savior.

This kind of truth has an affinity with Luther's argument that righteous works can come only after one is made righteous by the grace of God. The affinity lies in a way of knowing. Since Luther throughout equates "truth" with a dynamic, true knowledge of ourselves and God, our human nature and his, we cannot persuade others of this truth by discursive reasoning. One understands the truth only by experiencing it. The rationale for the truth reminds us of the common experience of trying to tell others of some great event that has transformed our lives or terrified us or brought us suddenly to the edge of mystical brightness—a vision of beauty, for example, or a sudden epiphany. No matter how rational our discourse, we cannot convey the power of that event unless we speak to someone already deeply and personally acquainted with that event—and then, paradoxically enough, we need scarcely speak at all. An enduring anomaly resides here—and it was to lie at the core of the Protestant Reformation. We cannot persuade those who do not agree with us about religion unless they are already willing to be persuaded or unless we can frame words to encapsulate their previous religious experience. To think otherwise is to believe that we can explain to a colorblind person the meaning of the word "green."

It is just at this point that Luther's early affection for German mysticism enters—including his enthusiasm, eventually cooled, for a warmhearted little work called the German Theology, which he edited in 1516, his first publication.[23] The mystical approach to religion involves a direct communion with God, an experience, sometimes an ecstasy that may be so strong that the soul or the mind, the entire consciousness of the self, becomes totally absorbed in the divine. But more often the mystical experience is milder, like the experience John Wesley described as his conversion when, on stopping by a chapel in Aldersgate on the evening of May 24, 1738, he felt his heart "strangely warmed" as he heard a reading of Luther's preface to the book of Romans. Luther was not one for ecstasy, although sometimes his language tips in that direction. His warmhearted mysticism was akin to a phenomenon found in many religions. The Quaker theologian Rufus Jones said it was the most universal religious experience. William James spoke of mystical moments as "states of insight into depths of truth unplumbed by the discursive intellect. They are illuminations, revelations, full of significance and importance, all inarticulate though they remain; and as a rule they carry with them a curious sense of authority for aftertime."[24]

The mystic seeking direct union with God may detour around Christ altogether to lose the self in the abyss of divine being. Luther could never do that. The nearest he comes to ecstasy is his awareness that God through Christ has forgiven him for his sins, but, as David Steinmetz has shown, that is not the same thing as climbing the ladder of contemplation until the world falls away and the self is absorbed in the divine presence.[25]

This view of truth—dynamic as it is—meant that Luther could never convey it to others by argument. It is almost purely rhetorical truth in that it may only be declared with energy, metaphor, analogy, eloquence, passion so that the person who perceives the declaration must assume that behind it stands a reality. The declaration has value to the person who makes it; while one declares the truth, one believes it—as a great actor may believe in performance the part he is playing on the stage. Yet if one chooses to reject that reality, all the passion and eloquence in the world cannot by themselves create belief in it. So it was that four years before he wrote his Ninety-five Theses, Luther was launched on a course that would determine his direction in the Reformation once he had decided to embark upon it.

We must see also that this dynamic truth has an unhistorical quality. Or it may be that it is raised above history. At least it begins without much attention to history. Any modern scholar of the Psalms or any other book of the Bible feels compelled to elucidate the historical context that produced the text and finds every text shaped by the historical moment when it was written and edited. The modern scholar also acknowledges that texts are unstable and that even simple questions about them come laden with ambiguities. This sort of historical interpretation lay at the heart of the biblical work of Erasmus that came to fruition in his *Novum Instrumentum,* the edition of the Greek New Testament published first in 1516. The modern biblical scholar can still profit from Erasmus's notes affixed to his New Testament text and discovers that his intuitions about style are remarkable for their plausibility and understanding. Modern biblical scholars agree with most of them.

In Luther's exegesis, the modern scholar learns much about Luther but little about a historical or philological approach to the Bible. Luther calls on history when it suits his purposes. But he is not interested in history as an encompassing, interconnected web of smaller truths, each joined to the whole and changing the whole whenever one is reinterpreted or called in question, as when an anachronism is discovered. For Luther the scriptural text is always powerfully *present,* a voice speaking *now,* a past that lives in God as Augustine found all time embraced in the divine being. It is one reason he emphasizes always the spoken *word* as the most powerful manifestation of God, for the spoken word is always present, always here and now, always addressed from a living being to living beings. The word was to become Luther's most powerful metaphor of God himself.[26]

Luther uses commentaries from the past to buttress his thoughts about the text. But he does not pile up bibliographical references in the traditional habit of scholars convinced that the one who has the most footnotes when he dies wins. Even in 1513, three years before he was to begin discarding the fourfold interpretation, Luther approached the text directly, giving considerable attention to Augustine, Nicholas of Lyra, Faber Staupelensis, and others who had written about scripture—yet never falling into unrestrained praise of a holy church that by its infallible tradition certified these commentators who mean so much to him. They are certified by the agreement of his heart with their fundamental message. Armed with his dynamic truth, Luther cultivates the Psalms like a confident farmer knowing his way in his own field. He expects Christ to be in every text, and he finds him.

What drove him? Luther's rhetoric is on the surface one of certainty. He has no room for scholarly ambiguity, for doubt, for tolerant consideration of views not his own. In a deconstructionist age, schooled to look beneath the surface of texts and to tease out deeper patterns of meaning, we must ask some questions about that firm rhetoric—especially since he later confessed terrors not visible in these early lectures. At the least we must suggest some motives to help explain Luther's theology.

One of Luther's fundamental assumptions in these lectures is usually overlooked. That is, lectures have to be given; the truth of Christ that comes dynamically from God has to be *taught.* But doesn't he teach that scripture is clear in itself? Here might seem to be a major contradiction. We may resolve it by saying that Luther addresses an audience that, he assumes, will have had his experience and will understand it, will clarify it by his words. He seems to work not to persuade but to define, to cause his students to recognize truth when they possess it already themselves and perhaps when they perceive it in others. To use again the metaphor of color, Luther may be said to be naming the colors we perceive and showing relations among them to tell us something we may perceive for ourselves the moment he speaks.

Luther's teaching is of a Christ who is his own validation. We cannot know

Christ's truth by the reasoning of the mind, especially not by the discursive logic of Aristotle. The mind turns away from Christ, Luther writes, both by ignorance and by too much wisdom.[27] That is, the mind is ignorant of the nature of itself and the nature of Christ, and it is too puffed up by worldly knowledge. Here are the first bubbles of the hatred of human reason and wisdom that will come to full boil in his mighty debate with Erasmus.

Yet without depending on reason, what could Luther accomplish? When later he thundered against his multitudes of opponents, he knew on his own assumptions that he could never convince them. We may therefore have at least one explanation for his habit of hyperbole, his fury, and his verbosity. Unable to trust reason, he would depend on a divine rhetoric, a Word given him like a hammer by the Holy Spirit, who alone could convey truth. The Word would do everything; Luther could only preach it, and if auditors did not receive it, well, they were damned. The hammer does not reason; it drives nails to hold things together, or else it shatters old forms.

The dangers of reason can be lethal. That is a message of these lectures, and Luther preached it all his life. His is a common Christian attitude—that we do not reason our way up to Christ step by step but rather that we accept historical event as present reality, a God alive in the past and ready now to receive his people. The scholastic response was that yes, we cannot discover revelation by reason, but once revelation comes, we can by reason find it plausible and consistent. Luther would have none of that. He thunders this message in these lectures. When the mind tries to think its way to God, it arrives at a dead end. By reasoning, we contradict faith. Here is a paradox about a man who continually extolled the paradoxes of God: Luther rejects reason in divine matters, but he cannot dismiss it; he must talk ceaselessly about it as if it were a viper coiled at his door, striking continually, a snake he cannot finally kill.

Throughout these lectures on the Psalms runs another theme, complementary to Luther's hatred of Aristotle. The revelation of God through Christ is mysterious, paradoxical, a hidden truth, a divine act not recognized by the world at large. This view is a commonplace in the New Testament, where the adherents to a small and struggling sect in the Roman Empire must take into account not only persecutors who might do them bodily harm but, more daunting by far, the indifference or scorn of multitudes who reject the gospel. Mystery early became a trope of Christian rhetoric, but with the victory of Christianity over the pagan world, the clarity of the gospel was assumed by those in authority to be well enough established to grant assurance to everyone who sought it. The medieval notion had been that souls perished not because the gospel was mysterious but because they failed to live up to what they knew. The Luther of these lectures felt compelled to emphasize the mystery of God and the necessity of submission to a mystery beyond human fathoming. We may judge from his later comments that part of that mystery was that those who sought God suffered agonies in their quest. Luther's spiritual world at this time seems shadowed and dark, but one scarcely sees the darkness in these lectures. The explanation may be simple: perhaps like most lecturers Luther developed a persona for his students and hid the struggles within his own heart behind it.

The triumph of Christian faith in the sixteenth century was to be celebrated by Baroque art, by huge churches and huge statues and huge paintings, by the spectacle of the church as visible empire led by an imperial pope and served by a clergy in glorious ritual splendor. Luther argues that the truth of God is interior, dynamic, alive, and writes as if great numbers of people are under the judgment of God because they do not have spiritual life. He also writes as if they do not care. The mystery of God goes on around them and leaves them inert. Luther judges his times to be Christian only in name. In his commentary on Psalm 91 in the Vulgate, he says that it is no wonder that foolish men *(insapientes)* do not understand, for the acts and counsels of God are hidden under a veil, and in them God works altogether contrary to appearances.[28] Within the spirit and the interior of a Christian man, God works glory, salvation, riches, beauty, and inestimable virtue. So God hides himself from these fools—whom he has allowed to be fools.

The mystery of Christ provided an *exemplum* for the larger mystery of the world. Wherever Luther looked, he found no visible evidence that God worked in society. Disorder and hypocrisy ruled. Those who claimed to be Christians were not. Did that mean that God does not rule in his creation? Could it possibly mean that God does not exist? Luther may have known Thomas Aquinas well enough to know that Aquinas held that one could not finally prove the creation of the world out of nothing; for it is not necessary that the creating cause precede its effect by duration, that is, that God must have existed before he called creation into existence. One may know that God exists *before* his creation only by revelation. (Aristotle had not taught creation out of nothing.) And one could not know one's final end, heaven or hell, by reason. William of Occam, the great progenitor of nominalist philosophy, held that even the existence of God could be scarcely more than a probability if one stood on reason alone.[29]

We have had several occasions already to see that Luther and others of his time had many examples of unrestrained reason in the great writers of classical antiquity. The flood of classical literature introduced into Europe by the humanists bore on its crest the skepticism of the Greek and Roman world.

Epicurus, Lucian, Lucretius, Cicero, Pliny, and Seneca the Younger, virtuous as they may have been, provided no hope for life after death and in fact regarded the hope for immortality as childish and unworthy of mature men.

Twentieth-century historians, many of them clergymen, many born during the losing battle for faith in the nineteenth century, have taken the curious position that the humanists of the Renaissance could absorb the pagan classics without being threatened by pagan skepticism. They declare that the Christian humanist enterprise tamed classical skepticism and brought it safely into Christianity in much the same way that Aquinas supposedly baptized Aristotle, pulled his rational teeth, and made him acceptable to Christian faith. I wonder. Erasmus found such virtue in the pagans that he made a character in one of his colloquies say, "I can hardly help exclaiming, 'Saint Socrates, pray for us!'"[30] Were these scholars so set in Christian faith that it did not occur to them to suppose that classical philosophy might offer not something complementary to Christian faith but something contradictory?

Modern thinkers often forget that for the humanists of the Renaissance to espouse publicly whatever doubts might be raised by classical texts would have been to destroy the possibility of humanism and most likely to ensure the destruction of the humanists themselves by a society unwilling to tolerate any overt expressions of religious skepticism. Yet surely to imagine such bizarre selectivity in the Christian apprehension of pagan literature is to suppose a dullness of mind that contradicts the admiration for the humanists generally prevalent among modern scholars or at least those in the English- and German-speaking worlds. As a modern Shakespearean critic has said of the supposition that atheism in the sixteenth century was "unthinkable," "It was not so much 'unthinkable' as unprintable. Yet any modern historian or critic who forgets about the censors becomes their accomplice, some four centuries too late to receive his pieces of silver."[31] The French have never been so eager to deny that skepticism of a fundamental religious sort existed in the fifteenth and sixteenth centuries. From an early time French scholars accepted Jacob Burckhardt's thesis that the Renaissance was pagan and that it was a threat to Christian belief and practice. Indeed Lucien Febvre's great affirmation of the sixteenth century as an age of faith was directed against a mass of French scholarship that made much of the skepticism of the age.

Luther always praised the role of reason in daily life, but he renounced reason about divine things, with its reliance on the empirical world that could not produce any certainty about God. It was part of his renunciation of the world of appearances, and he succeeded in making God more mysterious than ever. Surely it took a mysterious God to preside over a world like this; Luther would submit to the mystery rather than accept the alternative, which was that God did not exist or perhaps, as the classical Epicureans taught, that God or the gods took no interest in the mortal world. His work on the Psalms provides a quasi-mystical vocabulary, words that exalt the mystery and bring the soul to wondrous contemplation of it.

Christ himself was mystery—a man and yet the incarnation of God. Flesh and blood, Christ said, could never see that Christ is God.[32] No one could tell how this incarnation came to be, and when theologians tried to draw up formulae to describe it, they always fell into more conflict. Luther's solution was to speak of Christ as a living presence and rhetorically to make that presence felt, not to discuss the incarnation in any discursive way.

In Luther's works, the world partakes of the mystery of God that enshrouds the incarnation even as the incarnation becomes our revelation. To know anything of God is to know that the mystery exists and that deep within it God lives and works. It exists in scripture itself. Luther said that some read scripture merely by the letter, much as they might read one of the classical histories, and they do not receive the power of God that lies under the literal understanding of the words. So do the Jews and the heretics. So in fact, he implies, do most Christians. Faith is a mystery, and the mystery is everywhere that faith is.

Scriptural interpretation for Luther becomes a mystical experience in that it appeals to our inner relations with God immediately perceived. It is not an ecstatic experience but rather a warm, living communion with God in the act of interpreting the sacred text. His lectures are an act of worship. His exegesis creates a model of theology in which we may place all we want to believe about God or all that we think we ought to believe about God. Yet despite all the effort to expel it, reason remains with its implacable questions, its pale and melancholy light seeping into the holy gloom of the divine presence. How do we keep reason at bay and God with us? The question runs through his life's work like a flood, and it may not be too much to say that his answers to it gave him his theology and his significance in history.

7

THE LECTURES ON ROMANS, GALATIANS, AND HEBREWS

ROUND Easter of 1515 Luther began lecturing on the book of Romans and continued until early September of the next year, taking altogether three semesters to complete the book. This commentary is interesting, not least for its having reposed in Luther's original manuscript in the Royal Library in Berlin, catalogued and sometimes on display in exhibitions while scholars in the rest of the world presumed that it had been lost.[1]

In his autobiographical commentary in the preface to his Latin works in 1545, Luther said that his great discovery of the meaning of justification by faith came in his pondering of Romans 1:17, "For the justice of God is revealed from faith to faith in that it is written, for the just shall live by faith."[2] Yet in his consideration of this text in his lectures on Romans, Luther passes over it in a few sentences without giving it any special emphasis and does not read into it any stupendous enlightenment.[3] Nor in the entire set of lectures does he make any special point of the place of faith in acquiring the righteousness that justifies.[4] When his Latin works were published in 1545 Luther did not include these lectures on Romans. And with good reason, as we shall see. In them he had not yet arrived at his discovery of the "gospel."

The Epistle to the Romans is the longest of Paul's letters. In it he addressed the church at Rome that he had not yet visited. Writing to Christians in the teeming and polyglot capital of the empire, he set out to explain why the world at large did not know the Christian God and how it was that a God who revealed himself first to the Jews had now revealed himself in Jesus, whom so many Jews had rejected because they remained devoted to the Jewish law. On one level Romans is an explanation of the relation of Jewish law to the gospel, but in larger measure the epistle is a rationale for monotheism in a world of competing religions.

Throughout these lectures, Luther continues on the same course he has pursued during his lectures on the Psalms. The truly righteous recognize that sin always dwells in them; those who assume that they are righteous are hypocrites. "For inasmuch as the saints are always aware of their sin and implore God for the merciful gift of his righteousness, they are for this reason also always reckoned righteous by God."[5] "Faith" seems largely to be belief that God is correct in declaring the depravity of humankind. The depravity of humankind and the futility of good works are proved in the inevitable death that comes to all, the "good" and the bad. No good works can prevail against the ultimate penalty for sin, a corpse that rots and dissolves into dust.

In his consideration of the sixth chapter of Romans, Luther touches on the resurrection of Christ and the victory of the resurrection over death. He makes two points that seem to confirm that much of the energy in his quest for God came from his fear of death, not torments in hell. In quoting Augustine's *On the Trinity*, Luther proposes a twofold resurrection—the physical resurrection of Christ in historic time and the resurrection of Christ in the sacrament of the Eucharist when Christians partake of the body of Christ. He then considers death:

Hence, we must note that there is a double death, namely, the eternal or, better, temporal one, and the eternal one. Temporal death is the separation of body and soul. But this death is a symbol and a parable; it is, in comparison with eternal death (which is spiritual), like a picture of death painted on a wall. This is why the Scripture very frequently calls it sleep, rest, or slumber.

Also eternal death is twofold. One is a very great good. It is the death of sin and the death of death, by which the soul is freed and separated from sin and the body from corruption, and the soul is united by grace and glory with the living God. This is death in the strict and proper sense of the word (for in every other death some mixture of life remains, but not in this one, in which there is nothing but life itself: eternal life). It is only this death that the conditions of death fit absolutely and perfectly; whatever dies in it, and in it alone, vanishes entirely into everlasting nothingness, and nothing ever returns from it (indeed, it inflicts death also upon eternal death). Thus sin dies, and also the sinner when he is justified, for sin does not ever return, as the apostle says here:

"Christ dies no more," etc. . . . . This is the principal theme of the Scripture. For God arranged to take away through Christ whatever the devil brought in through Adam, and the devil brought in sin and death. Therefore, God brought about the death of death and the sin of sin, the prison of prison and the captivity . . .

The other death is eternal and a very great evil. It is the death of the damned. Here it is not sin and the sinner that die, while man is saved, but it is man that dies, while sin lives and remains forever. This is the "very evil death of the wicked."[6]

This is not an easy passage to interpret, but we can draw some inferences from it. At no point in these lectures does Luther mention hell. He says specifically that the penalty of sin is death.[7] This is, to be sure, the opinion of his source, the apostle Paul. But the church had gone beyond Paul's views to an elaborate theological vision of hell's torments in darkness and fire, and therefore it is noteworthy that Luther feels no compulsion to follow the church's traditional lead. His interpretation of death in this passage is that it is "everlasting nothingness." True, he is speaking here of the sins of the justified person that vanish away forever, but he does so by saying that this "everlasting nothingness" is what death means. In the "death of the damned . . . it is man that dies, while sin lives and remains forever."

If Luther felt profoundly the fear of hell, it would seem logical that here he should make an excursus, that he should say something about hell as the "second death," that he should comment on it in some way. But he remains silent. He seems to be saying that the damned depart into everlasting nothingness and that "sin lives and remains forever" in that the penalty of sin abides in that nothingness. Sin is everlasting because the nothingness is everlasting—an idea akin to the Augustinian idea that sin is itself depravation, that it is nonbeing. If sin is nonbeing, the penalty for sin could also be nonbeing, that is, annihilation. We find no echo here of the dreary pages and pages that Augustine spends in *The City of God* arguing against Origen's teaching that the fires of hell are not literal. For Augustine hell is an everlasting furnace, the damned eternally conscious of the flames, and he is triumphantly and vindictively pleased to contemplate its torments.

Later in his lectures on Romans Luther shapes an idea of the fear of death that he will change in later meditations on the subject. "We should not dread sin and death, not because they are not to be feared and abhorred at all but for the purpose of putting the prudence of the flesh in its place by recognizing it for what it is, so that the weak may get busy freeing themselves from this horror and by the grace of God receive the hope of security. Those weak in this way are still under the law, unless they longingly turn their face toward grace that they may be torn away from their troubles."[8] But remember: The later Luther said frankly that the fear of death always remains with us, and his own expressions of the horror of death continued until close to the end of his days. In this passage he seems to be aspiring to the notion that one might be freed from the fear of death in this life, that the fear of death indicates a person still under the "law," and that grace would allow the Christian to face death without terror.

Luther also strongly emphasizes predestination in these lectures, presenting the doctrine in an uncompromising way. He admits that we do not understand it; we shall understand it only in the future. He rejects any effort to mitigate predestination, for to assume that anything other than God's will guides the cosmos is to suggest that everything turns by chance. Predestination is how God lets us know "that he saves us not by our merits but by sheer election and his immutable will." He mocks the notion of some in the *via moderna* that we may come to God by a faint spark from our will and that in response God will rush to us to make up for our inability to do more than wish to be saved. This was the issue in his later battle with Erasmus. God wills to save only the elect. Inevitably the question rises: How can I be sure that I am among the elect? The greatest assurance lies in Luther's comment, "For whoever hates sin is already outside sin and belongs to the elect." His conclusion follows naturally: "Therefore, if a man is overwhelmed by the fear that he is not one of the elect or if he is assailed and troubled about his election, let him give thanks for such fear and let him rejoice over his anxiety." Anxiety seems to be a sign of election, for those not elect are not anxious about their destiny. He was to hold this view all his life. Yet the mystery of election remains troubling, and Luther deals with it in one of the traditional mystical ways. The highest form of faith is held by those willing to go to hell if that is God's pleasure. These are Christians so completely cleansed of their own will, their own wisdom of the flesh, that they surrender entirely to God.[9]

These ruminations might offer several consolations to a youngish man under an emotional stress focused on the power of God to save him from death. Why should he suffer so much while others seem indifferent to the matters that create his anguish? This is one of the most persistent and tormenting questions of the clinically depressed. Luther's answer is that those who do not suffer are not among the elect. Why are such multitudes not among the elect? Because God in his hidden counsel wills it to be so as part of the mystery of predestination. Then why is one tormented? Because one is among the elect, and the torment signifies grace. Why does God act this way? We do not know, but the life of Christ, especially the agony of the cross, shows us that this is how God works with humankind. In identifying with the historical Jesus as he did all his life, Luther makes suffering bearable as part of the hidden plan of God for redemption.

Already in his lectures on Romans, he prepares his way to stand alone or seemingly alone against centuries of Catholic tradition. His Catholic foes would argue passionately that God promised to keep the church from all error and that he confirmed his presence with the church with miracles. In his lectures on Romans, Luther sets up within himself a defense for a war that has not yet begun. God's ways cannot be found out by examination of empirical proofs like history or miracles. God wraps himself in mystery and reveals himself only to the elect, whose election is certified by torments such as those Luther himself has experienced. Jean Wirth has observed that with his lectures on the book of Romans, Luther establishes the principle of justification by faith, but its consequences are not worked out.[10]

It is also evident in these lectures that the elect comprised only a small number of the whole body of professing Christians—a view not uncommon among theologians throughout the Middle Ages and in the New Testament itself. Luther attacks the "utterly stupid and incompetent persons whom bishops and abbots nowadays promote everywhere to the pulpit." He attacks "spiritual rulers" who excommunicate those who protest the wealth of the church. He goes so far as to attack the "liberties" of the church whereby clergymen were free from taxation or any other control by the secular authorities.[11] He was in effect criticizing the consequences of the controversy over investitures that racked the eleventh century, and to this topic he would return with a vengeance. More important, he was already beginning to see the institutional Catholic Church as a den of thieves. This was not an uncommon vision among the devout aroused to righteous indignation at the corruptions in the church. Luther did not attack the sacraments or hold that the essence of the institutional church was evil. Nor is there any sign that he rejected the monastic vows of chastity and obedience. Our bodies, he said, are ordered for honorable marriage or still more honorable chastity, and the cure for lust is prayer.[12] All this is compatible with the monastic life, and the lectures on Romans remain well within the perimeters of orthodoxy.

In October 1516, beginning another school year, Luther began his lectures on Galatians, Paul's fierce letter to the church at Galatia in Asia Minor condemning the apostle Peter for seeking to force gentile Christians to observe the Jewish law. Galatians is a short letter that can easily be read in a half hour. Luther lectured on it until mid-March of 1517.[13] He came back to it time and again in later life. Once in his table talk he called it his "Katy von Bora," the name of his wife.[14]

It is a vehement little epistle, addressed to Christians divided by competing visions of the relation of Christianity to Judaism. Apparently Judaizers, including Peter, wanted adult gentile converts to Christianity to be circumcised. Paul thundered against Peter's views. The way to God was by faith in Christ, not by forcing gentiles into Jewish observances. Luther defends Paul's vehemence. If anyone tells empty lies, Luther says, someone taken up by the zeal of God is obligated to refute him.[15]

The Jews, says Luther, did not believe in Christ because they demanded visible signs. The gentiles did not believe because they thought the Resurrection was foolishness. The true Christian does not demand signs (that is, miracles) or a demonstration but follows the persuasion of the faithful— which is not to understand but to believe.[16] The controversy over the law was, Luther says, not precisely about the works of the law. Paul's point was not that all the works commanded under the Jewish law were forbidden but that none was to be forced on Christians. Circumcision was not to be required of any new convert. Paul did not say that he did not want people to be circumcised or that it was not lawful to be circumcised but rather that circumcision was not necessary.[17] Jews could do as they wanted, but they could not compel others. Luther was already defining a view of scripture and tradition that would set him apart from later rigorists—Ulrich Zwingli in Zurich, for example—who would hold that if something was not commanded or obviously practiced in the New Testament, it should be forbidden. Luther held that to tear down all the structures of piety in church tradition and to leave scripture alone would disrupt practices that helped Christians toward reverence. He was no primitive Christian demanding an impossible recreation of the remote past in the present.

Throughout these lectures he became more emphatic in his view that all sins could be reduced to unbelief. The presumptuous imagine that they will be saved because they are good and do not need Christ; those who despair suppose that Christ cannot save them from their terrible sins.[18] The thought here is striking—although it is such a commonplace of Christian preaching that we sometimes miss Luther's point. What makes anyone despair of salvation? The common modern view is that some people feel themselves too guilty of sin to be within the reach of God's forgiveness. God becomes in that way of looking at things a sort of cartoon psychiatrist who, on hearing the confessions of a patient, rises in outrage and orders the patient from the room. Doubtless many people in all ages are overcome by feelings of worthlessness and despair, and it seems plausible enough to suppose that some feel so guilty that they think no pardon is possible. Yet it is also possible that the despair comes from a sense of loneliness in an empty universe, an inability to believe that a God can exist who can love the helpless and raise the hopeless from the grave. The attitude is complicated—more complicated than preachers in all the centuries may make it. To the devout, even the expression of such thoughts may seem blasphemous, as if to give them utterance is to speak (or write) the unspeakable.

Often I imagine that here is the real gulf fixed between the centuries, that in our age we are eager to express our religious doubts, which include doubts about God's existence. Only those rare souls who have both intellectual acquaintance with a world hostile to their religion and personal yearning to believe literally in the God of the Bible, a God inspiring both terror and desire, can know what it is to be afraid to utter explicitly the doubts that consume them. Neither Luther nor most modern scholars of his work can be called "fundamentalists" in the twentieth-century understanding of that term. But it may be that those who have experienced modern fundamentalism, with its paradoxical psychology and its confusion of assertion, rationalization, mystical love, and abject fear, can best understand Luther's mind and heart, and his quest for God. Typical fundamentalists assert a roaring confidence in their faith—and run colleges and seminaries where not a breath of dissent is allowed lest their faith be swept away. Luther's mentality was not far distant from that.

Throughout the lectures on Galatians, Luther seems to have heightened the mystery of faith and its superiority over reason. The existence of mystery is testimony to the difficulty of faith, and Luther seeks to arrive at a definition of religion to fit the totality of experiences he absorbed in his time and place. It is almost as if his lectures on Romans with his lengthy attention to predestination made him pay all the more attention to the place of faith in God's relations with Christians. Predestination provided a means of talking about mystery, of the inability of the human mind to fathom reasons for the way God directs the world.

Luther's lectures on Hebrews began on April 21, 1516, and continued until March 26, 1518. He was therefore lecturing on Hebrews when the controversy over indulgences made him famous, and so this text provides a window into his soul at a great moment in his life. The book of Hebrews was late in being accepted into the canon of scripture, and when he came to translate the New Testament, Luther rejected its apostolic authority. By then he had been influenced by the Greek New Testament of Erasmus, and I shall take up his change of heart a little later.

Hebrews came into the canon under the fiction that it had been written by Paul, although, unlike Pauline epistles, it does not claim Pauline authorship or mention Paul by name. Debate about the matter was intense among the early fathers of the church. Eusebius (260–340?), the great historian of the early church, doubted that Paul wrote it. Erasmus came to the same conclusion. Modern New Testament scholars agree. Luther commented briefly on those, such as Jerome, who said Paul did not write it, but he seems to defend Pauline authorship.[19] Later he would change his mind.

Hebrews is the first book of the New Testament that speaks of Christ as a priest and aims to show that he displaced the priests of the old law. That is, from now on, we are to come to God not through the old priesthood with sacrifices in the temple of Jerusalem but through Christ, who has sacrificed himself for us. Hebrews makes much of the death of Christ and the conquest of death effected by his resurrection. Luther follows his text with fervor. Christ has destroyed death, and it is impossible for those who believe in Christ to die—that is, to remain dead once the earthly body has perished. "For just as Christ, by reason of His union with immortal divinity, overcame death by dying, so the Christian, by reason of his union with the immortal Christ—which comes about through faith in Him—also overcomes death by dying."[20]

At this point Luther rushes into a rhetorical flood of relief that death has been conquered. Yet at the same time his commentary is peppered with allusions to those who do not sufficiently believe. What do they not sufficiently believe? Again Luther makes a close association between the terror of death and its anodyne, faith. "He who fears death or is unwilling to die is not a Christian to a sufficient degree; for those who fear death still lack faith in the Resurrection, since they love this life more than they love the life to come."[21] He does not say here that those who fear death are afraid their sins will not be forgiven at the day of judgment; rather he says something like this: To fear death is to disbelieve in the Resurrection of Christ; to believe in the resurrection is to have confidence in the face of death. All this he has said in one way or another in his lectures on Romans. But now he makes a turn that, I think, is more important than is sometimes recognized. He says:

> Those who fear death should not despair, but they should be encouraged and exhorted as people weak in faith, who as the apostle enjoins in Rom. 14:1, should be welcomed. For that contempt for death and the gratitude for it, proclaimed by the apostle and the saints, is the goal and perfection toward which the whole life of Christians should strive, even though very few are so perfect. Thus in the Epistle to the Romans Paul

also calls Christians righteous, holy, and free from sin, not because they are, but because they have begun to be and should become people of this kind by making constant progress. For even saintly men have been frightened by death and the judgments of God . . . Therefore such people should be consoled and encouraged, first through Christ himself, who, in order to omit nothing that one could desire from the most pious priest, not only underwent death for us to overcome it for us and to make it deserving of our contempt but also, for the sake of the weak in faith, took upon himself, overcame, and sanctified the very fear of death, lest such fear be scorned to our damnation. Otherwise it is truly a sin to be unwilling to die and to fear death.[22]

The sense of these words seems to be this: The fear of death is part of our sinful nature, but Christ himself took on the fear of death, overcame it, and sanctified it. That is to say, he made the fear of death an acceptable part of our human experience. The fear of death should then be used to make us draw close to God; the fear of death that does not draw us to God is sinful; a righteous fear of death that emphasizes our need of God is not a sin.

Elsewhere in these lectures Luther is more insistent on tranquillity before death, so that it seems that a willingness to make room for the fear of death is not yet fully grounded in his thought, and that indeed he may have been preaching to his own soul. "We Christians ought to learn how to die with joy for as it is impossible that Christ, the victor of death, should die again, so it is impossible that he that believes in him should die."[23] And again; "Whoever fears death or does not want to die is not yet a sufficient Christian, for he fails in resurrection faith, so long as he loves this life more than that which is to come . . . for it is true that only the conscience aware of sin makes death horrible, for the 'sting of death is sin,' but this consciousness of sin nothing takes away save faith in Christ who gives us the victory."[24]

This preoccupation with the fear of death and the equation of death with the wrath of God may have influenced Luther's steadfast teaching that we can do nothing at all to please God on our own. Obviously nothing we do can raise us from the dead. Only God can perform so grand a miracle; only God can therefore grant us the grace of faith and forgiveness that allows us to hope for the resurrection of the dead. Luther's fear of death may lie at the heart of his doctrine of human impotence before the powers of darkness.

When Luther gave these lectures Thomas More had just published *Utopia*. The denizens of that New World island ruled by reasonable men held that those who died in terror of death were to be buried in shame and silence. But those who died happily were carried to their funerals with smiles and singing and, in a classical mode, were cremated and remembered with a column whereon were carved the distinctions of the deceased. "No part of his life is more frequently or more gladly spoken of than his cheerful death," said More through his foil, Raphael Hythlodaeus.[25] The view of the calm death as testimony of confidence in God was a medieval trope. Artists painted the death of the Virgin Mary as though she were going to sleep, surrounded by the disciples of Christ, all of them serene and ungrieving at the demise of the mother of Jesus.[26] Death is the gateway to paradise. Real believers do not fear it.

More's Utopians are proto-Christians—virtuous pagans who have taken what More considered to be the best from Greek and Roman culture and have made of it a society based on reason, ready to take the additional step of Christian revelation conveyed to them by Hythlodaeus and others in his European band who have come upon them. Their view of life has many affinities with that of Luther—and many differences. Utopia is built on the premise that although individuals left to themselves are tainted with pride, the consequence of original sin that infects all human beings, a community of reason may be agreed upon to keep the badness of individuals in check. We shall see that Luther believed that the real states in Europe had a similar function, but never did he imagine that an earthly state could be as virtuous as More's Utopia.

More seemed to be concerned throughout *Utopia* to show Christian Europe that its ugliest habits could be condemned by reference to a reasonable society where they had been overcome. One of these was terror before death. We may see evidence in both More and Luther, despite their admonitions against the fear of death, that a great many Christians acted as if they did not believe the fundamental profession of their faith, that Christ rose from the dead, gaining victory over death for all his own. Our view of our own death is indissolubly joined to our confidence in Christ's resurrection. If we have *real* faith, we should not have terror before death; that we have this terror means that our faith is not complete.

In Luther, the fear is not of judgment and hell to follow but merely of death, which he, following Paul, seems to take as annihilation. Indeed he says, somewhat ambiguously, "Hell is hell not because punishment is there, but because praise of God is not there, as Ps[alm] 6:5 states: 'For in death there is no one who remembers Thee.'"[27] He has nothing important to say about the great Judgment Day in any of these passages, and his use of the word "hell" seems scarcely more than metaphorical.

Throughout these lectures as in the others Luther had given on the Bible to this date, no special emphasis is placed on the institutional church. He does not mention the pope once during his lectures on Hebrews. Nor does he advance any theory of an oral tradition existing alongside scripture and justifying the church's nonscriptural beliefs and practices.

One of the most difficult texts of Christian scripture is Hebrews 6:4–6: "It is impossible for those who once illuminated and having tasted of the heavenly gift and being made part of the Holy Spirit and having tasted the good word of God and the glory of the world to come who have then fallen away to be renewed to penance, having crucified themselves again the Son of God." Here was the text that seemed to spell out the dread "unpardonable sin" that was certain to lead to damnation. What did it mean?

The Novatians of the third century used this text to prove that no one who renounced faith during the persecutions inflicted on Christians by the Roman emperor Decius could be received again into communion once the persecution had ended. Many Catholic commentators held that "impossible" here meant "extremely difficult," and Luther mentions them in his commentary. Later, in his great controversy with William Tyndale, Thomas More used Hebrews 6:4–6 to prove that the oral tradition of the church was superior to scripture because tradition had mellowed this text that otherwise would stand against the rest of Christian faith.[28] Luther tackled the issue head on and did not try to prove too much. He recognized the patristic tradition that made "impossible" mean "difficult," but "because it is dangerous to twist clear words of scripture into a different meaning, one should not readily permit this, lest in the end the authority of all scripture vacillate, except where the context demands it."[29] In the end the sentiments of this text made him reject the book.

For the time being Luther accepted Hebrews, including this text so contrary to his belief in predestination. But he could not resist citing other texts of scripture at length to prove that repentance after sin is possible for the Christian. He took a stab at interpreting the verse to conform to these other texts, saying that to fall into "unbelief" is to fall back into the belief that one may be saved without Christ. It is not a satisfying solution to the problem, and Luther seemed to know it. He left the issue quickly.[30]

Late in the lectures, when he considered the eleventh chapter of Hebrews, with its resounding definition of faith, Luther came on Hebrews 11:6, with its demand that anyone who pleases God must believe that he exists. It seems easy to some to believe that God exists, he says. But this is not so. "Human faith," he says, "is just like any other thought, art, wisdom, dream, etc., of man. For as soon as a trial assails, all those things immediately topple down."[31] It is a forthright acknowledgment that when one is in tribulation— as, for example, when one is wrapped in the terror of death—one may be tempted to believe not merely that God is angry but rather that God does not exist. Surely these lectures are enough to lay to rest the modern dogma that unbelief was impossible in the sixteenth century. We do better to accept Febvre's designation of the time as "a century that wanted to believe," but we might add that just as the desire to live forever does not mean we will, so does the desire to believe not mean that we always can. Luther confronts the issue with gloomy knowledge that belief is hard, that it was not the blissful unquestioning credence that modern expositors have imagined in their romantic conviction that our devout ancestors lived in a rosy certainty of faith that has in modern times receded like the cool and refreshing edge of a drying lake amid a desert of skepticism. Luther would have seen this vision as fantasy, and he would have regarded Matthew Arnold as one of the many "rotten spirits" he felt he had to combat in his own time.

We have seen that in Romans Luther advanced the idea that the highest form of faith was to be resigned to hell if such was the will of God. Evidently this was not a subject that he could let lie, probably because his own uncertainties dogged his soul. His solution seemed to concentrate on the work of the Jesus who had shared suffering and death and whose resurrection promised triumph over death to those bonded to him. By fixing one's attention on Christ, one received comfort. "Therefore a Christian must be sure, yes, completely sure, that Christ appears and is a Priest before God in his behalf. For as he will believe, so it will happen to him."[32]

Luther's emphasis that the Christian must be sure that Christ speaks directly to the individual heart, promising forgiveness of sins, raises a number of questions. Where does the certainty come from? What is its nature and degree? He speaks in these lectures on Hebrews of the invisible quality of faith—as does the author of the epistle. So one cannot be as certain of anything in faith as one is certain of propositions in Euclid's geometry—to use one of Thomas More's analogies. Does one then have a sweet, mystical certainty within, born of one's meditation on Christ and his works, a certainty that might be likened, for example, to the intuition of the exact place of a musical note on the scale by those who have perfect pitch? Is it then a certainty that comes unbidden, flowing in entirely from the outside? Is this his way of describing the epiphany that he was later to relate in the preface to his Latin works? Or is it a willed certainty, a dogged determination to believe, an aggressive discipline of the spirit set like a wall against torrents of doubt? If so, by Luther's developing theology, he would have to say that the discipline of faith does not *really* come from human striving but that it is the gift of God. Luther has already clearly declared that the longing for God is a sign of

God's favor; therefore it might appear that he is resolved to yearn for God at every instant with an overpowering heartfelt dedication. This longing may then grant him certainty under the umbrella of his own conception of grace. His effort to struggle against doubt about his salvation confirms his election.

Or may we take a deconstructionist tack to suggest that we have yet another understanding of "certainty" here? Is Luther using certainty as a means of encouragement, speaking of certainty when he knows that many doubt, that the doubts continue to rage within his own heart and that he cannot surmount them? Is he the general shouting conviction of victory to an army that feels itself defeated, rousing his troops so that his prophecy may be self-fulfilling? In that sense he would be emphasizing his evolving theology of the cross, that spiritual torment is a sign of God's blessing, and given that assumption, certainty is possible. Is he the spiritual coach telling the despairing human heart, "Think that you will win, and you will win," an assertion of certainty to attain a result that at the moment the assertion is made is not certain at all? It is a paradox: assurance comes out of doubt. But then Luther was nothing if not paradoxical. By raising the topic of certainty in this uncompromising way, he makes a frontal attack on the *via moderna,* which, as we have seen, prized uncertainty. Luther's thumping repetitions of the need to be certain of salvation would be one way of asserting the sole power of God over salvation, eliminating the supposed merit of any particle of human striving, including a striving to perfect belief.

Certainty of salvation was obviously not in his view an arrival at perpetual peace with God, since his later life demonstrates clearly enough that he never arrived at that blessed tranquillity himself. Nor was it certainty that he himself had been redeemed. It was certainty, rather, that he was doing the only thing he could do, following the only course he could follow. In this as in so many of Luther's texts, we see that a rousing affirmation was more a weapon against doubt than a sign of victory over fear and the threat of unbelief.

In almost the same breath that he extols certainty, Luther assaults the Catholic teaching that the sacraments are effective transmitters of grace and that "they do not require any disposition in the recipient except that he should put no obstacle in the way."[33] The sacrament, he says, putting emphasis on the Eucharist, requires a pure heart or otherwise it will bring judgment down on the participant. Such purity comes only by faith, and faith is the condition of validity for any sacrament.[34] By this time in his lectures, he must have begun pondering indulgences, and the lectures reflect his efforts to define the theology of penance within which he lodged his protest.

His lectures in these so-called silent years demonstrate that Luther's break with the church is less shocking than it might have seemed without these documents. His progress seems to have gone something like this: He went into the monastery to be saved from sin and the penalty of sin, which is death. His fear of death, the doubts that it aroused, and his anguished yearning for salvation through bouts of *Anfechtungen* continued to preoccupy him. He found his only solution in Christ and in the faith that made the believer know that Christ had died for the believer's sins and had risen again. Increasingly this faith in Christ was to be fixed on the marvel of Christ's suffering for sinful humankind, the loneliness of Christ in his death, and the example Christ had given of the torments that every true Christian also had to endure. Or perhaps we can suggest that his solution to his problems was to talk and write about the faith he yearned to have, the talk and the writing becoming surrogates for the serenity that eluded him.

Although he talks much about sin and sins, Luther does not tell us in detail what these sins are. We do not have here the catalogue of transgressions that are the stuff of penitential manuals or of sermons—no laments over sloth, gluttony, anger, envy, covetousness, pride, and lust, the deadly sins of Christian tradition. These, too, are outward things, and he is not much concerned with them. Rather he sees sin as a state, a continuing condition, especially the pride that assumes salvation is possible without full reliance on Christ. Both in his sermons and in his lectures on the Bible, he went behind external acts to the heart and found it wanting unless touched by grace. He never again lectured on either Romans or Hebrews, although he cited Romans again and again in lectures, sermons, and polemics. Neither series of lectures was published during his lifetime. His unwillingness to publish the lectures on Hebrews doubtless came from the lowering of esteem he felt for the book. He probably did not publish the lectures on Romans because he recognized that in them he had not reached the ripeness of thought he would later gain in pondering Paul's words. He had not reached the clear understanding of justification that he would shortly attain and for which the Epistle to the Romans was essential.

Luther also preached regularly during these months when he lectured to his students, and we may read his sermons to see something of his own development. In a sermon preached in February 1517, he spoke on the storm on the Sea of Galilee in Matthew 8:23–27, a storm calmed by Jesus. In the scriptural text Jesus, who has been asleep in the ship, berates his disciples for having so little faith that they fear the tempest will destroy them. Luther interprets the text to declare that the person who feels danger is blessed, that the person who feels no danger is in the gravest danger of all because he will not call for help.[35]

Once again we find him interpreting inward torment—doubtless his own—in such a way that it becomes a sign of God's grace. The indifferent ones are those most susceptible to damnation. Yet as I have argued earlier, the constancy and the vehemence of this assertion reflect a continuing tension. Continuing fear of death and its consequent melancholy might seem to a young man evidence that he had been predestined to be damned. Why did he keep on being afraid if he was not predestined to an eternity separated from God? Here are yet more signs of the development of his theology of the cross.

Some of the most tender and moving letters Luther ever wrote were to those anxious about their salvation and troubled by unbelief. In later years he often fell back on autobiographical reminiscences to support his advice. In 1531 he wrote to one Barbara Lisskirchen in Freiberg; she was the sister of a friend, and she lived in torment that she might be predestined to be damned. "I know all about this affliction," Luther wrote her. "I was myself brought to the brink of eternal death by it . . . I shall show you how God helped me out of this trouble and by what means I now protect myself against it every day." He advised her to fix in her mind that such thoughts were the temptation of the devil, to recall that we are nowhere told to think of such things or to seek answers from the mystery of God, and to trust God to take care of her. Under the onslaught of the temptation to despair, she should refuse to entertain such thoughts. Above all, he said, we must remain fixed on the image of Jesus Christ to see how much God loves us. "If you believe in Christ, then you are called. And if you are called, then you are most certainly predestinated."[36]

Yet Luther recognized that the fears return. The Christian requires mental discipline to eject them. "If they enter your mind, cast them out again, just as you would immediately spit out any filth that fell into your mouth."[37] We should recall that Luther said that these terrifying thoughts still entered his mind, and we have already noted that some of his longest and most powerful reflections on death as the penalty of sin and the wrath of God were written or spoken in the 1530s. He describes here a lifelong quest for religious peace that can never be entirely attained. The calm of his words of consolation indicates that he had achieved much more tranquillity of spirit than he knew as a younger man, but his words show that the struggle went on. Indeed the words seem to be his therapy against the terrors that required consoling.

Whether these anxieties afflicted him when the controversy over indulgences erupted is difficult to say. We know that in the months before he became notorious, predestination occupied his thoughts, and his sense of it directed him against scholastic theology, with its pretense to know more than human beings could know about the secrets of God. Late in August 1517 Luther wrote out his "Disputation against Scholastic Theology," to be used in a debate by one of his students. It represents an attack against nominalist theologians, who held that human beings have just enough free will to want to welcome God into their lives. Against them Luther maintained that we have no free will at all. As we have noted above, he touched on this point in his lectures on Romans.

The human will, he said, was like every other part of human nature; it was created good, but it had become "evil and corrupt." All our nature is self-centered, even our love. We cannot love God for himself alone. The preparation for grace is not something we will within ourselves. "The best and infallible preparation for grace and the sole means of obtaining grace is the eternal election and predestination of God."[38] The doctrine of predestination cannot be considered apart from everything else happening in Luther's life and thought here in the late summer of 1517 on the eve of the controversy over indulgences.

Predestination provided comforts in addition to its anxieties. The anxiety was evident—the fear that one might not be among those predestined to salvation. As many commentators have held, Luther was much influenced by the mystical tradition and in particular by St. Bernard, who had so vehemently opposed Abelard's introduction of Aristotelian doubt into Christian theology. In Abelard's view, the way to knowledge begins with doubt, for doubt makes us question, and questions lead us to knowledge.[39] Bernard's way was toward mystical contemplation of Jesus, especially the sufferings by which Jesus had redeemed the world. Yet the supposed end of the mystical way was perfect peace with God. As Steven Ozment has argued, an essential part of mysticism is the belief that man and God are somehow alike, and mystical experience was a foretaste of the future life, when man and God would be fully one as they were before the creation of the world.[40]

Luther's concept of the holiness of God put him a thousand miles away from this mystical familiarity with deity, for in Luther's view God and man were radically different, and nothing in the human soul could claim title to divinity. Nor did he ever have the perfect peace that mysticism claimed to be the end of religious striving in this world. Why could he not be freed of this fear and enter into the mystical peace with God so extolled by those in the mystical tradition? Did his continuing torments not mean that he was predestined to damnation?

In his table talk of about 1532 we have a question posed to Luther about those people—they were apparently many—who thought they might be predestined to damnation because they did not experience peace with God. Luther's reply was the essence of the theology of the cross. "The Christian life is to be lived amid sorrows, trials, afflictions, deaths." These vexations are signs that God cares for them, for sinful people who feel no anxiety are spiritually dead. Christians always feel these fears. "Therefore, it is the prime precept of God that we encourage and console the afflicted who are in sorrow. And on the other hand, those who are thus tempted should allow themselves to be cheered and should put an end to their depression and fear."[41]

It seems clear here that many were taking "depression and fear" as signs of predestination to damnation and that Luther replied that anxiety remains at the heart of Christian life and that it cannot be eliminated. It sounds like the wisdom of experience. The essence of the theology of the cross would seem then to be a never-ending battle of faith against unbelief, with all the torments that such ceaseless conflict and anxiety brought in their train. Luther himself, having learned to live with his struggle, could write tender letters of encouragement to those who felt the pangs of unbelief. Religious suffering was a sign of God's favor and that the Christian life was a travail of faith and doubt, assurance and fear, so mingled that the Christian went through agonies to understand the gospel. Increasingly clear in Luther's writing is the notion that spiritual agony is proof of God's favor and that easy faith is spiritual death.

To one young man, Valentine Hausmann, Luther wrote to comfort him for being "assailed by terror and unbelief." "How many there are who have less faith than you have!" said Luther. "Yet they are not aware of it and remain in their unbelief. The fact that God makes you sensible of this is a good sign that he wishes to help you out of his condition. The more you are aware of it, the nearer you are to improvement. Cling calmly to God, and he will cause everything to turn out well."[42] Time and again he said that those tempted to melancholy should shun solitude. To his younger friend Jerome Weller, who tutored Luther's children and took down much of the table talk, he wrote in 1530 to cure his depression. The letter deserves to be quoted at length for the insight it throws on Luther's early days.

You say that the temptation is heavier than you can bear, and that you fear that it will so break and beat you down as to drive you to despair and blasphemy. I know this wile of the devil. If he cannot break a person with his first attack, he tries by persevering to wear him out and weaken him until the person falls and confesses himself beaten. Whenever this temptation comes to you, avoid entering upon a disputation with the devil and do not allow yourself to dwell on these deadly thoughts, for to do so is nothing short of yielding to the devil and letting him have his way. Try as hard as you can to despise those thoughts which are induced by the devil. In this sort of temptation and struggle, contempt is the best and easiest method of winning over the devil. Laugh your adversary to scorn and ask who it is with whom you are talking. By all means flee solitude, for the devil watches and lies in wait for you most of all when you are alone. This devil is conquered by mocking and despising him, not by resisting and arguing with him. Therefore, Jerome, joke and play games with my wife and others. In this way you will drive out your diabolical thoughts and take courage.

This temptation is more necessary to you than food and drink. Let me remind you what happened to me when I was about your age. When I first entered the monastery it came to pass that I was sad and downcast, nor could I lay aside my melancholy. On this account I made confession to and took counsel with Dr. Staupitz . . . and opened to him what horrible and terrible thoughts I had. Then said he: "Don't you know, Martin, that this temptation is useful and necessary to you? God does not exercise you thus without reason. You will see that he intends to use you as his servant to accomplish great things." And so it turned out. I was made a great doctor (for I may with propriety say this of myself) although at the time when I suffered this temptation I never would have believed it possible. I have no doubt that this will happen to you too. You will become a great man. Just see to it that you are of good courage in the meantime, and be persuaded that such utterances, especially those which fall from the lips of learned and great men, are not without prophetic quality.

I remember that a certain man whom I once comforted on the loss of his son said to me, "Wait and see, Martin, you will become a great man." I have often thought of these words, for, as I have said, such utterances have something of a prophetic quality. Be of good courage, therefore, and cast these dreadful thoughts out of your mind. Whenever the devil pesters you with these thoughts, at once seek out the company of men, drink more, joke and jest, or engage in some other form of merriment. Sometimes it is necessary to drink a little more, play, jest, or even commit some sin in defiance and contempt of the devil in order not to give him an opportunity to make us scrupulous about trifles. We shall be overcome if we worry too much about falling into some sin.

Accordingly if the devil should say, "Do not drink," you should reply to him, "On this very account, because you forbid it, I shall drink, and what is more, I shall drink a generous amount." Thus one must always do the opposite of that which Satan prohibits. What do you think is my reason for drinking wine undiluted, talking freely, and eating more often if it is not to torment and vex the devil who made up his mind to torment and vex me? Would that I could commit some token sin simply for the sake of mocking the devil, so that he might understand that I acknowledge no sin and am conscious of no sin. When the devil throws our sins up to us and declares that we deserve death and hell, we ought to speak thus: "I admit that I deserve death and hell. What of it? Does this mean that I shall be sentenced to eternal damnation? By no means. For I know One who suffered and made satisfaction in my behalf. His name is Jesus Christ, the Son of God. Where he is, there I shall be also."[43]

This fascinating letter is about as far as anyone can go from the monastic version of mysticism and the monk's solitary quest for the vision of God. Now company and alcohol replace solitude. It is also a long way from Luther's somewhat conventional advice in his lectures on Romans to seek silence. It helps us understand Luther's comments about his late-night vigils and the torments of monastic life that Catholic writers since Heinrich Denifle have almost routinely doubted and even scorned. We may imagine a young man alone in the dark, seeking to carry out the prescribed prayers and meditations of the monk in solitude and being overwhelmed by melancholy. The source of melancholy for the depressed person is difficult to locate. Everything seems to bring about the same consequence—a black, bleak inability to find good relief anywhere and the sense of death everywhere. Death is where the weight of Luther's most lengthy discussions of sin and judgment fell throughout his life. He belonged fully to that world view described by Jean Delumeau in the term "un homme fragile," fragile man.[44] In this view human knowledge can answer none of the important questions about the meaning of life, and those who follow the dictates of reason are bound to arrive at a profound pessimism.

Luther discovered for himself that monastic solitude allowed doubts to pour in on him until he nearly drowned. In this sense his comment in his preface of 1545 takes on a stronger meaning, for he said *ita ebrium, imo submersum in dogmatibus papae,* that is, he was "drunk, or rather submerged in the doctrines of the pope."[45] He finds himself in fact choked with these doctrines. Since we can find no evidence in his early commentary on the Psalms that he had any great affection for the papacy in these years, we must look elsewhere for the definition of these choking "doctrines of the pope."

A plausible candidate is the traditional monastic version of the mystical vision whereby solitary contemplation of God leads to peace of heart. This was a teaching not created by popes, of course, but by the church presided over by popes. Here was the papal church that through the centuries extolled solitary contemplation and commissioned artists to paint St. Jerome and St. Francis and legions of other saints experiencing the mystical rapture of visions in the wilderness or in a darkness illuminated only by holy light. Yes, the saints went forth to serve the multitudes, but their strength came from their solitary encounter with God. Luther found a different experience. In solitude his terrors—including his terror before death—only increased. In his preface of 1545 he says *Ego . . . qui diem extremum horribiliter timui,* "I who horribly feared the last day."[46] The sentiment is deliciously ambivalent. *Diem extremum* usually means the day of judgment. But the term can also mean the day of one's death. The ambivalence may have a theological grounding in ways that I have suggested. To fear death without being able to win the battle of faith against that fear might well give to a young man the presentiment that he was predestined to damnation, to the penalties of the last day because he could not approach his own last day with serenity. Luther wrote young Weller that the anxieties never go away.

That is another important declaration in this letter. Eat and drink, he says. Play and jest. He drinks undiluted wine; he eats often; he talks freely. At least one Catholic writer has said that Luther suffered from the poisoning of alcohol.[47] Various images of him in his later years show him as grossly fat. By this text from his own hand we may have a key to his personality, that he was employing every agency he knew to stave off the terrors of melancholy. Yet Luther was one of those resolved to believe no matter what reason might tell him. That resolution to believe now stood with him as he entered the controversy over indulgences and his destiny.

Some biographers have pointed out that the Luther of these years seems to be coming closer to the humanists, those scholars interested in drawing on the rhetorical tradition of the Greek and Latin past and applying the wisdom of classical literature to the task of shaping virtue among clergy and laity alike. Humanism is often set over against scholasticism, although on examination one finds a "humanist" such as Pico della Mirandola respectful of much that he found in scholasticism. Luther's denunciation of Aristotle, the Neoplatonist Porphyry, and the scholastics was especially fierce in a letter to his friend Johann Lang in Erfurt on February 8, 1517. The study of these writers is worthless, he said; their interpretations better lie in the eternal silence of the dead.[48] In these years Luther was drifting further and further away from the scholastic mood that sought to explain everything and toward a common humanist perception that there was so much mystery in God's universe that it was only vain curiosity to try to unravel it. The true Christian was to cultivate devotion to God, a preoccupation with the moral life, with doing good, and a willingness to wait until God chose to reveal his secret ways. Logic could not lead to certainty. Erasmus agreed. Humanist piety and Luther's piety seemed to converge in these years. But that seeming convergence would shortly be shown to be illusory. Already by March 1517 Luther wrote Lang about Erasmus. He was reading "our Erasmus," he wrote, but "my soul toward him declines." He appreciated the erudite attacks of Erasmus on ignorant priests and monks. "But he does not push forward enough Christ and the grace of God . . . Human considerations [for him] are much more important than the divine"[49]

All this is to say that by 1517 Luther had wandered far from the customary emphases of official church piety, especially as that piety was directed toward ordinary Christians. He did not rebel against the teachings of the church. He did not suppose himself to be a heretic. He was working out a vision of God and humankind, a little like a man sailing a small boat, thinking of the wind and the water and having no real consciousness of how far out to sea he had gone. On the surface he was a young man rising quickly in the comfortable routines of his profession and in the esteem of his peers. He was becoming known beyond his immediate circle in Wittenberg. He preached regularly; he was general vicar for his order in the region, called upon to settle petty disputes and to make recommendations. In a letter to his friend Lang, written on October 26, 1516, he complained bitterly—but perhaps with the busy man's eternal tincture of pride—that he worked all the time, doing some things he found trivial, not only writing letters but being charged with supervising the fish pond in Litzkau. (A fish pond was important for monks, who could eat only fish on Fridays.) He was so busy, he wrote, that he scarcely had time to say his prayers or to deal with the temptations of the world, the flesh, and the devil.[50]

He published a little commentary on the Seven Penitential Psalms and passed it around among his friends. He published the *German Theology.* He planned to publish his lectures. By now he had become the friend of Georg Spalatin, the red-haired private secretary of Frederick the Wise—a friendship that may have saved his life. Luther complained gently about the thickheadedness of the Saxons when he wrote to his friend Christopher Scheurl at Nuremberg. They had to have everything chewed and digested before he could give it to them, he said. In the same letter he reported that he had responded to a book sent to him by another up-and-coming young theologian, Johann Eck.[51]

In his sermons he attacked aspects of popular piety foreign to his own theology, centered as it was on his sense of absolute dependence on the grace of God. He castigated practices that carried with them the notion that by doing them, Christians built up credit that God was obligated to reward. He began his sermon on St. Bartholomew's Day on August 24, 1516, by saying, "We scorn the story of St. Bartholomew." His auditors were then treated to a historical critique and blistering ridicule of the story as it was told in the Golden Legend, where saints neither hungered nor thirsted nor felt fatigue nor fear—and perhaps did not defecate.[52] Bartholomew was a popular saint, one of the apostles, said by the early church historian Eusebius to have carried a Gospel of Matthew in Aramaic to India. Various legendary accounts made him the enemy of demons in India and portrayed him as sumptuously dressed in clothes and shoes that never got old or showed stains and that, consequently, he was never required to remove. In the most popular legend (the one accepted by Michelangelo in his painting of the Last Judgment in the Sistine Chapel), he was said to have been martyred by being skinned alive. Not surprisingly he was the patron saint of skinners—those who tanned leather and worked it—and in icons he is shown holding a knife or a razor. Representations of him in Germany were especially popular and gory, showing him being flayed without flinching.[53]

Luther's brief but fierce little sermon was in effect an assault on the legendary paraphernalia of superhuman saintliness in the Golden Legend. Scripture showed Christ and the apostles in a more human light, without these ostentatious displays attributed to Bartholomew. "They are Jews," he said, "who wish to justify themselves by their own works; they do not wish to hear that Christ is their righteousness."[54] In a brief letter to Spalatin he assaulted the silliness and the lies of these saints' tales.[55]

His sermon may have had a hidden agenda. Frederick the Wise had himself painted with St. Bartholomew by Lucas Cranach. In the painting the saint stands behind the elector with one hand on Frederick's left shoulder and the other hand holding the knife that was the symbol of St. Bartholomew's martyrdom. The painting graced the altar in the castle church, which was crowded with paintings and sculptures of the saints.[56] Perhaps even before the indulgences controversy Luther was trying to send the elector a message about the nature of true religion.

This attack on the supernatural powers of the saints was an implacable working out of the logic of his earlier lectures. If Christ was our sole righteousness, the huge and ramshackle edifice of saint worship tumbled to the ground, for neither we nor the legendary saints could claim to have earned righteousness by good works. Catholic theology made a strict distinction between worshiping saints and worshiping God. (Modern Catholics speak of "venerating" the saints, but Catholics in Luther's time, including Thomas More in England, spoke simply of worshiping them—seeing them as divinely exalted high above the normal human status.) In the religious lives of ordinary Christians the saints occupied a prodigious place. Luther felt a particular affinity for some, finding their lives exemplary. But even they could not do more than God required for salvation, and they had no supernatural powers. He shows himself in this sermon on the verge of following his premises to their inevitable conclusion—with consequences both for theology and, more important, for the liturgy with which ordinary folk cultivated their feelings toward the divine.

In none of these thoughts had Luther traveled beyond the boundaries of orthodoxy. Yet just below the surface, he seems almost to have been waiting for something to happen, something to take him across the lines that he had drawn for himself within the church by the summer of 1517. That "something" was to be the quarrel over indulgences that broke in the autumn.

8

THE CONTROVERSY OVER
INDULGENCES

IN AUGUST 1513—the same month that young Dr. Martin Luther began
his first lectures on the Psalms—a younger brother of the Elector
Frederick the Wise died. The brother was Ernst, and he was archbishop
of Magdeburg. His untimely death was a blow to the ambitions of Frederick's
family, the Wettins, to expand its influence in Germany. Standing in the
wings waiting to enjoy his time onstage was young Albrecht of Brandenburg
(1490–1545), a member of the rival house of Hohenzollern from which
eventually would come the kings of Prussia. He was a second son—plump,
genial, ambitious, addicted to women and to comfort, and in need of a
living. The open bishopric offered an opportunity, and he was quick to
seize it.

Albrecht's family was influential. A brother had founded a university at
Frankfurt on the Oder. Like Frederick the Wise, Albrecht collected relics and
corresponded with important men, including Erasmus. A family friend was
Ulrich von Hutten, a humanist and rabid German nationalist who hated all
things Italian, a fluent hack who wrote extravagantly about Albrecht's supposed virtues. In August 1513 Albrecht got himself appointed archbishop of
Magdeburg with the lucrative perquisites of that high office and its grand old
cathedral not far from the Elbe. Here was the tomb of Otto I, founder of the
Holy Roman Empire, and beyond the city lay the plains and forests border-
ing the Elbe north of Wittenberg. Within a month Albrecht became also
administrator of the monastery attached to the cathedral of Halberstadt, and
in 1514 he succeeded through various intrigues in getting himself named

archbishop of Mainz, thus becoming one of the seven electors of the empire and one of the most powerful men in Germany. All this cost a fortune, and to pay for it he borrowed heavily from the great banking house of the Fuggers in Augsburg. He was too young to exercise these offices in 1514. The canon law of the church required a bishop to be thirty years old. Albrecht was twenty-four. But popes could dispense with canon law if they found good reason for doing so, and Leo X found an excellent reason to give a dispensation to the young archbishop: both needed money.

On the German side, political considerations played a role. The city of Erfurt, part of the territory of the archbishopric of Mainz, had huge debts, and because of its precarious financial condition seemed ready to fall into the hands of Frederick the Wise. The town fathers wanted Albrecht as their archbishop because the Hohenzollerns were traditional foes to Frederick's house, and they thought Albrecht would protect them. In the end he did so—at huge cost. But his election required Rome's cooperation.[1]

Pope Leo X was a member of the house of Medici, the energetic Florentine banking family with a talent for profit. His father was Lorenzo the Magnificent, one of the greatest patrons of the arts of all time, and the new pope—elected in 1513—had tastes of his own to pursue. He wanted to finish the great basilica dedicated to St. Peter over the supposed first pope's supposed grave in the Vatican. The foundation for new construction was laid during the reign of the warrior pope Julius II, but the design was not agreed on—the great basilica still gives the uncomfortable impression that it was designed by a committee—and building on such a scale required money and energy. To finance this mighty project, Leo issued a sale of indulgences and with a dispensation he certified Albrecht's elections. In exchange Albrecht agreed to the sale of indulgences within his territories and to split the profits with the pope fifty/fifty.

By this time Albrecht had collected some 8,933 relics of his own, providing in sum several million years of released time from purgatory. The common people valued papal indulgences more than the garden-variety sort dispensed by mere archbishops. Albrecht welcomed papal hucksters, knowing that with his profit-sharing plan with the pope, he could pay his debts. On his side, Leo X could build his church as a monument to himself and share in the Renaissance thirst for enduring fame that motivated artists, kings, writers, and even popes. The entire enterprise was suspect, not only morally but theologically, and this on several counts. The most questionable issue was that of indulgences themselves.

The indulgences that provoked Luther to begin his public career were attached to the sacrament of penance, the sacrament itself devised to allow

Christians in the early years of the church to return to the communion of faith after they had committed grievous sins.

The worst sin for early Christians was to renounce Christ under threat of torture and death in sporadic persecutions by pagans—whom Christians did everything in their power to mock and condemn. As we have noted in considering Luther's lectures on Hebrews, the writer of that book said flatly that Christians who fell away from Christ once they had tasted of the "heavenly gift" could never be pardoned. Persecution began early because Christians refused to acknowledge any god but their own and publicly scorned the civic religion of the Roman Empire, where tolerant people paid their respects indiscriminately to all the gods. The early attacks on Christianity seldom continued long, but for months in this city or that, and especially in Rome itself, they could be severe. In any persecution, many Christians fell away before the threat of painful death.

When persecution faded, fallen Christians clamored to be readmitted to fellowship. Many had suffered and stood firm, men and women who had endured prison, torture, and the sight of faithful comrades put to death with ingenious and spectacular methods. These brave souls were reluctant to welcome cowardly apostates back into communion. Rigorists took the attitude of the book of Hebrews that no restoration was possible, that those who had given way to persecution could expect no salvation.

But the social forces and the needs of the church were too much for fastidious rigor. It was hard for believers in a loving God to say that he would not forgive a contrite heart. Besides, Christians needed numbers to be successful rivals to the great pagan majority in the empire. The sacrament of penance developed slowly to accommodate the needs of reconciliation, and it went through many permutations over the centuries. By the high Middle Ages penance involved several steps. First the sinner must feel genuine sorrow for sin. At its best, this sorrow became contrition for having offended God. The Christian acknowledged having broken a bond of love that united the soul to a loving father. An inferior sorrow was called *attrition*—the fear of punishment rather than grief for having offended. The sinner sought reconciliation with God to avoid the penalty of hell at the day of judgment. In theory this sorrow was not sufficient for valid penance. In practice it was almost impossible to tell the difference between the two. Here in the late Middle Ages the doctrine of *facere quod in se est*—doing the best one can— fitted a need. The penitent did all he could to develop genuine contrition for sin; God accepted his best as enough.

The next step was confession, an oral confession to a priest, the priest being the mediator between God and humankind. The priest was set apart from ordinary society to be God's special agent to reconcile sinful humanity to himself, and the power of the priest over confession confirmed the superiority of priests over the laity. The priest heard the confession, judged how serious the sins were, estimated the sincerity of the penitent, and pronounced absolution—God's forgiveness.

Eventually satisfaction became a ritual part of penance and remains so to this day. About the tenth century it was common for the priest to absolve the sinner of guilt immediately on confession and to impose a satisfaction to be performed afterward. Indulgences developed from satisfaction, and their history is complicated.

Bishops in the early church, and later ordinary priests, defined satisfactions performed by penitents. In the barbarian age, penance may have restrained violence, since superstitious Germanic chieftains with no curb but religion might be coerced by priests and the fear of God into some semblance of moral and orderly behavior. Catholic clergy sometimes required prominent barbarian chieftains to make long and spectacular satisfactions for their sins. Even so, it was not easy to get these rough-and-ready folk to obey priests. Therefore before the tenth century, priests in barbarian kingdoms accepted substitutions—sometimes payments of money—for satisfactions they had imposed. Usually a compromise was involved. The penitent performed part of the satisfaction imposed by the priest and did something else—such as pay a fine—in lieu of the rest.[2] The pope was considered the supreme priest, and in urgent times he could summon Christians to special duties and promise special rewards. Peter Kawerau has said that the true first offer of indulgences came from Pope Leo VI (847–857) when an Arab raiding party plundered St. Peter's Church in Rome in 853. For all Christians who would come to Italy to help expel these muslims, the Pope promised heavenly reward—the first example, according to Kawerau, of a pope's proclamation of his own power to affect the afterlife.[3]

A new step came with the proclamation of the first crusade by Pope Urban II at the Council of Clermont in 1095.[4] The crusade was a holy war, and Urban needed soldiers to redeem Palestine from the Turks. He decreed that to go on crusade would be substitution for any satisfaction imposed on any penitent by any priest. The indulgence depended on a contrite confession made before the crusade. The indulgence was not therefore a mechanical transaction that took the place of the entire sacrament of penance. It depended, in Urban's view, on heartfelt renunciation of previous sins. But there was a major change here: Before Urban's pronouncement, the decision to issue an indulgence had been made by a bishop on an individual basis. Now any crusader was guaranteed an indulgence relieving him of any other satisfaction. The pope thereby asserted his sovereignty over the entire penitential system and created a use of indulgences that would prove useful to papal politics and finance. Indulgences continued to be offered by bishops, especially for relics venerated on pilgrimage. The great pilgrimage tides of the high Middle Ages, including visits to famous shrines such as St. James of Compostela, St. Thomas Becket at Canterbury, and Rocamadour in the south of France, were driven by the promise of indulgences.

In theory indulgences were given to contrite penitents with good reason for asking for them, and in gratitude the penitent gave alms—a freehearted contribution to the church. Technically therefore indulgences were not bought and sold. But money and indulgences changed hands, and in time the transfer of indulgences was regulated by suggested tables of contributions. The system offered chances for abuse. Enthusiastic salesmen in all the centuries may make exaggerated claims for their goods. Already in 1246 during the Albigensian controversy, a council at Béziers, in what is today Mediterranean France, condemned unscrupulous purveyors of indulgences who claimed that the purchase of an indulgence could free a damned soul from hell.[5]

The passion for indulgences among ordinary folk and the loose theory about them made expansion of their scope and power almost inevitable. The church claimed to administer a treasury of merit gathered from the deeds of the saints. At bottom was one of the essential mind-sets of medieval Christianity: nothing in the divine economy of salvation could be lost. This attitude was in part behind the cult of relics. The crib of Jesus, the wood of the cross, the crown of thorns could not have remained unknown after they were hallowed by a divine presence, and because they were found and venerated, they had to be enshrined. To prove their validity, they produced miracles. So it was with the shed blood of the blessed saints, blood that by the high Middle Ages had swelled to crimson floods gushing from the mortal wounds of thousands of martyrs certifying the truth of the Christian gospel by their faith, validating their faith and the gospel by performing miracles of those who served them.

The surfeit of saintly blood could not be lost in the burning sands of the Roman arenas. It had to count for something eternal. So the merits of the saints were miraculously assembled in a treasury that could be applied to indulgences to make them efficacious. A Christian may not have the faith of martyrs and may not achieve purity of heart when he performs a penitential satisfaction. But God transfers excess merits of the saints to him when he gives alms for an indulgence and does with an obedient heart what the church requires. The church is one body, its members joined in mystical union. The good performed by one part of the body radiates to the whole. The merits of the saints pour into the church, and the pope and other bishops can direct them to where they can do the most good.

But once the idea of the treasury of merit was established, how could it be limited to the earthly realm of this life? In the developing doctrine of purgatory, the pains of that dreadful place represented a continuation of satisfaction for sin. Purgatory is temporal in that its sufferings are limited by time— although they may last for thousands or millions of years of agony. But since they are temporal, what was to stop the church from applying indulgences to them? Both Thomas Aquinas and Bonaventure in the thirteenth century argued that the benefits of indulgences applied to purgatory. They did not say that a living person could buy an indulgence and free the soul of a dead person from the purgatorial fires. Rather they held that an indulgence won in this life might extend into purgatory after death.[6] In this respect the hierarchy of the church lagged behind theologians in that popes refrained for a good long time from applying indulgences to the afterlife.

But whatever the theology, Popes found indulgences lucrative. In 1300 Boniface VIII, one of the more unsavory popes of the later Middle Ages, proclaimed a jubilee year in Rome, granting a plenary indulgence to all pilgrims who came to the holy city with its huge stores of relics. Boniface's proclamation seems restrained, given the historical importance accorded it by many writers. Those who received indulgences were to demonstrate true penitence and to confess their sins fully, and only the satisfactions of venial sins were covered.[7] The seven deadly sins required penance in the old way. We may doubt that fine theological distinctions were observed by the crowds of pilgrims who swarmed into Rome from all Europe to take advantage of this spiritual largesse. Bishops and popes regularly condemned the abuses of indulgences—sign enough that abuses went on, that indulgences had become patent medicines for the soul hawked by unscrupulous pitchmen evaluated by their superiors on how much money they brought in. The Council of Vienne in 1312 attacked in appropriately horrified language claims that indulgences could free from both guilt and penalty those guilty of murder, perjury, and other mortal sins.[8] Obviously the indulgence peddlers exceeded their commissions. Just as obviously the continual financial crisis of the Avignon papacy made popes willing to wink at the extravagant claims of unscrupulous salesmen as long as the cash rolled in. The fourteenth and the fifteenth centuries witnessed the expansion and trivialization of indulgences. Perhaps the onset of the great plague cycles made people more anxious to prepare their souls for sudden death that could strike those who seemed young and healthy. Supply rose to meet demand. In melancholy and terror before uncertainty and death, an anxious population flocked to any relief it could get, and indulgences were snapped up by the masses. With the profit, bishops often built new churches or repaired old ones.

The greatest expansion of the power of indulgences issued to the living came in 1476, when Sixtus IV applied them to the dead in purgatory. He surrounded this claim with qualifications. Nevertheless he declared that after buying an indulgence in the name of a dead person, it was unnecessary to mention that person any longer in prayers explicitly for the dead.[9] The Sorbonne did not agree. The University of Paris, in the shadow of the king of France, was always skeptical about papal claims, and became a center of conciliar thought, the idea that councils were superior to popes and could depose popes for whatever reasons a council deemed sufficient. The Sorbonne was a critic of popes throughout the fifteenth century. In particular the theological faculty of the University of Paris objected to the notion that a soul flew out of purgatory as soon as the indulgence was purchased. Indeed it condemned the idea that popes had any jurisdiction at all over purgatory. But popes enjoyed a popular authority the University of Paris lacked. A bull market in papal indulgences held up. Popes were unable to do without the profits from indulgences regardless of the spiritual consequences.[10] Protests continued. In an Advent sermon preached at Nuremberg's Augustinian cloister in 1516, Johannes von Staupitz expressed his reservations.[11]

By then Pope Leo X had proclaimed his sale of indulgences in 1515 on behalf of his construction project over the tomb of the apostle Peter. The conditions of the sale had to be negotiated with the various governments involved. The Germans resented the flow of gold from their lands into Italy, the Emperor Maximilian had to be coaxed into an agreement to allow indulgence hawkers to circulate in his lands, but we have seen that Albrecht of Brandenburg welcomed them into his territories. The emperor and the archbishop of Mainz could not, however, compel the Elector Frederick the Wise. He refused to let indulgence sellers enter his part of Saxony. One reason was surely that papal indulgences would cheapen the value of his own huge collection of relics with their indulgences attached. Another was perhaps annoyance that Albrecht of Mainz and the house of Hohenzollern were rising so high on the German scene.[12] Whatever the reason, Frederick's resolve held, and the indulgence seller destined to infamy because Luther attacked him, Johann Tetzel, had to skirt the elector's territories and set up his standard and his collection box at Jüterbog, a few miles beyond the nebulous Saxon border.

Tetzel was a Dominican friar. The Dominicans had, like the Franciscans, fallen to low esteem. They depended for their living on their ability to sway crowds and to pass the hat for contributions, and their methods were often unscrupulous. Tetzel was forty-eight in an age when men were considered old at fifty, and he had been peddling indulgences of various sorts for fifteen years. Many of his alleged claims seem preposterous today, but they carry the smack of religious reasoning in a superstitious time. "Even if you have deflowered the Virgin Mary, an indulgence will free you from punishment in purgatory!" So he is supposed to have said. The claim was not so farfetched when we consider that the Virgin was often painted with voluptuous naked breasts and that Christ had said that whoever looks on a woman to lust after her in his heart has already committed adultery. (Tetzel later denied vehemently that he had made any such claim.)[13]

"When the coin in the coffer rings, a soul from purgatory springs!" Another supposed line from Tetzel. Well, why not? We have seen that high churchmen had opposed teachings of instantaneous release from purgatory by indulgences—indicating that some salesmen all along held out that hope. Augustine had taught that all time is present to God, and one could argue that the indulgence did its spiritual work on God's time and not ours. It was an age of exalted spirituality combined with the grossest sensual excesses, superstition, and the confusion of religion and magic. Why should the solid and comforting ring of the coin not be a sign of the flight of an imprisoned soul just as the ringing of a little bell at the Mass was a sign of the transubstantiation of the bread and wine into the very body and blood of Jesus? Tetzel may have claimed that indulgences were good for sins not yet committed—a position abhorred by good Catholics and nowhere claimed by any pope. But again, what was time to a faith that considered past, present, and future to be but a single moment to God, for whom all being was eternally present?

Everything that Tetzel is supposed to have claimed for indulgences may be justified on theological grounds that some Christians professed to believe and that Christian tradition revered. Tetzel's alleged promises therefore had a plausibility at the time that they now lack. He combined these serious issues with a superficial spirit and a mercenary lust that contradicted Luther's experience with God. All this ground irritably against Luther's emerging theology. He had by this time relentlessly proclaimed that no human being could do anything on his own to gain merit before God. He ignored legends of the saints and their reputed power to do miracles. In his silence about benefits from saints, he implicitly rejected the vow to St. Anne that had made him a monk. Usually when he mentioned saints, it was to speak in a general way of the totality of the redeemed, and although he spoke of St. Bernard and St. Augustine and others, his reference is to their teaching and their lives of devotion and not to any notion that by praying to them one might partake of their merits to gain privileged admission to God. Here was a radicalism that passed almost without notice in his academic lectures, and it may be that his silence about saintly miracles and merits indicates an uncertainty in Luther himself, a hesitation at renouncing a well-established tradition that in his religious experience he found superstitious and perhaps pernicious. Whether conscious or unconscious, his unwillingness to make much of saints betokens a rationalizing theology with profound implications.

Throughout the medieval centuries the saints were venerated like local divinities. Their shrines numbered in the thousands; houses of worship from tiny chapels to grand cathedrals bore their names, and their effigies stood in carved stone and wood in such numbers that in scarcely any town in Christian Europe could a citizen cast an eye up or down or around without seeing some reminder of them. In painting they gravely suffered the pains of their martyrdoms or else they stood by as solemn observers of sacred scenes, witnesses to the pride and piety of patrons who paid to have the paintings done. In their effigies, they appear dispassionate, almost detached, even when they are suffering the tortures of martyrdom, an attitude implying that to cry out in pain for what they endured or to show surprise for the miracles they witnessed might be to indicate a previous lack of faith in the almighty power of God, a lack demeaning to their superhuman holiness. While printing was in its cradle, books retelling the stories of the saints enjoyed great sales. But already in his lectures on the Bible before 1517 Luther had taken his theology to the point where he was bound to reject saints with their surpluses of merit. Therefore from the moment Tetzel set foot in the region, Luther was at odds with the fundamental concept of indulgences.

Indulgences contradicted Luther's experience. He was already shaping his theology of the cross. The crude barter of indulgences went against everything he understood of true religion. Everything came from God, in his view, and yet the Christian was in unceasing tension with God. Karl Holl put it this way in describing Luther's religion: "So is the very idea of God, especially the idea of a personal God, directly bound up with an inescapable sentiment of obligation."[14] It seemed clear from reports of Tetzel's preaching that no spiritual obligation at all was laid on the buyers of these certificates of blessing.

Luther did not shape his opposition to indulgences all at once. He seems to have wavered, trying to reconcile the pope's claims with his own developing theology as Tetzel moved across the German lands in the spring and summer of 1517, hawking his wares.[15] But when Tetzel set up shop in

Jüterborg and Wittenbergers went out to buy indulgences, Luther was faced with a pastoral issue. He felt obligated to intervene when his people were led astray. He did what ecclesiastical etiquette of the time required when one was offended with an abuse in church practice. He wrote a humble letter to his archbishop, Albrecht of Brandenburg. Luther enclosed ninety-five theses or propositions for debate for the pious consideration of the man who was splitting the take of the indulgence traffic.

A heated scholarly debate has raged in recent years over how Luther's Ninety-five Theses came before the public. The traditional view holds that on the eve of All Saints, October 31, 1517, Luther nailed a copy of the theses to the church door at Wittenberg. It is said that such a posting was normal procedure when one wished to announce an academic debate, and beyond that, those entering the church on All Saints' Day to view the relics exhibited by the elector would see the theses. The magnificent picture frequently drawn of dauntless Martin Luther pounding the theses to the door with a great hammer is irresistible, the symbolism overpowering. One man with a hammer knocks the old order down, and in a motion picture made by the Lutheran Church in the 1950s the pounding hammer resounds like a cannon in the ghostly church on the other side of the door. For many years it was supposed that someone copied the theses off the door, translated them from Latin into German, and had them reprinted so that they flew over Germany and made Luther a hero overnight.

Certainly the theses were quickly translated and circulated and Luther suddenly was propelled into fame. But in 1961 a German Catholic scholar, Erwin Iserloh, raised a question: Were the theses posted? In the current mood of Catholic ecumenicity, Iserloh was sympathetic to Luther. But he considered these facts. Nowhere in his table talk in later years did Luther speak of posting the Ninety-five Theses on the church door. In none of his own works reviewing the beginning of the controversy does he mention any public posting. He recalled that he preached to his people about grace and remission of sins against the shallow proclamations of the indulgence sellers, and he seems to have discussed the matter in private with associates and to have sent copies of the theses to learned friends. But none of this resembles a public act of hammering the theses onto a church door and calling for a disputation.

Iserloh holds that the story of the nailing of the theses to the church door comes from the pen of Philipp Melanchthon, who wrote a short summary of Luther's life a few months after Luther died. Melanchthon (1497–1560) was a professor of Greek, with a mind much more orderly (and commonplace) than Luther's, and one of Luther's closest colleagues. He was to become celebrated as the "teacher of Germany" when he tried to restore public education to German children after the Reformation in the Protestant lands had virtually destroyed the old system of ecclesiastical schooling. But Melanchthon had not yet come to Wittenberg when the theses were written, and he could not have witnessed the event. He arrived only in August 1518.

The argument made by some that he surely would have been corrected by eyewitnesses had he been mistaken about the posting is an unwarranted inference from silence. Nearly thirty years had passed by the time Melanchthon wrote. It is not at all certain that eyewitnesses abounded. Melanchthon made other errors in his account of Luther's life, but no one corrected him. Even if corrections are offered, they are no guarantee that any author will think enough of them to embody them in a revision.

Luther always claimed to have gone through channels, and Iserloh takes him seriously, concluding that the theses were not posted. Protestant scholars have reacted with dismay at the shattering of an icon. They have made elaborate arguments to prove that the theses were indeed posted as Melanchthon says they were.[16] We are handicapped because Luther himself never regarded the indulgence issue as important as his "discovery" of the gospel that came afterward. He frequently regretted that he had been a convinced papist when he fired his opening salvo against indulgences—meaning that he did not suppose the Ninety-five Theses represented a radical break with the essence of Catholic tradition.

We can do no more than attempt a plausible reconstruction of the fragmentary evidence, to explain as much as possible without tumbling into inexplicable contradictions with our incomplete sources. In October 1516 Luther complained to his friend Johann Lang of needing two secretaries because he was writing letters all day long;[17] yet from that year we have today only twenty-one letters from Luther's hand.

My own attempt to fit together the fragments of evidence has led to the following view of events. Luther was enraged at what he heard about Tetzel's indulgence hawking at Jüterbog. In that angry mood, he did what one might expect from so vehement a temperament: he fired off a letter on indulgences to his archbishop, the man supposed to oversee the religious life of the entire region. Nothing indicates that he wanted a public quarrel with Albrecht of Brandenburg or that he wanted to embarrass the Elector Frederick. In early November he wrote to his friend Spalatin that he did not want his theses to come into the hands of the elector before they had been received by those against whom they were directed, an indication that they were not meant for an academic audience in Wittenberg itself. He did not want anyone to suppose that the elector had anything to do with writing them. Apparently such rumors were already abroad as if to make it seem that the theses were an attack by the elector on Albrecht of Brandenburg.[18] It is difficult to imagine how the theses could have been posted on the door of the castle church without someone's having shown them to the elector. Luther seems to have written to Spalatin in the certainty that no one could have communicated his work to Frederick. Such assurance would seem absurd had the theses been already public. The theses seem to have been meant for Albrecht alone, a warning shot fired across the bow to make the young archbishop take stock of his course.

Even without posting, the theses represented a dangerous move. Albrecht of Mainz was a noble of the church while Luther was only a little monk, a nobody in a little university in a little place. Bishops could put monks in prison if they chose. Certain conventions of the time had to be observed for any communication between men of such disparate ranks. Luther's letter to Albrecht heaped flattery on the archbishop's head and humility on his own— customary conventions of late medieval Latin letters.

Luther began by calling himself a little shit of a man *(fex hominum)* daring to send a letter to someone as exalted as Albrecht. He was conscious of his low status and his sinfulness, he said. He also refrained from accusing the indulgence preachers, whom he claimed not to have heard. But he grieved, he said, at the false ideas that everywhere agitated the vulgar. He summarized many of the ninety-five theses he had sent along.

A bishop had duties, and a bishop was not saved by his office, Luther said, his humility the velvet glove on his steel fist of righteous indignation. Salvation of souls was, he declared—following the Old Testament prophets Amos and Zacharias—like plucking smoldering brands from the fire. Indulgences did no good in bringing the soul to salvation or to sanctity. Christ did not command us to preach indulgences, but he vehemently commanded the gospel to be preached. The gospel was drowned out by the thundering of indulgences.[19] Luther may have planned to send the letter and then, almost as an afterthought as he wrote, conceived the idea of the Ninety-five Theses. They allowed him to present his views in terms far more pungent and detailed than would have been possible in a letter to so esteemed a prince of the church. By presenting his arguments in the form of serial theses for debate in academic surroundings, he could avoid disrespect to his spiritual lord, and he could also make the claim that nothing he said was a firm tenet of his beliefs.

It was a safety device often employed by writers of dialogues during that century and afterward, and both Erasmus and, later, Galileo resorted to it. One could say something potentially dangerous, but, if pressed, one could retreat. The theses were not a dialogue, of course. But we know that Luther was reading the *Julius Exclusus* of Erasmus about the time he wrote them.[20] Here Erasmus had written a thunderously satirical dialogue against the old warrior Pope Julius II, who arrived at the gates of heaven only to be turned away by St. Peter, who did not recognize him in armor. Erasmus had not signed his name to this dialogue, although he never flatly denied writing it, and Thomas More wrote him discreetly inquiring what was to be done with a manuscript of the work in the handwriting of Erasmus himself that had come into More's possession. From this satirical little opus, Luther might well have taken the notion of phrasing his thoughts on indulgences in a form reasonably safe in a world where heresy was punished by horrible death. He could—as he later did—represent them as matters for discussion rather than as positions firmly adopted, and he could even if need be present them humorously. Hence he could utter such sentiments as these:

When our Lord and Master, Jesus Christ, says "Repent," he means that all the life of the faithful man should be repentance.

The pope cannot forgive any sin; he can only make known and testify to God's forgiveness.

The priests who, when someone is dying, issue penances for him to do in purgatory act stupidly and wickedly.

These weeds—namely, penances changed into the pains of purgatory—were sown evidently while the bishops were fast asleep.

Christians should be taught that if the pope knew the greedy crookedness of the indulgence preachers, he would prefer to let St. Peter's Cathedral be burned to cinders than have it erected with the skin, body, and bones of his flock.

Christians should be taught that in conferring indulgences, the pope needs and yearns for fervent prayer for himself instead of their money.[21]

Each thesis was alleged to be a point in an academic debate. The supporting evidence supposedly would be brought forward in the debate itself. At the moment they constituted a short, pungent, witty, and provocative position paper that might be an introduction to a serious discussion of the matter. His aim seemed to be to call attention to an annoying and pernicious abuse in the church. Even an archbishop could understand them. They have the look of ideas dashed off to vent his spleen, but they were powerful nevertheless, and they fitted easily into the theology he had been developing in his lectures. They struck at the roots of papal sovereignty, and they were bound to create a scandal among churchmen in high places.

Luther said that the pope could not remit any penalties except those he imposed himself. This meant that the pope might tell a Christian to go on a pilgrimage and change his mind and tell him to stay home. Or the pope could impose a penalty for eating meat on Friday but revoke it if there was a reason for doing so. But nobody ever claimed that the pope could send anyone to purgatory. Consequently Luther's thesis meant that the pope could not free anyone from purgatory, since such release was in the hand of God. Luther's statement was mild enough, but its meaning was sharp, given the claims of popes from Sixtus IV on. Sentiments limiting papal power are repeated several times in slightly different ways in the Ninety-five Theses. I rather think that this repetition lends credence to the notion that the theses were not designed for formal academic debate but were a succession of running heads, meant to be easily understood and to stand by themselves. In any case the debate over indulgences never took place because the issue quickly became whether the pope had authority over purgatory and then whether the pope had authority in the church.

Luther was cautious in the Ninety-five Theses. He was agitated and even impetuous, but he was not foolhardy. He expressed doubt on the "treasures of the church, out of which the pope distributes indulgences." They were, he said, "not sufficiently discussed or known among the people of Christ."[22] He referred to the excess of merit supposedly earned by the saints and deposited to a heavenly account to be drawn upon by the pope for distribution to less worthy Christians on earth and in purgatory. Luther had no place for merits of the saints and therefore no place for a treasury of merit. Yet neither in these earlier works nor here did he deny outright the Catholic teaching about saints. We don't know enough about this treasury of merit, he said; therefore, he implied, even a pope cannot make pronouncements about it. He suggested that the pope was ignorant of the abuses propagated by the indulgence sellers. In reading this proposition, one could suppose that he recognized some good in indulgences, that he castigated only the lies of the indulgence sellers. But he never explicitly conceded to indulgences any validity at all.

In time he was to reject purgatory. Like indulgences, the doctrine of purgatory had not been of ancient belief in the church. It arose from the habit of praying for the dead, a practice that does go far back into Christian antiquity and that probably came from the example of pagans, especially the Egyptians.[23] Such prayers were intended to help the dead attain blessing in the hereafter. Augustine believed that some of the dead passed through a purgatorial fire where they might be aided by the prayers of the living—but only if they had lived lives of faith before they died.[24] Not until the high scholastic period, however, did the rationalizing tendency of medieval Christendom work this rather primitive and simple practice into a full-blown doctrine of purgatory. Through the intervening centuries various ideas concerrning the fate of the dead contended with one another among theologians and in popular piety. By the thirteenth century purgatory had become a place, measured out and mathematically linked, says Jacques le Goff, with new conceptions of space and time. Le Goff supposes that the detailed building up of purgatory in the twelfth century corresponded with a growth in the joy of life and, alongside this joy, the fear of death. The twelfth century, he suggests, featured an enrichment of memory. The great aristocratic families made much of their genealogies and of family solidarity. Death became less of a frontier. "Purgatory then became an annex of earth and prolonged the time of life and memory."[25] The living on this earth and the dead in purgatory have intimate connections that the grave does not sever.

One might suggest a further thought here. Purgatory focused attention on time. Purgatory was temporal because it had an end. We have already noted the millions of years of time released from purgatory by veneration of the relics preserved by Albrecht of Mainz. I am not aware of any writer from the classical age of Greece and Rome who spoke of "millions of years." Certainly there is no such rhetoric in the Bible, either in the Old or New Testament. The Bible speaks of "ages" and "everlasting" and "eternal," but the longest time mentioned in Old or New Testaments is a "thousand years." All these terms might be interpreted as meaning only a good long time without being able to convey a sense of infinite time that we now take for granted with our own sense of the immensity of space and the billions of years extending back to the beginning of our universe. Could ancient or medieval people imagine such numbers? I am not sure they could. Medieval chronicles habitually begin with the creation of Adam and march forward in smooth progression to the lifetime of the chronicler who puts all this down in a smallish book. It all seems restricted, almost cozy.

But with the advent of more complicated speculations about purgatory and the power of indulgences, time begins to be talked and written about under new and perhaps horrifying expressions. If my conjectures here have any validity, I am still unable to guess which came first—the talk of purgatory in terms of millions of years, or broadening conceptions of time that were transferred to the theology of purgatory. But I believe we have a new kind of expression here, a vast expansion of the imagination to ponder infinite succession to an extent unknown in Greece or Rome or the early Middle Ages. In the seventeenth century Blaise Pascal could shudder with horror at the contemplation of infinite space. A shudder before infinite space seems natural to our ancestors in the revolutionary world of Galileo and Newton, the world of the telescope and mathematical law. Can we suppose a similar horror toward the discovery of infinite time? Is it possible that our more remote forebears had no conception of what it is to inhabit time that can be measured in millions of years? And is it then also possible that the awakening of such a conception might bring with it a horror akin to Pascal's before space? Certainly that horror might be translated into a sense of how long we are dead, how all that we know and yearn to have is dissolved in the immensity of time, and how futile our own existence is before the ceaseless flow of infinite years. This is, to be sure, an existential awareness of modern times. But I think it just possible that the rhetoric of purgatory, now usually noted only to be ridiculed, marks one of the great watersheds of our history, and that the sense of years by the million that it betokens can help explain Luther's sense of the horror of death as annihilation.

The doctrine of purgatory obviously contradicts other ideas of Christian faith. Does purgatory continue after the resurrection of the dead and the great day of judgment? Christians routinely expected the end of time to come soon—certainly not a million years from now. The artists who depicted the resurrection showed the dead coming out of their graves, not out of purgatory. Would purgatory continue after this great event? The idea seems strange. But for the moment, purgatory encapsulated a growing sense of the immensity of time and indeed of the idea of infinity itself. Luther did not treat all these questions.

In the Ninety-five Theses Luther seemed to reject the notion of purgatory as an extension of life. Death is death, its horrors so awful that one does not need further torments. Said he in Thesis 14: "Imperfect piety or love on the part of the dying person necessarily brings with it great fear; and the smaller the love, the greater the fear." The idea seems akin to Luther's lectures on Hebrews, where he taught that those who loved God did not fear death. And then in Thesis 16 we have a puzzling remark: "Hell, purgatory, and heaven seem to differ the same as despair, fear, and assurance of salvation." What does he mean? Can it be that the sufferings of hell and purgatory are nothing more than the dread of death and the damnation of the grave that we feel in this life as we contemplate our natural end? Is hell then a psychological affair? It would seem so.

His sudden and inflamed notoriety required Luther to publish a little book of *Explanations of the Ninety-five Theses*. This enlarged tractate did not appear until August 1518, although Luther had completed a draft by February of that year. By then he was being roundly accused of heresy, and the pope had been forced to take note of him. Luther sent copies to Staupitz and to Leo X, addressing the pope respectfully. The aim of the *Explanations* was to prove Luther's orthodoxy against his accusers, and we see him making more definite statements about purgatory than he had before. Yet they are ambiguous.

In considering Thesis 14, Luther alludes to 1 John 4:18 in saying that perfect love eliminates fear. But, he says, even among the redeemed, vestiges of the carnal man remain, and neither faith nor love is perfect. Terror and horror before death arise from defective faith; assurance arises from faith. The assumption is that distrust and faith exist together in Christian life—a far cry from the spirit of the legends of saints who approached death with total confidence in God and paradise.[26] Some may face death unafraid when they confront martyrdom, Luther suggested a little later on in these *Explanations,* but they were not typical Christians.[27] Now he says in his explanation of Thesis 15, "I say nothing of fire and the place of purgatory, not that I deny them but that this disputation is about something else." He does not know the place of purgatory, he says—though he recalls that Aquinas said it was under the earth, (as did Dante). He agrees with Augustine that the state of souls after death is beyond our understanding, but he believes most certainly *(Mihi certissimum est)* that purgatory exists because in the *Confessions* Augustine noted that he prayed for his mother and his father after they had died.[28] Then he makes a revealing comment that cracks a window onto the innermost wrestling of his soul: What if in the time of the apostles purgatory did not exist, as a certain heretic had declared some years earlier? Should anyone believe a heretic born scarcely fifty years ago and disbelieve the tradition of the church going back to St. Augustine eleven hundred years before?

Here was the crux. By the sixteenth century, churchmen knew that the only persuasive proof for church doctrine lay in tradition, the continuation of belief for hundreds of years. As Thomas More and battalions of other Catholic foes of Luther would say, Christ had promised to be with his people the church until the end of the world. If the church erred in any particular and if the error continued for a long period without being eradicated by divine intervention, Christ had broken his promise, and the world would be plunged into a chaos of meaninglessness where it would be impossible to know the way of salvation and perhaps even impossible to know the difference between right and wrong. The assumption that tradition defined faith was to the Catholic Church of the sixteenth century what the theorem that parallel lines never meet was to Euclid.

Luther demonstrates by his statement of the issue here that he knew the consequences of rejecting a traditional doctrine like purgatory. Yet he says, "But even if purgatory did not exist at the time of the apostles . . ."[29] Why did he not say, "But even if the apostles did not teach purgatory," or "But even if there was no doctrine of purgatory"? Was this a slip of the pen? It seems plausible that we have caught him here in the midst of his pondering the ultimate issue of his Reformation, whether authority came from the church and its hold over revelation, or from scripture alone.

Throughout these comments on the afterlife, Luther tends to interpret the suffering of purgatory and hell psychologically rather than "geographically" or physically. The sufferings of the impious are seen to be terror, horror, trembling, and apprehension.[30] It is possible to have such agony of spirit in this life, even the torments of hell, without assuming that hell is a place to be located on some celestial map of divine things. Here, in his exposition of Thesis 15, Luther says, "But even I once knew a man who declared himself to have suffered these torments indeed during an interval of the briefest time, but they were so great and so hellish that neither tongue could say nor pen write nor the inexperienced believe, and had they lasted for a half hour or ten minutes, he would have perished utterly and all his bones reduced to ashes."[31] Was this an autobiographical utterance? Most biographies have taken it to be so, though some scholars have doubted it.[32] Whether autobiographical or not, it seems in this context to be a statement of terror before death that was so hellish no torments of hell beyond the grave were needed. The fear of hell becomes psychological, existential, part of this life, this time without reference to eternal suffering after death.

It is perhaps significant that Luther's explanation of Thesis 16 is brief and does not answer the questions the thesis seems to raise in its original form. The souls in purgatory despair, he says. They groan and tremble and do not know whether they should hope or embrace despair. But then he breaks off. He will not speak more on these abstruse topics, he says. He will not speak as the indulgence sellers do of something he knows nothing about.[33]

Throughout the *Explanations*, Luther seems to have found himself wrestling with problems that became more complex, profound, and troubling as he pondered them. When he wrote the Ninety-five Theses, he had not been forced to think them out. Like most writers, he discovered that the process of setting down thoughts on paper changed them, expanded them, made him weigh them more carefully, perhaps made him see things that he had not seen at all when he began to write. As he worked, he realized how far he had traveled from official Catholic Christendom. In later life Luther often said that he entered the fray against indulgences without knowing where he was going. Had he known the consequences of his theses, he would not have thrown himself into battle. The wisdom of God, he said, had made him like a blind horse.[34] It was his picturesque way of saying that he had been an unknowing tool in the hand of God, going where God meant him to go rather than where he himself intended. But all that was later.

One element is constant in this work. He was resigned to accept God's will. In his *Explanations* he alluded to the desire of Pope Leo X to sponsor a crusade against the Turks. The Turks, said Luther, were what the Assyrians had been to Israel, God's scourge to punish wickedness. We should rather, he said, be fighting our iniquity rather than the rod of God's anger represented by the Turkish threat.[35] (He quickly changed his mind as the Turkish threat loomed closer. By 1532, when he sat at table one evening with students and friends, he said he wished he could be Samson. Then he would kill a thousand Turks a day, and in a year that would be 350,000 [*sic*] Turks.)[36]

The Ninety-five Theses made Luther famous within a month after he wrote them. They were picked up (perhaps by someone in the court of Albrecht of Mainz), translated into German, and carried from town to town in a rush of printing and reprinting. The reason for their overnight popularity was not so much theological as economic and national. Luther's fierce and mocking attacks on the papacy struck with bludgeoning irony and wit. Yet throughout, Luther was careful not to attack the pope himself. He took the standard tack of rebels in the later Middle Ages, that they revolted against evil counselors, not the ruler himself. Even his most scathing theses, he posed as the honest man unable to answer embarrassing questions asked by honest folk. He wrote his questions as if to report them. But there they were, as bold as a lash laid on the backs of arrogant and grasping peddlers of fraudulent goods: If the pope could empty purgatory by fiat, why would he not do so out of love rather than for money? If indulgences released people from purgatory and conveyed them directly to paradise, why did priests continue to pray for the souls of those who had left them endowments to do so? Why did the pope not return these endowments to the families of the deceased? In this thesis Luther was cleverly returning to the original claim of Pope Sixtus IV that once a plenary indulgence had been granted, it was no longer necessary to pray for a dead soul. Obviously priests paid to pray for the dead continued their efforts after papal plenary indulgences had been acquired for those departed spirits—and to collect their fees. Why didn't the pope, whose wealth was enormous, not build St. Peter's with his own money instead of collecting money from poor Christians? Given the wealth pouring into Rome from all the Christian world, the question might seem natural; but it was also a statement.

Read even today the Ninety-five Theses are sharp and witty. By December, when they had been translated into German, printed, and distributed throughout the empire, Germans everywhere were laughing and nodding their heads, and Luther's name was a household word. We cannot know precisely what was on Luther's mind in each of these theses when he wrote them—not even when we have his explanations of almost a year later. Were they heretical? The answer is no—not at least in themselves. Many extremists in the church claimed that popes were infallible, but that tangled issue was not settled even by the First Vatican Council of 1869–70, which defined the doctrine of papal infallibility. The pope is infallible when he speaks *ex cathedra* for the whole church. Fine and good. But when does he do that? The decree of July 18, 1870, affirming the doctrine is notoriously exalted and notoriously vague.[37] A century after the Council of Constance, when the church had accepted the superiority of the council over the pope, Luther's theses would have seemed altogether proper to multitudes of educated Christians, especially those offended by tales of open immorality by popes and members of the papal curia. Yet in Luther's lectures on the Bible, he was already a world away from the popular practices of Christian piety represented by indulgences and the paraphernalia of saint worship and concern for the state of the dead in purgatory.

It is worth repeating that Luther had not explicitly denied any of these popular practices at the time he penned his theses. He had had no reason to define his evolving positions publicly over against the complex and contradictory doctrines of the church universal. The controversy over indulgences forced definition on him and therefore makes sense of his claim in the preface of the 1545 edition to his Latin works that when he became notorious, he had been the maddest of papists, submerged in papal doctrines.[38] It is simply to say that like most of us Luther had managed to profess his beliefs in contradictory ideas because he had not been forced to compare them and choose one over the other. Between the time of his visit to Rome and the outbreak of the controversy over indulgences, purgatory received little mention. He appears to have thought very little about it. Even in the Ninety-five Theses he seems not to take the doctrine seriously, and the horror of death looms much larger than the penalties of purgatory.

Now there was no turning back. By December he was famous—or notorious, depending on one's point of view. Apparently indulgence sales fell off dramatically in the months that followed. Papal forces gathered themselves for counterattack.

9

✠

PREPARING FOR BATTLE

M EANWHILE, Luther threw himself into a frenzy of work. His correspondence flourished. He communicated with the Elector Frederick through Spalatin—in Latin. Now and then prince and professor exchanged letters—in German. Luther was humble but forthright, always willing to give annoying advice. His first letter to Frederick in November 1517, immediately after the Ninety-five Theses, begged him not to impose a tax that Luther had heard was imminent.[1]

With the elector's backing, Luther undertook reform of the curriculum of the university, drawing it away from scholasticism and more into the Renaissance mode of asking students to study the ancient texts of Christianity—the Bible and the church fathers—rather than the Aristotelian dialectic of the scholastics. Many biographers speak of this reform movement as "humanist." But we should be careful about using the words "humanist" and "humanism," since they were not coined during the Renaissance. They often carry a freight—even among scholars—that Luther would scarcely have recognized or condoned. The faculty of arts undertook to teach Aristotle's philosophical texts according to the best translations, especially his scientific works such as his physics, filled with errors and nonsense but representing the best that the classical world had to offer to explain natural phenomena. The logic of Aristotle was also taught, Luther agreeing with the consensus of his time that syllogistic reasoning in Aristotle's logic was the key to sorting out arguments about things of this world.[2]

But such logic had no place in theology. In a letter to Spalatin of February 22, 1518, Luther considered his friend's question: Is dialectic worthwhile *(arbiter)* for the confirmation of faith it allows the theologian? Spalatin had probably posed the question as part of the discussion over what kind of curriculum the university should have. The word *arbiter* literally means "witness" or "judge," and indicates that Spalatin was thinking of dialectic as the scholastics did, not as source of revelation but as support, a witness to the truth.[3] Luther's answer was a crashing negative. Dialectic might be a children's game. But it could be of no value in studying scripture. Syllogistic reasoning must be left behind when Christians came to faith. And here Luther—the "literal" interpreter of scripture—used an allegory. He referred to Genesis 22:5, where in preparing to sacrifice his son Isaac, Abraham left his servants behind while he led Isaac beyond to the place where he intended to kill the boy. There God sent an angel to stay his hand. Syllogisms, said Luther, must be left behind like the asses of Abraham when we interpret scripture. The metaphor suggests that syllogisms might be useful in bearing worldly burdens, in reasoning about the affairs of this life—an idea that Luther picked up later when he was forced to consider whether his renunciation of reason was absolute or whether it applied only to matters of faith. But for scriptural study he found dialectic unambiguously useless. We become students of scripture only by listening to an inner voice, heeding enlightenment from above, not by reasoning our way to understanding by logic alone.

Luther thus limited his arguments to quotation from scripture—the interpretations of the quotations certified by the authority of the inner voice speaking in the heart of the true Christian. His method of interpreting meant that he would always be unable to accept any major disagreement from his convictions. He felt that he had illumination from above, not by his own merit, to be sure, and not by ecstatic revelation, but by the grace of God working quietly in his own experience, and if anyone should disagree with him on an important matter, he could only pile up scriptural quotations and consign his opponent to God's judgment. Often, as foes would gleefully point out, he could use the same scriptural text in contradictory ways.

This is mysticism of a sort, getting to God through experience, but the most exalted mystical state involves a warm feeling of union with God. The most radical mystic yearns for the soul to disappear into the divine as a drop of water may disappear in the sea or a spark may vanish in the sun. Ecstatic mysticism with its dissolving of individual consciousness in the divine was never congenial to Luther. He used mystical language not as an end in itself but rather as a tool to understand scripture. The effect was to place his gospel beyond compromise or debate, and it was to some degree to deify his voluble intuitions.

At the moment he was rapidly developing the implications of his own theology of grace. Staupitz apparently wrote him in some anxiety in March

1518 that Luther was being widely condemned for renouncing the cult of the rosary and liturgical prayers, especially those prayers that monks chanted again and again. Luther was also accused of rejecting all "good works." It would seem that the *bona opera* Luther condemned were ritual practices intended to pile up merit on the part of those who performed them mechanically—works such as repeated prayers and saying the rosary. Luther took his stand with the warmly mystical *German Theology*, which he had edited and which Staupitz himself had given to the printer. This little book emphasized submission to God. The key words in it are "obedience" and "peace." It does not expound any general articles of faith as one might expect in a creed; neither does it assume that Christian faith is a matter of argument.

In his letter to Staupitz, Luther took the same line. He submits himself to Christ. But unlike the author of the *German Theology*, he is unable to do so without castigating the scholastics for what they pretend to know about God. He judges the scholastics only as they judge each other, he says; he neither rejects nor accepts everything they say—just as they neither reject nor accept one another. His adversaries hate him, he says. No matter. Words can do him no harm. He closes with a note of trust—or fatalism. The issue is in God's hands. If God works in a cause, no one can withstand it; if God is silent, no one can give the cause life. He asks Staupitz to pray for him "and for the truth of God, wherever it may be." He signed the letter "Fr. M. Eleutherius," making a Greek pun on his name to become "Brother Martin the Most Free."[4]

Whatever restraint he had felt about publicity for his Ninety-five Theses dissolved under the force of the attacks on him, and Luther struck back. Early in 1518 he published his first controversial work in German, his *Sermon on Grace and Indulgence*. It was popular, reprinted quickly some twenty times, sweeping through German's important cities.[5] Here he made a frontal assault on the entire doctrine of indulgences. Indulgences, he said, were for lazy Christians who did not want to do good works. Far better to take the money spent on indulgences and give it to the poor.

Now Luther was caught up in a torrent of feeling and argument. In reading this little work and in pondering Luther's impatient temperament and the furious drive amply evident in his life, we may see him here already launched on the tide that would carry him out of the Catholic Church. As the general supervisor of Augustinian monks in his region, he attended the triennial meeting of the Augustinian order in Heidelberg in April. He was the man of the hour, with all the prerequisites for literary fame—popular acclaim, furious enemies, and angry reviews. Over the next three years, Luther's enemies made every mistake that would ensure the conversion of protest into permanent rupture.

Johann Tetzel's Dominican order rushed blindly to his defense against Luther the Augustinian. Since the Cathar heresy, the Dominicans had become expert inquisitors, seeking out heretics and witches, refining psychological and physical tortures guaranteed to make any suspect confess anything, afterward triumphantly herding their victims to the secular authorities to be put to death. The Dominicans and other heresy hunters played an ambiguous role in forming the religious consciousness of the time. On the one hand their willingness to raise the cry of heresy at the slightest provocation certified them as rock-hard and implacable defenders of the church and made them feared. But their habitual shrillness convinced many that they were not to be trusted. Consequently their vitriolic attacks on Luther seemed to persuade many that Luther's ideas might be worth considering. "The dogs of the Lord," people called them, making a pun on their Latin name "Dominicanes." Now they sniffed over Luther's Ninety-five Theses and began to bark as if they had treed a heretic. In so doing they elevated Luther in public opinion and gave him a wider audience.

On April 11 Luther set out on foot across Germany to Heidelberg, keeping Spalatin informed of his progress and complaining mightily about the fatigue of walking. At the Augustinian monastery at Würzburg the local bishop came to see him and supplied a wagon to convey him the rest of the way. The Elector Frederick and the Saxon court feared for Luther's safety. The elector posted letters to various dignitaries along his professor's route, asking them to look out for him. But Luther was received everywhere as a celebrity, and the convent at Heidelberg saw him as a champion against their Dominican rivals.[6] Luther was officially at Heidelberg to support one of his students, who was to debate theses written by Luther. So the disputation was to be an exercise in apprenticeship. It appears from Luther's report of the affair to Spalatin that he participated fully in the discussions and that his formal opponents were courteous and even admiring, even as they rebutted his views.[7] The theses he argued were not about indulgences but about grace and human nature. By this astute move Luther was able to settle on some of the well-known doctrines of Augustine himself and in some degree to defend his own orthodoxy. Moreover, if the Augustinian view of grace was accepted in its purest form, the doctrine of indulgences would topple of its own weight.

Luther spoke in a mode that was to become common to him—paradox, the opposite of the scholastic habit of linear reasoning intended to iron out contradictions. Luther's paradoxes were filled with contradictions exuberantly asserted. Human works may seem "attractive and good," he said. But they are likely to be mortal sins. God's works are "always unattractive and appear evil," but they are nevertheless eternal good. After the fall, free will can choose only evil. When we do the best we can or what is in us *(facere quod in se est),* we do not gain merit as the theologians of the *via moderna* taught. Rather we commit mortal sin. The true theologian is not one "who looks upon the invisible things of God as though they were clearly perceptible in those things that have actually happened. He deserves to be called a theologian . . . who comprehends the visible and manifest things of God seen through suffering and the cross."[8]

Although we have the theses that Luther and his student advanced at Heidelberg, we lack a transcript of what he and his formal opponents said during the disputation. Even so, his intentions seem clear enough. He attacked the fundamental definition Aristotle gives for the reasoning process. Reasoning, says Aristotle, is a process of inference, of going from the visible and the obvious to what logically follows from what we observe. In the *Prior Analytics,* Aristotle describes syllogistic reasoning as a sequential process by which we begin with an assumption—either an observation or some proposition previously gained by reasoning or by the common opinion of the wise—and proceed like this: "Because A is true, we may infer that B is also true." If I observe that you have walked into my office carrying an umbrella and wearing a raincoat with water cascading off your clothes to puddle on my floor, I may infer plausibly that it is raining outside. As I have said earlier, both Aristotle and Aquinas believed that one could use this sort of reasoning to infer many qualities about God—including his existence—though Aristotle and Aquinas defined God in radically different ways.

By Luther's time the Catholic Church had moved to affirm this sort of reasoning to support its own authority, by no means as a substitute for revelation but as a tool to confirm the teachings of the church by demonstrating their unity and perseverance through the centuries. In the controversy Luther stirred up, a Catholic polemicist such as Thomas More would fling the same charge against Luther time and again. Christ promised to be with his church until the end of the world. Only the Catholic Church could claim unbroken existence from the time of Christ to the present. Heretics had broken away, but their heresies had soon withered and died. Therefore only one church—the Catholic Church—could claim to be the recipient of Christ's promise. This was Aristotelian logic applied to a Christian assumption, a logic based on the conviction that the parts of a rational whole could not contradict one another. By rejecting the logic and by using paradox as argument, Luther was mentally prepared to reject the claim of the church for its own validity even before his overt break with Rome.

It is the theme that he had worked out in his lectures on the Psalms. Nothing we see in the outward world, either in nature or in history, tells us anything about God. God hides in mystery. Why does he hide himself? That is part of his mystery. No inference can reveal what the mystery conceals. Suffering and the cross reveal God. Here we must take Luther to mean that the suffering of the true theologian is the desire for peace with God, a desire not easily satisfied, one that can be met only by bonding with Christ. This peace with God includes confidence that God is what Christian faith says he is, the all-powerful personal spirit able to resurrect believers from death. Luther loved Christ for sharing death with all its horror and darkness and for the triumph of the Resurrection. For Luther to trust in Christ was to count on recapitulating ourselves in his life, death, and resurrection to life again.

Throughout the Heidelberg disputation, Luther equates the wrath of God against sin with death and not with a hell beyond Judgment Day. In his discussion of the universality of sin, Luther directly joins our corrupt human nature with the fear of death. "We are created good," he says, following Augustine closely, but we are diseased by sin, and we cannot but yield to its effects. We cannot comfort ourselves by the admonition of the theologians of the *via moderna* to do what is in us. "Do what is in you, and do not fear death," they say. But, says Luther,

> I ask, what man does not shudder, does not despair, in the face of death? Who does not flee it? And yet because God wishes that we endure it, it is apparent that we by nature love our will more than the will of God. For if we should love the will of God more, we should submit to death with joy, indeed we should consider it a gain, just as though we considered it to be our will. Therefore we are discussing figments of our imagination. He loves God less than himself, even hates him, who hates or does not love death (that is, the will of God).[9]

This seems to be a clear definition by Luther of his *Anfechtungen*. One's relation to God is defined by one's relation to death. To be terrified by death is to admit to oneself that one does not love God, does not accept God's will, does not perhaps even believe in God. And yet the terror before death, for Luther at least, is inescapable. The continued presence of the terror is thus a continued witness to damning unbelief, to the worst kind of sin. Luther seems more in control of himself here, able to speak what was earlier unspeakable. This is human nature, the way we are, he says. As frail human beings we do not love God more than we love our own life and our will. This terror is proof and symbol of our depravity. Almost as an afterthought, he adds, "What shall I say then about hell? Who does not hate it?" Does he mean that hell, too, is part of the will of God for some? His theology adds up to that point of view. But he seems disinclined to pursue it, and, as usual when he feels compelled to make some reference to hell, he fails to expatiate on it. Perhaps he does not wish to define it. Hell does not concern him; death devours his mind.

In the latter theses of the disputation he attacks Aristotle directly. Among other things Luther condemns Aristotle for his materialism. "It was easy for Aristotle to believe that the world was eternal since he believed that the human soul was mortal." For if all things are material, the soul must be material, too. If all things are finally matter, the world must exist forever, or else it could not come into being out of nothing. "If Aristotle had recognized the absolute power of God, he would accordingly have maintained that it was impossible for matter to exist of itself alone."[10] The burden of the Heidelberg disputation seems to be that one knows God directly through the experience of seeking him or else one knows him not at all. In the brief notes appended to the theses themselves—notes perhaps used as prompts for Luther during the debate—we find an enthusiastic abnegation and rhetorical assurance that must have made Luther seem to his audience humble, heroic, and invincible.

He made a great impression at Heidelberg. Martin Bucer, later the reformer of Strasbourg, was in the crowd. He was enthralled. "His sweetness in answering is remarkable, his patience in listening is incomparable . . . his answers, so brief, so wise, and drawn from the Holy Scriptures, easily made all his hearers his admirers."[11] We could wish that Luther had kept that tone throughout his life. He did not.

He stopped at Erfurt on his way home. There he discovered that his former colleagues had continued their hostility toward him since his defection to Staupitz. Luther tried to be reconciled with them. He wrote to Jodokus Trutfetter, one of his old teachers, who had sent him a biting letter accusing him of ignorance and too stringent a criticism of the church. Luther seemed stung. He tried to placate Trutfetter, citing the intelligence and goodwill of colleagues at Wittenberg who supported him. But he held his ground. Reform of the church was impossible, he said, unless the canon law, the decretals, scholastic theology, and logic were rooted out and replaced with other studies, especially the Bible and the church fathers. He begged Trutfetter not to consent to the abuse of the "poor people of Christ" by the vexations of indulgences. He pleaded with his old teacher not to believe every slander heaped on his head.[12] Trutfetter at first refused to see him, but after this letter apparently relented. Reconciliation proved impossible.

Still Luther arrived back in Wittenberg in a confident mood. On May 15 he wrote to Spalatin, telling how he had been treated everywhere with kindness and respect. He had eaten and drunk well, and he said that some told him that he seemed healthier and heavier. Since his early portraits show him as skin and bones, even a little weight added to his frame would have been noticeable. He told how one of the young doctors among the theologians at Heidelberg had made everyone laugh by saying, "If the peasants heard this, they would certainly bury you with stones and kill you."[13] We do not know what utterance brought about this outburst. Perhaps it was Luther's insistence on suffering and lowliness. The peasants had had enough of such talk. They wanted more in this life, and in a few years those around Heidelberg would rise with others in Germany in the great revolt that would be a turning point in Luther's career. For the moment such negative thoughts were no more than a cloud the size of a man's hand against a sunny sky. The storm they portended was now about to burst on Luther and on Europe.

10

BEYOND HEIDELBERG

BEFORE he started to Heidelberg, Luther undertook his *Explanations of the Ninety-five Theses*. He continued it when he returned and published it in August—although his bishop, Jerome Scultetus, had ordered him not to put it in print. Already Luther must have begun to have confidence enough in the elector's protection to disobey his bishop's orders.

It was his longest publication to date. In it he argued his ninety-five propositions against indulgences one by one—though toward the end he lumped some of them together and considered them in a cursory way. It is useful to see this treatise as Luther's effort to work out his conviction that the Christian life is a matter of continual repentance, that true Christian faith is therefore an attitude rather than a system of ritual religious works. But what did this view of doctrine mean to the Catholic doctrine of tradition, which sanctioned any practice that had endured a long time in the church?

At heart here was a fundamental conviction that God was a person, a personality who moved invisibly in his creation, the mysterious director of history's great play on the stage of the world. This conviction was inevitably undermined by the drift of a recovered classical literature that posited fate or destiny or fortune as the blind, impersonal force that drove the world along. To deny the validity of Catholic tradition was to run the risk of denying that God was active in the human arena, for how could a living God have allowed the church to fall into depravity, the church that claimed to serve him, that numbered in its ranks so many saints, and that was confirmed by miracles done at its shrines?

In effect Luther had already abandoned the appeal to tradition in the way he went about interpreting scripture. In his biblical lectures he demonstrated large knowledge of other and earlier commentators, but his chief interest was human nature over against the holiness of God, and his chief rhetorical tool was quotation from scripture. Scripture was to him like a play to its audience, always present, not something merely confirmed by tradition or dead on a page but reenacted in his mind and heart in the present as he read it. Now he was forced to consider in more detail his attitude toward the authority of the church.

Where was the authority of the church located? Or, to put it another way, who spoke for the church in time of controversy? The extreme papalists replied that the pope was the only safe authority and that he was sovereign, that the power of the keys given to Peter in Matthew 16:18, the power to bind or loose in heaven and on earth, was passed on to Peter's successors the popes. All other voices in the church were too problematic. Papalists held to the sacred fiction that the pope had never erred in any of his official pronouncements on dogma. They also maintained that the papal authority had been established by Christ and that the sanctity of the pope's official acts was guaranteed by this divine fiat. This teaching Luther began to reject in the long work explaining his Ninety-five Theses.

He did so with obvious trepidation, even if we allow for the calculated rhetorical effect of his assertions of humility, his requests for instruction, his professions of obedience. He claims throughout to believe in the goodwill of the pope. But from the first he denies the jurisdiction of the pope over souls in purgatory. The pope cannot reduce or remove any punishments imposed by God on sinners. The pope can remove only penalties that he has imposed himself. This line of argument led Luther into more dangerous waters. As high priest of the church, the pope laid claim to incarnate to the fullest the powers of priesthood. From early times in the church, priesthood had been endowed with the authority to mediate between God and humankind. The issue of indulgences involved the role of priesthood in the sacrament of penance, the sacrament in which a priest conveyed the forgiveness of God for sins done after baptism.

Now Luther came close to saying that the pronouncement of forgiveness by the priest was only psychological, that God granted forgiveness as soon as he saw contrition in the sinner. The priest only affirmed what God had already done. The true Christian might feel despair and continued self-reproach. The word of the priest offered comfort, assurance of the forgiveness God had already granted. The priest, then, was not so much the instrument of grace as the person who persuaded the sinner that God was merciful.[1] The

pope could do only what any other Christian could do for souls in purgatory—pray for them.[2] These sentiments touched not only the papal primacy
but the doctrine of priesthood itself. Luther was now at the edge of heresy if
not beyond, whether he knew it or not, and in Rome the wheels intended to
grind heresy to powder now began slowly to turn.

Yet for many in Germany and elsewhere, Luther was a hero. Many admirers did not understand him. Many thought he was only a cruder version of
Erasmus, and it may be that at this time Erasmus himself saw Luther as an
amusing and interesting ally in the fight against abuses in the church. Erasmus was assaulted on every hand, accused of heresy and duplicity. On
March 5, 1518, he sent his friend Thomas More the *Conclusions on Papal
Pardons,*[3] obviously Luther's Ninety-five Theses. As late as October 17, 1518,
a year after the indulgences controversy broke, Erasmus could write Johann
Lang—one of Luther's best friends—that he had heard that Luther (whom
he called "Eleutherius") was supported by all the best men without exception. Some disapproved of Luther's comments on purgatory, Erasmus said,
but, he added, these people wanted to keep purgatory because it afforded
them a living.

As we have seen, Luther had already recognized the differences between
himself and Erasmus. Throughout Erasmus's work Luther found the classical
impulse, the notion that human beings gain virtue by a disciplined life and
that piety and decent living among one's neighbors in the world amount to
much the same thing. The wit, the immense learning, the pure Latin style of
Erasmus together with his astonishing scholarly output had won him friends
and admirers all over Europe. To be one of his correspondents was a mark of
status, and his correspondence was immense, in its modern Latin edition
taking up eleven fat volumes. To be considered an Erasmian was to some
degree to be safe.

The Dominicans defending Tetzel pushed accusations of heresy on the
grounds that Luther had questioned the authority of the pope. Pope Leo X
had a low opinion of monks, and he seems at first to have regarded the whole
affair as another dispute of the sort perpetually breaking out among the
quarrelsome monastic orders. He asked an official of the Augustinian order
in Rome, one Gabriel Venetus, to look into the matter.[4] But a little over a
month later word came to Rome that something more serious was afoot, that
Luther was questioning papal power itself. The heresy process speeded up.

Due process required that anyone under suspicion of heresy be summoned
before a clerical court to remove all cause of suspicion. The suspect was to be
given a charitable warning and offered either the opportunity to recant or the

prospect of a formal judicial examination. By June a formal process was begun in Rome to determine if indeed Luther was a heretic. Within a few weeks Luther was summoned to Rome to give an account of himself.[5] He was anxious. The summons arrived in Wittenberg on August 7, 1518. The accusations of heresy infuriated him. He felt himself a loyal son of the church. He wanted a formal, public disputation in which he could prove that his views were orthodox, supported by the Bible and the fathers of the church. If he was to have a hearing, he wanted it in Germany before German judges.[6] Frederick the Wise agreed and stood by his professor and his fledgling university. It was a good thing. Gabriel Venetus on August 25 sent word to the Saxon Congregation of Augustinians to seize Luther, "have him bound in chains, fetters and handcuffs," and sent immediately to Rome.[7] As Wilhelm Borth has demonstrated, Frederick was continuing a historic policy of Saxony—to expand the power of the territorial prince while reducing the administrative authority of the papal courts in his territories. Saxons were not to be tried in foreign courts, such as those of Rome and of bishops in the empire beyond the boundaries of Saxony.[8]

Luther's defense was that he was offering propositions for debate and that if he were proved wrong, he would abandon them. It was for him a matter of academic freedom, permission to turn over questions within the classroom so that the university might do the job expected of it by the church, examine the doctrines of Christianity so that they might be correctly defined and sorted out. "I shall never be a heretic," he wrote to Spalatin on August 28, and he continued to believe that a fair debate would vindicate him.[9]

An imperial Diet convened in the south German town of Augsburg during the late summer of 1518. Here the territorial princes met with the emperor to consider common topics of governance in the German lands. And here Emperor Maximilian, the "German Hercules," made his last appearance at a Diet before his death a few months later. He seemed to feel the end coming, and he sought to ensure the succession to the imperial office for his grandson, the eighteen-year-old Charles, who had been king of Spain since the death of Ferdinand of Aragon in 1516. As a compromise worked out by the court of Frederick the Wise, Luther went down to Augsburg to meet Jacopo di Vio de Gaeta, who called himself Thomas Cajetan (1480–1547) in honor of Thomas Aquinas and his own native town in Italy.

Cajetan was a cardinal and papal legate at the Diet. He did not come to Augsburg for a theological argument. He was sent by Pope Leo X to persuade the Germans to support a crusade against the Turks. The Turks had captured Constantinople in 1453, destroying the remnants of the Byzantine Empire.

Now they were moving steadily and lethally up the thick Balkan peninsula toward the rest of Europe, and the pope sought to raise the huge sum of 800,000 ducats to finance an army to beat back the Turkish threat. To ensure European concentration on the crusade, the pope sought a truce among all Christian princes, one that would stay in effect for fifteen years. Under the circumstances of Luther's protest against indulgences and the outcry raised all over Germany against papal financial exactions, the legation of Cajetan could hardly have been more inopportune. As a biographer of the Emperor Maximilian has written, at this Diet "for the first time all the enemies of Rome came together and agreed with each other within the narrow walls of one city."[10]

Cajetan was no diplomat. Still, he was highly respected and paradoxical. He was a Dominican and had devoted his life to the study of Thomas Aquinas, also a Dominican, with such intensity that under his influence Aquinas began to displace Peter the Lombard as the most important theologian in scholastic circles. Cajetan was a devoted Aristotelian, a logician, a supporter of papal supremacy in the church, and yet a reformer.

He could also change his mind. Early in his career he argued that the immortality of the soul could be demonstrated by reason alone. But perhaps persuaded by Aristotle himself, he argued later that immortality could not be proved by reason and that like the doctrines of the Trinity and the Incarnation, it had to be accepted solely on the basis of revelation through Christ. Revelation could be trusted only if the authority of the church was to be believed. It looks as if part of Cajetan's dogged insistence on papal authority arose from a conviction that only by this means could certainty of faith be ensured and the promise of life after death confirmed.

Yet Cajetan was also deeply offended by the immorality of clergy in Rome. He had worked hard for reform, demanding that priests under his jurisdiction practice charity in the cure of souls, and he fulminated against clergymen who frequented indecent entertainments. Later he was to be a major influence in the election of the reforming pope Adrian VI at the death of Leo X in 1522, and he had the courage to tell Pope Julius II that he should not merely claim that his power came from God but that he should also imitate the spirit of God.[11] It is too bad that Luther and Cajetan did not meet at a moment when they might have put their feet up and talked away a night as fellow seekers after truth, for they might have found much in common along with their differences.

Such an opportunity was not to be. It seems likely that Luther was allowed to see Cajetan only because the pope and the Roman curia were anticipating the death of Maximilian and feared the succession of his grandson to the imperial title. Maximilian had scored a great diplomatic coup in marrying off his son, Philip the Handsome, to the eldest daughter of Ferdinand and Isabella of Spain, Joanna. The first son of this union was Charles, born in February 1500. When Philip the Handsome died young and when Ferdinand and Isabella passed from the scene without leaving a male heir, Charles was left heir to vast territories—the Duchy of Burgundy, Spain itself, and (when Maximilian died) the territories of southeastern Europe that were eventually to form the Austrian Empire. Already the mighty Spaniards were engaged in conquering the richest and most populated regions of the New World, and although the flood of gold and silver from the New World to Spain had not yet begun, the legends of wealth to be found in this El Dorado now called America surged across Spain and Europe. The Emperor Maximilian must soon pay his debt to nature. For young Charles to succeed him was to pose danger to the pope's independence in Italy. Charles VIII of France had proved how weak Italy was. Everyone knew the wealth of the Italian cities. Both Spain and the empire kept oiled and shining in their armories of tradition their claims to parts of the Italian peninsula. Frederick as one of the electors would play a major role in choosing Maximilian's successor, and he might be persuaded to stand as a candidate himself. The pope did not wish to alienate him by seeming unfair in attacking Frederick's professor.

Luther arrived in Augsburg on October 7, constipated and sick at his stomach. He walked all but the last three miles, then hitched a ride on a wagon. He wrote to Spalatin on October 10 saying he had not yet met with Cajetan. Many years later he said that he refused to see Cajetan until he had a written safe conduct so he would not be hauled off to Rome and burned.[12] He first saw an Italian, Urban de Serralonga, who had for a time represented the pope at the court of Frederick the Wise. Serralonga was the kind of smooth-talking diplomat Luther hated, eager to patch things up without resolving anything, filled with diplomatic advice and foolish comments about indulgences and the power of the papacy. He wanted Luther to confess his heresy, recant, and go home. "Do you want to have a joust?" he demanded of Luther. "He is an Italian, and an Italian he remains," Luther said. "Italian" was the most insulting name he could call the man. Referring to indulgences, Serralonga said with a laugh, "Lies are good as long as they fill the box."[13] It was not a promising start.

Luther finally saw Cajetan on October 12 after the Diet had broken up. Then he spoke with the cardinal on three consecutive days. Each time he was accompanied by advisers, including, on the second day, his old friend Staupitz. He entertained few hopes for the meeting. Already on October 10 he told Spalatin that he was resolved to appeal to a future general council if the pope did not listen to him or if Cajetan threatened him with force rather than with argument.[14]

His forebodings proved correct. At their meetings, he prostrated himself before Cajetan. He was then allowed to rise to his knees. Finally he was allowed to stand. Apparently he was not allowed to sit during the entire interview. Luther himself doubtless came prepared to be slighted by an Italian Dominican, and he expected little good from one who revered Aquinas as Cajetan did. For his part, Cajetan had failed to get the Diet to cough up more than a pittance for the proposed crusade against the Turks, and he could suppose that the furor Luther had aroused over indulgences was largely responsible. Frederick the Wise had seen Cajetan near the end of August and asked him to treat Luther "like a father, not like a judge."[15] Such a request might depend on how one expected fathers to act. Cajetan expected the father of all the church to be obeyed.

So when Luther and Cajetan met, their conversation quickly turned to the authority of the pope: Could the pope by fiat conveyed through indulgences release souls from purgatory? Did the power of binding and loosing extend so far? Was the papal bull *Unigenitus* by which Pope Clement IV had claimed to preside over a treasury of merit accumulated by the saints in harmony with scripture? Here was the sticking point on which neither Cajetan nor Luther was willing to concede—papal authority. According to an account Luther wrote to Spalatin shortly after the meeting, Cajetan lost his temper. He screamed at Luther to recant, and when Luther tried to argue, the cardinal shouted him down. Luther saw Cajetan as yet another arrogant Italian trying to intimidate and denigrate a pious German. Much later on in his table talk, Luther said that he had appealed—seemingly informally in conversation—to a council in his conversations with Cajetan. The cardinal called him a "Gersonist" after Jean Gerson, the great conciliar thinker of the University of Paris, who had been a leader in summoning the Council of Constance. Luther took the opportunity to extol Constance, to which Cajetan replied angrily, "Oh, that council was reprobate."[16] Finally Cajetan ordered him out and told him not to return until he was ready to recant.[17] Luther wrote home to his colleague Andreas Bodenstein von Karlstadt that the legate wanted to avoid debate and subdue opposition by "might and power."[18] The words were pregnant. For one thing they were a biblical allusion to the demonic force of Satan. Luther's use of them also suggested he was about to raise the stakes of the confrontation by making a formal appeal from the pope to the general council—the kind of appeal that Pope Pius II had declared heretical in 1460. If the papal authority would not accept debate that might lead to a true definition of the doctrine under question, the good Christian had no recourse but to appeal to a higher office.

It is a mistake to assume that all Cajetan and Luther argued was the place of the pope in the church. The nature of the church itself was the more important problem. Luther had already begun to shape a view of the church as the community of redeemed Christians, not an institution with visible officers and a hierarchical form. The institutional church then lost its position as mediator of grace to the world through the sacraments and through the guarantee of pure doctrine that the church offered. Cajetan told him that his beliefs would mean "that one must build a new church."[19] It is just possible that he saw the point before Luther did.

Cajetan and Luther met on October 12, 13, and 14 or 15. Neither budged an inch in his argument. Luther's mistrust of Cajetan remained strong, and on October 16 he made a formal appeal to the pope himself, an appeal certified by a notary.[20]

Indulgences, he said, were based on uncertain doctrine. These uncertainties should be resolved. On October 17 and 18 he wrote Cajetan two appropriately meek and reverential letters. In his first letter, he confessed to speaking too sharply and irreverently about the pope, and he offered to remain publicly silent on the matter of indulgences if his foes would remain silent, too. Yet he remained firm on his fundamental position. He must stand on his conscience. The arguments of Aquinas and others did not suffice to prove that indulgences were valid. He asked for an official ruling from the pope on their efficacy.[21] In his letter of October 18, he announced that he was leaving Augsburg, appealing, he said, from a pope badly informed to one better informed.[22]

The days following the last meeting with Cajetan were tense. The example of John Hus was in every mind. Luther might well have been seized and carried off to Rome to be burned. Staupitz took some precautions; he released Luther from the vows of obedience that bound him to the Augustinian order.[23] This act gave Luther some right to resist the commands from Rome that he be seized by superiors in the order and conveyed south in chains if necessary. Staupitz left town; the Elector Frederick had already departed. Luther was left alone, feeling deserted, hopeless about support in Germany, supposing that France would offer him no help on account of the threats of the pope. Finally he gave up, slipped out of town at night, and walked home to Saxony, feeling gloomy and anxious.[24]

By All Hallow's Eve, a year after he had written the Ninety-five Theses, he returned to Wittenberg preparing to write an account of the meeting. The key player in the drama besides Luther himself was Frederick, and he continued to stand by his professor. Cajetan wrote the elector giving him an account of the meeting with Luther and expressed his astonishment that Luther was so damnable. Cajetan's position was simple. Popes had certified the virtues of indulgences, and that ought to be an end to it. In addition Cajetan made a more telling point. Luther claimed that he was merely propounding propositions for debate, an academic practice that could not be considered heretical, at least within limits. But, said Cajetan, he had heard that Luther was asserting his beliefs in sermons and in writings in German spread among the common people. Cajetan gave Frederick a choice—send Luther to Rome or expel him from Saxony.[25]

Luther replied with a long Latin letter to Frederick giving his side of things. For Luther the issue was as simple as it was to Cajetan. Whereas Cajetan stood on the papal primacy as his rock of argument, Luther stood on scripture. "He produced not one syllable of scripture!" Luther wrote. Cajetan, said Luther, depended entirely on the opinions of the "doctors," by which Luther meant the scholastic theologians of the later Middle Ages, especially Thomas Aquinas. Clearly by this time he had become convinced that to recant was to renounce the plain meaning of scripture and his own hard-won understanding of Christian faith. At the end of his letter, Luther threw himself on the mercy of the elector. If Frederick wanted him to leave Saxony, Luther would do it and go where God willed.[26]

Frederick hesitated, and in the meantime Luther made good his plan to launch a formal appeal to a general council yet to be called. It was an overt summons to the tradition that had brought Constance into session a century earlier to resolve the scandal created by three contesting popes.[27] He also published *Acta Augustana,* his account of the meeting with Cajetan.[28] He wrote Staupitz that the elector had reluctantly given permission to publish it. Luther knew that he would be in great danger if the pope officially condemned him. Would the elector protect him then? Apparently becoming more optimistic about refuge in France, he told Spalatin that he would go to Paris—where the Sorbonne had been at odds with the papacy throughout the later Middle Ages and where conciliar theory continued strong.[29]

It seemed that the elector was about to cave in. In the summer of 1535 as he talked at table Luther told a dramatic story about Frederick's final decision to stand with him. A German nobleman named Karl von Miltitz arrived at the Saxon court three days after Christmas, having traveled from Rome to confer on Frederick the Golden Rose, the highest distinction the pope could confer on a layman. It was part of the pope's courtship of Frederick looking toward the imperial election after the death of Maximilian. Miltitz brought with him, Luther said, some seventy legal briefs written by the pope to bishops and princes, ordering them to bind Luther and send him to Rome. Would Frederick protect him? Luther seemed uncertain. He called his friends together for a dinner to tell them farewell, and in the midst of it came a letter from Spalatin saying that Frederick marveled that he had not departed from the city. Luther said he felt deserted by everyone. Shortly afterward, while Luther still sat at supper, came another letter from Spalatin. If Luther had not already departed, said the elector, he should remain.[30] It seems to have been the last time Frederick wavered. If there is any date that marks an essential point in Luther's reformation, it is this one, for thereafter the elector stuck with him through thick and thin.

The story may be overly dramatic. Miltitz stayed in Saxony and met both with the elector and with Luther himself. It appears that he had been sent to spy out the land, to persuade Frederick with a mixture of cajolery and threat to hand Luther over, or to persuade Luther himself to submit. Miltitz tried to be all things to all people. He berated Tetzel to his face and spoke condescendingly of Cajetan and like some Germanic Colonel Blimp talked confidently about things he did not understand. He wanted to work out a compromise, silence all the parties, and end the conflict. All this would have given him great credit in the curia and in Europe at large, and such credit would open the way for his advancement in the higher diplomatic levels where he thought he belonged.

The sticking point was Luther's attack on papal authority. Luther and the elector wanted the matter decided by impartial judges, preferably trustworthy German bishops.[31] But obviously for the pope to allow such a move would be to renounce his sovereignty over the church and, in effect, to subscribe to the hated decisions of Constance that bishops in council could judge a pope, even remove him, for whatever reasons the council might define.

Luther tried to temper his words without compromising his convictions. After meeting with Miltitz in January, he published a small pamphlet in German sometime in February that showed how far he could go in reaching accommodation with the papal church.[32] In it he declared that he held fast with all Christendom that everyone should venerate the saints and call on them. Who could doubt, he asked, that even today God did miracles in their name through their beloved holy bodies and graves? This was a great concession for a man who had never in any surviving work of his to this time extolled the saints. Even here he made a distinction. Christians should call upon the saints for spiritual gifts, not physical ones. It was, for example, unchristian to call on St. Anne for wealth. The saints had no power of their own; they were but pleaders before God, and God had all power. He affirmed his belief in purgatory, where, he said, he believed the poor souls suffered, requiring us to pray for them and fast and give alms to help them. But what kind of pains they suffered and the purposes of their suffering were mysteries known only to God. He declared in a somewhat musing tone that he did not know how anyone could prove that indulgences had any power to change God's secret judgments about purgatory.

Making a distinction that would become important throughout this conflict, Luther said he thought it was all right for the "common man" to believe that an indulgence could provide satisfaction for sin. He meant "satisfaction" in the formal, sacramental sense. But, he said, indulgences were worth far less than good works. Christians could use indulgences or leave them alone. Luther does not spell out his definition of the "common man." But it is easy enough to know what he meant. The common man was that nebulous and ignorant creature, ruled by passion, made obedient only by fear or by hope of reward, always ready to rebel and to plunge the good order of society into unimaginable chaos. This "common man" was the monstrous phantom who haunted political literature in the sixteenth century and much of the religious controversy as well and made his seditious and tumultuous way into Shakespeare's history plays. Luther here joined himself to that family of ideas—and never wavered from it.

In a section on the "Commandments of the Holy Church," Luther exercised a certain irony. Yes, he thought that the commands of God given through the church should be obeyed. But it was a misfortune for the world, he said, that many people feared the pope and his word more than they feared God and his word. A man could be an adulterer, a robber, and a liar without being accused of sin if only he paid to have a Pater Noster said for him, undertook a fast, or venerated some special saint. In his most potent remark, he made a distinction between the laws of God and the laws of the church. If God's command did not hold within the church, the church's authority was only a harmful and shameful cover that might look good outside but had nothing good within. Good works, he said, were required of the Christian, but in doing them every Christian recognized that they were possible only through the bottomless grace and mercy we receive from God. This is one of Luther's most powerful thoughts; here the ability to do good works seems to be an honor that we gain only because God picks us out to perform them.[33]

Finally he declared that the Roman church was to be revered above all others. There Peter and Paul had come; there were the popes, there a hundred thousand martyrs had poured out their blood and had conquered hell and the world. That evils were also present in Rome was no reason to forsake that church. But where the power and authority of the pope were concerned, let scholars decide. Christ did not rule his church through visible authority and temporal things as did the rulers of the world. Christ had grounded his church on love, humility, and unity.[34]

Luther concluded by affirming his allegiance to the Roman papacy. He had left himself plenty of room to dissent from the absolute primacy claimed by papal champions busily damning Luther as a heretic. The document could satisfy none of them, and it did not change the direction of the conflict. If anything it showed how far Luther had come in a little over a year and how difficult compromise was becoming. Even someone as thick as Miltitz had to recognize that Luther's pamphlet offered no balm for the wound in the church.

The Miltitz episode is commonly viewed by Luther biographers as a foolish intervention by a petty and bumbling German nobleman. It was more than that. As Wilhelm Borth has demonstrated, it placed Luther and his prince firmly in opposition to the principle that the pope spoke for the church. To claim that Luther and his prince were thereby heretics was to ignore the conciliar movement and especially Constance, with its decrees subordinating popes to conciliar authority. But the papacy had given the energies of a century to subverting Constance, and for all practical purposes it had succeeded. The Fifth Lateran Council, called by Pope Julius II to meet in 1512 and finally sent home by Pope Leo X in 1517, was a lapdog to papal interests. Now Luther threatened to resurrect this dangerous ghost the papacy had laid. It was a move the pope could not allow to go unchecked without losing the game on which the religious fate of Europe was suddenly staked.

II

THE LEIPZIG DEBATE

Throughout Germany people were taking sides. An army of pestiferous pamphleteers flung print at Luther, and he needed allies. On December 14 he wrote a short and effusive letter of appreciation to Johann Reuchlin (1455–1522). One of Reuchlin's grand-nephews, the brilliant Philipp Melanchthon, joined Luther at Wittenberg in the summer of 1518. Like many others of those classical scholars we call humanists, Melanchthon's origins were commonplace without being lowly. His father was an artisan, a maker of fine tournament armor for aristocrats. His mother was the daughter of a successful merchant. They could afford an education for their son, and they gave him a good one. He became professor of Greek in Wittenberg and Luther's most trusted and valued assistant, prized by successive electors of Saxony for his Greek learning and European reputation as a scholar. Luther's choice of this moment to address Reuchlin seems to have been an effort to establish himself in the ranks of those who had been attacked by the conservatives in the church. In that way lay the safety that successive popes had allowed critics as diverse as Lorenzo Valla and Erasmus to flourish despite charges of heresy raised against them.

Reuchlin was old and tired in 1519. He had been at the center of one of the great controversies that swept across academic Germany before Luther's notoriety. Like many interested in classical studies, he visited Italy on several occasions and early in his life came under the influence of the great Florentine Neoplatonist Marsilio Ficino. Like all Platonists, Ficino believed that the physical universe was an inferior reflection of the more enduring reality lying behind what we see and hear, touch, taste, and feel. Reuchlin's profound interest in scholarship carried him to the study of Hebrew, and in 1506 he published a Hebrew grammar. It seemed natural to those preoccupied with classical philology that Christians should study the original language in which most of the Bible had been written, and interest in Hebrew had been growing in Christian circles for a couple of centuries.[1]

Much more daring was Reuchlin's interest in the Jewish Kabbala. The Kabbala is a body of texts and teaching and a way of religious life. It is usually called "mystical" because its various documents propound the idea that God is to be found by contemplation rather than by dialectical thinking. But it goes further.

In the Christian mystical tradition, to know God is to be brought into an intimate and heartfelt union with the divine. In the Kabbala, the mystical consciousness leads on to secret or esoteric knowledge about God. In general Kabbalists affirmed that in his essence God was beyond thought, beyond human power to make positive statements about him; however, it was possible to know some of the relations God had with creation. In this area the speculations of Kabbalists were bold and as nonsensical as astrology. The knowledge was to be kept secret among a closed group of initiates; thus in some of its manifestations the Kabbala resembled a kind of Masonic religious order with secret symbols and gestures, signifying cosmic obscurity and portentous vagueness.

Many of these symbols, assumed to be almost magical, were Hebrew words and various other combinations of the Hebrew alphabet. These symbols supposedly opened direct avenues into the divine. It was supposed that the Kabbala had been passed down by an esoteric oral tradition alongside the sacred texts so meticulously copied by Jewish scribes. In this respect the Kabbala somewhat resembled the idea of an oral tradition in the Catholic Church, and it offered similar benefits: troublesome written texts could be reconciled, difficulties removed, and continuing revelation offered of truths not found in the original sacred writings. Above all, the Kabbala allowed an emotional religious life more satisfying to some than the literal understanding of the Jewish Law. Kabbalists believed their understanding of the Torah was more profound and more direct than that of scribes who pondered the words without seeking mystic enlightenment.

Reuchlin was among those Christian scholars who thought that the Kabbala offered a better understanding of both Christian and Jewish scriptures—all leading to further proof that Jesus was the person the Catholic Church and the Christian tradition claimed him to be. Reuchlin was a disciple of Pico della Mirandola, who took on himself to reconcile the great religions of the world, supposing that they all fundamentally agreed and that Christianity embraced them all. Should he succeed, he thought that honest Jews would come to Christ, and honest Christians would have their own faith confirmed. Pico used the Kabbala in that process.

Erudite men like Pico and Reuchlin felt the need for yet more confirmation of Christian doctrine. Reuchlin put great stress on the resemblance between the Jewish Tetragrammaton, JHWH, and the frequent abbreviation of the name of Jesus, JHS. At this distance he and other Kabbalists look like prospectors in search of an underlying code that would demonstrate the certainty of things in doubt, the relation of apparently disparate phenomena, a vision of impeccable order where confusion had seemed to reign, a bit like the quest of Mr. Casaubon in George Eliot's *Middlemarch*. As in all religious seeking, the excitement of Kabbala lay in the imminent revelation of truths, not in their actual discovery.

Reuchlin came under fierce attack in 1510 from a converted Jew named Johann Pfefferkorn of Cologne. Like many converts Pfefferkorn became a zealot and turned vehemently on his former faith. He wanted to destroy all Hebrew books in Germany. Reuchlin opposed this projected wanton destruction, and Pfefferkorn accused him of heresy. The subsequent controversy became a fierce battle of books and pamphlets resolved only when Pope Leo X imposed silence on both sides. In most treatments of the Reformation, the Reuchlin affair is made to seem part of the ferment that produced Luther. But although Luther took Reuchlin's side in Wittenberg, he was a mere spectator, more opposed to Reuchlin's enemies than a fan of Reuchlin's ideas. Luther had little interest in the Kabbala, for as he contemplated the mystery of God, he asked not for esoteric knowledge to draw back the veil but rather for faith to accept the mystery and go on living without falling victim to the curse of vain curiosity.

One of Reuchlin's devoted defenders was Egidius Canisius of Viterbo, the general of the Augustinian order in Rome. Reuchlin pulled strings to get his grand-nephew Melanchthon appointed to his professorship in Wittenberg. Melanchthon may have suggested that Luther write his letter of December 14 in which he called Reuchlin "the most erudite and cultivated of men," expressed his love for him, and placed himself firmly in Reuchlin's camp.[2] This apparent bid for friendship against a common enemy may have been an effort to enlist Luther's order, the Augustinians, against the Dominicans. It is as flattering an epistle as Luther ever wrote. All this indicates that Luther still thought of himself as fighting a battle within the church, a battle he believed he could win. The overture to Reuchlin failed; the older man never left the Catholic Church, publicly rejected Luther, and broke with Melanchthon over the Reformation. Franz von Sickingen, a German knight with a mercenary army at his command, offered Reuchlin his protection during the prolonged battle over Hebrew books; instead Reuchlin found refuge in the home of Johann Eck at Ingolstadt.

The Emperor Maximilian died of a chill in January 1519 during a hunt in the mountains, fatuous to the end. Over the next several months a storm of nervous diplomacy blew through the papal curia, and the Luther matter became not merely a religious preoccupation but a political issue of the first order. For the moment the proceedings against Luther for heresy fell into the doldrums in Rome as the pope did everything in his power to fend off the heavily bribed election of young Charles of Hapsburg to the imperial office on June 28.

By this time Luther was on his way to Leipzig in ducal Saxony with his friend and colleague Karlstadt to face the redoubtable Eck in debate. Eck may have been sincere enough, although Luther called him a "glory-hungry little beast" in a letter to Spalatin of February 7, 1519.[3] He was one of the first to accuse Luther of heresy and to start the name-calling that provoked Luther into using his own copious talent for vituperation. Given the brief but bitter history between the two men, the debate at Leipzig seemed destined to make things worse, and so it did.

Luther seems not to have wanted to quarrel with Eck at first. The two had corresponded, disagreeing without breaking relations. While Luther was away in Heidelberg in April 1518, the impatient Karlstadt forced the issue by writing a sharp defense of criticisms that Eck had written of Luther. Luther seemed to want to keep the Ingolstadt theologian neutral in the developing controversy, and Heiko Oberman thinks that Eck at this time was disposed toward both German nationalism and a moderate view of papal authority. Luther may have thought that Eck could be won over.[4] But once the quarrel began, it accelerated as quarrels will do. Luther wrote sharply against Eck, and the Leipzig debate marked a watershed for both men. They met now as enemies. Eck became an ardent papalist; Luther turned irrevocably toward separation from the Catholic Church.

In theory Luther was not supposed to debate at all, since at Augsburg Cajetan had imposed silence upon him, and it seems that Frederick the Wise objected to Luther's participation.[5] From the beginning, Duke George, Frederick's cousin, despised Luther, and his university followed his lead. Karlstadt was to carry the flag, Luther to stand by as an adviser. All along Luther had asked to be heard, to have his case judged by impartial observers, and to settle by public debate the pressing questions he had raised. A debate seemed his chance. Yet he was not happy with the prospect. He was not to speak, and he knew that the theologians at Leipzig would side with Eck. He made a daring proposal: let all the university take part! Here would have been a startling act—laymen allowed to sit in judgment on a theological matter. Duke George turned that idea down.[6]

Duke George was in a difficult situation. He seems to have been naturally conservative, and he may have been jealous of the sudden notoriety that the rival university of Wittenberg had won because of Luther. The bishop of Merseburg, with jurisdiction over Leipzig, tried to prevent the disputation altogether. Since Pope Leo X had on November 9, 1518, reaffirmed the application of indulgences to purgatory, the bishop thought the disputation was unnecessary.[7] The duke overruled the bishop—perhaps because he wanted his university to have the credit for demolishing Wittenberg's champion. Whatever his motives, Duke George and his university made no effort to hide their enthusiasm for Eck. From the beginning of the disputation the notion of a debate to decide the truth was undermined in favor of Eck's position that the truth was known and had to be defended against evident disobedience if not heresy.

In the event the debate was a great affair. Eck came to Leipzig about June 22; Karlstadt arrived with Luther and a great crowd of other Wittenbergers, including some 200 students, a day or so later.[8] The preparations went on with the zest and ceremony that might attend an intercollegiate football game in America today, and there seems to have been something of that sort of rivalry in the air despite the seriousness of the occasion. Europe at that time functioned in accordance with sun time, and these were among the longest days of the year; it did not seem early to contemporaries when the debaters assumed their positions at 7:00 A.M. The sun had been up for three hours, and the air was still cool. Monks and university faculty members were expected to be up early.

The contestants set out to pound each other according to the carefully prescribed rules both had agreed on, rules that required courtesy in the midst of conflict just as the codes of chivalry did for knights in the joust. Part of that agreement was that the debate was to be between Eck and Karlstadt, and so it was from June 27 until July 3. Yet everyone had come to see Luther and Eck, not Karlstadt and Eck. Luther had in the beginning asked permission from Duke George to join in the debate if Eck attacked him. The duke consented, and finally on July 4 the audience got its wish. On that morning in the great hall of the ducal castle, the two men squared off.

The Latin transcript of the debate as we have it in the great Weimar edition of Luther's works shows the issue settling immediately on papal authority.[9] Eck's position was simple. Scripture and history proved that Christ had established the papal primacy over the church. He quoted Dionysius the Areopagite, supposedly converted by Paul in Athens, to show that God worked in hierarchies throughout heaven and earth and that hierarchies supposed a sovereign at the top. In the church that sovereign was the pope.

Eck's use of Dionysius was probably disingenuous. Lorenzo Valla had attacked the works of this Pseudo-Dionysius, as he is now called, in a devastating analysis that argued that they were forgeries, probably from the sixth century. Erasmus had published Valla's work in 1505. "Dionysius" quickly lost support among Catholics acquainted with classical scholarship.

Eck tried to prove that anyone who opposed the papal primacy had already placed himself outside the church and was therefore a heretic. It was a strategy of all or nothing, and it set Luther on fire. He vehemently objected to the proposition that those who denied the papal primacy were heretics— as well he might, given the history of the conciliar movement of the previous centuries.

Eck dredged up old arguments from analogy, the sort of argument that fitted Pseudo-Dionysius with his conception that the world was a mirror of the divine and that analogy was the key to understanding the mysteries of heaven and earth. The militant church on earth, Eck said, was made in the image of the triumphant church in heaven. The church in heaven had God at his head; for good order the church on earth must also have one head, and that was necessarily the pope, whose place was appointed by Christ himself. Luther dismissed the argument briefly as not pertaining to the issue at hand. Eck stormed back, perhaps bewildered by Luther's dismissive response. He cited ancient doctors of the church to support the dogma that the church on earth was a monarchy and that Peter's successors the popes were the divinely ordained monarchs of this spiritual realm.

But then Luther struck hard. Yes, the church required a head, but that head was Christ, not the pope. To support his stand he fired off a barrage of scripture and attacked the patristic texts that Eck had adduced, claiming that Eck had misinterpreted them. If any one bishop was to be granted authority over all Christians, Luther said, it should be the bishop of Jerusalem, for this church was the proper mother of all Christendom. And then Luther made an adroit move that linked him to the conciliar tradition. The real monarchy in the church lay not with the bishop of Rome or with any other bishop; it lay with the consensus of all the church of the faithful. True doctrine was what the masses of Christians believed to be true doctrine. It was not defined by the head any more than life in the body belongs to one part of the human anatomy.

Here was the theory of church authority that Thomas More was to advance against Luther a few years later. Imagine, said More, that all faithful Christians from all parts of the world were "vpon one fayre day comen into some one fayre playne feld" such as the plain of Salisbury. What that body agreed was the true faith was indeed the true faith, and all that was necessary was to discover what that common consent might be.[10] Some scholars have argued that this conviction that authority lay in all the Christian community taken together is an essential part of the movement toward constitutional government in the West—the notion that rulers have authority by the consent of the governed and not by direct appointment from God and that therefore the authority of public officials must operate within a consensus.

It is a simple idea, filled not only with complications but also with contradictions. Its fundamental notion was that the spirit of God worked mysteriously in the church to bring Christians into consensus about what doctrines ought to be believed. When controversy over doctrine arose, it was to be resolved by a representative assembly, the general council—a gathering of the bishops representing the whole Catholic Church. In the council God inspired the members to a consensus that defined the dogma at issue. After that definition the decisions of the council became received doctrine, and to contest them was to be come a heretic.

One of the many questions that plagued conciliar thinkers was whether the pope was essential to the council. No pope had been at Nicaea, the council that had defined the doctrine of the equality of Jesus to God the Father and prepared the way for formulation of the doctrine of the Trinity. Was the pope sovereign over a council? The Council of Constance said no and ended the Great Schism by deposing three rival claimants to the papal throne and choosing another. So when Luther argued that Christ and not the pope was the head of the church and that all the people of God were inspired by the Holy Spirit, he was taking a safe stand on language that had been defined by conciliar thinkers to suit themselves. Had he stayed there, his affair might have turned out very differently. But he did not.

Eck doggedly maintained the papal primacy by a learned appeal to tradition. Here for the moment the antagonists were on common ground. The sanctity of tradition rested on the assumption that God had always been present in his church, inspiring it to true doctrine, protecting it against error. God could not or would not contradict himself from one time to another. Or would he? Eck called up cherished authorities from the distant past to prove that the consensus of the church to which Luther appealed had through the centuries supported the Roman primacy. He hammered away at his major theme, that the fathers of the church a thousand years and more in the past had looked to the Roman pontiff as the source of judgment in disputed cases.

Hour after hour the debate rolled on, at first observing the formal courtesies but also trading barbs that were part of the show. The transcript demonstrates on both sides a remarkable command of patristic literature, the Bible, and the decrees of councils. Both men had phenomenal memories, sharpened by debate in the prescribed university customs of the day, and they used their minds well, sometimes like broadswords, sometimes like daggers.

Luther brought up the Greek Church, which had endured for centuries and had thousands of saints, all without allegiance to the papacy, and he struck hard at Eck's view that popes had always defined doctrines correctly. At least two popes in the fourth century, he said, had had Arian leanings. Eck replied with the arrogance of a religious man early in the age of discoveries with no idea how big the world was or how many non-Christians lived in it. He said that if we could argue that only a few among all the Christians in the Catholic Church would be saved, it was possible that fewer or even none would be saved in the Greek Church, which did not obey the pope. And, he said, no Roman pontiff had officially defined doctrine contrary to the faith of the Catholic Church.

Luther was on firm ground with respect to the Greek Church—if any firm ground existed in this slippery debate. The great councils of the fourth and fifth centuries—First and Second Nicaea, Ephesus, and Chalcedon—had all been held on the territory of the Greek Church. The Great Schism of 1054 permanently dividing Greek East from Latin West was far in the future then. All these councils were more or less under the auspices of the ruling eastern emperor, and none showed deference to the bishop of Rome. If it was granted that the Greeks were true Christians, Eck's arguments might be undermined.

Eck fought back furiously—and fatally for prospects of compromise. He tried again to tar Luther with heresy. John Wycliff and John Hus—both notorious heretics—had denied that to obtain salvation it was necessary to adhere to the church of Rome. The implication was clear—although Eck was using a well-known logical fallacy: Because Luther was like these heretics in one particular, he was like them in all—and therefore a heretic. Luther replied with a careful analysis of New Testament and early patristic writings to prove that the apostle Peter and his successors the popes were not considered superior to the other apostles or *their* successors, the bishops of the church. Eck had argued that as punishment for their secession from the Roman Communion, the Greeks had lost their empire to the Turks. Luther mocked this assertion. But the most important part of his argument was much more subversive of Eck's position and the tradition of the church. On the question of the papal primacy, Luther said, the fathers were divided. Some were for it; but many more were against it. As for Matthew 16, where Christ said to Peter, "Thou art Peter, and on this rock I will build my church," Luther noted that Augustine had often expounded that text to mean that Christ was the rock and that the most revered of all the fathers had scarcely ever interpreted the rock to mean Peter. He might also have quoted the notes on the Greek New Testament published by Erasmus in 1516 and in a new edition of 1519, but he did not.

At the end of the second morning of debate, Luther commented on the charge that he stood close to the Hussites of Bohemia. Let Eck write against them if he would, Luther said. But he was amazed, he added, that no one had tried to win these heretics from their error by brotherly charity. The comment seemed almost deliberately couched to antagonize his audience. The Hussite wars had ravaged the south of Germany in the previous century. In their vengeful anger at Catholics for burning their leader at the Council of Constance, Hussite armies were unrestrained by the quality of mercy. In an age when even recent history tended to blend quickly into legend and the vagaries of the folk memory, Luther's comments about charity to the Hussites must have clanged as discordantly as a modern suggestion that Hitler might have been made more reasonable by a charitable response to his program.

Luther was walking close to the edge here, perhaps not quite seeing, in the heat of debate, the implications of his words. On the one hand he pointed out that the fathers of the church had disagreed among themselves about a major doctrine—the primacy of Peter and the popes after him. This was hardly secret information. Abelard had collected patristic disagreements in his *Sic et Non* of the twelfth century. He had rankled people in the same way that Luther now did, for to call attention to the divisions and the lack of unity among the fathers of the church was to subvert one of the most treasured bastions of certainty in a time of religious doubt—that the grand unity of the church proved its divine infallibility. Luther suggested that the Bohemians had not been malicious in their heresy, and so in his way he was subverting another Catholic tenet. For to Catholic thinkers, part of the evil of heresy was its malice—the stubborn adhesion to error by those who knew better. The heretics "knew better" because an infallible church and their own consciences taught them so. To declare that heretics were not malicious—or else fatally ignorant—was to assume that the teachings of the church about salvation were not clear and that, therefore, the chilly doubts rising around the knees of Christian society had no remedy.

On this ambiguous note the contestants adjourned for lunch on the second day and resumed at two o'clock. Luther still had the floor. He began by saying that his aim was not to defend the Hussites but rather the Greek Church. Yet he could not resist responding to the fallacious argument that Eck had propounded in the morning, the implicit claim that if Luther believed in one article shared by the Hussites, he accepted all their errors. Luther commented that among the beliefs of these heretics had been some that were "most Christian and evangelical," and he mentioned some of them—that there were one universal church, a Holy Spirit, a holy Catholic Church, a communion of the saints. Whether Wycliffe or Hus said, "It is not necessary for salvation to believe that the Roman Church is superior to others," Luther cared not. He did care that Gregory Nazianzen, Basil, and innumerable other Greek bishops and church fathers who had not acknowledged the papal primacy were true Christians.[11] Here was Luther at his tempestuous and undiplomatic best. He would not shilly-shally; he would seek no compromise; he would not equivocate; he would plunge ahead even if in so doing the shattering of medieval Christian unity was made inevitable.

When Eck took the floor again, he had a weapon forged from Luther's own words—or so he thought. In his view Luther's comments about the Hussites amounted to praise, and he accused Luther of perverting the Greek saints into allies of the Hussite heresy. This distortion so angered Luther that he interrupted Eck with a denial and called him a liar. Eck continued smoothly after Luther's outburst. He pointed out that not merely Constance but many regional synods had condemned Hus and that many devout Catholics had written against the Hussites. Then Eck moved to a more important issue. He accused Luther of denying the authority of the Council of Constance, which he called holy and praiseworthy, speaking the consensus of all Christendom. Constance had condemned Wycliffe and Hus. How dare Luther call some of the articles of Wycliffe and Hus "most Christian and evangelical"? Again Luther broke in with a furious cry. He had not, he said, spoken against the Council of Constance. Indeed he had not. Or at least he had not objected to the final decisions of the council in its long deliberations. Eck was cheating and cheating outrageously. But he had gained an advantage. He cited Augustine. If any lie were to be admitted to sacred scripture, the truth of all would become suspect. Now if Luther became the defender of John Hus, a condemned heretic . . . Luther again broke in, outraged, calling Eck an impudent liar. Eck rolled on, drawing a parallel with Augustine's comment on scripture. If a council of the church erred in two articles of Christian faith, its authority must be shaken in all. Here was the crux; Eck considered that he was fighting a battle for the credibility of the Christian faith. So did Luther.

When Luther's turn came again the next morning, he set out to state his arguments in unmistakable terms. He flatly denied that he had called "the most pestilential errors of Hus's most Christian teaching." He then returned to his main point, that neither the early church nor the Greek Church had recognized a Roman primacy. Had he been another kind of personality he might have continued in that direction because it was both safer and more arguable than to mix it up with Eck over the Hussites. But in a while he came back to the Hussites as though drawn by the vortex of a whirlpool. Eck was a liar, Luther said, to accuse him of being in the company of the Hussites. He acknowledged that Catholic authorities had written against the Hussites. But what had been written, he said, had been lacking in fraternal affection. "I believe," he said, "that the Bohemians are men and that they may be attracted by gentle words and by compromise but that they are only hardened by being called criminal and by the opprobrious name of heretics."[12] Obviously Luther sympathized with Hus because like himself Hus had been accused of heresy and denied opportunity to defend himself. But by his later testimony we know that he had at this time only the vaguest idea of Hus's doctrines.

In a few moments he came back to the Council of Constance. The issue was simply this as Luther saw it: Constance had condemned Hus in broad, sweeping statements. The problem seems in Luther's mind to have been rhetorical. The thirty Hussite articles condemned at Constance in 1415 were seen as a unit in which each article reinforced the whole. The first article held that the universal church was a congregation of the predestinate; the fourth, that the one Christ had two natures, divine and human, and so on.[13] Read in context, these articles were "condemned" because Hus's interpretations of them added up to heresy. The council did not mean to condemn them individually but only as the parts made a heretical whole. It looks as if both Luther and Eck had fallen to quibbles, much as weary boxers will fall into a clinch when they are not quite certain what to do next. Luther had been forced to change positions. He had at first claimed vehemently that he did not reject Constance—that is, he did not deny the validity of its final judgment against Hus. Now he was maneuvered by Eck into holding that a council could err in the track that it took to judgment.

On the morning of July 6, Luther took up the question again, moving against Eck's citation of Augustine that if one part of scripture was found in error, all scripture might thus become suspect. (It was the same argument Eck had used against annotations of Erasmus in the 1516 Greek New Testament.) Eck extended that logic to the councils of the church; if one council erred, the decrees of all were thrown into doubt. Now Luther drew the line sharply in the sand. Augustine, said Luther, was speaking of divine scripture, "which is the infallible word of God." The council, he said, was "the creature of this word."[14] Injury was done to scripture by Eck's comparison, he said. The council could err, he said flatly—and he quoted for support Panormitanus, otherwise known as Nicolaus de Tudeschis (1386–1445), a Sicilian Benedictine and canonist who was also a conciliar thinker. Both the Roman pope and the members of a council were men. Therefore they, too, were to be tested by the word of scripture. Everything stood under the judgment of scripture, and now Luther's bent was clear: Scripture could contradict the long-received traditions of the Catholic Church in major ways, and if such contradictions were manifest, the Catholic Church had erred. What happened then to the notion that God had been continuously with his church from the resurrection of Christ? Luther had yet to work out the answer to this fateful question.

Luther's renunciation not only of the Roman primacy but also of the authority of the general council is the great moment recorded by all biographers. Here was the fruition of Luther's years in the monastery, his inner anguish, and his lonely wrestling with scripture as a means of finding his own way to truth. From his lectures on the Psalms and other books of the Bible, we might have expected him to go in this direction. But then this question inevitably arose: Who was to be the interpreter of scripture? Every heretic who had ever risen against the Catholic Church had claimed the authority of scripture. The dogma of conciliar thinkers was that God's spirit was in all the faithful and that when representative faithful came together in a "true" general council, whether or not convened by the pope, the decrees of that council were inspired by God and were thereby infallible. The tradition of the church might then be regarded as an ever-expanding body of inspired truths, not necessarily revealing new truths—although a Catholic thinker such as Thomas More thought new revelations might be possible. But most Catholics believed and believe today that all revealed truth is implicit in scripture and that councils and the growing consensus of the faithful made these implicit doctrines explicit. Whatever happened, Catholic theologians, popes, and bishops as well as educated laypeople who understood what was at stake believed in a body of tradition holding divine truths that the faithful could accept with certainty.

Now by saying that councils could err, Luther removed an essential foundation stone of this edifice of tradition. The surprise is how casually all this was done. Luther attacked conciliar authority almost as an aside. When Eck's turn came, he did not begin at once to attack Luther on this point. After again accusing Luther of holding doctrines similar to those of the Hussites, Eck turned back to his principal concern—his defense of papal primacy.

Constance was particularly difficult for the papalist party, given the council's thumping antipapal stand. Had Eck not been striving to tar Luther with the Hussite brush, Constance would probably not have entered the debate at all unless Luther had used it to strike at the papal primacy as he had against Cajetan. When Eck finally came back to consider the decrees of Constance he pointed out that they condemned the heretical interpretations Hus had put on some doctrines that in themselves seemed to be what Luther said they were—sound Christian theology. The only councils that had erred were not true councils at all but false *conciliabula,* Eck said, using the traditional Latin diminutive in a pejorative sense. It was "stinking," Eck thundered, to say that a council comprised men and that therefore the council could err as men erred.[15] For when a legitimate council assembled to determine and define faith, it was certain that it acted not according to human sense but by the spirit of God. Once the council had acted, we were bound to stop disputing the issue it had decided. Rather we were to accept its decrees as part of our own faith. Again Eck quickly turned away from the discussion of the council and went back to his larger effort to prove the papal primacy. By receiving the stigmata, Eck said, St. Francis of Assisi had proved to his fellow friars and all the world that obedience was due the pope.

The debate dragged on. On the morning of July 7 Luther insisted on speaking briefly in German to declare to the "common people" what the debate was about.[16] It was, he said, whether the Roman primacy had been established by divine law. On that point, speaking also in German, Eck agreed. It is a fascinating little vignette—the crowd pushing its way into the great hall to hear a debate in Latin that it did not understand but drawn by the excitement of the event in the way that people today might be drawn to witness a game whose rules they could not fathom but watch it because it is the only game in town. Luther said that his aim was not to overthrow the papacy but simply to say that popes could err and to presume that they could be corrected. This was a position solidly within the conciliar position, for not even the Council of Constance had presumed that the papacy could be purged from the church. He likened the pope to the German emperor—by this time a "constitutional" monarch in that his power was limited by the German princes. The emperor, Luther said, was not an absolute monarch by divine law; neither was the pope.

The debate returned to Latin, and Luther might well then have reverted to the traditional conciliar position that the bishops in a council were the natural agents to limit papal power. Instead he went back to his stubborn argument that Constance had declared heretical some beliefs of John Hus that Luther considered orthodox. He did not praise Hus or accept all his beliefs, for, as I have said, he probably did not know Hus's doctrines well enough to affirm them. That would come later.

Luther returned briefly to the authority of councils. He agreed, he said, with Eck that the decrees of councils were to be embraced by all the faithful. He made one major reservation: A council could err, and councils had erred, and no council could create a new article of faith. For then, he said, we would have only the opinions of men. He dismissed Eck's appeal to the stigmata of St. Francis and, instead of taking it seriously, attacked the mendicant orders. He could wish, Luther declared, that no mendicant orders existed. The insult brought Eck out of his seat in protest. Luther plunged ahead. He argued that the letter to the Galatians, with its account of Paul's denunciation of Peter, was proof that Peter enjoyed no primacy over the other apostles. When his turn came, Eck argued vehemently that Luther had misinterpreted the text, and he cited various fathers of the church to support his own interpretation.

The disputation had now reached its high point, and although it lasted another week, the most significant arguments had been made. Eck brought up the subject of purgatory and whether any good works done on earth could influence the condition of souls confined there. Luther declared that scripture had nothing to say about purgatory, that it spoke only of heaven or hell. He said he believed in purgatory, and he granted that its existence might be inferred from a few texts of scripture. But it could not be proved from any canonical book in such a way as to convince the stubborn. One of the major "scriptural" texts to support the belief in purgatory was 2 Maccabees 12:43–46, where the warrior hero Judas Maccabaeus speaks of those who sleep for whom prayers will bring salvation. Luther dismissed Maccabees as noncanonical. Here he was on firm ground, for the church never considered the books of the Apocrypha to be authoritative for doctrine. Luther quoted Jerome in support of his view that only the fully canonical books could be used in debate.

Luther's argument came down to this: One might accept purgatory as part of the tradition of the church. Augustine had assumed the existence of such a place. Yet Luther insisted that it could not be proved by scripture. His response opens a window into his mind. For Luther to say that purgatory could not be proved by scripture was tantamount to denying its existence altogether, even if Augustine implied that existence by praying for the dead and especially his dead mother. Luther seemed torn here, but his mind was moving, and he could not stop it. He would not yet deny purgatory, but he could say that only God knew the states of souls in that place. He followed this bold declaration by pointing out contradictions between texts used to support the existence of purgatory, including some that suggested that only the saints were in such a place. Then he suggested that purgatory might be a place where the souls of the dead slept. Whatever purgatory was could not be proved. When the disputation turned to indulgences, Luther could argue that they were sought chiefly by the ignorant; the fact that multitudes went to shrines or to Rome to obtain them proved nothing about their validity.

Crowds of the ignorant were not to be set against scripture. Luther's conviction came down to this: Christ alone was the key to salvation. Only faith in Christ counted for anything. The church's acceptance of certain opinions did not make them true.

Luther and Eck debated the nature of true penance without surprising results, and on July 14 the disputation came to an end. Already on June 28 the electors of the empire meeting at Frankfurt had given their votes to young Charles of Spain, the nineteen-year-old boy on whom the fate of Europe would depend. Duke George required his palace to receive the elector of Brandenburg returning from Frankfurt. Luther and Eck parted. To many, Eck seemed victorious, for he had defended the status quo with verve, armed with his prodigious memory. The universities of Paris and Erfurt were supposed to decide the winner on the basis of transcripts of the debate. For various reasons they never got around to it.

The real verdict was delivered by public opinion, and that was divided. Eck wrote crowing letters to friends and assorted dignitaries, including the pope, trumpeting his victory and calling Luther various uncomplimentary names. He even wrote Frederick the Wise, claiming good intentions and saying, oddly, "I do not mean to reproach Dr. Luther with all this, nor do I write to injure him, but only to excuse myself to your grace who would otherwise hear untruths to my dishonor."[17]

Back in Wittenberg on July 20 Luther wrote his account of the affair to Spalatin. He acknowledged bitterly that the people of Leipzig had cheered Eck as victor. They had feasted Eck, followed him in the streets, embraced him, and given him a fine gown.[18] Eck was, in Luther's view, a deceitful, double-faced hypocrite, and he expressed disgust that Eck had not truly disagreed with him on indulgences though in Luther's mind indulgences were the heart of the matter. Rather, Luther thought, the debate had turned too much on the authority of the pope. Luther mentioned almost casually that the Council of Constance had erred in condemning some of the articles of John Hus.[19]

Leipzig is rightly regarded as a major moment in Luther's life and in the Reformation. Now it was a matter of public record that he stood in radical opposition to the received doctrines of the Catholic Church or at least to the power of the institution of the church as it was incorporated in the bishops, the mendicant orders, and the pope. It would be hard indeed to imagine that after Leipzig the centers of power in the church could have considered Luther as anything but an enemy. But it is not certain that Leipzig represents anything but a working out of ideas already germinating in his early lectures on scripture. Leipzig made explicit some of the content of the silences in those lectures. We may also say that it was the prototype of all the debates and polemics of Catholics against Protestants through the rest of the Reformation and for centuries afterward until recent times, when a happier, ecumenical spirit has prevailed. Leipzig was a benchmark. It failed on both sides because both men hardened positions already taken. To use an expression about theological debates that Thomas More used in another connection, they were like naked men throwing stones at each other.[20] Neither could avoid injury.

When he arrived at Leipzig Luther carried the assumptions that would develop into his capital doctrines. One was that human beings, doomed to death and annihilation—God's punishment for sins—had no resources within themselves for salvation. The greatest saints and the foulest sinners came equally to death. The best deeds and the worst crimes differed more in how they were perceived than in motivation. Both arose from pride, the sin that denied humankind's true condition of utter wretchedness and helplessness before God.

In Christ, in particular the suffering and risen Christ, Luther found all his comfort. Christ had lived a man as Luther lived. Christ had died in torment and apparently forsaken in the loneliness that Luther felt as the inevitable sorrow and fear of the human condition. He found that Christ most abundantly in the Bible and most particularly in the Psalms, where the cries of an anguished soul were most intense, and in Paul's epistles. As Gerhard Ebeling has said of Luther's attitude, "God reveals himself to us only in the flesh of Jesus Christ. If God is not there, He is nowhere. If Christ is not God, so is neither the Father nor the Holy Spirit God."[21] If we take these pronouncements seriously, we have a Luther tormented by doubts that arise naturally from our observation of the world in itself. The world makes no sense; it has no pattern. It testifies to no benevolence or to no purpose. Aristotle taught that everything that existed had a purpose, an intelligible end, a teleological cause, but from Luther's point of view that purpose was ultimately meaningless because it was nothing but an endless cycle of birth and death. Only Christ's incarnation offered humans a way out of the cycle, and Luther found the incarnate Christ in the words of scripture. The gospel was the story of Christ as it was written throughout scripture, and that story read again and again provided Luther's fellowship with Christ, protecting him from onslaughts of doubt and the fear of death. As Ebeling has said, this encounter with Christ in scripture made revelation a continual "present."[22] That is, it was an immediate sense of the redeemer who comes to the reader of the sacred text and in the moment of reading joins the words to the reality they signify.

Eck came at Christian belief from another direction, as did most Catholic polemicists in the Reformation. Like Luther, Eck recognized the weakness of reason standing alone, the impossibility of assuming that to observe the world without the light of revelation was to find a mirror of God's action in creation. Against the danger of unbelief, Christians needed a sure authority, and that authority was the Catholic Church. In Eck's view that authority stood on the sacred and unbroken tradition running back to Christ himself. It was a sacred history, and in the history God had revealed himself by never allowing the church to err.

How could truth or error be defined in a world where no philosophical system could arrive at a standard of truth accepted spontaneously by all? In Catholic Christianity the *only* way to define truth was to say that it was a teaching or a practice that did not contradict another teaching or practice that had enjoyed consensus throughout the centuries. God could not be God and allow his people to fall into error. He himself was the guarantor of this sacred tradition. Catholic tradition included the proper interpretation of scripture. Only by measuring one's own interpretation of the sacred text by the consensus of the doctors throughout the ages could one be sure of proclaiming the true word of God.

Luther showed at Leipzig as Abelard had done in the twelfth century that this consensus was a fiction. Eck's view was that yes, there had been division and contradiction among Christians but that the infallibility of church pro-nouncements lay with the popes who in their *official* statements never erred, that is, never contradicted one another or the true thread of Christian tradi-tion. Moreover Eck maintained that the consistent tradition of the church had supported the view that the pope was the final judge in matters of belief and practice.

Given the importance of the papacy in Luther's revolution, it is worth saying that the fiction of papal infallibility represents a fortress to which the church might retreat at a time when the intense study of history, the quest for documents, and the growing sense of anachronism were providing tools for a Lorenzo Valla, for an Erasmus, and for a Luther. The more scholars under-stood the past, the more untenable became the contention that there had always been a consensus of the faithful about the most important doctrines and rituals. The Leipzig debate was in itself thumping proof that such a romantic notion could not be maintained except by those resolved to pre-serve it because they had a stake in it. That stake could be ambition, greed, status, or reputation. It could also be the heart's desperate longing for certainty and meaning in this world and the next.

Leipzig also seemed to make Luther refine his attitude toward scripture. Now scripture assumed the only proper authority in the church. Ulrich Bubenheimer has argued cogently that the early Luther held scripture and the decrees of the church councils on approximately the same level; that is, scripture was supreme as it was interpreted by councils who brought a collective wisdom and spiritual authority to the sacred text. Karlstadt had previously held that scripture was supreme as it was interpreted by successive popes, and in that conviction had assembled arguments against the infallibility of councils. They had erred; Constance was an example. Luther, on the other side, proved to his own satisfaction that popes had erred. The two men convinced each other. Now both Karlstadt and Luther were moved to the belief that scripture had been misinterpreted by both popes and councils and that its clear texts could be used to judge both the papacy and conciliar degrees.[23]

It seems that Luther came to Leipzig hoping that enough true Christians would be in his audience to make the debate with Eck worthwhile. As his letter afterward to Spalatin shows, he found his audience largely unfriendly. He attributed this hostile attitude to the malice and stupidity of the Leipzigers and left the city undaunted in his conviction that fair-minded people would agree with him. It was this faith in the fair-mindedness of true Christians that stood behind his attitude toward the Council of Constance in particular and councils in theory. His comments to Eck indicate that he accepted at that moment during the debate the ultimate verdict at Constance, that John Hus was a heretic. In arriving at that verdict, however, the council made sweeping generalizations condemning Hus and thereby condemned some points of sound doctrine. It acted as any assembly of men of goodwill might be expected to act under pressure, in a mixture of truth and error as it moved toward a decision. Luther seems at this point to have envisaged the life of the church as a continually erring and self-correcting process in which belief and practice were always subject to review, using scripture as the standard.

The spirit of his view would fit the major decision of the council in its degree *Frequens*. This was to require conciliar review at intervals of the pope's use of his office, the assumption being that if papal policy and performance were unsatisfactory, the council could correct papal errors and steer the church back to the truth. Conciliar thinkers believed that popes could err, that popes might even fall into heresy, but that the council, inspired by the

Holy Spirit, could restore right thinking and good order at the apex of Christian society. Now Luther seemed to take the position that one council might err but be corrected by another—a view not unlike the belief in the United States about the Supreme Court. But the U.S. Supreme Court has never claimed to define the truths necessary for eternal salvation, and Luther's view seemed to open a chasm along the pathway to certainty that Catholic Christians felt necessary to eternal life.

Luther expressed no desire at Leipzig to rid the church of the papacy. When he declared in German that the issue between him and Eck was whether the pope ruled by divine law, the alternative was not that without the sanction of divine law the pope could not rule at all. No, the alternative was that popes could rule as secular rulers did, without supposing that everything they decreed was infallible. This had been the influential view of the great French conciliarist Jean Gerson, one of the leaders at Constance. Quentin Skinner has said that for Gerson the church was a political society in Europe, and no matter what might be said about the authority given by Christ to Peter, the popes were put in office by men for the good of the church and could use power but not claim to own it.[24] The general council, acting as a parliament in the church, could therefore call the pope to account.

Luther's position seemed set in March 1519 when he wrote to Spalatin that it had never been his intention to separate himself from the Apostolic See at Rome. He was content, he said, that the pope should be lord of all. So he would honor the Turk if the Turk were his political leader. For he was sure, Luther said, that no power could exist against God's will. But he would not permit papal champions to drag the Word of Christ anywhere they wanted or to contaminate it.[25] His position would seem to be that the church was a living body, continually seeking to define and refine its teaching and conduct by reference to scripture.

Eck's crowing letters after the event declared that Luther opposed the sacred and solid tradition of the church with the appeal to the conscience of the individual. Men of Eck's conviction foresaw—rightly, as it turned out— that once the individual conscience was granted freedom to seek its own definition of truth, Christian faith would become so fragmented that no consensus would be possible and that the uncertainties inherent in any religion would then become part of the spiritual equipment of humankind.

It is worth saying one other thing about the Leipzig debate: Luther was evolving toward a conception of God outside of Christ in that unrevealed depth of the divine mystery that seems more and more like the Greek idea of fate or destiny. When Eck brought up the stigmata of St. Francis, Luther countered sharply that he wished all the mendicant orders might cease to exist. He did not therefore respond precisely to this well-known claim to miraculous confirmation of St. Francis's character and mission. But I have already noted the absence of any sign in his lectures on the Psalms of special veneration of the saints or attention to the miracles attributed to them. Once launched on preaching his gospel, he would deny that the miracles said to take place at the Catholic shrines were works of God, and he was to remain skeptical of miracle claims by his own followers. God's purposes became for him too secret for miracles. Rather, God works silently in what appears to be the natural course of the world, and even in these historical events is so hidden that with human sight we cannot see him at all. Everything happens according to God's consent. But nothing any mortal can do will influence God to move to the right hand or to the left. At times God's will outside of Christ seems to become for Luther the intellectual principle of creation, not unlike in effect the god of the hated Aristotle. Christ alone shows the merciful face of God—but only in the sacred text and then only in the encounter of the heart as the Christian assents to the text and reads it. The act of reading, the moment of feeling "This word is for me," provided for Luther comfort that became the center of his religion.

He was moving toward his mature position. Gerhard Ebeling has described this as the conviction that no other mediator was necessary between God and humankind except the Christ who spoke in scripture. He was unwilling to grant that the promise of Christ to send a "Spirit of truth" to lead his disciples into all truth was, as Catholics claimed, a promise to a legal institution, the Roman Church. Christ speaks not to an institution but to the heart.[26]

The immediate consequence of the debate at Leipzig was a war of books and pamphlets. The papalist side was now convinced it had a notorious heretic by the tail. Luther and his friends struck back in kind. Neither side could argue down the other. Therefore the arguments rolled on as fast as the slow-moving printing presses of the time could crank them out. Luther complained to Spalatin on August 18 that Eck was lying about him to the bishop of Brandenburg and grumbled that he and his allies at Wittenberg lacked a printing press swift enough to answer these assaults.[27]

The Hussite issue would not go away. From Prague on July 17, only a few days after the disputation at Leipzig ended, an advocate of Hus's views sent a glowing letter to Luther. The writer, one Wenzel von Rozdalowski, was overjoyed to have had news from a witness to the debate at Leipzig who reported that Luther had conquered his foe. Rozdalowski said that he himself had read Luther's works thoroughly and daily discussed them with friends. Now he had heard that Luther wanted to read Hus's book on the church.

This was the book, he said, that had caused Hus to be burned at Constance.[28] Luther had read the work by the following March, as had others, and a new edition was being printed by an Alsatian printer.[29] The reading of Hus's words confirmed opinions Luther had formed from reading the decrees of Constance. Now it seemed clear to him that Constance had erred not only in condemning too many of Hus's tenets but also in its final condemnation of Hus himself.

The papalist writers stirred Luther to furious response and to dark murmuring about the papacy itself. In a letter to Wenzelaus Link on December 18, 1518, Luther mused that it seemed that the Antichrist of which Paul had spoken now ruled over the curia in Rome.[30] To Spalatin on March 13, 1519, Luther again brought up the subject: The pope might be the Antichrist or, if not the Antichrist himself, perhaps the possible forerunner of the Antichrist who was to come before Christ returned to judge the world.[31]

The Antichrist in Christian mythology was the Beast of the Apocalypse who in the last days would reign upon the earth and subject the righteous to a great tribulation that would cause many Christians to fall away to devil worship. Christ would come again to earth to destroy this dark kingdom of the Beast, and so history would end. The Antichrist would not openly reject God but would instead pretend to be God's messenger to subvert true religion and lead the world into apostasy.[32] The notion of the Antichrist fitted one of the underlying obsessions of the age, that the most horrifying wickedness and destruction could mask itself with an appearance of purity and beauty. Here was somber evidence that human beings live in a world of shadows and illusions that if not carefully studied and judged may be traps to snare the unwary and send even those who wished to do good plunging into the abyss.

As expected, the University of Leipzig issued a summary condemnation of Luther and Karlstadt. The condemnation was tinctured with insult and offered no compromise.[33] Miltitz remained in Germany futilely trying to bring things to a good end by forcing Luther to appear before some sort of German ecclesiastical tribunal that might condemn him as a heretic and force him to recant. Eck stirred the universities of Cologne and Louvain to declare against Luther and to call on Christians to burn his works. Eck also wrote the pope to hasten an official papal condemnation of Luther and his doctrines.[34]

Throughout this onslaught, Frederick the Wise remained constant. He wanted a hearing for his professor before a German Diet. He was willing, he said, to revere and obey the pope "in just matters," but as a pious German prince, he was not willing to grant Rome authority over his professor until Luther could defend himself before the Reichstag. Luther continued to work, to study, to preach, to write letters, and to think. His thoughts became more radical. On December 18, 1519, he wrote Spalatin in response to a request to preach on the sacraments. He had by this time already preached on baptism, the Eucharist, and penance. Spalatin wanted him to continue with the other four—confirmation, ordination, marriage, and extreme unction. Luther refused. He did not believe they were sacraments. They carried no express promise of God; that is, they were not affirmed by scripture. Ordination especially troubled him. He had read in 1 Peter 2:5–9 that we are all priests. Priests and laity differed only in that priests were ministers of the sacrament and the Word.[35] So ended the decisive year 1519 with Luther resolved to find in scripture alone a standard for Christian doctrine. Almost a year before his *Babylonian Captivity* made public his renunciation of the traditional understanding of the sacraments, he was holding scripture up to them and finding tradition in error. Whether he fully understood his position vis-à-vis the rest of Catholic Christendom or not, he had moved beyond any possibility of compromise with the hierarchy. By 1519 his revolution was irrevocable unless he died before he could fully define it. That prospect loomed over him as he took up his work.

12

THE DISCOVERY OF
THE GOSPEL

W E CAN now discuss with proper caution one of the most perplexing and debated issues in Luther research in the last four decades—the date of his "tower experience," Luther's momentous discovery that inspired his rebellion against Rome, his understanding of the term "the righteousness of God." When did it happen? United to that question but often taken for granted is another: What was it? It is a difficult topic, made more difficult by Luther's inconsistent use of words.[1]

The tower in question included the little third-story office where Luther studied and wrote. It stood against the city wall, and in 1532 the tower had to be torn down when the wall was strengthened. "If I live another year," Luther said in March of that year, "my poor little room will be gone. From there I stormed against the papacy, and for that reason it's worthy to be remembered forever."[2] In the same tower was the monastery's latrine[3]—a matter Eric Erikson found portentous, for he interpreted a part of Luther's table talk to mean that a constipated Luther was on the privy and defecating when the great insight struck him.[4] Luther's release from the constricting bondage of fear corresponded to the release of his bowels. So Erikson. Most of us suppose that Luther was referring to the room where he worked, pondering the Bible and his soul. In mentioning the proximity of the latrine to his study, Luther seems to have been indulging in a characteristically paradoxical reflection, the meanness of the place and the greatness of the find.[5]

Luther wrote the story as completely as he ever did on March 5, 1545, in the preface to his selected Latin works published later that year, a few months before he died.[6] He was not enthusiastic about putting these works before the public in a fresh edition. He was happier, he said, that the Bible had been translated into most European languages than that his own books should be spread abroad. He called these early efforts "confused works done in the night"—pedantries.[7] Yet it was inevitable, he said, taking a sidelong look at his place in history, that they should be published. Moreover, his prince had commanded this edition. He warned that his writings should be read with caution and even with pity for the man he had been but was no longer.

He had been a monk, he said, the most insane papist, drunk with the pope's doctrines, so immersed in them he would have killed anyone who detracted one syllable of obedience from the pope. He was not, he added, like that frigid piece of ice, Johann Eck, who had defended the papacy out of greed and insincere motives. Indeed, he thought, Eck and others of his ilk seemed to laugh at the pope like Epicureans. Here again he seems to call "Epicurean" those who believed death ended human existence for everyone, the righteous and the unrighteous alike. As for himself, he wrote that he had pursued these issues with the greatest seriousness as one "who horribly feared the last day and from the very marrow of my bones desired to be saved."[8]

Out of his passion for the papacy, Luther lamented, he had in some of these early writings made concessions to papal authority that he had afterward renounced and now despised as the worst blasphemies. This was a pose, at least in part. Luther in his later years habitually represented himself as a loyal Catholic driven out of the papal communion, against his will, by the wickedness that he observed there. So he countered accusations by his foes that he itched for rebellion because he had a proud spirit and lusted for a wife. Yet we have seen that nowhere did he make much of the papacy in his early lectures on the Bible. The topic did not interest him until the conflict over indulgences forced him to consider the pope's authority. At Leipzig he spelled out a view of the pope as limited monarch in the church—limited by custom and consensus. To the old Luther, hardened in his fury against the pope, even this concession to the papacy evidently seemed intolerable.

Following this preamble, he passed into a brief chronological summary of the indulgence controversy—Tetzel's preaching, Luther's Ninety-five Theses in response, the uproar that followed, his appearance before Cajetan, the Leipzig debate with Eck, and the storm that came after that. He did not say that he *posted* his Ninety-five Theses in 1517. Rather, he said that he wrote a letter of protest to Albrecht of Mainz and another to Jerome Scultetus, the bishop of Brandenburg. When these were ignored or scorned, he said, he published *(edidi)* them together with a German sermon on indulgences and his resolutions. Here for the honor of the pope, he said, he did not renounce indulgences but said that good works were better. He represented himself as a lonely monk seeking truth and by innocent effort bringing down on his head the wrath of the pope and an army of stubborn and unsavory minions. In the meantime, German popular fervor, revolting against Roman greed and exploitation, rose to support him.[9] It was his version of consensus. Given their freedom, Christians would rush to his gospel, and in his recollection of his salad days as he wrote a few months before he died, they did.

Only after he carried his account all the way through the debate with Eck at Leipzig and with the discussions with Karl von Miltitz did he write this: *Interim eo anno iam redieram ad Psalterium interpretandum*—"Meanwhile in that year I had returned to interpreting the Psalms."[10] He had, he said, already lectured on Paul's letters to the Romans, to the Galatians, and "that one which is to the Hebrews." Clearly the year in this account was 1519, resulting eventually in the publication of the *Operationes in Psalmos,* commentaries on the Psalms printed in a series of volumes beginning in 1519 and concluding in 1521.[11] The reference was then not to his first lectures on the Psalms with which he began his teaching career in Wittenberg.

One word stuck in his way, the word "righteousness" in Romans 1:17—"For the righteousness [*iustitia*] of God is revealed from faith to faith, for the just [or righteous] shall live by faith." "I hated this term 'the righteousness of God,' for by the use and custom of all the doctors, I had been taught to understand 'righteousness' philosophically as they say, the formal or else the active righteousness by which God is righteous and punishes the unrighteous."[12] The juxtaposition of the righteousness of God and the righteousness of the Christian was troubling. It implied that the "just" were to have some righteousness in them that might be defined in some comparable way to the righteousness of God. He had lived, he said, as best one can *(utconque)* as an irreproachable monk, and yet he felt himself a sinner before God with the most anxious possible conscience, without any confidence that God could be pleased by his satisfaction—the word *satisfactione* here in Luther's vocabulary probably refers to that part of the sacrament of penance in which the absolved sinner goes his way resolved to sin no more, demonstrating a redemptive sorrow for sins for which he is forgiven.

He was secretly angry with God, he wrote, that even after sinners were doomed to eternal perdition by original sin and in every kind of calamity oppressed by the law of the Ten Commandments (which in his view no one could keep), God should add sorrow to sorrow by the gospel and by the gospel itself assail us with his righteousness and wrath. "I raged in a furious and stormy conscience; a rudely demanding man, I beat upon that place of Paul's, ardently thirsting to know what Saint Paul might wish."[13]

But then, said Luther, in his misery, hating God for his universal vindictiveness, he meditated on the forbidding text both night and day. By the mercy of God he received his great revelation. As he examined the joining of words "righteousness of God," he saw that this righteousness or "justice" was not something that God did *against* sinners; it was something that God gave *to* Christians. In legal terms, Luther saw that *iustitia* was not to be defined in Cicero's way, "that which conforms to law." *Iustitia*—justice, righteousness—did not mean that God judged people according to the Ten Commandments; rather, *iustitia* was equity, a favorable verdict given by the judge because of special circumstances, the circumstances here being helplessness and faith on the part of the Christian. Justice or righteousness is then *passive* for the person who receives it. "Passive" means that the redeemed person does not will and do anything on his own. The justified person can do nothing to merit divine mercy—not even have faith by himself. God becomes righteous because he is merciful—demonstrating the kind of God he is. Luther had absorbed from nominalism the belief that God was supremely free to be anything he willed to be, including a God of vindictive and merciless wrath. The willingness of God to grant righteousness to sinners was not therefore merely a transaction; it went to the nature of God himself and made the supreme force of the universe a benign being. Luther was overjoyed at his discovery. "I felt myself absolutely reborn," he wrote, "as though I had entered into the open gates of paradise itself."[14]

Afterward, he wrote, he discovered that Augustine had said much the same thing in his *On the Spirit and the Letter*. And, he said, he would have written another commentary on the Psalms had he not been overtaken by the Diet of Worms.

This righteousness of God did not mean that the Christian became righteousness in any objective sense. Luther's doctrine cut the ground from beneath the cult of saints and the monastic ideal whereby the monk disciplined himself through life, purging away sin and arriving at a higher level of righteousness than anything possible in the secular world. His definition of righteousness meant rather that God accepted the goodness of Christ in lieu of the wickedness of the sinner, for Christ had conquered the powers of darkness, in particular the power of death, by his resurrection, and by God's mercy the Christian was joined to that cosmic triumph. Thus the Christian could be *simul iustus et peccator,* justified before God and a sinner at the same time. Christ substituted himself for the sinner, and God gave mercy rather than justice.

Everything Luther says in this preface to his Latin works seems straightforward, and if we take him literally, we find no difficulty locating his discovery of the gospel *after* the Leipzig debate in 1519, during his lectures published as the *Operationes in Psalmos.* Yet few scholars have taken Luther at his word. Some have placed Luther's discovery as early as 1508, only a year after he was ordained to the priesthood. Most scholars of a generation ago held that his Reformation awareness could be found in the pages of Luther's first commentary on the Psalms and certainly in his lectures on Romans.[15] One exception during that period was a German scholar named Ernst Bizer, who in a 1958 monograph, *Fides ex auditu,* argued with great cogency and power for taking Luther's 1545 preface literally.[16]

Bizer's book stirred up a scholarly debate that four decades later shows no sign of resolution. Why is agreement on the matter so difficult? The main reason is Luther himself. He talked about his discovery often, yet only in the preface to the 1545 edition of his Latin works did he date it precisely. Could he have been confused? We know his memory slipped sometimes. Once he said he had stayed in the Augustinian house when he met Cajetan at Augsburg, but in fact he stayed with the Carthusians because there was no Augustinian house in Augsburg in 1518.[17] But that was a mere bagatelle, tossed off in his table talk. The preface to the Latin writings is carefully detailed and circumstantial. Could he have erred so much in a matter so important?

Or could he have made the whole thing up? In a time when we recognize more than ever before that all autobiographical utterances are fictions of a sort, an effort at self-fashioning, we are less willing than our scholarly predecessors to believe everything that anyone writes about himself, even if we are speaking of a religious hero. Some have suspected that there was no "breakthrough," that Luther's account was part of his own self-fashioning, and that in fact his theology was a gradual development of efforts to free himself from the dead end of monastic life.[18] Or could Luther have compressed the resolution of his suffering into one dramatic moment to make a good story, one that would locate him with Paul and others through the centuries since who have told triumphant conversion tales? It is not an impossible thought.

No doubt there is a certain logic in dating the discovery of the gospel before the indulgence controversy because of how Luther talked and wrote about it elsewhere. In his comments about his *Anfechtungen* during his table talk, he often mentioned the helpful responses of Staupitz, and his association with Staupitz was closest between 1508—Luther's first teaching at Wittenberg—and Luther's doctorate in 1512. Staupitz resigned his professorship in 1512, leaving his teaching duties to Luther, and began a peripatetic existence that kept him on the move throughout Germany. In 1515 he became general vicar for the Augustinians in the empire, and afterward Luther saw him seldom, although, as we have seen, he accompanied Luther to Augsburg for the stormy interview with Cajetan and left Luther there alone when the interview was finished. Given Luther's frequent affectionate references to Staupitz, we might conclude that the older man was present at Luther's breakthrough. But Luther never says so. According to Luther's frequent stories, Staupitz comforted him in bleak moments of depression. He remembered Staupitz's consolations with affectionate gratitude, but there is no evidence that they immediately led Luther to his discovery. Nor is there any textual evidence to let us suppose that Staupitz was even nearby at the moment of Luther's great conversion experience.

Another, more important reason for the common belief that Luther's discovery came early should be apparent from the content of Luther's early biblical lectures. Nowhere in them does he suggest that human beings can please God by their good works. His fully developed doctrine of justification by faith holds persistently that human beings have no righteousness of their own and must depend on Christ for all their hope. Augustine held that all humankind represented a mass of perdition with nothing good within itself, not even the desire to do good. So the longing for justification on the part of a few was itself a gift of God's grace, not caused by our impotent human will. The young Luther was thoroughly grounded in this Augustinian tradition.[19] This Augustinian view of our inability to do anything to save ourselves shows in all his early lectures, including those on the Psalms. Since Luther in his 1545 preface made much of Augustine's *On the Spirit and the Letter*, it would seem that at the very least we might date his "tower experience" to 1515 or 1516, when he was lecturing on Romans, for he mentions the little book there many times. Augustine makes the explicit point in *On the Spirit and the Letter* that the righteousness of God in Romans 1:17 refers to the righteousness with which God clothes the sinner whom he has made righteous.[20] Yet it is a common experience of all of us who spend our lives with books that we may know a text well, even teach it and cherish it, and after a long while suddenly find a meaning in it that we have never seen before. Luther could very well have done the same.

Then what about the role of faith in his thought? Faith is, after all, at the heart of his discovery. He had much less to say about faith in his early lectures on Psalms than he did in his later expositions of Romans, Galatians, and

Hebrews, but human depravity and helplessness are choric elements in all of them. He is not silent on the subject of faith. So also is Christ a recurring theme. Luther's interpretation of Psalm 102 is particularly resonant with a passion to condemn the works of the flesh and to cling only to God in Christ. He comments on Psalm 102:3, "Turn not your face from me." To know Christ, said Luther, "is to know and to have everything. For the face [in the text] is knowledge of the Lord which now by faith is in us, but then by direct sight."[21]

No wonder that scholars as learned as Roland Bainton and Karl Holl before him confidently assumed that Luther's great enlightenment came *before* the indulgences controversy began.[22] No wonder also that some modern scholars persist in dating Luther's breakthrough as early as 1515, when he was bringing his lectures on the Psalms to an end.

How then do we deal with Luther's unequivocal description of his experience, locating it as he does in 1519? Bainton's biography ignores the problem. Holl assumes that Luther's memory slipped, an opinion concurred in by many recent scholars. Bizer took hold of the other horn of the dilemma posed by Luther's 1545 preface: If we accept it as a true report, how do we interpret the earlier works where scholars have so confidently located Luther's discovery of justification by faith? How was the recognition that he describes so powerfully in his 1545 story different from the theology of his early lectures on the Bible? So the question of *when* Luther arrived at his idea of justification cannot be separated from *what* Luther meant by it, and here the 1545 preface to his Latin writings is maddeningly difficult.

Just what brought Luther the ecstasy of relief he described in 1545? The essential text was Romans 1:17, "For therein is the righteousness of God revealed from faith to faith, as it is written, the just shall live by faith." In his later works, Luther comes back to this text countless times to extol its central place in his idea of redemption. He dwells on it with loving enchantment as the immaculate and powerful lens through which all scripture becomes radiantly clear. Yet in his lectures on Romans before the indulgence quarrel, he dismisses this text with a few conventional words.[23] This minimal comment on a text that later resonated in Luther's works like a chorus of trumpets is proof enough that we should take his 1545 statement literally, that he recognized the full meaning of justification by faith only in 1519. It seems also important that Luther did not include his lectures on Romans in his collected Latin works when one of the express purposes of the edition was to reveal how his thought had developed. It seems likely that he found these lectures unessential in his own development.

Yes, the lectures on Romans emphasize the helplessness of the natural man before the power of sin. That was by no means a new idea. In the Catholic academic theological tradition, the human ability to merit salvation was strictly limited or nonexistent. In the Augustinian view, even faith is not our own act. In his most predestinarian mode, late in his life when he battled the Pelagians, who championed free will, Augustine held that we lack any power to turn to God unless God first enters our souls and calls us to himself. God elects us; *then* we have faith. In Augustine's view, the only free will humankind possessed outside grace was freedom to sin.[24] Faith came to the believer as an act of God's mercy, and only by faith alone could anyone be saved. Small wonder that the great early twentieth-century Catholic debunker of Luther's story, Heinrich Denifle, wrote with biting scorn that Luther's supposed "discovery" was old Catholic doctrine and that his story in the preface to the 1545 edition of his Latin works was a complete fabrication![25]

In the teaching of the *via moderna* in which Luther had grown up, the sharper edges of Augustinianism were blunted. Even so, this school held that the best the sinner could do was to recognize his sin and helplessness and beg God for forgiveness. Free will, insofar as it existed, was limited to this plea for help and to the willingness to receive help when it came. One might make the plea or not. Thomas More, who became Luther's most powerful English antagonist, summed the matter up in his frequent quotation of Revelation 3:20: "Behold I stand at the door and knock, if anyone hears my voice and opens the door to me, I shall enter to him and dine with him, and he with me."[26] God's grace comes before salvation in that God knocks, but the choice to open remains the sinner's. Ever afterward, in this "scholastic" scheme of things, the Christian maintained a spark of free will, however faint, that allowed him to accept or reject God's grace in the sacraments until the end of life. Insofar as the Christian was capable of any "merit," it lay in that tiny motion of free will toward God's enveloping grace. It was "merit" only because God agreed in his mercy to accept it as such. The longer human beings lived in that grace, the stronger it became and the less likely free will was to allow the Christian pilgrim to fall from the way to paradise.

Some theologians joined even this limited view of free will to a scheme of predestination, for they held that God knew from the foundation of the world those who would exercise free will to seek him and because of his foreknowledge predestined these chosen ones to salvation. Saving faith was said to be "formed faith," faith infused with love that required the believer to do good works. Even this formed faith might be predestined so that good works were part of the machinery God used to grant salvation to individuals.[27] An analogy would be that God might predestine a watch to tell the correct time by the precise motions of its parts rather than by a time signal sent directly to the watch face at intervals from heaven. The doctrine of predestination under any guise becomes much like a snake that bites its tail. Once we begin to ponder the implication of an all-powerful God who knows future, present, and past, for whom all time is present, predestination of some sort becomes almost—if readers will forgive the word—inevitable.

The conundrum of predestination offers helpful clues to just what Luther discovered in his Reformation awareness. We know that later in his life he warned Christians off the topic with a fervor that burns on the page all these centuries later. He told his followers to leave the subject alone. Predestination, he wrote to one disciple,

> is like a fire that cannot be extinguished, and the more he disputes the more he despairs. Our Lord God is so hostile to such disputation that he instituted Baptism, the Word, and the Sacrament as signs to counteract it. We should rely on these and say: "I have been baptized. I believe in Jesus Christ. I have received the Sacrament. What do I care if I have been predestined or not?"[28]

Here is a significant comment about the power of liturgy to remove us from some contradictions of systematic theology—the discipline that tries to eliminate contradiction and to fit together the various things we believe about God and so bangs our heads against predestination because we cannot finally reconcile God's omnipotence and his omniscience with our free will and God's justice. In these liturgical acts—baptism, hearing and reading the Word, and receiving the Eucharist—we are brought close to God as a comforting presence. We do not participate in the liturgy like philosophers seeking to resolve contradictions and expose fallacies; we participate in a drama that is emotional and mystical, that assumes the presence of the God we seek. In sharing the liturgy, only the most skeptical of us fail to suspend disbelief—just as we suspend disbelief in our participation in a work of literature or in our immersion in some other form of art. Thus are we comforted. This dynamic comfort should drive out of our minds the torments associated with the doctrine of predestination. This attitude would become a major part of Luther's spiritual arsenal against despair.

We can infer from many other comments by the later Luther that predestination deeply troubled him as a young man. Since one of his strongest expressions of the doctrine came in a disputation of September 1517—only two months before the indulgences controversy broke out—we can assume that he pondered it during the events that he describes as the context for his discovery of justification by faith. We may infer that his doctrine of justification freed him from the taunting fear that he was one of the damned.

Did it then give him full assurance of his salvation? Sometimes he could write so powerfully about grace that we may almost conclude that certainty about salvation was possible. But Luther never claimed absolute certainty that he was predestined to salvation or that we can be certain that anyone is one of the elect. To George Spalatin he wrote in 1522, "My opinion is this: we should trust the grace of God but remain uncertain of the future perseverance or else predestination of ourselves or others as he says: Let he who stands watch out lest he fall."[29] Here Luther sounds very much like his Catholic antagonists who warned against presumption at one extreme and despair on the other. His attitude toward the subject is consistent with his later admonition, quoted above, to leave predestination alone. (If my argument is valid that for Luther damnation was annihilation, no life after death for someone still left God's existence intact and with it a providential understanding of the world.)

But if Luther's discovery that he sketched in 1545 was not the assurance that he himself would be saved, what was it? Bizer reinterpreted Luther's early lectures on Psalms and Romans as examples of a late medieval piety of humility. It is a complex and erudite argument; I believe it can be roughly summarized in the following way: God has told us that we are utterly unworthy of redemption. Our sins have so separated us from God's holiness that we deserve nothing but condemnation. The world and our own pride conspire to make us believe that we have some worth of our own, even if it is only our desire to please God. The visible signs of our good works, whether good deeds done for others or the ritual piety of religious observance, allow us to be puffed up with pride and to imagine that we deserve some reward. According to the theology of humility, Bizer said, we should wholeheartedly agree with God about our unworthiness. Luther's early works, with their iterations of profound abnegation, fit into this theological scheme of things. The living good news of the gospel—ever renewed in our reading of scripture—exposes the depravity and the helplessness of our true nature, and if we are redeemed, we accept its judgment instead of the verdict of the world and our own proud minds, which see only the outward appearance. The gospel in its full message includes the law and reveals the righteousness of God in that it accuses us and annihilates us, sets its demands before us, and thereby kills our pride because we cannot meet these demands.[30] "Faith," says Bizer, elucidating this scheme of things, "is the behavior of the entire man that corresponds to the judgment of God."[31] That is, to believe is to accept God's verdict on our wickedness in every part of our being. In that flattened state, we call out to God, and he is merciful to us. This view is consistent with Luther's fervent declaration in his early exposition on the Psalms:

> The soul which uninterruptedly hates itself, the person who "hates his life in this world" [John 12:25], who is displeased with himself and hates his deeds, this is the one who bears this judgment and always rises again. On the contrary, those who set up their own righteousness and excuse themselves for their sins (like Saul, like Adam and Eve) do not judge themselves or accuse themselves but think they are doing well and are pleased with themselves and love themselves and their own life in this world. "Therefore the ungodly will not rise in the judgment," because the Jews do not confess their wrong and do not accuse themselves. But as the righteous man is the first to accuse himself, so the ungodly man is the first to defend himself.[32]

Bizer's interpretation of Luther's early works allows us to fit together many of Luther's autobiographical recollections. It also helps us see some problems of the theology of humility that could torment an ultraconscientious monk. Luther often wrote in these early works of the necessity for an inner acceptance of God's verdict on our worth. In a sermon on indulgences, probably preached in October 1516, he declared, ""For interior penance is true contrition, true confession, true satisfaction in spirit. When the penitent most purely dislikes himself in everything that he does, and is truly turned around to God and completely recognizes guilt and trusts in God with the heart, by his inner detestation he chews and punishes himself, and because of that very same thing, he satisfies God.[33]

The demand, frequently expressed, is not for mere formal agreement with the judgment of God but for a heartfelt consent that in Luther's language requires an active conviction that he describes in emotional terms. It is an "existential awareness," a judgment in which not merely reason but our whole consciousness participates in full agreement with God's condemnation of our sinfulness. Although he does not use the metaphor, Luther seems to demand an intuition about one's own condition not unlike the intuition we have when we perceive that blue is not red or that yellow is not green. We must *know* that we are precisely what God tells us we are.

But such inner certainty in abnegation of the self is not continuously possible for anyone of honest and sound mind. Luther knew how quickly the human heart can gild humility with pride. If indeed he tried to become perfectly humble, we can understand his obsession with the confessional. He said later that he confessed sometimes as long as six hours in a single day.[34] At the end of that time he would think of still other sins that he had forgotten. He said in his table talk that he fasted as long as three days without a drop of water or a bite of food.[35] We may see in these rigors an effort to create within himself certainty that he had fallen to a level of abnegation sufficient to allow him to claim the mercy of God. It would then appear that as this regime failed, Luther saw the quest for humility to be a "good work." We all know that we can be proud of our humility; Luther knew that, too.

Bizer saw the Reformation awareness begin to take shape in Luther's increased emphasis on Christ in his lectures on Romans. Christ through his suffering and death was humiliated to nothingness and so became exalted.[36] Not through might and strength are death and evil conquered, and not through flight and fear can anyone flee away from them. They may be overcome only through weakness—that is, an absence of strength—in that one bears them patiently and willingly.[37] Yet, Bizer maintained, even with this growing emphasis on Christ, Luther remained set on humility as the proper response of the Christian. The Christian is to believe in God's judgment against him; faith is not here extended to the belief that God has forgiven the sinner of his sins. In the exposition of Romans, says Bizer, for Luther the one who is humble according to these rigid strictures is the one who has received grace.[38]

Not until the lectures on Hebrews—given as Luther plunged into the controversy over indulgences—so Bizer says, can we see a clear change in Luther's theological expression. Faith by then had become the trust that God will forgive one's sins. Faith begins for Luther to be the means by which one attains the peace that passes all understanding, and this awareness came by about December 1517. This peace lies in the certainty of the forgiveness of sins certified by the shedding of the blood of Christ, which, says the book of Hebrews, establishes a new covenant and a new priesthood by which Christ himself becomes our high priest before God.[39] With the forgiveness of Christ, we need not fear any punishment for our sins.

In this inner development, Luther was drifting away from the medieval sense of economy. In a world presided over by a divinity who knew everything and who shaped the visible cosmos into signs of the eternal and the invisible, nothing could be lost; everything had to be accounted for in a heavenly balance sheet. Everything from Christ's cradle to stray drops of milk from the Virgin Mary's breast to the head of John the Baptist had to have some continuing sacred witness to give to the world. If Peter and Paul had died in Rome, their tombs had to be found. Sacred history had to have a symmetrical shape. The great historian of Gothic art and architecture, Emile

Mâle, wrote that in the thirteenth century it was held that in the Annunciation, the angel Gabriel appeared to Mary on the very spot where God had formed Adam out of earth and that Jesus died over the grave of Adam "so that His blood should flow over the bones of our first parent," and the cross itself was constructed from the tree of the knowledge of good and evil whose fruit, eaten by Eve, had been fatal to the human race.[40] Our sins also took their place within a divine economy. Every sin had to be numbered, listed, and remembered in God's books and to be paid for by its precisely appropriate punishment. Purgatory, by this reasoning, became inevitable because even redeemed Christians had to have sins punished in precise ratio to the seriousness of the offense. And what of the merits of the saints, those who had by divine grace managed to surmount sin and to do more than necessary for their salvation? Those merits could not be strewn away and lost. They required a place in this economy of the divine where nothing goes astray. So as we have seen, they were accumulated in a treasury of merit that could be applied to those in need of merit in purgatory. As Bizer points out, Luther in these early years still affirmed belief in purgatory, but he had in fact already undermined the doctrine by his conception that the death of Christ was sufficient to forgive all sins and that forgiveness meant that the sins of the Christian would not be punished.[41] Bizer follows the texts carefully to his conclusion that the "gospel" became for Luther not only the revelation but also the medium by which the Christian achieved righteousness. The gospel wakened faith.[42] The faith was that Christ dwells in us and has forgiven our sins. As seen in Christ, the face of God is merciful and not angry. The symmetrical economy is forever broken; we gain something from God that overwhelms any human sense of proportion.

Bizer's argument takes account of Luther's character—a man who from 1513 onward was caught on a treadmill of duties and, with the indulgences controversy, was swept up in a fury of notoriety, writing, and speaking. Like many others from time immemorial Luther probably did not know what he thought until he spoke or wrote his ideas. In him the hand seemed to inform the brain—as it does for many of us. He wrote swiftly for the moment to meet the issue that confronted him. His works usually have an ad hoc quality. It seems inevitable that he needed time to understand the implications of many of his own ideas.

If we are to look for the text that signals Luther's discovery, the logical place would seem to be the *Operationes in Psalmos* that, according to his own testimony in 1545, became the focus of his studies when the justification awareness fell upon him. Early in this series, in his exposition of the Third Psalm, Luther came on the text "I went to bed, and I slumbered, and I woke up again since the Lord sustained me." He made sleep into an allegory of death, and his exposition became a prose poem of exultation in Christ who had weakened the horror of death and the tomb by making death a sleep from which we shall waken at the resurrection, sustained by the hand of God stretched down from above.[43]

Shortly afterward, in his exposition of the Fourth Psalm, Luther wrote, "Who does not believe, makes [God] a liar; whoever does not hope either from inability or ignorance or willfulness fashions the necessary consequence, which is horrible to think about, of contempt of God." Later on he spoke of the silence of the Christian, calling in Isaiah 30:15, "In quietness and hope shall be your strength." Said Luther, "Here, to be silent means nothing other than to have a still patience."[44] It is a counsel of immobile tranquillity, waiting for God to do what no human being can do for himself.

Then in his exposition of the Fifth Psalm, he came to verse 8, *Domine, deduc me in iusticia tua propter inimicos meus, dirige in conspectu tuo viam mean*—"Lord, from above lead me in thy righteousness because of my enemies; make my way straight before thy face." The word *iusticia* turned him to Romans 1:17, a verse he had scarcely considered in his first lectures on the Psalms, and it seems that here, very suddenly, everything came together for him. "We shall have much to say below about the righteousness of God," he wrote, and without further ado he defined the term. "It is not that a just God condemns the wicked, as is the most common opinion," he said. It is, as St. Augustine has said in his work *On the Spirit and the Letter*, that which God pours into a man which justifies him.[45]

It is here, as Luther himself was to say in 1545, that we are to date his Reformation breakthrough—in 1519, or perhaps the winter of 1519–20.[46] As he streamed on in these expositions, the meaning of his discovery seemed to become more and more clear to him. Part of that clarity was his recognition that the true Christian life was filled with pain, temptation, doubt, and fear. In his exposition on the Fifth Psalm, he declared, "Living, no, on the contrary, dying and being damned makes the theologian, not understanding, reading, or speculating."[47]

It may seem almost redundant to pose yet another question: Why was Luther driven on this absorbing quest for clarification? The answer, I believe, lies in his devouring fear of death. His discovery of the gospel was his means of reconciling his fear of death with a saving faith. The consequence of the wrath of God is death. Death, hell, the grave, and wrath are almost synonyms in Luther's rhetoric. The formal content of faith was that Christ redeemed us from death. Forgiveness meant resurrection. If God did not forgive, the dead could not be raised.

If Luther was terrified of death, was his terror not then proof that he did not believe sufficiently? He said as much many times. Here was his dilemma. If have faith, I should not fear death; if I fear death, I do not have faith. I fear death; yet I yearn to have faith. His "Reformation breakthrough" was, I believe, his discovery of a theological and existential means of transforming the dilemma into a paradox. Just as he could not will himself into perfect humility, so he could not will away his terror before death.

Part of the transformation involved the equation of faith to the promises of God. Bizer's student Oswald Bayer has argued that in the earlier Luther, God's promise was to save the sinner who fully condemned himself in fear and trembling. The motto *simul iustus et peccator,* which appears in the lectures on Romans, would then simply describe the state of the contrite heart condemning himself. The sinner who accused himself had God's promise of ultimate redemption.[48]

But we know how difficult self-condemnation and submission were for Luther, for we have his witness that he rebelled, that sometimes he hated God and wished that God did not exist. This sort of rebellion is obviously not the attitude that demonstrates perfect contrition for one's depraved state. Now, with his "tower experience," a different conception of promise asserted itself. It involved a deeply personal identification with the crucified Christ and the questing Christian. The seeker no longer perceived Christ as a stimulus to condemn himself, but saw Christ dying and became united with the suffering Christ in the loneliness of death and in the promise of resurrection.[49] Often afterward, he used the image of Christ as victor over death, the innocent son of God unjustly taken by death. In a sermon of 1526 Luther spoke of Christ, holy and guiltless, killed on the cross unrighteously by sin. Sin, here a synonym for Satan, became then God's debtor and must pay for his injustice, and so Christ has with his blood won the right over all the sins of the world.[50] It is hard to know how literally to take utterances like these, but their importance is clear. Christ hangs on the cross not merely as a example to prove our own wretchedness that we require such a sacrifice. Instead he is our warrior chieftain, fighting on our side against the powers of darkness, and we participate in his victory.

But promise includes a further meaning. A promise is a sign of a reality to come. It is not the reality itself; it depends on the one who makes it. Oswald Bayer has pointed out how important Christ's death is to Luther's 1519 sermon on baptism and how closely repentance and baptism go together in his thought. Baptism is a sign that carries in itself the substance of victory over death, and the gospel and the sacraments are testaments of an inheritance that God freely gives us because of what Christ has done.[51]

Although in Luther's theology sign and substance are present both in the preaching of the gospel and in the sacraments, we locate the substance only by faith. Since God makes the promise, we can affirm to ourselves that the substance is present in those agents that he has ordained to signify it. But God is hidden from our immediate sight, and the substance of his promise remains hidden, too. Its full disclosure will come only at the end of time. A promise by its nature looks to the future, something not yet complete. In this life, God does not lift the Christian out of human nature, and God does not reveal himself beyond any shadow of doubt. Weak human nature will not let us believe in the promises of God with a confidence that purges from the soul the anguish of fear and unbelief, the *Anfechtungen.* Suffering agonies of doubt is part of the Christian way. Therefore, in Luther's discovery of justification the Christian was liberated from the self-imposed requirement to present a perfect mental attitude to God, to confuse belief with knowledge, faith with the direct intuition of an observed world. Whereas in the earlier Luther the fear of death was the ultimate form of unbelief, the Luther who discovered justification by faith understood that no matter how great our faith, it cannot be strong enough to stave off terror before death. In Luther's particular case, the Christian was not required to have such faith that horror at death and annihilation and corruption could be considered a sign of unbelief and damnation.

Throughout the *Operationes* Luther comes back time and again to the dialectic of hope and despair, the two colliding continually in the Christian life. In the midst of despair, the Christian is to pray, knowing that hope will come again. To surrender to despair is to deny God, an act "that is horrible to think."[52] Despair here would seem to mean resignation to a denial of God's very existence. The Christian must accept his own fears, with their undercurrent of ultimate and abysmal unbelief, as part of the human condition for which grace is necessary; and here, in Luther's theology, the human Christ became all-important because in looking at him, the Christian saw grace, mercy, and welcome rather than a calculating divine judge inspecting every human thought and act for its imperfection, inscribing every thought and act in his own doomsday book. Moreover, the Christian saw a human Jesus suffering from loneliness, forsaken before God in the moment of death. The Christian could identify with that Jesus, love him, and trust him just because that divinely human figure had taken on himself the common human experience of isolation in the cosmos. In Jesus, God himself validated that experience and presented it in the Gospels as the tragic earthly destiny of humankind. Having accepted this tragic dimension as both inevitable and inescapable in this life, Luther could live with his own tumultuous ups and downs, his recurring, raging melancholy, his radical introspection, his fear of what reason said about faith, his bouts with stark unbelief, all combined in his day-to-day life with a frenzy of ceaseless activity that even in our busy world of today seems incredible.

Luther's "discovery" seems to embody a radical willingness to accept anxieties—including the extreme human difficulty of believing that the Christian God exists and that Christ rose from the dead and that we shall all be raised. That the difficulty of such belief continued is clear in hundreds of Luther's later pronouncements; indeed, they are so numerous that we are likely to read them as a stylistic tic, a habit that may numb us to Luther's passion in asserting them. They help to explain his antipathy toward human reason, for many thinkers in this time, including Luther himself, said flatly that reason offered no hope at all that the soul could survive death. These deep and abiding agonies become part of Luther's theology of the cross—the notion that doubt and anguish are conditions the Christian must expect.

In his lectures on Romans and Hebrews, Luther was still teaching that the fear of death was a sign of lack of faith, a fear the Christian should overcome: "So then, if you feel that you dread death, instead of loving the thought of it, you can take this as a most certain sign that you are still involved in the 'prudence of the flesh.'"[53] Yet by the time Luther wrote his *Explanations of the Ninety-five Theses,* he was saying that the fear of death was natural to all human beings. When he looked back on this part of life in his later letters of "spiritual counsel," he made much of his own horror in thinking of death in this period and afterward. He made no effort to excuse himself for this horror or to pretend that he had outgrown it. So the Luther who told his auditors in his lectures on Romans that they should not fear death was, by his later testimony, engaged at that moment in horrific interior conflict surely exacerbated by his own preaching that such fear was a sign of unbelief. In a sermon preached on March 19, 1525, he declared, "Because I always fear death, my faith is feeble, and it is indeed a sin. It does not damn me if I die in that sin; still faith will draw me forward to God."[54] Here is the "Reformation breakthrough" in all its maturity, crashing across the late medieval teaching that our eternal destiny depends on our psychological attitude toward God in the moment of our death.

At the heart of the Reformation awareness seems to be a falling in place of ideas incubating in his mind and heart for years. Bizer, who has interpreted this process as well as anyone, points out just how much Luther emphasized the sacraments in 1519 and afterward—an emphasis lacking in the early expositions of Psalms and Romans. Indeed, says Bizer, "In Luther's early days one can very nearly speak of an antisacramental mood."[55] But then the joining of word and sacrament became fundamental to Luther's theology so that he eventually said that "all the stories of the gospel are indeed sacraments."[56]

This notion that the stories of the gospel are sacraments and that the sacraments themselves are part of the Word brings me back to Luther's attention to baptism and the Eucharist. While engaged in these liturgical acts, we are not in the rational/systematic mode that inclines us to tease out and resolve contradictions in our religious confessions that may make us question and doubt. We are in a participatory mode; we are actors in the collective drama of redemption.

In the same way, to hear the gospel proclaimed as Luther defined it—Christ bearing to us the forgiveness of sin and victory over death—or to proclaim that gospel ourselves is to place us in a mode whereby the experience validates itself. The gospel story has the power of all good stories to draw us into itself and to make us live it as we hear it. Once Luther discovered that the essence of the gospel is that Christ has forgiven our sins, the discovery was not "historical" in that it became something like the discovery of America, happening on a given date and, like all historical events, limited to that date. It is rather a discovery that to be validated must be repeated again and again so that it becomes present each time the story is told. The gospel is never a story told once and for all; it is always a story *being told,* always a story *in progress.* It is told powerfully in the sacraments—especially in the Eucharist but also in baptism, the reenactment of death, burial, and resurrection.

It is also told in words. Luther's prodigious output has something of a sacramental quality, the vigorous repetition of the story that in the telling affirmed itself and buried the doubts that reason raised against faith. Gordon Rupp long ago pointed out that from 1517 until his death in 1546, Luther published an average of one work every two weeks—and many of these works are large and important treatises.[57] I believe that we understand somewhat better this furious and gargantuan production if we see it as Luther telling the stories of the gospel repeatedly to himself as well as to others and by that ceaseless retelling ceaselessly reliving the experience of Christ forgiving him his sins and reassuring him of resurrection and the life everlasting and triumph over death. His preaching and writing became a ministry of the sacrament of the Word and, to a large degree, somewhat mystical acts binding his soul to the God who was beyond the power of reason to comprehend. At the same time that he spoke and wrote, his affirmations kept the dogs of reason and doubt at bay.

We are left with a paradox—the problem of predestination for Luther. On the one hand it seems clear that he had been deeply preoccupied with his own salvation during the terrible *Anfechtungen* that assaulted him in his early life. And yet as we have seen, after his experience of the discovery of justification by faith he was to say habitually that it was dangerous to dwell on predestination and that also no one could be certain of his own election. Time and again he was to speak to those troubled by predestination as if their torment was in itself a sign of their faith and that God had elected them.

We shall return to predestination when we examine the great controversy between Luther and Erasmus over freedom of the will. For now, it seems safe to say that from 1519 on the problem seemed less acute for Luther. From the time he met Cajetan at Augsburg in the fall of 1518 until the conclusion of the debate with Johann Eck in the summer of 1519, Luther had discovered that the papal church would not move an inch to accommodate the gospel he was defining during those months. He passed through a period of intense and brutal tribulation. On February 20, 1519, Luther wrote a confessional letter to Staupitz, speaking of the array of enemies massed against him. He asked Staupitz to pray for him. "I am a man exposed and rolled up in society, in drunkenness, in titillations, in indifference, and in other evils, beyond those evils that press upon me out of my official duties."[58]

As noted earlier, Luther's letter to Spalatin on March 13, 1519 expressed his first grim presentiment that the pope might be the Antichrist or at least his apostle. The remark may have been spoken half in jest; Luther told Spalatin, "I speak in your ear" this idea about the Antichrist, perhaps a confidential witticism.[59] But by December 1519 in a letter to his friend Johann Lang, Luther referred almost casually to the pope as the "Roman Antichrist."[60] Whenever troubles had seemed ready to overwhelm the church, speculations about the imminent appearance of the Antichrist swept the Christian world. Pierre d'Ailly, whose conciliar view of the church was akin to Luther's expressions at Leipzig, believed that the Great Schism, with two and then three rival popes bitterly excommunicating one another, portended the Antichrist and the end of the world.[61]

Now with increasing conviction Luther saw the Antichrist possessing the Catholic Church in the person of the pope. By the time he came to full understanding of justification by faith in the summer or early fall of 1519, he believed that he was God's instrument to resist the Antichrist in the congregation of the faithful. The Reformation awareness may have been, in part, this sense of divine validation forged in the strain of battle and shaped finally into a willingness to stand alone for the truth of the gospel against the papal church. I surmise that this sense of an outside enemy to fight with all his strength took his mind off the enemy within and relieved from his *An-*

fechtungen. As Bizer points out, when Luther saw that the papal church—in the person first of Cajetan and later of the pope himself—would not answer him with scripture but responded only with fiats drawn from tradition, he defended scripture, the Word of God, against the words of men.[62]

Given the stress Luther was under in 1519, we may liken his ecstasy at the discovery of the gospel to the well-known human experience of being in an agony of anxiety over some difficult moment in life over which we seem to have little or no control and then of coming—often rather suddenly—to a feeling of unexpected relief at the thought that our very powerlessness liberates us. What will be will be; we must do what must be done. With Luther this relief fixed on the human figure of Christ, who revealed the merciful face of God.

The fear of predestination seemed to be one of those doubts, one of the *Anfechtungen,* that was purged away by hearing the story of the gospel again. Predestination referred to the future; the gospel story repeated in Word and sacrament was now. Here it is worth returning to one of Luther's later letters that we have considered earlier, his epistle of consolation to his children's tutor Jerome Weller in July 1530. Weller had been overwhelmed by melancholy. Luther went back to his own early depression and to Staupitz's comforting words: You will see, said Staupitz, that God "intends to use you as his servant to accomplish great things." On another occasion, he said in the same letter, a man he had comforted told him, "Wait and see, Martin, you will become a great man."[63] He told another version of this same story in his table talk two years later, quoting the man directly: "Dear baccalarius; don't worry; you will yet become a great man." In this version Luther said, "So have I also heard a prophet."[64]

At first reading, such comments sound like intolerable boasting, but we should not take them so. His story had now become one of the stories that conveyed the gospel and made it live in the present. Such remarks as those he made to young Weller show rather that Luther's ultimate consolation was to believe that God was using him, despite his fears, that he had a destiny. That being true, he might have a fair degree of assurance that his faith was sufficient, that his sins were forgiven, and that he was one of the predestined. Since God was using him to tell and retell the story of the gospel, the gospel was continually renewing that assurance against the horrifying presence of death in the midst of life—the paradox of *simul iustus et peccator,* justified Christian and sinner, believer and doubter, fearful and serene, all at the same time.

Why then did Luther say that Christians should not trouble themselves over predestination and that no one could be certain of his own salvation? Is there not here an insoluble contradiction? I think not. When Luther preached the gospel and partook of the sacraments, he felt the assurance of the story, of being caught up in it, of living it as a character in the drama. When he let himself dwell on predestination, he left the field of the story and its good news about the revelation of God in Christ and fell into a speculative, rational mood, becoming spectator rather than participant, and in that mood—inevitably detached from the story of the gospel—no assurance was possible. It was impossible to prevent that rationalizing mood from pressing into the mind from time to time. But it was possible to focus one's eyes and heart on the stories of the gospel, of Christ's life, death, and resurrection, and in that story to subdue the terrors that arise from the rational scrutiny of life, conscience, sins, death, the grave, and the fatal roll of the cosmic dice that mean predestination to damnation.

In many respects the conflict between the gospel with its stories about Christ and the rational speculation about predestination reminds me of children's books being sold as I write. In these books, we are presented at first with an apparent random design that may seem as monotonous as wallpaper. But we refocus our eyes as though to look *through* the picture, held just in front of our noses, and the picture suddenly changes dramatically, becomes three-dimensional, reveals designs we could not perceive in our early, "rational" inspection. By blinking or refocusing our eyes, the image again disappears, but when we renew the process of discovery, we see that it is always there, waiting for us.

In a similar way Luther thought we can look at the great gulf fixed between God and ourselves and perceive only the certainty of our damnation. But when we refocus and look at Christ in the distance, beyond our speculations about ourselves, the design shifts, and we see a gracious God. The superficial design is always there, seemingly chaotic, likely to reshape itself and push aside the dimension in which we see the benign face of the redeemer. But if we keep our eyes fixed through superficial appearance, we perceive another picture, that of the victorious Christ, always ready to comfort and forgive.

The paradox then was that Luther found peace with God by accepting inner turmoil and doubt as part of the human condition. His ultimate rebellion against monastic piety was to reject the supposition that the prayers and other pious routines of the monastery could lead to serenity in this life. All life to him was an existential dialectic between hope and despair, the proclamation of life against the stark reality of death. Most interpreters seem to put the emphasis on faith in his great text, so that if we say it aloud it becomes, "The just shall live by *faith*." In my view we should change the emphasis to make the text in his mind read, "The just shall *live* by faith." Faith, like life itself, is not a milestone that can be located on a map of existence, but is continuing consciousness, the mind in the stream of time swept by the current through pools of tranquility but then through raging torrents in unpredictable variation.

Faith is nurtured by repeated hearing of the Word—the story of the gospel told in scripture but especially efficacious as it is spoken aloud by ministers. It is, as Luther said, a passive righteousness, and vivid images of passivity abound in Luther's description of how the Christian apprehends God's justification. Already in his lectures on Romans Luther had argued that in receiving the first grace, which makes us seek God, we should be as passive as a woman is in the moment of conceiving a child.[65] Images of passivity are frequent in Luther's attempts to describe the discovery of justification by faith. Later, in his *Church Postils,* a collection of sermons to be read by ministers in churches, he wrote that the only way humans could receive God was to accept him. The experience was, said Luther, like the sun warming still water. When water is running swiftly, the sun cannot warm it. Mary held herself still and silent at the Annunciation, considering herself the lowliest maid in town.[66]

Yet despite these images, the passivity does not result in prolonged serenity. That seems evident from his own stories told time and again. The passivity includes acceptance of suffering, pain, anguish, knowing that torments of fear and doubt will come, knowing that the Christian cannot will himself into fending them off. All of Luther's theology is shaped by his conviction that all true Christians must endure the same anxiety he experienced to find peace with God—and that the anxiety does not stop. The receptive calm of the justified Christian comes amid turmoil and doubt combined with feelings of sublime abnegation born of a profound sense of sin. The experience as recorded in his preface to the Latin works of 1545 is one of boundless joy, release, the skies opening. But the joy did not represent the end of the battle. The joy lay rather in the promise of ultimate victory.

It has been common to link Luther to the mystics, with their alternations between joyous illumination and the dark night of the soul. And Luther's rhetoric does include some mystical elements. Yet the bond between Luther and mysticism does not ultimately seem essential or even very strong. The mystical experience was likely to involve some sense of unity with God, the merging of the soul with the divine so that in extreme varieties of mysticism all separation between divinity and humanity vanished, and individuality disappeared in ecstasy. Even less extreme forms of mysticism seem to be too cozy to coexist with Luther's sentiment that divinity and humanity, holiness and sin, are separated by a profound gulf that only Christ can bridge and that we cannot cross over by the emotional and mental discipline that the mystics savored. I wonder if Luther's experience of justification was more akin to the catharsis that has been a traditional part of the tragic experience in the Western world. Tragedy involves ultimate questions posed to the universe about the meaning of life. It includes tumult and violent conflict, death, and a certain stillness when at the end of the drama peace returns with the removal of the corpses from the stage.

Catharsis in the tragic experience involves an acceptance of what has happened together with a wisdom born of resignation to the will of the gods, a wisdom that affirms implicit values held by the society where tragedy is enacted. For the audience at least, it results in peacefulness after pain, the sense that unbearable turmoil has ended, the battle concluded so that we leave the theater and go about our lives both reduced and exalted by what we have learned about the human condition. At the end of *King Lear* the storms inside the soul and on the heath of the stage have subsided, and we have learned of the abyss into which a great character can fall because of a foolish narcissism, an inseparable part of his character from which he can find neither escape nor redemption until he falls at the verge of death. Yet an additional part of catharsis is the relief that comes to the audience when it is all over. I have often wondered if part of the development of the sense of catharsis in tragedy came from the primitive experience of death, whether within the family or in human sacrifice, when the survivors, the spectators, felt the terrific sense that at last the tension was broken, the fatal drama played out, and they could now go about their business, accepting death and taking up life once more.

Certainly Luther's description of the passivity of the Christian receiving the justification awareness has within it a determined acceptance of the character flaw, the state of sin, the being unto death, that is an essential, inescapable, implacable fact of human existence. As he describes it in the preface to the Latin works, it includes the somewhat paradoxical sense of emotional cleansing from storm and stress. It is this striking willingness to accept simultaneously his own nature and peace with God that makes him differ from mystics who sought to transcend human nature to achieve unity with God. It also brings him closer to the experience that became classical catharsis.

Bizer argues that Luther began to arrive at his understanding of justification in the winter of 1517, and he gives an impression that Luther developed this idea somewhat slowly. This interpretation seems to fit Luther's own account in his preface to the Latin works and to correct a misunderstanding—the notion that Luther fell on the idea of justification by faith in a lightning flash, like Paul on the road to Damascus or like Augustine in his garden when he heard the child singing nearby, "Take and read; take and read."[67]

Such stories of sudden conversion have been a staple, a topos in Christian tradition. Because we read everything by the light of what we have read before, it is not surprising that generations of scholars have taken Luther's conversion to be similar to other lightning flashes that mark the conversions of great men and women. Luther himself sometimes used language that accorded with this Christian trope, without ever quite saying that the justification awareness came on him in a blinding flash. In Erikson's theory that the perpetually constipated Luther's conversion came while he was defecating, we have the ultimate theory of abrupt discovery and revolutionary change.[68]

It seems more plausible that the "discovery" grew over a period of months or years, and that like most sudden insights it was not something utterly new so much as it was an abrupt understanding of a cumulative experience. This was the story of Augustine as he recorded it in his *Confessions*. The voice of a child drove him to the Epistle to the Romans and the promise of the help of Christ, and Augustine took the moment as a divine intervention in his life. But before he heard the child singing beyond his own garden wall, he had been long torn between his desire to become a Christian and his potent sexual desires. He wanted to become a Christian to escape the terror and the gloom of death, but he lacked the strength to give up lust and embrace eternal life. When he heard the child's voice and picked up the Epistle to the Romans, Augustine was already in a turmoil of anguish and tears, and his conversion seems almost inevitable.

So with Luther. To his inner anxiety of conscience and fear of death was added the anxiety of the circumstances of 1519. Now he labored forward in a way that could lead to public death at the stake following condemnation as a heretic. Despite his fear of death, he embraced mortal danger. Like a soldier who has had nightmares about death, he discovered in the sound of battle the courage to do his duty.

In May 1519, while Luther prepared for the Leipzig debate with Johann Eck, he wrote out a German "sermon" on getting ready to die. It is not clear that he preached this "sermon." It was written at the request of Spalatin on behalf of a friend troubled at the thought of death. It captures Luther's mind when, according to his later testimony, he was on the verge of his discovery of the gospel. It is much longer than his usual sermons, showing the importance he gave to the topic. At times it has a classical, Ciceronian tone of admonition: The best way to prepare for death is to face it squarely in the midst of life and health and to get used to the idea.

A major theme is that death is a terror but that the terror may be mitigated and endured by a number of steps. The devil, he says, "conjures up before man's eyes all the kinds of sudden and terrible death ever seen, heard, or read by man . . . In that way he fills our foolish human nature with the dread of death while cultivating a love and concern for life, so that burdened with such thoughts man forgets God, flees and abhors death, and thus, in the end, is and remains disobedient to God." Luther does not go from this thought to the notion expressed earlier in his lectures on Romans, where he saw the fear of death as lack of faith pure and simple. The emphasis has subtly changed. He says:

> We should familiarize ourselves with death during our lifetime, inviting death into our presence when it is still at a distance and not on the move. At the time of dying, however, this is hazardous and useless, for then death looms large of its own accord. In that hour we must put the thought of death out of mind and refuse to see it, as we shall hear. The power and might of death are rooted in the fearfulness of our nature and in our untimely and undue viewing and contemplating of it.[69]

Young man Luther was obviously not alone in his obsession with death. Here is a fear that some have in a much higher degree than others, that seems to preoccupy some ages more than others, and Luther appears to have been hypersensitive to death's terrors, especially to the terror of annihilation.[70] For whatever reason, he was unable to build up the wall of denial that allows most of us to lead relatively "healthy-minded" lives, at least up until that moment when a doctor tells us that we have a fatal illness. Luther's fear seems to have led him into a state of mind that we call today clinical depression. He called it *tristitia*. I am as skeptical as anyone about extreme claims by Freudians—including Erik Erikson—to explain historical figures in confident, schematic detail. As Roland Bainton used to say, there are grave difficulties in psychoanalyzing the dead. But even historians most doubtful about the use of psychology cannot deny that all human beings are affected by the irrational within themselves, that their fears condition the way they view reality, and that some obsessive fears are even reasonable. Yossarian in Joseph Heller's World War II novel *Catch 22* has what a medical man calls a paranoid fear that someone is trying to kill him; but Yossarian is also flying bombing missions over Germany, where thousands of German fighter pilots and anti-aircraft crews are trying to kill him every time he comes over. Luther, like the rest of us, was faced with death—real and inevitable death. We have abundant texts from Luther that testify to his black misery of soul before death, and if we cannot call this misery "depression," we have scarcely another word for it in a modern vocabulary.

Drugs to alleviate depression today are routinely prescribed. Our forebears had to suffer through it until something dramatic within themselves relieved it, or else until it wore itself out. Augustine was driven by the death of a friend to see death everywhere and to begin his transit from Manichaeism to Christianity.[71] Like Augustine, young Luther turned from his despair to the church and more particularly to the monastery, where the combination of companionship, a ritual life, and communal prayers effected an antidote to depression that serves some well in every age. The novelty and the ceaseless activity of monastic ritual worked against the loneliness of uncontrolled introspection and solitude that Luther in his later life found so perilous to the afflicted.

In all these early lectures on scripture neither hell nor purgatory is much on his mind, whereas death very much is. Nor does he speak in any extended and excessive way about either the Last Judgment or Satan. (I have come to think that usually when Luther spoke of God's judgment it did not mean the calling of the living and the dead before the great white throne of the book of Revelation, the text that inspired all those romanesque and gothic judgments on the facades of churches, but that God's judgment was death itself.) Mention of the devil is almost casual, without the dark loathing that marked his attitude later on when he equated Satan with all the forces ranged against himself. His Reformation awareness therefore included growing acceptance of the fear of death as the human lot, its implications of unbelief a cross to be borne, and a refusal to look on death with Socratic tranquillity part of the Christian acceptance of fallen human nature. The Platonic attitude required the triumph of human will over human nature, and it was just this dependence on the will that Luther had already rejected. He had proved to himself that he could will neither faith nor serenity in his own heart. Now, as he seemed to do so often in his early academic life, he saw implications of beliefs already affirmed. If the human will has no power, we cannot will away terror before death. But we can affirm that as God will save us through his grace though the sins of the "flesh" remain within us, so God can also save us even if we remain tormented by a horror of annihilation—a fear that implies doubt about the power of God to do what he promises us in scripture.

In his Latin sermon on twofold justification of 1519, we find Luther making a characteristic declaration that Christ has done for us what we cannot do for ourselves.[72] A major text in this scripture-filled sermon is

John 11:25, "I am the resurrection and the life; he who believes in me will not die in eternity." The Christian can claim to possess "what Christ lived, did, said, suffered, and died" although the Christian has not done those things himself.[73] They belong to the Christian, says Luther, as all the possessions of the wife belong to the husband.

This is an "alien righteousness," one infused in us by grace and not by any act of our own, not unlike original sin, which comes to us by birth and not by our acts. By this alien righteousness Christ expels Adam from us more and more, as faith grows in us. This faith does not come all at once, says Luther, but it begins, it grows, and it is perfected in us finally by death. Here is the final paradox. Death, the most feared enemy of the Christian, becomes the entry into fulfillment that eludes us throughout our lives. In this life, ultimate fears remain and yet do not destroy the validity of our faith in Christ. This faith brings fruits in the mortification of the flesh and in the "crucifixion of concupiscence" so that the Christian does good works and loves the neighbor.[74] In our humility and fear of God we hate ourselves for the sin that is in us, living soberly, justly before our neighbor, piously before God.

The weight of this sermon lies on the person of Christ—Christ who did not think it robbery to be considered equal to God. This is the theme with which Luther begins the sermon and to which he returns again and again throughout. Christ is God, who not only has done everything that we could not do ourselves, but who has also suffered death and experienced resurrection. Hence the Christian must cling to Christ through all the seasons of life—but with a faith never complete until death. Luther's faith then allowed the presence of fear and trembling through all of life. To contemplate Jesus is to be reminded in the midst of the most radical kind of doubt and fear that God is with us. This is the message of the *Operationes in Psalmos,* and I believe in this work more than any other we can trace the culmination of his understanding of justification by faith. Indeed I think that here is the place where one sees his mind working clearly, stepping from stone to stone across the river of tribulation and despair, to arrive at acceptance of the human condition and clear definition of what God has done in response.

But with his amazing capacity for work, Luther was writing other things as well. During 1519 he also undertook to revise and publish his lectures on Galatians. The importance of this little epistle to his own rejection of the "law" is obvious. Paul wrote his letter to the church in Galatia when he fell into a dispute with the apostle Peter over whether gentile converts to Christianity should be required to obey the Jewish law. In furious prose, Paul announced that faith in Christ's resurrection was the only requirement for admission into the congregation of the redeemed. Luther found this sentiment a blessed freedom from compulsion in religion, and his *Galatians* of 1519 resonates with the conviction that the Christian life is a spontaneous attachment to Christ and not a requirement to do good works of any sort— including the ritual good works of Catholic piety—out of fear. The Christian was to go directly to Christ:

> Therefore I like the practice that nothing but the crucified Christ is impressed on those who are about to die, and that they are exhorted to faith and to hope. Here at least—no matter to what extent the deceivers of souls may have deluded our whole life—free will collapses, good works collapse, the righteousness of the Law collapses. Only faith and the invoking of God's completely free mercy remain, so that there are either more or better Christians in death than in life.[75]

When he gave these lectures, Luther was well launched on his break with Rome, advancing with more daring on the principle that religious compulsion of any sort was injurious to faith. By the end of lectures on Galatians in 1519, he was denouncing priestly celibacy, implying that celibacy might be good for some priests but not for all.[76] He was on the threshold of reinterpreting the entire sacramental system of the church.

What we call his discovery of the gospel looks very much like release from his efforts to be a stoic. Now he would go forward as a Christian against all his fears to take his leap into the dark—depending on the everlasting arms of the human Jesus to pluck him up and lift him aloft. He would spend his life and work *as though* the gospel were true, *as though* the promise would be fulfilled, taking Christ by faith to be what the Bible said he was. Biblical exposition became an act of liturgy and worship to cultivate the presence of the Christ in whom Luther willed to believe no matter what reason and the world might say to the contrary.

Much later on Luther spoke and wrote with thoughtful wisdom about the dangers of solitude to the melancholy soul. "Solitude produces melancholy," he said in his table talk. "When we are alone the worst and saddest things come to mind."[77] By 1519 he had little time for solitude. The busy life now thrust on him was therapy for his melancholy. In looking back on this period from 1545 and compressing his experience somewhat, he seems to have found in the totality of events his great discovery, and he remembered it as a moment fated to make him what he became, something God did for him, leading him along and bringing him home to his destiny.

Although this analysis of justification by faith bears many similarities to the concept of tragedy as it has developed in the West, it differs in an essential point: Luther's entire effort was, like Paul's, intended to see death as an enemy to be conquered by faith in Christ. Luther both affirms the horror of death and yet denies death's ultimate victory. Yet as Richard B. Sewall argued decades ago, the vision of tragedy comprises a sense of terrible finality about death:

> The tragic vision is in its first phase primal, or primitive, in that it calls up out of the depths the first (and last) of all questions, the question of existence: What does it mean to be? It recalls the original terror, harking back to a world that antedates the conceptions of philosophy, the consolations of the later religions, and whatever constructions the human mind has devised to persuade itself that its universe is secure. It recalls the original un-reason, the terror of the irrational. It sees man as questioner, naked, unaccommodated, alone, facing mysterious demonic forces in his own nature and outside, and the irreducible facts of suffering and death. Thus it is not for those who cannot live with unsolved questions or unresolved doubts, whose bent of mind would reduce the fact of evil into something else or resolve it into some larger whole. Though no one is exempt from moments of tragic doubt or insight, the vision of life peculiar to the mystic, the pious, the propagandist, the confirmed optimist or pessimist—or the confirmed anything—is not tragic.[78]

Luther felt forces that contribute to the tragic sense. Yet by embracing Christ as he did, he pulled back from the darkest implications of tragedy and the vision that was to come to dominate serious secular literature in his century.

13

THE PLUNGE INTO
THE UNKNOWN

L UTHER'S rejection of the pope and the papal church was well-nigh complete by the end of 1519. He was now convinced that the traditions that gave the papacy its authority had been mistaken (and possibly satanic), that the pope and his minions had maliciously built up these errors, and that true Christians must be liberated from the tyranny of sterile forms and human corruptions of the divine Word.

As the year 1520 came on, rumors flew. Luther was said to have fled into Bohemia. Yet Archbishop Albrecht of Brandenburg was said to be sympathetic to him. A shower of meteorites streaked through the skies over Vienna in January, provoking much foreboding. When word of this cosmic event arrived in Wittenberg, complete with drawings and fervid descriptions, it coincided with news of condemnations of Luther's doctrines by the faculties of theology at Louvain and Cologne. Luther wrote to Spalatin on March 19, commenting briefly on the "asses" at these two schools and remarking that he was reading the work of John Hus, not agreeing with all of it but amazed at Hus's erudition. He commented briefly on the flames in the sky over Vienna and wondered if these might be omens of his own "tragedy." He did not believe that the stars or other heavenly bodies caused events on earth as the astrologers said; that would be to ascribe to the stars the works of God. But he always believed that unusual celestial events were portents, sometimes good, sometimes not.[1]

One of his supporters, Crotus Rubianus, wrote him from Bamberg on April 28 that Franz von Sickingen had offered Luther sanctuary and support and a place to do his work.[2] Sickingen had a string of castles scattered across Germany. He was a leader of the "knights," those inferior lords whose territories were no match for the great domains of the dukes, margraves, and electors of the empire. But he had a head for money, increased his own properties, sold his services to other noblemen in need of mercenaries, and for a time was a man to be feared. In what seems to have been a nationalist impulse—frequently romanticized by German historians since—he offered to protect Luther as he had offered to protect Reuchlin. To his friend Wolfgang Capito on April 30, Luther wrote that the more he was attacked, the more he felt the Holy Spirit flow into him. He was furious with Eck for his malice and pride and mocked Eck's habit of beginning his works with the words, "In your name sweet Jesus, Glory only to God." His enemies at Louvain and Cologne were "Epicureans," but Capito need not fear that he, Luther, would "retreat."[3]

Early in the Reformation, Duke George of Leipzig said of Luther and his disciples, "They do say what they really mean."[4] The essence of religion was "meaning it," an inner, spiritual relation of words to reality through the Christ found in the gospel. The principle of "meaning it" now had to be applied to every aspect of Christian life, both in the soul and in society. Luther did not—and could not—consider this task as a program in the way that an architect might survey the site of a recently demolished building and set himself to drawing blueprints for the edifice that would replace it. On the contrary, he labored piecemeal as issues arose, often as others requested his opinions. Georg Spalatin was one of his most persistent questioners and for that reason one of the most important motivators of Luther's thought. Doubtless behind Spalatin stirred the curious and perplexed mind of the Elector Frederick the Wise, seeking to understand where his professor was leading his university, electoral Saxony, and the elector himself.

Despite the almost random way in which Luther was forced to address issues, a remarkable consistency ruled his prodigious output during the year after the debate with Eck at Leipzig. He preached regularly; not all his sermons were published, but auditors took notes, and many of these have been preserved. One faithful auditor who jotted notes on Luther's sermons had been secretary to Johann Eck and accompanied Eck to Leipzig for the debate with Luther. He was John Graumann, called Poliander, and he was so impressed by Luther that he deserted Eck and followed Luther back to Wittenberg. Later he became a Lutheran pastor.[5] Most striking about these brief notes, many of them extracts from sermons, is how frequently Luther resorted to allegory. In one the drunkenness of Noah became an allegory of the Crucifixion. Noah was drunk on wine; Christ was drunk on the chalice of the Last Supper. Noah, naked, was mocked by his sons; Christ, the son of God, was crucified between two thieves and mocked by the multitude that looked on.[6] Luther considered these sermons literal interpretations of the Bible because they presented Christ, but they seem less than literal to us, and later he was to castigate himself for how wedded he was to allegory in these early years of his fame.[7]

He kept the printers in Wittenberg busy. Yet the channel that directed the flood of his words was deep and definite and may be charted with confidence. His driving definition of religion was that it was an earnest experience of God by Christians thirsting for peace in their souls, like his own experience in his quest for justification. As Karl Holl long ago demonstrated, Luther sought union with God not in some mystical melting into God's being but rather in a harmony of will between the Christian and the divine.[8] Luther hated casual religion, religion as habitual rite, religion with hollow forms, empty of substance, religion that bargained with God for worldly benefit. Religion was not something one got easily from another; it was not mere obedience to the rules—whatever the rules might be. True religion was a profound, unceasing life with God conducted through the story of the Christ of the Gospels and the letters of Paul—a Christ that he constructed, as any reader does, both from the text and from his own experience.

All these qualities were expressed in various treatises he wrote in 1519 and 1520 on matters as diverse as economic policy, prayer, good works, the role of the secular princes, and the nature of the sacraments. He became a radical in the eyes of the papal church, but he saw himself as trying to conserve a Christianity buried by novelties and unnatural usages laid on by wicked human beings. To him papal doctrines were no longer believable; he would replace them with a believable faith.

His positions were misunderstood by many who leaped from Luther's words to positions so radical in comparison that he loathed them. For the moment he wrote with the enthusiasm of a man convinced that multitudes would heed his voice and find the liberation that he had found in the gospel. Heiko Oberman has argued that Luther never expected to see his movement reform the whole church. In Oberman's view, Luther spoke rather as a voice of truth proclaimed for truth's sake against the expectation of the end of the world, when God himself would wrap history up like a scroll and bring judgment on the earth. Luther never intended, says Oberman, to "reform" the world in the sense of making it a morally better place.[9] Oberman's description fits the later Luther much better than the Luther in the wake of his discovery of justification by faith. The thunderous early tractates voice an expectation that Christians will follow him and that the papal church will be exposed and be made a byword among the nations. There are a grandeur to his vision, a confidence, and a willingness to face in radical clarity implications of beliefs beaten into shape on the anvil of his suffering and his experience with the Bible.

In late 1519 he had preached a sermon on usury. Usury was formally forbidden by canon law, but clever canon lawyers found ways to evade the prohibition. Dissatisfied with the first version of the sermon, Luther issued it in a larger edition early in 1520.[10] He hated the excesses of emergent capitalism. He shared the older Christian view, derived from Aristotle, that money was lifeless stuff and that to charge interest on lending it was exploitation. Interest was yet another device used by the rich to crush the poor; Jews were allowed to lend money at interest since they were accursed by God anyway. The frontispiece of the 1520 edition features a crude woodcut caricature of a Jew gloating over receiving interest.[11]

In these months Luther preached often and wrote several brief works on prayer. As an example of the genre, we may look at his *Sermon on Prayer and Procession during Cross Week,* preached during the so-called Rogation Days of late May and early June 1519—a few weeks before the debate with Eck at Leipzig. The Rogation Days commemorated the last three days before Christ ascended into heaven after the Resurrection. It was a period of feasting, carousing, and processions in which an entire village might take part. It had long since become a spring festival to celebrate the greening of crops in the fields and fruit in orchards after the last killing frosts of winter. Such festivals in all the centuries have their share of drunken revelry and a sexual *joie de vivre* that affront the righteous.

This little sermon went through at least twelve printed editions in little more than a year, a record that seems to attest its popularity at least among the authorities charged with keeping their people from riot.[12] Luther undertook to teach Christians how to pray and by the bye to restrain drunken and licentious behavior during the festival. Christians, he said, must be drawn by God himself. We can claim no power of our own—not even the power to pray—for all good things must come from the abyss *(Abgrund)* of God's goodness. We are to pray without doubting that God will hear our prayer and answer it, and Luther cites several texts from the Gospels that promise that our prayers will be answered. Unless we come without doubt, we make God a liar. Confidence in God's faithfulness means that we have no confidence in our own merit. "We pray after all because we are unworthy to pray. The fact that we dare to pray confidently, unworthy as we are but trusting only in the faithfulness of God, lets us have our prayers answered."[13]

But having spoken boldly about confidence in God, Luther imposes a caveat. "Your trust must not set a goal for God, not a time and place, not specify the way or the means of his fulfilment, but it must entrust all of that to his will, wisdom, and omnipotence."[14] God will answer our prayers, but only on his own terms and in ways that we may not perceive as answers. God cannot be predicted or bound by our expectations or desires. In the Old Testament he did unexpected miracles, Luther said, to answer the prayers of his people. Although he was careful not to promise miracles, he assured his auditors that God will bring about a good result to their requests.

By condemning the scandalous misuse of the Rogation Days processions, Luther opened a window onto the folk piety of the time. We can pray to God to "protect the crops in the fields and cleanse the air—not only that God may send blessed rain and good weather to ripen the fruit, but rather that the fruit may not be poisoned and that we, together with the animals, eat and drink thereof and become infected with pestilence, syphilis [Luther calls syphilis the 'French disease'], fever, and other illnesses." Pestilence and plague come "from the evil spirits who poison the air." So, he says, "the Gospels are therefore read publicly in the fields and in the open so that through the power of the holy word of God the devils may be weakened and the air kept pure and, subsequently, that the fruit may grow vigorously and be a blessing to us."[15]

This purification of the air and blessing of the crops are the only *external* requests that Luther seems to sanction in prayer. It is akin to "give us our daily bread" in the Lord's Prayer, a plea for the regularity of a life that includes sustaining the body with food. In no way does he suggest that the processions and the reading of the gospel are *necessary* if these good effects are to be granted by God. Rather he suggests several times during the sermon that, given the rowdiness of the crowds, the processions could be abolished. But if the processions must be held, he will provide a pious and spiritual rationale for them. Part of the rationale is to ask God to purify the air by quelling the evil spirits that may corrupt it and bring on dearth and pestilence.

Absent here entirely is the mood of prayer associated with pilgrimages to shrines and veneration of the saints, prayers directed toward specific and personal requests. Luther does not mention the saints at all, and we have seen that his earlier writing and preaching shows him to have been uninterested in their miraculous stories or in their legendary power to do good or evil. We find neither here nor elsewhere in his early works the saint worship that called on St. Apollonia to cure toothache or St. Christopher to protect the traveler or St. Sebastian to protect from plague or St. Wilgefort to rid a pious woman of a cruel and unwanted husband. Indeed, we find scarcely any specific requests and nothing that resembles petition for special blessing of the sort that still brings thousands of Catholic pilgrims to Lourdes and other shrines or that still inspires votive plaques for answered prayer in many churches. Luther confines himself to the traditional spring rites where God is called upon to protect and nourish the crops in the field—a prayer that in the normal course would be answered nearly every year. In dearth or plague, blame could be placed on the sins of the people, sins that had caused God to withdraw his protecting hand and to let the evil spirits have their way until sinners had repented. To conclude his sermon, Luther once again takes prayer inside, as it were, making the point that the abundance that God normally gives in the fields leads people to the "plague of the soul" that is sin. While we flee from physical pestilence, "we indulge in drunkenness, idleness, followed by unchastity, adultery, cursing, swearing, murder, quarrels, and every other evil."[16]

God here plays a mysterious role. He uses the gift of abundance to make us presumptuous, to allow us to sin more so that we may be all the more worthy of the divine wrath that will come down on our heads. "God, who now sees and recognizes the thoughts of our hearts and our scorn for this plague, closes his eyes and lets matters take their course, gives plentifully to us, blinds us, and immerses us so deeply in our sins that sin thus becomes a habit and a custom, and we no longer regard it as a sin."[17] Those who don't "mean it," whose religion is casual and sprinkled with peccadilloes and worse, are allowed by God to kill their own souls.

Here is a sermon to ponder. Luther was at pains to put God in a darkly mysterious realm beyond any human effort to prove or disprove his existence or to define his nature by external evidence—including divine intervention in the physical world. Luther's God comes to us in darkness except for the light in Christ. Attached to saint worship was a multitude of legends to feed the commonplace Catholic belief that saints worked miracles at shrines dedicated to them and did so in response to the pleading of their devotees. Augustine had taught that miracles confirmed the doctrines of the church.[18] But Augustine also said that evil men could do miracles with the aid of demons. Faith was much stronger, he said, when it did not require miracles.[19]

Luther would make more and more of this thought. By the time he wrote his treatise *On the Abrogation of the Private Mass* in 1521, Luther saw "miracles" at Catholic shrines as "works of Satan, permitted by God to tempt your faith."[20]

Luther was constructing a theology in line with his experience as well as his authority—scripture. His experience, as he interpreted it, showed God working with a certain regularity in nature. Augustine held that nature itself was a continuing miracle. The miracle that Jesus performed in turning water into wine was no greater than the yearly miracle that turned water from the clouds to wine when rain fell upon vineyards.[21] Luther was on his way to the belief, quickly assumed by mainline Protestants after him, that miracles apart from nature's persistent miracle had ceased.

Yet demons flourished in the ghoul-haunted world of the earthly life. In this sermon Luther made demons responsible for the irregular, unpredictable evils that interrupt the goodness of nature's sublime regularity. As though in an almost reflexive reaction against the notion that God may be seen in earthly abundance, he rejected the idea that a bountiful crop signifies the blessing of God—although he had sanctioned prayer for that blessing a moment earlier in the sermon. On the contrary, a bountiful crop may mean that God wants to confirm the wicked in their wickedness so that he may punish them more in his wrath.

The upshot is that God's *overt* acts in the events of life are concealed in a nimbus of mystery that no one can penetrate, that indeed makes them almost irrelevant to religious doctrines. No one can point to any specific happening and declare that in it God is showing himself, proving to us that he is sovereign over the world and active in the cosmos. (The events recorded in the Bible in which God revealed himself are, of course, exceptions.) We cannot come face to face with God in the physical world; we can meet him only in the inner response of our souls to the Word or the gospel.

Although like most others of his time Luther could ponder signs and omens, his more constant judgment is that external events can neither confirm nor destroy the testimony of the Word. Theology is therefore liberated from the skepticism or at least the detachment created by any effort to create a "natural theology," a theology that rises in tiers from inferences drawn from what we observe in nature. Here is Luther the nominalist again, refusing to see any way that reason can prove the existence of God as "creator" or "first cause" or "first mover" of the cosmos. But as his theology is liberated from the external, it is made captive to his own experience. To accept Luther's theology, one had to believe that his experience with God was normative. Otherwise, Luther thought, the devil was at work.

Satan and his minions now became more and more prominent in his sermons and his writing. Before the controversy over indulgences, he preached a series of sermons on the Ten Commandments. In his Latin notes for these sermons, presumably preached in German, he took up the damages witches could do. They could wound and blind the eyes, weaken the body, wound the legs, and cause other suffering. Witches could cast spells by using a picture or a piece of the garment of the person they wished to harm. They could cause storms, make thunder, ruin crops, kill livestock, and spoil butter, milk, and cheese. He condemned also fortune telling and consulting witches to find lost items or hidden treasures. He believed that Satan could take the shape of a woman and accept the seed of a man in the rectum and so conceive. His list ran on, yielding another insight into the popular culture of his time, in which black and white magic lay at the fingertips of common experience.[22]

This sentiment of being surrounded by dark powers was to become inseparable from his sense that he had been chosen by God for a great work. In theory Satan and his minions, including witches, had only the power that God permitted them to have. Luther called on the book of Job and its contest between God and Satan for Job's soul as proof that God used these forces for his own ends. But Luther wrote increasingly as if the world were in contention between God and Satan and the outcome for the individual soul perpetually in doubt.[23] After 1519 Satan cluttered Luther's letters and other works and smoldered in his mind.

Luther's evolution forced him to consider the sacraments. Of these the most important was the Eucharist, with its daily, invisible miracle, the transformation of the elements of bread and wine into the body and blood of Christ. Among his outpouring of publications came a sermon extending a conciliatory hand to the moderate Hussites. They demanded the cup for the laity in Holy Communion. For centuries the cup had been restricted to priests, and during communion the laity took only the body in the form of bread placed in the mouth of the communicant by the priest. The soiled hands of the laity, filthy with mundane concerns, might not touch the sacred element. Catholic liturgical theology taught that both the blood and body were present in both "kinds" or elements, the bread and the wine. But in the rite as it was practiced, the laity seemed inferior to priests. Hus objected to this segregation, and his followers continued to do so. Luther thought that a council might rule in favor of the Hussites, but in the meantime he thought it better to continue the old practice.

On January 24, 1520, a functionary in the chancery of the bishop of Meissen upriver on the Elbe from Wittenberg issued a brief note condemning Luther's *Sermon on the Sacrament of the Body of Christ*. Spalatin sent a copy to Luther, who fired off a response in German that he labored over for half a day. The official had misunderstood the sermon; Luther had not called for communion in both kinds. He had only said that the matter should be discussed.[24]

Karl von Miltitz was still blundering about, trying to solve the Luther matter. He happened to be at a supper with the bishop of Meissen when a printed copy of Luther's sharp response arrived. The bishop read all four pages of it, laughing as he went along—much to the annoyance of the functionary who had written the note Luther attacked and who happened to be present also at the table. Miltitz wrote all this to the Elector Frederick and added that he had sent Luther's little pamphlet on to Duke George of Saxony, who had read it himself and laughed out loud over most of it.[25]

The little tractate allowed Luther to exercise one of a writer's sweetest pleasures—to assault a reviewer who has not understood or even read the book. Luther was also able to protest his own orthodoxy, saying that the presence of Christ was in all the sacrament. Christ does not come in pieces, he wrote; he is completely present in each part of the sacrament. Thus Luther could accept communion in only one kind for the laity, at least until a council could make a ruling.[26] Finally, in a fierce coda, Luther took up a serious practical matter: Was he, by his answer, being "proud and arrogant" in writing against "great prelates"? Anybody could see, he said, that he had written against a shamefully wicked and envious nobody who had torn away the bishop's name and wrapped it around himself like a cloak.[27]

At the very end he made a pregnant mention of the Reuchlin affair. The authorities at Cologne, he said, had burned Reuchlin's books and supposed that would be an end to the furor Reuchlin had raised. "When a man cannot withstand the clear truth and cannot allow it, then fire is the best protection against books and death against the writer."[28] Even in this hard-hitting blast of wit and invective, he could not put out of his mind the possible consequences of his dangerous course. He was almost literally playing with fire. Given the cruelties of the day, his boldness exposed him to threats of torture that might make burning at the stake seem merciful.

Yet if the threats to Luther accomplished anything, they made him throw off restraints. Enemies swarmed on every side. Luther—encouraged by Spalatin—responded to them in ever-expanding detail, giving them even more opportunity to assault him. To a modern reader trying to be sympathetic to both sides, the most lamentable aspect of these exchanges is their stubborn unwillingness to concede anything to the opposition. Each side demonized the other. Two irreconcilable and finally undemonstrable approaches to religion went to war with each other, and the result was animosity that fueled religious wars that would burn and bloody Europe for generations after Luther died.

Luther wanted a religious communion where everyone meant it, where good works and rituals of faith came from the heart. Catholics held that although such a life might be possible for saints, the church had an obligation to ensure the providential meaning of history by a continuous, occasionally miraculous validation of itself and to provide enough hope for the masses to keep them obedient to laws that made society possible. In Catholic practice one brings such faith as one can muster to the sacraments and trusts the church's teaching as guide to the life everlasting.

Early in 1520 Luther developed his ideas in a small treatise called *Confitendi Ratio,* the "Reason for Confession." This work grew out of a brief German sketch called *A Short Instruction in How One Should Confess.* Luther had given the manuscript to Spalatin; it circulated, and an admirer begged Luther to put it in print. This he did. It appeared in Latin on March 25, 1520, and was quickly reprinted and soon translated into German.[29] Here Luther's audience is the Christian who, like himself, has been tormented by sin and seeks peace with God in confession. He is intent throughout to discard any quality about confession that makes it magic, an external rite that may force God into some sort of bargain to forgive sins. Luther rejects and mocks the fears of scrupulous priests that if they stumble over the words of the canon of the Mass, they have committed some monstrous horror. He also rejects the notion that Christians should dig deep into their hearts to dredge up every sin in detail and lay it before God, the penitential practice that had grown up in the wake of the Black Death. Such an exercise is finally impossible, he says, and futile. Nor is anything to be gained by making elaborate distinctions between mortal and venial sins. He rejects the propensity of Christians of his time to make vows to God—vows such as a promise to go on pilgrimage to the Holy Land, to Rome, or to the shrine of St. James of Compostela, or a vow to chastity taken by a young man under the age of puberty. Confession is a matter of coming to God with confidence that God will forgive those who seek forgiveness. True confession is based on the certain conviction that God is loving and merciful.

Gone from this view is the Catholic sense that the church is like Noah's Ark, including both the clean and the unclean to be separated at the day of judgment. In Catholic thought, the rituals of confession and indeed all the ceremonial observances and ritual requirements of the faith served to order moral thinking and to reinforce the foundations of society. No Catholic ever taught that the condition of the heart did not matter in the sacrament of penance; yet it was assumed that performance of the act with a desire to achieve its benefits disciplined the will and strengthened the Christian pilgrim in this world. Luther had experienced enough futility in the rote repetition of ritual pieties to believe that emphasis on the external was more menace than help.

He followed the small work on confession with a larger and more complex essay in German, *On Good Works*.[30] This was a long exposition of the meaning of the Ten Commandments. Here were both attack and defense. Catholics claimed that Luther's emphasis on justification by faith alone reduced works to unimportance. This accusation was to grow into a storm. The demand for good works was considered a civilizing impulse, necessary to check human evil, which would otherwise send society into chaos. No police authority was sufficient to control all the members of sixteenth-century society. Left to themselves without a religious motive to do good works, human beings, or a significant number of them, would indulge in secret sins—including conspiracies to topple order. More than a century before Thomas Hobbes published his *Leviathan,* educated Europeans feared the common herd that might overthrow government and return to the chaotic state of nature where war would be ceaseless "and the life of man solitary, poor, nasty, brutish, and short."

Thomas More would join a large and loud phalanx of Catholic literary warriors bent on convicting Luther of treason against organized society. The problem of how to reconcile sinful and selfish human nature with a good society had already occupied More in his fiction about the ideal commonwealth he called Utopia. He solved the problem by eliminating private life, even in a society where the social institutions were reasonable and good. In Utopia citizens watched each other all the time, and those caught having private talks about politics were put to death. The social structure was to be kept intact by relentless public scrutiny of every individual in the commonwealth.

In that climate of fear and suspicion directed toward the masses, Luther's thoughts on the Christian life had political impact. The German princes could be alarmed by any hint that a popular preacher might be tramping doggedly toward conclusions that in previous centuries had driven the poor to rebellion. To attack the pope was one thing; to undermine the delicate balance of fear and hope, reward and punishment, in traditional doctrines about good works was to raise an intolerable threat to secular authority and society.

Support by secular authority was essential if Luther and his gospel were to survive. Frederick the Wise was at risk; if he could be isolated from his princely peers and made to appear to champion a champion of chaos, Saxony might well become the object of a crusade in which the warrior caste of

Germany might enjoy historic pleasures—pillage and plunder under the glowing aegis of piety, followed by mass executions carried out with exquisite tortures. At Rome the process of excommunication rolled forward like a juggernaut, pope and curia moving with all deliberate speed to search Luther's writings for heresy and to present their case before the court of European public opinion. A high officer of the curia, Hieronymus Ghinucci, declared before the papal consistory in January 1520 that Frederick the Wise was an "enemy to the Christian religion" and was entirely responsible for the spread of the Lutheran heresy. Eck went to Rome in March to help stoke the fires. Frederick was kept informed by the curia itself of the process. Rome seemed resolved to let him know the dangers he courted by his stubborn unwillingness to surrender his professor.[31]

Driven by these circumstances, Luther set out to define the place of works in Christian life. It is a passionate treatise, a furious outburst of rage against disorders in both church and society. At the same time we see his vision of Christian passivity before the will of God—even when the will of God is delivered as the scourge of evil rulers. He dedicated the book to John, duke of electoral Saxony, younger brother of the elector, and affixed to it a prefatory letter in German—the act of an obedient subject. One by one he went through the Ten Commandments, interpreting them broadly to fit the concerns of his times. Most of his comments on secular authority, for example, came in his discussion of the duty of obedience to parents.

Throughout the work Luther made his central point that every good thing in the Christian life comes from faith. In a striking metaphor, he likened faith to health in the body. Without health, the body can do nothing. But to say that with health we *should* do nothing is nonsense. For the human being, "health must first be there to work all the works of his limbs. In the same way faith must be the master-workman and captain in all the works, or they are nothing at all." The Christian life should be one of active piety. If everyone had faith, he said, "we would need no more laws. Everyone would of himself do good works all the time, as his faith shows him."[32] But he knew that not everyone did have faith.

He classified people under four headings. First are the truly righteous, those who believe confidently in God's favor. They do what they know and what they can, and they do not require law. The second group is falsely confident and lazy; they are likely to use their freedom as an excuse to sin. These people should be guided by laws and teaching that will help them know what they should do. The third group comprises the truly wicked. They must be held in check by laws, like "wild horses and dogs," and if they will not submit, they must be killed. The fourth group includes the immature in faith. They need to be helped along by "reading, praying, fasting, singing, churches, decorations, organs, and all those things commanded and observed in monasteries and churches, until such time as they too learn to know the teachings of faith."[33]

His aim seems clear: he is not calling for revolution, for the overthrow of old rituals and ceremonies. He expresses confidence that Christians dependent on external observances can be taught and led toward a higher form of faith. In that higher faith, compulsion is not necessary. He demands obedience to temporal rulers and provides a view of the Christian life that is anything but riotous. On the contrary, the true Christian—in Luther's view—is passive, we might even say stoical in the face of oppression by the civil authority. Disobedience to parents or to civil authority, he says, "is a sin worse than murder, unchastity, theft, dishonesty, and all that goes with them." We should not only obey our parents, but we should also honor them. "Honor is higher than mere love, and includes within it a kind of fear which unites with love and has such an effect upon a man that he fears offending them more than he fears the ensuing punishment." These obligations to parents we owe also to our surrogate parents in the world, "friends, relatives, godparents, temporal lords, and spiritual fathers."[34] The Christian is not in Luther's mind an Achilles, rushing forward at the foe with drawn sword and deadly intent, thirsting for worldly honor and notoriety. The Christian is meek and lowly, ready to flee all earthly praise and fame. The response to a bad ruler is to submit to loss of life or property if necessary. Whether it does good or evil, temporal authority cannot harm the soul. Indeed, "to suffer wrong destroys no man's soul; in fact, it improves the soul."[35]

All of this portrays a Christian life that might seem to threaten no ruler on earth. But scattered through this long treatise are comments that might be taken in another spirit, that indeed would be scrutinized by literate peasants, some of whom might have read Luther's work themselves, since it was in German, or a majority who may have heard what they wanted to hear in it when its message was passed on to them by word of mouth. "The first thing to understand," said Luther, "is that no work is good except as God has commanded it, just is nothing is sin unless God has forbidden it."[36] But, he said, anyone who wants to do good works must first know what God's commands are. The first good work is to believe in Christ. In this faith must all good works begin, their goodness taken on loan from Christ. Given faith, all normal activities that sustain life are good works—including eating, drinking, and sleeping. Whoever is born of God, who believes and trusts God, cannot sin.[37]

Statements like these could sound inflammatory, for they wiped out the careful late medieval tension between presumption and despair. If we believe that we cannot sin, will we not live like the devil, presuming that God will hold nothing we do against us? Did Luther mean that every Christian was to decide for himself what was good or bad? If so, his teachings would be the worst nightmare of those who feared the anarchy supposed to smolder in the breast of the common man and woman in Christian Europe.

But again Luther was writing (as most writers do) to an imaginary audience made up of multiples of himself, to those who yearned to please God and who had discovered peace in God's assurance of love. Faith, he said, is like the relationship between a husband and wife. The size and number of works they do for each other are not the substance of the marriage; what counts is the attitude of heart that creates works great and small. Here was the essence of Luther's doctrine, that faith and the Christian life were to go forward as though the Christian belonged to the family of God through Jesus Christ. In a loving family was no compulsion; rather the family was knitted together by a spirit that made each want to please the rest. Quoting Romans 1:17 now with confidence, Luther declared that since the just shall live by faith, all righteousness resides in faith and that faith alone fulfills all God's commands and makes all its works righteous.[38]

All this was different from the ritual good works encouraged by the Roman Church as aids to the habit of piety—pilgrimages, prayers at specified times, chants, benefactions to churches. These exterior and, to Luther's mind, mechanical observances were not bad in themselves, but they were fatal to piety if they became rules. They could allow evil people to suppose themselves virtuous merely by practicing them. The true Christian could do without them; Luther counseled true Christians among his readers to be patient with those still enslaved to ceremonies and to educate them by precept and example to a freer and higher form of piety.

If I am not mistaken, Luther means by faith here that certain truths about God are taught in the Bible, in particular by Paul, and must become the premises of the Christian life. The objective reality of these premises cannot be substantiated by reason. But if we live, trusting that they are true, we discover a confirmation within ourselves that becomes sufficient to guide our lives, and we discover God responding to us in our hearts. The place to confirm these premises objectively is in the Bible; but our reading of the Bible depends on the spirit we bring to it—not what we necessarily find in the letter of the text.

In all this burns the image of Christ, dying for sinners. Before that awesome fact, we cannot claim any good works to earn merit before God. Here was the same message that Luther had preached in his early expositions on the Psalms—but now with an added emphasis on faith. If the treatise could be summarized in one imperative statement it would be "Mean it!" We must do with the spirit the praise and reverence to God that we owe him. Mere outer forms of piety will not do. In this work at least Luther was at odds with the Catholic experience that these "outer forms" of piety may cultivate a spirit in the worshiper that may be more open to the right-mindedness in the Christian life that Luther here requires. For the moment he was convinced that a resolute commitment to meaning faith, enlightened by the image of Christ in the Bible, is the essence of Christian devotion.

The tensions in this work, exploding off Luther's pen, are great. The Christian must be meek, heedless of worldly fame or praise for doing good. Yet the Christian cannot stand by while the powerful abuse the weak, and at times Luther sounds like the apocalyptic preachers of the later Middle Ages who found in the poor the true people of God, men like Jack Cade and John Ball in England who found much in the Bible to support revolt of the poor against the wealthy. "Look!" says Luther. "Lots of good works are here to be done! Most of the powerful, the rich and [their] friends commit injustice, impose force on the poor, weak, and anyone who resists. The greater they are, the worse they are, and when no one can do anything by force to help the truth, at least one can confess it and with words thereby do something, not to please the wicked or to concede their right, but to speak the truth freely."[39]

The main target in this passage is the Roman Church with its high authorities sucking away the substance of the poor. But the assaults on the powerful are sufficiently generic to embrace political leaders as well. For the moment Luther lambastes the pope and the Catholic clergy for false pieties and neglect of the spiritual health of the Christian flock. But later in the treatise he returns to the political theme. Temporal authority—the authority of governments over this world of time—is not as important as spiritual authority. Temporal authority rules only the body; the spiritual authority is supposed to nourish the soul. To suffer wrongs done by government does no harm to the soul, though it may destroy our possessions, and whatever government does, God wants it obeyed and does not want us to murmur against government in public or in private. But in almost the same breath Luther castigates evil governments for oppressing the poor and letting the rich go free, and he cannot resist admonishing rulers to do better. Governments should end gluttony and drunkenness and regulate spending on spices and fancy clothes. Governments should end the subterfuges by which Christians evaded the rules against charging interest. They should eliminate brothels.

None of this was much different from the counsel poured out on princes by earlier writers ready to give advice to the powerful. Erasmus had done something similar in his *Institution of the Christian Prince* of 1516, but Erasmus had a gentler voice. Nothing Luther said was seditious. In effect he made a distinction between speaking against the abuses of government and taking collective political or military action against those abuses. To speak against political abuses was an obligation; to rebel was among the foulest of sins. As we shall see when we discuss Luther's reaction to the Peasants' Rebellion of 1525, he seemed to limit bold speaking against the sins of governors to those whose station it was to be prophets in society—such as ministers like himself. He did not believe that every jack in the populace had the right to public criticism of the government.

He practiced what he taught about the obligations of ministers. Already litigants were appealing to him for help with the elector in cases where they felt abused, and Luther was obliging with letters to Spalatin and sometimes to the elector himself. This was to be a lifelong habit, although often his vigorous advice was ignored.[40]

It was clear by the spring of 1520 that nothing could stop the process of excommunication moving inexorably forward in Rome. Since Luther refused to submit, he had to respond in a double-barreled fashion, and this he did with huge and vituperative eloquence in German. First he assaulted the pope with a thunderous treatise, *On the Papacy in Rome against the Famous Romanist at Leipzig.* Then, almost immediately, he produced one of the greatest tracts of the Reformation, the *Address to the Christian Nobility of the German Nation Concerning the Reform of the Christian Estate.* Both attacks were aimed at convincing the German princes that self-interest should provoke them to resist the pope.

The blast against the pope came in response to a work by a monk in Leipzig, Augustine Altveld, arguing that absolute papal sovereignty over the church could be proved by scripture. Not for Altveld was the common conciliar notion that the papacy had been established as a convenient and constitutional office to be overseen by a council. Altveld's claims were extreme. No government, Altveld said, could be well run apart from submission to the pope, the sole vicar of Christ. Without such submission, riot, thievery, and other crimes would soon bring any government to an end.[41] He made the familiar argument that Christ had conferred the power of the keys on the apostle Peter and Peter's successors and that the popes held their power by divine law and that anyone who denied this fact was guilty of blasphemy. Luther's response was finished by May 5 and printed soon after in Wittenberg, then picked up by other printers in the German lands, who knew they could turn a profit by publishing anything Luther wrote. It is written in German so that even a prince could read it, and it is filled with biting sarcasm and bitter irony calculated to evoke laughter.[42]

This public attack on the papacy was in part an effort to put Luther in the tradition of the *gravamina* of the German Reichstag, the articles of formal complaint presented by the Diet for redress of grievances inflicted on Germany by the papacy. As we have seen, previous popes had routinely rejected them, usually spicing rejection with scorn and arrogance. By tying into this tradition, Luther could expect at least an informal hearing for his views in this, the first year of the imperial reign of the young and as yet untested and unknown Charles V.[43]

Luther set the problem quickly. Was the papacy ordained by God or by men? Was it heresy to refuse allegiance to the pope, even if in all other respects—sacraments, gospel, and all articles of faith—Christians were agreed? What did one do then with the Christians of Moscow, the White Russians, the Greeks, and the people of Bohemia, all of whom denied the papal primacy? Clearly, he thought, history had vindicated a genuine Christian faith existing apart from papal rule. He accused the papacy of selling ecclesiastical offices. An archbishop's or bishop's pallium (a cape with the insignia of office embroidered upon it) cost 30,000 gulden. It was said that the Antichrist would plunder the treasury of the world, he wrote; the Romanists had reduced Germany to misery, and if the princes did not do something about it quickly, Germany would become a desert.

He denied the contention that every human society should have one leader at the top. His main point was that the true church was not an institution, but a communion embracing all who confessed Christ; it was not centered in Rome but rather was present wherever faith lives in the human heart. Luther's consistent theme was that the church was a hidden communion, and one by one he attacked other definitions that emphasize institutional visibility. The church could have no earthly head, neither bishop nor pope; over the church ruled Christ alone. The only visible signs of the church were baptism, the Eucharist, and the preaching of the gospel.

Once more Luther took up the declaration of Christ to Peter in Matthew 16, "Thou art Peter, and upon this rock I shall build my church, and the gates of hell shall not prevail against it." The text could not apply to the papacy, said Luther, for history proved that the gates of hell had prevailed against the popes many times. Most who held to the authority of the pope were "possessed by all the power of hell, filled with sin and wickedness, and some popes have themselves been heretics and have issued heretical laws, and yet remained in authority."[44] The papacy had been subject not only to the devil but also to bishops and to the worldly power of the German emperor. Here Luther reached back to the early church history before the investiture controversy of the eleventh century, when German emperors routinely made and unmade popes. It was a use of the sense of history that humanism brought to the Renaissance, a historical awareness that granted depth perception just as the discovery of perspective made Renaissance painting a window through which the observer looked onto lines converging in a distance.

Luther's conclusion after this tirade may seem surprising, but it fitted his emerging conceptions of the power of God over human events, including history. The papal power was a fact, he said; it had come through the providence of God, but the papacy was a product of God's angry providence, that will on the part of God to punish the world. To live under the pope was like living under the Turk, a condition ordained by God and one we should not resist. Although Luther did not say it, this opinion mirrored the history of biblical Israel in captivity, when secular obedience to Babylonians, Persians, Greeks, or Romans was acceptable only to the point that no specific divine law should be broken. Daniel accepted the lions' den under Nebuchadnezzar rather than submit to a Babylonian law that contradicted his faith.

Even obedience to the Turk extended only to earthly matters; when the Turk or any other scourge of God required Christians to forsake their own faith, Christians were obliged to refuse, even unto death. Having said that Christians should not resist the pope, Luther immediately declared that the papacy had no right to call Christians heretics who did not accept papal authority and that everything the pope decreed should be judged by scripture.

Then he returned to his growing conviction that the pope might be the Antichrist. Roman rascals were trying to set the pope over Christ and scripture by saying he could not err, and in addition violating Paul's definition of faith in the book of Hebrews that it was something not seen. The pope and his minions, so Luther thought, sought to replace this invisible faith with their decrees and their physical community. But if the pope permitted such behavior he might be, "God forbid," the Antichrist.[45]

In what seems almost an aside toward the end of this treatise, Luther wrote that he would be content to see kings, princes, and nobles sweep the streets clean of the papal rabble and regain control of the bishoprics now under papal authority. Secular rulers could resist the pope in a way forbidden to private men. This idea he was to develop extensively in his *Address to the Christian Nobility of the German Nation Concerning the Reform of the Christian Estate.*

Several events converged to inspire Luther to write it. One was a pedantic and altogether uncompromising assertion of papal infallibility and sovereignty over the church published by a plodding Roman theologian named Sylvester Prierias. When it arrived in Wittenberg, Luther promptly had it published with a brief introduction of his own, a bold stroke that—as he intended—showed how exalted papal claims were. Luther commented on these claims in mocking notes, and gave up all pretense of hesitation in naming the pope the Antichrist.[46] Prierias held that among men, only the pope held his authority directly from God—a return to the position of Pope Gregory VII in his conflict with the Emperor Henry IV. Prierias also dismissed the decrees of Constance as unbinding on later popes. Luther had already decided that a general council offered the only hope of curbing or eliminating papal authority over the church, and the forthright denunciation of conciliarism by Prierias called for a response.

Another influence was the offer of help from Ulrich von Hutten. Hutten was one of many Germans who heard in Luther's strong voice a trumpet blast calling on Germany to awaken. He was not theologically sophisticated, and he was to die young, infected by syphilis. But for the moment he sent word to Luther that Franz von Sickingen stood ready to defend him, and Luther seemed ready to accept Sickingen's military aid against the authority of emperor and princes. Later he would vehemently oppose rebellion, but he would always give princes the right to protect their people from the pope. Perhaps he saw Sickingen as such a prince.

The book went to the printer on June 13; on August 18 some 4,000 copies were on sale. That press run was quickly exhausted, and Luther enlarged the book for another printing.[47] Presses in Leipzig, Strasbourg, and Basel, among others, quickly pirated the work and issued their own editions.[48] The book was hopefully dedicated to the young emperor. In it Luther called upon the German nobility—from small-time knights to mighty princes and Charles V himself—to do their Christian duty and defend the church against the pope and see to it that a general council was summoned to reform the church and the Christian estate. In doing so he essentially sought to roll back the consequences of Pope Gregory VII's reforms of the eleventh century that had asserted the superiority of the papacy over secular rulers and that had done so much damage to Germany. The effect of the Gregorian reforms was to exalt priests as a special class within society. It was just this exaltation of priesthood that Luther assaulted in his blistering treatise.

Luther claimed that no Christian priesthood can be found in the New Testament. His idea is historically plausible. Catholic legends of the Middle Ages made almost every Christian male mentioned in the New Testament a priest, and artists and writers read back into history vows of celibacy and sacraments and even the dress of medieval priesthood. From our vantage point, the early disciples of Jesus seem to have constituted a movement rather than an institution, with leaders arising spontaneously, assuming such offices as overseer, elder, presbyter, deacon, and shepherd in the disorganized way any movement is likely to cast up leaders in turbulent times.

Luther went back to the New Testament, where Jesus seemed to have gone out of his way to certify the validity of marriage and uttered no word against the institution in any canonical gospel. He is said to have had brothers, although the church ruled with tenuous philological authority that they were cousins—indicating that the Virgin Mary, even in the two gospels where her virginity is mentioned, was a virgin only until after Jesus was born. He healed Peter's mother-in-law of disease without then warning his disciples not to have mothers-in-law in the future if they intended to be priests. Paul the Apostle held that it was better to remain unmarried because the world was a troublesome place and wives only added to the troubles. Soon the church under the influence of a current of dualism running through the ancient world had converted Paul's advice into a universal law for the clergy. The body and passion were bad; spirit and dispassion were good, and by the end of the second century celibacy began to be imposed on Christian priests.

Clergy obligated themselves by vows of poverty, chastity, and obedience. In Christianity the vow-breaker was subject to the awful penalty of being considered unfit for the human community. In the Middle Ages, the terror of his vow probably lay on the average priest with more compelling weight than the burdens of chastity itself. To turn from priesthood once it had been assumed was to turn away from God and man, to be an exile in the midst of the earth. Among the fathers of the church in the first six centuries of Christianity, vow-breakers were considered to be committing adultery against God. Such was the rule of the canon law, and vow-breakers were consigned to hell by the church. The mentality lingered, so that pious Catholics were horrified later when Luther told clergymen that they could marry and set an example by marrying a nun. Luther came to consider religious vows as attempts to earn salvation, and considered them not binding. His foes took him to mean that promises made to God could be disdained. Thus he was seen as a blasphemer. This evolution would come later.

In Luther's view at this stage in his life, all Christians belonged to the same spiritual estate; that is, all Christians were priests. They differed only in the offices they performed for the benefit of one another. He supposed that human beings required organizations with leaders, but in religious affairs they were capable of arranging that organization themselves without depending on the pope. Suppose, he said, that a group of devout Christian laymen was set down on a desert island without a priest. They could, he thought, elect one of their number to administer the sacraments and preach the gospel, and he would be as much a priest as if he had been consecrated by a bishop. In effect Luther was saying that abilities differed; the congregation could discern who could be a good pastor, and Christians could therefore choose spiritual leaders without supposing that their choice imposed some indelible character of superior priestly status that could never be taken away. When a pastor proved unworthy of his trust, he could be deposed, and nothing of his spiritual dignity remained.

In the *Address* Luther used his doctrine of the priesthood of all believers to persuade the German princes to take the lead in reforming the church, arguing that the lay status of princes did not make them inferior to priests. Indeed, by proving that a special priestly status conferred by the institutional hierarchy was a deceit, Luther wanted to show the princes that they exercised a legitimate, divinely ordained power against the pope and his clerical subordinates, including bishops, who did not constitute a superior, spiritual estate. Princes possessed the same gifts as all Christians, for all Christians were priests, equal before God. The authority of princes came from God, who had ordained government. It was the Christian duty of every man to use his office in the service of God, and what better service could a prince do than to lead in the reform of the church? "Therefore," wrote Luther, "the secular Christian authority should use its office free, without restriction and without considering whether it hits pope, bishop, or priest. Whoever is guilty should suffer."[50]

Luther was far from asserting any special theological authority for princes. He had no Eastern coloration to his thought of the sort that had made at least one council in Byzantium declare that the emperor at Constantinople was inspired in theological matters with the same spirit that had moved the apostles to write scripture. In good Western fashion Luther always made a distinction between the man and the job, holding that a bad man could occupy a good office. In the *Address* he held only that the world runs by various orders, all necessary, all good as the various parts of the body were all good. Princes with legitimate secular authority should use it to do good in the church. Luther assumed that, in reforming the church, princes and all other Christians would be guided by the Word of God, understood by them as he saw it and agreed upon by all true Christians.

Here was the rub. Luther had no direct experience with princes. As far as I can tell, he had seen only two German princes by the time he wrote his *Address*. He had seen Duke George at Leipzig, and Duke George was to become his bitter enemy. But although Duke George was a curmudgeon, he was a religious curmudgeon, needing perhaps only proper guidance and the proper spirit, and in 1520 Luther still had hopes for him. The other prince Luther had seen was Prince William of Anhalt, whom he had observed in his student days—the prince begging his bread like a pauper in the streets, emaciated and in rags, having renounced all earthly goods to seek salvation. This noble young man, stooped, starved, and probably unbalanced by the terror of death, was hardly typical of his class.

Dwelling within the walls of the Augustinian cloister and sealed off from the rest of the world by the high and sturdy walls of Wittenberg, Luther seems to have imagined an audience of ideal princes waiting for his liberating words to free them to support reform. He lost this illusion soon enough; yet the hope deserves attention, for it provides a sign of Luther's optimism in this exuberant year. At the fiery apogee of his revolution, the horizons of the possible stretched away to a sunny distance.

It was a propitious time. In 1520 the German princes were not yet acquainted with their new emperor. He had not visited the German lands, and he did not speak German. They were wary of him—and largely uninterested in fine points of theology. It was Luther's great good luck to work within the jurisdiction of one of the few German princes with a streak of genuine piety and, it seems, of some theological sophistication. The secular princes—as well as the German cities—felt abused by the papacy, and they had economic reasons to resent the papal monarchy with its base in distant Italy among Italians, whom Germans envied and despised. It seemed to Luther that the princes had every reason to stand with him against the pope.

By now Luther saw satanic influence everywhere. The pope represented chaos in what Luther saw as the persistent papal conspiracy to subvert government and institute a papal tyranny in its place. The pope insisted on the right to make kings and emperors and, in essence, to depose them by excommunication. It was not really as simple as papal theory claimed that it was, and in Luther's time, politically minded popes seldom used the weapon of excommunication against monarchs. The weapon, used frequently in the Middle Ages, had lost its edge, and William Tyndale would remark later on that the Venetians had been excommunicated again and again but had discovered that they shat as well as they ever did. But simple people trembled before a solemn and official condemnation to hell, and princes feared excommunication because it could threaten their rule. In Luther's mind, therefore, the papacy represented demonic confusion in the secular realm.

He lived at a time when people looked to authority to settle great issues. He might be expected to see the authority of princes as surrogate on earth for the authority of God. For both prince and deity, the emblem of rule was order. He saw the German princes as natural agents of reform in a struggle to determine the fate of Christianity. Christian princes should, he thought, use their authority to restore order in the church. The first step was to call a council of the church. Luther envisaged a mass movement of Christians inspired by ripping apart what he called the "second wall" that the papacy had erected around itself.[50] This wall was the claim that only popes had the right to make final judgments about how scripture was to be interpreted.

We have noted that Sylvester Prierias, author of one of the first attacks on Luther, rested his case on papal infallibility. If Luther opposed the pope in the matter of indulgences, Prierias wrote, he was a heretic, for it was heresy to say that a pope could err in matters of doctrine. Such extreme claims, not shared by many Catholics (including Thomas More), played into Luther's hands. In the *Address* he wrote a sizzling attack on papal extravagance and papal wickedness and set over against such decadence his imagined masses of true Christians who read and understood the Bible and who were ready for reform. The princes were in the best position to lead these good Christians, and the first step should be a council.

It may seem strange that Luther could speak so positively about councils after he had rejected their binding authority in the debate at Leipzig. But at Leipzig Luther had condemned Constance for sending John Hus to the stake. He condemned most of all the notion that only the pope could call a council, that a council was valid only because the pope said it was, and that a council could deliberate only with the pope as the presiding officer. Such councils, including Fourth Lateran in 1215, Luther found to be contrary to the Word of God. But for years he retained the conviction that a council based on scripture and attended by honest and learned Christians under the protection of godly princes would assert the truth of Christian doctrine. He thought that some councils had done just that. He prized the Council of

Nicaea, which in 325 had proclaimed God the Father and Christ the Son to be of one substance and co-eternal—a council called by the Emperor Constantine, not by the pope. To Luther, Nicaea had defended the old faith, clearly set down in scripture, against the "novelty" of those who held that Christ was somehow less than God. Since the Christian prince could have no more competence in reading the Bible than could any other honest and studious Christian, the council would not be a meeting like the German Diet. The council would be called by the princes and defended by them, but its deliberations would be carried out among equals, led by the Word of God. The decision of the council would vindicate the true faith—Luther's faith. It would possess authority in Christendom by the eminence of its doctors and by its affirmation of the Word of God.

Most of the *Address* was given over to attacks on the immorality of the popes and the cardinals. He dwelled especially on the limitless thirst of the papal court for German money obtained by the papacy by various taxes on church lands in the Holy Roman Empire. Here was another astute effort to meld his cause with the *gravamina*. It was common practice for the pope to appoint Italians to German benefices so that these Italian clerics might reap the income without ever setting foot in Germany itself. Popes appointed cardinals, often to several German bishoprics at once, and collected from these new appointees lucrative fees.[51] Luther attacked these practices and the custom of annates itself.

Throughout the little book, Luther portrayed the "German nation," that is the virtuous German people, as abused and long-suffering and called on them to take their religious destiny into their own wise and virtuous hands. He exposed bureaucratic chicanery that allowed the papacy to fill its coffers with German money even while popes violated both the letter and the spirit of their own canon law. Rome itself he depicted as a sink of iniquity where every kind of foulness gathered. Rome could not bear a council, Luther wrote, because it would then be clear to all that Rome could not be more wicked if the Antichrist himself ruled there.

In the earlier part of his little book, Luther never quite called the pope the Antichrist, though he came close to doing so again and again. Toward the last he seemed to lose all restraint in the torrent of his own words. Here he denounced the papal legates who travelled in Germany and for fees dissolved contracts—including, presumably, the marriage contract. This paying of hard cash to be released from righteous obligation so infuriated Luther that he burst out, "If no other wicked treachery proved that the pope was the Antichrist, this piece would be enough. Listen to this, Pope, not the all holiest but the all most sinful, let God right now destroy thy seat and sink it into the abyss of hell!"[52]

Surprisingly enough, in the balance of this work, he did not demand the abolition of the papacy. The religious affairs of the ideal church that seems to emerge from this hot little tractate would be in the custody of the bishops within each nation. The pope would remain as a sort of presiding bishop but without sovereignty. The secular authority would protect the national bishops in their conscientious performance of their duties, and popes would be relieved of all coercive authority, including secular rule over the papal territories in Italy, where the pope acted as sovereign prince.

Neither did Luther demand the abolition of monasticism. He did call for the unification of the various monastic orders. He also wanted to end the unsupervised wandering of the friars, the begging orders—of whom the Franciscans and the Dominicans were chief—and whose emotional sermons and easy virtue had long made them an object of scorn. He wished these wandering orders could be suppressed altogether, but failing that drastic a step, he thought they should be banned from preaching and made to live under supervision in regular monasteries. Acknowledging that many priests lived with illegal wives and children, he wrote that they should be allowed to marry. Masses for the dead, all festivals except Sundays, indulgences, pilgrimages, and the shrines of saints should be eliminated.

Toward the end Luther called for the reformation of the universities and denounced "the blind pagan master" Aristotle and Aristotelian influence in higher learning within the church.[53] Aristotle's *Physics, Metaphysics, On the Soul,* and both *Ethics* should be dropped from the curriculum, for Aristotle taught nothing true about either the natural world or the world of the spirit. In a paradoxical way Luther called Aristotle's book *On the Soul* his best. But he expressed horror that Aristotle taught that the soul dies with the body—although, he said, many had tried with empty words to save Aristotle's reputation on this difficult score. Scripture tells us all we need to know, he wrote; and yet we have allowed this "dead pagan" to overwhelm the holy books.[54]

The rest of the book issues a miscellaneous call for reforms in university, church, and the world—abolition of canon law, reform of German laws, more attention to the Bible and less to theologians—and a final plea to use the empire God has given to the Germans for the good of all humankind and not to waste its substance in conspicuous consumption of exotic spices, gluttony, drunkenness, and elaborate and expensive dress. The urban brothels, tolerated nearly everywhere in Europe (many of them serving as bathhouses), also came under his condemnation. These matters of reform, he concluded, were things within the scope of secular government once it had been freed from papal tyranny.

Did Luther expect these sweeping reforms to be carried out? As any writer knows, writing can become a domain of infinite possibility where the writer not merely describes or explains but creates the world he addresses. In writing the *Address* and the other reforming treatises he produced in 1520, Luther was possessed by, even intoxicated with, his truth. Shaped by the pumping jet of his words, a new creation came shining out of the tohubohu of the corrupt previous centuries, and he was in his own view God's instrument.

Yet at the end of this extended and furious little book, he seems to have pulled up before the chasm of doubt that would separate his proposals from being put into practice. "I know full well that I have sung high and advanced many things that will be seen as impossible and that I have attacked many things too sharply. But what should I otherwise do!"[55] It was a cry from the heart. He was God's prophet, and the obligation of the prophet was to speak truth. Those hearing the prophet and heeding not would be judged; the prophet would be judged for doing what God commands. At the close of his denunciations of the papacy within the book and calling for the pope to give up the papacy, he said with a thump of satisfaction, "With this I am excused!"[56] He had done what he was supposed to do: he had announced the truth. The carrying out of the truth was for others, especially the nobility, to do.

Yet it is hard not to see in this fluent and powerful stream of language both optimism and hope that truth would be irresistible. In this and in the next work we shall examine, the *Babylonian Captivity,* Luther looks like a man who has seen into the glowing fire of truth and believes that others will spontaneously see its brightness once he has directed their eyes to it. If he had been terrified of death, the terror was now set aside in the heat of battle, and the Luther of 1520 looks like a revolutionary to whom the gates of the city are open and the people within ready to overthrow the tyrants and admit the liberator of their souls.

14

THE BREAKING POINT

A T THE end of his *Address to the Christian Nobility,* Luther promised more fireworks. He had in mind his *De Captivitate Babylonica Ecclesiae,* or *Babylonian Captivity of the Church,* with its subtitle *Praeludium Martini Lutheri.* The Latin word *praeludium* described the ceremonious maneuvering—that might include trumpet blasts—at the beginning of a battle. It indicates that Luther understood that this work represented an explicit declaration of war on the papal church, carrying far beyond his previous pronouncements.

The "Babylonian Captivity" in the title alluded to the exile imposed on the Jews by King Nebuchadnezzar after he took Jerusalem in 587 B.C.E. and carried the population of Judaea off to Mesopotamia. The pope and his hierarchy were seen as enemies of God who had carried the people of God— that is, the church—off into pagan Babylon. The term had also been used to describe the removal of the papacy to Avignon after Pope Boniface VIII died in 1305—an exile from Rome that led to the Great Schism in 1378. The title was therefore loaded with antipapal significance, heightened by apocalyptic overtones from the title's allusion to the book of Revelation, where, on the triumph of the Lamb, an angel cries with a great voice (18:2–8):

Babylon the great is fallen, is fallen, and is become the habitation of devils, and the hold of every foul spirit, and a cause of every unclean and hateful bird. For all nations have drunk of the wine of the wrath of her fornication, and the kings of the earth have committed fornication with her, and the merchants of the earth are waxed rich through the abundance of her delicacies. And I heard another voice from heaven saying, Come out of her, my people, that ye be not partakers of her sins and that ye receive not of her plagues. For her sins have reached unto heaven, and God hath remembered her iniquities . . . Therefore shall her plagues come in one day, death, and mourning and famine: and she shall be utterly burned with fire: for strong is the Lord God who judgeth her.

Luther wrote knowing that the papal bull threatening excommunication was soon to be issued against him in Rome. Eck was there, fulminating and maneuvering. On June 15, 1520, the bull appeared in its official form from the papal chancery, its grandiloquent prose supplied, so it is said, principally by Eck himself. Three official copies of the bull were made, impressively inscribed on parchment with the papal seal, or "bull," attached at the bottom. One of these was sent directly to Duke George of Saxony. Karl von Miltitz was to take only a certified copy to Frederick the Wise.[1] Pope Leo X received the first draft of the document while he was at his hunting lodge not far from Rome, pursuing one of his favorite hobbies—hunting wild boars.[2] The final draft showed the pope's preoccupation: "Arise, O Lord . . . A bellowing boar from the forest is trying to demolish thy vineyard . . . Arise, O Peter . . . Arise O Paul . . . Arise all saints . . ."[3] Forty-one articles of Luther's beliefs were condemned as heretical. The pope did not argue the points; he merely stated them. Among the articles condemned as heresy was Luther's belief that to burn heretics was against the will of the Holy Spirit. Luther was commanded to remain silent. His books were to be burned, and no Catholic was to read them, on pain of excommunication. No one was allowed to praise anything Luther had written. Luther was ordered to recant within sixty days or be excommunicated from the church. Anyone who helped him was also to be excommunicated.

In Wittenberg the bull was expected through the summer, although its precise contents were not known. Tensions were high. On July 13 students at the university got into a brawl with apprentices attached to the painter Lucas Cranach. Swords were drawn, the city authorities moved in, and order was quickly restored. Luther preached against disorder and wrote to Spalatin that Satan was behind the whole business; having failed to quench the revived word of God, the devil now turned to other means to spread reproach on it.[4]

Luther went on writing furiously, knowing he was surrounded by enemies thirsting for his death. On August 3 he wrote to his fellow Augustinian monk John Boigt in Magdeburg, "An ass in Leipzig is writing many books against me, and in Cremona in Italy an anonymous ignoramus whom I believe to be a member of the Preaching Friars does the same."[5] But, he said, Franz von

Sickingen, Ulrich von Hutten, and a German noble named Sylvester von Schaumberg had promised to aid him against all foes. Promises of help poured in from other quarters as well. He wrote that he was composing the *Address,* and again he declared that he thought the pope was acting like the Antichrist. Clearly he was in a mood to accept the support of those who would resist by armed force the pope and his minions.

Opposition to Luther was no longer limited to the perfervid papalists who wanted to hurry him to the rack and the fire. Erasmus was also getting worried. Luther tried to draw Erasmus onto his side. Even the Elector Frederick wrote Erasmus praising Luther. Erasmus resisted, and in May 1519 wrote to Luther advising restraint and announcing his own neutrality in the developing brawl.[6] As Luther became more radical, angry Catholics attacked Erasmus as the instigator of the whole business. Someone coined a famous proverbial sentence: Erasmus laid the egg that Luther hatched. Erasmus defended himself by saying he had read none of Luther's works.

From Louvain on July 6, 1520, Erasmus wrote to Spalatin, praising the elector and expressing gratitude for the gift of a gold and a silver medal with Frederick's image stamped thereon. He prayed to the all-powerful Christ, Erasmus said, that Luther's style and spirit might be softened so that he might render more service to evangelical piety. He sensed in those who attacked Luther, he said, more the spirit of this world than the spirit of Christ; and yet sins lay on both sides. He wished Luther could remain at the periphery of these broils and follow the pure gospel. But now, said Erasmus, Luther weighed down the cause of good letters with "a hostility fatal for us and sterile for himself."[7]

On August 1, 1520, Erasmus wrote Luther a long letter constructed with diplomatic care and a desire to throw water on the fires now blazing up around Luther's name.[8] He began with a little gossip as though in light-hearted banter among friends. He spoke of his troubles with young Edward Lee, an Englishman campaigning to condemn Erasmus's Greek New Testament, which by 1520 had gone through two large editions. Lee sniffed heresy in Erasmus's work, and Erasmus in turn found envious ambition and malicious mischief in Lee. The literary battle did little good to the reputation of either.

Erasmus relayed a chatty anecdote of how Thomas More had defended him before Henry VIII and Queen Catherine against Lee's attacks and the more absurd blasts of a Franciscan friar named Henry Standish. Standish claimed that Jerome had translated the Gospel of John from the original Hebrew! Erasmus skimmed over other quarrelsome people who had attacked him, and in so doing established that he and Luther were comrades in a common cause. That done, he could get down to business and give Luther some advice. His counsel reveals as well as anything Erasmus wrote the chasm between the two men.

Luther should not, wrote Erasmus, condemn all philosophy, for then he would have not only the universities against him but also the ancients. Even if one conceded that all philosophy was to be rejected, it was not wise to say so because that was to take on too many foes at once. Everywhere the "new teaching" had enemies. These enemies had infested all the royal courts. The king of England had asked Erasmus about Luther. Erasmus had answered, he said, that he lacked the skill to have an opinion, and the king had said that he wished Luther would write with more prudence and moderation.

That was good advice, Erasmus thought, and many who wished Luther well agreed with it. It was not good to provoke men who could not be made to submit without upheaval and conflict. Once conflict began, it could not be controlled, and it could spread far beyond its original causes for dispute. "Even so, I do not oppose your opinions," Erasmus wrote. "I fear, if they are inspired by Christ, to oppose Him." Luther had mentioned Erasmus as comrade in a fierce attack on the universities of Louvain and Cologne for condemning his own views. Erasmus begged him not to mix his name in such quarrels. "Otherwise you will make suspect those who might serve you better if they were not compromised."

Erasmus closed with the wish that Luther write about a part of the scriptures without passion—something devotional rather than polemic. Let things calm down, and disorder might dissolve. The undogmatic Erasmus believed in reform by education and a quiet piety. He felt none of the yearning for forgiveness that Luther felt, and by this time in his life he seems not to have seen death as a horror. He feared the masses. Throughout his life he believed that the educated should band together to advance "good letters" and to set a good example to the ignorant. The right sort of learning, joining the best of classical literature and the best of Christian theology, could gradually purify the church and reform society.

It was not a message to touch Luther. He was in a fighting mood. By August it was known in Wittenberg that the bull threatening excommunication was on the way. All ambiguity about the Antichrist evaporated from his mind; to him the pope was the Beast, the man of evil foretold by cloudy prophecies in the New Testament, and no compromise was possible. Popular support for Luther was strong. By September Eck moved into Germany, carefully avoiding electoral Saxony, scattering printed copies of the bull in every city and dispatching a copy to Wittenberg by a carrier from Leipzig on

October 3. Following a secret commission from the papacy, he added names now and then to those threatened with excommunication by the papal bull.

His task was not easy. When he arrived in Leipzig, he was greeted warmly enough, but Duke George's university refused to support official proclamation of the bull. Eck received so many threats that he had to take refuge in the Dominican cloister.[9] The papal nuncio Girolamo Aleandro, carrying the bull through the Rhineland and the Netherlands, had an easier time of it, but it seemed clear that the German people were unwilling to take the pope's word at face value. Translations of the bull into German appeared in city after city. The Elector Frederick the Wise had one done by Spalatin published in Wittenberg itself.[10] The elector probably supposed the bull would help rally support to his professor. So it did.

Along the way, in Leipzig, Eck published a defense of the Council of Constance and its delivery of John Hus to the flames. Eck's intent was to show that Hus had had a fair trial and had been fairly burned. It was not an example to be lost on Luther and his partisans. Luther responded with a savage little tract against Eck, the title implying that the bull was another of Eck's lies and not from the pope at all.[11] Luther's blast is filled with biting irony and insult against both Eck and the papacy. "You know, my dear Romanist, that you understand the Holy Scripture as much as an ass knows how to play the lyre."[12] Luther repeated his call to have his case decided by a general council dedicated to understanding scripture and including wise laymen as well as impartial clergy. His fiction that the bull was the product of Eck and the papal court was a strange fantasy. Luther kept expressing his confidence in the innocence of Pope Leo X as though he hoped that Leo might come to his senses and see how wicked the papal office was. Luther may also have been trying to buy time.

He was not about to back down. On October 6, his *Babylonian Captivity* emerged from the press of Melchior Lotther in Wittenberg—a forty-four page Latin bomb planted in the midst of the delicate machinery of the Catholic sacramental system.[13] The publication of the *Babylonica*, as it came to be known in English, shattered any lingering illusions that Luther was a reformer cast in the mold of Erasmus—although oddly enough Luther could write to Lazarus Spengler on November 17 a conciliatory letter saying, "Erasmus and I, if God wills, will certainly remain united."[14]

Luther said there was nothing new in the *Babylonica*. He was right. Everything here he had already either written explicitly or implied. Still, his tone and his radicalism jarred educated Europe. The pope was now unmistakably the Antichrist, the ruler of "Babylon."[15] The priest confessor of young

Charles V, John Glapion, told Gregor Brück, chancellor to Frederick the Wise, that he had first read Luther in hopes that some good might come out of all this for the church. But when he read the *Babylonian Captivity*, he could not have been more shocked and horrified if someone had taken a whip and split him from head to foot.[16]

The *Babylonica* redefines the sacramental system of the church. Luther makes three major points about sacraments: all sacraments should originate with a command of Christ in the New Testament for reasons unique to the Christian faith; they should be an aid and sign of the direct communion between the Christian and God; and they should be freed from all those ties that enslave the Christian to the corrupt tyranny of the Pope at Rome.

Luther had studied the Greek New Testament of Erasmus. He knew that the Latin word *sacramentum* translated the Greek word that we usually trans-literate as "mystery," and that it did not denote a "sign" of some secret and sacred act of God but that a "mystery" was the act itself.[17] He found only three sacraments in the New Testament that fitted his first rubric: baptism, the Eucharist, and penance.[18] He rejected four sacraments practiced for many centuries: confirmation, ordination, marriage, and extreme unction. He argued that the sacraments he dismissed possessed neither scriptural authority nor great antiquity. By this rejection he attacked the heart of the Catholic tradition, the faith that God would not let all his church err about something so essential to salvation. (In fact through the centuries the number of sacraments had varied. Only in the twelfth century did Peter the Lombard's great *Four Books of the Sentences* finally certify the dogma of seven sacraments.[19]) To Luther, scripture prevailed over any tradition, no matter how sacrosanct, and because he found only three sacraments in scripture, he was willing to reject the pious practices of four centuries. Here again Luther was the beneficiary of the historical criticism of the Renaissance, the sense of perspective and anachronism that made scholars aware of the differences between centuries and of the accumulation of new practices in both church and society. Luther's critique of the sacraments owed something to the notes Erasmus appended to his Greek New Testament of 1516, corrected and issued again in 1519.

Much of his attack was directed against priestcraft, the ancient notion that a sacred class of human beings stood between the laity and God. Like Hus before him, he thought the laity should have both the cup and the host in the Eucharist. His tone was insulting and fierce—as was the tone of every Catholic foe contesting with him. He recognized the nature of the battle and made a halfhearted effort to lift himself above virulence. "This I know for certain," he said, quoting proverbial wisdom, "if I fight with shit, conqueror or conquered, I am still stained."[20] It was too much to ask a man of Luther's temperament to restrain himself when he found so much excrement to fling at his foes.

To his opponents, Luther's most outrageous comments in the *Babylonica* involved the Mass, which had always been "the supreme sacrament."[21] He raged at the church's use of Aristotle to define the doctrine of transubstantiation. Aristotle had divided all things into "essence" or "substance" on the one hand and "accidents" on the other. The accidents were those sensual qualities available to human perception. Modern scientific thinking has junked "essence" and "accidents" as terms worthless to physics, chemistry, and any other experimental science. But for Aristotle the essence of bread was the quality that makes bread what it is and not merely flour and water or whatever. The accidents of bread are those several qualities we can perceive by our senses—its taste, its appearance, its texture, its smell, and the sound it would make if we dropped it on the floor. The doctrine of transubstantiation held that in the Eucharist, the essence of the bread and the wine are miraculously changed into the body and blood of Christ, while the accidents remain those of bread and wine.

Luther saw these philosophical terms as a conspiracy by the popes to enslave Christians to idolatry—the worship of bread and wine instead of God and a dependence upon a priesthood under the tyranny of the bishop of Rome. Here he used Occam's razor—without mentioning Occam. The words of Christ in the Gospels were simple. Jesus said, "This is my body . . . This is my blood." Explanations of texts should be only as complicated as the text required; elaborate and unnecessary explanations should be cut away. The text indicated a real presence of Christ in the elements. This joining, he said, was like the joining of heat to iron, an unseen but felt quality added to what was there already, not the replacement of one thing by another. Thus one adored not the bread and the wine but the body and the blood of Christ in the bread and the wine.

This doctrine of the Eucharist has been accurately enough labeled "consubstantiation," although Luther did not use that term. In the Eucharist, thought he, God was physically present, and in the liturgy of the Mass the believer could share an encounter with Christ, present in the same bodily world in which the Christian must live, and foretelling the resurrection of the body that would come at God's pleasure. In Luther's view, the Christian was not required to rationalize the process by an elaborate and unscriptural theory based on Aristotle. Here was more than a desire to simplify. Luther was extending the boundary between reason and faith, unwilling to send Christianity into an arena in a fight it could not win. Faith included propositions to be believed so that the Christian had to react to them in a profoundly existential way, just as one must breathe to live. To introduce philosophical reasoning into the process was to introduce a poison that suffocated the soul.

Moreover, Luther rejected the notion of the Eucharist as sacrifice and a good work. Here was a knot tied with barbed wire. Old Testament priests offered sacrifices on the altars of God. It seemed natural to many in the Catholic Church to say that priests of the New Covenant, that is, Christian priests, should also offer a sacrifice when they performed the sacrament of the Eucharist. By Luther's time, received dogma held that the Eucharist was a sacrifice of the body and blood of Christ and that it was also a good work in that masses offered for the living and the dead were assumed to aid the progress of the Christian pilgrim from earth through purgatory and on to paradise. To become a spectator to the sacrifice constituted a good work, even if one did not take communion.

At the very least, the notion of the Eucharist as sacrifice gave enormous power to priests as the mediators of this essential transaction between Christians and God. It raised theological problems as well, for it gave the Eucharist a physical quality that could be perplexing. Was the Eucharist a repetition of the sacrifice of Christ? If so, was the historical crucifixion and sacrifice of Christ somehow cheapened by not being unique? Was the body of Christ on the altar the same as the historical body of Christ? Could a mouse eat the body and drink the blood of Christ?[22] In time a somewhat loose definition of the word "substance" covered the difficulties but did not bury them forever.

Luther resurrected the difficulties with a fierce rhetoric. The conception of the Eucharist as sacrifice created ever-higher levels of ceremony for its observance. By eliminating the sacrificial quality of the Eucharist and by making it more a personal communion with God, he struck at elaborate ceremonies and at the power of priests who officiated at those occasions. All the substance of the Eucharist, he said, lay in the words of institution by Christ. He dwelled on the words, "This is the cup of the new testament in my blood which for you and for many is poured out in the remission of sins. This do in remembrance of me."[23] This was the testament, he said, of one about to die. The Mass is the promise of the remission of sins, a forgiveness that was a gracious act of God and established by the death of his son. The only difference between a testament and a promise is that the testament involves the death of the one who makes it. Christ could not have died unless he had been a man; so in the word "testament" are included both the incarnation and the death of Christ.

Only faith in the promise makes the sacrament, Luther said. First comes the Word of God, then comes faith, and after faith comes charity or love, which makes works good and fulfills the law. In effect, the Eucharist becomes here a paradigm of the Christian life. To have faith is to believe a promise that has been made but not yet fulfilled. With the death of the testator, Jesus the Christ, the inheritance has now been passed to the heirs. But the promise will not be completely fulfilled until the resurrection of the dead. It seems worth repeating here that for Luther, to believe a promise was not to say that one has an absolute certainty that the promise is to be kept, not at least the certainty that might see clearly the fulfilled promise in the distance as though one were seeing land from a vast sea. To believe a promise is to accept the statement of the giver, but it is not to rise to the superhuman power of having no possible doubts about the future. A promise is incomplete action, its fulfillment unseen. Doubts may come from all sorts of "reasonable" contingencies, but one fends off these doubts by repeating the promise. The repetition of the Mass for Luther may be likened to a continual return of the Christian to the origins of his faith for refuge, even momentary, liturgical refuge, from doubts that by Luther's own testimony remained always with the Christian.

Thus the *Babylonian Captivity* reiterates Luther's steadfast view of the Christian as *simul justus et peccator,* always justified and sinning at the same time—words that become his metaphor for human nature. If the only justification is faith, the only sin is unbelief, and these two strive continually in the Christian's heart, requiring the Christian to continual reaffirmations of faith, reaffirmations that come sacramentally in the Eucharist. The Christian, heeding the words of the promise and taking the sacrament in faith, "soon afterwards feels spontaneously the sweetest feeling of the heart in which the spirit is expanded and attached to the heart of man."[24] All this Luther described in emotional, even passionate terms. For him the Eucharist became a profoundly spiritual event, nothing like the dead ceremony administered by those priests whom Luther had heard in Rome less than a decade before, racing through the Mass and hissing at him, "Get on! Get on!"

The emphasis on promise occupied Luther for several pages. To make the Eucharist a promise with its validity dependent on faith was to remove from it the magical qualities that the church never sanctioned but that flourished in popular culture—including the legends that the host sometimes oozed with the blood of Christ. The word of promise spoken was spiritual and addressed the soul. It did not do tricks. It did not use spells or incantations to move the physical world. The Eucharist did not cure people of illness or lengthen their lives or give them a boost in worldly enterprises. In the Mass the priest could not do something for the Christian; everyone must make the sacrament for himself.

Luther's view of the Eucharist was to become one of the many walls dividing him from Ulrich Zwingli of Zurich, John Calvin of Geneva, and the "reformed" tradition that mightily influenced Protestantism in the United States. The Eucharist was for him part of the drama of faith, its liturgy the story of the gospel presented in a reverent ceremony, the ceremony telling the story of the gospel. For Luther an essential part of the eucharistic drama was that in it he met the invisible Christ in visible form, and the anxieties and doubts he might bring with him to the liturgy were cleansed away as he became a character in the play of redemption. Against the presence of Christ in this holy rite, reason could not prevail.

His views on baptism seem to contradict his scriptural principles. Everywhere he stresses the need for personal faith when we approach the ceremonies of the church. The Eucharist testifies to our faith in the incarnation of Christ, his Passion, and the bloody victory of the cross over sin, death, and the devil. Baptism testifies to the redemption we receive in faith from the curse passed on to us from Adam. Luther scorns the notion that baptism is magic, having in it some power apart from faith. "For if the sacrament give me grace merely because I accept it, truly it comes out of my own work, and I do not obtain this grace through faith, nor do I apprehend the promise in the sacrament but only the sign instituted and taught by God."[25] He likes immersion as a mode of baptism because it is most like the death, burial, and resurrection of Christ. He expects children to be plunged under the water. This was the medieval practice—as any baptismal font from the Middle Ages will indicate. As for those who say—as the Anabaptists soon would—that infants cannot believe God's promises, Luther asserts that he believes in infant baptism in the same way that he believes children are helped by the praying and believing church.

Here we can see Luther's sense of his own baptism as a powerful reinforcement in his battle against the fear of death. Baptism was from earliest times a reenactment of death and resurrection, made powerful and real by immersion, itself an active threat to life. The Christian lifted from beneath the waters of baptism is quite literally saved from the death that would ensue if the administering priest should hold him under. No one ever drowned by being sprinkled. In this passage on baptism we see the fervor of Luther's emphasis on the sacrament as a promise of justification fully consummated only in the death and resurrection of the body. Like the Eucharist, baptism is a sacrament, an incarnation of sorts, the spirit of God powerfully present in a physical way, just as Christ is present for Luther in the elements of the Supper. Baptism must therefore *do* something when it is used within the Christian community, and what it does is to bring the child's body into that community. The physicalness of both these sacraments, a physicalness that was to cause so much conflict among evangelicals, was for Luther part of his faith that the dead must be raised if the Christian faith is to mean anything. The resurrection is not a mere spiritual business; it is physical, as the sacraments are physical, and as the resurrection will be physical.

This message runs powerfully through the section on baptism, as though Luther's future co-religionist Johann Sebastian Bach had hit upon a powerful fugue that sent the contrapuntal themes of death and resurrection hammering together in a thunderous harmony that might crack the heart with hope and joy. Luther here makes no mention of salvation from hell or even of God's judgment. The enemy is death, and resurrection is not to judgment but to life. In everything he says on baptism, Luther sees the church as a community of life, faith, and death. The briefer our life, the more quickly we fulfill our baptism. The church was most happy, he says, when martyrs were dying every day and were accounted by pagans as sheep for the slaughter. We can feel a nostalgia for the communal quality of Christian martyrdom in the legendary days of the persecuted church when he compares martyrdom with the loneliness of death as he expressed it in so many of his letters of spiritual counsel. In an age when no one understood the nature of disease and when little children might cough themselves to death in the middle of the night or burn out their insides with some nameless fever or die some languid death like a frail white candle burning to a soft end without a sound, baptism was not a gift that Luther could withhold from them.

A few years later the lure of biblical literalism attracted large numbers of Anabaptists, who rejected infant baptism. In Zurich the town authorities with the full approval of Ulrich Zwingli had them drowned. Drowning seemed fit punishment for those who demanded that adults who had been baptized as children be baptized again when they were old enough to profess their faith. Luther was exasperated with them. But he did not think they should be killed. And in early 1528 he published an open letter *On Anabaptism to Two Pastors,* whose names are not known. In it he argued the case passionately for infant baptism. But in beginning his treatise he said,

> It is not just, and I am pained because these miserable people are so wretchedly killed, burned, and horribly slaughtered. One ought to let everyone believe what he will. If he believes incorrectly, so he will have enough punishment in the eternal fires of hell. Why will anyone then kill them also in time, so long as they only err in faith and do not then become rebellious or otherwise withstand the authorities? My God. How soon it is that one errs and with a blow is struck down to the devil?

With the scripture and God's word shall one defend against and stand up to such people. With fire one accomplishes little.[26]

It is one of the few places where Luther speaks of the "eternal fires" of hell, and he may have been speaking ironically, since foes of the Anabaptists commonly taught that they would be damned to eternal torment for their error. Hell is hardly the burden of Luther's thought here, but his tolerance for the Anabaptists would soon dry up. By 1529 he believed that those who spoke out peacefully against infant baptism should be exiled. By 1530 he had become convinced that the Anabaptist preaching against infant baptism inevitably led to sedition, and he saw their teaching as blasphemy against the Word of God. Although it was cruel to punish them with the sword, he said, it was more cruel to let them condemn the ministry of the Word and suppress sound doctrine and destroy the political order.[27] Yet to the end of his life he expressed grudging admiration for how Anabaptists died without flinching. They had, he said, no inner fear of death. Therefore the death of the body did not cast them down.[28]

Luther's doctrine of faith seems to be fully clarified in his comments on baptism in the *Babylonian Captivity*. It is here that he makes the statement hurled back at him in outrage by Catholic foes such as Thomas More: "For no faith can damn the Christian except unbelief alone." And, says he in another lapidary declaration, "I say therefore, neither pope nor bishop nor any man has the right to impose one syllable of law upon the Christian man except that the Christian give it his consent."[29] To Luther's foes these sentences meant anarchy.

To Luther they meant nothing of the kind. They expressed the life of tension between the promise given but not yet complete—to be completed only in the resurrection. They do not imply that belief is something done once and for all. Luther's rhetoric of baptism implies a Christian life in which fear and faith live in symbiosis, and faith is never sight and certainty, and the visible "sign" of the true sacraments is a necessary help for the faltering Christian—who always falters but who must never despair.[30] The powerful sacrament of baptism is given only once, but faith repeats it again and again as the heart requires it. When does the heart require it most? When confronted by the fear of death and the faltering of the heart that fear causes.

So faith throughout this exposition seems like continual resolve, strengthened by meditation on the sacrament, to take God's promises as if they were true and to live under that assumption, regardless of what temptations may assail the soul. Faith, Luther always said, is an *opus alienum,* a work not one's own, something done outside human power and within God's dominion.

Faith does not depend on our making either our emotions or our intellect over in such a way that all doubts are purged and serenity reigns. God accepts us even with our doubts that God may not exist, that he may not raise the dead. Luther wrote as though the soul were always in battle, always in need of the refreshment of contemplating the sacrament and symbol of baptism, claiming God's promise that this sacred rite is the story of redemption from death.

Several times in his table talk Luther mentioned the doubts of the apostle Paul as expressed in his epistles. When Paul wrote of the crown of life laid up for him in heaven, Luther wondered if he was as certain as he seemed. "I myself cannot believe as strongly as I write, and Paul did not believe as strongly as he spoke." The subject under discussion here was Paul's faith in resurrection and eternal life. Doubts about these matters were fundamental doubts about the validity of Christian faith. Luther confessed these doubts himself. Yet he believed that God accepts us, doubts and all.[31]

At the end of his discussion of baptism, Luther rolled into an attack on vows that he was to develop presently into a treatise against monastic vows. In part his denunciation of vows was driven by the claim of popes to be alone able to absolve Christians of vows they had made for whatever purpose. The entire structure of vows in the church was in his view only a mask of papal usurpation. In part, too, his antagonism to vows arose out of the injustices committed in their name. Suppose, he suggested, that one spouse might wish to dissolve the marriage ties by vowing to enter a monastery. Could the pope sanction such things in the name of vows? And are vows made by children binding? For him baptism was the powerful bond that made one a Christian; beside it, all vows were of little account.

Luther's attitude toward penance seemed to change as he wrote the *Babylonian Captivity.* Early in his discussion of confession, he said, "Secret confession in the way it is now practiced, even if it cannot be proved by scripture, I see as both pleasing and useful, even necessary, and I do not wish that it be discontinued but rather rejoice that it is in the Church of Christ since it is for the afflicted conscience the only remedy."[32] He always believed in the worth of oral confession, one Christian to another. He practiced this sort of confession regularly himself. The effects were important. Years afterward in his table talk, he remarked that in private confession one was not required to enumerate his sins. But to confess to another and to receive from a human mouth the assurance of God's forgiveness was to confirm one's faith and to be at peace. Therefore, he said, "This is the most powerful reason why we shall retain private confession . . . as long as I live."[33]

His experience made him keep the practice without calling it a sacrament.

The papal version of penance had, he said, turned it into another manifestation of tyranny, and it had been the zone of conflict where he had attacked indulgences. Confession as Luther held to it at the last became another of the less formal means he employed to make of life continual worship and reassurance. Stripped of its formal liturgical style and the somber confessional, with its anonymous and almost invisible priest hidden behind a screen, confession became an act Christians might perform in private conversation, even at a meal or on a walk, two Christians speaking to each other from the heart about sin, death, and the devil. All this broke the clerical monopoly on penance. By stressing simple oral confession and assurance of forgiveness, he eliminated the multitude of liturgical practices associated with satisfactions imposed by priests—the pilgrimage, the relic, the fast, the vigil, the funerary bequest to the church, the vow of service to God for oneself or one's children, and, of course, indulgences.

His enemies said he made confession easy and that therefore sin was now easy. But for Luther confession was for true Christians, and true Christians lived with a genuine abhorrence of sin and could take the comfort of forgiveness without any sense that they were getting away with anything. He allowed no place for the suggestion that a sinner could work off a penalty for sin by some sterling work of satisfaction. Pilgrimages and the rest smacked of works-righteousness and superstition. Christ had already won the battle against sin. Righteousness was faith in Christ. That faith was planted by God, and no power on earth could root it out once God had placed it in the heart of his elect. That was the absolution that one Christian could use to comfort another in the hour when sinful human nature outraged the pious heart of the true believer.

Almost by the bye, Luther declared himself on the subject of women. Speaking of Catholic priests and bishops, he said, "For the hearing of secret sins, let them permit it in the freest possible manner by brothers and sisters so that the sinner can reveal his or sins to whomever he or she might wish and forgive forgiveness and consolation, that is, the Word of Christ, out of the mouth of the neighbor when it is asked for."[34] This mention was to enrage Thomas More, who turned the whole idea into a lascivious joke.[35] But it was scarcely a manifesto by Luther to emancipate women from the bondage of the patriarchal late medieval culture.

Even so, if we take liturgy to be the set of rituals and ceremonies and other acts by which Christians worship God, Luther's radical redefinition of penance became the most important liturgical event of his Reformation. It made more visible changes in formal Christian practice than any other reform he made. Indeed, he made confession so informal that it became less than a sacrament in his own thought, and most Protestant churches abandoned it altogether.

He concluded by dismissing the other four sacraments—confirmation, marriage, ordination, and extreme unction. Because they were not scriptural, he regarded them as perversions despite their long tradition in the Catholic Church. Confirmation was made a sacrament, said Luther, only because it gave lazy bishops something to do, since they had abandoned the other sacraments to the lower clergy. Christ had given no promise about confirmation; he had not instituted it, and it should not be a sacrament.

Matrimony was more complicated. Since marriage had existed from the beginning of the world and among unbelievers, it could not be a Christian sacrament, he said. Again he turned to the Greek New Testament and the understanding he had gained from Erasmus. The scriptural support for taking matrimony as a sacrament turned on Paul's letter to the church at Ephesus, where the Vulgate said in apparently unmistakable clarity, *Propter hoc relinquet homo patrem et matrem suam, et adhaerebit uxori suae, et erunt duo in carne una. Sacramentum hoc magnum est, ego autem dico in Christo et in Ecclesia.* Several centuries of Catholic tradition had translated this passage thus: "For this a man shall leave his father and mother and hold to his wife, and they two shall be in one flesh. This is a great sacrament; and I say this by Christ and by the Church." In his annotations on the Greek New Testament of 1516 Erasmus had pointed out that *sacramentum* here translates the Greek word *mysterion*, meaning something holy, hidden, and therefore mysterious. Luther attacked the issue philologically, showing places in the Vulgate where *sacramentum* was not translated as "sacrament."

Turning from this argument, Luther attacked the vast and ramshackle provisions of the canon law for matrimony. These legal articles, mostly about blood relations within which marriage was forbidden, rules for divorce, definitions of betrothal, and so forth, made marriage into a Gordian knot of regulations where lawyers, theologians, and keepers of genealogical tables swarmed among the threads. For centuries church rules would not let two people marry if they shared an ancestor seven generations back. After the Fourth Lateran Council of 1215, marriage was permitted if the couple had no common ancestor earlier than four generations back.[36]

The change was not much of an improvement. Even today we have trouble discovering who our great-great-grandfather might have been. Since everyone has eight such male ancestors, the problem of keeping up with all their descendants is formidable. It was nearly impossible in the Middle Ages, when records were scanty. The canon law complicated things by holding that anyone who stood as the godparent of a child at baptism became spiritually related to that child's family. Since the church regarded this spiritual kinship as important as blood relation, canon law made godparents into family members, and their relations might never marry. Naturally enough, if a man got tired of his wife, the surest way to be rid of her was to discover that he and she had a common ancestor within the forbidden degrees of kinship. Such a crusty old ancestor, immobile in the grave for decades (or perhaps even nonexistent), might be summoned up to cut marriage ties supposed to bind till death. An unhappy husband might learn that his grandfather had served as godfather to his wife's mother—a relationship that made his marriage invalid. It was an impossible business made to order for the purveyor of false genealogies, able to manufacture an ancestor with a flourish of his pen, a wink of the eye, and a clink of the proper coin.

Luther was unsparing in his denunciation of these legalities and the bargaining over them in divorce cases. Through these laws, he wrote, "the Romanists of today have become salesmen. And what do they sell? Vulvas and penises."[37] Luther wanted to get rid of the sterile rules that hindered warm human relations. He wanted affection between husband and wife, unbound by the rigidities of ossified custom. To him marriage was a bond between two people, publicly assumed, marked by love, sexual intercourse, obligations, children, and a shared life. Husband and wife had responsibilities toward each other, but these did not require the definitions of the canon law. They were matters of spontaneous affection and common sense. So the canon law should melt away. But in this melting, the power of the institutional church over marriage was also dissolved.

Some of Luther's thoughts on marriage were radical. Suppose a man is impotent, says Luther, and unable to have sexual intercourse with his wife. He might give his wife her freedom to marry another. But at the very least he should grant her the liberty to have sexual intercourse with somebody else. If she has children from such a union, the impotent husband should happily bring them up as his own. Luther, always conscious of appearances, suggested that in such cases the intimate arrangements be kept from the public at large. If the impotent husband should not give his consent, Luther advised the woman to run off with another man to some far-off place where she would not be known.

Here is breathtaking radicalism. But it is rooted both in scripture and in Luther's sense of human relations. Marriage is not an institution where the husband owns the wife as though she were a slave. She has rights, including sexual rights. If the husband loves her, he should be willing to let someone else meet her sexual needs if he cannot do so himself. Here Luther not only exalted women relative to their lowly medieval status, but he also departed from the medieval Catholic view that sex was shameful, something always to be regarded with aversion or amusement and engaged in with as much dispassion as possible for the propagation of the race. On this matter Luther in particular differed from the teachings of Augustine, who saw sexual passion even between husband and wife as a threat of chaos. As Peter Brown has observed, "Augustine never found a way, any more than did any of his Christian contemporaries, of articulating the possibility that sexual pleasure might, in itself, enrich the relations between husband and wife."[38] Even between husband and wife, Augustine said, sexual intercourse had in it an element of shame.[39] Luther followed Augustine in a somewhat suspect sermon on the married state preached in 1519. Sexual love in marriage would have been beautiful if Adam and Eve had not fallen, he wrote. But since they did fall, it was in consequence never clean.[40] By the *Babylonian Captivity,* he seems to have had a change of heart.

For Luther sexuality was as much a part of life as eating. In line with a common prejudice of his day, he believed that women craved sex more than men did. Yet he knew the power of the sexual drive himself. He seems to have confessed openly and with apparent passion in his sermon on the married state that his own sexual desire was intense and painful, a true *Anfechtung.*[41] He spoke frankly in lectures to students and in his table talk of the problems of nocturnal emission and lust, all with the candor of a man who knows these to be part of the common male experience. When he made these jarring proposals in the *Babylonica,* he was carrying on that healthful propensity of his to see the biology of humankind as natural and therefore good. Sin for him never lay in the mere act of anything. Nature required its due. Sexual intercourse was part of God's creation. So he could hold that an impotent man should supply a sexual partner for his wife. He could make this suggestion without a shade of the jeering hilarity that would be provoked by such a notion today.

Luther touched briefly on divorce. He hated divorce so much that he would prefer bigamy, he said, though he was not sure that bigamy was right.[42] The notion was not farfetched to anyone steeped in scripture as Luther was. Nowhere in the Bible is polygamy condemned. The patriarchs and kings of the Old Testament had many wives. Paul in the New Testament said that an "overseer," or bishop, should be the husband of one wife, but he never suggested that the ordinary Christian had to be so limited. Monogamy is a legacy of the Greeks and Romans. By approving of bigamy, Luther was concerned to protect a wife from being discarded in a cruel world where a woman required a man to protect her.

Luther had already claimed that all Christians were priests. Now he attacked the sacrament of holy orders, or ordination. It came not from scripture but from the papal tyranny, he said. Scripture had not one word about it, and the only early church writer to mention it was Dionysius the Areopagite. Along the way Luther gave a thumping denunciation of "Dionysius" himself, mistakenly assumed by medieval scholars to have been the Dionysius converted by Paul's sermon preached on Mars Hill in Athens.

Luther also rejected a cherished traditional notion, that all the apostles became priests. Priesthood was therefore glorified by its antecedents, and legendary histories of the apostles extolled their virginity or celibacy and raised an impermeable wall between priests and laity. Luther's doctrine of the priesthood of all believers turned priests into ministers of the Word chosen by their congregations, permitted to marry, and commissioned to preach and to teach. He ridiculed the restraints on marriage imposed by the church on candidates for priesthood. A married man might become a priest if his wife had died, but if he had married twice and both wives had died, priesthood was forever barred to him. Neither could a man become a priest after his wife had died if she had not been a virgin when he married her. But, said Luther, a man might have had sex with hundreds of whores and defiled innumerable virgins and wives and kept male prostitutes in his house, and might still become bishop, cardinal, or pope. All believers were priests; the duty of priests was to speak the Word of God, and for that purpose no ordination by a papal church was necessary.

He approved of the practice of anointing with oil those on the point of death, but he would not call it a sacrament. He knew that his foes would cast in his teeth, as he said, the book of James, which advised Christians to call the "elders of the church" when anyone was sick so that the ill person might be anointed with oil and healed by God (James 5:14–15). Luther here spoke of the author of the book of James in almost the same terms that he had spoken of Dionysius the Areopagite. This book, he said, had no apostolic spirit, and many had suggested that it was not by the apostle James at all; but even if an apostle had written it, he had no authority to institute a sacrament on his own. Erasmus had doubted its apostolic authority; Luther may have been influenced by him, and he would become more definite on the matter later on. Now he proceeded to show that whatever it was that "James" advised did not fit the standard definition of extreme unction in Catholic belief and practice.

So he concluded this most radical of his works to date. Given the tendencies of later evangelicals who tried to read their beliefs and practices out of scripture alone, Luther's pronouncements seem almost conservative. Thomas

More blistered him for not making footwashing a sacrament. Jesus had done it with his disciples, according to the Fourth Gospel, and he had commanded them to wash the feet of one another, and More said that if Luther made his doctrines from scripture alone, he would have Lutherans scrubbing feet if they were to be consistent. More's argument was that the church controlled scripture and not the reverse and that even Luther accepted many beliefs and practices that were contrary to a literal understanding of the Bible.[43]

More's gibe indeed illuminates Luther's understanding of scripture and tradition. He had experienced many pious practices within the Catholic Church. He was not willing to cast them off merely because he found no sanction for them in the Bible. Infant baptism was one. In his letter of 1528 to the two pastors regarding infant baptism, he said it was "fools' work" to try to cast off everything the Catholic Church had taught. "Christ found in the Jewish people the misuses of the Pharisees and the scribes," he wrote. "But he did not then reject everything that they had received and taught. We confess that under the papacy much Christian good, indeed all Christian good is, and so it has come to us. Namely we confess with the papacy that there is a correct holy scripture, a correct baptism, a correct sacrament of the altar, a correct key to the forgiveness of sin, a correct preaching office, a correct catechism, the Lord's Prayer, the Ten Commandments, the articles of faith."[44] Always his aim was to reform the old, to make it more viable, more meaningful. He never tried to sweep everything away and begin anew with Christian teaching and practice drawn out of scripture alone.

The Anabaptists and others we shall encounter were true radicals. They looked on the New Testament as a law to be followed in every particular. Were only adults baptized in the New Testament? Then they would baptize only adults. Was there no instrumental music in the New Testament? Then they would not use organs to accompany their hymns. Did New Testament Christians practice a form of communism? Some Anabaptists would flee society, set up communes, and live unto themselves. Did Jesus forbid his disciples to swear? The Anabaptists would take no oaths; and so they would exclude themselves from public life, where oath taking was an official rite of society. Did Jesus forbid his followers to kill? Then the Anabaptists would not be soldiers. And did Jesus command the washing of feet? Well then, some of the Anabaptists would resurrect the practice. And so it went.

The Anabaptists and others sat down with a book and tried to generate a whole new world of religious experience out of it. Ulrich Zwingli and John Calvin, both much more conservative than the Anabaptists, hated the Anabaptists, but even they were more bookish than Luther in their attitudes toward scripture. Luther sought to redefine the old, not to create something entirely new. So he remained essentially conservative, seeking to reform the church rather than tear it all down and build a new edifice on the old ground.

But with the *Babylonian Captivity* he cut himself away from moderates who might have joined him to limit the power of the papacy. His redefinition of the sacraments was more than moderation could bear. In October 1520, only a few days after the *Babylonian Captivity* appeared, Erasmus wrote vigorously to Godescalc Rosemondt, rector of the University of Louvain, on the subject of Luther. He did not approve of what Luther had written, said Erasmus, but he disapproved of how the Luther case had been handled by the Catholic Church. "I have never admitted, nor will I ever admit, that a man should be so publicly overwhelmed under tumultuous cries before even his books have been read and examined to the bottom, before he had been warned of his error, before his works were refuted by proofs and by the testimony of the Holy Scriptures."[45] By February 25 he had read the *Babylonian Captivity.* "It alienated many readers," he said, "and from day to day his behavior becomes more violent. I don't know what he expects from his enterprise unless, perhaps, he depends on the Bohemians."[46] For a time Erasmus had to deal with accusations and innuendo that he had written the little book himself. Such suspicions drove him almost to distraction.[47] But no longer did he believe that he might mediate a reconciliation between Luther and the church. No longer did he try.

15

THE FREEDOM OF
A CHRISTIAN

THE most eloquent of Luther's 1520 works was his *Freedom of a Christian,* which appeared in November but was backdated to September to make it seem that it had been written and published before the *Babylonian Captivity.*[1] Luther had heard a rumor that the pope's attitude was softening toward him. Many Christians were urging compromise. The ever-hopeful Karl von Miltitz suggested through Luther's old mentor Staupitz and his friend Winzeslaus Link that Luther write a letter of apology to Pope Leo X.[2] If the pope showed himself amenable to reconciliation, Luther might be able to deny that he had written the *Babylonian Captivity.*

For Miltitz the bull threatening excommunication represented a disaster to his hopes of resolving the dispute. He insisted on meeting with Luther, and Frederick the Wise commanded Luther to agree. Miltitz and Luther met on October 12. Some gesture on Luther's part would be welcomed as a sign of Christian charity and Catholic unity. Under pressure from his prince, Luther agreed to write a brief and properly humble note to the pope in both Latin and German, in which he would make certain that Leo understood that Luther was not attacking him personally and that he wanted peace. Luther's letter to Spalatin reporting the meeting with Miltitz sounds almost curt.[3]

The work that emerged from these discussions was an open letter to the pope meant to be affixed as a preface to *A Treatise on the Freedom of a Christian.*[4] The letter is humorous in the heaviness of its irony. Its surface radiates conciliation and humility, but it is in fact a declaration that the differences between Luther and the papacy were irreconcilable. He whipped off the German version in a couple of days and followed it with a somewhat enlarged Latin version. Both went to press in November.

As urged, Luther professed willingness to make amends, claiming he had never spoken evil of Leo as a man, praising his innocence, blaming the pope's bad counselors for the troubles of the church, and begging for a hearing where the two of them might get their minds together. The attack on evil counselors was standard in medieval rebellions; the rebels seldom attacked the king himself. "Loyal servants" of the king felt compelled to take up arms to free him from his wicked advisers. So Luther here.

He never had much talent for apology. Now he addressed Leo in the firm tones of a good German schoolmaster admonishing an inept but well-meaning child. Although he had not attacked Leo personally, he nevertheless declared unremitting war against the papacy itself, he said. Leo was counseled to give up his "glory"—that is, the title of pope—to retire to the parish and live on the income of a simple priest, and to accept all the doctrinal definitions Luther had proposed. Then Leo could help Luther reform the church. In effect, Luther said peace could reign between them if Leo helped destroy the papacy.

The letter looks like a calculated insult, couched in a vocabulary of meekness and friendship but aimed at showing friends as well as enemies—the elector and Spalatin as well as Miltitz and the pope—that no compromise was possible between true Christians and the Antichrist at Rome. But who can tell? Maybe Luther was so swept up in the righteousness of his cause that his letter to the pope seemed to him only a statement of obvious fact to a world in danger. To Leo he said, "I called you Daniel in Babylon."[5] Yes, Luther agreed, he had used sharp language, but so had Paul, and what good was salt unless it could bite? Rome, he said, was Sodom and Babylon, and the Roman Church, once the most holy, was now a den of licentious thieves, a brothel of the most shameless, the kingdom of sin, death, and hell, so that it could not be worse if Antichrist came. Leo was a lamb in the midst of wolves, like Daniel in the lions' den, like Ezekiel living among scorpions. "Is it not true that under this vast sky, nothing is more corrupt, more pestilential, more hateful than the Roman Curia?"[6] Johann Eck, he said, was an adversary of Christ and a glory-hungry beast. (Luther seemed fond of describing Eck with this term; he used it often.)

Leo was in the most miserable and dangerous place imaginable; his enemies lied to him about his authority, and if the pope believed them, he was doomed to perdition. They erred especially when they exalted the pope over the universal church and the council. Luther made a fantastic play on words. The pope was styled "Vicar of Christ." A vicar acted only when the master was absent; so if the pope was vicar, Christ was absent, and what could such a vicar be, acting without the presence of Christ, except the Antichrist, an idol? The letter looks like satire of the first order, bitterly ironic, howlingly funny when we consider the stations of the principals and Luther's declaration that reconciliation between Luther and the papal church was impossible. But was Luther perhaps so confident that he meant it?

The body of the treatise on Christian liberty is perhaps the finest thing Luther ever wrote.[7] Here he sought to answer this question: If we have no power to earn merit by doing good works, why should we live ethically in society? Why should we not eat, drink, and be merry, knowing that what will be will be? His enemies posed these questions as if they had only one answer: Why indeed not? The moral issues were worrisome to rulers, who saw the masses as tinder to be set ablaze by any suggestion that good deeds were not required. Luther's exposition was written with princes in mind, intended to show that his doctrines must lead to an orderly and obedient populace.

Here he proposes his famous paradox: A Christian is utterly free, master of all, slave to none; a Christian is the willing slave of all, commanded by all. The freedom of the Christian is that Christ has done all the work to earn salvation and there is nothing left for Christians to do themselves. Christians are freed from the law and freed from the tyranny of perfection, from the fear of never being good enough. Christians know that God's commands humble mortals because no one can obey them. The commandments destroy pride— which in good Augustinian fashion Luther interprets as the quality that makes us put ourselves in the center of the universe and usurp the place of God. Only in humiliation do we perceive that we are not divine, and only then can we truly let God be God, to acknowledge that God rules all. Only when we recognize this essential truth can God give us the grace that saves us. Freedom consists in the faith that we have already been released from the bondage of sin and that we need not suffer anguish to win something we already possess. Our response to God for the gift of salvation is to love him with all our hearts.

Luther's intent may be fairly expressed by an analogy drawn from common experience. If I love someone and am assured of that person's love for me, I do not go to a rule book to see what bargain I must strike, what deeds I must perform, what dragons I must slay to provoke a love I already feel. Those human relations where someone says, "Do this, and I will love you," are cold and mechanical. Under conditions of trade and bargain, one can never be certain of love at all. If I know that someone loves me, I can enter a warm human bond and have real freedom. I do not have to prove my love by constant effort. Yet what sort of freedom is it? It is obviously not a freedom to do anything contrary to the nature of love itself. I am not free to slash my beloved's tires, to beat his children, to poison his dog, or to burn his house down. I am bound by love, but it is a bondage that I do not feel as bondage. For Luther, the cross proved for all time how much God loves us. Because they are assured of God's love, true Christians spontaneously act in immeasurable gratitude to the Christ who has redeemed them. Christ loves all humankind, and Christians reciprocate by sharing the love of Christ for all humanity. "Good works," he said, "do not make a good man; but a good man does good works." And again, "A house built badly or well does not make a good or bad builder; but the good or bad builder makes a good or bad house."[8]

None of this is to suggest that the Christian lives a perfect life. Early in the *Freedom of a Christian,* Luther makes a distinction derived from Paul and his own experience. Human beings have two natures, one spiritual and one "fleshly." These two are at war with each other—the spirit against the flesh and the flesh against the spirit.[9] Luther harps on this dualistic nature of human being. He sees the Christian life as a discipline in which the body is by continual spiritual exercise subjected to the rule of the spirit. The Christian cannot rest but must at all times seek to bring the body under subjection and to purge it of all its lusts. This effort may include restraining the body by fasting, vigils, and work. It is an ascetic impulse, not so different from the monastic discipline that sought to subject the body to the spirit by continual discipline. In time Luther was to leave this rhetoric of asceticism behind. His later comments on how to avoid the fear of death see the pleasures of the body, including eating and drinking, as ways of escaping the terrors of solitude.

For the moment his emphasis on the body as enemy to the soul served to make his moral teachings engagingly similar to the best in Catholic piety. He condemned not ascetic practices in themselves but rather the popular view— not held by any theologian that I can find—that extreme feats of self-denial are heroic and meritorious in themselves even if the only effect of such acts is to punish the body and even derange the mind. At the cost of making a caricature of monastic devotion and discipline, Luther repeated his lifelong theme, that no Christian could put God in his debt by doing good works that God was obligated to reward. He defined this theme to provide a rationale for good works and to show how his moral teachings upheld the orderly life that princes desired for their people.

If the spirit is to conquer the body, the spirit must be nourished. The food of the spirit is the word of God, and the nourished spirit responds with belief in the Word. Neither here nor elsewhere did Luther interpret belief as certain, intuitive knowledge of the sort that allows us to discern objects in the corporeal world. Rather for him faith is resolution to accept the Word of God in Christ and in scripture. We "know" that word is true no matter what agonies of doubt we must endure in consequence of being the dual creatures we are, bodies living in the world of the physical and unable to see the hidden realm of God. "Belief" and "faith" denote an attitude of heart and mind that leaves everything to God in the way that we might trust a promise from a loving father even when that father is distant from us and we have no visible proof that the promise will be kept.

Luther writes fervently about "promise" so that it becomes in his rhetoric identical with the word of God. The Word is a promise to be kept in the future, and by writing about it in ardent levels of repetition, he reassures himself that it will be kept. Belief in the promise translates responsibility to God, and therefore this faith, this intention to confide everything to God, is more than any good work can be. It is not surprising that the word "promise" recurs in this treatise like a grand chorus summoning Christians to belief and relief. Nor is it surprising that the weight of Luther's relief rests on salvation from death and the grave.

Since the dual nature of human being remains until death, it is not contradictory that Luther could make these thumping assertions of the reliability of the promise and yet sometimes sink perilously close to despair. Faith is the reaction of the will to the Word, the resolve of the will to trust the promise, no matter what the appearances. Despair rises from uncontrollable emotions and must be suffered as the Christian must suffer the various pangs brought on by this life in a body. We will not be freed from the obligation to subdue the body until the resurrection of the dead.

The immediate purpose of the treatise was to counter the Catholic slander that Luther's teaching meant that Christians could believe the propositions of the gospel and live like the devil and still be certain of salvation. For Luther faith was the presence of Christ in the heart, and it required the Christian to have the same selfless attitude toward the world that Christ had possessed. Luther expected discipline, love, and service from everyone who bore the name of Christ. The motives of this life could not be selfish. Christians did not love the neighbor out of slavish lust for reward; rather they loved others because Christ had already loved them. Good works did not make Christians good; Christ made them good, and Christians did good works out of gratitude in the changed nature that Christ had given them.

As Peter Kawerau has cogently argued, this little treatise on Christian liberty not only contains Luther's view of the nature of Christian life and morals; it also demonstrates the essence of Luther's view of the church, the community of Christians existing through time from its founding by Christ unto the ending of the world.[10] By releasing the Christian from the bondage of law, Luther also declared independence from the vast and complicated decrees of the canon law, the collection of authoritative statements by popes, councils, and theologians that had been sanctified by tradition and that kept good order in the church. The canon law defined Christian marriage, grounds for divorce, the relation of the pope to the church, the requirements for priesthood, the correct way of administering and understanding the sacraments, and almost everything else that one might imagine relating to the outward conduct of Christians in the church and the world. Given the Catholic attitude toward tradition, that any belief and practice observed for a very long time by Christians must be sanctified by God, canon law and divine law appeared to be identical in many minds.

Luther came back to an abiding theme—the priesthood of all believers. It meant that every Christian could stand before God without any intermediary except Christ himself. He was careful to say that the priesthood of all believers does not mean that every Christian has a divine right to preach and teach. As Paul said, "So one esteems us as ministers of Christ and dispensers of the mysteries of God" (1 Corinthians 4:1). The "us" refers to the ministers who administer the sacraments, the "mysteries of God," as Luther had called them in the *Babylonian Captivity.*

Here is a seeming contradiction: Luther sought to overthrow the institutional hierarchy of the Catholic Church with its priests, bishops, and the pope; yet he created another hierarchy, that of the ministers confirmed by congregations in the right to preach the Word, the "mysteries of God," that ordinary Christians might mistake unless they had an authoritative guide. In effect he conceded a major point. Yes, the Bible was clear and unambiguous in its teachings; but even true Christians, who could count themselves priests before God, might not understand this clear Bible. Therefore a class of ministers was required to explain it to the masses. Luther seemed to expect the well-meaning masses to see the clarity once they heard it explained, and if they did not, they would still live obedient and faithful lives and accept the word of their preachers.

Luther's caution was sound; if ministers of the Word were not carefully regulated by a community that certified their "gifts"—that is, their willingness to conform to "true" belief—fragmentation and uncertainty would result. Since neither Luther nor anybody else could control the large and amorphous group that became known as "Protestants," or "evangelicals," fragmentation was inevitable. In little more than a decade after Luther wrote the *Freedom of a Christian,* Thomas More described the disagreement of those he called "heretics" with one another and compared their disunity with the grand unity of the Catholic Church:

> But now these heretics be almost as many sects as men, and never one agreeth with another, so that if the world were to learn the right way of them, that matter were much like as if a man walking in a wilderness that fain would find the right way toward the town that he intended, should meet with a crowd of lewd, mocking knaves, which when the poor man had prayed them to tell him the way, would get them into a roundel [circle] turning them back to back, and then speak all at once, and each of them tell him, "this way," each of them pointing forth with his hand the way that his face standeth.[11]

Throughout his great treatises of 1520 Luther wrote as if Christian doctrines were perfectly clear in the Bible, at least to true Christians. He was sure by 1520 that the Catholic hierarchical church with the pope at its head was not identical with the "true church" of the faithful, a congregation known only to God. Yet the tone of his rhetoric did not allow him to distinguish between the "true church," a tiny remnant of true believers, and the great masses of professing Christians, and he affirmed again and again that no one could be certain who was a true Christian and who was not. His frequent identification of baptism as a mark of true Christianity added to the confusion of his position. In effect he taught that all Christians were baptized but that not all those baptized were Christians—simple enough as a proposition but of little benefit to efforts to make distinctions between truth and error.

The essential word throughout for Luther was "spirit," the living divinity that made the Word alive in the Christian heart. Spirit was the invisible force, the presence of the living Christ within the Christian. "Insofar as the Word is, so of itself it forms the soul just as the heated iron glows as it represents a union between itself and fire."[12] Christ and the soul become bridegroom and bride, one flesh. "Christ is filled with grace, life, and salvation; the soul is filled with sin, death, and damnation." With the Christian's faith, Christ assumes sin, death, and the grave.[13] Christ is God and man in one person; dying, descending into the grave (ad infernum descendens), and rising again, he conquers all in a stupendous duel (stupendo duello), "for his righteousness is stronger than all sins, his life more powerful than any death, his salvation more triumphant than all the lower region."[14]

Here is cosmic drama, and here are echoes of the ancient Mediterranean cults whence Paul, Luther's chief authority, developed his rationale for what Christ did by his life, death, and resurrection. It sounds very much like the cult of Dionysus or the other mystery religions of that old world. Salvation comes through a mystic joining of the initiate to the god, an interchange that is invisible, though it may be helped along by physical objects and ritual forms such as the elaborate and still largely unknown rites at Eleusis where classical and Hellenistic Athenians joined themselves to Persephone and hoped to share in her triumph over the underworld. Luther could declare such ideas because he was steeped in the Bible and because they were in accord with his own dramatic and turbulent experience of the fear of death, his yearning for salvation, and his sense of the victorious life promised in Christ.

This is hardly the stuff of which philosophy is made, and Luther did not try to shape into a systematic theology these dramatic images of death at war against God. They represented his experience—as they have represented the experience of millions of people from time immemorial for whom death and the grave are personified as forces at war with human existence. Reason rebels against such a confusing spectacle played out on a cosmic stage with contradictions galore. For Luther this inability of reason to systematize experience was enough for him to reject the role of reason in matters of the soul. Reason was for the earthly life; there it did well much of the time. But it had no independent authority in divine things. Once allowed to question faith, reason would destroy it.

This flaming experience of faith in Christ and victory over sin, death, and the grave was the mark of the true Christian. All true Christians had this experience. Luther wrote under that assumption, believing his words would harmonize with them as two strings tuned perfectly to the same note will resonate with each other when one is played. No Christian could tell who among his acquaintances was also a true Christian and who might be a hypocrite; here the Renaissance cleavage between appearance and reality reached its apogee. In 1521 Luther would write against Ambrosius Catharinus, one of his most dogged Roman antagonists, that were the apostle Peter present with us, we could not know if he might endure to salvation.[15]

His point against Catharinus was only an extension of his views in his great tractates of 1520. The true church was the community of those justified by faith and spread throughout the world, known with certainty only to God. That church had continued in an unbroken line from its founding by Christ until the present, the living resonance, one might say, of God's word spoken continuously to his creation. He strove to overcome a dilemma. On the one hand he attacked the institutional papal church as the church of Antichrist, captured by the devil. Yet he could not maintain that everyone in that church was corrupt. His notion of the hidden church of the faithful allowed him to posit multitudes of true Christians to whom he might appeal and who knew the enlightening faith of God in Christ. When Catholics held—as they did with a clamor of voices—that Christ had promised to be with his church to the end of the world and that only the papal church had so endured, Luther could reply that his church, known to God alone, had existed out of the sight of humankind but in the sight of God and that therefore Christ had kept his word.

Luther was never able to say with precision at just what moment the Catholic Church had fallen away from its divine calling.[16] As he grew older, he would push the time of the church's fall closer and closer to its beginnings, seeing, as one commentator has said, "the whole history of the church [seeming to be] under the enduring influence of the devil."[17] He was certain only that the history of the papal church demonstrated that the closer one came to his own times, the more corrupt the church had become. Yet the more corrupt the visible church was in his eyes, the higher his rhetoric could climb in his praise of the "true" church, the living congregation of true believers doggedly persisting on God's word and sustained by faith throughout the world. All this was a means of attacking the depravity of the papal church. At Augsburg Cajetan had listened to Luther and in response had said, "That would mean we must build a new church."[18] Now Luther was forced to acknowledge the fatal truth of that observation, for he recognized that he must busy himself with the construction of a visible institution. He would have to build a "Lutheran" church. Yet that was a contradiction to everything he had been seeking until now. No wonder that Jaroslav Pelikan has noted, "No trial oppressed Luther's spirit more often in his later years than this recognition that structure was inevitable, combined as the recognition was with a candid awareness that the institutions now being erected were not necessarily superior to those which had (often against Luther's advice) been swept away."[19]

For the moment Luther had to deal with the papal bull *Exsurge Domine,* threatening him with excommunication unless he recanted. For months Luther maintained the fiction that the bull was a crude forgery by Eck. By December such pretense was no longer possible. Luther's books were burned in many towns in ceremonies presided over by the public executioners and urged on by Aleandro, Eck, and other papal representatives. Luther's supporters would reply in kind. At around nine o'clock on the morning of December 10, 1520, Wittenbergers, summoned by Melanchthon, demonstrated in support of Luther.[20] They made their own bonfire near the gate in the Wittenberg wall through which passed the road to the nearby town of Elster. Onto that pyre they heaped volumes of canon law and an assortment of books written by Luther's foes, including Johann Eck. Standing by, Luther tossed onto the fire a copy of the papal bull. The affair seems to have been a deliberate reply to a recent burning of Luther's books at Leipzig, for, said Luther to Spalatin, the occasion was meant to show the papalists how easy it was to burn books they could not refute.[21] He could, it seems, demonstrate how easy it was to burn down the entire edifice of papal power.

Praise for Luther poured in from many quarters. He wrote to Spalatin on December 15 in wonder and exaltation: "Dear God! What will be the end of these new things? The papacy until now seemingly invincible may even be rooted out beyond all hope, or else the last day is near."[22] His words resound with the relief and ecstacy of a formal declaration of war against a hated enemy. For three years the conflict had smoldered and spread. Argument had not cooled passions; argument only convinced everyone that people on the other side would not listen to reason and were therefore malicious. Now the pope's bull and Luther's act of incineration constituted an exchange of declarations of war. The conflict was to be longer, larger, and more disastrous than either side could imagine on that wintry morning of festivity and fire.

16

THE PROGRESS TO WORMS

FROM the beginning of the quarrel, Frederick the Wise insisted that his professor have a hearing on German soil by German authorities. As early as the imperial election in the summer of 1519, Frederick and the archbishop of Trier had suggested that this hearing might be held at the next Diet.[1] That would be at Worms in the spring of 1521, and the young Charles V would preside, making his first appearance as emperor on German soil. In the spring of 1521 Charles visited Henry VIII and Henry's wife Catherine, Charles's aunt, in England and was treated to the pomp and circumstance that made Henry one of the most theatrical monarchs of the sixteenth century. The two monarchs had a common enemy in Francis I of France. Since 1494 the French had through war and diplomacy tried to gain a foothold in Italy from which they could dominate the Italian cities. Henry VIII lusted to undo the effects of the Hundred Years' War, which had excluded the English from France except for an enclave at the port of Calais. Charles wanted Italy to be an adjunct to his empire, and so Italy would occupy much more of his time and energy than Luther ever would. In their conversations Henry and Charles made vague overtures toward an alliance that would hold the ambitions of Francis and France in check.

Charles was an unprepossessing-looking twenty-year-old with an undershot jaw that made his mouth hang open so that in most paintings and sculptures of his person he seems to look at the world with mild surprise. His mother went insane early in her life and was finally confined to a monastery at Tordesillas, north of Madrid, where she lived until 1555, cared for like a child and, with her reputed mad stare, becoming a wildly popular subject for nineteenth-century Spanish painters. Charles may have inherited from her a tendency to melancholy. In 1556 he abdicated his many titles and withdrew to the Spanish monastery of Yuste to spend the last three years of his life preparing to meet God. Perhaps the unceasing energy and iron will of this redoubtable man were the consequence of a temperament not unlike that of Martin Luther, a man driven to superhuman labors by the demons of sorrow working within.

In 1518, when Charles was already king of Castile and about to become king of Aragon, he acquired one of the great men of the age, Mercurino Arborio de Gattinara, as "Grand Chancellor of all the realms and kingdoms of the king."[2] Theirs was to be a stormy career together. Gattinara shared with Charles and perhaps imposed upon him a vision of worldwide empire, not merely the restoration of the empire of Charlemagne but a government to embrace both the Old and the New World. Gattinara wrote to Charles on July 12, 1519, calling attention to the opportunities now open, recalling the grandeur of Charlemagne, and offering a vision of universal peace under emperor and pope.[3] At the moment Charles was elected to the imperial office, the troops of Hernán Cortez were already in Mexico; by August 1521 the great Aztec city of Tenochtitlán would fall into Spanish hands, and the Aztec empire would be no more. The raging epidemic of smallpox that killed more than half the Aztec population was seen by the Spaniards as God's judgment against the heathen. Already ships laden with treasure from Spanish conquests were making their way across the Atlantic to light Spain to a golden age, and nothing seemed impossible. Charles's imperial design took for granted a united church. Whether the emperor himself was as committed to orthodoxy as he was to politics has been debated since his time.

In October 1520 Charles was crowned emperor in Aachen, the city of Charlemagne. It was a grand occasion, begun on October 22 by a parade of hundreds of horsemen, including Spanish grandees in their full ceremonial regalia. Beside Charles rode the archbishops of Cologne and Mainz. The electors of the empire met him at the city gates and kissed the young man's hand while he sat bareheaded on his spirited horse, which, said witnesses, he controlled perfectly. In the evening Charles lay face down on the floor of the cathedral of Aachen, where Charlemagne was buried, while the archbishop of Cologne prayed over him. On the next day the young monarch was asked if he would protect the church, preserve traditional faith, rule justly, protect the poor, widows, and orphans, and remain true to the pope. Charles responded to each question in Latin, *Volo*, "I will." He was then anointed with holy oil on the head, the breast, the neck, the elbows, and the hands, and to the sound of trumpets, drums, and the cathedral organ, the crown was placed on his head.[4]

Erasmus attended in his role as occasional imperial counselor, vainly urging moderation on everyone. Frederick the Wise was absent. He remained at Cologne, a victim of gout, the affliction of the age of those who had plenty to eat.[5] The papal nuncio Girolamo Aleandro attended and tried to persuade Charles to see to it that *Exsurge Domine* was promulgated and enforced throughout the empire. From the beginning papal policy was to keep Luther from being heard by civil authorities, who, in the pope's view, had no right to judge theological matters.

Aleandro (1480–1542) played a major role in events. He was Italian, said by many—including Luther—to have been born a Jew. (In a speech delivered before the Diet at Worms in February 1521, he did not quite deny the charge.)[6] He was in his youth a serious humanist, reportedly a brilliant student of Greek and Latin, and a friend and employee of the Venetian printer Aldus Manutius and of Erasmus, who told him to go to France and provided letters of introduction. The advice was good; the letters worked. Aleandro went to Paris, became a member of the faculty of arts at the Sorbonne, where he boasted of the numbers of rich students and high-born men who flocked to his lectures. He discovered that fame did not translate into money and complained bitterly that he was not paid what he was worth. "I live but from day to day," he wrote a friend. "I have clothes, books, and some furniture, but you would find nothing in my purse but spiderwebs."[7] His fortunes improved. In 1513 he became the first Italian to be elected rector of the Sorbonne since Marsiglio of Padua, the famous conciliar thinker, had held the post in 1312.

He seems to have held an ambiguous opinion of the authority of the papacy, but he tried to avoid any conflict that might jeopardize his career. He was elected as one of the representatives of the university at a general council at Pisa called for the fall of 1511. He wavered and finally refused to attend. This council, supported by King Louis XII of France and some disgruntled cardinals, reasserted the decrees of Constance against papal absolutism in the church and went home. Its efforts called attention to the smoldering opposition to papal absolutism in the church. Aleandro disliked the warrior pope Julius II and privately wrote contemptuous letters about him.

Pope Leo X brought a different spirit to the papacy. The plump young pope liked scholars and made Rome more attractive for them, and when a lucrative opportunity came to return to Italy as secretary to the bishop of Liège, Aleandro took it. He apparently possessed an effusive personality and worked his way into the confidence of the pope, perhaps because the two were very much alike. In 1519 he became librarian of the Palatine Library, forerunner to the Library of the Vatican. In that capacity he helped draw up

Exsurge Domine, and from then on he was involved in the Lutheran affair until his death.[8] He turned on Erasmus and by February 1521 was writing to Rome that Erasmus was the source of all the evil of the Reformation.[9]

An odor of shallow opportunism hangs over Aleandro that the fragrance of his undoubted learning cannot quite cover up. He saw everything in political and institutional terms; not until late in his life did he begin to understand the powerful cravings for reform that had drawn so many to Luther. He also underestimated Frederick the Wise. In the meantime he used every political tactic to ensure victory for the institutional church over Luther's revolt.

Frederick met the emperor at Cologne in November. Erasmus and Aleandro were in town at the same time, and both had interviews with the elector. Erasmus said that Frederick persuaded Charles to allow Luther to appear at the Diet to defend his writings—a process that would, in effect, have ignored the papal condemnation of Luther's doctrines and given Luther a chance to win his audience over by argument.[10] Erasmus did everything he could to throw water on the growing fire. On November 9, 1520, he addressed a long letter to Conrad Peutinger, a trusted counselor of Charles V. In it he spoke of "this tragedy" of Luther, which might end in a "catastrophe extremely dangerous for the Christian religion."[11] Many suggested that Luther be suppressed with violence, Erasmus said. He pleaded against that course. If the disease were to be healed, its causes must be addressed.

These causes were, he said, anchored in hatred of good literature. Those who despised the study of ancient texts attacked them by attacking Luther, and many who wished to defend good literature took Luther's side without meaning to do so. Hatred of Rome and its immorality was widespread in many nations. The pope's counselors did him no good by serving their interests and not his. "Now, the pope should act only within the limits where his authority serves at the same time the interests of Christ and those of the Christian flock."[12]

He castigated Luther's style of combat; even when Luther wrote the truth, said Erasmus, he did so in such a way as to rob truth of its power. But those who had written against him by the clumsiness of their attacks would have done harm had they defended the best of causes. In his opinion, Erasmus said, the only success in this affair lay in seeking the glory of Christ. One might strike out right and left against foes, but nothing could move the stone where was engraved this "mystic sentence: The Lord knows who belongs to him." Nothing that came from the spirit of Christ could be repressed by human force, no matter how much one might try; nothing strictly human could endure, no matter with how much zeal it might be carried forward. "Some" regretted, said Erasmus, the lack of meekness in the papal bull

Exsurge Domine.[13] The times needed an exceptional spirit who might moderate events so that all good might not be submerged by the waves or cast in shipwreck along the shore. The pope himself should consent to having the affair judged by wise men of integrity who were above suspicion. The best place to realize this project would be at the coming Diet meeting at Worms.

Erasmus went out of his way in this letter to avoid attacking the papal primacy, but neither did he assert it. The pope, he said, would not be *constrained* to allow judgment of the Luther affair by independent arbiters; rather, he would be *voluntarily* allowing such a procedure out of his love for the church. He flattered Pope Leo X as a man who would seize the initiative from unworthy advisers and do the right thing for the sake of peace among Christians. The right thing would be a moderate course, to sift out the good from the bad in Luther, and to seek reforms that would rally the church again to unity. Erasmus's advice might have saved Europe from over a century of religious war and the habit of demonizing the foe. But his conciliatory pleas never had a chance of success. A pope doing what Erasmus suggested would have made concessions that every pope after the Council of Constance did everything possible to avoid.

Charles remained in Germany in anticipation of the Diet to open at Worms in January. Aleandro saw the issue now entirely as a threat to papal authority on which he hung the security of the church in the world and doubtless, too, his place in that world. On December 13 and 14 he spoke with the emperor, urging on Charles the opinion that only the pope had the right to judge Christian doctrine. In opposition, the emperor maintained that to condemn a German without a proper hearing would be a scandal. Luther had praised Charles in his *Address to the Christian Nobility of the German Nation,* and many humanists saw in Charles almost messianic hope for a rebirth of German liberty. Fears abounded. The drone of insurrection was in the air. The "common man," finding that Luther was unfairly treated, might rise in riot and rebellion.[14] Such fears helped Aleandro and the emperor patch over their differences in an agreement that doomed Luther's hopes for the Diet at the start. The emperor would demand that Luther recant his heresies. Luther would have no opportunity to argue his case.[15] Frederick the Wise doggedly argued that Luther should get a real hearing, an opportunity to debate. But now Aleandro had the upper hand.

Sometime around Christmas Spalatin wrote to Luther with question: Would he appear before the emperor and the Diet if given the opportunity? Luther replied with characteristic vigor on December 29. His letter has the feel of an anxious man thinking out loud, arriving at a firm decision, and encouraging himself in the obvious danger he ran.[16] If called, he said, he would go under his own power, or, if he were sick, he would be carried. No one could doubt that if the emperor called, it was the will of God. The example of John Hus was in his mind. But if the imperial authorities should use force against him, as force had been used against Hus, "My head," he said, "is a small thing compared to Christ, who was killed in the supreme ignominy to the scandal and destruction of man."[17] The gospel would be shamed if those who preached it were too afraid to die for it.

Luther knew that such a journey might be to his death and that his army of foes would then gloat that righteousness had triumphed over wickedness and that his cause therefore was the devil's work. Whatever happened he must commend himself to God, for in the end God would judge the wicked and vindicate the gospel and those who upheld it. Christ had died a felon's death; those who had ridiculed him had been lost. Luther put himself in Christ's place. He expressed the hope that the young emperor would not begin his reign with the shameful act of shedding his blood. He would rather, he said, perish at the hands of the Romanists alone than have the emperor shame himself by involvement in the affair. He recalled with grim delight the fate of Sigismund, the emperor who had rescinded the safe-conduct given to John Hus at the Council of Constance, permitting Hus to be burned. Sigismund had died without a son, and his widow disgraced herself through her immorality. God's will be done, said Luther. The letter represented a prayer with a hint of imprecation; twice Luther closed anxious paragraphs with the word "Amen."

The stream of events now became a torrent, rushing Luther, the papacy, the emperor, and Western culture to the destiny that we know as history. In a letter to the emperor written toward the end of August, Luther had already appealed for imperial protection from the papacy.[18] On November 17, 1520, he renewed his appeal to a General Council against the pope. He published his appeal in both German and Latin. The Latin version called the pope the Antichrist; the German did not.[19]

The pope and his advisers set themselves to defend papal power to the utmost. The emperor, heir on his mother's side to a centuries-long Spanish tradition of equating Catholic orthodoxy with divine right against stubborn Jews and schismatic muslims, rallied to the cause.[20] Charles seems to have been one of those dull and diligent fellows who have done much mischief in history by responding to the call of duty. The papal party urged on the young emperor the example of the devastating Hussite wars, an argument for destroying heresy before it could flame up into violence. Charles's fear of popular tumult was heightened by news of the bloody revolt of the Comuneros in Spain, where he had been unpopular since his curt treatment of

Cardinel Jiménez de Cisneros, who had acted as regent until Charles made his first trip there in 1517. The revolt was centered in the cities which had traditionally enjoyed a large measure of self-government and which Charles sought to bring under his authority by putting men loyal to himself—often from his native Flanders—in charge. The Spaniards therefore resented not only the financial exactions that Charles imposed on them for his imperial ventures but also the sense of being ruled by foreigners. Not until 1522 was Charles finally able to put down the Comuneros. The experience was not one to make the young emperor sympathetic to rebels. At Worms, the emperor's heart was all on one side, and it was not Luther's.

On the same day that Luther wrote his brave letter to Spalatin, the emperor issued an edict against Luther and anyone who adhered to Luther's doctrines. An envoy should proceed to Wittenberg and demand that Frederick burn Luther's books and jail Luther himself.[21] As though some invisible telegraph worked between Germany and Rome, Pope Leo X issued a bull of outright excommunication against Luther on January 3, 1521.[22]

Yet negotiations went on. The bull of excommunication was not immediately published because popular opinion stood firmly on Luther's side. Aleandro, one of two papal ambassadors to the Diet, thought that if he published the bull, the Germans would kill him. Even *Exsurge Domine* had not been fully published through the German lands, and publication proceeded hesitantly in many areas, as civil authorities feared to provoke the masses. The emperor hesitated, making other gestures of conciliation toward Frederick the Wise. He drew back from putting the weight of imperial authority behind further ceremonial burning of Luther's books—though here and there such burning went on.

Broadsides with woodcuts proliferated, some making Luther a hero inspired by the Holy Spirit, others condemning the pope in crude vehemence. About this time Hans Holbein the Younger created a woodcut drawing of Luther the German Hercules (the same title applied to the Emperor Maximilian) holding in his mouth a cord attached to a strangled pope, who hangs at his chest. With his mighty right hand, this furious Luther raises a club with which he has already beaten to death a host of foes including Aristotle, Thomas Aquinas, the medieval biblical commentator Nicholas of Lyra, and others upon whom the scholasticism of the Middle Ages had been formed. It is a fierce portrait, crackling with violence, portent of real violence couching at the door to German society.[23]

Hans Baldung provided a different Luther—a saint complete with halo and the dove overhead symbolic of the Holy Spirit.[24] Recall that Baldung was also the almost fervent painter of the macabre in all its horror, showing

implacable skeletons seizing voluptuous maidens, sign of the triumph of
death over all the pleasures of life and the world.

Before the point of no return, nervous and perplexed minds drew back.
Ominous fears of religious war hung over a landscape in suspense. Ulrich von
Hutten had written several times to Luther offering military aid against papal
tyranny and floating rumors of intended violence against Luther by papal
agents. Luther had for a time been encouraged by these pledges of support,
and he had corresponded not only with Hutten but also with the military
captain Franz von Sickingen. By January 16, 1521, he was experiencing a
change of heart. On that day he wrote to Spalatin mentioning a letter from
Hutten, apparently again offering armed force against the pope. But, said
Luther, he had no wish to take up arms for the gospel. The Antichrist would
not be overcome by human hands; rather he would be defeated by the
Word.[25] Nevertheless, Hutten's military threats continued, and Aleandro and,
it seems, the emperor took them seriously.

A mood of combative resignation seems to have come over Luther himself.
On January 25 he wrote the Elector Frederick in German that he would go
to Worms if he could receive an imperial safe-conduct, and again he begged
the elector to intercede with the emperor so that he might have a hearing
before impartial judges who would base their decisions on scripture alone.
Clearly Luther wanted to debate at Worms, and he was confident that with
scripture he would win the day. He had heard that Aleandro had said that the
Germans paid less than any other nation to the papacy and that if they did
free themselves from the papal yoke, they would be consumed in civil war.[26]
Against such Italian gossip, he saw himself as the savior of Germany.

By now the controversial literature directed at Luther had evolved into
something resembling the echoes that may resound and resound again within
a colossal cavern from a single shout hurled toward a ceiling hidden in the
dark. Luther's response to Sylvester Prierias, whom we have already met, was
filled with crushing invective that included one of the most ferocious and
bloodthirsty cries ever written against the papacy:

> It truly seems to me that if this fury of the Romanists should continue,
> there is no remedy except that the emperor, kings, and princes, girded
> with force and arms, should resolve to attack this plague of all the earth
> no longer with words but with the sword . . . If we punish thieves with
> the gallows, robbers with the sword, and heretics with fire, why do we
> not all the more fling ourselves with all our weapons upon these masters
> of perdition, these cardinals, these popes, and all this sink of Roman

sodomy that ceaselessly corrupts the church of God and wash our hands in their blood so that we may free ourselves and all who belong to us from this most dangerous fire?[27]

Here is a fierce tumble of language, a verbal fire seemingly consuming all before it. But now Prierias found a defender, a Dominican canon lawyer named Lancelotto dei' Politi, who called himself Ambrosius Catharinus (1484–1563). In December 1520 Catharinus published an *Apology* for Prierias and addressed it to the Emperor Charles V. It was a thorough, logical treatise that was to have tremendous influence among Catholic thinkers, including Thomas More, and it was written in a tone of scornful assurance that carried a weight of considered judgment.

Catharinus ridiculed Luther's doctrine of scripture alone. He argued that the visible Catholic Church was the recipient of all the promises of Christ to the church. Moreover the church had transmitted over the centuries the truths of God necessary to salvation, given by Christ, passed through the fathers, and continued to the present as a well-known consensus. Scripture was not always clear in itself; it required the church to provide correct definitions of doctrine, and papal supremacy in the church was the cornerstone of the consensus that distinguished true teaching from false. The consensus was not easy; Catharinus defended vigorously the sometimes minute definitions in both theology and the canon law. These, too, were part of God's revelation, and Christians could not unilaterally reject them. Moreover God had certified the authority of the church by miracles that confirmed its teachings. The church contained good and bad members. These would be separated at the day of judgment. But the church was not validated by the purity of its membership. Rather it received its validity from its historical development of a tradition that left human beings certain about beliefs and practices necessary for salvation.

This was a powerful argument, calling to its side the witness of history. In it lay embedded the fundamental conviction of Catholic tradition: Without the church to define doctrine, no one could discern between the true and the false. It was well and good to claim the authority of scripture, but scripture required an interpreter.

Luther took Catharinus seriously enough to reply at length, publishing his counterattack early in April.[28] It was an opportunity for him to think out his doctrine of the church. He might have helped his case by writing in a civil tone, given the growing fear that his movement might erupt in violence. But the importance of the argument and his talent for invective got the better of him. The sarcasm of his foe infuriated him, and from the start he threw insults at Catharinus, calling him in various places a Thomist, an ass, and, perhaps worst of all—an Italian.

The major theme of this sulphurous treatise was that the papal church was so corrupt in morals and in doctrine that it could not be the true church of Christ; it was rather the synagogue of Satan. The true church was the company of faithful Christians known with certainty only to God and thus hidden on this earth. Luther objected vehemently to the careful distinctions common to canon law and scholastic theology, and he mocked Catharinus for accepting them. For him scripture was clear and simple and spoke with one voice, and Catharinus with his distinctions was all wrong.

A major point made by Catharinus was that a hidden church, one not discernible to the eye and common sense, could not do the work of the church in the world. For him and Catholic polemicists who came after him, the church was a sort of grand sacrament, partaking of human nature in that it showed itself in a visible body animated, like the seven sacraments, by an inner and invisible divine power. For Catholics the sacraments and the church represented a kind of continuing incarnation in that the good of the physical creation was affirmed by God's dwelling in it. Luther's rhetoric against Catharinus is at times so radical that he comes close to sounding like a Manichaean, rejecting the physical, the visible, as unworthy of the divine, spiritualizing the true church to the point that no one could recognize its presence or its absence. Most ceremonial customs in the church were matters of indifference; Christians could use them as psychological helps to worship as long as they were not enslaved to them; but Christians could also reject them utterly. The true church had only three visible signs—baptism, the Eucharist, and, most powerful of all, the gospel. Wherever one saw these signs, there undoubtedly was the church—one faith, one baptism, one Lord. But one did not know who was a true member of that church and who was not. No one could be certain of another's salvation, not even the salvation of Peter, whose authority Catharinus exalted so that he could exalt the popes, Peter's successors.

All of this turned the history of the church and indeed God himself into a terrific mystery. What kind of God allowed the Catholic Church to flourish for so many centuries as the one true light of salvation when, if Luther was correct, it was infested by the powers of darkness? Luther's doctrine of the church drove him into making God more unfathomable than ever before— and if God was unfathomable, the only way to think of him was as possessing an absolute power by which he directed the world to his own mysterious purposes. Yet such was the natural end of Luther's idea of the church. His church was the consequence of salvation, not the necessary mediator of redemption. God's word needed no institution to convey salvation to the elect. They were stirred by the word of God speaking to them in scripture, and their church was not a visible institution but a congregation known of certainty only to God.

The theologians of the *via moderna* who had emphasized the absolute power of God were on this track long before Luther was born. But to them the mystery was made negotiable by the certainty that the institutional Catholic Church and its traditions threw a beam of unquenchable light across the centuries and that within this divinely illuminated pathway the Christian pilgrim could be safe and secure in faith. Now Luther was shouting that for much if not most of its history that church had been the devil's instrument to delude. What kind of God would play such a game with his creation?

Luther would quickly discover that his three infallible signs of the church's presence were subject to disparate interpretation. Should children be baptized? The Anabaptists would infuriate him by pointing out that no children were known to be baptized in the New Testament. What exactly was the Eucharist? Luther rejected transubstantiation, but he held onto the faith that Christ remained somehow physically present in the elements of bread and wine. And what was the gospel? For the rest of his life he quarreled fiercely with other dissenters from Catholic faith—many of them beginning as his disciples—over the definition of this most treasured of his signs. How could God be in charge of all this confusion?

Increasingly Luther fell into dark ruminations on the almost infinite branches streaming from this ultimate question: Where was God discernible in history? The ferocity of his assault on Catharinus may be taken as an indication of his frustration that the mystery was so deep. It does not require much insight to infer that he countered this frustration with a barrage of vehement language, railing on and on for page after ugly page as if he could hold all his fears and doubts at bay only by pouring liquid fire onto his foes, dissolving them and his doubts in one mighty holocaust of rhetoric.

Two related tendencies in the treatise are noteworthy. One is an apocalyptic strain that seems less pronounced in his earlier work. Now Luther wrote and spoke as if the world were in its last days and the Beast were about to appear in all its horror. His assault on Catharinus burns with quotations from the mysterious apocalyptic books of Daniel, Second Thessalonians, and Revelation, and some sayings attributed to Jesus himself. The other tendency is an emphasis on the power of Satan.

Toward the end of the world, so these books hold, evil will seem supreme, and chaos will reign; nothing will be what it seems to be. These prophecies were sufficiently generic to be applied to any period of unrest, and so they have been from the days of primitive Christianity to our own time. Luther equated this ultimate evil with the papacy and the church that obeyed papal decrees. Now false doctors taught their traditions instead of the gospel, and the impious followed them to damnation. Among multitudes of religious traitors, the few faithful followers of Christ held to their glorious and steadfast way. For Luther, as for the communities of faith, both Jewish and Christian, that had produced these thoughts, the notion of a faithful few among the scornful and damned multitudes vindicated the minority that would ultimately triumph. An unmistakable sign of the demonic church of the majority was its proliferation of laws that enslaved Christians to idolatrous customs. He castigated clerical and monastic celibacy, the veneration of relics, and the innumerable pilgrimages on which the foolish common people wasted time and money and neglected their homes, leaving wives and children behind. All these were abominations spread on earth by Satan's influence among the hierarchy of the church. Luther buttressed these views with a dazzling allegorical interpretation of Revelation 8 and 9, in which the Seven Angels of the last days blast their trumpets, heralding disaster over a suffering world. The smoke rising from the fiery abyss of Revelation 9:2 as though from a great furnace became the "naked words and opinions of Aristotle." And the sun that the smoke obscured was the truth of Christ. The angel Abbadon rising out of the burning and bottomless pit was not, Luther said, an angel of God but the angel of the dead and the damned. He was the angel of natural light or wisdom, Aristotle, the devastating force that ruined the church, Aristotle "dead and damned . . . in all the universities now raised above Christ."[29]

In his furious and unrelenting attack on the papacy he recapitulated many of his earlier arguments as if the continual repetition of words were an incantation that would bring down the enemy. Throughout the later parts of this treatise the apocalyptic rhetoric throbbed like a drumbeat. In all the ages since the primitive church and even before, apocalyptic declarations proclaimed a coming end to the age of troubles. And against Catharinus Luther predicted the return of Christ and fierce judgment on the doomed church, sounding a shrieking apocalyptic note.

This treatise on the church would seem to make the "true church" an article of faith that could be neither proved nor disproved, safe from refutation, in a realm beyond the range of reason's dreadful artillery. It represents a tour de force not only against the Catholic Church but also against the notion that history, tradition, or custom could be proof of the validity of any institution. In this direction lay perhaps Luther's most truly revolutionary impulse. The medieval mentality had been to say that anything long sanctioned by tradition was valid because tradition or custom represented the working out of the will of an almighty and invisible God. The Middle Ages much more than the age of Enlightenment might sing in almost unanimous chorus, "Whatever is, is right." This willingness to dismiss the authority of custom in favor of a scriptural text that might radically contradict custom—or tradition—could lead to the notion that all the institutions of society might be made over anew. These might include positive law—law as announced in statutes and royal decrees. They might include even the political order itself.

Yet this thundering treatise against Catharinus with its hidden church known only to God ran against a stronger impulse of Luther's that was soon to assert itself once it became clear that he would have no reconciliation with the Catholic Church. He was by temperament conservative in his political views, and like other educated people of his time he feared the common people.

Moreover, despite the apocalyptic fervor of this tractate, Luther was far from being one of those souls who look skyward every day expecting to hear the last trumpet and to see the heavens split with the return of Christ in judgment. The end times had begun; but he did not make predictions about how long they would last, nor did he claim that Christians might help things along by revolting against Catholic princes. He soon set about building institutions intended to last as long as the world did, and his supposition seemed to be that the world was here to stay for a while—though from time to time he declared that the end was near. The vision of the church that he held here did not preclude the notion of an institutional church on this earth that was to be a locus of gathering for the faithful and for the preaching of the gospel. But just as Augustine's City of God was never to be equated with any City of Earth until the return of Christ, so Luther's institutional church that would eventually be called "Lutheran" was not the divine but hidden entity without spot nor blemish whose outlines he sketched here against Catharinus.

The wheels now ground swiftly, bearing Luther to his historic appearance before the Diet on April 17 and 18, 1521. The Diet assembled for a formal opening on January 27. Its procedures creaked along. The agenda included long "Complaints of the Hard-Pressed German Nation" against the papacy for its treatment of Germans, complaints not directly related to the Luther affair but indicative of public resentment at the high-handed way in which popes and their Italian servants dealt with the German people. It might be supposed that these bitter and detailed protests, debated over several weeks, disposed the assembly to give Luther a sympathetic hearing. To some extent they did. But these were formal items debated in an assembly of leaders. Luther arrived in Worms already tarred with the brush of a popular following, which, for a monk accused of heresy, was regarded by princes with deep suspicion.

Luther completed his attack on Catharinus on Easter Sunday, March 31, 1521. On Tuesday, April 2, he set off to his fateful meeting with the emperor and the Diet at Worms. He traveled in a small "Saxon cart," sheltered from the rain and the sun by a cover. Ahead of him on horseback rode the imperial herald, Kaspar Sturm, bearing the Hapsburg coat of arms, the imperial eagle with its fierce beak and its outstretched claws. Aleandro thought that the choice of the herald was a disgrace, since Sturm was known to be an enemy of the clergy. Luther's progress took on the air of a triumphal march. A few students and colleagues from Wittenberg accompanied him, and all along the way crowds turned out to see him. In Leipzig, where Duke George's enmity continued, he was coldly received. But in Erfurt, where he had been shunned after the Leipzig debate not two years earlier, the university threw a huge party for him, and thousands pressed forward in the streets to catch a glimpse of him.

Part of the reason for his warm reception at Erfurt this time was Johannes Crotus Rubianus (1480?–1539?), newly elected to the position of rector at the university. Crotus had been a friend to Luther in their student days at Erfurt and afterward traveled here and there in Europe living the life of the wandering scholar. In the Reuchlin affair he teamed up with Hutten to write the *Letters of Obscure Men,* a hilarious concoction of deliberately illiterate letters supposedly written by stupid and ignorant monks against Reuchlin. Crotus was therefore one of those akin in spirit to Erasmus who turned against the corruptions of the church the most devastating weapon that can be used against a rich and powerful institution—ridicule. He was in Italy when Luther burst on the European scene, but there his energies were absorbed in the defense of Pietro Pomponazzi in the bitter quarrel over belief and unbelief in the natural immortality of the soul. When he discovered Luther's writing—in Rome, ironically enough—he became a passionate convert to the cause. It was he who first called Luther and his followers "evangelicals." His was not an enduring conversion, for in time he returned to the Catholic Church like others who in the beginning saw Luther as a leader of reform but not of revolution. But in his initial enthusiasm Crotus represented many educated Europeans in 1521. Luther was seen as a hero, speaking clearly against old and entrenched abuses, and to multitudes it seemed impossible that such a voice should fall on deaf ears.[30]

In Frankfurt, already the site of a great annual fair for printed books, Luther's writing had won many disciples. An elderly woman of the city, seeing him as a champion against the pope, sent him two bottles of Malmsey wine. Along the way, he preached several times. Anxieties abounded on all sides. Aleandro and others feared that the military force of Franz von Sickingen might fall on the Catholics, perhaps doing violence to members of the Diet and to the emperor himself.[31] Spalatin warned Luther of danger. Luther wrote from Frankfurt on April 14 that he would go on to Worms though opposed by all the gates of hell and the powers of the air.[32] Much later in his life he said that he had been resolved to go to Worms even had there been as many devils there as tiles on the roofs.[33] Aleandro, in the grip of panic, forwarded every wild rumor to Rome and was certain that the people of Worms, "always enemies of the priests," were ready to destroy the clergy to the last man.[34]

Amid these rumblings Luther came doggedly onward, and at ten o'clock on the morning of Tuesday, April 16, he entered the city to a fanfare of trumpets from the towers of the cathedral. Aleandro had wanted the authorities to usher Luther into the city quietly and to lodge him virtually under house arrest, but as he disgustedly reported to his superiors in Rome, Luther's arrival in Worms caused wild excitement. A priest hugged Luther, ritually touched him three times, and afterward crowed over his accomplishment with the glee familiar to those moderns whose only fame in life may be a brief encounter with a celebrity. Aleandro reported that the priest had been as pleased as he might have been to hold a saint, and he grumbled that soon, he supposed, people would be claiming that Luther did miracles. Luther, said Aleandro, had "demoniac eyes," but nevertheless after his lunch "the whole world flocked to see him."[35] In fact Luther was so tense that he felt ill.

At a little after three in the afternoon the next day, April 17, Luther appeared before the emperor, princes, and the emperor's younger brother Ferdinand, who would later become regent of the Hapsburg Austrian lands and one of Luther's most implacable foes. Aleandro and another papal nuncio in the city refused to attend; they stayed away to honor the official Roman position that the hearing was illegal. They missed a great show.

In charge was Johann von der Ecken—no kin to Johann Eck, Luther's foe at Leipzig. Von der Ecken was chief officer under the archbishop of Trier. Among his accomplishments was an efficient burning of all Luther's books he could locate in Trier so that Aleandro was convinced that none were left.[36]

The assembly was held in a meeting room of the bishop's palace—destroyed in the seventeenth century. The citizens of Worms seem to have had no wish to glorify their bishop, for even before Luther they had guarded with fierce resolve their independence from episcopal meddling in their political affairs. They commissioned no official sketches of the palace; at least none survive.

In 1540, Luther recalled that his books were piled up in a window of the room.[37] Von der Ecken asked if he would acknowledge that he had written them. They would have made a huge pile. Both Erasmus and Aleandro had expressed disbelief that Luther could have written all the works attributed to him. But with the certainty of the writer who knows his own children, Luther made a sign of affirmation before Hieronymus Schurf, one of his friends and advisers sent by Frederick the Wise, cried out, "Let the titles be read." So the titles were read, and we may imagine a startled silence as one after another the names of books and smaller treatises went on and on. At the end Luther declared aloud that all were his.

The next question was simple and implacable: "Will you then recant?" Here Luther surprised everyone—and puzzles many scholars to this day. He asked for time to consider. The case, he said, involved the word of God, the most exalted thing in heaven or earth, and if he put the word of God to shame, he would fall under the judgment of his heavenly father and his angels.[38] After some moments of deliberation the young emperor granted him a day, although von der Ecken expressed indignation at Luther's request. Having been summoned to the Diet, von der Ecken grumbled, Luther should have been prepared to answer.[39]

Why did Luther ask for the delay? Roland Bainton provides a dramatic and plausible explanation. Here Luther stood at the threshold of an irrevocable break with the church that for centuries had been seen as the sacred custodian of divine revelation. For a moment, Bainton supposes, Luther was caught up in the same terror of the holy that had nearly consumed him at his first mass.[40] Maybe so. But within an hour after this appearance he was importuned to write a letter to a poet and scholar, one John Cuspianus. Luther scribbled a few words. He had, he said, been allowed only to identify his books and to say whether he would recant. Tomorrow he would give his answer, he said. He would not revoke even a particle of his belief for all eternity, Christ willing.[41] This letter does not indicate a man caught up in awe by the drama of his decision.

Luther hoped until the last that he might have a chance to argue his case. That opportunity was flatly denied him. He was to be allowed only to answer "yes" or "no." He needed time to frame an answer that would also be an argument. So the stage was set for his magnificent appearance before the entire Diet the next afternoon. Because of crowds that pushed into the assembly, this meeting was changed to a larger room. Luther was to appear at four. Delays of various sorts intervened, and he did not rise to face the emperor and the princes again until six o'clock. The dim illumination from the sinking sun would have heightened the drama of the moment. He spoke first in German and then in Latin. The room was so full that only the emperor was able to sit.[42] The press of bodies made the chamber stuffy and hot, and later on Luther recalled that he was sweating so profusely that someone suggested that a declaration in German was enough. He insisted on speaking in both languages. In both tongues, his reply was unforgettable.

He acknowledged first that the books he had been shown on the day before were all his—and thereby cast off the opportunity to escape censure by denying that he had written some of his most radical works, notably the *Babylonian Captivity*. Now came the second question: Would he recant what he had written? His answer was a rhetorical tour de force. A simple "no" might have set loose on him all the pent-up hostility of the emperor and the Catholic party. The flat answer would have resounded rudely in the room like a slap, and what then? One blow deserved another; the emperor in pique might have ordered him seized. But Luther played skillfully on the moment. Instead of answering with a simple yes or no, he discriminated.

He could not, he said, renounce all his works because they were not all of the same sort. Some dealt with faith and practice, about which he had written simply and evangelically in ways that even his adversaries accepted, and these works were useful, harmless, and completely worthy of being read by Christians. (He may have heard the rumors that Jean Glapion, the emperor's confessor, had said as much.) To renounce these works would be unthinkable, for that would be to renounce accepted Christian doctrine—which would be a damnable sin.

A second group of his works, he said, was directed against the foul doctrine and evil living of the papists. But these offenses were well known by universal experience, he said, for papal laws and human doctrines—he meant ecclesiastical tradition—had trapped the consciences of men and in particular had bound the great German people under that intolerable tyranny. To recant what he had said against this tyranny would be an evil deed.

Aleandro—not present—wrote later that at this point the emperor himself intervened to tell Luther to drop this subject and to get on with something else.[43] But Aleandro's reports are so often demonstrably wrong that we may doubt this one, especially given that other accounts are silent on the matter; the nuncio may simply have indulged in wishful thinking. At any rate, the appeal to noble Germans against papal and Italianate perfidy could be expected to fall on fertile ground, given the long tradition of *gravamina* in the Diet, including this one; but it was not sufficient to bring the assembly unambiguously to his side.

Luther plunged on. The third group of his books, he said, involved attacks on private persons and individuals who supported Rome and who attacked his own efforts to build an instructed piety. In these attacks he confessed to having been acerbic in the cause of religion. These attacks he made not to elevate his own sanctity, he said, but for the doctrine of Christ. Yet if he had not attacked these people, tyranny and impiety would have increased in a realm that Luther was obliged to protect. He was but a man, he said, no more than a lump of feces, not a god, and he could err. Only let his errors be proved to him by scripture, the prophets, and the evangelists, and he would revoke any error and throw his books into the fire. Then he said:

So it is that because of my teaching danger, dissension, and conflicts have risen in the world. So yesterday I was admonished about them in the strongest terms. But I have seen what has happened and what is happening. And I must say that for me it is a joyful spectacle to see that passions and conflicts arise over the word of God. For that is how the word of God works! As the Lord Jesus said, "I came to send not peace, but a sword. For I am come to set a man at variance against his father, and the daughter against her mother, and the daughter-in-law against her mother-in-law." And so we must weigh carefully how wonderful and how awful our Lord is in his secret counsels. We must be sure that those things we do to banish strife (if in so doing we undertake to condemn the word of God) do not rather lead to a flood of unbearable evil. Then it might be that the government of this young, noble prince Charles (on whom next to God we hope for so much) would become sick unto death. I could call on many examples from scripture—pharaoh, the king of Babylon, the kings of Israel—that would show how they were brought utterly to earth when they tried to free their kingdoms from strife by means of their own wisdom. For God traps the wise in their own cunning and turns the mountains upside down in a moment. Such are the requirements of reverence toward God! I say this not because such exalted men need my teaching and my warning but because I must not shun the duty I owe my Germany. And so I commit myself to your majesty and to your lordships. I humbly beg you not to condemn me without reason because of the passions of my enemies. I have spoken.[44]

Luther had outfoxed his enemies; he had made the speech he was to have been prevented from making, and by his account at least von der Ecken was furious and shouted at him. He had not answered the question. The imperial officer attacked with a litany of names, heresies already condemned in the past that Luther was now resurrecting as if they were new discoveries. Heretics had always claimed the support of scripture against the church, he said. The worst heresies were those in which a little error was mixed with a lot of true doctrine—perhaps a slap against those in the room like Glapion who had said that Luther's books contained much good. Luther was a man who could stumble and err, and scripture could not be interpreted by one fallible man.

We cannot draw things into doubt and dispute that the Catholic Church has judged already, things that have passed into usage, rite, and observance, things that our fathers held onto with firm faith, for which they suffered pain and torture, for which even thousands suffered death rather than reject one of them! And now you want to seduce us from the way to which our fathers were true! And what would the Jews and Turks and Saracens and the other enemies of our faith say when they heard about it? Why, they would burst into scornful laughter! Here are we Christians beginning to argue whether we have believed correctly until now! Do not deceive yourself, Martin. You are not the only one who knows the scripture, not the only one who has struggled to convey the true meaning of holy scripture—not after so many holy doctors have worked day and night to explain holy writ! Do not set your judgment over that of so many famous men. Do not imagine you know more than all of them. Do not throw the most sacred orthodox faith into doubt, the faith that Christ the most perfect lawgiver ordained, the faith that the apostles spread over the world, the faith confirmed by miracles, the faith that martyrs strengthened with their red blood . . . You wait in vain, Martin, for a disputation over things that you are obligated to believe with certain and professing faith.[45]

Von der Ecken's assumption was one of the great medieval myths, a myth taken for granted for so long that only when it was sternly questioned did those who accepted it see how fragile it was. The myth was that history was a positive and progressive force, shaped by divinity, and that revelation became more certain and more detailed with the passage of time. It seems clear from this speech that von der Ecken recognized the fragility of the assumptions that give faith plausibility and how Luther's attack threatened to bring them all down. In a room now filling with darkness, the voice of the imperial orator must have been a cry against a greater darkness that von der Ecken saw creeping over the world. If Luther was right, was anything certain? How could one man set himself against history? This question always struck Luther in the heart. Perhaps its force helps explain his passionate outburst when von der Ecken demanded again that he recant "without horns or teeth"—which is to say, without equivocation.

> Since then your majesty and your lordships desire a simple reply, I will answer without horns or teeth. Unless I am convicted by scripture and by plain reason (I do not believe in the authority of either popes or councils by themselves, for it is plain that they have often erred and contradicted each other) in those scriptures that I have presented, for my conscience is captive to the Word of God, I cannot and I will not recant anything, for to go against conscience is neither right nor safe. God help me, Amen.[46]

A later printed version issued in Wittenberg added the words "Here I stand; I can do no other," before the words, "God help me, Amen."[47] They do not appear in the extensive stenographic accounts taken down as Luther spoke. But they express his conviction.

By then the room was very dark, and the proceedings broke up in confusion. A Spanish observer in the emperor's entourage reported that Luther lifted his hands above his head, giving the sign that German knights gave when they had triumphed in a joust. He also reported that the Spaniards shouted, "To the fire! To the fire!"[48]

The next day the young emperor handed down his own verdict in the Luther affair. It came in the form of a brief letter written in French—the language with which Charles, raised in the Burgundian court, was most at home. Apparently the emperor had written it with his own hand. Its long opening sentence provided the sense of the whole:

> You know that I am descended from the most Christian emperors of the noble German nation, the Catholic kings of Spain, the archdukes of Austria, the dukes of Burgundy, who have all been until now faithful sons of the Roman Church, having always been defenders of the Catholic faith, its sacred ceremonies, decrees, ordinances, and holy customs for the honor of God, the increase of the faith, and the salvation of souls according to the passage of time in which by natural law and inheri-

tance we have been left these sacred catholic observances so that we may live and die by their examples which as true imitators of them our predecessors have by the grace of God lived until now.[49]

The emperor was resolved to remain in the tradition of his ancestors. One solitary monk could not be right against all the opinion of Christendom for more than a thousand years. It would be a shame to the great and noble German nation to allow either heresy or the suspicion of heresy to infect the present. He would honor Luther's safe-conduct, he said, but once Luther had arrived home, Charles declared himself ready to proceed against him as a notorious heretic and to demand of those present that they comport themselves as good Christians in the affair—that is, that they, too, exercise all their force against Luther.

At first glance this imperial letter looked like complete victory for Rome. Not so. Notably absent from Charles's comment is any praise for the pope or any assertion of papal authority. Moreover, with the emperor's tacit consent—and much to the annoyance of Aleandro—private conversations went on with Luther for several more days in an effort to arrive at some compromise.

Part of the reason may have been a placard posted through Worms on the evening of April 19. It claimed that four hundred armed knights were ready to pounce upon Luther's foes, and it was signed with the words *Bundschuh Bundschuh Bundschuh,* the blunt symbol of a secret peasant society ready to revolt against aristocracy and order. The society was almost certainly mythical. But reality and fear are not necessarily proportional, and in a society that felt the fragility of public order, the placard inspired terror. Aleandro feared that private discussions with Luther would lead to a compromise in which Luther bent himself to some imperial demands while he maintained his fury against the pope.[50] Given the emperor's silence about the papacy in his remarks to the Diet, Aleandro's fears might seem justified. On April 20 the emperor received a petition, in French, from the "electors, princes, and estates" of the Diet that Luther have further discussion. He had said that he would recant if his errors were shown to him; it was important that the common people not believe that Luther had been condemned without hearing. If Luther refused after further hearings to recant, he should be allowed to return home under his safe-conduct, and then he might be treated as a hardened heretic.[51]

The discussions got nowhere. In them Luther was brought face to face with a man who would become one of the most prolific and dogged of his antagonists, Johannes Cochlaeus (1479–1552). Cochlaeus was of peasant stock, both scholar and priest, a man whose energy and zeal carried him farther than his intelligence and character might have merited. His encounter with Luther at Worms seems to have been heated, and Cochlaeus emerged from it with a lifelong detestation for everything Luther stood for. He wrote a library against Luther and in 1549, three years after Luther's death, published a scurrilous biography that for centuries colored Catholic attitudes toward Luther. In it he claimed that Luther protested against indulgences because he had not been granted the commission to sell them, and he told the notorious story of Luther's "fit in the choir" when, as a monk, Luther supposedly threw himself to the floor, demon possessed, shouting, "It is not I. It is not I." Erik Erikson made this tale the centerpiece of his psychological study of Luther, but it is almost certainly a canard. More substantial were Cochlaeus's reports in Latin of Luther's German publications together with the effort of Cochlaeus to refute them and to demonstrate their contradictions.[52] In England Thomas More studied the early, invective-clogged polemical works of Cochlaeus and presented this warped view of Luther to the English-speaking world. Cochlaeus was also one of the first to undertake to answer Luther in German, although it was not until 1522 that he could find a printer for his work.[53] Evidently Luther was so popular that no printer wanted to take the job of publishing anything against him.

Luther stayed on in Worms until Friday, April 26, when, after a final meal, he left the city about ten o'clock in the morning led by the herald Kaspar Sturm and guarded by twenty horsemen who, Aleandro reported, were said to have been sent by Sickingen at the urging of Hutten.[54] That same day, April 28, he wrote to his friend Lucas Cranach that he had consented to let himself be hidden, he knew not where.[55] On the same day he wrote to the emperor, assuring young Charles of his own goodwill and thanking him for the safe-conduct, but affirming once again his resolve to stand solely on the word of God.[56] He wrote a similar letter in German to the Diet. On Sunday he visited one of his father's brothers. Against the specific command of the emperor, he also preached. The next morning he wrote to Spalatin that he had dismissed Sturm.[57]

The stage was now set for Luther's "capture" by men sent out by Frederick the Wise to take him into hiding and safety. Luther later said that the entire episode was kept secret until the last so that only his friend and companion Nicholas von Amsdorf knew of it. In a forest outside Eisenach on May 4, his party was set upon by horsemen who trained bows on the others and took Luther away on the run. In the turmoil he lost a new gray hat. After a long day's ride twisting and turning to throw off any pursuit, they came late at night to the castle of the Wartburg, where, Luther recalled, he had picked strawberries as a child.[58] The castle stood on a high, broad peak above the walled city of Eisenach, where Luther had spent part of his childhood. His "captors" were Burkhard Hund von Wenkheim, who had made the pilgrimage to Palestine with Frederick the Wise in 1493, and Hans von Berlepsch, castellan of the Wartburg—trusted friends of the elector.[59]

He was settled in a small room with a high ceiling and modest furniture, and although he had the company of his keepers, he was plunged into a solitude and an inactivity that troubled him. He wrote letters to assuage his loneliness. News and rumors from the outside world filtered in to him. In Erfurt students rioted against the Catholic clergy; Luther was displeased, and wrote Melanchthon a grumpy letter on May 8 about the unrest. He was afflicted by painful constipation. On May 12 he wrote to Melanchthon, "The Lord has struck me in the rear end with terrible pain. My excrement is so hard that I have to strain with such force to expel it that I sweat, and the longer I wait, the harder it gets. After four days [without a bowel movement] I was able to go once, and then I couldn't sleep all night, and still I have no relief."[60] To Amsdorf he wrote in Latin on the same day but in German said, "My arse has gone bad."[61]

Yet amid his afflictions, he went to work. By May 14 he was writing to Spalatin, "I sit here idle and drunk all day long; I am reading the Greek and Hebrew Bible. I am writing a sermon in the vernacular on our liberty from auricular confession." He was also working on the Psalms and a collection of German sermons that could be read from the pulpit by priests, and he planned to finish a work on the Magnificat. In the same letter he told Spalatin that he was letting his hair grow long to cover his tonsure, and he was beginning a beard. He would soon be known as "Junker George."[62]

Meanwhile the Diet ground on to a conclusion. The princes began to leave. The gout of Frederick the Wise took him conveniently away on May 23.[63] The last session came on May 25 amid threats of war from France and declarations of the emperor's intent to go to Rome to follow in the steps of Charlemagne and to be crowned by the pope himself. Charles was left to shape a final edict against Luther, and this he did with Aleandro's help, being careful to guard imperial prerogatives against papal claims. Luther was declared a heretic and an outlaw of the empire. He was to be taken prisoner, his books to be burned, and his allies to be considered also outlaws and to lose all their property. Was the edict legal, given that the Diet had dissolved before the edict was issued? The matter is still debated. At the moment it was a lethal threat to Luther and his movement. One of the most important parts of the edict was that it condemned Luther not for withstanding the pope and the papal bull but for his stubbornness in refusing to renounce his heresy when commanded to do so by the emperor and the Diet. Frederick the Wise did not receive an official copy of the edict, and he could therefore treat it as a nullity.[64] The other princes and cities of the empire were left to decide whether they would enforce the edict or let it lie. The only certainty was now that the emperor did not have the military or economic power to enforce his will over the princes and the cities if they resisted him actively or passively. So for the moment the Luther affair became a matter of regional and local politics—giving Luther and his followers room to breathe and expand. In this expansion the stay at the Wartburg allowed Luther himself an astonishing productivity. In considering the works that he wrote there, we may suggest that it was as though he built the pyramids in a year.

17

EXILE IN PATMOS

LUTHER's first days in the Wartburg were filled with melancholy musings about Satan. He had in his earlier years constructed from the biblical text and his experience a comforting composite of Jesus Christ. This portrait became well defined in his biblical expositions following the Leipzig debate, especially in the *Operationes in Psalmos*. Luther's Jesus stood invisibly near, speaking words of comfort, assurance, and promise out of the experience of the incarnate God in human life, loneliness, and suffering. Now, alongside this consoling Christ stood the archfiend, Lucifer, rebel against God, cast out of heaven and hovering in the air at Luther's face, responsible for the doubts that buzzed through his head.

Like Luther's Jesus, his Satan was a composite, rising like some nightmare antagonist out of scripture, tradition, and his own soul. In letters written from his hiding place, he called it his Patmos—recalling the desolate and waterless island where "John" wrote the book of Revelation with its stirring visions of the apocalyptic final struggle between the lamb of God and the horrific beast with seven heads and its bestial allies. Years afterward in his table talk Luther recalled the torments inflicted on him by Satan in the Wartburg. A story he repeated often was of how Satan or a poltergeist snatched walnuts off the table and flung them at the ceiling all night long.[1] Once he found a dog in his bed. He threw the poor animal out the window. The next day he asked the keeper of the castle if he had a dog on the premises. The castellan said no. Luther was convinced that the "dog" was an apparition of the devil.[2]

Rumors flew about Luther's fate. Some thought he had been killed— although Aleandro knew better—but by July the opinion seemed widespread that he was at the Wartburg. Charles V had his hands full. He was once again about to go to war against France. The Turkish threat in the Balkans was dangerous to both Austria and Hungary, and the revolt in Spain was becoming more bloody and chaotic. He could not give much attention to a monk sitting alone in a room in a hilltop castle in Saxony.

Luther meanwhile went to work—and what a marvel of production he was! His first task was to respond to an attack on him by James Latomus (1475–1544), a theologian of the University of Louvain. Latomus eventually became an inquisitor. Out of his lifelong hatred of novelty, he had already attacked Erasmus. Without mentioning Erasmus by name, Latomus had in 1519 published *A Dialogue on Three Languages and Theological Studies.* In it he argued that Latin alone was sufficient for the theologian and that Greek and Hebrew were not only unnecessary but possibly dangerous.

In 1520 he published a long attack on Luther, justifying and explaining the condemnation issued by the University of Louvain. Latomus was a pedant and a bad-tempered one at that. Luther grumbled to Melanchthon in a letter that he found it a trial to read anything so tedious, prolix, and poorly written as Latomus's work.[3] Still he felt he must reply, and so he did. Latomus argued against Luther's central assumption, that sinful human nature was incapable of pleasing God. His position reflected the typical view of adherents to the *via moderna,* Gabriel Biel and others, that "grace is granted only if man does what is in him."[4] The premise was that man could do *something* to take responsibility for his eternal destiny. Faith was a gift of God; no Catholic could deny that. But Latomus argued that at some point, however minute our power to do good may be, we have the power to choose the good or the bad. Next to the question of the authority of the Catholic Church and its tradition, this was the most perplexing issue of the Reformation. If human beings had no good in them and no power to do anything whatsoever to help themselves toward salvation, what was the sense of any ethical teaching or striving, and what was the purpose of life?

This was the problem that would draw Erasmus into literary warfare against Luther two years afterward in one of the great intellectual debates of Western civilization. In his later years Luther delighted in slapping Erasmus with a rhetorical backhand by saying that Latomus was the best of all those who had written against him. "Erasmus," he said in 1532, "was not the equal of Latomus."[5] The strength of Latomus, Luther acknowledged, was his insistence that the church could not err and that what the church accepted was not to be rejected.[6] This was the strongest of the Catholic arguments, one that seriously troubled Luther, and the scornful invective poured out in his

Confutation of the Reasoning of Latomus may be a masquerade of sorts, an effort to bury the anxiety that Latomus created in him.[7]

Latomus had commented—as many would—on Luther's vituperative style. Luther did not apologize. He had, he said, never claimed modesty or holiness. He cared nothing for what people said of him personally; he cared only that they know the gospel. He said that he had defamed no one; he had attacked only those whose dogma, labors, and novelties stood against the word of God. Christ himself had called the Pharisees a "generation of vipers," and Luther claimed to follow the example of his Lord against enemies of the true faith. Having made these somewhat contradictory declarations, Luther called his foes—including Latomus—"ignorant, stupid, impious, committing sacrilege against the word of God, doing inestimable harm to piety and to souls, and wounding the whole gospel."[8]

The paradoxes here are numerous. Against Latomus Luther made an assertion that would become a commonplace in his thought. His movement was not to be judged according to the morality of his followers or himself; it was to be judged rather for the purity of its doctrine. Yet he laid down a barrage of objections to the Catholic Church on account of the moral failures of popes, bishops, and clergy. He was by this time persuaded that the sins of the papacy and the rest of the hierarchy were rooted in malicious unwillingness to acknowledge the contradiction between their teaching and the word of God as contained in the clear word of scripture. For him the Catholic Church and its universities had become "synagogues of Satan," a favorite biblical allusion of Luther's hostile to both Jews and papists.[9]

Luther also made a point that would play a role in later events. What should be the attitude of the preacher of the Word toward the sins of the great? Latomus had criticized him for using vituperation against the pope, for failing to exercise proper respect toward leaders of the church. Latomus's view was shared throughout Europe. Ordinary people who attacked the great seemed to be inciting commoners to sedition, and in many countries laws prohibited any speech against those in authority. Latomus had raised the specter of sedition. Luther responded that such cautions were like those of the Jews who feared that Christ would cause sedition and worsen rather than better their conditions. Superiors should be respected, said Luther, but not when they offended against the word of God, and in any case ecclesiastical authorities who strayed deserved harsher condemnation than secular rulers, for when a bishop neglected the word of God, he became "a wolf and an apostle of Satan" and led souls astray.[10] The private sins of magistrates did no harm to the souls of their people. Here is a signpost in Luther's developing sense of the place of the magistrate in human life—a signpost that the German peasants, hearing Luther's democratic religious pronouncements against the hierarchy of the church, were not destined to see. Luther's position early and late was that magistrates and church officials should be condemned for their sins but that on no account were commoners to lift up violent hands against them. The passivity that he upheld for the Christian in the process of salvation was akin in spirit to the passivity he advocated for the Christian in society in accepting the rule of secular authority.

Luther came down firmly on the side of authority in another important matter. "That erroneous books should be burned, I agree and approve." Recollection of this comment should deter moderns who might want to make Luther an apostle of liberty; he was no such thing. He claimed to be certain that absolute certainty could be found in the Bible. And, he said, books should not be burned until they had been proved to be in error. "Fire, as they say, resolves no arguments."[11]

On the ethical level, Latomus had argued that human beings must take some responsibility to do good works, for God would not command the impossible. This was to be an argument raised by Erasmus, and we shall return to it. As it developed early in the Reformation, the issue threatened to create a competition to see who could burn the most straw men. From our vantage point, all these centuries afterward and with the benefit of a mountain of biblical scholarship to stand upon, we can see easily enough that the opposing positions rested upon inconsistencies in the New Testament record. Luther stood with the apostle Paul, especially Paul's epistle to the church at Rome with its explanation of why the Jewish people had been cast away by God and a new Christian "Israel" had set in its place. Augustine had given Paul's letter to the Romans an emphatic and rigorous predestinarian interpretation. God saved whom he would, damned whom he would.[12] Luther followed Augustine.

But it is difficult indeed to find a rigorous schema of predestination in the Gospels—especially the synoptic Gospels of Matthew, Mark, and Luke. There Jesus looks like a miracle worker, crucified, dead, buried, and resurrected, proclaimer of the kingdom of heaven. The requirement of those who would follow him seem to be good works, faith that he was indeed triumphant over death, and participation in the cultic meal that joined the faithful to him in the drama of life, death, and resurrection. Catholics managed for centuries to affirm predestination when they were driven to make their theology entirely consistent and yet at the same time to use a rhetoric that implied some sort of free will in the Christian's response to grace. Yet grace was always necessary for salvation. This was essentially the position that

Latomus had defended. Luther in his vehement counterattack held that Latomus taught that salvation could be won without any grace at all. But this was hyperbole.

Luther's argument for the completeness of human depravity never changed from his early lectures on the Psalms. Against Latomus he argued for the continued presence of sin in the body after baptism, contradicting the Catholic assertion that baptism washes away the guilt of original sin and leaves the body weak and prone to sin but fully cleansed of condemnation for Adam's guilt. In theory, according to Catholic theology, the person who dies at the moment of baptism will be immediately wafted to paradise without having to go through purgatory. For Luther baptism represented pardon from sin, but sin remains, incessantly active, corrupting our will and our deeds as long as we live. When God forgives us, he does not impute our sins to us. That is, he does not judge and punish us for those sins we have committed and the sinful nature that underlies our entire being. The Christian acknowledges sin, does not consent to it, refuses to allow his will to conform to sin, and struggles daily in the blessed hope of the day when, in the presence of God, sin will be altogether annihilated. At some level in consciousness, the Christian stands apart from himself and sees sin present in every part of life, but in the upper level of the mind or heart, God's grace causes him to refuse to consent to sin and instead to trust in God for ultimate deliverance.

For Luther sin was not enumerated in specific acts such as whoredom, adultery, or fornication, theft, fraud, cursing, and murder. It was rather "almost a radical ferment" on the inside that produces the fruit of evil deeds.[13] The ferment endures as long as life, but grace controls its outward consequences. Faith kills the old man of sin within us—but not at one stroke. It is a lifelong struggle, and the power of sin taints the most noble of our works until the end, even such faith as we muster in God. It is not, Luther said, that a single passion burns within us, driving us mad. We do not always smolder with anger or go out of our heads with lust or find ourselves tortured with envy, but rather one of these vices succeeds the other, and when we feel no passion to sin, we are slothful and indolent and therefore sinning in a different mode. Sin is a condition, a weakness like mortality itself, that dwells with us in the midst of life, and its manifestations are like the various illnesses and other afflictions rooted in our mortality.

Along the way Luther admitted that many if not most of the fathers of the church disagreed with his view of the relation of sin and grace and the incapacity of human beings to do any good work. "And you say, 'Do you not believe in the sayings of the Fathers?' I answer, 'I believe? Who commands that they be believed? Where is the order from God concerning their faith?"[14] Near the end he attacked Thomas Aquinas, whom Latomus had cited: "Now as for Thomas Aquinas, whether he be damned or blessed, I most vehemently doubt. Thomas wrote many heresies and is the author of the reign of Aristotle, the destroyer of pious teaching." He ended with a caustic demand to his followers back in Wittenberg to get busy at polemics. The foes must be answered. Everyone must do his part. "I have crushed the head of the serpent; can you not stomp its body?"[15]

Anyone but the most case-hardened theologian or church historian must pause in awe before this volcano of vehemence. What was at stake here? Were not both Luther and Latomus finally arguing that the Christian depends on the grace of God and that the Christian life should be a struggle against the propensity to sin? Did not Luther himself write and preach as though his audience had some responsibility to respond? We may plausibly conjecture that Luther recognized that Latomus had struck him at his weakest point. He thought that to place any responsibility for salvation on himself was to plunge himself back into that world where he believed that he must combat reason with his own strength and have perfect faith. We shall return to these questions when we come to his watershed controversy with Erasmus over the freedom of the will. Other polemics poured from his pen during his exile; they were no less furious than this one.

One was against Jerome Emser, a vicar at the Elbe city of Meissen, south of Wittenberg. They had traded insults before in print. At the Wartburg Luther wrote an ironic reply to Emser's latest. He called it *Dr. Luther's Retraction of the Error Forced upon Him by the Most Highly Learned Priest of God, Sir Jerome Emser, Vicar in Meissen.* The irony is obvious from the title. Luther set out to prove that Emser was a fool. Distortions swarmed in the texts of both men. In defending his concept of the priesthood of all believers, Luther said, "I shall be glad to humble myself and hear women and children preach."[16] It sounds like a radical pronouncement, but it was not an opening for women preachers in Luther's movement. It was hyperbole. Luther's pastors would all be men.

Before Luther's vehemence many humanists and others desirous of reform in the church now began to lose confidence that he was the prophet for whom they so earnestly waited. Erasmus had committed himself firmly to neutrality. Now his hostility to Luther hardened. A Louvain theologian, Peter Barbirius, tried to coax him into an alliance against Luther. Erasmus replied bitterly on August 13, 1521. He said he had read less than a dozen pages of Luther, and he reproached those who had attacked Luther as a seditious person inciting the common people to revolt—as Latomus had done, although Erasmus did not mention him by name. His bitterness and hostility extended to the Lutheran camp and to those Lutherans who "by odious means" had tried to seduce him to their side. Yet, said he to Barbirius, "I fear that they are very numerous who with mighty invective attack secondary propositions among Luther such as, 'Although one may do good works, they are sinful,' although they themselves do not believe in that which creates the foundation of our faith, that the soul survives the death of the body."[17]

Erasmus called such a paradoxical statement a "secondary proposition," and we may be tempted to follow his lead. On one level Luther's declaration that all good works are tainted with sin sounds like modern questions based on sociobiology and psychological inquiry. Is selfless human action possible, or is there in the very performance of an unselfish act a superior sense of generosity and magnanimity that are desirable emotional rewards for benevolence? At a certain point such questions may seem to lead only to sophomoric squabbles over meaningless issues.

For Luther something grand and fundamental was at stake. That was that morality could not become a substitute for intimate involvement in the drama of redemption. To those satisfied with their conduct in the world (as most of us usually are) Luther's message was one of radical introspection, intended to drive us not to the enumeration of our sinful acts but to the examination of the spirit that motivated them. In the complexity of that infinite rejection of our own power of disinterested benevolence, we were to be driven to a saving despair about ourselves and into the arms of Christ, who alone could save us. Morality without Christ might have value in the world in helping people get along with one another, and Luther never denied the role of reason in helping human beings create orderly societies. By his assertion that we sin when we do good works, he made a frontal assault on Renaissance intellectuals enamored not only with classical literature but with the proud sense of culture that was part of it. He implicitly attacked the pride not only of those who found virtue in giving alms, going on pilgrimage, and the like but also of those who claimed to be good because they imitated virtuous men of classical times. Luther made Christ the only virtue and made it impossible to speak of goodness in any way without calling Christ into the argument.

It does not require daring psychological insight to see that the almighty necessity of Christ in the definition of virtue and the all-powerful God who thunders out of this treatise against Latomus met deep personal needs in Luther. He was riddled with an existential torment—fear that was part of his being so that for him life and suffering were one. He was afraid of death; he was afraid of his fear of death. He was afraid of that which he could not understand—including the stubborn refusal of so many people, among them the young emperor, to see in scripture the clear truth of God that he found there. Luther's loneliness at the Wartburg was a living metaphor for the loneliness he felt within Christendom.

One response to this fear and loneliness was to write as furiously as he could against his foes. As is so with most of us, Luther's fury was greatest when he felt himself threatened in the ground of his being. His vehemence was self-validation. Another response was to urge his followers in Wittenberg to do likewise, to fill the presses with their own literary efforts to crush the serpent, so that he would not be left alone in his battle. Still another was to create in his mind a God who took everything into his own hand so that Luther did not have final responsibility to make things come out right.

Erasmus, as we have seen, was appalled by Luther's language. Melanchthon in his funeral oration years later would regret publicly Luther's constant ire. But this aggressive outpouring of wrath was for Luther himself a form of faith. He did not have to advance the gospel by political cunning or deft, manipulative rhetoric. It was all in the hands of God. In a letter of May 26, 1521, to Melanchthon he expressed the abiding faith of his mature years: "Let the ignorant remain ignorant, and whoever perishes, let him perish, and let them not be able to say that we have not done our duty to them."[18] Luther was an instrument in God's hand, and his attitude was a kind of fatalism, although he would not call it that. He would say that all was in the hands of God working things out so that in the end all would be well.

In his effort to ensure good doctrine from the pulpit, Luther threw himself into writing a "German Postil," a collection of brief sermons in the vernacular intended to be read by pastors to their congregations. (These were not published until the following year.)[19] They are interesting for many reasons, not least for how he conveyed his Reformation to congregations. These homilies are taken from the New Testament and are, as to be expected, sharply focused on Christ. Luther's Christology has been the subject of many worthy studies that seek to shape a precise, systematic theological image of what Luther found in Christ. But perhaps it is best to see Luther's Christ as constructed from what Luther needed. That construction hung then on whatever scriptural texts seemed to fit those needs.

Christ was the human shape of the presence of God whom he could approach in prayer and in adoration, a Christ who provided divine approval, consolation, and hope. As Marc Lienhard has observed, Luther's Christ was shaped by the apostle Paul and was summarized in Colossians 2:9, "For in him the whole fullness of deity dwells bodily."[20] This is the Christ of these homilies, God hidden in the Incarnation so that no one who looked at Christ on earth with the eye of natural reason alone could recognize him as God. Only with the light of faith can the hidden God be revealed.[21] One looks in vain in Luther for any philosophical explanation of how the divine and human natures are joined in Christ, the sort of ponderous stuff that agitated Greek theologians in the early centuries of Christianity with their talk of "hypostatic union" and names such as "monophysites" and "monothelites." Christ is, said Luther, "true God and man, who has created all things, and he is given to men as light and life, although few received him among those to whom he was revealed."[22]

Christ's gift to the Christian is a free and spontaneously devout and charitable life without any of the compulsion that comes from making religion a set of laws to be obeyed. In some of these sermons Luther provided hints of what he means by the predestination he teaches in his more technical works of theology. "What we do not do with our will," he wrote, "that do we not but it is done by the one who compels us. Should someone take my hand by force and use it to strike another and kill him or else use my hand to give alms to a poor man, the work would not be mine although my hand did it, but rather [the work of] the one who forced it. So the work neither harmed nor helped me at all."[23] A corollary of this notion is that in predestination God does not damn or save souls against their will but rather moves their will to correspond to what he has decided for their destiny.

Throughout these homilies, the frequency of attacks on natural reason in matters of faith is striking. Luther personified reason, making it an expression of Satan. In discussing the divine command to Abraham in Genesis 17 that circumcision should be the sign of the chosen people, Luther wrote of how foolish, ridiculous, and useless this command seemed in the light of natural reason. Yet Abraham obeyed it. Natural reason is, said Luther, "Frau Jezebel."[24] For Luther the gospel was as contrary to reason as circumcision was when it was first announced to Abraham. His frequent utterances on the subject sound defiant. I suspect that in all of them was the gnawing worm of doubt, and that his shrieking against reason was in part a cry of pain. Otherwise why this ferocious vehemence?

Faith is the only way to God, and as Luther presented it, faith seems always to have a warmhearted, existential content. It involves a personal, emotional binding with Christ. True faith is not merely to believe that the stories recounted in the Gospels are true; such belief "is no help, for all sinners and even the damned believe that." True faith, that faith filled with grace, is to know "that Christ was born for you, that his birth was for you, that it was all for your good."[25]

Yet the recurring emphasis on the need to put reason aside in matters of faith seems to indicate that this universal belief in the historical veracity of the Gospels might be only lip service in the audience Luther addressed. Among people without much historical sense it was probably as easy to profess faith in the historical record of the Gospels as it might have been to believe any number of legends handed down as true accounts of the past. But to make that faith part of the fabric of life, to make it present and vital, the continual reference point of all consciousness, was rare.

The backside of the attacks on reason is that Christ is to be found only in scripture. False spirits are everywhere. The word of God is our only light in an otherwise absolute darkness. When the Magi came from the East following the star, they asked King Herod only one question: "Where is the newborn King of the Jews?" (In his discussion of the Magi he made a distinction between those who studied nature in a spiritual way and those who by the help of Satan became witches and learned the secrets of nature for purposes of enchantment.)[26] "Let Herod inquire from the priests and the scribes. We ask only for the one born king. Let the universities ask, 'Where is Aristotle?' 'Where is the pope?' 'Where is Natural Reason?' 'Where is Bernard?' 'Where is Gregory?' 'Where are the councils?' 'Where are the Doctors?' We ask, 'Where is Christ?'"[27]

Luther was not above finding elaborate allegories in the scriptural texts he expounded in these sermons. In Luke 2:22–38, the baby Jesus is presented in the temple, and an old man named Simeon appears on the scene to testify that this child will be the Messiah. A woman prophet named Hannah who prays in the temple night and day confirms Simeon's prophecy. For Luther Simeon becomes an allegorical figure of the holy prophets who wrote of the coming of Christ, Hannah an allegory of those who listen to the prophets and confess Christ. She is the holy synagogue, the people of Israel written of in the Bible; the temple where all this takes place is an allegory of the scripture; and Mary is an allegory of the Christian people after the birth of Christ.[28]

All these homilies are couched in an implicit paradox. They are addressed to audiences of common folk who may be reached by the voice of pastors who have come over to the Lutheran side. They are intended to displace the crude miracle stories so common in popular preaching. Yet they assume that most people will not follow the true way of Christ. They assume that life for true Christians is the same profound existential experience that it was for Luther himself, and yet it was shortly to become evident that this kind of Christianity was not to be adopted by the masses who followed Luther voluntarily or else who became nominal converts, swept along by the political currents of the time. The eloquence of the homilies is striking, the metaphors and images falling in flashes of brilliance. If writers write first of all for themselves, as Flaubert claimed he did, Luther preached first of all for himself, putting his own experience with the Bible and with Christ into his sermons. But in the world to which those sermons were preached, their passion fell with disappointing effect that was to cause him anguish in the months and years to come.

Luther also wrote a separate commentary on the Magnificat, the Virgin Mary's song in response to Elizabeth, her cousin and the mother of John the Baptist, who called her blessed among women for the child Jesus she was about to bear. The story is told in the Gospel of Luke, and Mary's song has been for centuries the heart of Catholic veneration of the Virgin. Luther translated the song into German and provided a long and detailed commentary.

He always had a special place in his heart for Mary, and late in his life preached a fierce sermon against the Jews in which he explicitly affirmed his faith in the immaculate conception, the teaching that she had been born without original sin.[29] In his commentary on the Magnificat Luther strove to make Mary an example of the Christian life rather than the demigoddess that she was in popular imagination. She was the supreme example of the *Nichtigkeit,* the passivity before God's intervention in the soul that Luther felt was the mark of justification by faith. She was abandoned to God, surrendering all her will to him.[30] In no place in Luther's view was she the mediatrix with God, and he cautioned against exalting her powers. "She does nothing; God does all things."[31] Luther never made much of the saints in his early lectures on the Psalms, although at least one scholar has claimed that his faith in them remained unbroken until 1513—when he began those lectures.[32] The commentary on the Magnificat represented his mature conviction that no one but Christ could serve as mediator between God and humankind, and Mary became only a glowing example of what the power of God might do with one of His own.

His view of Mary followed the logic of his experience with Christ and his insistence that Christ was the center of his faith. The popular theology of the Middle Ages saw Christ portrayed in one extreme in the agonies of the cross and on the other as the stern judge presiding over the eternal destiny of souls at the last day. The Virgin Mary exemplified maternal love for sinful humanity, pleading with her son to be merciful. Luther could see that Mary's exaltation in Catholic belief rested on shaky scriptural foundations. The virgin birth of Christ is noted only in the Gospels of Matthew and Luke. It became a powerful myth, but the intent was probably not so much to exalt Mary as it was to establish that Jesus was truly human, that he was not a phantasm without a real body. The story of the virgin birth was probably told originally for the same reasons that the doctrine of transubstantiation later became codified in the church, to contradict docetic interpretations of Christ put forth by dualist sects who held that the physical was evil and the soul good and that the goal of true religion was to free the soul from the body. Nothing in scripture shows that Mary was considered a mediator with God, interceding with the Almighty for mercy to sinners. After the fifth century she was sometimes called a mediator of grace, but the term seems to have meant only that she had been the means of bringing Jesus into the world.

By September Luther was pondering another implication of his theology—the status of monastic vows. Here his concern was personal. To keep a rash vow, made in terror during a storm, he entered the monastery. Monks and nuns having taken vows and afterward fled the monastery could be severely punished in both canon and secular law. As we have seen, some men and women were forced to enter monastic life because their families could think of nothing else to do with them. Erasmus always claimed that his guardians had put him in the monastery so they could steal his inheritance. Luther wanted such people to be able to choose freedom without fear of retribution. Yet he also recognized a principle of evangelical freedom. Some men became monks out of a desire for the monastic life because the monastery suited their temperaments. Certainly at this moment in his defining of the Christian life, he had no idea to force people out of the monastery. He merely wanted to eliminate the idea that monks were superior because they were monks and therefore more likely to be redeemed.

To Melanchthon he wrote a long, studious letter on September 9 sifting arguments he would make in his treatise *Martin Luther's Judgment on Monastic Vows,* finished in November and published in Wittenberg early in 1522. Luther did not reject all vows. Some, like marriage, could be assumed with the "Christian liberty" that he proclaimed as part of the gospel, and once a husband and wife made their vows to each other, they were not free to violate those vows by divorce. Melanchthon had argued that vows should not be made if they could not be kept. Luther replied, somewhat tartly, that reasoning like that might abrogate the divine commandments—canons of moral conduct even when they could not be perfectly observed. The principle Luther followed was not whether it lay within human power to keep vows but the purpose for which the vow was made. If the vow was made as a bargain with God to obtain salvation as though by barter, Luther considered the vow idolatry.[33]

In his letter to Melanchthon, Luther mentioned his father's comment made when young Martin, newly ordained, performed his first mass. Martin had explained his own vow. His father had replied, "Let's hope it's not a trick of Satan." These words took root in his heart, Luther wrote, and he never heard his father speak afterward without thinking of them.[34] In token of this recollection, Luther dedicated his *Judgment on Monastic Vows* to Hans and prefaced it with a long "letter" addressed to his father.[35] In it he recalled how he had entered the monastery against his father's will and how Hans had resolved to "chain me up with an honorable and opulent marriage." Again he told the story of Hans's disappointment and wrath, his own efforts to stand against his father, and Hans's crushing rejoinder, "And have you not heard that you should obey your parents?"[36]

As Luther saw things, they had all worked out to the good. Satan had been the source of his vow, but God had used Satan's evil for his own purposes. By becoming a monk and living a monastic life without reproach for many years, Luther declared himself fit to denounce monasticism free from the reproach of enemies that he did not know what he was talking about. In the attention Satan gave him, Luther had, paradoxically, proof of his divine calling.

The body of the treatise became a passionate argument against irrevocable vows by men and women committing themselves to the monastery or convent and, inevitably, the vows priests took when they were ordained.[37] All clergy took vows of poverty, chastity, and obedience. The vow of chastity was an interdiction on marriage for any priest, monk, or nun. Already Luther had approved marriages by his followers in Wittenberg. Both Melanchthon and Karlstadt, his closest allies at the university, had taken wives.

This was heavy business. At least since the twelfth century a formal vow of celibacy had set clergymen—and monks and nuns not ordained—apart from the masses of people. Even before the formal vow began to be required, celibacy was expected of all clergy. It is difficult to find any point on which the great fathers of the church were more agreed than the requirement that clergy abstain from sex. The notion that Jerome, Augustine, Ambrose, Gregory, or legions of other great ascetic doctors should approve of clerical marriage was manifestly absurd, but one might ask if their consensus had been inspired by God. Catholic ways of thinking almost required that the answer to that question be yes. Christ had been born of a virgin; the notion persisted in the early church that the gift of prophecy—that is, the ability to speak with God's word—came only to those who abstained from the filthiness and the distractions of sex.[38] For Luther to declare that all this was not Christian was to bring down on his head not only accusations of novelty, which were bad enough, but also the charge—repeated for centuries—that his Reformation was fueled only by an unchaste burning in his loins.

Another inconvenient fact rose out of scripture itself. Paul in writing to his disciple Timothy spoke of widows who had apparently vowed chastity and broken their vows by marrying again. It looks as if widows had a special office in the early church that they could accept only if they remained unmarried and chaste. Young widows should marry and look after their children, said Paul. Their natural desires distract them from devotion to Christ, he said, and he implies that when they break their vow to remain unmarried and instead take a husband, they "have turned aside to follow Satan."[39] It would seem then that he regarded vows once made to be binding. Paul himself cut his hair at one point in his missionary journeys because of a vow he had made (Acts 18:18). Later he seems to have made a vow to God along with other men to show himself a proper Jew (Acts 21:23–26). Yet it seems that formal vows did not become commonplace for many centuries, perhaps because they were assumed to be unnecessary, given the common assumptions about priesthood.

In the *Judgment on Monastic Vows* the central question is which vows are valid and which are not. Monastic vows, in Luther's view, stand against the word of God and against Christ because they violate the freedom of the gospel and make religion a matter of rules, statues, orders, and divisions rather than a spontaneous relation to God through Christ. Some can remain virginal and some cannot, he says, but he finds it ridiculous to assume that virginity is superior to marriage. It is more a practical matter; the unmarried man can serve God better because he can live without the responsibility of taking care of a family. The notion that the celibate person attains a higher stage of perfection is abhorrent because it involves unbelief that Christ has done everything sufficient for our salvation.

With respect to the development of Catholic religious practices through the Middle Ages, Luther's insight regarding the human propensity in religion to multiply observances so that they become justification for the observances themselves seems acutely correct. Wylie Sypher, in his *Four Stages of Renaissance Style,* made the point that baroque art and architecture was intended to create overwhelming feelings to counteract the attacks of heresy and doubt. "This art," he observed, "speaks with the voluminous tones of a new orthodoxy . . . the Council of Trent announced its decrees with majestic voice; it overwhelmed heresy by splendor; it did not argue, but proclaimed; it brought conviction to the doubter by the very scale of its grandeurs; it guaranteed truth by magniloquence. The baroque style reaches its decisions through spectacle."[40] How can one deny the validity of the saints when saints are pictured and sculpted in huge and emotional representations, arousing an awe that transcends doubt? Yet in a curious paradox the doubts are the origin of the art, for if the doubts had not existed, the art would not have been created to combat them, or at least it would not have taken the forms it did.

In like manner, Luther's point seems to be that some Christians deal with unbelief by multiplying observances such as monastic vows. If they have taken these vows and observed celibacy and followed all the other observances common to monks, their practice and outward professions come to be a substitute for faith itself. Since the issue of faith is avoided by being submerged in observance and "law," the religion that results is hollow at the core and results in hypocrisy that cannot distinguish form from substance. For Luther faith is the radical commitment to the belief that God has done everything in Christ, and that commitment goes alongside the equally radical knowledge that faith always includes the fear that it may not be true. Faith is a commitment to life while knowing that death couches at the door.

To subject faith to examination by reason is to kill faith. A significant pointer in Luther's thought occurs early in his attack on monastic vows. He has alluded to the teaching of the *via moderna* that it is good to be uncertain about one's salvation, for then we are not likely to plunge into the evil works that result from both presumption and despair. But in response to this teaching, Luther interposes Christ between the believer and God the judge. "If Christ is for us and is mine," says he, echoing and expanding the words of Paul to the Romans, "Who is against me?"[41] So, he says a few lines later, the thoughts of men are fearful, but God does not wish us to dwell on them. It is his acknowledgment that the Christian life is not free of doubts and of the most distressing and radical sort, but that in response to these doubts the Christian is to return again and again to Christ.

The issue goes far deeper than the traditional historical wisdom that Luther's doubts were only about whether God could save him. Rather, he had to fight off the persistent temptation to question whether a God exists who can save *anybody*. It seems plausible to link these continual fears that Luther describes to the fear of death, death that is always for him God's judgment on sin. These fears are made more intense by his frequently expressed comment—very much like Occam's—that reason cannot prove the existence of the personal God of Christianity. Reason without faith denies that the dead shall be raised.[42] Reason cannot assent to the belief that Christ was God incarnate and that the Trinity exists. But, Luther said in his table talk, "I learned out of scripture against the greatest agony and temptation that Christ is God and that he took on flesh . . . Therefore I do not so much as believe but know by experience that these articles [of faith] are true."[43]

So the essence of faith was to keep coming back to the invisible Christ and to renounce all the "rational" props—such as logic or a life lived out according to formal vows of poverty, chastity, and obedience—which were vain human efforts to push away the unbelief that they in fact symbolized. A major element of this faith appears to be continual talking and writing about it; thus every time Luther spoke or wrote he engaged in an act of worship that created anew in his mind in that moment the Christ who thrust back the ever-present doubt in every serious thought about God. Christ for Luther was like a campfire projecting a circle of light against the vast dark of earthly life. Whenever the darkness threatened to encroach upon that illuminated ground, Luther flung more of his volatile ink onto the fire, causing it to flame up again in his own heart, and keeping the darkness at bay.

For Luther virginity became an indifferent matter. Those who wanted to be virgins could be so; those who did not could marry and live as honorably before God as any virgin. If anyone made a vow to remain celibate, he or she could retract it at will. Luther made a distinction between vows made to God and contracts, such as marriage, made between mortals. A man was not free to desert his wife because he no longer chose to observe the vow he had made to her. "The liberty of the gospel governs only in relations between God and you, not between you and your neighbor."[44] Contracts were as necessary to human society as reason itself, although like reason they had no business in relations with an almighty God.

Luther's words rolled on and on. Erasmus, who hated monks and monasticism, decried Luther's vehemence, but a couple of years later, when Duke George of Saxony sent him a copy of the *Judgement on Monastic Vows* (which he had already seen), urging him to refute it, Erasmus replied obliquely that he had received the work and begun to read it. "I see it is verbose," he said.[45] He never wrote the refutation the duke George sought.

Somehow Luther also found time to write a couple of important and popular treatises on sacramental practice. One was a German work, *On Confession: Whether the Pope Has Power to Regulate It.*[46] Not surprisingly, the answer to the indirect question he poses is "no." He drew manifold examples from the Bible to prove that confession of sins did not require a priest commissioned by the pope to handle confession in a ritual, sacramental way. Christians were to confess their sins to one another. One of his citations was "James the Apostle who counseled his readers to confess their sins to one another."[47] Soon in his translation of the New Testament Luther was to say harsh words about this "James" and to deny that he was an apostle. But as we shall see, Luther was always willing to pick up a text of scripture that spoke to him, whether he found it in one of the lesser works or one in whose authority he firmly believed. For those who fell into open sins, Luther recommended that the pastor and the congregation admonish him openly in church "between the Mass and the gospel."[48] The sinner who refused to reform should be thrust out of the church, and no one was to have anything to do with him. So regulation of the moral life became a congregational responsibility, and the formal liturgical practice of penance was to be dissolved. With it would go the chain of legal relations that ran from the local confessional to the pope as supreme judge regarding matters of satisfaction and excommunication. Here Luther seems to have come close to the practice in the very early church.

In a warmly grateful preface, he dedicated the work to Franz von Sickingen, the petty German knight and warlord who had stood ready to come to his aid at Worms with a private army. Luther's attitude toward Sickingen looks ambiguous and raises a problem. Luther steadfastly opposed rebellion against authority by the common people. He still held out hope for the young Emperor Charles. He was grateful for the support of the Elector Frederick. But in all this was a nest of questions. Suppose Charles continued his fierce opposition to Luther—as he did. Did Sickingen have a right to armed resistance that a commoner did not have? Luther's dedication of a little book is not a theological statement. But it represents the beginning of a justification for the horrifying religious wars that went on well into the seventeenth century. Common folk without aristocratic leadership could not resist divinely ordained authority—such as an emperor or even a great prince. But a petty warlord like Sickingen seemed in Luther's mind to have a right to resistance and, some would say, rebellion.

In his other sacramental treatise, *The Misuse of the Mass,* published in both a Latin and a German version, Luther struck out at private masses.[49] Under this staple of medieval piety, priests were paid by an endowment to say masses for the souls of the dead. The theory that allowed such a practice was that the priest made a renewed sacrifice every time he lifted the host and pronounced the words of institution, and that sacrifice was a "good work" that could be transferred to the credit of the name of the person in whose name it was done. It was a comforting practice, implicitly assuming the existence of purgatory. Yet the doctrine of purgatory was probably not as important as the simple psychological benefit of assuring the living that they could reach beyond death to help the souls of those they loved.

Luther attacked the practice all the way down the line. Priesthood was not a special status. All believers were priests. The mass was not a sacrifice; therefore it was not a "good work" whose value could be assigned mechanically to someone else. Christ had made the one sacrifice necessary for our salvation, and priests had no power to repeat it. The mass could not be a good work to help us to salvation because no work we do was adequate for such a desire.

Much of this longish work is given over to denunciations of the Catholic clergy. Luther had not been so sharp earlier against the clergy as a whole, perhaps because he thought that many priests would come over to his movement. But now he extended his denunciations from the pope downward. A true priesthood and a false priesthood existed among Christians. In this treatise Luther saw no middle ground between them, and his general broadside against the Catholic priesthood is fierce.[50]

He was also concerned about an issue rising in Wittenberg—communion in both kinds, offering both the bread and the wine, the body and the blood of Christ, to the laity during the Eucharist. To those back in Wittenberg who wanted to get on with the Reformation, here was a matter of high symbolic importance. If the priest continued to partake alone of the wine, the superiority of priesthood over ordinary Christians seemed crashingly affirmed. If all believers were priests, why should all believers—both ministers and laity—not also partake of both bread and wine? Luther advised caution. Despite all his fulminating against priesthood, he knew almost instinctively that the power of sacred ceremonies lies in the comforts of repetition and familiarity and the sentiment that one is partaking of a rite that binds the ages together. He recognized how upset many religious people become when a particle of their time-honored rituals is changed, and for the moment he thought too many Wittenbergers were not ready for changing this fundamental observance.

Luther also began his most prodigious literary achievement in the Wartburg—his translation of the Bible into German. While he remained in hiding, the forces he had set in motion rolled on, and as he labored with almost incredible energy during what amounts to the only sabbatical he had in his adult life, events conspired to bring him back to Wittenberg.

18

BACK TO WITTENBERG

WHILE Luther remained in the Wartburg, leadership in Wittenberg fell into the hands of more radical spirits stirred by the divine logic of fanatics in all the ages: If we are certain of the truth, we should act upon it right away no matter what the consequences. Luther had uncovered the gospel. Hasty men now sprang up to claim divine sanction for breaking down the worn and corrupt old religious habits that had deadened the hearts of Christians everywhere and for raising in their place a cleansed temple of faith constructed stone by gleaming stone on the pure word of God.

Philipp Melanchthon was the jewel of the faculty left at the university, and he enjoyed Luther's trust and affection. In the months Luther spent in the Wartburg, Melanchthon wrote the *Loci Communes*, the "commonplaces" of agreement about the content of the new evangelical theology. It is a brief, clearly written compendium of Luther's teachings, and like nearly everything Melanchthon wrote, it went through many editions and innumerable printings. Throughout his life Luther praised it, saying it surpassed all his own work.[1] But Melanchthon was young and lacked the temper of a leader. Besides, he was not ordained and had no authority to preach, and he was in the faculty of arts rather than theology.

More than willing to take events in hand were two lesser men, Andreas Bodenstein von Karlstadt (1486–1541) and Gabriel Zwilling, both authorized to preach and both eager to plunge ahead in reform of the church according to their view of Luther's principles.

We have met Karlstadt before. He was the intended representative of Wittenberg's "new theology" for the debate with Johann Eck at Leipzig. In retrospect he seems to have carried through life the taint of failure and the second rate. Luther's later judgments of him were harsh. "He thought that he was the only learned man in the world," he said. "Whatever I wrote he imitated, but gave it another color."[2] A sympathetic modern scholar concedes that Karlstadt had an "exasperating and volatile personality."[3] Karlstadt joined the faculty at Wittenberg in 1505 as professor of scholastic theology. At the time he was devoted to Aquinas and opposed the teachings of the *via moderna* that had influenced Luther. He took his doctorate in 1510 and went to Rome in 1515 and took another doctorate in canon law early the next year. His interest in law seems to indicate a certain ambition to advance in the church. He may have hoped to become an archdeacon and thence to ascend to a bishopric.[4]

Like Luther he was appalled by the scandalous behavior he observed at the papal court. As Luther's influence waxed within Wittenberg University, Karlstadt opposed him, defending scholastic theology against Luther's Augustinianism. Luther remarked later on that when he became a doctor, Karlstadt did not own a Bible.[5] In January 1517 he journeyed to Leipzig to buy the works of Augustine to refute Luther, but his reading converted him to Luther's position.[6] He then became more Augustinian than Augustine himself, following Luther to the position that the person justified by faith nevertheless sinned in all his good works—although God did not charge the sin against a divine account.[7]

Karlstadt's conversion offers a key to his character. He seemed always ready to leap to the more radical side. Luther once said that Karlstadt had not experienced suffering in his quest for faith. It was Luther's way of saying that his colleague was superficial; he never thought much of Karlstadt's intellect. A modern student of his work, Erich Hertzsch, has said that Karlstadt was not much concerned with the question "How may I be certain of salvation?" Yet it seems clear that Karlstadt imbibed the spirit of a group of lay Christians in Wittenberg who saw possibilities in religious liberty opened to them by Luther's movement, possibilities that Luther himself rejected, just as he ultimately rejected the confidence he had so powerfully asserted in his cherished doctrine of the priesthood of all believers. Karlstadt was far more "democratic" than Luther. Hertzsch says that Luther loved the common folk but did not trust them. Karlstadt trusted commoners to lead the Reformation and tried to become a commoner himself. And why not? Most of the disciples of Jesus were fishermen if they were anything, and none was known to be an intellectual. Paul knew classical literature and had a good education, but he never knew Jesus "in the flesh." Through all the Christian centuries the lure of the simplicity of innocence has had powerful attraction to many.

Karlstadt was not a monk. He was a secular priest, an archdeacon, and his experience with the people of Wittenberg brought him close to them. His confidence in them was the foundation and cornerstone of his theological thought and churchly practice.[8]

Karlstadt seemed always unlucky, a man quick to persuade himself that he was about to become admiral of the ocean sea of theology, only to rush onto ships about to sink in ponds.

In Denmark King Christian II saw possibilities in Luther's Reformation. Christian was unpopular, with a streak of cruelty and a penchant for public adulteries. He found himself at odds with his nobility, who resented his efforts to reduce their feudal powers. He sought to give privileges to his cities and to build up their commerce. Given his will to power, it is not surprising that he came in conflict with the Catholic clergy in his land and saw in Luther's doctrines a means of undermining clerical authority. He sent a representative to Wittenberg in the spring of 1521 hoping to bring back Luther and Karlstadt. Since Luther was otherwise engaged, Karlstadt accepted the invitation in May and went to Copenhagen.

He set out to impose reformation as quickly as possible, changing the worship services to the vernacular, and allowing clergy to marry. Christian backed him until suddenly in June the king changed his mind. Christian was married to a sister of Charles V. He hoped to get from Charles imperial sanction to bind the black-soiled fields of Holstein more closely to Denmark, but to do so he had to enforce the Edict of Worms against Luther. Karlstadt was back in Wittenberg—not entirely welcome—by June 21.[9]

There he continued to seek leadership in Luther's absence. He raged against vows of celibacy and encouraged priests and monks to take wives. In his view, sexual abstinence caused desires that wrecked the purity of a priest's life and filled it with devilish lusts and inner conflict no matter what outward sanctity might seem to prevail.[10] (Luther came to have the same opinions.) Karlstadt warred against the use of images in Christian worship and attacked the use of Gregorian chant, which, he said, "separates the spirit from God."[11] In many respects Karlstadt's radicalism in Wittenberg mirrored his work in Denmark—an absolutist impulse that followed an iron logic, the fundamentalist mentality of all the ages and all religions. Since Truth was clear, society should be reformed in Truth's image.

Zwilling (1487–1558) took the Latinized version of his name, Gabriel Didymus. He was one of the first of the Augustinian monks in Wittenberg to accept Luther's doctrines, and in late November 1521 he was the first monk to leave the monastery. Soon the departure of monks from the Augustinian cloister became an exodus, and the cloister finally bade those who desired to leave to go in peace.[12] Zwilling was a powerful preacher, compared by auditors to Luther himself, and like Karlstadt he was impatient to reform church practice from the bottom up. When anyone saw a monk in the streets, he said, one should make the sign of a cross (as though meeting a demon), pull on his coat, and mock him.[13] Melanchthon seemed enthralled by him. It was said that Melanchthon never missed one of Zwilling's sermons.[14]

At the heart of Catholic worship was the Eucharist, and Luther had already argued for communion in both kinds, for the sharing of both bread and wine, body and blood, with the laity. Within the Augustinian cloister the monks began privately celebrating the Mass as a communal meal—as the institution of the sacrament is described in the New Testament—passing bread and wine to everyone whether ordained or not. Students harassed priests and monks who refused to come over to the new doctrines. The Elector Frederick wavered. His authority over the city was not absolute, since the city council was elected by citizens, controlled its own treasury, police, and administration, and also regulated the guilds of artisans.[15] The right to vote extended to most males, even to those who did not own property.[16] Now Frederick and Spalatin became worried that unrest might break into riot.

Luther slipped into Wittenberg late in the afternoon of December 4. He may have remained ten days—long enough for Lucas Cranach to make the sketches that he reworked into his portrait of Luther as Junker George. Luther had been impatient with Spalatin for delaying publication of his *Judgment on Monastic Vows* and wanted to push the work through the press. Since he seems to have left quietly to avoid letting the elector know he was there, he had little opportunity see how high passions were running. He offered no reproach to the rampaging students. Did he know what they were doing? It is hard to say. I suspect that he thought they would further his cause, and Melanchthon probably put the best possible light on things.

Luther's major concerns lay elsewhere. Archbishop Albrecht of Mainz was authorized by the pope to exhibit a prodigious number of relics in the monastic church at Halle and to sell indulgences to pilgrims who came to see them. The church at Halle had 9,000 relics, many of them body parts of saints, and forty-two complete bodies by which one might achieve thirty-nine million years of release from purgatory. The relics included some of the mud God had used to make Adam, part of the burning bush Moses had seen in the wilderness, several vessels of milk from the Virgin Mary, and the finger Thomas had placed in the side of the risen Jesus.[17]

Luther wrote a scalding attack on the exposition and on December 1 addressed a vigorous letter to Albrecht himself. The letter, written hastily in German on the supposition that Albrecht could not understand Latin, is couched in formal terms of respect. But it threatens the wrath of God if Albrecht should continue to display this "Idol at Halle"—that is, the relics with their accompanying indulgences. It contained an ultimatum. If Albrecht did not cancel the sale of indulgences, Luther promised to attack him directly "and show the world [the] difference between a bishop and [a] wolf. On this knowledge Your Highborn Princely Grace can decide what judgment to make and how to behave."[18]

Spalatin—doubtless acting on the elector's instruction—refused to let Luther's attack be published. About December 5, Luther wrote Spalatin a brief but defiant letter. "I want what I have written to be published, if not at Wittenberg then elsewhere. If the copies are lost or if you are holding onto them, my spirit will be all the more irritated, and I shall nevertheless set myself to write much more vehemently on this subject." Almost as a postscript he said of his brief visit to Wittenberg, "Everything that I saw and heard pleases me mightily."[19] Perhaps his wrath made him wink at the uproar in the city—or he may have had only a slight idea of the seriousness of the situation.

That uproar was considerable but by no means riotous. The day before Luther arrived in town, students disrupted the mass at the castle church. As tempers rose, they went further, threatening the Franciscan monastery, which remained obdurately against Luther. It was said that some students drew knives, but no blows seem to have been struck. Partisans of Luther presented other demands for reform. The elector and the council became increasingly alarmed. From the Wartburg Luther wrote an open letter titled *A True Admonition to All Christians to Guard against Insurrection and Rebellion*.[20] The editors of the Weimar texts think it probable that he was pushed into writing it to clear himself from the suspicion of favoring insurrection, and they hint that he did so somewhat reluctantly.[21]

We know that Luther was furious with Spalatin—and by extension with the elector—for withholding publication of the *Judgment on Monastic Vows*. Given his previous expression of mighty approval of all he had seen in Wittenberg, he may have thought that the uproar was God's way of pushing the elector more firmly toward the gospel. Whatever his motives, he now took note of the danger of riot, although he refused to panic. For the moment he retained his confidence in the goodwill of "true Christians," who should know that rebellion was always wrong. But he sought to apply the brakes on the rush to freedom from Catholic practices. Give God's word time. Shortly it would triumph without need for force and violence. God's wrath would come on the papacy, he said. Artists showed Christ on the rainbow with a rod and a sword in his mouth. The government of the papal

Antichrist would be destroyed with the word of Christ, which was the spirit, rod, and sword of his mouth, and his crimes and shame would be exposed to all the world. So Christians should be patient and not rush to do what God would accomplish. Already that destruction had begun; the crimes of the papacy were revealed to all. No man was such a fool as to follow open lies and falsehood rather than hate them. In the meantime, Christians should remember the weak and not offend them. Altogether it was a remarkably calm, almost serene statement. It is a benchmark by which to measure his expectations and so to understand his later disappointment, pessimism, and depressions.

Even while Luther was writing this appeal for calm, Karlstadt became more the biblical literalist. Since New Testament Christians had not been said to use musical instruments in worship services, he wanted to abandon organ music in church. Increasingly he exalted the working man as the Christian paragon. A craftsman, he said, knew more about the Bible than a bishop.[22] His impulse was toward a more democratic Christianity in which class differences might be broken down. On Christmas Eve a huge crowd pushed its way into the traditional celebration of the Mass and disrupted it. It was a raucous affair. Some people threw lead balls—probably bullets—at a priest. Instead of traditional hymns, the crowd burst out with folk songs, including one called "A Maid Has Lost Her shoe."[23]

On Christmas Day, dressed not in the vestments of a priest but in a plain gown, Karlstadt presided at a mass in the castle church, and the 2,000 to 2,500 people packed into the building partook of both the bread and the wine.[24] James Preus has pointed out that even hostile accounts of this service do not report riotous behavior. The size of the crowd indicates hearty popular support for Karlstadt and a religious fervor on the part of those not in the habit of attending church. Preus thinks that Karlstadt may have kept the situation orderly by yielding to public opinion, which desired a lay-centered mass.[25] For those who remained loyal to traditional Catholic practices, the spectacle was abhorrent—especially since in the inevitable confusion some of the bread fell to the floor.[26] Moreover, Karlstadt had not required those who partook of the Mass to confess to a priest or to fast beforehand—another scandal to traditional believers.

The next day Karlstadt accompanied by Melanchthon and Justus Jonas went out to the village of Segrehna and publicly celebrated his engagement to a fifteen-year-old girl, Anna von Mochau. She was the daughter of a penniless nobleman and by some reports not pretty. The marriage followed with great fanfare on January 19.[27] Karlstadt invited the elector; Frederick did not come. Karlstadt intended his wedding to be a grand affair. He sent printed invitations to everyone he could think of, and eventually these were reprinted and circulated all over Germany with mocking commentary by Catholic wits ready to scorn the alacrity with which Luther's followers forsook vows for the pleasures of the marriage bed. Luther approved of the wedding. He knew the girl. He thought Karlstadt would be a good example to other priests contemplating marriage.[28] As chance would have it, on the day after Karlstadt's marriage, the representatives of Charles V in Germany ordered Wittenberg to give up its reforms and to return to old practices. Was there power among the imperial forces to back up such commands? No one could be sure. The threat seemed dangerous.

In the meantime, shortly after Christmas more radical men came into Wittenberg, drawn by the possibilities of a fluid situation. Among them were some from the weaving town of Zwickau, the wealthiest town in electoral Saxony, three times larger than the city of Dresden.[29] Zwickau included a class of wealthy merchants and industrialists, but it also numbered a large and motley working class suffering unemployment, burdened with debts, and often reduced to begging. Added to the mix were silver miners who had been thrust out of their holdings by associations, precursors of the joint stock companies that would become a common feature of European capitalism.[30] These disgruntled, hopeless people provided fertile ground for radicalism. Perhaps the fact that Zwickau was also a great brewing town helped things along.

The radicals included one Nicholas Storch, a weaver able to quote the Bible at supendous length although he may have been illiterate. Another, Marcus Stübner, claimed to be able to read minds. Weavers had radical leanings throughout Europe in the later Middle Ages. The looms in their great sheds brought weavers and their helpers close together, allowed them to talk, to share a sense of abuse and hope, and provided a classic example of the Marxist view of how the instruments of production serve to organize labor against rich and powerful owners of the means of production. Storch and his friends represented one of the perils of depending on the Bible as sole authority for faith. They rejected the baptism of infants because throughout the New Testament, faith was the essential prerequisite for baptism, and babies were not capable of asserting faith. Yet to abolish infant baptism seemed to deprive children of the benefit of the sacrament that most typified victory over death and to lessen the communal bonds of the church itself.

More threatening was the claim of Storch and his allies of immediate divine inspiration, that God spoke to them directly to interpret scripture and through them uttered commands to his people. And why not? Throughout the Bible God speaks directly to his prophets, telling them his will for the moment. The God of the Bible is living, and he speaks. Why should he keep silent in the Sixteenth Century while great events were afoot? How *could* he keep silent? But what would he say? Karlstadt never claimed special revelation of the sort touted by these "prophets."[31] But Melanchthon saw the logic of their theology, and he seems to have been impressed by Storch. He thought they might be God's messengers. He wrote to Luther asking for advice.

Luther replied in a cautious letter of January 13. What was the proper Christian response to those claiming private revelation? He said it was to ask whether those claiming it had suffered anguish of spirit by their encounter with God. He reeled off biblical quotations to demonstrate that those who met God in biblical accounts were terrified. God was a consuming fire. Those who claimed private revelation and spoke sweetly, calmly, zealously, and in scrupulous detail even if they were caught up into the third heaven should not be approved. Worthy Christians had experienced God as Luther had—as a threat to one's very being. He also declared that from what he had heard these "prophets" had done nothing to prove they were not inspired by Satan—again showing one of the essential problems of the age, the sense of illusion everywhere, and the corresponding inability to discriminate between divine revelation and satanic plot.[32]

In a curious paradox, this letter revealed some of Luther's weaknesses against the storm of Catholic attack rising against him. He himself would be regularly accused of claiming private revelation against the tradition of the church for centuries. Once upon a time, he said, anyone who claimed private revelation had it certified by someone else. When the child Samuel heard the voice of God calling him, Eli the priest testified that it was so. Luther placed himself in this line so that the truly godly men of his own time would affirm his divine call. But as Catholics were to point out time and again, this attitude begged the question. These ancient prophets of the Hebrew Bible also had their prophetic mission validated by "signs," *signa*. "Signs" as used in the biblical text, especially in the Fourth Gospel, denote miracles, and Luther could claim no miracles to confirm his divine mission. Even Erasmus would throw this barb at him. Perhaps the constancy of these attacks moved Luther to the opinion that the word of God came to the church through its appointed ministers, those able to interpret with their own voices the Word for their time.[33] As Heiko Oberman has observed, Luther never grounded his own authority either in special revelation or in deep mystical experience.[34] He claimed only to be an expositor of scripture. Yet his reading of scripture at this time involved tortured and allegorical interpretations, and his reasoning had a circular quality that foes were quick to point out and ridicule.

A further problem rose about the baptism of infants—another issue raised by the Zwickau prophets and soon taken up by Karlstadt. Luther affirmed the position he had taken in the *Babylonian Captivity*, and it was not strong. He quoted Mark 16:16—as it happens, a spurious text, one that does not appear in early manuscripts: "He that believeth and is baptized shall be saved." He seemed to equate baptism with belief, as if the act of immersing a child in water introduced the infant to God's protection. "That these little ones do not believe by themselves absolutely does not move me in any way," he wrote. And then, as if pondering the matter further, he said in the next sentence, "And by what way can they [the Zwickau prophets] prove that they [the children] do not believe?"[35] God preserves our faith in us while we are asleep; in the same way he may give faith to children in their infancy as though they were in a kind of sleep. The notion may refer to predestination. Predestination stands above time, in the timeless realm of God's will. The predestined child is redeemed already by God's grace; why should it not be baptized? Luther pointed to numerous ways in which biblical characters had prayed for others, bringing them to God. Why could parents not do the same for their children?

We can follow his frustration through one sentence after another, as if he found himself wrestling with an insoluble problem. He could not deny the gift of baptism to children—this in an age when every family expected to lose children to disease in infancy, as Luther himself would eventually lose a beloved daughter. But infant baptism is not sanctioned by scripture. Finally he appealed to the authority of tradition. He considered it a singular miracle of God that the doctrine that infants should be baptized had never been denied by any heretic in history and that it was the accepted doctrine throughout the world. It was a contradiction within his own thought. On the one hand he stood for scripture alone as the authority for belief and practice, and the New Testament seems unambiguous in its association of baptism and salvation—even in texts other than the spurious command Luther quoted from Mark. Luther stood for faith alone as the response of the Christian. So if children were to be saved, they had to be baptized, and some means had to be found to allow them faith for this initial sacrament. His own uncertainty on the issue emerged at the end of the letter. "I always expected Satan to touch this ulcer," he wrote. "But he did not wish to do it through the papists. It is among ourselves and among our own that this grave schism is set in motion, but Christ truly will quickly crush it under our feet."[36] In fact the issues raised in this letter were to plague Luther and his movement and to divide evangelicals from that time to this.

Not everything in Wittenberg was chaos. On January 24 the governing council of the city, led by Karlstadt, passed an ordinance intended to put into operation its own view of reformation. It established a "common chest" intended to provide help for the poor and the sick in the city—taking seriously the assertions of Luther and others (including Catholic writers such as Erasmus and Thomas More) that it was better for Christians to take care of the poor than to support lavish ceremony in the church. Images were to be cast out of the churches. The Mass was changed; communion was to be in both kinds: both the bread and the wine, the body and the blood of Christ in the Eucharist, was to be given to both clergy and laity. The bread and the wine were to be passed from hand to hand among the communicants and not distributed to each by a priest. Begging by monks was forbidden, and the brothels were closed.[37] Frederick moved quickly to frustrate these measures; nothing official was to be done about religion in Wittenberg without his consent. For Luther this ordinance was too much too soon; it regulated worship by law, and he felt worship should rise spontaneously from the heart. He must also have been disturbed at the elector's antagonism to many known to be Luther's friends and at Karlstadt's seeming willingness to defy Frederick.

Karlstadt and the others pushed forward. Their aim was to make Wittenberg a Christian city in profession and deed. Between January 27 and February 5 some images were apparently destroyed, perhaps cut up and burned. Karlstadt declared that Christ had not set aside the Old Testament law, and that law had been sternly against idolatry, against worshiping the creature rather than the creator.[38]

Bound up with this sentiment against "idolatry" came new and dangerous attitudes toward the Eucharist. In the ritual of the Mass, the priest traditionally adored the elements, the body and the blood of Christ in the form of bread and wine. Drifting into Wittenberg now were fervent spirits from various places in Europe, including some from Holland, where a layman, Cornelisz Hendrixz Hoen (c. 1460–1524), had propounded the belief that the bread and the wine in the Eucharist remained as they were, untransformed by miracle during the Mass. Bread and wine were only symbols of the body and blood of Christ. The Eucharist should provoke in Christians a vivid memory of the sufferings of the son of God for the sins of humankind, but it was idolatry to adore the elements and bad doctrine to teach even the "real presence" of Luther's theology, that the body and blood of Christ were physically joined to the bread and wine in the Mass. Whatever the origins, these ideas spread in Wittenberg. Zwilling and Karlstadt took them up, and even Melanchthon wavered.[39]

Meanwhile Luther's stature was acknowledged in a somewhat inverted way by Albrecht of Mainz. In response to Luther's letter denouncing him for the display of relics at Halle, Albrecht wrote Luther a respectful letter on December 21, beginning with the salutation "Beloved Doctor." Albrecht said that the abuses Luther condemned had already been halted, and he promised to behave as "a spiritual and Christian prince ought to conduct himself, as far as God will grant me grace, strength, and reason." Continuing, he said, "I confess that I need the grace of God because I am a poor, sinful man who can sin and err and that I daily sin and go astray I do not deny. I know that without the grace of God nothing good is in me and that I am nothing more than a stinking piece of shit."[40] The brief letter in Albrecht's own hand is a remarkable epistle from an archbishop to a man condemned and excommunicated by the pope for heresy. It shows Luther's charismatic authority at that moment in Germany.

On the same day, Wolfgang Capito, Albrecht's chancellor, wrote a longer, conciliatory letter to Luther.[41] It was also a letter of admonition. Capito was a friend of Erasmus, and he followed Erasmus's view that vehement religious controversy could incite the masses to violence and cause infinite bloodshed. He defended Albrecht's sincerity and piety and suggested that the archbishop might help Luther, perhaps obliquely, with Rome. Albrecht was striving to do better, and many men in his court were devoted to Luther's welfare and his teachings—although Capito thought the marriage of priests would lead to trouble. He advised Luther to be patient with Albrecht and to trust him, and not to attack him.

The idea that the archbishop might come over to Luther's side was not farfetched. Albrecht was a protean character, interested in learning, eager to seem Erasmian in his interest in reforming the church. For a time Ulrich von Hutten was his secretary, and the call of Capito to his court in 1520 was a sign of Albrecht's reforming interests. (Capito would soon leave the archbishop's service and go over wholeheartedly to the Reformation.) Albrecht withstood the foes of Reuchlin in their frenzy to burn Hebrew books. In the same spirit he asked Erasmus in the fall of 1519 for advice about Luther, unwilling to accept at face value the fulminations of Rome. Erasmus responded with a long epistle written as though to one interested in reform and absorbed with "good letters" rather than useless debates of scholastic theology.[42] Maybe Albrecht was faking and maneuvering, trying to work out his advantage. A recent scholar has declared that he never felt personal involvement with the theological issues of the Reformation.[43] He may have considered the possibility of taking his bishopric out of the church and turning it into a hereditary territory—a practice later followed by several German bishops who converted to Luther's doctrines. Albrecht never went so far. His plump effigy remains over his tomb in the cathedral of Mainz to this day, testimony to his decision to stay with the old church.

Luther was no political manipulator. He replied sharply to Capito. Albrecht continued to forbid priests in his domains to marry, to separate priests already married from their wives—and to keep open the brothels in towns subject to him.[44] (Albrecht would eventually keep a kind of harem for himself in Halle.)[45] Luther's letter to Capito burns with righteous indignation—combined with protestations of respect and obedience. Luther was willing to obey any command unrelated to his developing faith; but he was unwilling to compromise or to be patient or to mitigate his language when something important to faith was at stake.

Very much in that mood he continued to refuse to declare himself wholeheartedly against the movement toward ever more radical reform in Wittenberg. On February 22 he wrote a somewhat jocular letter to the Elector Frederick, who had for so long been avid to collect relics. Now, said Luther, Frederick had a new relic, a whole cross—meaning the tumult raised in Wittenberg by the gospel. It was the nature of life that Satan was among the children of God, that Judas was among the apostles.[46] Perhaps his "Judas" was Karlstadt.[47] Again Luther's mood was active resignation. God was working; troubles would come; but things would work out, for God was finally in charge.

Frederick was not amused. Occasional riotous attacks on images and conservative clergy made it seem that Wittenberg was in anarchy. Duke George at Leipzig was fulminating against Wittenberg, and Frederick feared a military alliance, perhaps even a crusade, against himself. He despatched a messenger, John Oswald, to speak with Luther, giving him a memorandum on what to say. The elector was worried. People were observing the Mass in different ways, some wearing the priestly garb, some not; the divisions were unseemly. Students were leaving the university on account of the turmoil. Above all, Frederick feared isolation. If Luther were to return, the emperor might enforce the Edict of Worms, and the elector would be unable to help more than he had already. It would perhaps be better for Luther to remain in hiding until the upcoming Diet at Nuremberg, when perhaps the affair might be settled to Luther's advantage. The elector saw positive signs, especially in Meissen, where the bishop seemed to be in a reforming mood. It would seem better for Luther to stay put. Yet in the end Frederick expressed the attitude that had carried him thus far on Luther's behalf. He would not be pleased, he told his agent, to stand in the way of God's will and work. He concluded with expressions of goodwill to Luther.[48] He did not forbid Luther to return. It may be, as Preus suggests, that the city council of Wittenberg itself extended an invitation to Luther to come back.[49]

Luther responded humbly enough and even with apology. He was unwavering in his resolve, and his letter illustrates his lifelong habit of dealing with princes whom he did not find malicious. He spoke firmly and boldly and with a confidence in his own convictions that modern readers will find heroic or arrogant, depending on their taste. He wrote passionately and unequivocally against the unrest among his partisans in Wittenberg. It had brought the gospel into disgrace. He would willingly have given his life had it been possible thereby to avoid this calamity. It was enough to make him despair and renounce the whole cause unless he was certain that he and his followers possessed the true gospel. Of that Luther had no doubt. "Yet for my part, gracious lord, I answer thus: Your Highborn Princely Grace knows—or, if you do not know, receive herewith this message—that I have the gospel not from men but only from heaven through our Lord Jesus Christ, that I might be able to declare and write, as I shall henceforth, that I am a slave and evangelist."[50] His claim, of course, was only to be authoritative in interpreting scripture; he did not say he had a special revelation. Yet it is still an assertion worth pondering. Mark U. Edwards has suggested that before 1522 Luther had never presented himself as anything other than a doctor of theology expounding scripture. Afterward Luther saw himself increasingly as a prophet raised up by God in a special time.[51]

Luther did not ask Frederick to protect him. God would do that if he so willed, and the elector should have faith. If Luther should be taken and killed, Frederick would not be responsible. If the emperor moved against Luther, Frederick should not resist. Only God, who had ordained the emperor's power, could resist it; but if God protected Luther, no one could harm him. The way to answer the devil was with courage and faith. He recalled the warnings he had received before going to Worms. Satan, he said, "saw my heart well, that I would enter Worms even if I had known that as many devils lay in ambush for me as there were tiles on the roof; then would I have sprung into the midst of them with joy." In comparison with the demonic adversaries that Luther now found everywhere, he considered Duke George's continuing enmity. Duke George was not equal to even one devil, he wrote. If this affair were in Leipzig rather than in Wittenberg, Luther said, he would go there at God's call even if it rained Duke Georges for nine days and if every one of them were nine times more furious than this one.[52]

And so he returned to Wittenberg, arriving on March 6, dressed like a knight and wearing a full, black beard. He was quickly commanded to write the elector a letter that Frederick could show around to prove that Luther had come back of his own volition against Frederick's will and that he would not do anything rash. In all this, Luther was the obedient servant as long as obedience coincided with his devotion to what he considered the will of God. He professed no doubts as to what that will might be. Satan had entered the fold at Wittenberg; Luther felt compelled to drive the evil one away. At the end of this letter, he made a declaration about the relation of the spiritual and the secular realms. Frederick in his role as prince was lord only of goods and bodies; "Christ is however also the lord of souls, to whom he has sent me and for that reason raised me up; I cannot forsake these souls."[53]

Frederick continued to be anxious. Luther wrote several letters to him over the next week, seeking to assuage his worries. Luther continually asserted his submissiveness and yet continued also to claim his mission. Wittenberg was his flock; God wanted him there, and he would stay, even unto death. Meanwhile Spalatin came over formally to the new evangelical doctrines, inspiring a grateful response from Luther. Spalatin's conversion was yet another proof that Frederick's support for Luther was firm. Perhaps he held onto Luther's early faith that the old church might yet be reformed.

On March 9 Luther began a series of eight daily sermons in German that quickly restored order in Wittenberg—backed as they were by the authority of the elector. He appeared with his hair cut, the top of the scalp shaved like a monk's, and in black, clerical dress. He began the first sermon with a stark sentence: "We are all held to death, and no one can die for another, but each in his own person must be harnessed and armed for himself to fight against the devil and death."[54] We are all children of wrath, he said. God has given us his Son, that believing on him we might be saved. Our task is to believe and to love one another. We must have faith in God, but all people do not have equal faith. Indeed, faith wavers from day to day for everyone. Love should make us bow to our weaker brothers and patiently tolerate their weak faith. This was his theme through the week—that love and faith were marks of the Christian and that in the rush to reform, the weaker brothers—those who held to the traditional means of worship—should not be left behind or cast aside.

The battle, Luther said, was not against popes, bishops, and secular princes, but against the devil, the spirit of wickedness under heaven, as Paul had taught. Changes must come, but not in disorderly ways. He called upon the advanced Wittenbergers to exercise tolerance and patience with those who had not come so far so fast. In this first sermon he asserted his own authority. "I have not taken my office as preacher myself nor force myself into it, but I was commanded and even against my will raised here to preach."[55] Here was a statement not entirely unlike the claim to authority by the radicals who claimed direct, divine inspiration. As Luther had earlier suggested, certification of this divine mission had to come through the response of godly men. Yet who were the godly men? That was a matter of dispute, finally decided by a consensus for order mandated by the elector. The radicals had acted in the spirit in which Luther himself had bravely complained a year earlier at Worms. There he had thundered:

And I must say that for me it is a joyful spectacle to see that passions and conflicts arise over the word of God. For that is how the word of God works! As the Lord Jesus said, "I came to send not peace, but a sword. For I am come to set a man at variance against his father, and the daughter against her mother, and the daughter-in-law against her mother-in-law." And so we must weigh carefully how wonderful and how awful our Lord is in his secret counsels.[56]

But that was Luther as public orator. Now he was Luther the pastor and Luther the diplomat, aware that weighty matters hung on the outcome of events and unwilling to break the delicate thread of negotiation that held prince, people, and preachers together.

The other sermons continued in the same spirit. Some reforms in faith and practice were necessary, he said. The Mass as it had been observed, as a sacrifice and a meritorious work, was evil and should be cast away. This article was no more doubtful than the belief that God should be worshipped. But what about private masses, which Luther had also condemned? Here was a different matter, something desirable but not essential. Yes, private masses should eventually disappear. Christians should proclaim, preach, and write that such masses are sinful. But masses should not be torn out by the hair. One should leave such things to God so that his word might work without our efforts or our work. People could not be forced to have the correct belief.[57] He had, he said, stood against the pope, indulgences, and all the papists—yet without force, with no outrages, with no riots; he had preached only God's word, and otherwise had he done nothing. "Had I acted with force and violence, I could have begun such a game that would have made all Germany gush with blood."[58]

These were powerful words, including explicit confidence and implicit threat. So far Luther could say that his entire Reformation had been brought about by the word of God—spoken through himself. The revolution he had wrought through God's word was there for everyone to see. It validated itself—and Luther as God's minister. Yet all along Luther understood how much violence he might have unleashed had he wished. His rhetoric has

many layers. We can read these sermons—immediately published and distributed widely—as a caution not only to the Wittenbergers not to use force
but also to the rest of Germany to consider well before force was brought
against Wittenberg and Saxony. He was implying that if violence came, it
would not be his responsibility—but the consequences would be bloody and
spread not merely in electoral Saxony but throughout the other German
lands.

Luther sought to make his gospel inclusive without dissolving it into
unmeaning. Some religious matters depended on taste or preference. It was
indifferent whether people used images in worship, became nuns or monks
or left the cloister, refused to eat meat on Fridays or not, whether pastors
took wives or not. God had made these matters free. Christians could do as
they pleased. Monks were free to break their vows of poverty, chastity, and
obedience, since vows were against God's command. If he vowed to hit his
father in the mouth, said Luther, God would not be pleased if the vow were
kept. But one might choose to live in a monastic community and to follow
the old traditions. It was all right to use images in a worship service; it was
not all right to pray to them. If some did pray to these images, Christians
should not break them up with riot; the secular authority should forbid
them.[59]

At this point, in the third of these sermons, Luther seemed to lose something of the staunch, confident reliance on God's word that marked his
earlier comments. The people acting riotously should not undertake to do
away with practices that Luther found objectionable. They should let the
word of God hold forth and wait patiently for God's will to be done. Here
was Christian resignation. But suddenly interjected into these confident sermons, almost as an aside, came the dictum that the magistrate could do what
the common people could not. King Hezekiah of Judah had destroyed the
brass serpent that Moses had lifted up in the wilderness to cure the Israelites
of snakebite. The people in Hezekiah's time had begun to worship it. Secular
rulers could do the same to keep their people from idolatry. Perhaps Christians were not to wait—so long as the magistrate led them.

Although he often said that no conscience should be compelled, he was
perfectly willing to compel practice, and the magistrate became the agency of
the compulsion. Luther elevated the magistrate, made it a mysterious instrument whereby God worked in unfathomable ways to do his will. Ordinary
Christians were not such instruments. They could preach the word of God
and not use force, but when the secular authority used force, God had
ordained it for good or for ill. In practical terms, Luther meant that "prophets" from Zwickau or wherever had no divine sanction to lead tumult while

claiming to obey God's command. Luther's assumption throughout was that the scripture was clear and coherent about all the important doctrines; the fair-minded prince could see that clarity, especially when taught by the person God had chosen to teach—in Luther's view, himself.

Within the complexities and contradictions of Luther's views lay a couple of clear and important points. One was that the heart was more important in religion than outward practice, and some hearts required longer than others for enlightenment. The other was that true Christians were a minority and could not create the kingdom of heaven by forcing conformity on the majority. This is an essential tenet, one that set a great gulf between him and Karlstadt. Karlstadt could take the priesthood of all believers to a radically democratic conclusion. Since all true Christians were equal, they could withstand the elector himself because they could, in a certain sense, vote his views down. Luther disagreed. All his days he held that the majority of professing Christians might not correspond to the scattered "true Christians" who were always a hidden minority, known only to God. The hiddenness of the true church kept him from espousing radical theories of Christian democracy. No visible crowd of revolutionaries could claim to be so pure that they could take on themselves the inauguration of the kingdom of God. No group could be taken as true Christians merely because they said they were. Luther would not make Wittenberg a theocracy that could serve Calvin as a model later on in Geneva.

The only outward signs Christians could count on, he said in his sixth sermon after his return, were baptism and the Eucharist. These signs must be accompanied by faith that Jesus Christ was God's son and the only satisfaction for our sins. There was always in Luther a powerful sense, paradoxically terrifying and comforting at once, of the individual standing alone before God. That being so, he did not think Christians could establish any single, binding form for the Eucharist or any other church practice.[60]

Christians were to love one another. In his seventh sermon Luther told his flock that they now had the gospel "clear and bright," but they were not demonstrating love for each other. If they did not learn to love, God would "send a great plague on you, for he will not have his word preached and revealed in vain, and he will not permit anyone to scorn or contemn his Word."[61] What would this "plague" be? literal plague? to be overcome by enemies from without? Luther does not say. His language is vague enough to allow the interpretation that would become standard in mainline Protestantism, that the judgments of God are seen as miraculous only by the real Christians, while to others they appear as part of the endless shifting of the historical process.

Luther's sermons were brief, pungent, and delivered with both force and gentleness. They demonstrate many of his personal concerns. In his seventh sermon he spoke feelingly of the sacrament of the body and blood of Christ, which was "for those in whom is the fear of death, whom the devil hunts, who possess a despondent, foolish conscience and who are afraid of sin and hell."[62] Here all in a bundle were Luther's great fears, beginning with the fear of death and ending with hell, which for Luther usually meant the grave rather than a place of fiery torment. And here was the Eucharist, which gave him the physical presence of Christ to strengthen him on his way.

The sermons were also vague, staying carefully away from any effort to examine specifically the claims to immediate revelation made by the Zwickau prophets. He seemed to know instinctively that if he got into the arena of debate to confront them directly, he would end in an argument that would resolve nothing. They could adduce biblical examples on their side; the debate would turn into a clash of biblical interpretations without any accepted standard to declare who had won and who had lost. Instead Luther defined Christian practice so as to exclude the radical consequences the prophets drew from their own revelations. Given his penchant for polemics, the sermons seem remarkably gentle, an exhibition of the attitude he sought to inculcate in his congregation.

He could afford to be gentle. Frederick quickly moved against the prophets and against Karlstadt. Karlstadt was blamed for inciting riotous behavior and, as Preus holds, became a scapegoat for what was in fact a large and fervent popular movement, led not only by Karlstadt but by the city council. Preus thinks that Luther came back to Wittenberg because he felt his movement slipping away from him and that he could not bear to lose his position of leadership.[63] Throughout the rest of his life Luther was to be *the* leader of his own movement, and he was always to claim that this was the destiny that God had given him. If he were not the prophet of God endowed with true understanding of scripture, all his tormented life would become meaningless.

By appealing to the "common man," Karlstadt made himself odious to anyone who feared and loathed commoners. He was left without allies and banned from the pulpit in Wittenberg's city church.[64] He responded with a vigorous tract against Luther, essentially asserting once again his trust in the "common man." For this offense he was hauled before a committee of the university and condemned, and publication of his tract forbidden. He would remain in Wittenberg another year. Now and then Luther mentioned him in letters without unfriendly comments. But he was no longer a player in the drama there.

The Zwickau prophets received more summary judgment. Luther condescended to speak with a group of them. On April 12 he wrote in exasperation to Spalatin that Satan had shat on himself to produce their "wisdom." They talked so fast that he could hardly get a word in. He commanded them to do miracles to prove their claims of direct conversation with God. They refused. He said, "My God keeps your god from doing a miracle."[65] Soon they were gone. Luther was now the pope of Wittenberg, and so he would remain to the end of his days more than two decades later. He demanded and got the repeal of the ordinance passed by the Wittenberg city council on January 24. He had resisted the effort of the papal church, as he saw it, to compel consciences. That he would not do himself. Or so he said.

He still held to his claim, made in the *Babylonian Captivity*, that no law could bind the Christian, but his ordinary Christian was passive and spontaneously lived at peace with his neighbors. In Wittenberg, whatever else might happen, the Catholic Church was gone, new, moderate practices were installed, worship and preaching went on, children were born and baptized, marriages were celebrated, people died and had to be buried, and the other rites of Christian passage had to be observed. Willy-nilly Luther found himself presiding over an institution, and Wittenberg became his world where he had to work out some compromise between the rule of conscience among the "true Christians" and the rule of force over the ignorance and willfulness of the "common man," who had to be taken into account regardless of the state of his heart or the destiny of his soul. This was to be a daunting task with contradictions and paradoxes and confusions that he never successfully resolved.

19

TRIBULATION

Luther did not see his return to Wittenberg as a triumph. Rather he found much to discourage him, enemies and dissenters on every hand. Written sometime after his secret visit to his city in December 1521, his calm *Admonition* seems to have been written without genuine knowledge of what was going on in the city. Now on the scene, he saw Satan at work in unexpected corners and opposition where he had expected support. He was annoyed to see—apparently for the first time—a collection of letters published by Erasmus a year earlier. In these epistles, in which Luther's name appeared frequently, Erasmus held himself at a discreet and disapproving distance. "I acknowledge Christ," he wrote to one correspondent. "I do not know Luther." He acknowledged the Church of Rome, which, he thought, did not dissent from Catholic faith. Erasmus was no believer in papal sovereignty over the church. He had already made that point clear in his annotations to his edition of the Greek New Testament. He expressed his horror of sedition and earnestly hoped that Luther and the rest of Germany might not slip into rebellion. It was amazing, he said, how Luther's foes seemed to be in league with Luther himself. No one harmed Luther, said Erasmus, as much as he hurt himself with his hateful books. But those who attacked Luther were so stupid, so arrogant, and so seditious that they could only raise sympathy for him.[1]

Luther's reaction within his own circle was to grumble that it was better to have an open enemy like Eck than someone like Erasmus posing as a friend.[2] Since Erasmus had declared forthrightly that he was not Luther's friend, Luther's comment seems misplaced.

Despite his condemnation at Worms the previous April, Luther kept hoping that the young Emperor Charles might yet rally to his side. His *Address to the Christian Nobility of the German Nation* rested on hopes of reform supported by good Christian rulers. In Spain the Comunero revolt turned into class conflict. Out of fear of the rabble, the nobles reluctantly turned back to Charles, whose power they had tried to limit. Charles descended on the country with an army of German mercenaries. The rebels were butchered, and by the summer of 1522 the revolt was over. Charles did not have a subtle mind; the revolt taught him a simple lesson: Opposition should be crushed before it could become danger.

He set out to destroy any Lutherans in his personal domains, which included Burgundy—most of today's Belgium and the Netherlands and part of today's France. Luther heard a false rumor that one of his followers there had been burned at the stake. Within a year, such rumors would have substance. Luther kept searching for glimmers of hope. In June he wrote a pastor named Paul Speratus in Moravia that God had given Charles and the persecutors in the Low Countries a fatal sign that perhaps might make them repent. A whale had been cast ashore at Harlaam, seventy feet long and thirty-five feet wide. This spectacle was, by ancient examples, a sure sign of the wrath of God.[3]

Sometime in June he received a letter from his old mentor Staupitz. Staupitz, seemingly overcome with sadness and anxiety for what Luther had done, had left the Augustinian order in 1520 to become a Benedictine. In 1522 he became abbot of the Benedictine monastery in Salzburg, and two years later he would be dead. In his letter (not now extant), Staupitz said that Luther's doctrines were being hurled about by men who frequented brothels and that Luther's books had been a cause for scandal.

Luther replied sorrowfully but without retreating. It was his job to publish the pure word without tumult, and whether his words were used for good or for ill was not in his power. He was sure of his destiny. "It is up to me, my father, to destroy that kingdom of abomination and ruin that belongs to the pope along with his whole order of things. And yet that is happening without us, without raising a hand; his end is coming in the providence of God."[4] Luther sounded an apocalyptic note, citing New Testament predictions that in the last days tumults would come. God's mighty hand would be revealed. With fierce confidence—or perhaps yearning—Luther wrote that at first his message had been scorned by everyone, but now it grew stronger and stronger.[5]

Later in 1522 Luther heard that Staupitz wept at the necessity of his transfer to the Benedictines. Silence descended again between the two until September 1523, when Luther wrote affectionately to Staupitz, wondering that he had not heard from his old mentor, and expressing his gratitude that under Staupitz he had first begun to see the light of the gospel break through the darkness. The friends of Staupitz at Wittenberg, said Luther (including himself among them), had not been pleased that he had become abbot in his Benedictine monastery. It would be a wonder, said Luther, if in his present position Staupitz did not run the risk of denying Christ. His friends prayed for him and hoped always that he would return to them. The occasion for the letter was to request that Staupitz give something to a monk who had fled the abbey, a man now destitute and with no means of support. Luther begged Staupitz not to take the monk back but to provide for him out of the riches of the monastery. He implied that Staupitz might, too, be a prisoner, and expressed hope that Staupitz might stand up against the pope and Staupitz's cardinal, a man named Mathaeus Lang. He yearned for Staupitz to become "as you once were."[6] The letter conveys the insolence of pain. He yearned for Staupitz to reconsider and to join the movement that Luther always maintained Staupitz had inspired, but Luther seemed resigned that the conversion of his old friend and guide was not to be.

Only affection could have made Staupitz reply to such a letter, couched as it was in condescension. As it was, the older man waited until April 1524 before he wrote again, full of warmth and a Catholic spirit. He gently reproached Luther for confusing superficial evils with the substance of faith—a common attitude among devout adherents to the Old Church who never denied that many priests were evil and that much in the practice of Christians needed reform. This attitude supposed that Luther's reform was chiefly moral rather than doctrinal, and nothing in Staupitz's letter can be clearly interpreted to mean anything else.

Staupitz did not approve of Luther's wholesale rejection of the old understanding of vows. For the benefit of a few—perhaps for the benefit of only one—Luther had cast away all vows, said Staupitz. The remark was quietly given, but it had bite. Staupitz implied that Luther might have attacked monastic vows only as a means of justifying his own wish to be free of them. Yes, some monks were corrupt, Staupitz admitted, but many persisted in true faith and piety. He asked Luther to remember the "little ones," the simple Christians confused by all that Luther had done, and, he said, "We owe you much for having led us from the dried bean shells [fed to] pigs to the pastures of life and the words of salvation." The allusion was to the story of the prodigal son who lived for a time on fodder fed to pigs before returning to the bountiful table of his father at home. Staupitz reproached the evangelical movement for its "liberty of the flesh" of which he saw "innumerable" examples. Perhaps he meant simply clerical marriage. In the most touching comment of all, Staupitz wished for one hour together so that he might open to Luther the "secrets of my heart." The letter was borne by a student whom Staupitz was sending to Wittenberg to study at the university. He asked Luther to take him in. He closed by saying he still detested the "Babylonian Captivity," perhaps an oblique reference to the sovereignty of the papacy over the church.[7]

For all its gentleness, this letter rejected Luther's movement as Staupitz understood it, and it seems to indicate that he did not clearly understand Luther, although I cannot think that understanding would have made Staupitz come over to his old disciple. If he did not understand Luther, we may also say that in their early time together Luther did not understand him. The letter seems to have been the last communication between them. By January 1525 Luther had learned that Staupitz had died and commented briefly on how short a time he had been abbot.

Staupitz is mentioned far more frequently in the table talk than Luther's father, Hans. Again and again Luther praised the consolation Staupitz had given him, repeating several times his counsel that no one should debate predestination. But I have not found any comment Luther made on Staupitz's defection. A reader (or hearer) of the table talk might suppose that Staupitz had become a convert. Perhaps Luther could not bear to touch on a subject so painful as Staupitz's final rejection of "the gospel."

Formidable enemies continued to rally against Luther. One of the most formidable of all came on the scene in the person of Henry VIII, king of England. Luther had reason to think that his message had been well received in the English court. In May 1519 Erasmus had written him that his books were greatly admired by some of the highest people of rank in England.[8] It was not farfetched to suppose that these important admirers included the king, who fancied himself both pious and scholarly. Henry seemed the sort of devout ruler Luther had in mind when he wrote his *Address to the Christian Nobility of the German Nation.* He was English, but then Luther hoped for European-wide acceptance of his gospel.

Henry had other ideas. He itched to receive a title from the papacy to put him on equal footing with the king of France, whom the pope had named "Most Christian King." He was also innately conservative in theology. Luther's *Babylonian Captivity* enraged him and offered an opportunity. Helped by various learned courtiers and churchmen, he put together his *Assertio Septem Sacramentorum,* an "Assertion" of the standard understanding of all seven sacraments against Luther's efforts to reduce them to only baptism and Eucharist. Thomas More was one of the helpers, although his precise contribution remains unclear. Later on in his troubles with the pope

Henry blamed More for the work—though he and his successors kept the title won from the pope for it. Henry's anger at More for the book would seem to indicate More's considerable influence. One thing is certain: Although he thunderously declared the validity of the seven sacraments, Henry was vague in his definition of the papal authority.[9] If Luther had read the book carefully, he would have noted that the king, perhaps steered by More, neatly evaded affirmation of papal sovereignty over either doctrine or administration in the church. Behind the thumping declarations of papal primacy and attacks on Luther for his pride in denying it lay no definitions of what primacy meant. The volume was published in London in the summer of 1521. On October 11, Leo X issued a bull granting Henry the title *Fidei defensor,* "Defender of the Faith." It was one of the final acts of the pope's troubled reign, for he died on December 1, shortly before Henry's book was republished in Rome.

By June 28 a German translation by Jerome Emser was on sale in Meissen.[10] Luther had seen Henry's book for the first time in the spring of 1522 while preparing his German translation of the New Testament for the printer. He guessed that Henry's book was inspired by Pope Leo X, and he suspected that the real author was Edward Lee, a sharp critic of Erasmus's editions of the Greek New Testament.[11]

Luther should have let Henry's book go. It was not original, and it lacked the eloquence that might have made it worth attacking. But it was written under the name of a king, one touted by Erasmus as intellectual and devout. The German translation made it seem dangerous to Luther's cause. In it Henry also spoke of Luther with contempt. Luther, the miner's son who had made his mark in the world as prophet of God, felt driven to reply.

Henry's real theme was not the authority of the papacy but the truth of Catholic tradition. Jesus had not written a book; he had founded a church, and as the author of the Gospel of John declared, if all that Christ had said and done were written down, the world itself could not contain the books. Christ passed many doctrines on orally to his disciples. These doctrines were received by the apostles and preserved in the church. If the scripture had never been written, said Henry, the gospel would remain in the church, written in the hearts of the faithful.[12]

Sometime in early June Spalatin wrote Luther posing a number of questions seemingly related to Henry's *Assertio.* What did Christ mean when he told his disciples, as recorded in the Gospel of John (16:12), that he had much to tell them that they could not now bear, that would be taught them later by the Holy Spirit? When was the Spirit to do this teaching? Questions such as these evidently sprang from the Catholic teaching of an oral tradition that supposedly controlled the interpretation of scripture, and it also comprised doctrines that had not been written down for centuries, some of them kept secret until they could be understood. Both Henry and, later, Thomas More appealed to the oral tradition to justify elements in Catholic faith that Luther had attacked.

Luther replied in detail. These words of Christ had been spoken before the Resurrection. The disciples had been unable to understand them fully until after Christ had risen from the dead, and that fuller understanding was to be found in the later epistles, especially those of Paul. Then Christians knew that Christ did not plan an earthly kingdom but a heavenly one—something they might not have understood before this greatest of all miracles. Thus everything Christ wanted his disciples—and his church—to believe was contained in scripture. In addition Luther suggested a belief that he would later harden into one of his major doctrines—often neglected by modern scholars—that miracles had been necessary to confirm the mission of Christ until the gospel was established and the law was abrogated, but that afterward they were no longer needed.[13] He would never go so far as to deny that supernatural wonders happened in the Catholic Church; but he ascribed them to the power of Satan.[14]

When it came, Luther's public answer to Henry VIII was a tirade of invective scarcely to be equaled by another hostile communication addressed to a royal figure in the sixteenth century. Luther meant to offend and was delighted when he did. His *Against Henry, King of the English* came from the press in a German version on August 1. A Latin version followed shortly afterward. His vehemence made his friends anxious, but Luther seemed as proud of it as a child who has learned he can break windows with rocks. To his friend Johann Lang he wrote late in the summer, "My book against Henry of the English offends many, just as I wanted."[15] A German friend wrote—obviously in consternation—to ask why Luther had struck at Henry so hard. Luther responded with the example of invective in the Bible against Jews and others by Christ, Peter, and Paul. He had tried mildness, he said. All it had got him was rage and slander from his enemies.[16] He would have no more of mildness against those who distorted his views. Given Luther's habit of furious polemics from the start of his public career, we must wonder which of his works he considered mild. The letter to "X," as it is listed in the Weimar edition, and Luther's fury suggest a deepening frustration that the world was not listening to his proclamation of the Christ given us by a Bible with a clear and simple gospel.

The blast against Henry together with its dedicatory letter to a friend, Count Sebastian Schlik, betrays a sense of isolation. Henry expected Luther to flee Germany for Bohemia and the Hussites. Luther raged because the English king equated him with John Hus and declared him a heretic without weighing the possibility that Luther's teachings might be true. Luther's tone is dark and displays a bravado that came across to some (like Thomas More) as insufferable arrogance. He seemed to have lost faith in all rulers and, by extension, confidence in the human, secular authority that would destroy the papacy and bring the gospel to Christians everywhere. The princes of Germany, once of the most praiseworthy faith, he said, had learned in servile fawning to the Roman idol do nothing other than scorn the faith to the perpetual ignominy of the German nation. Luther had invited antagonists to come to Wittenberg to debate, but no one had accepted. And now came this king with a book filled with droolings about Luther's supposed flight to Bohemia, and the effeminate and mad king believed that such a flight would mean victory for the papists.[17] (The charge of effeminacy must have been especially galling to the English king, who had begun his *Assertio* by calling attention to his prowess as a warrior, mentioning that the pope would be surprised to know he also had studied theology.)[18] If the papists killed him or left him alive, he said, he was given to them as a portent from Christ his Lord that no grace, no peace, no solace would they have from the Furies of their own conscience so that they deserved to suffer the eternal tortures of hell.[19]

Luther accused Henry and the papists of begging the question, of claiming that the traditions of the church should be observed merely because they were traditions, without considering whether they came from God or from human invention. "I cry gospel, gospel, Christ, Christ; they respond fathers fathers, custom, custom, laws, laws, where as I say truly that the fathers, custom, and law have often erred . . . Christ cannot err."[20] Perhaps Luther's greatest insult was to say that no one imagined that Henry had written his book by himself.[21]

On Luther rolled in a torrent of abuse. "Draw near to my rod, you vainglorious Thomist," he cried. "I will teach you how to argue about dogma."[22] At the end he crowed that he had been victorious over the king by opposing God's word to human custom.[23] "Here I stand," he wrote,

> here I sit, here I remain, here I glory, here I triumph, here I contemn Papists, Thomists, Henricians, sophists, and all the gates of hell all the more in that they are led astray by the sayings of holy men or customs. God's word is over all. The divine majesty works with me, and I do not care if a thousand Augustines, a thousand Cyprians, a thousand

churches of Henry stand against me. God cannot err or fail; Augustine and Cyprian like all the elects can err, and they did err.[24]

The issue, as any Catholic knew, was not whether the fathers could err as individuals; it was whether they had reached consensus on a core of doctrines necessary to be believed. Luther's furious language indicates a willingness to attack that ancient consensus in the name of the gospel and to elevate his own understanding above the agreements of centuries.

None of the fathers was exempt from his strictures, and that attitude remained all his life and is significant for his development. In his 1545 preface to the edition of the Latin works, he could still praise Augustine's *On the Spirit and the Letter* for its help in giving him his great revelation about grace. But he could be surprisingly harsh on his favorite ancient saint. In the beginning, he said, he had devoured Augustine, but when "Paul opened the door for me so that I understood what justification by faith was, it was all over with him [Augustine]." Augustine had two worthwhile opinions—that sins are forgiven—not that they disappear but that they do not damn us—and that the law is fulfilled not that it is kept but that it is acknowledged, and recognized as impossible for us. "The *Confessions* set us on fire and tell a lot of stories, but they don't teach anything. St. Augustine became a pious sinner who no longer had his little whore and his son with him."[25] The target here is obviously the strict celibacy that all the fathers of the church agreed upon. Augustine tells us in the *Confessions* of putting away the mother of his son as part of his conversion—and never speaks her name. Luther's bravado in such statements barely conceals a troubled soul. He had posed the question to himself in his treatise on abrogating private masses: "Are you alone wise? Has everyone else been mistaken? Have so many ages dwelled in ignorance? What if you are wrong and in your error draw so many into eternal damnation?"[26] The question came back to him early and late.[27] It seems that one of his ways of combatting it was to assert his calling with all the more vehemence. His words to Henry about the fathers were picked up and flung back at him as an example of his insufferable arrogance.

Henry's dull little book provoked Luther to more wrath than anything so far written or said against him. Why? The most plausible reason is that Henry's book made him see that his hopes for general reform in the church might be vain. The rulers of Europe would not flock to him to join a crusade against the papacy. The gospel would not overcome its adversaries in an outburst of enlightenment and faith firmly and justly led by princes. Luther's assault on Henry was the reflex action of a man afraid not for his own life but for what his life meant. He was alone with the word of God and a scattering of followers. All he could do was preach the Word as hard as he could in hopes that the Word would win its own battles and defeat the papacy by supernatural means rather than through the natural agency of princely power. But would it?

One effect of his tirade was to give foes another cudgel to use against him. By turning his rhetorical broadside on Henry VIII, Luther seemed to savage royalty itself. Heresy throughout the Catholic centuries had been associated with sedition, riot, and a chaos thought to be satanic, the opposite of the orderly system God had created. Already Luther stood accused of inciting the common folk. Now the accusations of sedition fell thick and fast on his head.

In England Thomas More undertook to write a reply to Luther's attack on Henry, and in it More accused Luther of a willingness to destroy all laws.[28] The rumor spread that Erasmus had helped him write against Henry VIII. Erasmus denied this slander vigorously to friends in England. Among them was Cuthbert Tunstall, bishop of London and friend of Thomas More. Tunstall wrote on June 5, 1523, expressing joy that Erasmus had publicly denied having anything to do with Luther or his response to Henry. But, said Tunstall, it was time for Erasmus to write directly against the German heretic. Throughout the history of the church, Tunstall declared, those skilled in knowledge of the Bible had taken up their pens against heresy that threatened the church in their time. Now Erasmus must do the same. Erasmus held out. He feared that by attacking Luther directly, he would encourage the "Pharisees" within the Catholic Church. Yet in the end he could not resist pressure brought to bear on him by so many influential people. To a friend in Germany he wrote late in August 1523, "All the princes urge me to write against Luther."[29] He delayed, but pressure was building in response to Luther's assault on Henry VIII.

In the meantime Luther was busier than ever. From all over Germany people great and small wrote him for advice. Towns near Wittenberg asked him to recommend pastors to preach the true gospel. Pastors in place got from him letters of counsel. Late in April he undertook a preaching tour. He returned early in May. Among other towns, he visited Zwickau whence those "prophets" had come. He preached at least four sermons there. These sermons—brief by later standards of Protestant pulpit oratory—defined justification by faith and castigated false religion. His major theme was to uphold Christ as victor over "death, sin, and hell," and he said that the true believer, clinging to Christ in faith, had no reason to fear any of this terrible trinity.[30] It was not a statement that Christians did not fear. It was only consolation against those fears, and once again, "hell" seems to be a synonym for the grave. He emphasized love of one's neighbor as the fruit of faith, as he had earlier, making good works the consequence rather than the cause of redemption.

At Zwickau he proclaimed the validity of baptizing children, adducing the story of the men who in the Gospel of Luke broke through the roof and lowered the palsied man to Jesus who preached within, surrounded by crowds so thick that the bearers of the man could not pass through. Through their faith, the man was healed, and Luther used the example to demonstrate how the faith of friends could help one another—including children. He seems not to have considered the contradiction here with his constant refrain that each of us must have faith for himself.

On May 3, near Zwickau, he preached at the village of Borna commemorating the discovery of the true cross by Helena, the mother of the Emperor Constantine. (Helena's good luck on that trip to Palestine was stunning; she also found Christ's seamless robe, brought it back to Constantinople, and thence it came to Trier. In May 1512 the "Holy Robe" was exhibited in the presence of the Emperor Maximilian, and within a few days over 100,000 pilgrims came to see it.)[31] He was careful in the presence of such a venerated relic. This was a traditional celebration, popular with the masses. Luther thought, he said, that the true cross should be esteemed, but it was subject to much misuse. It should not be venerated for itself; that was idolatry. He was also skeptical. So many pieces of the true cross had been found, he said, that one could have built a house with them. The practice of venerating the cross had gone so far, said he, that he thought it would have been no sin had the cross remained buried under ground.[32] His visitations let him brace up his followers and exclude radicals who charged beyond the limits that he had drawn. His sermons explained his doctrines, including a rejection of the notion that any conduct was acceptable so long as the Christian professed true belief. In his sermon on the finding of the true cross, Luther emphasized the need for every Christian to bear his own cross.

In another sermon at Borna, Luther raised another issue. What did the Christian do if commanded by his prince to go against the gospel? Luther counseled disobedience. Let the Christian say to such a prince, "You are no longer a prince to me; I am no longer obligated to obey you, as Peter declared in Acts 4, 'You must recognize then whether we should hear you rather than God.'"[33] This was dangerous stuff. Luther did not summon the people to armed rebellion; but to counsel disobedience to a prince on religious grounds could seem like an appeal to the masses against princely authority, and, as in the past, others might make of these injunctions more than Luther made of them himself.

His activity was unceasing. Back he came to Wittenberg to write, to preach, to counsel. If any proof were needed against the old Catholic slander that Luther made his Reformation so that he could marry, it is here. Unlike other priests, who rushed to take wives, Luther worked night and day, seemingly without any private life at all. He seemed able to take on a thousand tasks at once; one wonders how he found time to sleep. Nor was any end in sight, for now he had to concentrate on what he considered his most important task—to translate the Bible into German. With such a translation, he could prove to true Christians in the German world, at least, that he was right, that his rebellion against Rome was justified, and that they should follow him.

20

THE SEPTEMBER
TESTAMENT

LUTHER made his first draft of the translation of the New Testament during a period of eleven weeks in the Wartburg. His letters through the spring and summer of 1522 are filled with his labors. By May 10 he sent proof sheets to Spalatin, and by September 21, when he had finished his last revisions to his preface to the book of Romans, the printing of the "September Testament" was complete. It was a large, expensive book, sold at the price of a good horse, so Luther himself said, beautifully illustrated by woodcuts, some carved by the court artist, Lucas Cranach the Elder—one of Luther's best friends.

Like writers from the beginning of printing, Luther became enraged with his publisher for carelessness and neglect. He accused the Wittenberg printer Melchior Lotther of inept work and broken promises. Still, the work was *there*—and so popular despite its high price that the 3,000 or perhaps as many as 5,000 copies of the first edition sold quickly; and by December another, corrected, edition was ready for the public.[1]

The German Bible reveals as clearly as anything what Luther wanted to believe and where he felt he had to struggle to overcome problems and doubt. He founded his gospel on scripture. He was sure that scripture radically contradicted many traditions of the Catholic Church. In his view the papal church represented "novelty," and scripture was the fountain whence flowed the uncorrupted truth of God. He maintained with thumping certitude the clarity of scripture to those not ignorant of mind or malicious of heart. Already in a German commentary of 1521 on the Thirty-sixth Psalm he had declared, "There is on earth no clearer book written than the holy scripture, which compared to other books is like the sun compared to all lights."[2] He was sure that if the common people read scripture in the vernacular, they could see how alien Catholic belief and practice were from the pure word of God delivered to prophets and apostles.

Yet scripture in the vernacular was not intended to be a mere polemical effort against the papal church. Luther had found his own sacred history, his salvation, in scripture, and he believed that Christians everywhere could be spiritually nourished by the sacred text. Scripture had made him what he was. He believed it would transform others in the same way. He had made his university career as a teacher of the Bible; he would now extend his vocation to include the whole German people.

He had help, especially from Melanchthon. He also had the incalculable aid of the second edition of Erasmus's Greek New Testament with its Latin translation and its erudite annotations. Some detailed consideration of it will help bring Luther's achievement into focus. It seems probable that Erasmus intended to publish only a Latin translation, a revision of the Vulgate.[3] To establish the validity of his new translation, he felt compelled to publish the Greek text that was his authority for editorial selection. Then, to demonstrate his thinking about various problems represented in the text, he appended a hefty collection of philological, theological, and historical notes.

The notes were explosives wrapped in discreet Latin. Thomas Aquinas had delivered the medieval judgment on the Bible in his emphatic sentence: "The author of the Bible is God." This notion of inspiration naturally led to the opinion that God had hidden in the sacred text all sorts of esoteric truths about various subjects. In a paradoxical way, the belief that God had dictated the various books of the Bible to inspired writers contributed to the medieval habit of not reading the Bible as a book—or as the collection of books that it is. It became rather a treasury of proof texts to be used as needed for the support of this or that doctrine propounded by theologians and preachers. God was everywhere equally in it. With the allegorical interpretation, anything could be found in all of it. We have seen that Luther saw the Bible as a mirror held up to the sacred history of sin and redemption where the central event was the incarnation of God in Christ, the Crucifixion and the Resurrection. Luther had a higher sense of history than the scholastic theologians. But in many respects his biblical world was outside history, a word of God speaking an eternal present in the words of scripture. This transhistorical sense of the Bible is evident, as we have seen, in his early lectures on the Psalms.

But then came Erasmus with his successive editions of the New Testament, applying a critical, historical understanding of the sacred text. Erasmus knew how long a century was, how long a millennium, and he knew how different the centuries were from one another. Luther was, to be sure, not ignorant of these differences, but he never felt them with the profundity of discrimination that we find in Erasmus. Erasmus recognized several qualities of the Bible, all to some degree related to an advanced understanding of history and now considered commonplaces by biblical scholars. Lorenzo Valla had used his ability to recognize anachronism to expose as a forgery the so-called Donation of Constantine. Many of the words used in the Donation were much later coinages. Valla had also written philological notes on the New Testament, subjecting parts of it to critical historical analysis. Erasmus published these notes early in his own career. They furnished part of the inspiration for his New Testament, where Valla is quoted frequently in notes explaining Erasmus's choices of Latin words to translate the Greek text. His notes helped readers understand the intention of the authors. Inevitably some textual notes took on theological meaning.

Erasmus's labors contributed to Luther's translation and almost certainly to several theological positions Luther had taken before he translated the Bible. We have noted that in his notes to Ephesians 5:32, Erasmus undermined the traditional Catholic teaching that marriage was a sacrament, a teaching on the Vulgate's rendering of *sacramentum magnum* to describe marriage. Henry VIII used this Latin reading in his attack on Luther's claim in the *Babylonian Captivity* that marriage was not a sacrament.[4] But Erasmus coolly pointed out in his note here that the word *sacramentum* translated the Greek *mysterion,* which does not mean sacrament in the common, ecclesiastical sense but rather a sacred mystery, something the human mind cannot fathom. Not content with this philological consideration, Erasmus assembled the testimony of many fathers of the church, including Augustine and Jerome, who in their listing of the sacraments did not include marriage. Further, he said that if marriage was a sacrament and virginity was not, marriage might seem to be a more elevated state than virginity—an idea contradicting the almost unanimous Catholic tradition of centuries that for those who could heed the call of virginity, a special grace elevated them above the common herd of those whose fleshly call to marriage could not be resisted. Erasmus declared that he accepted the sacramental status of marriage because the tradition of the church taught it. After reading the long note with its powerful arguments that this sacramental status was not set in either scripture or important patristic sources, we may be permitted to wonder if we have here a supreme ironist at work, the author of the *Praise of Folly* turning his temperament to the interpretation of scripture.

As for Ephesians itself, Erasmus said that the thought and spirit of the book was absolutely Pauline but that the style was not. He doubted that James the Apostle had written the book of James. He thought the writers of the New Testament had made errors in their quotations from the Hebrew Bible, which they had received by way of the Greek translation called the Septuagint. He said little about the book of Revelation. What he did say was not complimentary. The book's repetition of "I, John" irritated him. This way of talking about himself lacked the modesty of the apostle John, who in the gospel attributed to him never mentioned his own name but rather called himself only the "disciple whom Jesus loved." The repetitive "I, John, I, John," said Erasmus, made it sound as if the author were writing a legal contract rather than a sacred book. More radically, Erasmus revived an ancient suspicion that Revelation had been written by an early Christian heretic and planted in the canon to lead the faithful astray. After an exposition of this startling thought, he declared that he could not believe that God would allow Satan to deceive his people to such a degree. Having cast these doubts on the book, he said that he would keep it in his New Testament because it reflected the life and thought of the early church.

The ever-quarrelsome Johann Eck wrote Erasmus a sharp letter of protest in February 1518. Eck began with sugary flattery but passed quickly into annoyed and detailed criticism of what Erasmus had done with the sacred text.[5] In particular he attacked Erasmus for saying that now and then the authors of the New Testament had suffered memory lapses and made mistakes in quoting the Hebrew Bible. He was also offended because Erasmus said that the apostles had written in a vulgar Greek not up to the standards of eloquence set by some classical writers. To Eck these comments indicated that the Bible, as Erasmus saw it, was of human origin and not divine.

In May 1518 Erasmus replied to Eck with an annoyed letter of his own. His considered the nature of divine revelation. He categorically rejected the notion that every word in the New Testament was inspired by the Holy Spirit. "It is perhaps not for us to know just in what way the Spirit joined itself to the instrument of the apostles." The "instrument" *(organum)* here is the New Testament. "But," continued Erasmus, "however it did so, it was in such a way as to work best toward the salvation of the human race. So the Spirit was with them insofar as necessary for the business of the gospel, and yet elsewhere leaving them free to be men. Neither do I say these things that I might suppose that the apostles had ever made errors but that I might deny that all scripture might be shaken for whatever errors there might be."[6]

From this statement I infer that Erasmus believed the apostles were inspired but not all their words. We have in this view a foretaste of the modern notion that words only feebly convey the reality they signify. Erasmus grounded the superiority of scripture on the superiority of the men who wrote it and on their reliability as witnesses to the events they described. In this light, scripture is inspired as its authors were inspired, but since they were feeble human beings, their texts partake of their human fallibility. The history behind the text is inspired, for it comprises the teaching, life, death, and resurrection of Christ, and a spiritual reading of the New Testament brings us into living encounter with those events. All these events may be allegorically interpreted to heal and nourish the Christian soul in its struggles with this earthly life. But none of this redeeming action requires us to believe that scripture is textually infallible.[7]

At times Erasmus could be bolder. He found much in the Hebrew Bible, the Old Testament, to scorn. God in the Hebrew Bible, as it emerged from its editing process, is almighty; he creates heaven and earth with a word, and he is above all other gods—but he creates a serpent who undoes all his creative work. Often he acts like a large and powerful and somewhat bad-tempered human being. Like any landlord, he walks in the Garden of Eden in the cool of the day. He gets angry. He bargains with his people. He changes his mind. He falls into vindictive rages, as in the case of Noah's flood or the Tower of Babel or the unfortunate cities of Sodom and Gomorrah, and he plays atrocious games, as in the case of his command to Abraham to sacrifice his son Isaac. He has a somewhat bizarre preoccupation with the length of Samson's hair. He performs prodigious wonders, such as slaughtering the first-born sons of Egypt and leading the Israelites to safety through the parted waters of the Red Sea—only to discover that those who have witnessed those stupendous miracles quickly forget them and turn to complaint and the worship of other gods. Like all of us, the God of the Hebrew Bible is a mess of contradictions.

Erasmus recognized the problems. Lucien Febvre notes with admiration the "daring" of Erasmus in pointing them out in his commentary on the adage "Sileni Alcibiadis," the object that is ugly on the outside but when opened reveals something of surpassing beauty. The Bible was such a "silenus," ugly on the outside, and Febvre summarizes Erasmus on the subject:

Adam formed by a divine sculpture with the help of wet clay; the soul breathed into him; Eve manufactured from a rib of the first man; the Garden of Eden; a serpent who speaks a language that can be understood by human beings; the miraculous, nursery-tale tree; a God who strolls in his garden in the cool of the day; the angel who stands guard with a flaming soul . . . What mythology! exclaims Erasmus. It is what one would say about the fables that come out of old Homer's inexhaustible workshop in such naive abundance.[8]

Erasmus was here influenced by Origen, one of the most thoroughly educated of the early Greek fathers of the church, a Neoplatonist, and historically suspect within the church in his willingness to cover the difficulties of scripture with allegory. Throughout his little book called the *Enchiridion,* first published in 1503, Erasmus championed the use of allegory in interpreting scripture, especially the Old Testament. Water, for example, became a symbol of God's law—by which Erasmus meant the spiritual righteousness God wanted from his people. Wherever water, rivers, wells, or washing are mentioned, we have allegories of divine wisdom. "The frequent references in sacred writings to wells, fountains, and rivers suggest to us nothing less than a diligent scrutiny of the secret meanings of Scripture. For what is water hidden in the heart of the earth but mysterious truth hidden under the literal sense? And what is this same water bubbling up as a spring but that mystery opened up and illuminated?"[9]

All this is related to a platonizing rhetoric that Erasmus used in making religious distinctions. Spiritual truth lay concealed in a material covering. For him, the key to scripture was Christ. The texts of the Gospels "mirror the living image of that most holy Spirit and Christ himself as he speaks, heals, dies, rises again and makes him finally so fully present that one might see less of him if he stood before our eyes."[10] This principle allowed Erasmus to declare, as he did in the *Enchiridion,* that "all the Holy Scriptures are divinely inspired and originate with God as the Author." Yet always there was a "husk," the material text, and always there was a "spiritual meaning" that must be dug out. And Erasmus could advise readers of scripture to choose those interpretations of "divine Scripture" that "go as far as possible beyond literal meaning."[11]

The problem with allegory is, of course, that what emerges from the process depends on what the reader brings to a text. Erasmus brought to his allegories the Christ he found in the Gospels. The appearance of scripture often contradicts the reality of God. When that happens, the Christian reader is to bring Christ to the text, and then the ugly exterior will be cast aside, and the true beauty of meaning will be revealed.[12] In effect scripture becomes a substitute for the incarnation of the risen and ascended Christ of the Gospels. All this is to remove the literal *text* of scripture at a length from the medieval conception that it was dictated by God in the way of paintings of St. Matthew, pen in hand, looking attentively at an angel who is whispering the words of the gospel into his ear. (The angel was the traditional symbol of Matthew; the notion of the dictating angel thus came naturally.)

Erasmus brings the Bible down into a human landscape even while preserving the divine mystery. It inevitably reduces the literal certainty of the biblical record, although Erasmus's thoughts on the book of Revelation may be applied here. Just as God would not allow a deceitful book of heresy to be admitted into the canon of holy scripture, neither would he allow erroneous or seemingly unworthy scriptural texts to impugn the fundamentals of the Christian faith.

Although Erasmus's New Testament influenced Luther's translation, it was contrary to Luther's spirit. In particular Luther objected to the relish with which Erasmus showed the fathers of the church at odds with each other. "We should have nothing to do with the translation of Erasmus," he grumbled once. "It is not serious. It is ambiguous and sophistical. In his New Testament he brings in all the Fathers. So thinks Ambrose. So reads Augustine! Why? To perturb the reader so that he may suppose that this doctrine is absolutely uncertain. He abuses all us Christians without discrimination. He makes no exception for Paul or any other pious Christian."[13]

Still, many of Luther's interpretations matched those of Erasmus. In addition to following Erasmus's reading of Ephesians 5:32, he agreed with Erasmus that the command of John the Baptist to repent did not imply the developed Catholic doctrine of penance with its steps of contrition, confession, and satisfaction. From Erasmus, too, he would take his doubts about the authorship of the book of James, a book Luther detested because it had been written against Paul's doctrine of faith as the sole necessity in salvation. The book of Revelation, the Apocalypse with its lurid images and its depiction of a final, cataclysmic war between God and Satan, posed special problems for Luther. It had fascinated medieval monks, and some of the most beautiful manuscripts we have from the Middle Ages are copies of this mysterious book lovingly illuminated by monastic artists.

In his early lectures on the Psalms he had quoted Revelation often, some fifty-four times—more than most of the historical books of the Hebrew Bible, more than the Gospel of Mark, more than most of the shorter epistles of the New Testament.[14] But by his stay in the Wartburg, he expressed doubts about it in his treatise *The Misuse of the Mass*.[15] With its vivid and spectacular prophecies of the coming Antichrist, the book offered Luther a rhetorical hammer with which to pound the papacy, which in Luther's view was the fulfillment of all those dire visions. So he used it, but he did not otherwise try to define doctrine with it. Later on, as life closed in on him and he found himself beset by rivals in the evangelical movement, confronted by a papacy that had gathered remarkable new strength, he found new worth in the book of Revelation and came back to it now and then. In 1532 he remarked that with the Turks on the move and the papacy clearly the Antichrist, "All things in scripture have now been fulfilled."[16] The great apocalyptic books of Daniel and Revelation now seemed to fit together. The end of the world was near.

Like Erasmus, Luther found himself making a revolutionary shift in his evaluation of scripture. The books of the Bible were not all of the same worth. The divine was not found equally in all its parts. Therefore a translation could not be a mere release of the bare text upon the world. Luther's translation came with many helps to ensure that readers understood it as he did. The most important of these helps were prefaces and sidenotes. He affixed to the front of his New Testament a general preface in which he explained how the work was to be read.[17]

The New Testament, he said, carries the good news of the gospel that raises a cry of joy from those who receive it and know that it represents victory over sin, death, and the devil. It is called a "testament" because Christ in dying gave to believers all his property, which is to say his life, with which he conquered death; his righteousness, with which he canceled sin; and his salvation, with which he overcame eternal damnation.

The emphasis throughout the preface on the conquest of sin and death is strong and constant, and when Luther speaks of sin, death, and hell, it is without any suggestion that hell is a place of torment. The Old Testament contains the law, although for Luther it also resonated with prophecies of Christ. The New Testament contains the gospel in all its fullness but also precepts about right living. Yet despite these precepts that guide our moral life, Christians should take care not to make Christ a second lawgiver. The gospel, he said, is not a law book but a sermon about the good deeds of Christ given to anyone who believes. Luther's rhetoric through this and the other prefaces throughout his translation pounds his message home with a force that for many has proved sufficient to overcome some of the inherent difficulties of his position. Committed Catholics were in no such mood. The core of these difficulties lay in a selective reading of scripture with no canon to regulate his judgment except his sense of which books conformed to the gospel.

This selective reading shows in sharpest focus in the boldness with which Luther asserts his own canon of scripture within the larger corpus of the New Testament. He tells us that the Gospel of John, Paul's epistles—especially Romans—and 1 Peter are central to all the rest and ought to be read daily by

Christians. These books, he says, are to be prized above even the Gospels of Matthew, Mark, and Luke. Luther's preferences exhibit a penchant for exalting books that explain the mission of Christ over those that tell only what Christ did. Some books he comes close to dismissing altogether, but he stops short of such radicalism—as did Erasmus, who made similar judgments. In his general preface Luther calls "James" a "right strawy epistle without any evangelical sense."[18]

In addition to his general preface, Luther set marginal notes at key texts where he wanted to be certain that readers not take a wrong turn. He did not affix a preface to any of the four Gospels or to the book of Acts. But to the Epistle to the Romans he wrote a long introduction, calling it the high point of the New Testament, worthy not only to be learned by heart by Christians but also to be considered the daily bread of the soul; It can never be read too much; the more it is considered, the more precious it becomes.[19]

He followed this fervent expression with an eloquent description of the relation of law and gospel. The law spoken of here, he said, represents all that a man can do by his own free will and strength, and it is not sufficient to earn the righteousness God requires for salvation. That salvation can come only through the grace of God in faith. Faith is a divine work in us, a new birth from God that kills the old Adam and makes us completely different men in heart, spirit, being, and all strength. "Oh, it is living, creating, acting powerful thing concerning faith that it cannot but do good."[20]

He made a distinction between "flesh" and "spirit" to explain Paul. "Flesh" is not external and "spirit" is not internal; rather the flesh is a principle in human life, both external and internal, that attends to life in time on earth. The "spirit" is all that is human existence, both interior and external, that serves the eternal life to come.[21] Having made this distinction, he delivered a chapter-by-chapter summary of Romans with a fervor that must be read to be appreciated.

Each of the following books of the New Testament got its own preface. Some are perfunctory; others raise interesting historical questions. Erasmus cautiously rejected Pauline authorship of the book of Hebrews. Luther was bolder. He found internal evidence to persuade himself that the epistle had been written by someone who knew Jesus and the original apostles. He spoke of the "hard knot" in the claim of the author of Hebrews that those who commit sins after baptism cannot repent and be restored to the Christian community—a teaching that Luther rightly pointed out contradicts the epistles of Paul and the four gospels. Hebrews is, said Luther, an epistle that has its gold, silver, and precious stones; but its wealth does not keep us from finding mixed in with it some wood, straw, and grass.[22] So far had he come since the lectures on Hebrews that he gave while the controversy over indulgences broke out.

In his prologue to "James," he returned to the theme developed in his general preface. He praised "James," he said, but it was not apostolic. It stands against the apostle Paul and all the rest of scripture in teaching that works justify. It contradicts Paul directly, said Luther, in that "James" declares that in his willingness to sacrifice his son Isaac, Abraham was justified by his works; Paul said in Romans that Abraham in that moment was justified by his faith. Moreover, said Luther, "James" mentions Christ several times but teaches us nothing about his suffering, his resurrection, and his spirit and, instead of speaking of faith in Christ, speaks rather of a general faith in God. The touchstone of any book, Luther wrote, was whether it preached Christ or not. "Whatever does not teach Christ is not apostolic even if Peter or Paul teaches it. On the other hand, whatever teaches Christ is apostolic, even if it is done by Judas, Annas, Pilate, and Herod."[23]

This "James," Luther wrote, was probably some good, pious man who seized upon something said by some of the disciples of the apostles and set it down in writing. Or, he suggested, perhaps the book was from his preaching as taken down by yet another.[24] Luther's condescension is clear. The book might be three generations removed from Christ, and it was third rate. He had here fallen into the historical critical mode used by Erasmus whereby scripture was subject to dissection by the tools being sharpened by humanism, helped along by James's demand that "faith without works is dead." (Erasmus, while rejecting the apostolic origin of James, heartily approved its ethical message.)

His comments on Revelation are much more severe. "I say what I feel," he wrote in 1522. The book was neither apostolic nor prophetic, and its imagery and unclarity had nothing in them like the simplicity and directness of the language of the apostles. People could do with the book what they wanted, he said, but his own spirit was uncomfortable with it. In it Christ is neither taught nor proclaimed. He preferred, he said, to stick with those books of the Bible that gave him Christ "bright and clear."[25]

Ironically, the most striking feature to the casual examiner of the "September Testament" is the array of woodblock prints portraying the visions of Revelation and carved by Lucas Cranach and artists/artisans under his direction. These prints were heavily influenced by a series of prints on Revelation issued by Albrecht Dürer in 1498. The mythic pictures show the firm grip apocalyptic visions had on the popular mind, and someone thought they would help sell the book. Luther may not have had much to do with them.

Some did illustrate Luther's viewpoint by placing a papal tiara on the heads of the beast and of the whore of Babylon representing the Antichrist. Duke George of Saxony was so incensed by Luther's Bible that he forbade its sale in his domains, and even the Elector Frederick seemed upset by these images of the papal tiara. When Luther's New Testament was reprinted in December, the papal tiara in these prints had been modified to become an ordinary and therefore nondescript crown.[26]

Other illustrations also helped carry the message. In showing an altar within the temple, Cranach set it not in the choir but in the main part of the building. The altar was not surrounded by a railing. The message was the priesthood of all believers and the supposed end of the exaltation of priesthood over the laity. Equally clear was the tiara-crowned beast threatening the entire scene.[27]

Luther's grading of scripture deserves commentary. The great Luther scholar and admirer Heinrich Bornkamm pointed out some years ago that Luther's attitude toward the Bible, finding the gospel within the Gospels, represents a revolution.[28] The medieval notion that all parts of the Bible were equally inspired was cast aside. As we have seen, Erasmus had gone far in the same direction, raising doubts about both the book of James and the book of Revelation, but his final word on each sounds much more moderate than Luther's condescending disapproval of James, Jude, and Revelation, not to mention his grave doubts about the message of Hebrews.

Luther's judgments have been frequently admired. Except for fundamentalists, few if any modern New Testament scholars hold that Revelation, "James," and Jude were written by men close to Jesus in time or place. Revelation—the "Apocalypse" as it was called in the Middle Ages, using a transliteration of the Greek word for Revelation—remains the esoteric darling of zealots in every age who use it to prove that the world will soon be transformed by the Antichrist, the Great Tribulation, and finally the return of Christ.

Yet the step Luther took—as Erasmus had before him—was inevitably to undermine the movement he had willy-nilly founded. He claimed to rely on scripture alone for his advice. Catholics mocked him with the charge that Christ had not written a book but had rather founded a church and that without the authority of the church, Luther had no way of telling what was scripture and what was not. Now with the prefaces for the "September Testament" he seemed to concede their argument. Beyond the protective wall of Catholic tradition, scripture might seem to dissolve into its parts, and only private judgment was to be the standard for which parts were valid and which not. Naturally enough Luther claimed that his was not private judgment at all but the testimony of the Holy Spirit. For him the best parts of scripture proclaimed and explained the mission of Christ, especially his suffering, his resurrection from the dead, and his grace and promise to those who clung to him in faith. This suffering Christ mirrored Luther's own experience, and whenever that Christ appeared, nails in his hands and feet and crown of thorns on his head, Luther knew that here was an apostolic word, the word and work of God.

It is worth emphasizing, too, that Luther was selective even among the Gospels. He did not reject the synoptics—Matthew, Mark, and Luke, generally held by scholars to have been written within a generation of Christ's death. Yet he valued them less than he did the Gospel of John, now considered to have been written perhaps two generations after Christ's death and perhaps later than that. His reasons are clear enough. In Matthew, Mark, and Luke Jesus seems to be a miracle worker and ethical teacher who proclaims the mysterious "Kingdom" and who is crucified and resurrected. In Matthew and in the oldest copies we have of Mark, Jesus does not ascend into heaven. He seems rather to fade away (as he does in the Gospel of John). Only in the book of Acts, an extension of Luke, do we have the story of his ascent to the skies, although the Gospel of John implies that he ascended immediately after the Resurrection and then returned to appear to his disciples (John 20:17, 27–28).

With the Fourth Gospel, we have a fully developed religion of salvation from death, the teaching that Jesus is the Logos—the divine, creative principle of the cosmos—and that he will incorporate his followers into himself to live with him in the life to come. The great miracle of this gospel is the resurrection of Lazarus—unknown to the synoptics. This is the culmination of the religion of Paul, who never saw Jesus but who had his famous experience on the road to Damascus and became the apostle of Christ the victor over death and for whom the ethical teachings of Jesus became a collection of generalities summarized in his exaltation of love above all other virtues.

Luther seems to have had little continuing interest in miracle stories except for the grandest miracle of all, the resurrection of Jesus. Magicians were common enough in the ancient world. For Luther as for Paul, the major Christian proclamation was not that Christ healed the sick, opened the eyes of the blind, multiplied loaves and fishes, or walked on water and calmed storms. Rather that proclamation was that Christ rose from the dead and incorporates his followers into himself so that they, too, will rise from the dead.

Jesus the ethical teacher, who seems to the common reader to offer heavenly rewards in exchange for earthly good deeds, the Jesus of the Sermon on the Mount as recorded in Matthew and Luke, does not fit Luther's view of the gospel. The Jesus of the synoptic Gospels tells his disciples that the Kingdom is soon coming, that it will belong to the poor or to the poor in spirit, that it is harder for a camel to go through the eye of a needle than for a rich man to enter heaven, and holds out a divine carrot and stick to coax or drive humanity into virtue. This is the Jesus of Erasmus. Luther's Jesus was Paul's. As noted earlier, in his table talk Luther did not disagree when one of his students remarked that Paul taught more clearly than Christ himself.[29]

Many Christians in the early church, it seems, considered dropping the Hebrew scriptures altogether from the canon. But for Luther the Old Testament and the New Testament were complementary parts of a divine miracle of revelation, and the Old Testament had to be translated into German. Still, his selective principles of interpretation became the avenue that would in time lead to the "higher criticism" of the Bible that in the nineteenth century would become supreme in Germany and virtually demolish among the educated the notion that such inspiration as the Bible possesses enjoys a magical, supernatural quality. The fundamentalist movement that arose in reaction to higher criticism and other modern currents of thought, including Darwinism, was a renunciation of a selective evaluation of the Bible that Luther himself advocated.

Luther had hardly seen the "September Testament" off to the printer before he started work on his translation of the Hebrew scriptures. It was to appear in three volumes. The first two were finished and published by early 1524. Controversies and illness then intervened, and he did not complete the Old Testament and the Apocrypha until 1532. Thereafter he revised continually almost to the eve of his death.

He never claimed to be a profound scholar of either Greek or Hebrew. He regretted throughout his life that he had not begun his study of both languages earlier, and he never developed the intuitive feeling for Greek possessed by Erasmus. He lacked the sweeping knowledge of Greek literature that allowed Erasmus to say with authority that the writers of the Gospels did not rise to the eloquence of the best Greek writers and to suggest that the style of Ephesians was not Pauline although the substance was. Most of Luther's Old Testament translation is heavily dependent on the Latin Vulgate, his basic source text.

He had a working knowledge of both Greek and Hebrew, and it got better as he went along. He sought help everywhere he could find it from friends and other scholars. He required help even in German, for he had spent his adult life in the monastery, and his German vocabulary was largely religious and theological. He needed help in finding the right German words for things as diverse as jewels and animals mentioned in the Bible. His German improved as he worked, and his Bible became one of the great milestones in the development of High German, the language that eventually won out in popularity over the various dialects spoken in the German lands—though its victory has never been complete. German remains notoriously "dialektisch."

In his preface to the Old Testament, published in the first volume issued in 1523, Luther took into account those who had devalued the Hebrew scriptures, including Jerome and Origen. He quoted Jesus, Paul, and Peter that the Old Testament prophesied Christ, his death and resurrection, and that Christians should read it, for, he said, "What else is the New Testament except an open preaching and proclamation of the prophecies set down in the Old Testament and through Christ fulfilled?"[30]

He was also cautious. His German Bible was going to the laity, to people uneducated in the complexities of theology, and who could easily misunderstand the message Luther believed scripture held. The literate masses included perforce many Christians in name only, the multitude whom Luther scorned and feared. Scripture, he said early in his preface, must be read by those who would not stumble on their own wisdom and vanity. Scripture turned the wise and the intelligent into fools, and often the humble and the foolish understood it best. Here was a circumspect appeal not to rush to judgment on scripture, not to find things in it that were not there, not to approach it with vanity and pride. We in the Protestant tradition have heard words like these so often both in hundreds of sermons and in the New Testament itself that their cautions roll off us like water on a tile roof. Yet in Luther's preface, they appeal against the extremes of interpretation that had already burst out among his own followers and reveal a sense of risk taken with this mass-produced biblical text. He insisted on seeing the value of the Hebrew scriptures in their testimony about Christ.

The Old Testament was a law book, telling people what they should do and providing examples for the consequences of disobedience. The New Testament was a book of grace and showed how the law might be fulfilled. Yet amid the law of the Old Testament was the promise of Christ to come, the proclamation by the prophets of grace and peace and the forgiveness of sins in Christ. In summarizing the first books of the Old Testament, he followed Paul in the teaching that the purpose of the law of Moses was to define the true nature of sin and to establish also the Jews as the people of God. But all this only confirmed by historical example the impossibility of fulfilling the law—which finally came down to the commands to love God and to love the neighbor as the self.

The Mosaic law was of three sorts, he said. One sort governed strictly earthly matters—such as the laws of marriage and divorce. Moses permitted bigamy. As Luther saw it, bigamy had nothing to do with divine matters; it was an earthly arrangement. Another sort of law dealt with the outward worship of God. The forms of worship were not eternally defined; true worship required only faith and love, and the forms might change with time and circumstance. He castigated the Jews for their dietary laws, for Moses had given them, he thought, for his times and not for eternity. He pointed out several places in the historical books of the Old Testament where people had taken the law into their own hands. King David had extended mercy to several people who, according to the law of Moses, deserved to die, and thus he had broken the law. Whoever set out to rule a people by law, he said, must treat them like asses, for law was a matter of compulsion. To live under the law was to recognize a sickness, and the experience of Israel under the law helped prepare for the grace that would come in Christ.

That finally was the main purpose of the law, to make the people of God recognize that it does not suffice. Quoting Paul, he declared that by law can no one please God. Moses could do no more than to show us what we ought to do. But in the law is no strength to do what we ought. The law leaves us in sin, and death then comes on us as revenge and punishment for sin. And as Paul said, sin is the sting of death.

Then Luther made an important point, one he was to hold for the rest of his life, one of his great consistencies amid the inconsistencies of his turbulent career. Without the law, our blind reason cannot know what sin is. Without the law no one can recognize that unbelief and doubting God are sins. Without the law human pride turns to the notion that good deeds make the good man when these good deeds done for such a motive are in fact sins, an inclination to the "flesh," which in Luther as in Paul stands for all those impulses that have as their purpose a better mortal life without regard for the life hereafter. In effect Luther was attacking one of the major impulses of classical Greek and Roman philosophy so beloved by many humanists, including the Christianized version that became the "philosophy of Christ" for Erasmus. Both the stoic and Epicurean ethical philosophies were built on self-control and restraint, on a certain detachment that, in some forms of stoicism, might lead to doing one's duty to one's society—however duty was defined—without the expectation of any reward except the consciousness that one had done one's best.

But more here was at stake than a judgment on classical philosophy and the humanists of the Renaissance. How do we have any sense of what is "right" or "wrong" in human conduct? What is the ground of any ethical system, the primary assumption from which we may extract all the rest?

Amid the genocide and total war of the twentieth century, this ultimate derivation of right and wrong becomes an issue of basic survival that we can define in a negative way as "crimes against humanity." In a positive sense we come up with words such as "tolerance" and "humanity" and "justice" and even "pity" and "love." But the content of these words lies concealed in the fuzziness of our thinking and in the fervor of those who claim the right to do what they want because they have a power that no one can or will effectively resist.

Luther appears to be saying here that we can have no ultimate sense of right or wrong, no solidly grounded ethic, unless we are religious people and unless we believe that God has defined right and wrong by the law. Our inability to obey the law does not subtract from its value; in fact the purpose of the law is to reveal our weakness to us by providing standards of virtue. In the recognition of our inability to be good, we become humble, unwilling to assert our power over others unless we are magistrates charged with suppressing those who would otherwise use power for private ends.

What happens to natural law, the law planted in our hearts by our nature to tell us the difference between right and wrong? According to Luther, in nature we find "certainly neither trust nor faith, neither fear nor love for God."[31] These qualities are the essence of the law, lying behind the law's outward rules and regulations, which, in Luther's view, can be lifted if in particular moments they conflict with love and faith. In legal terms Luther was applying a principle of equity to all the Old Testament law, which, though given by God through Moses, could be suspended for suitable cause.

The preface is filled with the brooding over death as the curse of the law—Paul's great theme in 1 Corinthians 15. Luther speaks from time to time of both death and hell, and again hell in these passages may be only a synonym for the grave, although he does not define it. He says nothing about hell as eternal torment. He delivers a striking allegory of how the law brings death by commanding that which we cannot do. He likens the law and the punishment of death that is attached to it to the Philistine giant Goliath, "whose spear was like a weaver's beam" with an iron point weighing 600 shekels, so that all Israel fled before him. But then came David alone, like Christ, and Goliath fell. Without Christ to bring clarity to the law of Moses, no one could bear the blinding glare of the law and the fear of death.[32] It is a striking image—death standing before us like a giant with an iron-tipped spear, the shining of the blade so intense that we are blinded by it, but Christ comes and gives us "clarity" by which we see through the glare to the grace he provides.

Luther made of the entire history of Israel an allegory of salvation. The promised land was the Israelites' if they obeyed the law, but since they could not obey, they lost their land. Christ then came with the New Testament guaranteed by God himself, a land of promise that will never be lost. The Levitical priesthood, he said, was a figure of the priesthood of Christ. Whereas the Old Testament priests killed and offered sacrifices, the priests of Christ—all the Christians of earth—preach the gospel by which the old man is killed and offered to God and by love in the Holy Spirit is burned and consumed and sends up a pleasing odor to God.

He closed the preface of the 1523 edition with some comments on the difficulties of the Hebrew text. The Jews had corrupted it, and Christians had not learned the language as they should. Still, he said, his German text was much better than the Latin Vulgate in many places—so long as the printer did not mess it up—something, said Luther, the printer had promised to avoid. He knew he would be criticized. Others should try their hand at the task of translation. He had not worked alone, he said; he had taken help wherever he could find it. Anyone with suggestions to make should "help me where he can." He concluded by expressing the desire of his heart: "May God will to complete his work that he has begun."[33]

In the midst of this gigantic labor lies a paradox: Only those who already accepted at least the outline of Luther's concept of religion could accept his reading of scripture. His reading of the Bible was not to be proved by the bare text; it was rather to be validated by the experience of the "true Christians" whom he addressed, an experience very much like his.

Soon enough Luther was to discover to his chagrin and alarm that "true Christians" were not as numerous as he supposed and that, as Catholic writers such as Thomas More had scornfully predicted, agreement on the meaning of scripture was impossible, even among the devout. He argued eloquently that true religion could not be imposed by force. In the end force ruled after all. His tragedy was that the intensity of his own experience and his demand for certainty blinded him almost completely to the experience of others.

21

THE AUTHORITY
OF PRINCES

As luther's New Testament circulated in the German lands, Catholic authorities tried to suppress it. Duke George of Saxony fulminated against this professor who was turning the world upside down, and he now campaigned against the spread of this heretical translation. As early as September 1522 Luther had been reconsidering the role of secular authority in the Christian life, and he had preached on the subject. His attack on Henry VIII and the sharp criticism he received about it from some quarters naturally stayed on his mind despite the bravado with which he justified it.

Now Duke George demanded that his people surrender copies of Luther's testament so the book could be destroyed. Should the duke's commands be obeyed? Luther thought that the question deserved an extended answer, one based on a full theological consideration of the relation between the Christian who lived by the gospel and the secular authority that ruled by the power of laws supported by the force of arms—including the headsman's ax, the hangman's noose, and all the other common instruments of mutilation and torture that put iron teeth in the law of the times.

So he wrote *On Secular Authority and How Far One Should Be Obedient to It.* He wrote in German to be certain his thought gained the widest currency among the people, even among the literate peasants. The peasants were restless. Among them stirrings of revolt trembled like leaves before a storm. The treatise could also be read by the knights of Germany, who were having a hard time economically and who looked for leadership to Franz von Sickingen. Many knights and peasants saw Luther as a messiah, the prophet of their own interests. Had they read the treatise with care, they would have felt otherwise.

Luther dated his preface in a letter to Duke John of electoral Saxony, Frederick's younger brother—January 1, 1523. The book was doubtless still at the printer's when Luther wrote to Duke George himself on January 3 in response to an indignant letter from George a few days earlier. A private letter Luther had written to a friend had been published. In it Luther referred to George as a "bladder," that is, someone full of urine. In the original letter, Luther had left the name of the alleged "bladder" blank, but in the published version, the friend had thoughtfully filled in Duke George's name. The duke was furious and wrote Luther to tell him so. Luther responded with his usual tact. The duke demanded to know if Luther would admit to writing the slanderous letter. The German idiom for "admit" was *geständig sein,* "to stand for something." Luther replied that as far as the duke was concerned, it was all the same whether standing, lying down, sitting, or running. "I volunteer to serve your ungrace in any way I can as long as your request is not altogether wrong. If that's contempt, I can't do anything about it. But I'm not going to be scared to death over any bladder if God and my Lord Jesus Christ will it."[1] In 1540, within a year after Duke George died, Luther was still calling him a "bladder." Of the duke's ten children, only one, a daughter, survived, and she was married to Philip of Hesse, by then a Lutheran prince. Luther saw the end of the duke's male line as sign of the judgment of God for seeking to destroy the Word.[2] Shortly after Duke George died in 1539, Leipzig and ducal Saxony came over to Lutheran doctrines, but Luther was never popular there.

Luther's *On Secular Authority* is in some degree an extension of his retort to Duke George.[3] Rulers had authority that went only so far. They commanded earthly things for the good order of the human community. But they could not claim jurisdiction over things of the spirit pertaining to the soul and its destiny. Luther had arrived through his own independent reasoning and experience to a position reminiscent of the views of Pope Gregory VII in the investiture controversy of the eleventh century—views that had created the politically powerful papacy that Luther detested. Like Gregory he considered most princes to be miserable human beings, filled with greed and pride and without proper reverence toward God. "You must know," wrote Luther, "that from the very beginning of the world, a wise prince is a rare bird, and even much rarer is a pious prince."[4] Princes are, he said, usually the biggest fools or the worst rogues on earth. Therefore one should always expect the worst from them and only exceptionally a godly deed that pertains to the salvation of souls.

Then why do princes rule? For the same reason Pope Gregory decreed in the eleventh century—following Augustine seven hundred years earlier and Paul shortly after the time of Christ. Princes rule by force because the prevailing wickedness in the world among the multitude is so great that without the prince's power to suppress evil, the world would tumble into chaos. Two kingdoms live intertwined with each other on earth—the kingdom of God and the kingdom of earth. To the kingdom of God belonged the true Christians, Luther said, those who like tame animals need no law to keep them from devouring one another. If Christians were the only people on earth, no prince, king, lord, sword, or even law would be necessary or useful. Why? Because Christians have the Holy Spirit in their hearts to instruct them and to keep them from doing harm. Where every right thing is done, every man is loved and every wrong is suffered, even death, there is no contention, hatred, court, judge, punishment, law, or sword required.

But the world is not made up of true Christians. In fact among thousands of people scarcely one true Christian may be found. The wicked would tear each other to pieces if the world were ruled by the gospel alone. So the two orders must remain, and the true Christians must serve secular government whenever possible because in so doing they help keep the peace. By taking part in worldly government, they demonstrate their love for the neighbor. As Paul said in Romans 13, the secular authority is ordained by God and does not bear the sword in vain. Can hangmen be true Christians? Yes, said Luther, as long as they serve not their own interest but rather the law. When power and sword serve God, Christians do good by wielding them, even if they must put others to death.

Yet secular authority has its limits. It can rule only the externals, body and goods. It has no authority over the soul. No government can decree faith. Everyone has the responsibility for his own belief and must see to it that he believes correctly. Luther quoted Augustine: No one should be compelled to believe. Luther specified the lines of disobedience. If the prince or secular Lord commands the Christian to stay with the pope or to believe unchristian doctrines or takes away your godly books you must say, "It is not possible to seat Lucifer with God." The Christian must refuse to obey such a command. Luther named several territories where "tyrants" had ordered the surrender of his translation of the New Testament.[5] Those who *willingly* gave up their copies were murderers of Christ. But resistance should not be active. If the authorities came to their houses and took away the New Testament by force, the people should not resist.

Luther not only exhorted the "true Christians" to make only passive resistance; he also held over the heads of the princes the threat of vengeance for injustice by the mob. The common people could take only so much. If princes did not rule with justice, they might face the wrath of the unchristian multitude. Luther closed with some fairly conventional advice on how princes ought to govern. Throughout he was steadfast in his counsel that rebellion was a sin and could never be Christian.

This work has always been considered a foundation stone in the edifice of Luther's opinions about how the Christian should deal with government. Many parts of it were traditional. The belief that force was necessary to keep in check the greed of individuals went back at least to Augustine and beyond him to Paul, who seemed proud of his Roman citizenship and extolled "the powers that be" as divinely ordained. The small number of true Christians relative to the multitude of the wicked was a staple of the New Testament, and even in the Middle Ages, the so-called age of faith, estimates of the final number of the redeemed were discouragingly low.

Luther was also in accord with the dominant medieval tradition holding that the Christian served God in serving secular government in its effort to keep order. The prevailing sentiment of the church before Constantine had been different. Although now and then some Christians had served pagan Rome, they were few. Most Christians, though willing to pray for the success of Roman fortunes, had not been willing to take part in government. Already by 1523 some radicals stirring in the wake of Luther's movement were teaching that the world was the realm of Satan and that true Christians should isolate themselves in conventicles and have nothing to do with worldly authority. Many of these sects became pacifist, a development that did not prevent Catholics and evangelicals from slaughtering them for their deviations from orthodox doctrine. To many of these peaceable radical groups, the world was the sphere of the devil, and as far as they were concerned, it could go straight to hell. As Heinrich Bornkamm pointed out long ago, these separatist attitudes were not absent from the Middle Ages. The spiritual Franciscans among others wanted the church to withdraw from politics into its own realm of purity and apostolic poverty.[6]

Luther, like Augustine before him, affirmed his belief in the essential goodness of creation by upholding the divine ordination of secular authority. God had made the world; he had not given it over to Satan merely because humankind had sinned. God had a purpose for creation; he had not renounced that purpose. Secular government that kept the peace and allowed the gospel to be preached was part of that purpose. In this treatise Luther not only argued against the "tyranny" of Catholic princes but also shored up his beliefs against the radicals who would read the German New Testament he had given to them and come to the plausible conclusion that the true Christian was an anarchist.

Other qualities of *On Secular Authority* are more problematic. Luther posits an almost mythical "true Christian" here. In his more pastoral works and in his exegesis of scripture, he gives us a Christian always at war with himself, the Christian who is *simul justus et peccator,* as he has it in his early lectures on Romans. This Christian bears the cross of his own sins and suffers attacks of unbelief and perpetual pain for sin until finally redeemed out of this life by the Resurrection. But the Christian in the treatise on secular authority is a saint, passive in persecution, willing to obey and even respect foolish and malicious tyrants who are the princes of Germany. These true Christians are so nearly perfect in Luther's description of them that if the world were full of them they would have no need for government at all. It is as though the Luther who had begun his rebellion against old forms by positing a Christian always aware of sin in the midst of grace had now begun to extol an idealized Christian for whom sin might somehow lurk in the heart but whose saintly outward demeanor was such that the Holy Spirit freed him from all the necessity of secular government. That redeemed paragon of virtue needed no external force to make him do the right thing. The "true Christian" of this work thus becomes a stranger to the true Christian in the rest of Luther's theology of grace so that the sinner who coexists with the justified soul almost disappears. It seems likely that Luther's "true Christian" here is a rhetorical construct intended to stand over against growing numbers of his pretended followers who were leaning toward a more radical way than his. He seems unwilling to admit the tragic dimension that some of us might see here, the true Christian yearning to do the right thing but driven by weakness and circumstance into doing terrible deeds unless the restraints of government apply to him in the same way that they do the rest of us sinners. His conception of the "true Christian" represents both an exaltation of an ideal and a failure of imagination.

His scorn of princes was another matter. In the biting insults that he heaped upon their heads, he enumerated with great rhetorical power their outrages against the common people and the poor. Yes, he counseled obedience to these powerful rogues and fools. The contradiction was too much for ordinary folk to take in. If we know anything about the encounter of people and print in the twentieth century, it is that the masses see in a long discourse only what they want to see. The sound-bite is not the creation of television news. The great ideas of history have always had to become sound-bites of one sort or another before the multitudes could live and die for them. After Luther's tirade against the evils of the ruling class, it would have required superhuman sophistication and restraint in a half-literate population to make the common reader of sixteenth-century Germany believe that it was Christian duty to be passive before the miserable and stupid wretches sketched in Luther's denunciation of princely wickedness. Luther's final admonitions to the princes could make people already disposed to unrest measure the distance between his ideal for princes and his description of the crass and wicked reality.

Luther threatened the princes with the contempt and wrath of the common man, and he called the mob a scourge that might be God's punishment. The reference was to the biblical judgment on the Assyrians who conquered the northern tribes of Israel because the latter had forsaken the true worship of Yahweh. The Assyrians by this biblical reading were not righteous servants of Israel's God; they were merely tools. God could use the wicked for his own purposes, which, the purpose accomplished, could be tossed away. In the end God doomed the Assyrians to the destruction that came on them with terrible speed and finality, celebrated ecstatically by the prophet Nahum. When Luther presented the threat of the wrathful common people as a scourge to princes, he specifically declared that they would not be acting without guilt. They would be tools of God, subject to God's wrath once their purpose was accomplished.

The treatise on secular authority represents an emotional response to unyielding princes determined to stamp out Luther's gospel without giving it a hearing. He needed them. God required them to act as pious Christians. They were not responding. On the one hand he reassured the princes of the harmlessness of his gospel; on the other he threatened them for the hardness of their hearts and their oblivious hostility to his New Testament.

Luther's *On Secular Authority* has always been considered of major importance both in his own evolution and in his influence on the development of German attitudes toward the state. The stereotypical qualities attributed to Germans—obedience, orderliness, passivity before the dictates of government—have been almost routinely attributed to Luther's doctrine of the two kingdoms spelled out in this treatise. Admirers and detractors alike have sought to resolve the eternal dilemma that he here so cogently expressed, the responsibility we have as individuals to our own conscience and our responsibility as citizens to and for the collective will of the nation as defined and set in motion by those who govern.

The horrors of Nazi genocide against the Jews have been almost routinely blamed on Luther's teaching that the Christian should be ultimately passive before evil government, trusting God to avenge himself against wicked rulers. Hitler's twelve-year Reich has become a lens through which Luther's attitudes have been observed, magnified, and inevitably distorted. Whatever Luther was, he was not a progenitor of the Nazis. To him they would have seemed much more like the radical enthusiasts whom he despised. The German tradition of obedience to rulers probably owes far more to Germany's location in the center of Europe, surrounded by enemies, than it does to anything that Luther said or wrote.

Luther's treatise on secular authority shows that he was anything but passive before princes. He railed against their evils and foibles. He always stood ready to assault not only the Duke Georges of the world but also his own successive princes in Wittenberg when they did things—such as raising taxes—that he regarded as immoral and unjust. Yet these protests remained individual and pastoral, and Luther never saw himself as the leader of a rebellion that might organize itself politically to force a government to accede to its wishes. The Christian minister should speak out and be willing to suffer for his opinions, trusting that God was sovereign. Always Luther remained fixed on the admonition of Jesus in John 18:36, "My kingdom is not of this world."

Luther was caught in a dilemma. His message and appeal aimed at a democratic understanding of the church in which all Christians stood on equal ground as priests. In this church, hierarchy would disappear, and in this early period he favored allowing congregations the right to choose their own pastors—an essential tenet of the later "Congregational" churches, heirs to the Puritans in the English-speaking lands. He loved an abstraction called the "German people," but he mistrusted the masses, and his experience with the Zwickau prophets and others increased his apprehension. The masses operating on their own with no authority to control them stood ready to run amok, and evil men with their own purposes lurked ever in the shadows ready to take advantage of the propensity of the masses to violence.

To some degree his dilemma was resolved by his conviction that among the multitudes, only a few true Christians could be found—and even the identity of these true Christians was known only to God. All the rest required force from above to make them obey the restraining wisdom of the law. Thus Luther could in effect extol a democracy of true believers and at the same time certify the need for governments to rule by power and coercion. In the end this fragile solution proved too subtle to be grasped by most people in his own or any other time.

Later, when a few princes came over to his doctrines, he argued that they were in a practical way the successors of the bishops in the Catholic Church. It was up to them to select pastors, to ensure that the pastors were paid and that they preached sound doctrines from their pulpits. Princes were also to enforce rules against idolatrous practices left over from the old church and to curb the preaching and writing of fanatics who threatened the true gospel. Princes became quasi theological officers in that they had it in their power to decide what was good theology and what not. The role of the prince was to be a continuing problem in Germany and the Scandinavian lands where Lutheranism took root.

22

ON THE JEWS

I N JANUARY 1523, when Luther wrote *On Secular Authority*, he published another treatise in German on a subject destined to become one of the darkest stains on his historical reputation. This brief work, *That Jesus Christ Was Born a Jew*, has often been advanced as proof by scholarly partisans of Luther that his attitude toward the Jews was better than many of his critics have claimed. In fact Luther's expressions about the Jews varied over his lifetime, but it seems foolish and even immoral to seek to mitigate or explain away or cover over his prevailing hatred of the Jewish people.

Luther knew few Jews personally, for few Jews remained in Germany to be known. Successive waves of persecution in the German lands had driven Jews toward the East. Persecution was particularly savage in the wake of the Black Death, when Jews were accused of poisoning wells to spread the disease—an accusation helped along by the reputation of Jews, which Luther noted, for skill in medicine.[1] During this hysteria some 2,000 Jews in Strasbourg were herded onto a crude wooden platform erected in the Jewish cemetery, the platform was set afire, and the Jews were burned alive. Jews were mercilessly assaulted in every major German city, and in some, such as Mainz, they burned their houses over their own heads and died in order to escape being hideously tortured to death by angry Christians. In Luther's time Jews could live in the empire only in Worms, Frankfurt am Main, and Prague.[2]

Throughout his life Luther met occasional Jews, some of whom he asked for help in translating parts of the Hebrew Bible. Twice in his table talk he mentioned a visit by three rabbis who sought to convert him. One of them told Luther, "We rejoice that you Christians learn our language and our books such as Genesis and the rest. We hope that in future you will all become Jews." Luther replied that he hoped all Jews would become Christians and said, "Christ can do many things." Luther gave them letters of introduction when they parted, putting in them "In the name of Christ." The rabbis were offended, but later one of them sent Luther a copy of Psalm 130 written in Hebrew letters, which pleased him very much.[3]

Yet through most of his life the Jews remained a people whom Luther did not know face to face. He therefore constructed "the Jews" in his imagination, pouring the abstraction full of his boiling rhetoric as the needs of the moment required. Usually those needs were polemical, but not always. He wrote *That Jesus Christ Was Born a Jew* first to defend himself against slander by Catholics and only as a secondary matter to urge Jews to convert.

The immediate motive for the little work was a rumor spread at the imperial Diet at Nuremberg a few months earlier that Luther had denied the virgin birth of Jesus. The Emperor Charles had not attended this Diet. He sent in his place his brother Ferdinand—if anything a more ardent Catholic than the emperor and a man willing to believe any evil report of Luther and his followers. Ferdinand said that Luther taught that Jesus had been born from the "seed of Abraham" and had therefore rejected the virgin birth—a remark Luther took as a joke when it was first conveyed to him.[4] How could such an innocent statement be contrary to the doctrine of the virgin birth? Who was Jesus if not a Jew? But these accusations took a more serious turn when it appeared that many believed that Luther was teaching that Mary was no virgin when she gave birth to her son.

Luther's attitude toward the Virgin had been warmhearted but circumspect. Like Erasmus he chided those who sought favors from her, but he spent little time and energy on the subject. He seems to have thought it better to preach the gospel and let the cult of the Virgin take care of itself. Meanwhile he extolled the mother of Jesus as an example of Christian humility, especially with regard to the submission and industry women should practice at home and in life. Now he had to defend himself against the widely circulated charge that he had attacked one of the most cherished of Christian beliefs, the perpetual virginity of Mary revered in images of the Madonna and child, a wildly popular religious icon of the Middle Ages.

To consider the doctrines about Mary herself in such a circumstance might have been impolitic. His theology required Luther to maintain that Mary was God's instrument and not the quasi-deity she became in Catholic popular piety. In 1522 he said that to call her "Queen of Heaven" was to give her too much reverence.[5] Yet he never wavered in his conviction that the birth of Jesus was miraculous and that Mary was a virgin when Jesus was born and remained a virgin throughout her marriage to Joseph.[6]

To defend himself he wrote *That Jesus Christ Was Born a Jew.*[7] In it he attacked the evident foolishness of the notion that it was heresy to say that Jesus was born of the seed of Abraham. (It would sound as silly to "accuse" George Washington of being born an English citizen.) To object to saying that Jesus was born of the seed of Abraham was to imply that Jesus had not been born a Jew. Luther picked up on the Christian hatred of the Jews implied in such a declaration and turned it into an accusation against the Catholic clergy and princes whose animosity toward Jews could feed on so ridiculous a thought. He could thereby capture the high moral ground by saying that "they" had acted as though the Jews were dogs and not men and that "they" had done nothing with the Jews other than mock them and rob them of their goods. When Jews were baptized, what did they see in Christendom? Papistry and monks! The Jews saw their own religion as fixed in scripture while they saw Catholics abjure scripture altogether. Luther claimed to have heard from pious, baptized Jews that had it not been for the preaching of the gospel "in our time," they would have remained secretly Jews while pretending to be Christians.[8] He hoped, he said, warming to his task, that if Christians now behaved in friendly fashion to the Jews and taught them soberly from holy scripture, many would be converted and, like their ancestors the prophets and the patriarchs, believe in Christ. If the apostles—who were Jews—had treated the gentiles as Christians treated the Jews, he said, no one among the gentiles would have been converted.

Luther's main purpose in the early part of the treatise was to exercise his rhetorical gifts to turn the tables on his Catholic foes, whom he saw as foolish, malicious, and cruel. He used the Jews as a mirror to hold up to Catholic malice. But he also saw an opportunity to draw the Jews toward conversion. Among Jews in Europe, messianic expectations had been on the rise through the fifteenth century. Many rabbis had predicted that the messiah would come in 1500.[9] Some Jews had rejoiced in the fall of Constantinople to the Turks in 1453, seeing in that Christian catastrophe an event similar to the fall of Babylon to Persia in ancient times. (The Persians had granted religious liberty to the Jews and allowed them to return from exile to Jerusalem.) With Christians in collapse, the messiah would arrive to bring in a new and glorious kingdom on a rejuvenated earth. Luther set out to prove that the messiah had already arrived in Jesus, and he settled into one of his habitual themes, that the New Testament was the fulfillment of the Hebrew Bible, that the messiah foretold in the Old Testament was the Christ proclaimed in the New. For a few pages he developed the theme announced in the beginning—that if Jews were treated kindly by Christians and lovingly instructed out of Holy Writ, they would be converted. Then he shifted to a labored exercise to show prospective Jewish readers—not the audience he first had in mind—that their own scriptures proved that Jesus was the messiah.

His intent was eschatological. An ancient Christian tradition held that the Jews were to be converted before the return of Christ—a belief still staunchly held by many Christian fundamentalists in the United States today, making many of them at once ardently Zionist and harshly anti-Semitic. They love the Jews for what they will be but hate them for what they are. The conversion of the Jews was to become a certain sign of the last days. This expectation of Jewish conversion was not universally held among Christians, and Luther seems to have ignored it in his early lectures on the Psalms. Then the suffering of the Jews, including their diaspora through the nations, seemed to him proof of the wrath of God against them for the Crucifixion. But in his lectures on Romans in 1515–16 he pondered whether a few or all the Jews might be converted, and he suggested that Christians should be kind to them so that they might be attracted to Christ.[10]

By the end of the lectures on Romans, Luther accepted what he called the "common opinion" that at the last day the Jews would be saved. This conviction seems to have grown on him. His translation of the Magnificat into German, published in March 1521, expressed these sentiments even more forcefully, and the conviction became more passionate as he saw that the Catholic Church would not be reformed as he wished and that the power of the papacy would not be broken. The hopes for the Jews expressed in *That Jesus Christ Was Born a Jew* perhaps represented consciously or unconsciously his hopes for his own vindication in a world that was rejecting his gospel and assaulting his character. What a miracle it would be if the Jews were converted and Christ returned in glory to vindicate the gospel that Luther preached!

His arguments that Jesus was the foretold messiah are uninteresting to most of us. Here and there he made a noteworthy judgment. Christ had to be an ordinary man, for he had to crush the power of the devil, sin, and death, and all ordinary men are under the power of sin. He reached back to the patristic age to echo Augustine in his view of biological conception. Christ had to be born of a virgin because even among Christians the sexual act is driven by lust that corrupts it, and lust is the medium by which original sin is transmitted. One might say that according to this teaching, Christ escaped original sin because God the Father engendered him in Mary with the same absence of passion that, according to Augustine, characterized the sexual life of Adam and Eve in Eden, when to engender a child required no more lust than to shake hands.[11]

Luther might have proclaimed Mary's immaculate conception here—a widely shared popular belief that Mary had been freed from the stain of original sin. He had earlier said that the belief was unimportant.[12] Here he left it alone. Later in life he affirmed it.[13] The doctrine was not defined as official dogma until Pius IX proclaimed it in his decree *Ineffabilis Deus* on December 8, 1854.

Luther knew that Paul does not say that Christ was born of a virgin. Paul alludes to Jesus' mother—not by name—only in Galatians 4:4, where he says that Christ was born of a woman. Since Paul does not mention a man's involvement in the process, Luther thought he implied the virgin birth. It was a traditional Christian rationalization of Paul's uncomfortable silence on this doctrine. Luther also knew—as did Jerome and Erasmus—that the celebrated text of Isaiah 7:14, used by Matthew to make the birth of Jesus the fulfillment of prophecy, rested on a suspect translation. The Greek text of the Septuagint used by the author of the Gospel of Matthew reads: "Behold a virgin shall conceive and bring forth a child." The Hebrew word that the Septuagint translators rendered "virgin," *parthenos,* may be transliterated from Hebrew into English as *almah,* a young woman of childbearing age. The Hebrew word for virgin is *bethulah.* Jews traditionally scorned this mistranslation and used it to argue that the story of the virgin birth from Matthew was a hoax. Luther struggled to refute them by saying there was nothing momentous about a young woman's bearing a child in the normal way. To be a divine sign, the young woman had to be a virgin.[14] To anyone reading Isaiah 7:14 today in the context of the biblical book (thought by most modern scholars to be a composite) and the events it describes, the suggestion that the child here prophesied would be the messiah seems far-fetched indeed.

Luther finally did some elaborate calculations from prophesies in the Hebrew bible to show that the messiah predicted then had to appear during the time of Christ. Since the Jews admitted that no other messiah had yet appeared, Christ was ipso facto the true messiah. Luther is nowhere more tedious than he is here in these elaborate chronological calculations; we may be excused for supposing that he is locked in an argument to prove something to himself.

Luther did not organize any great campaign to convert the Jews. The treatise was written as though his duty was to tell the truth and to let God do the rest. The little work proved to be remarkably popular. In Wittenberg alone it went through nine editions in 1523, and it was reprinted in Augsburg, Basel, Strasbourg, and Hagenau. Luther's good friend Justus Jonas translated it from German into Latin.[15] This popularity was probably born of eschatological hopes among Luther's followers. The world they knew was caught up in turmoil and revolution; some divine climax must be portended in all this, and the conversion of the Jews—if it came—would be a sure signal from on high. People with escatalogical impulses will read anything that confirms their obsessions, the more dramatic and filled with numbers and calculations, the better.

Luther's hope for the conversion of the Jews waxed and waned. In 1533 in his table talk he was still hoping for their conversion. The wrath of God still reigned over them, he thought, offering proof of the suffering of the Jews, their exclusion from so many countries. He puzzled over the adherence of so many Christians to the papacy. Why should the Jews not remain in their own faith? If he were a Jew, he said, he would a hundred times rather remain so than to turn to the papacy. "I think many Jews will be converted if they hear our preaching and our interpretation of the Old Testament."[16] Even late in his life he could express pity for how Jews were forced to live crowded together, sometimes fifty to a house, stacked up together in what amounted to a steam bath.[17]

Yet always beneath his pity ran the assumption that the Jews deserved their fate because they had rejected Christ. Time and again his anger erupted at what he considered the natural deduction that Jews made from their rejection of Jesus—that the Virgin Mary was a "whore" and that Jesus was a whore's son.[18] As years passed and the Jews steadfastly refused his or any other gospel, his wrath occasionally flamed into vehement hatred, culminating in his merciless tirades of 1543. Roland Bainton in his effort to make the best of Luther declared that Luther's view of the Jews "was entirely religious and by no means racial."[19] True; the crackpot version of social Darwinism that gave rise to "racial" anti-Semitism was a creation of the nineteenth and twentieth centuries. Luther hated the Jews because they rejected Christ. But his fury was no less cruel and vicious because its underlying motives were different or because his suggestions for carrying his cruelty to some final solution were less comprehensive and efficient.

His fury culminated in his vicious book of 1543, *On the Jews and Their Lies*. In late 1542 Pope Paul III had issued a call for the great reforming council to assemble at Trent beginning in 1545. It was to become a Catholic and papal triumph. What Trent would become was unclear in 1542, but Luther could see clearly enough that it represented a defeat for the evangelical cause. Through these years his attacks on foes of all kinds became even more vulgar and inflammatory because, as Heiko Oberman has said, he felt his work threatened on every side.[20]

Personal issues may also have been an influence. His beloved daughter

Magdalena died in his arms on September 20, 1542. Afterward his grief was intense, and he spoke feelingly of the terror before death while affirming his trust in Christ.[21] This combination of woes may have driven him to lash out at someone, and the Jews were there, testifying to his worst fear, that Jesus had not risen from the dead, and that Chrisitians would enjoy no victory over the grave. Whatever the cause, his outrageous attack in *On the Jews and Their Lies* represents one of those rhetorical horrors that may be explained in the various ways that we explain the cruelties that human beings inflict on others when the tormentors feel their own place in the universe threatened with annihilation. Yet explanation cannot finally excuse the horror.

After raging against the Jews for dozens of pages of tedious vehemence, Luther recommended what should be done with them: Their synagogues should be burned down; their books should be taken from them, "not leaving them one leaf"; they should be "forbidden on pain of death to praise God, to give thanks, to pray, and to teach publicly among us and in our country"; and they should "be forbidden to utter the name of God within our hearing."[22] Christians were guilty for not taking vengeance against the Jews for having killed Christ and for having killed innocent Christians for three hundred years after the Crucifixion, for not "striking them to death."[23]

He was not done with the Jews in this tract. Later in 1543 he published in German *On Schem Hemphoras and the Lineage of Christ,* a vile little assault on the supposed claim of some Jews that Jesus had done his miracles by sorcery, especially by using the supposedly magical incantations called "Schem Hemphoras."[24] This formula Luther thought to be taken from a magical use of the Hebrew letters of the name of God. His work, Luther said, was inspired in part by a stone effigy of a "Jewish sow" nursing her piglets and Jews, carved on the wall of the Wittenberg parish church. Behind the sow was a rabbi, lifting her tail as though to peer into her rectum, which in Luther's mind represented the Talmud. (Before the image today in Wittenberg is a modern, apologetic inscription set in the pavement of the sidewalk.) Above the sow was the inscription "She Mhemphoras." Luther seemed delighted to write down to the level of this carving. The book was so vulgar that evangelicals in Zurich declared that no one had written anything more coarse, more wild, more unseemly against Christian discipline and modesty in handling the faith and large and serious matters.[25] Andreas Osiander, one of Luther's good friends, wrote to another friend expressing unhappiness with Luther's outburst. A copy of Osiander's letter and the reply came into the hands of Melanchthon, who burned them without showing them to Luther. He persuaded Osiander to suppress it. He wrote that he hated the flattery that poured out on Luther's every work, but he still thought it was better to suppress the letter against him.[26]

Oberman relates this fury of Luther's as part of an apocalyptic expectation that became more and more pronounced as Luther drew near the end of his life.[27] I would add that the increasing ferocity of these apocalyptic hopes represents the nadir of Luther's expectations for his movement in time and history. It had been done in by the forces of darkness represented by Jews, papists, defectors from within his own ranks, and the Turks, whose threats both to the empire and to Christian faith seemed near and overwhelming. In such dire times, only the direct intervention of God himself by the return of Christ could redeem both the world and Luther's gospel. Here Luther became a railing prophet akin to those in all ages who believe that if they speak in wild boldness, they will force God to act. It seems possible, too, that Luther was drinking too much, continually ill and in discomfort and pain as well as in grief for the death of his daughter. He released on the Jews the rage created in him by the combination of all his defeats. At the beginning of *On Schem Hamphoras* he said that he wrote against the Jews much as one might write against the devil, hell, death, and sin—not that they could be changed into their opposites but that we might beware of them. "So I write against the Jews," he said, "for a Jew or a Jewish heart is a wooden, stone, devil heart that can be moved by nothing."[28] If Moses and the prophets had performed in vain all those miracles before the Jews' eyes to make them leave their hard hearts—as had Christ and the apostles—so it would be vain to try to convert them.

At the very end of this vicious book, Luther announced almost plaintively that he would have nothing more to do with the Jews. He would not write against them again. He could hope that through God's grace some of them might be converted and praise God the Father our creator together with our Lord Jesus Christ and the Holy spirit forever. This valedictory has something both desperate and forlorn about it. The last sermon that he preached, three days before he died in February 1546, was an attack on the Jews.

His continual harping on the suffering of the Jews as certain sign of the wrath of God contains no hint of the possibility that the suffering inflicted by one group of human beings upon another might arise from the depravity that he saw in unredeemed human nature. Nor does he ever seem to have pondered how contradictory it might seem to see the sufferings of Christians as a sign of the blessings of God to those he loved but the sufferings of Jews as testimony to God's wrath against those he hated.

Luther's virulent railing against the Jews seems to reflect an aspect of his character. As a man capable of giving complete devotion to the task at hand, all the power of his amazing personality was directed at whatever object was in front of it. Something about him calls to mind a high-pressure fire hose with a reservoir of enormous volume and force behind it, directed by the small focus of the nozzle and so delivered with shattering intensity. He could rage against the Jews or the pope or rulers who displeased him or his foes on every hand so that one might suppose that these antagonists commanded his life and all his energy. But then his attention could shift, and away from his pulpit or his writing desk he could turn the same intensity toward good humored conversation at table or the delights of his garden or the pleasure he took later on in his much beloved wife. Luther never organized any campaign against the Jews, and, as Heiko Oberman has said, despite the ferocity of his tirades against them he never truly renounced the notion of coexistence between Jews and Christians.[29] But the fact that Luther's hostility to Jews was not the same as modern anti-Semitism does not excuse it. It was as bad as Luther could make it, and that was bad enough to leave a legacy that had hateful consequences for centuries.

23

WORSHIP AND ETHICS

B OTH Luther and the civil authorities had an interest in making religious institutions in Saxony conform to the gospel Luther was preaching. The disturbances in Wittenberg during his absence in the Wartburg convinced conservative evangelicals that, in the absence of religious uniformity, anarchy was certain to reduce society to chaos. In shaping an order of worship, Luther was forced to become *the* authority, a role he played with the assurance that he would be backed by the secular sword wielded by the hand of the Elector Frederick and by the city council of Wittenberg. His tactic was change with restraint, all based on his sense of what could be deduced from scripture.

Luther also had to become lawgiver in areas where the canon law of the church had reigned supreme throughout the later Middle Ages. The canon law was an effort at a code, a systematic presentation of ecclesiastical authorities—conciliar decrees, statements by popes, declarations by theologians, and pronouncements by the fathers of the church—on matters as diverse as governance of the church, wills and testaments, disputes between clerics and laymen, vows, proper forms of legal appeal, marriage, and divorce. One reason for the expanded authority of the papacy in the fifteenth century after the Council of Constance was that in legal cases litigants appealed to the pope as the supreme judicial authority in the church, the supreme court of Christian law. For centuries various compilers strove to gather the various authoritative pronouncements in books with the contradictions weeded out and the related canons arranged together for easy reference. To Luther in his early days the canon law seemed to be a pyramid supporting the pope at the apex, and at the ritual book burning before the Elster Gate in December 1520, Luther threw onto the flames a printed copy of the canon law.

But the needs treated by canon law remained in society, and Luther had to address them—finally returning to the canon law himself for guidance in the teeming mass of complex legal issues presented for his judgment. But in the early days of Luther's movement, he and his associates struggled to replace canon law in ordering the lives of Christians in the innumerable ways that human beings can graze or transgress the boundaries of acceptable conduct and belief.

Karlstadt, who had been trained in the canon law, had an easy solution. The Bible, both Old and New Testaments, contained a law code, binding on Christians. The law was there, written down for everyone to see in the Ten Commandments and in the practices and demands of Jesus and the apostles. It was objective, and Christians were required to obey it. As one commentator has said, the sense of the Bible as law for the Christian runs like a red path through all Karlstadt's acts in Wittenberg in 1521 and 1522.[1]

Luther took a much more subjective tack. Faith was everything. For Luther the Mosaic law was for the Jews in their own time and place; it was not binding on Christians. Even the Ten Commandments did not bind Christians except insofar as they reflected the generally accepted principles of human conduct that forbade murder, adultery, lying, and dishonor to parents. Despite his fulminations against reason, Luther never entirely gave up the notion of natural law, that human nature required society and that society must function according to rational principles judged on how they helped or hindered in the effort of human beings to live together. The Ten Commandments comprised some of these principles. But nothing in the Jewish ceremonial law had any validity for Christians. The Christian life was to be directed by a warmhearted relation to Christ and a loving attitude toward others.

In Christian worship Luther made the sermon the centerpiece—a sermon preached from scripture, after the Eucharist on Sundays. It is not farfetched to say that the sermon was his real sacrament, that Christians came to sermons and went away strengthened and refreshed to make the decisions of life within the glow of a renewed faith. Sermons were therefore to be readily available. He felt none of the legalistic compulsion toward keeping Sunday as a holy day, the dreary rigor that was to mark the Calvinists in Geneva and later in England and America. Christians had no sabbath, he said. For the sake of the sensibilities of the common people, he did not wish to change Sunday as a special day of worship. But he was not legalistic about it, and when some evangelicals, reading the Bible literally, wished to treat Saturday as the Sabbath, Luther scoffed. The sabbath was for the Jews, he said, not for Christians. Those who wished to observe the seventh day as the sabbath ought to follow their logic and be circumcised, too.[2] Luther held that the Bible should be read through in church services until it was all read, and where it was not understood, the preacher should pass over that text and give God the glory. Sermons were to be about a half-hour long or even shorter.[3]

In Wittenberg during Luther's time, sermons could be heard every day. Students had to attend. Citizens in the town were not compelled to do so. Services on weekdays were simple and brief, not unlike the noonday worship services offered by many urban churches in the United States today. Similar services were offered in the evening, although the tradition of evensong that was to become such a rich part of Anglican worship never became as popular in Germany as it was in England.

Luther recognized how much depended on preachers, in preaching to the simple, the uneducated. One must sit on the pulpit as though on a milking stool, he said, and pull hard and drink milk with the people, for every day a new church grows up that needs instruction in first principles. Thereby should the minister diligently teach the catechism and pass out the milk. Higher thoughts and elements one should speak only to the knowledgeable and then in private.[4] In short: Keep it simple for the simple. Difficult matters of faith should be left to those able to deal with them. Before going into the pulpit, the preacher should pray, "Dear Lord God, I want to preach to glorify Thee. I want to speak of Thee, praise thee, and glorify Thy name. If I cannot do it well and God, make thou good of it."[5]

As his movement expanded, he feared a scarcity of preachers. About 1530 he grumbled that soon Christians would have to go about looking for preachers, raking them up out of the earth when they heard of them. There were too many doctors and lawyers, he said. They could rule the world. One needed two hundred pastors to stave off one lawyer. One lawyer would be enough for Erfurt—a large city—but every village ought to have one pastor. Soon, he said, "We must make doctors and lawyers into pastors. Then you'll see something!"[6] He was joking, of course, but the problem was real.

He often complained bitterly about how poverty-stricken pastors were and how little respected by the populace at large. "The world will never believe us poor preachers," he said in 1532. "But if we had money like the papists, we would easily convert the world; because we're poor, we have no respect."[7] In 1538 he said, "If I wanted to be rich, I'd not preach, but I'd become a juggler and go through the country. Then for money I might have many spectators."

The peasants would not feed their pastors. Some ministers hired themselves out as shepherds to make a living. When the peasants were asked why they were so stingy, they replied, "But you see, we have to have shepherds!"[8]

Luther often complained about preachers and preaching. He suffered impatiently the long sermons of his good friend and confessor, John Bugenhagen, "Dr. Pommer." "Every priest has his own sacrifice," Luther said. "With his long sermons, Pommer sacrifices his auditors."[9] Over the years his complaints about preachers became bitter. He warned steadily against pride and popularity. The true preacher must preach the cross. "The world loves what belongs to it," he said. "We are called to another life."[10] Again a paradox is evident. Luther taught that true Christians were a tiny minority in the world. Yet his concern with preaching and his sometimes caustic remarks about the problems of getting good men and sustaining them in their ministry demonstrate a yearning to bring as many into the fold as possible.

The bitterness and disappointment that came into his comments as the years passed reveal a sorrow that often expressed itself in anger. The quietism that evolved later in some offshoots of Lutheranism could assume that God was in charge and that no matter how bad things looked, the goal of the Christian in this life was peace within and serenity in outward things. Luther's sense of the all-seeing providence of God was that he was a tool in God's hand, called to act as an instrument in God's purpose for the world. The hard note of anguish and wrath that comes through his comments on preaching and preachers seems to betoken a continuing struggle to persuade himself that God was indeed with him.

One of Luther's most enduring contributions to worship arose out of his love of music. Lutheran congregations could enjoy lusty singing of stirring hymns in harmony, accompanied by musical instruments that included the pipe organ—to become as the sixteenth century progressed a piece of technology that was a wonder of the age. In this spirit Luther was different from other reformers rising to leadership in other cities, respecting Luther but not slavishly obeying him. Luther's efforts to establish coherent worship were in part directed against other evangelicals whose interpretations of scripture were different from his own. By 1523 the course was set toward the fragmentation Catholics had predicted from the first. We have already looked at parts of it.

In Zurich by 1523 Ulrich Zwingli, a pastor and one of the most unpleasant men in the century, succeeded in leading the city out of the Roman Church. Zwingli tried to follow the New Testament to the letter. He was a spiritual cousin of Karlstadt. He banned instrumental music because no New Testament evidence exists that primitive Christians used musical instruments in worship services. Since early Christians met in private homes, this lack of instruments to make music seems hardly surprising. He was not consistent. He baptized infants, and his congregations did not engage in the communal foot washing enjoined by the Gospel of John. We have noted that he approved the drowning of Anabaptists. Most Anabaptists were poor and inoffensive people, no more fanatical in belief than the mainline reformers but usually of a lower social class. They were pacifists because Jesus had told Peter to put up his sword and commanded all his followers to love their enemies and forgive them. Zwingli did not follow New Testament pacifism; he died fighting for his Swiss canton in battle in 1531 in a war he had provoked himself. Catholics and evangelicals joined in ridiculing and rejoicing at his death.

Zwingli's motive for banning musical instruments went beyond scripture. His was a puritanical impulse stemming from a radical form of Christian Platonism. In his view the physical was not worthy to bear the divine, and veneration of the physical or the sensual was akin to idolatry. Instrumental music in the worship service was a sensual element unworthy of the true Christian—although in the secular world of the everyday life, music was as acceptable as a host of other secular activities one would not bring into church.[11] He had churches whitewashed, stained glass smashed out of windows, and religious statuary pulled down and broken up. This puritanical simplicity formed another motive for silencing instrumental music, leaving Zurich congregations to sing droning versions of unaccompanied metrical translations of the Psalms. In this tradition—later adopted by most Calvinist churches—the consequence was some of the dreariest stuff in the history of religious music. Zwingli understood what anyone listening today to Beethoven's Ninth Symphony knows intuitively, that we may delight in the sublime pleasures of music without sharing belief in the religious doctrines that music presents. Could he see Christmas congregations of all degrees of faith and unfaith crammed into churches to hear Handel's *Messiah,* he would utter a fanatical and rueful "I told you so," historically the puritan's dour last word and everlasting revenge against godless pleasure.

Luther at the heart of his religious being believed in incarnation, the goodness of creation, the capacity of physical and spiritual to be joined together. That belief was the foundation of his doctrine of the Eucharist. Sin might infect creation, but Christ would finally restore God's work to its original purity. In part this quality of his personality influenced his view of the definition of life. Life took place in a body, and if there were no genuine resurrection of a physical body, there was no everlasting life. He often expressed puzzlement at what life after death might be. That was a mystery, but he knew Christians had to affirm faith in a full bodily resurrection.[12] He could make no sense of the notion that when the body died, the soul somehow rose to an ethereal realm. In his relish for the physical, aesthetic delight could be summoned to the service of faith. In the sublime harmonies of music, God could speak to the human soul. The sensory world and the world of the spirit were not necessarily at odds with each other, but both were under grace.

He wrote hymns to be set to music, and by the end of 1523 he was preparing a hymnbook for German evangelicals. Sometime near the end of the year he wrote Spalatin about the project, asking for help. Spalatin was both poet and translator. He should exercise himself, Luther said, to translate some psalms into German verse to be set to music. He should avoid hifalutin words used at court and new coinages. These hymns were to convey the word of God in German verses that everyone could understand.[13] He had, he told Spalatin, already done some such work of translation himself. A book of eight hymns appeared in print early in 1524. Later that year, an expanded collection contained twenty-four hymns, sixteen of them written by Luther. He wrote only the words, leaving to others the task of setting the words to music.

The only hymn for which we know with certainty that Luther wrote both words and music is the unforgettable "A Mighty Fortress," which appeared in 1528. It embodies in stirring song his militant theology of struggle with Satan and victory by God's matchless and invincible grace. He reworked some medieval hymns, including one that began "In the midst of life, we are seized by death. Who can give us help that we can grace receive?" By 1537 this hymn in Luther's translation (unacknowledged) began to appear in Catholic hymnbooks rushed into print to compete with the popularity of congregational singing among Lutherans. Luther's interest in music never waned; he wrote it and sang for the rest of his life. Tradition associates him with a lute that he is supposed to have strummed sometimes among friends in the evening.

The Eucharist was not observed daily but was usually reserved for Sundays. It took second place to the sermon in Luther's view of worship. He thought it was a sermon in sacramental form. The Eucharist represented the physical advent of Christ in the world of believers, and it remained part of the main service of the week held on Sunday. The daily masses of the Catholic Church now gave way to the primacy of daily preaching, and the Eucharist was to be celebrated on any day but Sunday only in special circumstances. Always for him the sacrament was validated by God's word preached about it; without preaching it was better "neither to sing, nor read, nor come together."[14] He did not want masses said for dead souls or with the intent of persuading God to grant various kinds of aid.[15] Yet in his efforts to make worship uniform and regular, Luther was cautious. Always he wanted to bring the common people along with him voluntarily. In his *Formulas for Mass and Communion* of 1523 he claimed that he did nothing by force or command but proceeded in all changes with fear and hesitation. He was concerned, he said, for those unclean spirits who liked novelty for its own sake, people who had no real faith at all.[16]

For the moment, the Eucharist remained in Latin, a language mysterious and seemingly magical to late medieval Christians, doubtless giving multitudes a sense of the sacred to the rite that a cautious reformer might jostle only with circumspection. Not until 1526 did he provide a German Mass, this after other German evangelicals had led the way. He permitted the elevation of the host, a devout gesture that more radical reformers abandoned and forbade because to them it smacked of idolatry. He thought all the words of the eucharistic service should be said in a loud voice by the minister so that the entire congregation might share them. So he abandoned those secret whispered prayers in which the Catholic priest had spoken alone to God at the altar with his back to the congregation. Because Luther denied the special priestly status of ministers and made all believers priests, and because he denied also that the Eucharist was a sacrifice, the altar in Catholic worship was replaced by a communion table set at floor level, and the congregation gathered around the table for the service.

The Eucharist in Luther's view was only for those judged to be pious. The pastor should take it on himself to exclude from communion open sinners such as fornicators, adulterers, drunks, those not serious, usurers, blasphemers, and those guilty of infamous crimes unless they professed willingness to change their lives. Those who sincerely repented of gross sins should be quickly readmitted to the table, for the Mass was for them. Luther allowed communion in both kinds to be introduced in Wittenberg in early 1523 after a decent interval following his return from the Wartburg. He delayed so that the townspeople could be instructed and not disturbed by the innovation. The laity could now partake of both bread and wine, body and blood. In the heady optimism of 1520, he expected a general council to make a formal decree allowing such a practice—permitted to the Bohemian Hussites in the peace made between them and the Catholic Church in the previous century. The hope for a general council to be called by the young emperor was one of his great, driving illusions in the early days of his movement. Now, losing faith that such a council would ever take place, he permitted his followers to go ahead with communion in both kinds.[17]

All of this flowed naturally from Luther's belief in the priesthood of believers. Here was a democratic impulse in his thought—to be short-lived. All Christians were seen to stand on equal footing. The heartfelt prayer of the solitary Christian in pain for his sins went directly to God wherever it was uttered. Confession of sin did not require formal absolution by a priest to be stricken from the accounting presented to God. It should be said that at no time in the history of Catholic Christendom did formal theology hold that the ordinary Christian man or woman required a priest to approach God. Yet in the popular imagination, the priest could easily seem necessary since all the sacraments except baptism required a priest to make them efficacious, and the Christian who did not confess formally in the sacrament of penance and receive absolution could be accused of the deadly sin of pride. In Luther's idea of a community of the devout sharing spiritual burdens, Christians continually reassured one another of God's gracious benevolence, confessing sins to one another and receiving mutual confirmation of God's forgiveness. This ideal assumed that true Christians grieved for their sins and yearned for the restoration of spiritual fellowship with the Almighty. As Christian history worked out, this ideal was broadly realized only in the ranks of various emotion-ridden enthusiasts whom Luther detested as much as he did the pope.

If everyone was a priest in Luther's view, experience quickly proved that not everyone was a minister able to interpret the Bible for the congregation, preach regularly, and administer the two sacraments remaining in Luther's theology. "Priests are born," Luther wrote in 1523, meaning that anyone born into Christian faith was ipso facto a priest. But, he said, "Ministers are made."[18] Since Luther thought that the preaching of the Word was a matter of faith, he had no patience with the notion of an apostolic succession through the laying on of hands. In the papal church—and in the schismatic Church of England that Henry VIII was to establish—the notion remained that priestly authority came through the sacrament of ordination whereby hands were laid on the head of the candidate by men who had had hands laid on them in a succession of men all the way back to Christ. In Thomas More's mythical Utopia, sailors from an expedition of Amerigo Vespucci brought the Christian religion to the virtuous pagans on the island commonwealth, but, lacking a priest, Utopian Christians could not observe the sacraments. Luther held a contrary view, that if a group of Christians found themselves without someone to administer the Eucharist, they could choose one of their number to be their minister. If the word of God was present and everything else lacking, the Word was sufficient to make a minister.[19]

His conception of ministry was to evolve as the Reformation developed and as he found his doctrines threatened by impulses more democratic than his own. The minister was made by his ability to preach the word of God truly—a task that despite the alleged clarity of the Bible required careful education and examination of candidates for the office of pastor. In 1523 Luther was still arguing that a Christian congregation had the authority to judge all doctrines and to call its own pastors.[20] In effect he called upon Christian parishes to expel Catholic priests who taught doctrines contrary to the word of God and to install in their place preachers of the gospel. But when peasants demanded the right to choose their pastors and installed preachers whose doctrines differed radically from Luther's, he quickly and with characteristic vehemence retreated from this dangerous democratic impulse. The puritans who followed the teachings of John Calvin continued to insist on the right of congregations to choose their pastors—and so contributed mightily to the ideals of democracy in Scotland, England, and the United States. Germany was to go in another direction, and although Luther cannot be blamed for this authoritarian German bent, his growing distrust of the common people was so great that his Reformation did not oppose a broader national evolution to rule from the top.

During this time Luther's war against "blasphemy" and his confidence in his own interpretation of scripture led him in another crusade in Wittenberg itself, a crusade that belies his occasional affirmations that he wanted no compulsion in religion. Frederick the Wise associated with his vast collection of relics a religious foundation of priests supported by the revenues taken from the devout who came to venerate these holy objects. The priests, called canons, said masses regularly at the castle church, continuing under the elector's protection to follow the old ways in the belief that repeating masses did something to channel the grace of God into those pious souls who paid for the endowments.

From his eyrie in the Wartburg, Luther thundered against these priests. He said they were like the priests of Beth-Aven, Israelite priests in the time of schismatic King Jeroboam who served golden calves set up as gods, an idolatry that according to the books of Kings and Chronicles brought destruction on Israel. Luther's fury was limitless, and some of these priests came over to his point of view. But despite Luther's fulminations, the elector kept his canons, and they continued to observe the Mass in the old way. The elector did cease to exhibit his precious collection of relics following a last display on All Saints Day, November 1, 1522. In December, in a letter to Spalatin, Luther referred to the foundation as a whorehouse.[21] Did he mean the term metaphorically in the sense of priests whoring after strange gods? Perhaps. But in January 1523 Luther cited testimony from his friend Nicholas von

Amsdorf that all but three of the canons were fornicators who had sex with women almost every night and impudently and unfeelingly celebrated their masses in the morning.[22] We have no way of knowing whether these charges were true.

Luther felt that continued masses under the elector's protection represented an insult to him and his gospel and weakened the power of the gospel in the world. He attacked the foundation in sermons of increasing vehemence in both German and Latin during August 1523, saying that its continuation was "to our ridicule." The prince, he said, allowed the foundation to continue although he knew the apostolic injunction that we ought to obey God rather than men.[23] In a somewhat rambling Latin sermon—with a few German phrases thrown in—Luther spoke of the foundation as a "whorehouse of the devil's before our eyes."[24] He went back in this sermon to some of his thoughts about the secular authority. Christians should not resist a prince by force. God punished princes who did not do his will. The people had to wait for God and not take matters into their own hands.

Wittenbergers still faithful to the old church went to the castle church to celebrate the Eucharist. The elector maintained his foundation with the stubbornness that had earlier saved Luther's life and position. Luther continued to rage against the foundation as an insult to himself, a sign of the elector's unbelief, and a portent of the judgment of God. He succeeded at last in setting the city council of Wittenberg against the elector in this matter, and in December 1524 Frederick consented to the abolition of the foundation rather than face tumult in the city.

In this trivial affair we see as though in a red crystal ball the bloody future of religious war that in the century after Luther would plunge Europe into a barbarism that makes the so-called barbarian invasions of the late Roman Empire seem like the summit of decency. In his treatise *On Secular Authority,* Luther carefully distinguished the "two kingdoms" where Christians served God and government. Separate though they were, nothing could keep the realms from overlapping. The Christian prince was both Christian and prince. When he saw God's word violated by "idolatry," he was obligated as a Christian to use the power of the sword to enforce God's approved way of doing things. Eternal life and death hung on the outcome; toleration was inconceivable. Luther kept saying that he opposed the use of force against the foundation—and vehemently called on the elector to close it down until Frederick did so to avoid tumult in his dominions. The elector never eliminated the foundation; the priests remained after they ceased to say mass. By then he was only months away from death.

Luther concerned himself with questions about marriage because so many monks, nuns, and priests were throwing off vows of celibacy, coming over to the Reformation, and taking spouses. In the spring of 1522 he brought out a sixteen-page treatise in German, *On Married Life*.[25] It was reprinted many times. He developed his opinion expressed in the *Babylonian Captivity* that marriage was a natural state and clerical celibacy was inspired by Satan. Some might choose not to marry because of circumstances at a given moment. But no one should undertake to vow celibacy for life, for circumstances might change. Monks and nuns should feel free to forsake their vows whenever they pleased to enter into Christian matrimony.

He repeated some of his daring ideas. A woman married to an impotent man should have the right to take another husband—her legal husband's brother, perhaps, or a close relative. In essence Luther was counseling bigamy on two grounds. One was that a woman had a right to sexual intercourse and to children; the other was that polygamy was sanctioned in the Old Testament and never condemned in the New—although we have no clear text to show that any Christian male mentioned in the New Testament had more than one wife. The rationale was much the same as for instrumental music and infant baptism: In the absence of explicit prohibition, a practice was permitted—in this instance a kind of polygamy. Luther also did away with the system of degrees of kinship within which marriage was prohibited in the papal church, as he had advocated in the *Babylonian Captivity*. Siblings, of course, could not marry, and he followed Leviticus in forbidding marriage to aunts and uncles. He seemed intent on making marriage a matter of love and common sense.

He took a tough line on adultery. If either partner in marriage committed adultery, the innocent person was permitted to divorce and to marry again. The Old Testament law provided that the guilty party be put to death. Luther was in favor of capital punishment for adultery but recognized that most governments were too soft to carry it out. At the least the Christian community in his view should publicly rebuke the adulterer. More surprising, Luther permitted divorce if one spouse refused to have sex with the other, but he refused divorce in the case of a spouse prevented by illness from having sexual relations.

He concluded by praising marriage because it produced children, for creating mutual affection between husband and wife, and for the healthiness of sexual intercourse for both parties. Physicians, he said, were right to teach that the forcible restraint of the natural sexual drive caused the body to become poisoned, presumably with the unreleased sexual fluids, so that it became unhealthy, weak, sweaty, and stinking. Anybody could see, he declared, that a childless woman was weak and unhealthy compared with those women who bore children and were healthier, cleaner, and more energetic. Even in this affirmation of bodily desire and the propagation of children within marriage, Luther could not quite forsake the Augustinian tradition within which he had learned his theology. Sexual intercourse even within marriage, he said, was never completely without sin. Concupiscence, said Augustine, was the means by which original sin was passed on through the human race, and Luther agreed.

Luther showed no inclination to marry. On April 8 he wrote a brief, jolly letter to his friend Wenzelaus Link agreeing to come to Link's forthcoming wedding. Link was one of Luther's oldest friends, their amity dating perhaps to their school days. He had come to Wittenberg almost as soon as the university opened and had like Luther fallen under the influence of Staupitz. He became professor and general vicar of the Wittenberg cloister when Staupitz departed. The cloister shut down in 1522, and now Link, like Luther aged forty, was about to marry. Luther mentioned several others who would attend, including Lucas Cranach. At the end he mentioned that he had on the day before received nine nuns "from captivity" in the Cistercian convent in the small town of Grimma.[26] One of these was a twenty-four-year-old named Katherine von Bora.

24

✠

OPPOSITION AND DIVISIONS

MEANWHILE Luther found himself embattled, not only against the Catholic side but from within, from dissident Christians who had followed him but who now wanted to go beyond him. In addition he lived so frugally as to be sometimes close to utter poverty. He never received money from his books. He lived almost alone in the Augustinian cloister now that the monks had departed. He earned a small stipend from preaching at the city church, but he received no salary from his professorship. He had been supplied to the university by the Augustinian order, which was supposed to pay for his needs. That source of income was no more, and the Elector Frederick could not be prevailed upon to make up the difference. Evidently the elector supposed that the Lord would provide.

It is easy to wonder if Frederick even liked Luther. Yes, he stood by his professor, but that might have been a combination of caution, stubbornness, piety, and pride. Nothing indicates that he felt any special warmth toward him or that he even accepted Luther's doctrines, although it was said that on his deathbed he took the Eucharist in both kinds for the first time.[1] His delay in this quintessential Lutheran act is fascinating and yet finally unfathomable. Was it a conversion? Or was it something urged or even forced upon a dying man by zealots seeking some final affirmation of their own faith? Something about Frederick's attitude suggests that he thought Luther *might* be right. So he would protect him and wait upon the Lord. He never showed himself generous to his professor, allowing Luther to go about in a worn monk's cowl until it became so shabby that Luther gave it up in October 1524 and began to dress as a simple citizen, usually in an academic gown.

Only with the advent of Frederick's successor, his brother Duke John, did Luther receive a salary from the Saxon treasury, and it was meager.

On July 1, 1523, the first martyrs to Luther's cause—Heinrich Vos and Johan van den Eschen, former members of the Augustinian cloister at Antwerp—were burned at the stake in the great market at Brussels. Their deaths testified to the Catholic resolve of the young Emperor Charles in whom Luther had misplaced so much hope. In this part of his Burgundian inheritance Charles ruled in absolute authority, able to override any opposition and to pursue heretics to the death without consulting a Diet or any other kind of representative assembly.

Luther responded with a German *Letter to the Christians in the Netherlands*.[2] The Weimar editors of Luther's works commented on the tone of jubilation in the letter. This triumphant spirit should not surprise us. The Christian tradition venerated its martyrs from earliest times. Anyone who died in witness to the faith validated with his life the faith itself. "Oh how contemptibly were these two condemned!" Luther cried. "But how gloriously and in eternal joy will they come again with Christ and justly judge the very ones by whom they were so unrighteously judged . . . What is the world against God? With what desire and joy have the angels looked after these two souls . . . God be praised and blessed for eternity that we have lived to see and to hear real saints and true martyrs, we who until now have exalted and prayed to so many false saints."[3] Once given his own martyrs he was ready to back away from the bold statement he had made against Catharinus, that no one could know the state of another's soul, that even if the apostle Peter were among us, we could not know if he were among the redeemed. These men were guaranteed entry into paradise. He later wrote hymns in their praise.

On May 7, 1523, Luther lost one of his strongest supporters when "the last German Knight," Franz von Sickingen, died of wounds suffered in a futile defense of his castle, the Ebernburg, against the combined forces of Philip of Hesse, Ludwig of the Palatinate, and Richard von Greiffenklau, elector and archbishop of Trier. Sickingen's rise and fall represented the passing of the old order of feudalism. The knights he sought to unify and lead were the odd men out in the evolution of Germany. They held so little land and wealth that they could not compete in status with the great dukes, counts, and electors of the empire. Their military importance had lessened with the revolution in the technology of warfare. Mounted cavalry had long since given way to masses of foot soldiers, and the advent of gunpowder, the musket, and artillery made war so expensive that it could be successfully waged only by strong governments able to raise the money to put an army into the field. The price revolution of the sixteenth century caught the knights in its gold and silver jaws. They could raise taxes on their peasants or borrow money (usually at exorbitant interest rates) or else rob and pillage. Nothing they did helped for long.[4]

Neither could they compete with the wealth of the booming cities of the empire. Perhaps more important, they did not share the ethos of either those who enjoyed high princely authority or the rough-and-tumble of urban commerce. Most seem to have been barely literate, and some were unable even to sign their names.[5] They had no standing in the imperial Diets, having failed to see the wisdom of an alliance with the towns that the knights of the shires in England had pursued to gain representation in Parliament. The German knights doggedly held on to their pretensions, including their old tradition of ragtag private armies that went to war on the claim of vindicating themselves when someone violated an oath. The Diet had outlawed such private wars but lacked the power to enforce its decrees. The knights formally extolled the emperor as the hope of German unity, but their disorderly habits made them a nuisance rather than the van of national revolution. They were like old gunfighters in the American West struggling to find a place in a society becoming accustomed to law and order and the comforts of a new day. No emperor wanted anything to do with them, and if anything Charles V was more hostile to them than Maximilian had been.

In the fall of 1522 Sickingen picked a fight with the archiepiscopal city of Trier in western Germany. Now he was declared an outlaw of the empire, and the three princes of Trier, the Palatinate, and Hesse combined forces to destroy him. The enmity of the Elector Louis of the Palatinate must have been especially galling to Sickingen, since Louis sympathized with Luther and had been Sickingen's friend and supporter.[6] Philip of Hesse was also leaning toward Lutheranism, but he hated Sickingen's lawlessness. Sickingen's castles fell one by one. On May 1, 1523, commanding the defense of the Ebernburg, he was wounded by a cannonball made of stone. On May 6, as he lay dying, he surrendered the castle, and the next day he gave up the ghost. In a letter to Spalatin on May 23, Luther called it a "miserable story."[7] Sickingen's death left the territorial princes in command of Germany and ensured division and disunity to modern times. The division allowed Luther's Reformation to take root; now it was to shape the way Luther's views expanded in Germany.

In the meantime the imperial Diet at Nuremberg came up with a surprising compromise. Pope Leo X died in December 1521 while Luther was in the Wartburg. His successor was the father confessor of the Emperor Charles, a devout, stern Dutchman, Adrian of Utrecht, who took the papal name Adrian VI—the last pope not to change his name on election to the papal office and the last non-Italian pope until the elevation of Pope John Paul II in our time. When Charles became king of Spain in 1516, he appointed Adrian regent. The future pope helped provoke the revolt of the Comuneros with his harsh polices. He represented a sea change from the luxury-loving Leo X, whose favorite pursuits were arts and the hunt. Adrian set out with grim resolve to reform the church and suppress heresy. Consequently he was despised by the Italians. He saw the relation between reform and the allegiance of the German lands, and he demanded that the coming Reichstag at Nuremberg enforce the Edict of Worms against Luther and his followers. In exchange he promised to make things right in the church and presumably to give relief to the Germans for some of their worst complaints against the papacy.[8]

The representative of Frederick the Wise at Nuremberg was a canny diplomat, Hans von der Planitz, trained as a lawyer in Italy, a man whom Luther called friend. Planitz had discussions with a papal nuncio in Nuremberg in December and advanced an important idea. It was not possible, he said, to suppress Luther's movement in Germany without religious war. The Lutherans had to be met by arguments carried on with goodwill in a brotherly and friendly spirit. Planitz argued that the Lutherans could no longer be treated as heretics with the Catholic Church presumed to have all the right and all the arguments on its side. No, Lutheranism now represented a schism in the church, and a schism could be healed only by a general council.[9] This step would in effect make Luther and the papacy equal contestants in a religious debate—and for the time being it would take the initiative away from both of them. To the Lutherans the scheme offered advantages.

In the end, Planitz carried the Diet. The complaints, the *gravamina,* of the German nation against the papacy and the papal court were reasserted. Until the abuses that had provoked these complaints were ended, Luther's popular support could not be put down. The Diet called for a general council to meet in some peaceful German city within a year. In the meantime, Frederick the Wise and the other parties were to see that nothing else was written or printed. It was an effort to throw a blanket onto the religious fire and smother it. Neither side obeyed this command to silence. The greatest victory at Nuremberg for the Lutherans was that the Edict of Worms was declared unenforceable, and the question of whether Luther was a heretic was now declared undecided.[10] The projected German council to settle the religious issue was never to take place, but for the moment both the Elector Frederick and Luther had room to breathe. As it turned out, they needed it.

Luther's popularity grew by leaps and bounds. In early June 1523 he sent a letter to printers begging them not to print any of his sermons unless he had prepared them for the press himself or unless they had been published at Wittenberg under his personal imprimatur. Careless unauthorized editions could bring the gospel into mockery, he said. Besides, it was better if people read scripture and let his own work go. Preferable, he said, to drink from the spring than from the book that had led people to the spring.[11] The circular reveals humility and hope—humility before the pure source of the word of God and hope that readers could find the gospel for themselves if they perused scripture on their own without Luther's guidance.

But sometime in July 1523 Luther received a letter from Thomas Müntzer, a man who would quickly demolish all these hopes for unity in faith. Müntzer defended himself against the charge of causing tumult and claimed to be an unmovable friend of Luther's. Yet in a rambling and sometimes obsequious exposition he hinted at the radicalism soon to grow into a thunder on the left that would threaten Luther's Reformation with disaster. In reaction against Müntzer's radicalism, Luther's movement would change direction, the fervid popular support for Luther's gospel would dissolve, and Luther's most daring creative stage of life would end.

Although he had spent time in Zwickau, Müntzer was not in the same camp as the ecstatic "prophets" of that city. For one thing, he was a well-educated man. In his letter he sought to deny any association with the ignorant fanatics who had earlier plagued Wittenberg. Yet the denial had a hook to it. He did not uphold ecstasies and visions, he said—unless God compelled them. He would not believe in such things unless he saw them.[12] Just as clear as this declaration of circumspection was his faith that overt manifestations of the divine did occur. To support his views, Müntzer had no trouble adducing scriptural texts from throughout the Bible.

Luther called such people *Schwärmer,* a word often translated "enthusiasts" but more correctly rendered as "fanatics." The word suggests also the swarming of insects that sting and bite, an implication that they disturbed the peace. Here Luther was a prisoner of his own culture. In many respects the *Schwärmer* were much more akin to the disciples of the New Testament church than Luther's carefully regulated institution in Wittenberg. New Testament Christians went into ecstasies, spoke in tongues, made prophecies, enjoyed direct inspiration, and performed miracles. The difference between the *Schwärmer* of Luther's day and the Christians of the New Testament was that the *Schwärmer*—or at least some of them—were willing to use force to attain their religious ends just as Old Testament prophets and kings had done in Israel against the foes of Yahweh, especially royal foes such as Ahab and

Jezebel. Luther was painfully learning that anyone who makes the Bible a supreme authority has trouble deciding where to stop. Müntzer became his first dangerous enemy in the evangelical camp.

Müntzer's origins are obscure.[13] He seems to have come from the eastern part of Germany, where Slavs and Germans mingled on the forested plains cut by rivers that eventually poured into the Baltic. He got himself a good university education, perhaps at the University of Frankfurt on the Oder, and when Luther burst on the scene, Müntzer quickly became one of his disciples, drifting into Wittenberg during the winter of 1517–18. Early in 1519 he was pastor at Jüterborg just beyond the fringes of Frederick's territories, enjoying Luther's vigorous support in controversies that immediately swirled around him. He seems to have attended the Leipzig debate, moving afterward to a succession of preaching positions and perhaps stopping several times in Wittenberg, even sitting in on lectures at the university, though apparently without being close to Luther or Melanchthon.[14]

Müntzer sought certain faith in a world where doubts abounded. Norman Cohn says that Müntzer "was a troubled soul, full of doubts about the truth of Christianity and even about the existence of God but obstinately struggling after certainty—in fact in that labile condition which so often ends in conversion."[15] His road to that faith passed through mysticism, the way of direct spiritual union with God. And somewhere he seems to have come under the influence of the Anabaptists. By the spring of 1520 he found his way to a pastorate in Zwickau, where he seems to have preached in a fierce and uncompromising rhetoric against abuses he saw in Catholic belief and practice. By December of that year he had won a following strong enough to threaten violence to priests who opposed him. He also preached vigorously against the leading pastor of the town, an Erasmian moderate named John Egranus who seemed to treat Müntzer as a joke. Some sort of disturbance broke out, and Müntzer fled the city in April, apparently in the middle of the night.[16]

He wandered to Prague and mingled with disciples of the martyred John Hus who then controlled the city. The conviction grew in him that God still spoke directly through his chosen prophets. He said often that the true prophet must suffer within. But the suffering validated the ministry, and he was sure that God would work miracles if people would only listen to him. The people of Prague listened, but they did not heed. Something about Müntzer frightened them, and they forced him to leave the city. He again took up a wandering life, landing in 1523 in the hamlet of Allstedt in the territories of Frederick the Wise. There on Easter Sunday, April 5, 1523, he began preaching at St. John's Church while the citizens decided whether to make him their permanent pastor. He quickly dominated Allstedt as Luther dominated Wittenberg. Allstedt was a quiet town, but it was located in a region where gold, silver, and copper were mined. To appeal to its people Müntzer reformed the liturgy, and before Luther had done so in Wittenberg, Müntzer gave his town services completely in German, including German hymns sung by the congregation.[17] His preaching pleased the people but frightened the local count, Ernest of Mansfeld, who reported his concern to the Elector Frederick.

Müntzer propounded rigorous ethics, showing himself akin to the primitive church of the New Testament. Christians throughout the New Testament demonstrate an ethical rigor supported by radical demands from Jesus himself—especially the Jesus of the synoptic Gospels, including the Sermon on the Mount. One might say that Müntzer commanded his followers to be the ideal Christians who populate the pages of Luther's 1520 treatise *On the Freedom of the Christian*. For Luther, Christian perfection was usually a matter of desire, not of real perfection. The Christian yearned to attain the ideal but knew he could not and therefore lived in continual tension between desire and failure. Müntzer wanted moral perfection in this life.

By 1523 it seemed clear to people of Müntzer's disposition that Luther's Reformation had not wrought the ethical rejuvenation of the church in Wittenberg. What to others might appear to be brilliant compromises on Luther's part, holding a community together under the auspices of prince and city council, appeared to biblical literalists like Müntzer to be a promenade with the devil and the powers of darkness. It is easy to see why he felt so frustrated with Luther. Luther could on one level assert the word of God as he saw it with unmitigated and uncompromising force as though it had the power to sweep aside all resistance, destroy the old order, and raise up a new Christian community. But on the practical level, faced with a real ruler and real people ever ready to pervert his teachings, Luther compromised. It is a paradox not unknown in the history of revolutions and their rhetoric.

In Allstedt, Müntzer married a former nun who remained one of his most fervent supporters through his life and violent death. She soon bore him a son, and he settled there for a time—if indeed the quiet verb "settle" can be justly applied to so stormy and relentless a character. Infant baptism was banned. Belief in a real presence in the Eucharist was replaced by the more radical view that the sacrament was a commemorative meal that only recalled the sacrifice of Christ and that it did not include the real presence of Christ. More dangerous than anything else in the minds of sober authorities was Müntzer's vision of a level society where emperor, king, pope, bishops, and other officials in a social and economic hierarchy gave way to pure democracy where all Christians were equal in the sight of God and one another, a universal society of love and kinship. Those who refused to lower themselves from their commanding heights would be pulled down by force of arms.[18]

Müntzer's appeal to the poor brought an immediate and enthusiastic response—and fear and hatred from many who saw in him a harbinger of revolution, although, as in the French Revolution much later, some of the wealthy heard him gladly and were ready to throw in their lot with him. Müntzer seemed to go from peak to peak of certainty and fanaticism. He began organizing recruits for the great apocalyptic war that would inaugurate the thousand-year kingdom of Christ. In March 1524 he preached a fierce sermon, using as a text Deuteronomy 7:5, "Ye shall destroy their altars, and break down their images, and cut down their groves, and burn their graven images with fire." His followers rushed out to set fire to the Mallerbach Chapel near Allstedt, where a picture of the Virgin was said to have miraculous powers to cure the sick. The nuns in charge of the chapel took refuge with the brother of the Elector Frederick, Duke John.[19] Both Duke John and the elector commanded that the perpetrators be brought to justice, only to learn that armed miners had streamed into Allstedt from surrounding towns and were prepared to resist.

In July 1524 Duke John and members of his court came to a castle near Allstedt and ordered Müntzer to appear and preach before them. Müntzer obliged and took his text from Daniel 2:1–48, a passage beloved of apocalyptic prophets throughout the ages, Daniel's interpretation of Nebuchadnezzar's dream of a great image with a head of gold and feet that were part iron and part clay. In the dream a great stone falls on the image from heaven and breaks it to powder. Müntzer found all this made to order for him, and he preached a hair-raising sermon on the adultery of the church and its coming judgment by Christ, who would fall on it like this stone from heaven.

Just as Daniel had interpreted Nebuchadnezzar's dream, so the prophets of God in Müntzer's time could interpret the will of God to the people. A new Daniel must lead. Those who did not heed the call of these prophets would be ripped out by the roots and thrown into the fire, and he found abundant examples in the Bible to prove that idols should be broken and idolaters destroyed. All princes must heed the call of God or be exterminated. The ungodly have no right to live.[20]

For the moment nothing happened. Duke John and his courtiers went away. Müntzer remained in place. The elector hesitated, and Müntzer had his sermon printed.[21]

Luther was enraged, but he kept silent, hoping the controversy could be settled quietly so the disunity in the ranks of those opposing the Catholic Church should not be manifest. But after Müntzer's sermon defending violence, he felt he had to enter the fray publicly, and this he did with his *Letter to the Princes of Saxony Concerning the Rebellious Spirit*.[22] The letter is revealing on several counts. It is addressed in respectful terms to princes who might be tempted to believe Müntzer's claims. He mocked Müntzer for not taking his bold claims of direct revelation into the territories of the bilious Duke George or to some other Catholic land where, Luther implies, hostile authorities would make short work of such a satanic pest. Luther advised his own princes to let Müntzer preach as much as he wanted, for time would show what was true and what false. He scoffed at Müntzer for refusing to come to Wittenberg to face Luther in face-to-face debate. Yet he expressed his confidence that if the conflict was left to words alone, truth—Luther's interpretation of the Bible—would win out. Still he urged the princes to take strong action if Müntzer threatened violence. A minister of the Word—such as Müntzer claimed to be—could not use force. If Müntzer tried to use force, the princes must banish him or else face sedition.

All this was standard Christian teaching, but Luther appeared to think that the Saxon princes—and especially the Elector Frederick—required exhortation to see the light. We may ask if Frederick, whose earlier reluctance to banish Luther seems to have been founded on a devout conscience seeking divine truth, may have been seeking still. Did he and his younger brother find in Müntzer's bold and charismatic preaching something that made them wonder if this man armed with such certainties might be preaching a fuller revelation? The elector at least seemed to waver.[23]

The letter also shows Luther's growing propensity to stand outside himself to view his break with Rome as a heroic epic. He reviews his own career, his humility, his courage at Augsburg, at Leipzig, and finally at Worms, the suffering he endured, the dangers he faced, the meekness of his spirit. Luther wrote as one self-conscious and proud of his humility and grateful to the God who has accomplished great works through him—all this in contrast to the haughty spirit of Müntzer, who would appear only before audiences who agreed with him already. Finally Luther said that God worked in the Old Testament days among the Jews when they had direct inspiration from God and were required to destroy idols by force. The Jews had such a command from God, but we do not, he said. The Jews, he implied, received authority through miraculous intervention, but Müntzer, he said, has done no miracle at all. It was a breathtaking charge, given that Luther had been mocked on the same grounds by Catholics. How could he claim that he brought a new revelation when he did no miracles to prove his authority? His answer was that he had the word of God—scripture as he interpreted it. But that was Müntzer's claim, too, pushed to the conclusion drawn from the New Testament that the preachers of Christ's resurrection continued to do miracles with no suggestion that God might call a halt to them.

With Müntzer Luther was now seriously engaged with the greatest single issue of the Reformation—the reception of his preaching that the word of God was revealed in scripture alone. For the moment his advice may have helped stir Frederick and John to take measures against Müntzer. They were also doubtless roused to action by an outbreak of violence when some of Müntzer's followers were massacred by a petty German princeling who owed nominal allegiance to Duke George. Müntzer threatened retaliation, and Frederick, prodded by George, summoned Müntzer to Weimar for a hearing in August. Before this tribunal Müntzer was accused of fomenting sedition. Supporters who had accompanied him from Allstedt fell away. When he returned to Allstedt, the city fathers who had backed him now turned against him, and he fled the city on the evening of August 7, 1524, leaving his wife and infant son behind. He landed in Mühlhausen in central Germany, an imperial city where the city council had more liberty than in towns where the controlling lord lived nearby. It was a textile town populated by weavers, as we have noted, a traditionally revolutionary group and ready to listen to his proclamation of a gospel of the people.[24] There for a moment we can leave him and take up again the career of another early follower of Luther's now turned enemy—Andreas Bodenstein von Karlstadt.[25]

We have already noted Karlstadt's drift away from Luther and his radical departures in worship at Wittenberg. He lingered in the city when Luther returned from the Wartburg, but he was increasingly persona non grata, pushed into the shadows. In February 1523 he renounced his academic life, dressed himself in the rough clothes of a peasant, and seems to have given farming a try.[26] Not surprisingly, he—like Müntzer—turned his attention to the German mystics, those late medieval thinkers who found the true way to God through experience rather than through reason, though, unlike Müntzer, Karlstadt did not hold that the divine spirit encountered through prayer and meditation gave him special revelations.

In the summer of 1523 after some negotiation and a little sleight of hand, Karlstadt became archdeacon and preacher—though not pastor—of the church in a small town called Orlamünde not far from Wittenberg. Here he became more radical, unrestrained by Luther's personality and authority. He purged the church of images, halted the baptism of infants, and, in a step that shocked Luther, denied the real presence of Christ in the elements of the Eucharist. The Eucharist, he said, was nothing more than a vivid symbol intended to make communicants remember more vividly the sacrifice of Christ on the cross.[27] Moreover, he committed the unpardonable sin of a thinker of thoughts against the grain of the times: he published them. Publication was a violation of the truce called in the Diet of Nuremberg the previous year and threatened the concessions granted then to the Lutherans.[28]

Karlstadt was ordered to give up his position at Orlamünde and to return to his university position at Wittenberg. The alternative was to be cast adrift in the world without income or recommendations. His congregation supported him and formally elected him pastor. Luther had vigorously supported the rights of congregations to choose their own pastors, but now he had second thoughts. This congregation had called a pastor opposed to some of Luther's fundamental tenets of doctrine and worship, and he would not let this challenge go unanswered. Already Müntzer was fomenting armed uprisings among peasants, and the authorities were alarmed. Luther tarred Karlstadt with the revolutionary brush. In a letter of July 4, 1524, he named Karlstadt as one of those taking up arms against civil authorities—although not a particle of evidence exists that Karlstadt ever acquiesced in Müntzer's call to arms.[29]

To Luther and the princes, the threat seemed palpable. Müntzer's followers seemed to be growing, and Müntzer was ready to declare Karlstadt an ally, a move that Karlstadt did not welcome but one obviously worrisome to Luther, who tended to see both men as a team harnessed by the devil. Karlstadt's affectation of peasant dress was seen in court circles as a dangerous sign of adherence to the ripe old German tradition of peasant rebellion symbolized by the *Bundschuh.*

In late August, Luther and Karlstadt came face to face in Jena, where Luther had been sent to preach calm to a restless population. Karlstadt, wearing a hat to disguise himself, came to hear Luther preach on August 22. Luther preached against the spirit of violence manifested by Müntzer and others of his ilk, the "spirit of Allstedt." Afterward Karlstadt asked for a meeting, and the two men sat down together in an inn. Their confrontation was angry. Karlstadt found it slanderous that Luther lumped him and Müntzer together, and Luther was forced to agree that Karlstadt had not been a prophet of rebellion. On the matter of the Eucharist, they could not compromise. Luther's fury mounted. He whipped out a gold gulden and gave it to Karlstadt like a knight handing a glove to another in a challenge to meet on the jousting ground. This was a literary challenge. The two men were to debate their views on the Eucharist in print.[30]

The rest of Luther's trip was troublesome. He spoke the next day in a church at a village near Jena, stepping over a large crucifix shattered in pieces "by the Karlstadtians" as he ascended the pulpit. Luther took the shattered cross as a deliberate provocation and years later enjoyed telling how he did not mention it at all in his sermon. "And so against the pride of Satan, I outdid him in pride."[31]

The next day Luther went to Orlamünde itself to meet with members of Karlstadt's congregation. Karlstadt tried to attend, but Luther refused to speak as long as Karlstadt remained in the room. From first to last the conversation was hostile on both sides. Much of it turned on the use of images in worship. The Orlamünders wanted them cast out of the church entirely; Luther said images were tolerable if they were not worshipped. A cobbler undertook to engage Luther in debate, quoting as "scripture" the sentence "I wish my bride to be naked and do not wish for her to be wearing her gown." Apparently he meant that one should approach God directly without the gown of images, but the absurdity of the "quotation" made Luther put his face in his hands.[32]

He quickly changed his mind about the wisdom of a literary debate. When he got back to Wittenberg, he advised the princes to expel Karlstadt from Saxony without delay, and by September 18 Karlstadt was ordered out of the elector's territories. Ronald Sider has summarized the differences between the styles of Luther and Karlstadt. Luther wanted to go slowly; Karlstadt was in a hurry and maintained the activist faith that (in my view) resonates in the great works published by Luther in 1520, that if right doctrines were clearly proclaimed and argued from scripture, preachers could be bold, God would do the rest, and the gospel would take care of itself.[33] In a letter of October 1520 to a friend about the uproar caused by publication of the *Babylonian Captivity,* Luther wrote confidently of the tumults that must come when the gospel was truly preached.[34] That continued to be his opinion at Worms. His attitude in that heady time was clearly to let justice be done though the world fall. But by 1524 Luther was thinking as a tactician; Karlstadt was booming ahead, in expectation not that God would open the skies and do miracles to vindicate him but that God would act through the common folk to make right doctrine prevail. Luther's passion for order was such that he could brook no threat of tumult, and Karlstadt's reliance on the common people was alarming, especially when armed rebellion shouldered its way into German society. Luther could argue for Christian equality in a somewhat abstract form in 1520 when he wrote *The Freedom of a Christian* and the *Babylonian Captivity.* In 1524, when it came to flesh-and-blood peasants and other commoners, he changed his mind.

Sider has demonstrated that with regard to the essential doctrine of justification, Luther and Karlstadt substantially agreed. With regard to one doctrine, the Eucharist, they remained furiously apart. As early as 1521 Karlstadt had admitted that his "Old Adam," that part of him prone to rebellion, had a hard time accepting the notion of a physical presence of Christ in the Eucharist. By 1523 he had given up any effort to believe in the real presence. The bread was bread; the wine was wine. No grace came from these elements. The purpose of the Mass was to inspire emotional recollection of the sacrifice of Christ on the cross.[35] It sounds a bit like Proust's description of how the madeleine dipped in an infusion of tea brought together the whole life of his narrator in *A la recherche du temps perdu*. Karlstadt's view was in part a mystical conception of religion. In the ceremony of the Eucharist, we are to be elevated to God by having aroused in us profound feelings stirred by the recollection of what Christ has done for us. All apart from theological definitions, we can probably say that the feelings of some are roused by memory and the feelings of others are stirred by the belief that they are taking the body and blood of Christ into their bodies and that the intensity of our participation is probably part of our psychological state at the time.

Karlstadt feared the mechanical and the ceremonial in religion more than Luther did. Here Karlstadt presages a strand of modernity shared by Ulrich Zwingli of Zurich that the physical world is mere stuff, created by God, part of the divinely ordained universe, but still inferior to spirit, especially to the Holy Spirit, who motivates our hearts in our relations with the Almighty. Bodies of all sorts changed, decayed, and passed away with time; spirit was eternal. Karlstadt's view of the Eucharist, shared by Zwingli, looks like another sign of creeping rationalism in the sixteenth century. By rationalism I mean the tendency remarked by Henri Busson, among others, to see the world moving in an orderly progression of cause and effect, Nature self-sufficiently moving according to its own laws, a bit like the clock in William Paley's famous eighteenth-century metaphor of creation. Confronted by ordinary sight and sound, taste, smell, and touch, a certain kind of temperament could not persuade itself that something extraordinary was secretly happening in the physical world; the extraordinary had to happen in our hearts. If it looked like bread and wine, tasted, felt, smelled, and sounded like bread and wine in the mouth, it must be only bread and wine. Karlstadt, Zwingli, and perhaps Calvin would have found much to discuss in the later religious views of René Descartes and his concept of the division between that which can be measured and that which can be known only by direct intuition in the ways that we know color—and God.

Karlstadt was of this temperament—all the more reason for him to reject the apocalyptic fantasies of Thomas Müntzer. Luther stood on the other side of the great gulf fixed between those who see in the physical world the shine of divinity and those who cannot. As Karlstadt's rumination about the "Old Adam" indicates, he tried to believe in the real presence but felt forced to admit that he could not. Karlstadt believed that scripture conveyed the gospel and that the Holy Spirit elucidated the word of scripture. But he did not share Müntzer's belief that the Holy Spirit gave new revelations in the present.

For Luther—who as a young priest trembled to hold God in his hand at his first mass—the Eucharist was a kind of incarnation, a union of God and matter ritually renewed every time it was observed by believers. It continued to be a miracle, yet one that did not take place in a manifestation of visible supernatural transformation. His view of the miraculous represented another paradox: His profound yearning for the miracle of the Eucharist combined with his rejection of miracles at shrines worked to stand the traditional order on its head. When God intervened in the world, he did so not with storm and fire but with signs that could be understood only by those prepared by grace to receive them.

Luther himself tended to see "nature" as part of the created order, given to us by God's grace, operating under its own rules, and we humans were supposed to use nature for the purposes for which God intended it. Nature moved in cycles of reproduction, continuation, and death, and human beings were supposed to create orderly lives out of nature to ensure the continuation of human existence. We serve God by doing our part to serve nature's purposes. Since human beings are fallen creatures, work in the world is accompanied by hardship, but the work itself is all to the good and part of the reason we were created.[36]

He was one of many in his century who found that the orderly working of nature itself in procreation, birth, and growth was one of the greatest miracles of all, and he steadily castigated Catholic demands for clerical celibacy as "against nature" and therefore evil.[37] Here, despite his preoccupation with the demonic powers and his devotion to the idea of God's almighty power, he fell into the mood of classical authors such as Cicero who found in the self-perpetuation of nature all the miracles they needed in the daily life. Catholic claims of divine intervention in the miracles at shrines were demonic delusions whose reality he did not deny but whose value he did not accept. But he could not give up the notion of a miraculous presence of Christ in the Eucharist. The sacraments were not "natural." They were incarnations that helped lift the Christian from nature and time and death to the transcendent and eternal realm of God.

Karlstadt blamed his troubles on Luther, and in his wandering exile attacked his old colleague as turncoat and oppressor. He drifted to Strasbourg, thence to Zurich, thence to Basel, and to Heidelberg and to Strasbourg again. His writing continued, including a pamphlet giving his side of his expulsion from Orlamünde, blaming Luther for it, and it had an effect. We surmise that only a few people could read—perhaps only ten percent of the German population. Books were meant to be read aloud, and if the subject was of consuming interest, they were.[38] We may surmise that the reading might be done passionately by someone who cared enough to speak the text aloud to a group, and we may surmise, too, that the reception of the oral text was both varied and somewhat simplistic, with the audience retaining parts of the most startling thoughts and retaining also something of the passion of the reader if indeed reader and auditors were already disposed to agree on the worth of the text. The oral reception of doctrine and the tradition that flowed from it seemed to become a kind of megaphone broadcasting the loudest sounds without subtlety or hesitation. Karlstadt's arguments about the Lord's Supper and believers' baptism struck many as both scriptural and sensible. The Gospels are filled with metaphorical utterances by Christ as he explained his mission of salvation. Christ was a door, a vine, a shepherd. That the declaration "This is my body" was one of those metaphors seemed plausible. It did not have to betoken an actual change in the elements of bread and wine. The sixteenth-century world, cut off from detailed knowledge of cultic meals essential to some mystery religions, could not see their connection to the Eucharist, to the ancient conviction that the communicant actually ate the body of the dying and rising god. Even so, for Christians bonded to a centuries-old tradition of a miraculous transformation in the Mass, Karlstadt's doctrines were deeply troubling. Luther wrote to various correspondents attacking Karlstadt, but he acknowledged in late October that Karlstadt's teachings were gaining adherents.[39]

He smarted over the charge that Karlstadt had been expelled from Orlamünde "without being heard and, without being vanquished." But Karlstadt was not his sole problem. In Bavaria Duke William pushed hard to exterminate Luther's followers in his territories, burning some at the stake, beheading others, and according to several accounts, mutilating still others. Luther hoped that the blood of the martyrs would choke the persecutors.[40] But although he could put a brave face on things, these were not good times, and the divisions among those who had started as Luther's followers seemed scandalous. He was also discouraged because he could detect no growth in piety in the Wittenbergers who accepted his gospel. He could impose rules for those who could or could not participate in the Eucharist. But he could not remake the spirits of his congregations.

As if these internecine combats and persecution from the Catholics were not enough, Luther faced attack from yet another quarter. In the fall of 1524 Erasmus published a little book called *A Discourse on Free Will,* an attack on Luther's doctrine of predestination. It was not something Erasmus wanted to write; he would have preferred to remain above the fray. Although he regarded the Luther affair as a tragedy and hated Luther's vehemence, Erasmus would not renounce the sharp criticisms he himself had made against the papal church and its corruptions of both life and doctrine. He could not sympathize with Luther's vehement spirit; Luther's poisonous attack on Henry VIII seemed to be the last straw. Pressure from friends and authorities within the old church became irresistible, and Erasmus had to take sides. We shall adjourn our own consideration of the controversy that then erupted between the two men. Luther apparently first saw Erasmus's book in late October, for by November 1 he was expressing his disgust for it, calling it the unlearned product of a learned man.[41] He promised a reply soon. For the moment Karlstadt occupied his mind.

From Strasbourg on November 22, Nicholas Gerbel wrote to Luther reporting on Karlstadt's activities. He had made himself, his wife, and his infant child public martyrs at Luther's hand, creating a following among the lower classes always avid for some new thing. Not even the Catholics, including Johann Eck and others, attacked Luther as vehemently as Karlstadt, Gerbel said. People were asking for a response, he said. He asked that Luther write not briefly but copiously and soberly.[42]

The next day a number of ministers in Strasbourg, including Wolfgang Capito and Martin Bucer, joined their names to a similar request. They affirmed their devotion to scripture, but Karlstadt had shaken their convictions about what scripture meant. Karlstadt had come up with an ingenious theory, that when Christ said, "This is my body," he pointed to himself in a gesture intended to say that his body would be sacrificed for humankind. Only after that gesture, said Karlstadt, did Christ shift his attention to the bread and the wine. By that ingenious interpretation—worthy of the director of some play searching for a new slant on old lines—Karlstadt left the bread and the wine in the supper intact, a commemoration of the sacrifice of Christ without being an incarnation of Christ in the elements. He had come up with a clever analogy that obviously troubled the Strasbourg pastors. By Luther's interpretation—held also by Erasmus—Christ had made a similar rhetorical shift when he told Peter in Matthew 16:18, "Thou art Peter, and on this rock I will build my church." That is, he had begun the sentence addressing one object, Peter, and finished the sentence by shifting the direction to himself. By the interpretations of both Luther and Erasmus, we can imagine Jesus flinging his hand out in a punning way to Peter, declaring, "You are Peter, a rock," then shifting his hand back to himself, declaring, "and on this rock I will build my church." Why should not Christ have made a similar shift in discussing the relation of the Eucharist to himself?[43] Why not indeed?

The Strasbourg pastors, fundamentally conservative men, did not like or trust Karlstadt. But they were at a loss as to how to refute him. They called on Luther to respond both to what Karlstadt said about the Eucharist and to what he said about infant baptism. The pastors asked Luther to make his reply without bad humor, "without stomach," as the Latin has it. They wanted a calm and dispassionate exposition of scripture, and they knew enough of Luther to caution him against his own temper. They felt themselves in the midst of tragedy, the foes of the papalist church divided among themselves in the face of their satanic adversary. "Help us," they begged.[44]

All this was disturbing. Luther fretted that Ulrich Zwingli, who shared Karlstadt's idea of the Eucharist, was gaining converts. When the letter from the Strasbourg pastors arrived in Wittenberg on December 14, he was infuriated by its reports of what Karlstadt was saying about him—that Luther was a second pope and that he had nothing sound in him. Luther saw his own cause as the cause of Christ, and in almost every letter on the subject he called Karlstadt the surrogate of Satan.[45]

At first Luther tried to curb his "stomach." He replied with a brief, mild letter to the pastors, recalling Karlstadt's insults and threats against his person when he had gone to Orlamünde to preach against Karlstadt's doctrines. Mildness was not enough. Increasingly Luther heard reports of the spread of Karlstadt's influence, and he read printed works by Karlstadt, including a dialogue on the Eucharist in which a character representing Karlstadt trounced a Lutheran. Late in December Luther threw off restraint and set himself to writing a furious attack on his old colleague. It appeared from the press in two parts over the next months, the first part dealing with what Luther regarded as Karlstadt's teaching about authority and images, the second dedicated to refuting Karlstadt on the Eucharist. He called it *Against the Heavenly Prophets* and he wrote in German—a sign that he supposed Karlstadt's doctrines had their greatest following among the lower and less literate classes.[46]

Throughout the tractate, Luther hurled insults and mockery at his former associate. It must have been a choice experience to hear Luther's unmitigated scorn and vehemence read aloud, but it did nothing to advance Christian charity. Karlstadt was now "our worst enemy." He and his disciples had now replaced faith with a doctrine of works—an obligation to make external things such as food, clothing, and images the central part of the gospel. He accused Karlstadt of wishing to be "the greatest spirit of all, he who has devoured the Holy Spirit feathers and all." He claimed that Karlstadt used riotous breaking of images as a secret means of accustoming the people to revolution. Only the authorities should be allowed to take such steps. In a backhanded slap, Luther thundered, "Though I have not said that Dr. Karlstadt is a murderous prophet, yet he has a rebellious, murderous, seditious spirit in him which, if given an opportunity, would assert itself."[47]

Luther contended that one should destroy images in the heart; when that task was accomplished, the physical images would be of no consequence. He meant that if preachers instructed their congregations about the inward nature of faith, the people would on their own give up false reverence to stocks and stones. His plea was for a conjunction of order and spontaneity, for he had given up the notion that only one order of service could be imposed on all true Christians and congregations. The outward means of worship would vary according to temperament and taste. The essential was Christ, and no one group could force its ways on others. Compulsion in religion was anathema—unless compulsion was exercised against those who by Luther's lights taught unsound doctrine.

Luther defended the real presence, attacking Karlstadt down the line and adducing context, grammar, and philology to support his doctrine that the bread and the wine were the body and blood of Christ. *Against the Heavenly Prophets* is a tedious work for all but those most persuaded that Luther was right in all his acts and deeds. Melanchthon at the time was disturbed by its rhetoric. The editors and translators of the American edition of Luther's works record their embarrassment at the hateful tone of the treatise, and weary readers can only agree with them. It is informed by Luther's conviction that in the essentials of Christian doctrine he was right in everything and that anyone who disagreed was a tool of the devil.

Throughout the first part of the work Luther tarred Karlstadt with the brush of sedition, charges based on nothing more than iconoclasm and ugly words and gestures flung at Luther on his visit to Orlamünde. He had not, he said, been responsible for the expulsion of Karlstadt from Orlamünde. Here he claimed that he had never spoken to the Elector Frederick, that indeed he had seen him only once in his life and that was at the Diet of Worms in

1521. But Luther also said he was happy that Karlstadt had been driven away and that "insofar as my entreaties are effectual, he shall not again return, and would again have to leave were he found here" unless he should become another man.[48]

Luther was enraged that Karlstadt had appealed to the masses, the common people—an appeal that might once have seemed perfectly consistent with Luther's teaching about the priesthood of all believers. Not so now. Authority, Luther said, lay with princes, and Karlstadt had violated the confidence of the elector by leaving his post at the university and becoming the pastor at Orlamünde, pushing aside the designated pastor. True, the congregation at Orlamünde had eventually called Karlstadt to be their minister. Luther was not embarrassed that he himself had shortly before spoken out for the right of congregations to choose their own pastors. Now he declared that even if the prince had appointed a godless minister to Orlamünde, the people would have had no right to resist. It was a stunning reversal, but a furious Luther seemed scarcely to notice it.

Three major problems for Luther come together in this treatise. One is the place of the Hebrew Bible, the Old Testament, in Christian faith; another is the difficulties of consensus about the Bible; the third is the relation of princely authority to the masses, especially in religious matters. Karlstadt took literally the consistent, furious, and often bloodthirsty outrage of some writers of the Hebrew Bible against images and other forms of idolatry in worship. Zwingli, Calvin, and the English puritans were to follow this path. As we have noted, Luther felt that the use of images was harmless as long as one remained clear that they were neither necessary nor endowed with special divine attributes that might compromise reliance on the gospel.

Beyond this particular question lay the larger issue of the Old Testament, the Hebrew Bible, itself. What did Christians do with it? The problem lifted its head at the dawn of Christianity and remained lively until the church developed a tradition able to absorb the Old Testament as a set of types and archetypes of Christ. The allegorical interpretations of Origen helped the church in this direction. The Old Testament became a collection of proof texts, esoteric and arcane unless understood as prophecies and types referring to the coming of Christ—in which case they became miraculously clear, a stimulus to wonder at the mysterious workings of God. Church tradition gathered firmly around the Old Testament and imposed a Christian interpretation upon it to prevent dangerous readings—although in the later Middle Ages popular revolts were often helped along by the example of Israel's holy wars.

Luther's appeal to scripture alone tore away the protective mantle of

Catholic tradition and left the Hebrew Bible open to reinterpretation. We have seen that Luther believed he had special insight into those parts of the Old Testament that were abiding and Christocentric and those that were time-bound, intended to regulate Israel's religious and social life within a historical context and to be cast aside when circumstances changed—as when Christ fulfilled Old Testament prophecies. But in a humanistic age when the languages—including Hebrew—and history of the ancient world were emerging from the blurred focus of a more naive time, the unity of the Old Testament became more and more problematic. Later puritan literalism about matters such as the sabbath, images, and holy war illustrate difficulties that are endemic to dependence on the Bible. What in the Old Testament was still binding? What could be cast aside? Under the prodding of Paul, New Testament Christians agreed that circumcision, the everlasting covenant with Israel, according to the book of Genesis, would not be required of new gentile converts—a decision that made evangelism much easier around the Mediterranean. The dietary laws fell by the wayside early on. Many difficult areas were left to be decided upon by evangelicals. Karlstadt—scarcely important in himself—was an early and implacable demonstration that consensus on the Old Testament would be impossible among evangelicals.

Consensus about the Old Testament was part of the larger problem of the Bible itself. Karlstadt's arguments about the Lord's Supper as sign and memorial rather than as real presence may have been more clever than profound, but in time most evangelicals accepted them, leaving the doctrine of the real presence to a minority of non-Catholics—including Lutherans and some Anglicans. Consequently in most churches in the evangelical tradition, the Eucharist remains a brief commemoration occasionally tacked on to the rest of the service. Whether this development contributed to an advancement of piety or a sense of awe and wonder may be debated. Luther declared his preference for the Gospel of John over the other gospels, but it does not include the Eucharist at all. Instead the "sacrament" Jesus seems to institute at the Last Supper is that of mutual foot washing. The problems pile up on examination of the biblical text.

These two issues dissolved into the third, that of authority. The contempt that Luther felt for the masses or the "common people" shows vividly in this long and ugly treatise, this despite his earlier professions of love for the German people. The idea was not new to Luther; his view was that the "true church" true Christians were a scattered group, known finally to God alone. Here his argument turned on the notion that the godly prince somehow intuited from the Bible what true Christians believed and put his power behind them, casting into exile (but not killing) those who disagreed. Luther had to acknowledge that the people at Orlamünde finally wanted Karlstadt to be their pastor, no matter how irregular his first coming to them had been. Luther's response was to say that the elector was in charge of such things and that even if the prince had sent a godless minister to Orlamünde, the people would have had no right to resist. His retreat from his early enthusiasms and trust in Christian congregations was here complete and more than a bit ridiculous. The reformer who had in 1520 and 1521 believed that the word of God would sweep all before it and batter the papacy into oblivion or at least defeat was now confronted by bitter division within his own ranks and, more important, the growing consciousness that God was not going to intervene miraculously to resolve disputes and carry the gospel to victory throughout Christian Europe. From this period on, Luther was to shrink his expectations and, if anything, see life as darker, God as more mysterious and inscrutable, and Satan as more active. For the rest of his life he was to fight a two-front war, one against the Catholic Church and the other against the myriad contradictory voices rising in the implacable centrifugal forces within the movement he had begun. He would have confidence in neither pope nor people. Instead, he would be forced to put his trust in princes—and most of them he did not trust either. So was to evolve his ultimate tragedy.

Karlstadt deserves a final word. At the height of the Peasants' Rebellion, adrift with his wife and afraid for his life, he capitulated entirely to Luther in exchange for safety. For eight weeks in June and July he hid in Luther's house. As many have remarked, Luther could assault his enemies with the fiercest polemics, but on face-to-face contact he could be a different man, kind and merciful. Karlstadt remained unchanged by his experience. When danger died down, he tried his hand at farming and then at being a merchant. He resumed his "sacramentarian" belief about the Eucharist, that it was merely a symbol and a remembrance of the sacrifice of Christ and that it contained no real presence. He took refuge in Switzerland in 1530, threw in his lot with Zwingli, and remained in Switzerland after Zwingli's death in battle until his own in 1541. His views became more mystical, more in tune with the warmhearted devotion that would later be part of German Pietism and, by that vehicle, be translated to English and American Methodism. His doctrines haunted Luther, and Luther's frequently expressed scorn for him was in part indication of Karlstadt's success.

25

THE PEASANTS' REBELLION

L UTHER worked amid a tempest of demands through the winter of 1524–25. His correspondence shows him giving advice on topics as diverse as establishing the Reformation in Danzig to dealing with an alleged Jewish plot to poison him and to giving counsel to a woman who claimed that her legal husband was impotent and wanted to know what to do. In many letters he raged against Karlstadt and promised time and again to deliver a blow against Erasmus's *Discourse on Free Will* when more important business did not press.

His letters tended to be brief, a few lines in haste with apologies and protestations of overwork. In February Karlstadt wrote asking for a safe-conduct from the elector to allow him to return to Saxony. The elector refused—with Luther's approval. From Strasbourg on March 23, Nikolaus Gerbel, one of Luther's most loyal and scholarly followers, wrote him a letter gently protesting the ugly tone of the treatise *Against the Heavenly Prophets.* Increasingly evangelicals in other cities following Luther's lead in orderly secession from the papal church found his fierce and volatile anger disturbing and embarrassing.

Lacking in Luther's own letters from this time is any preoccupation with sporadic outbursts of violence among peasants of Thuringia and southern and southwestern Germany—isolated outbursts that were to grow into the great Peasants' Rebellion of the spring of 1525. Peasant risings erupted now and then throughout western Europe in the later Middle Ages—and were quickly and savagely suppressed by the authorities.

The causes of peasant unrest were complex—as causes always are—and doubtless class and temperament combined with various passions to induce them to listen to some leaders rather than others. Charismatic men such as Thomas Müntzer were somehow able to assume the tragic role of command that, given the realities of the time, could end only in violent death for many and utter defeat for their cause.

The evidence is clear on one point: the peasants represented a volatile conglomeration, and until the catastrophe of 1525 they burst out in occasional explosive revolts that frightened the ruling classes out of their wits. Often rebellious peasants joined forces with discontented city dwellers, as in the Wat Tyler revolt in England in 1381, a rebellion that came close to overthrowing the government. Religious icons and rhetoric permeated society. It seems natural therefore that these uprisings were usually urged on by charismatic preachers who found in the Bible ample proof for their fervent belief that God was on the side of the poor and that the rich were wicked and deserved to be cast down from their high places and their estates broken in pieces.

Their interpretation of the Bible was probably on the mark—at least as far as the Gospels relate the life and ministry of Jesus. Much modern scholarship carried on in cool detachment from traditional Christian dogma finds in Jesus and in Paul the Apostle prophets who saw the end of the world about to come in a storm of fire. In many of his supposed utterances Jesus tells of a divine finale that will incinerate privilege and give to the poor their just inheritance. Blessed are the poor, for they shall inherit the Kingdom of Heaven. It is easier for a camel to pass through the eye of a needle than it is for a rich man to be saved. The book of Acts, the earliest history of the church after the disappearance of Jesus from the scene, tells us that Christians in Jerusalem practiced communism among themselves. "And all who shared the faith owned everything in common; they sold their goods and possessions and distributed the proceeds among themselves according to what each one needed."[1] We can read these utterances in safely symbolic terms, but we can also choose to read them literally as doubtless they were intended to be read by the authors of the New Testament works.

It is not amazing that masses of people untutored in the subtleties of conservative Christian orthodoxy found revolution in the scriptures at various times during the later Middle Ages. The Franciscan movement of the thirteenth century emphasized voluntary poverty, and from almost the moment St. Francis himself died, some Franciscans drifted into heresy. Kindred movements extolling poverty spread into Germany and the Low Countries. "Brethren of the Free Spirit" became numerous in the Rhine Valley, especially in and around Cologne, and, as Norman Cohn has observed, became the targets of "the first regular episcopal inquisition on German soil." Many of these free spirits adopted a version of Neoplatonism that found God in every created thing, but, as Cohn has said, "It was the eternal essence of things, not their existence in time, that was truly God; whatever had a separate transitory existence had emanated from God, but no longer was God."[2] This view would work against transubstantiation or the real presence and may have contributed in some indirect way to the discomfort of those like Zwingli, Müntzer, and Karlstadt who rejected a "real" presence. Some of these medieval "free spirits" practiced sexual promiscuity, and most believed in some form of direct divine inspiration apart from the rituals and doctrines of the Catholic Church.

In Germany in 1476, a young shepherd of Niklashausen announced that the Virgin Mary had appeared to him in a dream and told him to preach that both pope and emperor would soon be overthrown and all other secular authority would dissolve and all taxes, usury, forced labor, and rents be abolished. Woods, water, and pastures would be free to all.[3] His name was Hans Böhm, and when he was not keeping his sheep, he entertained people by drumming and playing the pipe. Having begun by preaching repentance, he soon gathered huge crowds, and, inspired by them, he decided that he was a new messiah with powers over heaven, earth, and the life to come.[4] He was condemned as a heretic and burned at the stake, singing hymns to Mary as he died, but before his drama was done, some 34,000 peasants stood to arms and threatened the higher orders. Lacking effective leadership after Böhm's death, this motley peasant army quickly dwindled away.

It was a portent of things to come. Peasants throughout Europe remained in various levels of bondage to feudal lords who held legal title not only to the land but to obligations owed them by peasants who lived in villages and worked the soil. At every moment these obligations intruded on peasant life in annoying ways. Many peasants could marry only with the consent of their lords. They were forbidden to hunt in the lord's forests or fish in his ponds or pasture their cattle in his fields, and they might be summoned to work for him when they had their own crops to plant or to tend or to harvest. Peasants were not usually hunters—although they might poach game at the risk of a death sentence if caught. Fishing was more important, since fish offered the most easily obtained relief from the monotonous diet of bread and pulse in the winter months.

Perhaps as much as any grievance felt by peasants was humiliation endured at the hands of the higher classes. They were the niggers of their time, mocked, scorned, and held to be incorrigible examples of the worst of humankind. Luther later on quoted a German proverb: "A peasant is a pig; hit him, and he's dead. He thinks nothing of the life to come."[5] He viewed the peasant as grasping, devious, stupid, and incorrigible, frequently quoting another common proverb, "A peasant is a peasant," akin to another German saying, "Put a gold collar on a pig, and he is still a pig." Another declared, "Peasants and pigs are one and the same." Yet another proverb said, "Don't grieve for a peasant or a Jew."[6]

In parts of France peasants were required to beat ponds with rods to keep the frogs from singing at night and thereby disrupting the slumber of the lords and their families.[7] Hunting was the sacrosanct pleasure of the noble classes, and peasants had no recourse when hunting parties on horseback plunged through fields in pursuit of wild boars or deer or other prey. Sometimes peasants were summoned to beat the game out of the forests in the direction of hunters waiting for the kill. In many areas of Germany free peasants were forced into serfdom throughout the fifteenth and sixteenth centuries. A free peasant might have the right to choose his lord in much the same way that a tenant farmer in the southern United States in an earlier time had the right to choose the owner on whose land he lived and worked. Free peasants were at liberty to marry spouses of their choice. But the serf was bound to the land and was scarcely more than a slave. Throughout the fifteenth century the German nobles felt themselves under increasing financial pressures, and doubtless many felt the panic that seems to come on any group threatened with the loss of status. They reacted by tightening the rules, and peasants found themselves operating in a world where the legal walls seemed to be inching in on them, the plight of each generation worse than that of the one before.[8]

With all their disadvantages, many peasants were well off by the standards of the day. Despite taxes and other financial burdens imposed on them by the nobility, some peasants had surpluses to sell, and if they were close to a large city they had a ready market for their crops and produce, especially grain and wine.[9] Some social thinkers have argued that a class is most likely to become revolutionary when its living conditions have been improving and it encounters some blockade that threatens to stop its progress.

Anticlericalism appears to have run deep in peasant culture. The church, including the monasteries, owned vast lands. Literate churchmen kept careful records that could be brought into play with great and unanswerable effect when disputes arose over the interpretation of who owed what and to whom. In any age people who live close to the land and its mysterious uncertainties are instinctively religious—though equally instinctively heterodox. Their sense of injury at the hands of the established church would naturally have roused peasants to welcome Luther's proclamation of reformation and renewal directed against the papacy and all its minions. Their relative illiteracy would prevent a clear understanding of the intricacies of Luther's gospel, but when they heard that he had written something called *The Freedom of a Christian,* they could believe that here was a prophet risen to liberate them from feudal obligations. When they heard also that in the *Babylonian Captivity* he had declared that no Christian was obligated to obey a law imposed on him by another, they could as readily believe that he stood on their side against impositions from the German nobility. Other radical statements pepper his works of 1520. One of the most extreme appears in his "Short Form" of the Ten Commandments and the Lord's Prayer. In it he said of the church:

> I believe that no man can be redeemed who does not belong to this community, who does not walk single-mindedly in it in one faith, word, [belief in the] sacraments, hope, and love and that no Jew, heretic, heathen, or sinner will be redeemed with it, for it must be that he becomes reconciled, united, and like-minded with it in all things.
>
> I believe that in this community or Christendom, all things are common, and all the goods of one belong to the other and that no one owns anything entirely of his own so that to me and to every single believer every prayer and good work comes to the aid of the whole community to confirm and strengthen it for all times, in life and in death, and also that everyone must bear the burdens of one another as St. Paul teaches.[10]

It is scarcely any wonder that peasants reading—or, more likely, hearing—these words assumed Luther was their champion. Müntzer developed in his own way thoughts that Luther himself had vigorously expressed, and his movement may be seen as a natural development from many of the same premises that drove Luther himself.[11] They were different in what they did with those premises, and Müntzer, rootless and lacking the kind of protection that Luther enjoyed from the Elector Frederick, was driven to try the main chance. Perhaps Müntzer's doubts were even more gnawing and terrible than those of Luther so that he was all the more compelled to put God to the test that might draw divine intervention.

The vast pamphlet literature with its garish woodcuts and simple captions could be passed from hand to hand among the illiterate, and anyone could see that here was the German Hercules come to smash to blood and bone the enemies of the good common people. Luther's fierce temperament with his fondness for extravagant assertion appealed to an uneducated populace whose emotional range tended to run from fire to ice with not much subtlety in between. From the beginning of his notoriety, foes predicted that he would stir the common people to rebellion. Just as regularly Luther responded that the gospel always caused tumults. How could the peasants not believe him to be on their side!

In Zurich, Ulrich Zwingli's radical doctrines stood for a program of reform that bound church and government in a republican order, embracing many of the vague goals of the peasants for the "common man."[12] Zwingli was not, however, of a temperament to see in the lower classes the hope of the world. In Marxist terms, Zwingli represented a bourgeois revolution that would later be taken over by John Calvin. Nevertheless, in the confused religious atmosphere of 1525, Zwingli must have seemed to riotous peasants to be one more pillar to their movement. His republicanism, conveyed with the inevitable distortions of word of mouth, would have been another element in the rising expectations of peasants that all this religious unrest had something special to do with them.

We've already seen enough to know that from the beginning Luther had no interest in leading a secular reformation of society. A man preoccupied with the horror of death, avid to believe in a Christ holding the key to resurrection and the life everlasting, was not made of social revolutionary stuff. He was more likely to wish for social stability so the gospel might be preached and the way prepared for death and the life beyond—much as the medieval church remained content to let kings do what they wanted as long as they upheld dogmas deemed necessary for salvation, including moral precepts, narrowly construed, that indicated obedience to ecclesiastical authority. Yet Luther's extravagant language with its raging hyperbole was like a military band of trumpets and drums drowning out the piping notes of his distinction between secular expectation and Christian hope.

The sticking point was Christian equality and sometimes more than equality, even the superiority of the poor over the rich—a doctrine that finds ample warrant in the New Testament. Mary sang in her Magnificat as recorded in Luke 1:46–55: "He hath put down the mighty from their seats and exalted them of low degree. He hath filled the hungry with good things; and the rich he hath sent empty away." And in Luke's version of the Sermon on the Mount (Luke 6:24), Jesus himself says, "Woe unto you that are rich, for ye have received your consolation." That is, their wealth is their consolation, but God will console the poor.

Luther seemed to emphasize equality with radical abandon in his thumping treatises *On the Freedom of a Christian* and the *Babylonian Captivity of the Church*. The radicals who came after him pushed these teachings about equality to the limit—and found plenty of biblical texts to support their enthusiasms. Philipp Melanchthon, as we have seen, was at first receptive to and perhaps enthusiastic over the message brought to Wittenberg by the Zwickau prophets. Thomas Müntzer and his disciples could never renounce the conviction that equality applied not only in religious affairs but also in civil and political society and that consequently the true Christian should work, with God's help, for a comprehensive social revolution in church and nation. God, he thought, was not to be encountered in books but through direct experience.[13]

In numbers the peasants represented a formidable force, and these multitudes haunted the imaginations of the ruling classes. The mood was similar among the planters of the Old South in the United States who contemplated with anxiety masses of slaves, knowing that if those masses could unite under one command, doom for the planters and their society would be violent and final. In the event, the peasants proved to be fatally divided among themselves, and although they drew some of the dissatisfied from all classes of society, especially the miners, they never succeeded in making a solid alliance with artisans among the city dwellers who could have added immeasurable strength to their cause. Yet fear has its own logic, and to tell the ruling classes that such unity among the oppressed was all but impossible seemed paltry comfort against the visible evidence on every hand of hordes of human beings whose brute appearance concealed not merely hostility but hatred. Cruel proverbs and jokes directed against blacks in America and peasants in sixteenth-century Germany were the backside of fear.

Müntzer was the sort to turn this fear into terror. He came to believe that the "elect" included many non-Christians—a view shared by Zwingli. Turks, pagans, and Jews were Christians without sometimes knowing it. The Spirit acted through all the world, and people in all religions had freedom within themselves to respond to it. Throughout the world, the "elect" were the poor, always forced to contend against the wealthy, who in satanic force lorded it over the righteous. The coming age of the Spirit would sweep these evil souls all away.[14]

Müntzer's thoughts here illustrate a creative effort to deal with the growing knowledge of how many non-Christians lived in a world becoming larger and more complicated than anyone had believed. When the rebellion collapsed in May 1525 and he was tortured by his captors, he was said to have declared that all things were to be held in common: "Everybody should properly receive according to his need. Any prince, count, or lord who refuses to do this even when seriously warned should be hanged or have his head chopped off."[15] Müntzer's "communist" ideology was akin to the views expressed by Thomas More in his *Utopia* published in 1516—except that More placed his communist society on a mythical island in the pagan New World and recoiled at the notion that any rebels should overthrow European government to establish such a system among Christians. And More wrote in Latin, not the language that might inspire ecstatic thoughts of revolution among the masses.

As his sermon before Duke John shows, Müntzer took literally the glowing account of Old Testament warriors and prophets who massacred idolaters, and his biblical justification for violence would seem to have been as great as Luther's biblical justification for resignation in the face of oppression. The Bible itself is divided on that score. The book of Revelation—regarded suspiciously by Luther, as we have seen, but part of the New Testament canon—portrays a great holy war at the end of time in which blood shall run up to the horses' bridles and the defeated battalions of the Antichrist shall be not only slaughtered on earth but condemned to everlasting torments in a burning hell. Many scholars have pointed out that the peasants and their leaders had little sense of what they would do once they overthrew existing authority. Planning was not their forte or their concern. They saw their cause literally in apocalyptic terms, expecting the direct aid of God to slaughter their foes, and God himself to reveal what do do afterward. They were to demonstrate their faith by acting, and God would not fail them. God would meet their acts with his own and fulfill his plan for the world. Cohn suggests that Müntzer's millennium would be the state of nature of the time before Adam fell, when all things were held in common and no one wanted for anything.[16]

But Müntzer was not the only spokesman for the peasants. Many of them had more peaceable and more humble desires. Like Luther and his foes, the peasants found in the printing press the means to propaganda that made their revolt a true mass movement. They published lists of grievances that demanded relief. The most significant of these documents in 1525 was called the Twelve Articles. It seems to have appeared first in Upper Swabia and then to have been reprinted with many variations throughout many of the German lands. Peter Blickle has compared many local grievance lists with the Twelve Articles and finds that in many respects, especially with regard to taxes, the latter are milder, less radical.[17] They are pacific, explicitly renouncing force and violence. In a version published in early March the first article proclaimed obedience to both civil and ecclesiastical authority, but the document also called for obedience to the law on all sides.[18]

Here was the rub. The lords were breaking down law and custom—and in the Middle Ages custom had an authority that, if anything, was higher than statutes, since long-standing custom in civil as in religious affairs seemed blessed with divine authority. Blickle concludes that the largest complaints were directed against the effort of German lords to squeeze peasants into more restricted forms of serfdom, lessening peasant freedom, and taking a larger portion of what peasants produced. For the inconvenience of his death, the peasant owed his lord a death tax, which might be as high as a third of the serf's estate. These taxes increased throughout the fifteenth century, making it almost impossible for peasants to leave anything to their children. Yet it seems clear that population was increasing among the peasantry, making the peasants seek more land and causing them to feel all the more threatened with taxes and rents on lands they already possessed.[19] Throughout the Twelve Articles runs a plea against arbitrary conduct by both lords and clergy. The peasants wanted legal provision for a voice of their own in the affairs that touched them closely. Behind their pleas ran the powerful and dangerous conviction that all men are born free.

Amid grievances about labor, taxes, and law ran demands for religious reform. In one of the most common versions of the Twelve Articles, the first request was the right of congregations to choose their own pastors[20]—a request that, as we have seen, Luther had originally made part of his program for reformation. The peasants also wanted assurance that their tithes to the church would be used to support their pastors and not the luxury of prelates. Throughout the Twelve Articles the appeal is for Christian charity from the lords to peasants rather than for any truly revolutionary program that would have flattened all class distinctions. In some editions Luther was named as someone who might mediate between peasants and nobles. And why not? His teachings about Christian equality and Christian unity against oppression would have seemed exactly the sort of credo that embattled peasants could espouse with enthusiasm.

The variety of versions of the Twelve Articles and the even larger variety of other remonstrances from peasant communities throughout the German lands demonstrates a truism of mass movements, that they are likely to become many-headed, trying to pull the body in different directions. And— it should be emphasized—not all the discontented souls in Germany were peasants. Blickle has shown that a number of middle class citizens of various southern German cities expressed support for the Twelve Articles—but not enough to create a mass movement from German towns, although many towns welcomed the rebels. Albrecht of Mainz was so uncertain of the loyalty of his own city that he fled when the rebellion was at its height. Nevertheless, the center of gravity for the revolt lay on the land, and despite the pacific tone of the Twelve Articles, some peasants and others sympathetic to their aims were ready for violence. Müntzer thundered for months against the wolves of privilege among the nobility. "See what a stew of usury, theft, and robbery are our princes and lords. They turn all creatures into property—the fish in the water, the birds in the air, the produce of the earth. Everything shall belong to them. And then they preach to the poor the command, 'Thou shalt not steal.' They, however, take whatever they find. They scrape the hide off the peasants and the artisans."[21]

Müntzer was joined by other radical and eloquent preachers, including Balthasar Hubmaier (1480–1528), once a student and follower of Johann Eck. Hubmaier was for a while chaplain of the cathedral of Regensburg and in 1519 zealously took part in expelling the Jews from that city and tearing down their synagogue.[22] He was one of many in religious history who have put a fundamentally nasty disposition to work for God. He swept into the Reformation through the influence of Zwingli. In 1524 he preached the evangelical gospel in the town of Waldshut, where he sided with rebellious peasants and seems to have helped them shape some of their demands. The ideas of Müntzer and Karlstadt converted him to a further radicalism, and he passed on to Anabaptism—a natural evolution for those who believed in the civic and spiritual equality of all Christians. He apparently became a fervent preacher of rebellion, and afterward regretted his participation in it. He finally fell into the hands of the Hapsburgs and was burned at the stake in Vienna in 1528. His wife was drowned in the Danube.

Miners in some parts of Germany resorted to sporadic violence early in 1525—a continuation of desultory outbreaks that had flared up and died away since the summer of 1524. Mercenary infantry clashed briefly with peasants in December 1524 near the hamlet of Donaueschingen, at the source of the Danube in southwestern Germany. As the weather warmed in the spring of 1525 a number of monasteries in various parts of Germany were sacked, and, judging from woodcuts of the uprising, we may assume that the peasants treated themselves to the monastic wine cellars. The movement spread. Eck, Luther's old antagonist, noted with grim irony that the troubles had split the Lutheran movement. "The poor Lutherans support the peasants," he wrote, but "those who are not Lutherans and those Lutherans who are rich say that the peasants are in the wrong."[23] By mid-March reports circulated that peasants in various locales were destroying castles.[24] These rumors were exaggerated, but the feverish spirit of the times provided a greenhouse for atrocity tales. The peasants did destroy some cloisters. Some seemed to delight in burning books and destroying libraries.[25] Erasmus saw the peasants' rebellion as being as much against monks as against the nobility. To his friend Willibald Pirckheimer he wrote a long letter on August 28, 1525, lamenting the miserable state of Christendom. He thought it was a horror that the peasants had sacked monasteries, but he thought also that the monks had brought violence on themselves by their corrupt lives and their refusal to be regulated by any law. As Heiko Oberman has said, Erasmus abhorred violence, but he steadfastly maintained that the grievances of the peasants were justified.[26] In Mühlhausen in Thuringia, Müntzer raised a rainbow flag, symbolizing the covenant God had made with Noah after the Flood, and preached fire and blood against the godless.[27] By this time he seems to have gone quite mad with hatred. He seemed to be the incarnation of the most deeply rooted and perhaps even subconscious fears of the ruling classes.

Sometime in early April Luther saw a version of the Twelve Articles. Since the peasants mentioned him as one they trusted, he had to make some sort of response, or important people might suppose he supported them. In his region the peasants seemed quiet. In a letter to Spalatin written on April 16, Luther joked about rumors of his own impending marriage; apart from a line of gloomy rumination about the presence of Satan in a dispute about establishing a school, the letter betrays no anxiety.[28] But he acted promptly, and by early May his answer to the Twelve Articles was published and widely reprinted.

It is a fateful document, not only because Luther rejected the idea that his gospel applied to any worldly aspirations toward the equality of all Christians but because it represents a Lutheran position that hardened into the notion, preserved by the Lutheran tradition in Germany, that Christians must adapt themselves to the social and political conditions in which they find themselves. Historically speaking, the vast majority of Lutherans in Germany have never been on the side of organized political resistance to the powers that be, and without such organized resistance, backed by a willingness to use force against oppressive governments, criticism by individuals of this or that injustice remains mere carping, and those holding power can usually ignore it. Luther's doctrines never attracted a majority of the German people. But they fitted in nicely with the view expressed years ago by Hajo Holborn in his seminar at Yale on the Reformation, that the Germans did not have revolutions because the police would not let them.

Luther called his tractate *An Admonition to Peace on the Twelve Articles of the Peasantry in Swabia.*[29] The manuscript survives, and the editors of the Weimar edition note with some asperity that its punctuation conforms to no rules—perhaps an indication that Luther wrote in white-hot temper. The tone of the opening is surprisingly mild given Luther's penchant for fury when things did not go his way. He was obviously trying to be diplomatic. In their twelfth article the peasants expressed a desire to be instructed if their interpretations of scripture and fairness were incorrect. Luther was happy to give them the instruction they sought. The mildest of peasants could not have been pleased with his detailed response to their grievances.

Luther began at the heart of the matter. Without doubt, he said, some among the peasants expressed their fine Christian sentiments only for "paint and show," since "it is not possible in such a great host that all should be true Christians and have good intentions."[30] His abiding conviction that true Christians formed a tiny minority among those who professed faith would seemingly force him to conclude that even among his own disciples, most were damned. If true Christians were always an unknown few, no political order was possible that assumed all nominal Christians to be equal. The majority of professing Christians would always live by selfish principles, and any program with specific details that claimed to be Christian could be only be "color and shine," pretense and appearance.

This principle applied to the princes and other nobles just as it did to peasants, and Luther lashed out at them, first for obstructing the gospel, and then for living in "display and pride," which the poor people could no longer bear. "The sword is at your throats," he said. Yet despite this wrathful declaration, it is clear that Luther does not justify the peasants for their rebellion; they are here seen in much the same light in which the Old Testament prophet saw Assyria, as the scourge of God, a tool in God's hand, not to be praised for their own motives in violence and revolution. Like an Old Testament prophet, Luther thundered, "It is not the peasants, dear lords, who fight against you now and will fight against you in the future; it is God himself who sets himself against you to bring down on your own heads your fury." He urged kindness on the lords and commented on the fairness of some of the peasant demands, and he made a startling concession. The peasants should be allowed to choose their own pastors, although they should not pay these pastors from the tithes paid by the whole region. Their main desire, he said, was to hear the gospel preached. "No authority," he said, "should decree what anyone should teach or believe, whether it be the gospel or lies. It is enough that authority condemn riot and breaking the peace."[31] Luther had, of course, intervened in preventing Karlstadt from being chosen pastor—but under color of the trumped-up charge that Karlstadt threatened the peace.

When he turned to address the peasants directly, he seems to have been carried away by a zeal and fear that increased as he wrote, and his mild tone dissolved into vehement wrath. He offered the standard Christian teaching against rebellion: it was a mortal sin. He quoted Paul in Romans 12:19, "Vengeance is mine; I will repay says the Lord," one of the basic proof texts against both rebellion and private vengeance. He followed the teaching of Augustine that if government—even bad government—were destroyed, unutterable chaos would result. He urged Christian passivity from the gospel—going the second mile, turning the other cheek, suffering as Christ suffered on the cross, trusting God for vindication and reward. "Suffering, suffering, cross, cross is the Christian law, that and nothing else," he thundered.[32] Yes, the lords had done terrible things, but the Christian would wait for God and not take up the sword to defend himself. Natural law and God's law alike condemned rebellion.

After this long peroration, when he turned to a more detailed consideration of the Twelve Articles, it is as though he had changed his mind from his early praise. He was never one to revise his work for the sake of consistency, and if we may judge from his frequent boasting about his capacity for drink, he may have poured himself another flagon of beer in the midst of his composition. "The one who set down your articles," he said, "is no devout and sincere man."[33] Then one by one he took on the articles. Did the peasants want to choose their own pastors? Fine, if they could pay their pastors out of their own funds and did not expect the lords to pay. If the lord gave them a bad pastor, what could they do? Why, they could flee away to another region where they could find a pastor to their liking. Either Luther was here being disingenuous or else he was strangely unacquainted with those tightening laws that turned free peasants into serfs and bound them to the land.

What about the second article, requesting that the surplus of tithes after pastors were paid be distributed to the poor? Outright robbery, said Luther. The peasants had no right to say what should be done with tithes paid by the lords. Here was no consideration of the possibility that the lords paid their tithes from the grinding taxes they collected from the peasants. Now with the property of the lords threatened, the author of the Twelve Articles became in Luther's prose a "lying preacher and a false prophet" who smeared scripture on the margins of the articles.[34]

And then for the third article, protesting serfdom, only a page or so removed from his advice to peasants to flee a pastor they did not like, came Luther's response to the peasants' claim that Christian equality meant that no Christian should own the body of another. Slavery was recognized in the Bible, said Luther; slaves could be Christians, and yet their bodies were the property of their lords. Social and civic equality had nothing to do with Christian equality. So, we presume, if serfs took Luther's advice in response to the first article and ran away from a bad pastor to a good one, they would violate his counsel on the third article where he told them they were robbers if they took their bodies away from the lord who owned them. The other eight articles Luther treated in summary. They were worldly matters, he said, for lawyers rather than a preacher like himself. No one had warrant to claim any earthly right as a Christian, and those who did so were in danger of damnation.

In the end Luther called down a plague on both houses, nobles and peasants, and exhorted them to peaceful discussion and arbitration. Conflict would mean the destruction of both sides, Germany would become waste-land, and blood would flow until the life of the people had departed. Most lords were tyrants; most peasants were robbers. Again Luther's assumption was that Christians were a tiny few and that it did no good to view this conflict over earthly matters as a battle between right on one side and wrong on the other.

In this passionate jungle of rhetoric is a consistent position. The world cannot be Christian or even very good, and those who try to make it so are deceived. It runs according to its own rules, and the end of those rules is not salvation but order. There can be no such thing as Christian social reform because not enough true Christians exist in the world to make reform pos-sible. The pride and greed of the many corrupt any movement, no matter how lofty its announced aims. On a practical level, lords can help preserve order by being more generous to their peasants and by allowing free access to the gospel. But the world is such that social and political inequality are necessary, and no one has the right to turn society topsy-turvy in the name of Christ.

Luther asserted "No one may sit as judge in his own case." It is an odd statement, given the circumstances. The peasants were not in a court of law; they were appealing for justice and compassion by government, and the Twelve Articles represented an appeal to conscience in the same spirit that Luther's own appeals were made to the conscience of his readers, including rulers. The difference is that the peasants wanted social justice and appealed to rules on the basis of multitudes of biblical texts requiring mercy to the weak. Luther insisted on seeing the threat of violence in all peasant protest and in writing as if they had no legal right to make the protest at all. They were to submit and to wait for God to act.

What would Luther have thought of the American Revolution, the trade union movement, or the quest for civil rights by his namesake, the Reverend Martin Luther King Jr? Perhaps he would have attacked the abusers of privilege as he did the princes in his own time. But although it is unfair to transplant him into a historical context not his own, it is difficult to find anything in Luther favoring practical organization of the abused to gain a better earthly life for themselves. And since all our great movements toward equality under the law have been accompanied by violence or the threat of violence, it seems difficult indeed to take much inspiration for these causes from anything in Martin Luther. This world was not his home, and Christ existed not to give us a better life here but to offer hope against the certainty of death. In his mind arguments about timber, fishing, land rights, and all the rest were as nothing against the looming shadow of the tomb and the troubled hope of the life everlasting.

In mid-April, before publication of the *Admonition,* Luther went to Eisleben and preached in several churches in the region. He called for order and tranquillity and blasted fomenters of unrest. He privately exhorted rulers to strike the peasants hard, to kill them without mercy if they revolted. His sermons were greeted by sullen congregations and visible anger. One congregation rang bells while he preached so he could not be heard. He returned to Wittenberg convinced that the peasants now wished him personal harm, and he prepared again to be a martyr should their forces take the city. He was also fiercely angry.

As Luther's *Admonition* emerged from the press in Wittenberg, old Frederick the Wise died on the evening of May 5 after receiving the Eucharist in both kinds. He had been ailing for a long time, and now he expired in gloomy rumination on the disorder spreading through Germany. He had no kin around him when he died. He said to a servant, "Dear child, if I have ever injured you, I beg you in God's will to forgive me. We princes do to the poor people much that is not good."[35] Spalatin asked Luther for advice about the funeral. Luther counseled doing away with any forms that might recall the old Catholic observances such as singing during a vigil over the corpse lying in state.

Luther preached two funeral sermons for the elector, the first on May 10, the second at the burial the next day.[36] Of course he preached on death. It may be noteworthy that many of his other sermons during this turbulent spring dwelled on death—a sign perhaps of depression in the lurid light of the peasants' uprising and the revival of his own expectations of martyrdom. These are especially eloquent. Gone entirely was his early view that to mourn the dead betokened lack of faith. Abraham had mourned for his wife, Sarah, Joseph for his father, Jacob, Israel for Aaron and Moses. Paul the Apostle assumed that Christians grieved for their dead. The difference between pagans and Christians was that Christians had hope while the heathen did not. Luther praised the prince, lamented the turmoil in which Germany now found itself on account of the peasants, and recalled the peace that had marked most of Frederick's reign. Thanks to Frederick, Luther said, Germany had been blessed with the gospel, which since the time of the apostles had never shone forth so clearly as now.

The sermon of May 10 dwells on the resurrection of Christ and its promise to Christians, who in the sleep of death await the resurrection, when they shall receive bodies brighter than the sun. It was a certain hope, he said. Even so, it was hope and not yet reality, and he dwelled on Paul's comment to the Corinthians that unless Christ had been raised, both Christian preaching and faith were all in vain. Belief was haunted by the possibility of unbelief, and in his style and the style of the faith he represented, Luther held that we must cling to Christ. The assertion of trust in Christ was itself a kind of worship, a litany intended to comfort.

In the sermon on May 11, Luther returned to the theme of resurrection and dwelled on Paul's comments to the Thessalonians that at the sound of the last trumpet, the dead in Christ should immediately rise, immortal and incorruptible. He passed to ruminations by Christ reported in Luke 18. At the return of the Son of Man at the end of the world, would he find faith on the earth? The question gave Luther an opportunity to expound on the ills besetting Germany, raging evils so great that he wondered how society could stand under their weight. Now the evils came not from the pope alone but to people who had gone against the faith that had been delivered to them. At the last day, all these sins would be punished.

Luther's words about death pour out in a rush of passion and hope. What a mystery it is, how contrary to reason, he said, that when the trumpet sounds, the dead who have been carried away, reduced to dust, burned to ashes, drowned in water and eaten by the fish, and those devoured by wild animals on earth shall all in an instant over the whole world live again and be changed to immortal being! He tried hard in this sermon to draw together all the New Testament teachings about Christ's return and the resurrection of the dead. He showed his ability to note inconsistency in scripture and to resolve it by using the authority of his more favored books to correct the less favored.

What will happen to those who are alive at the moment of the Second Coming? It would seem to be a strange topic for a funeral sermon, but Luther felt it important enough to dwell on—perhaps a desire to smooth all parts of his theology of death and resurrection to himself. The book of Hebrews says that all men must die; Paul told the Corinthians that we shall not all sleep, but we shall be changed. Luther, believing in soul sleep at death, held here that in the moment of resurrection, when, as Peter predicted, the whole earth will burn in fire, the righteous then alive will die but be instantaneously transformed into immortality. But whereas the righteous will rise to meet Christ in the air, the ungodly will remain on earth for judgment, where they will hear the dreadful sentence, "Depart from me into everlasting fire."[37]

Luther did not dwell on this punishment, but his mention of it does stand out, given his lifelong reluctance to speak of hell in the traditional Christian mode. Only a few months later in his comments on Jonah would he seemingly retreat from teaching that hell was a place eternal fiery torment. Will the dead be conscious in the everlasting fire even in this utterance? It is hard to say. In his exposition of the Apostles' Creed that was part of his comments in 1520 on the Ten Commandments and the Lord's Prayer he had said he believed that both the righteous and the wicked would be raised in the same flesh that had died, been buried, decayed, and been scattered. "It will come together and live again." After the resurrection the righteous would go into the eternal life of the redeemed, and the sinners into "eternal death."[38]

Yet even here, Luther's preoccupation was not hell and the judgment of the damned but death in itself. His comments were addressed mainly to Christians mourning and tempted by doubt in the presence of death, and he offered a detailed and systematic exposition on the Christian hope of resurrection. That attitude is so pronounced that his almost ritual remarks about the damned sound like an afterthought, and he offers no exposition at all on their condition after judgment. Given his life story, it seems significant that he says unequivocally that all this stands against reason and that he calls the fear of death an *Anfechtung*, the word he used to describe his youthful torments of terror before God.[39]

Luther's journey to and from Eisleben and the hostility he encountered along the way had, along with further reports of peasant violence, excited him to fury. By that time these reports were widespread. A few castles were being plundered; some peasant groups were making demands that wealth be shared until all classes of society were equal. Luther believed the worst. At about the time Frederick died, when Luther had returned from his round of sermons, frustrated and angry, he penned the most vitriolic tractate of his vitriolic career, a brief and burning *Against the Robbing and Murdering Gangs of Peasants*.[40] The little work disgusted many of Luther's would-be admirers at the time, and it has been a perpetual embarrassment to those who in modern times have cherished him as hero and prophet. These words from it have been branded into his own historical reputation:

> They raise up rebellion, rob and plunder with criminal violence cloisters and castles that do not belong to them, and so they deserve punishment of death in body and soul two times over as we punish robbers and

murderers. For when we can establish that someone is a rebellious man, he becomes an outlaw before both God and emperor, and who ever can first kill that person does so legally and well. For every man becomes both judge and executioner of the rebel, just as when a fire breaks out, the first man who can put it out is the best man for the job. For rebellion is not merely murder; it is like a great fire that burns up and lays waste a land. Rebellion brings with it a land filled with murders, the pouring out of blood, and makes widows and orphans and destroys all, which is the worst misfortune imaginable. So then anyone who can should smash, strangle, and stab, secretly or openly, remembering that nothing can be more poisonous, harmful, or demonic than a rebellious man, just as when one must kill a mad dog, for if you do not strike him, he will strike you and the whole land with you.[41]

This furious little pamphlet, reprinted often in Luther's time, made his name a byword among the peasants and others who, though perhaps not sympathizing with rebellion, found his merciless demand for death offensive and shocking.

Even as his call to slaughter the peasants came from the press, the lords of Germany were putting the rebels to rout and massacre. On May 15 about 8,000 peasants met an army led by several German princes at Frankenhausen in Thuringia. One of the princes was young Philip of Hesse, in his twenties, acquainted with Luther since Worms. He would soon publicly convert to Luther's doctrines. Our sources for what happened that day are skimpy. By one account, Philip of Hesse, commanding the high ground, offered terms— life for the peasants in return for Müntzer. But a rainbow appeared around the sun, and since Müntzer's banner carried an image of the rainbow, God seemed to have given a sign. Müntzer convinced his troops that if they fought, they would prevail. The princely army had artillery and cavalry; the peasants had no cavalry and little artillery, but Müntzer is said to have told them he would catch the cannonballs in the sleeves of his cloak. He seems to have expected the battle to be the prophesied Armageddon, where Christ would return in a rage of glory in the midst of the conflict to slay all the enemies of God. The heavens remained shut. The concentrated artillery fire of the princes terrified the insurgents. The princes and their army butchered 5,000 peasants and captured Müntzer. Six men in the princely army were killed. Müntzer was tortured and, when he had confessed various sins, be-headed.[42] At the last he recanted his heresies and confessed his adhesion to the old church. Did he mean it? I think so. Having failed to make God respond to his bold act of faith against doubt, he had no place to go but to the ancient faith or else profess at the moment of his death that there was no God at all.

Frankenhausen was only one of many successive massacres of peasants by soldiers under princely direction throughout the German lands. Once years ago when I was on a walking trip near Colmar in Alsace, an old peasant pointed out a low hill which he called the *Blutberg*, the blood mountain, because, he said, the skulls of hundreds of peasants were heaped up there after they were killed by the princes. We cannot know how many perished. But there can be no doubt that whenever experienced troops encountered bands of peasants, the peasants were slaughtered like sheep.

Compared with these "battles," the relatively few examples of peasant violence pale to random outbreaks where few were killed or seriously injured. The peasants were far more likely to burn a cloister or a stronghold than they were to kill the people who lived there. Even Luther admitted as much after the peasants had been defeated.[43] Most scholars agree that the Twelve Articles in their various forms, all of them moderate, were far more representative of peasant opinion than flaming rhetoric from Müntzer and others. But rulers in all ages find it convenient to believe that the most radical elements represent a broad movement that must be crushed if society is to be preserved. Yet in their own way, the Twelve Articles threatened the nobility with a force greater than violence, for they called for negotiation between the nobles and the peasants who worked the land. Who could tell where such ideas might end?

The nobles did not require Luther to urge them to massacre; they were entirely capable of inspiring themselves to the bloody business that they pursued for several months. The Margrave Casimir of Brandenburg-Ansbach had introduced Luther's Reformation into his territories. The peasants looked on him as their friend. When the rebellion was suppressed, he went through his lands in what one scholar has called "a sadistic campaign of revenge." He put out the eyes of sixty citizens of one town, he declared ironically, because they had neglected "to look upon him" as their lord.[44] Some Catholic lords, on the other hand, used the rebellion as an excuse to kill any Lutherans they found in their territories.

Luther was not responsible for these atrocities. Yet to many people, the timing of his diatribe against the peasants made him seem a cause of the slaughter that followed. Many fellow evangelicals reproached him for his savage rhetoric. In mid-June he felt compelled to reply to these complaints with a longish German response, *An Epistle on the Hard Little Book against the Peasants*.[45] In it he retracted not a word, and he accused those who had reproached him of being rebels themselves in their hearts. He did condemn the massacre of both guilty and innocent together that was going on as he wrote this defense. As long as the rebellion continued he said he thought princes had the right to kill both the innocent and the guilty; once the princes were victorious, they should be merciful. In their quest for vengeance, they were now bloodhounds who did not care whom they killed. He said he had heard that a German nobleman had had the pregnant widow of Thomas Müntzer brought before him, gone down on one knee in a parody of pro-posal, said, "Dear lady, let me fuck you," and then raped her.[46] Luther raged against the tyranny of the nobles in books and pamphlets over the next year or so and blamed their merciless conduct for continued peasant unrest. Although he conceded that the peasants had destroyed property rather than people, he was fully in accord with the sentiment of his times that those who robbed others, especially under the threat of violence, were as worthy of death as any murderer. Not for him the compassion expressed by his contem-porary Thomas More through the character Hythlodaeus in *Utopia*: "It seems to me absolutely unjust to take away the life of a man because he has taken away somebody's money; In truth I think that all the wealth of the world cannot equal the price of human life."[47] Later in his table talk of 1532 Luther remarked that preachers were the greatest killers because they exhorted mag-istrates to do their duty. "In the rebellion, I struck all the peasants," he said. "All their blood is on my neck. But I know it from our Lord God that he commanded me to speak."[48]

He thought that some benefits had arisen from the rebellion and its suppressions. The peasants, Luther said, had learned how well off they had been before their revolt, and now they would be content with peace. Better one cow with peace, he said, than two with the continual menace of thieves and murderers all around. Some things in his defense of the "hard book" help us see why his Catholic foes at the time could ridicule the contradictions in his doctrines. The riotous peasants had coerced others into joining their bands, and many of these "others" were killed along with the guilty. Should those forced to participate not have been judged with more lenient measure? Luther scoffed at the idea. "Whoever heard of anyone forced to do good or evil? Who can force the will of a man?"[49] Those forced into the fighting ranks should have resisted with body and soul, and then they would have been guiltless.

Never at any time could Luther have sympathized with the peasants, and although his Catholic foes blamed him for the rebellion and condemned him for turning so savagely on the rebels, his relation to the entire episode is much more complex and probably finally unfathomable. His gospel was essentially otherworldly, aimed at salvation from death rather than improvements of life on earth. Since the Christian lived in this world until death, the gospel had some secular implications. Luther hated usury and the greed of those who coined all human values and lived in conspicuous display of wealth, and he wrote frequently against the excesses of the mercantile mentality. Usury to him was always theft. His doctrine of vocation was an offshoot of his belief in the priesthood of all believers. On one level it struck at the elevated status of monks and priests by sanctifying the common life. Luther's view was that people should work at the honorable tasks God had given them to do without feeling shame for their lowliness or pride for their high status. Carpenters, peasants, housewives, cobblers, hangmen, and all the rest had their jobs to do in preserving society, and they served God by doing these jobs happily and well. It was a way of telling people to stay put in their condition, not to use religion to better themselves through revolution or uncontrolled ambition. His conception of a social world would remain relatively static, and in it was no room for any episode like rebellion or, for that matter, any organization that workers might join to better themselves. Worldly ambition of that sort did not fit Luther's hope for a Christianity that looked beyond this world to resurrection from the dead.

He felt compassion for those abused by authority, and his rage was unfeigned against the cruelty of the nobles in crushing the peasants in blood long after the rebellion was over. Yet if the peasants misread Luther and used him for their own ends, so did the nobles. In his static view of earthly life, he was no threat to their place in the world. Catholics everywhere blamed him for the rebellion—although, as Luther pointed out, no uprisings had occurred in or around Wittenberg. In July 1525 several Catholic princes in northern Germany—including Duke George and Archbishop Albrecht of Mainz—banded together in a pledge to destroy Lutheranism. Philip of Hesse and John of Saxony joined forces in the League of Gotha to defend the evangelical doctrines. These religious alliances and their successors would bloody Germany for more than a century.

Other princes found advantages to going over to the Lutheran side, and for once they read Luther aright when they pondered his demand for obedience among the people. Luther's stress on obedience became a monotonous theme in his preaching ever afterward. It is far too simple to explain these conversions by any one influence. But at least it could be said that these transformations would not have happened had the princes not had proof that Luther supported their right to authority no matter how cruel their authority might be. He could rage against the sins of the nobles; they were content to ignore him since he had proven that his way was finally resignation rather than rebellion.

For their part, good evidence exists that the peasants took little further interest in his doctrines even in those regions where Lutheranism became the official religion. Gerald Strauss has amply shown that the ultimate result of the Lutheran reformation among the common people was to take away from them many of their common practices and to leave them in religious ignorance and indifference.[50] We have noted earlier Luther's bitter comments on the unwillingness of peasants to support pastors in the village churches. In that sense the Peasants' Rebellion proved to be a disaster for Luther's gospel. Lutheranism ceased to be a large popular movement and became an affair of princes. Luther's ugly language proved clearly enough to those who read his words that he was neither a saintly prophet able to lead Christians to a higher plane of spirituality nor a Moses able to save his people by appeals to God to do miracles.

His ravings about the wrath of God visited on the peasants for their uprising and the wrath of God to be visited on the nobles for their fury have something powerless and pathetic about them; they seem to signal a fiercely angry man screaming defiance with no one to listen or to heed and few beyond his own circle to care. Although Luther could speak with surpassing eloquence about the mystery of God and tell the peasants that the Christian life was "suffering, suffering, cross, cross," the most oppressed the most blessed, the mystery seemed to dissolve into a clear, hard light when he saw his enemies in pain and the agony of death. No mystery now! The defeat of the wicked was the consequence of the anger of the Almighty. His rage troubled his friends and stirred in his foes gleeful charges of hypocrisy. Luther would have taken all those consequences as part of the inscrutable will of God in a world ruled by Satan and the dark powers of the air. His theology by now could justify anything he felt he had to believe.

26

MARRIAGE

IN JUNE 1525, while peasants were still being hunted down and massacred, Luther took himself a wife.[1] She was Katherine von Bora (1499–1552), a nun who had fled a convent near a town called Grimma in the territories of Duke George and taken refuge with others in Wittenberg in April 1523. Luther himself had engineered the escape of the group, sending over a covered wagon to pick the women up and transport them to freedom and safety.[2] Like many another young woman of the time without dowry and marital prospects, she seems to have been thrust into the convent without any vocation of her own to be a nun. A nunnery was a convenient place to dump women of good family but with no dowry to make them attractive to men who saw marriage as a business proposition. She fled with eight others—among them the sister of Johannes von Staupitz—to Wittenberg for refuge, and Luther undertook to find them husbands or else to lodge them in families where they might have a normal life.

Katherine found a place in the household of the court painter, Lucas Cranach the Elder, whose bearded self-portrait shows a man of solid middle-class decorum. Someone has described the unclothed women in Cranach's paintings as naked rather than nude. Luther, who had little sense of painting or sculpture, did not so far as I can see ever comment on Cranach's work. Cranach was wealthy, respected, and inclined toward the new doctrines, and he was Luther's friend.

Luther strove without success to find Katherine a husband. She may not have been attractive enough; the few extant portraits of her are not encouraging on that score. She was apparently crotchety—not an advantage in a day when husbands expected wives to be submissive or at least to pretend to be so until the time of marriage. For a time she developed a friendly relation with the son of a well-to-do family in Nuremberg, a young man named Hieronymus Baumgärtner devoted to Luther's teachings. She and Baumgärtner apparently had serious talks about marriage. But because she had no dowry to bring to the altar, his parents talked him out of the match. Luther tried to win him back to her with a letter written on October 12, 1924. "By the way," he wrote, "if you want to hold on to Katy von Bora, get busy before she's taken by someone else who is at hand. She has not yet conquered her love for you. I would rejoice for this marriage on both sides."[3] Baumgärtner showed no interest. Luther sought to push his protégée on another, much older man, but Katherine objected vehemently. She said she'd be happy to marry Luther's friend Nicholas von Amsdorf or Luther himself. Amsdorf, a nephew of Luther's mentor Staupitz, was Luther's age, but he had the advantage of an aristocratic background, which may have elevated him in Katherine's opinion. But he was not interested; he remained a bachelor all his life. Luther was eligible and increasingly willing.

He was urged to marry by many of his friends, including George Spalatin. He had urged marriage on others; why should he not marry someone himself? He resisted. In a letter to Spalatin of November 30, 1524, he explained his reluctance to take a wife. It was not that he had no sexual desire; he was neither wood nor stone, he said. But he expected a heretic's death. Under those circumstances, he would not marry.[4] In April 1525 he joked about marriage again with Spalatin, at the same time urging his friend to get on with his own plans to take a wife. Spalatin had been hesitating for months. Said Luther, "Watch out that I, who have not thought of marriage at all, do not someday overtake you too-eager suitors—just as God usually does those things which are least expected."[5]

The least expected happened. When Luther broached the idea of marrying, friends were shocked, not that he should marry, but that he should choose Katherine. He went ahead, and on June 13, before a small company of friends, including Lucas Cranach and his wife, the couple took their vows of betrothal. These vows represented marriage in the eyes of God, and Luther and Katy had their wedding night afterward, followed by a public wedding service performed a couple of weeks later by Johann Bugenhagen, Luther's confessor.[6] Melanchthon was not invited to the ceremony of the vows, and he was hurt by the slight and angry at the marriage itself, finding it ill timed; but then Melanchthon had a propensity to feel neglected and unappreciated. He got over his annoyance.

To three friends Luther wrote on June 15 that he had married according to the wish of "my dear father."[7] To Spalatin he wrote next day, giving him the news, and saying he knew that he would be attacked for the marriage.[8] On June 21 he wrote to his friend Amsdorf and invited him to the feast that customarily confirmed the wedding to the public. This would be held on June 27, and he said his parents would be there. He described the wedding as "sudden." He wanted to do his duty to his father's hope for children to carry on the line. "I neither love nor lust for my wife," he said, "but I esteem her."[9]

His forecast that his enemies would reproach him was on the mark. Then and for centuries afterward Catholic antagonists had proof that all Luther had ever wanted was sex, and since he married a former nun, it seemed he had now lived out yet another of the bawdy stories told of nuns and monks lusting for one another. His most bitter foes crowed over the marriage in monotonous fury in print. Erasmus knew of it by October and wrote to friends ironically about it. He passed on the canard that Katherine had given birth to a child a few days after the wedding.[10] By March 13 he had learned that the rumor was false, although he understood (correctly) that Katherine was now pregnant. He ruminated on the "popular legend" that the Antichrist would be born to a monk and a nun—a tale probably circulating about Luther's coming child. If that prophecy were true, he said with bitter wit, "How many thousands of Antichrists had the world already known!"[11] He expressed the wistful hope that marriage might make Luther more gentle, but by this time he had seen Luther's vehement *On the Bondage of the Will,* and he had given up all hope that Luther might moderate his language.

Comments by Luther and others about Katherine suggest a no-nonsense quality in her character—which may have been the reason Luther came to adore her. She was what she was without affectation or regret. She was twenty-six years old when they married; he was in his forty-second year. She took care of the house, the garden, and the accounts. She cleaned up his living quarters. She brewed beer, and doubtless she went to the river with the family laundry to wash clothes in the company of other women of the town. She gave her husband her utter devotion, spiced with scolding commentary on his lack of concern for finances and his generosity to those close to him.

On Luther's side it was a remarkably happy union. Later on he remarked that the first year of marriage required adjustments. Sitting at the table you think, "I was alone, and now there's someone else here. In bed you wake up in the morning and see a couple of pigtails on the pillow." He recalled that when he was trying to concentrate on his work, Katy sat next to him prattling and asking him, "Herr Doctor, is the Hochmeister the Margrave's brother?"[12] The comment was a joke on Katy's ignorance. Markgrave Albrecht of Brandenburg had among his many titles "Hochmeister des Deutschordens in Preussen," Supreme Master of the German Order in Prussia.

(The "German Order" was the religious Teutonic Order that installed celibate, warrior monks in eastern Prussia to fend off the Slavs. The Albrecht in question came over to Luther's views, led his men in giving up celibacy, and made eastern Prussia one of the most Lutheran of the German lands.)

She was a consolation to him in his bouts with *tristitia,* a word meaning "sadness" that I think is here best translated by "depression," attacks that he said in 1533 were greater afflictions than all his enemies and his labors. These assaults of *tristitia* were the "weapons of death," he said. Others had them and asked his counsel. He advised them to declare, "I shall not die but live!" Sometimes, he said, when these attacks came on him, he embraced his wife naked in bed, and these depressions sent from the devil fled away.[13] He had these attacks often, he said; Satan filled him with such thoughts that he had to run away from them. But then he said the greatest victories over such thoughts he had in bed with his Katy.[14]

In June 1526 Katherine gave birth to a son. Luther named the child Hans, after his father. His next child, Elizabeth, was born December 10, 1527; she died within a few months. In May 1529, a girl, Magdalene, was born. She died in Luther's arms in 1542, and Luther sobbed at her funeral. Son Martin was born in 1531, son Paul in January 1533, and the last child, Margaret, in December 1534.[15] Luther's greatest biographer, Martin Brecht, tells us, "Luther certainly was never a passionate lover."[16] Perhaps the comment represents the biographer's fallacy of assuming that his subject never had an unpublished thought. This succession of births coming about as rapidly as one child may be born after another would suggest that Luther was passionate enough. When Hans Cranach, one of the painter's sons, died in Italy in October 1537, Luther spoke at length of love for children and of Adam and David, who had wept for the loss of sons. He himself had five children whom he loved dearly, he said, but when he saw how evil the world was and how little hope there was of improvement, he could wish them all dead.[17]

In a happier mood before the birth of his son Paul, Luther said, "I am rich. My God has given me a nun and three little children. I don't care that I have a lot of debts, for when my Katya counts them up, another child comes along."[18] Luther never had much money, even when the Elector John finally granted him a salary. It was barely enough, and later benefactions were never opulent. In 1540 Katherine noted that students taking down what Luther said at table sold his "table talk" and made money from it. Luther should not teach them for nothing, she said. Luther responded, "I've taught and preached for nothing for thirty years. Should I now begin in the decrepitude of age to sell something?"[19]

The Augustinian monastery where he lived as a monk now became the dwelling place of his family—often shared by relatives, friends, and student boarders. Katherine somehow had to manage the household. She often seems grasping and even petty in her quest for money, and we have many hints that Wittenbergers did not like her. She succeeded in adding considerably to the property Luther held, and she was evidently a tight manager of her servants as well as her husband. Luther was indifferent to such matters and showed always a personal generosity that is one of his finest traits. Katherine kept her eye on the bottom line.

Luther's views on marriage took into account bodily and spiritual needs. We have noted already his seemingly radical advice on the subject in the *Babylonian Captivity* and other works. He always stood against divorce, by which a man might thrust a wife defenseless into the world. This opposition to divorce helps explain his consent to the bigamy of Philip of Hesse in 1540. Philip became one of the great champions of Luther's cause. His portrait by Hans Krell in 1525 shows a fine-featured, almost pretty young man. His marriage in 1523 to a daughter of Duke George of Saxony produced seven children. By 1539 he was tired of his wife, and his many adulteries had given him syphilis, a disease rampant in the sixteenth century. He wanted to marry a seventeen-year-old girl. It seemed to him that he could commit bigamy since polygamy runs through the Old Testament and is not forbidden in the New. Luther and Melanchthon reluctantly agreed—so long as the second marriage was kept secret. It was not. The second wife naturally wanted recognition. The scandal broke, and Luther was ridiculed everywhere.[20] Yet his major aim was to protect Philip's first wife from being thrown to the wolves. If one takes the Bible as the norm of behavior it is hard to see how Luther can be condemned.

He hated adultery, and on many occasions expressed his stern belief that adulterers should be punished with death. When in 1525 a newly married Lutheran pastor was deserted by his wife, Luther said the man ought to be able to marry again. Marriage was in his mind the best defense against sins arising from natural sexual desire, and he regularly pilloried the Catholic Church for making virginity superior to the married state. His own happy marriage confirmed him in this view to the end of his days.

He did not grant equality to women in religious matters. When some of the radicals permitted women to preach, Luther found the idea ridiculous. A woman's place is in the home, he said. Women talk a lot, but they have no understanding, and when they attempt to speak about serious things, they speak foolishness.[21] The radicals with their belief in direct inspiration were naturally much more open to women preachers. Luther saw women as adjuncts to men, as Eve had been intended for Adam. Although he considered that inferior role to be their natural state, he was at least concerned that they be treated with fairness, compassion, and even with heartfelt love and that they not be cast out helpless into a hostile world when men had got through using them. In his own time and place, such a view represented progress.

27

THE ATTACK ON ERASMUS

L UTHER said in 1540 that Katherine had persuaded him to write against Erasmus, herself urged on by one of Luther's friends, John Camerarius. Luther claimed he had intended to remain silent.[1] It seems dubious that he had to be urged to reply to the man whom he probably hated as much as any enemy he encountered in his lifetime. Already in March 1525 he was preaching against *liberum arbitrium,* freedom of the will, as though he had Erasmus in mind.[2]

In that sermon he laid down his uncompromising position, taking the words of Christ in Luke 11:23, "For who is not with me is against me." There is no middle ground, Luther said. One is either with God or with the devil in both spirit and mind. Obviously Erasmus had touched him at the most tender part of his theology. At various times Luther likened Erasmus to Judas Iscariot; to Caiphas, the high priest who engineered Christ's crucifixion; and to Arius, who denied the Trinity.[3] Time and again he called Erasmus a Lucian and an "Epicurean"—synonyms in that age for "atheist."[4] "I vehemently and from the very heart hate Erasmus," he said.[5] Often as he sat at table, mention of the name Erasmus sent Luther into a paroxysm of loathing.

The intensity of this hatred is striking, even in Luther, for whom hatreds seemed as common as rocks in a quarry. I suspect that much of his fury came from a combination of disappointment and a sense of betrayal. Before Luther became notorious, Erasmus was in the field attacking many of the abuses that Luther later castigated himself. Why did he not then go all the way? Luther could only attribute malice and cowardice and ambition to him. Perhaps, too, Luther felt a little jealousy at the depth of Erasmus' learning and the renown he enjoyed all over Christian Europe. I surmise, too, that part of the hatred of Erasmus involved a kind of projection. Luther was sure that human reason if followed in theological matters would lead to atheism and licence. He saw Erasmus as the epitome of human reason. He therefore forced on Erasmus his own conceptions of where reason led if followed to the end.

The temperaments of the two men were radically different. "Erasmus is an eel," Luther said once. "No one can grasp him except Christ himself."[6] Others have made similar judgments in modern times. I recall a conversation with the great Canadian scholar of the Renaissance Arthur Barker, who in frustration threw his hands into the air and said that sometimes in this text or that he found the Latin style of Erasmus "pellucid" but the meaning of the passage completely ambiguous. Luther's ambiguities were few, and he shouted his certainties in vehement, hyperbolic repetitions in a deliberate effort to incite his foes. Luther was the preacher, the proclaimer, the trumpet of the word of God no matter what he might be writing or saying. Erasmus loved peace. He was the scholar and critic, more fitted for the study than for the crowd, and I am not aware that he ever preached a sermon or gave a speech or said a mass once he was out of the monastery.[7] His favorite trope was irony—the most difficult rhetorical device to interpret. In his *Colloquies* Erasmus presented dialogues in his pure Latin style, supposedly intended to teach good Latin to young people. Style requires some substance. In these exercises, his characters mocked superstitions attached to shrines, relics, prayers to the Virgin Mary, and veneration of the saints. We might suppose Luther would have relished these sallies against targets that he himself hit time and again. But in March 1524, only a few months before Erasmus published his *Discourse on Free Will* against Luther, he brought out his colloquy called *An Examination Concerning Faith*.[8]

This little dialogue between "Aulus" and "Barbatius" represents a discussion of the Apostles' Creed—but under the rubric that the creed is the only test of a true Christian. Here Erasmus offers a way to peace between the warring religious factions with their angry and sometimes hysterical definitions of doctrine. The Apostles' Creed says nothing about authority in the church, nothing about justification by faith, and nothing about the sacraments. It announces that God the Father Almighty is creator of heaven and earth and that "Jesus Christ his only Son our Lord" was conceived by the Holy Spirit, but it makes no effort to define the relations among these three as was done eventually in the very complicated Christian doctrine of the Trinity. It posits a relatively undogmatic Christianity centered on Christ as son of the creator God, incarnate among human beings, victor over death, judge of the earth, and champion of the resurrection of the dead. It says nothing about free will or predestination. Luther said that if he were dying, he would order his children not to read the *Colloquies* of Erasmus. "He speaks under the cover of other persons his own impieties against faith and the Church. Lucian is much better than Erasmus, who mocks everything under the pretense of piety."⁹

The attitude of Erasmus toward the doctrine of the Trinity seems ambiguous. Of course he never denied it. But it was not a topic that interested him. His theology was fixed on the image of Christ in the Gospels, the Christ who lived, loved, died, and through his death poured out a transforming mystery onto the world, available to those who would receive it. The greatest part of the mystery was what he called the "foolishness of God," the *stultitia dei,* by which in Christ God lowered himself to our human condition. Those who follow Christ find his spirit born within them, and so their lives are changed into a simplicity and a humility in keeping with his example. Christ was not for Erasmus merely a model for our behavior like some ancient hero whom we might emulate. By his death Christ rent the veil of the temple and made the knowledge of God available to us through the spirit released in us by contemplation of the mystery of scripture. The "philosophy of Christ" was to make that spirit active in our own souls as we find Christ revealed in holy writ. In scarcely any part of his enormous literary output is this ideal more clearly revealed than in his preface to his revised "Paraphrase" of the Gospel of Matthew, published in 1522.¹⁰

Absent from Erasmus is the thundering drama of sin and redemption that made Luther see human salvation resulting from divine victory in a cosmic struggle with death. In one of his *Church Postils,* also published in 1522, Luther commented on Luke 2:21.

Christ was placed under the law to deliver those who were under the law. For just as death fell on him and killed him and had neither right nor cause to kill him and because he willingly and without guilt gave himself over and let himself be killed, so is death become his debtor, and having done him wrong and sinned against him, has lost everything so that Christ has fair title to him. So is now this unlawful act so great that he has worked against him that death can neither buy himself out of it nor make up for it. So must death then forever be under Christ and in his power forever. And so is death by Christ overcome and throttled. Now has Christ done this not for himself but for us and has given us this same conquest of death in baptism so that all who believe in Christ become death's master, death their subject, their criminal whom they judge and condemn.¹¹

Here was Luther's dramatic vision of cosmic battle between Christ and death personified, a battle that the Christian shares and from which he emerges victorious over death and all the powers of darkness. Such violent imagery fits Erasmus neither in temperament nor in style.

For Erasmus God was spirit and so mysterious that it was only vain curiosity to attempt to work out his anatomy by trinitarian speculation. In Erasmian simplicity, moral rectitude went hand in hand with a quiet and humble spirit. Small wonder that many Unitarians in the sixteenth century took their lead from Erasmus, including Michael Servetus—burned at the stake in Calvin's Geneva in 1555 with the approval of Philipp Melanchthon back in Wittenberg. Small wonder, too, that Erasmus had enormous influence in Spain, where Jews and Muslims forced to convert to Catholicism wrestled to define a faith that would not renounce their heritages but also that would not bring them to the tortures of the Spanish Inquisition. Most Spanish scholars see an overwhelming influence of Erasmus on Miguel de Cervantes, author of *Don Quixote*.[12] And if we turn upside down the miraculous world of the mad knight errant and set in its place the view of his sidekick Sancho Panza, we have an orderly universe where wisdom is skepticism combined with empirical judgment.

Lucien Febvre has summed up as well as anybody has the essence of Erasmus's religion:

> There are few articles [of faith], in one place and the other. There are no theological subtleties. Christ is at the center of religious life—Christ and the Gospel, interpreted with sincerity. Between this God and man there are no useless intercessors: the Virgin and the saints, reduced to the ranks, play only a secondary and remote role. There is no pessimism. The stain of original sin is learnedly attenuated; confidence is proclaimed in the proper virtue and fundamental probity of human nature; finally, moral duty is placed in the forefront. The sacraments are reduced in number, dignity, and value; ceremonies and observances are judged to be inefficacious by themselves and subordinated to rectitude of conscience; finally the monastic life is judged mercilessly as to its theory and its practice. This is the basis of Erasmus's religion as described in the *Enchiridion, The Praise of Folly,* the *Adages,* and the *Colloquies.*[13]

Like Luther Erasmus had been a monk, and his hatred for monks and monasticism is if anything more single-minded than Luther's. The guardians of Erasmus put him in the monastery when he was an adolescent, after his parents died of the plague in 1484. Yet Erasmus did not leave the monastery as an overt rebel against the old church. He left as the secretary to a bishop and then because of his recognized brilliance allowed to attend the University of Paris to further his education. He made important friends. He became a tutor to rich young men. He learned Greek. Through an almost incredible energy, industry, and intellect, he brought the world of ancient Greek literature and both the Greek and Latin fathers of the church into his mind and heart to a degree that few scholars in the history of the West could match.

We have already noted that Luther depended on the edition of the Greek New Testament that Erasmus published first in 1516 and continued revising for as long as he lived. Luther used the 1519 edition for his first translation. Erasmus in turn carefully studied the biblical scholarship of Jerome, and quoted this great father of the church and translator of the Vulgate often in his own notes on the New Testament. He shared Jerome's love of philology and his sense that Christianity was not only divine revelation but the embodiment of the best of classical language and wisdom. Erasmus admired Jerome so much that after 1496 he gave himself the name Desiderius after one of Jerome's dearest friends.[14]

Luther detested Jerome and lambasted him with monotonous regularity in his table talk. Jerome knew nothing about faith; Jerome could be read for historical reasons, but for faith and doctrine in true religion he had scarcely a word.[15] Jerome ought not to be numbered among the fathers of the church because he was a heretic, Luther said. Jerome never spoke of Christ spontaneously; he spoke of fasts, food, virginity, and he did not mention charity or good works. Doubtless too Luther was annoyed by Jerome's steadfast belief in some freedom in the human will.[16] He said that Staupitz used to wonder whether Jerome had been saved, but Luther professed his own belief that even Jerome had been saved by faith in Christ. Still, he said, he did not know any writer who should be hated as much as Jerome.[17]

Although Luther depended heavily on the biblical scholarship of Erasmus, he hated Erasmus's attitude toward the Bible expressed in the annotations of the Greek New Testament. It was not a serious work, Luther said. Erasmus says, "So thinks Ambrose. So reads Augustine. Why? To disturb the reader and make him think that this doctrine is absolutely uncertain. He shows us Christians in all our differences, not excepting Paul or any devout person."[18]

Many of these judgments came later on, but they seem to be consolidations of differences in temperament that ran through their lives. In 1524 and 1525 they came to a head in the prolonged exchange over the freedom of the will. Erasmus had no desire to engage Luther in debate. Although, as we have seen, he at first tried to use his influence to get Luther a fair hearing, he detested Luther's vehemence and hyperbole. Yet he was favorably impressed by Luther's reading of Paul and his devotional studies of the Psalms. If only Luther had not turned so vehement and so radical, Erasmus could have seen in him a comrade.[19]

Luther's radicalism carried risks for Erasmus himself. Catholic hard-liners had accused Erasmus of preparing the way for Luther. Now from every quarter of Catholic Europe, defenders of the old church, including many friends of Erasmus, called on him to unsheathe his polemical sword and help slay the dragon and save his own reputation. Erasmus resisted the call, but by 1524 he could remain aloof no longer. Luther's ferocious attack on Henry VIII provoked Thomas More and Cuthbert Tunstall, bishop of London, to beg Erasmus to write against Luther. Still he held out until early in 1524, when he sat down and in five days (by his own account) turned out his little work, *A Discourse on Free Will*.[20] Erasmus usually dedicated his work to important people, hoping for their goodwill and patronage. He dedicated this little book to no one, seemingly flinging it off his fingers like mud so he could get on to more important and more congenial things.

The novelty of the work was its approach. Luther in attacking the sacraments and traditions of Roman Catholicism, including the papal office, caused most other Catholic defenders to rally around the authority of the church. Yet apart from the issue of the authority of the pope was the ultimate question raised by Luther's Reformation, the authority of tradition. In effect two powerful myths came head to head in Luther's Reformation. On the one hand was the Catholic myth that its ceremonies, its doctrines, its governance, its sacraments, its interpretations of scripture, and its other usages all ran back through the centuries to Christ, and that those elements that could not be found explicitly in scripture gained their authority by an oral tradition passed along from Christ through the apostles and their followers to become explicitly incorporated in the church. Catholics argued that Christ had promised to lead the church into all truth and to be with the church until the end of time. These promises were embedded in the papal bull *Exsurge Domine* in 1520. If the church taught or practiced error, Christ had broken his word. Therefore, everything the church did and taught with general consensus had to be true if practice or teaching had endured a long time; otherwise God would have acted to correct it.

On the other side was Luther's myth that all necessary doctrines were embraced in scripture and that scripture could be readily understood by the spiritually enlightened Christian. Within that myth lay another—that of the

godly Christian community, hidden from sight in the world but always eager
for the word of God and holding within itself the ultimate purposes of God
for creation. If one differed from Luther on scripture, one was simply ignorant or malicious and not a member of the true community of Christ. That
narrow view was uncannily similar to the position taken by Luther's Catholic
foes who held that those who differed with Catholic tradition could not
know the true faith. But the true church in the Catholic sense was a visible
institution. So the center of gravity in the Reformation rested on definitions
of the church and finding the locus of authority within the church.

Erasmus tried to outflank this frontal warfare and to discuss not the
church but human nature. He chose to attack Luther's teaching about predestination, a view put forth in uncompromising terms in Luther's *Assertion
of All the Articles,* written in December 1520 in response to *Exsurge Domine.*
The choice makes sense, given Erasmus's career. He had throughout his
scholarly life sought to turn Christians from grosser forms of material piety
that stressed ceremonies, literalism, and rules over the piety of the spirit.
How did one separate "tradition" from the various "traditions" within the
church? Pilgrimages, prayers to saints for benefits, ceremonies of all sorts,
days of fasting and days of festival, monasticism, and many other things that
Erasmus had attacked were doubtless of long duration in the church. Were
they valid expressions of God's will for his people? As opposition to Luther
continued, Catholic sanctification of traditions hallowed by time became
ever more rigid and uncompromising, embracing usages that to Erasmus
were pernicious, superstitious, and opposed to the spiritual devotion that for
him constituted the "philosophy of Christ." The ironic, witty scholar of the
classics and translator of Lucian who mocked the practice of going on pilgrimages and praying to the saints for material benefits and who found most
monks contemptible hypocrites could not choose a battleground that make
him seem to renege on his critique of materialist superstition in Christian
life. To debate human nature offered Erasmus opportunity to remain faithful
to his lifelong quest for spiritual reform and at the same time to go on record
against Luther. He seemed off the mark to more ardent defenders of the old
faith. Yet he had with unerring judgment chosen his ground well not just for
his own concerns but also because human nature and divine grace lay at the
heart of Luther's consciousness of his own calling—an issue that in secular
guise still arises in modern discussions of choice and responsibility, freedom
and fate.

For both men the issue was central, but it was also insoluble. How we read
the debate almost five centuries afterward depends on our own religious
suppositions, our faith or our lack of belief, and the last word on the matter

will never be said. The greatest modern scholar of the controversy, Harry J. McSorley, who happened to be a devout Catholic, sought to define in his study some grounds for ecumenism, and he titled his careful and scholarly book *Luther: Right or Wrong?*[21] McSorley assumed that there *was* a right and a wrong, that scripture provided a consistent message, and that Catholic orthodoxy through the centuries had come to the correct understanding of how to reconcile God's almighty and predestinating power with human responsibility. McSorley concluded that by this canon both Erasmus and Luther finally erred in their statement of the "truth," though he found Luther's book more profound. Yet with great patience and care he compiled divergent scholarly views to show, empirically at least, how thorny and incapable of final resolution the problem was.

Erasmus approached the debate with three major aims. He wanted peace in the church in the cool shade of a divine mystery better adored than argued about. He wanted to vindicate the righteousness of God as well as his conviction that human beings are responsible for their actions. Luther's assertion of grace and predestination made God, in the view of Erasmus, seem both unjust and unlovable. "Who will be able to bring himself to love God with all his heart when He created hell seething with eternal torments in order to punish his own misdeeds in his victims as though he took delight in human torments?"[22] Erasmus, like many another, missed Luther's almost complete silence on "eternal torments," but even so, he believed that Luther's doctrines would make God unjust, and the damned became victims of divine caprice.

And how could the always dangerous common people hear Luther's teaching without believing that they might as well live like the devil? If our fate is already sealed by God, what good is morality? "What evildoer will take pains to correct his own life?"[23] This utilitarian reason for religion seemed obvious to sixteenth-century thinkers. We've met it before. Thomas More required his Utopians to believe in God and a future state of rewards and punishments for the same reason. Of the atheist, More's narrator Hythlodaeus declares, "Who can doubt that he will strive either to evade by craft the public laws of his country or to break them by violence in order to serve his own private desires when he has nothing to fear but laws and no hope beyond the body."[24]

To support his view that free will must count for something if human beings are to be moral, Erasmus resorted to several authorities. The most important was scripture, and Erasmus had no difficulty in finding biblical statements and commands that implied free will. Indeed one can argue that obedience is what the Hebrew Bible is about almost from first to last and that people are rewarded or punished according to their heeding or rejecting divine commands. The Gospels of Matthew, Mark, and Luke portray Jesus as an ethical teacher and miracle worker and harbinger of the kingdom of God. A commonsense reading of these texts would seem to find everywhere an implication of responsibility on those whom Jesus addressed. Choose the right path, and you will join the redeemed in the great day of judgment when the kingdom comes; choose wrong and face eternal death. Exhortations to obedience imply that we can choose whether to obey.

Erasmus offered another authority—the fathers of the church and the tradition they established, although here he was less expansive and comprehensive. From the time of the apostles, he said, no writers except Manichaeus and John Wycliffe "have totally taken away the power of freedom of choice," though he claimed Lorenzo Valla almost did so.[25] Then he manfully attacked those parts of scripture, so dear to Luther, that seem to stand against free choice, interpreting them in his favor. In the end he returned to his major premise, that to strew the predestinarian opinions of Luther among the common folk would lead to moral turmoil.

Despite his efforts, Erasmus found himself wedged against a wall of tradition in Luther's favor and had little room to maneuver. He could not escape the iron logic that Luther was to impose upon him. Erasmus wanted a simple, Jesus-centered faith that involved both ethics and a gentle mysticism as well as human choice. Yet he had to deal with orthodoxy, born of the insistence of the early church after Jesus to draw out the implications from Christ and scripture and to make those implications consistent with one another. Scripture did not tell believers everything they wanted to know. So in the end both Luther and Erasmus had to go outside scripture to prove their points, and the arguments on both sides became necessarily speculative and unprovable.

The trouble lay in the history of the church itself. The great German church historian, Adolf von Harnack, believed that Jesus began by proclaiming an ethical religion of reform in the Jewish prophetic tradition but that this simple message was quickly transmogrified after the Crucifixion into a religion of salvation from death and mixed up with Greek philosophy so that the history of theology became a continual and creative effort to reconcile the two—the religion of Jesus and classical categories of reasoned thought, philosophical speculation, and a yearning for life after death. In Harnack's view, Jesus' teaching that he was the Jewish messiah gave substance to the new religion by claiming to illuminate the Hebrew Bible, the Old Testament, and at the same time cut the new faith away from Judaism. That process of affirmation and distinction became complete within two generations of believers.[26] These early Christians, scattered in communities around the eastern

Mediterranean, lived in expectation that the kingdom of God was imminent. Within 150 years, Harnack says, the detachment from Judaism was complete, and the church—now essentially a religious commonwealth within the Roman Empire—had to turn elsewhere for sustenance. Says Harnack, "The Christian Church and its doctrine were developed within the Roman world and Greek culture in opposition to the Jewish church."[27]

Without accepting Harnack in every detail, we can still posit his view that the New Testament as we have it teeters between the Hebrew Bible and Greek categories and that conceptions about Jesus and the meaning of his life and death are inconsistent and contradictory. Yet there can be no doubt that philosophical speculation on beliefs held by Christians led to dogmatic formulations that would have bewildered both the historical Jesus and his early followers who wrote the books of the New Testament. The doctrine of the Trinity is one of these. The doctrine of two natures in one person in Christ is another. The precise relation of the Holy Spirit to God the Father and Jesus is yet another. I believe that Erasmus understood early on that such beliefs were no part of New Testament faith. The shaping of the doctrine of the Trinity, with its attendant dogma on the relation of the divine and the human in Christ, betrays absolutist tendencies that early shaped Christian doctrines about both God and humankind. God in the Hebrew Bible, as it emerged from its editing process, is almighty. But what did "almighty" mean? Greek Christian thinkers invented speculations to explain this omnipotence, speculations that had no place in the Hebrew Bible. For example, God was stripped of his emotions since emotions seemed to demonstrate a lack of something, and God in his omnipotence could not lack anything. God cannot be truly angry because anger is emotion that betokens our lack of control over something. What then of God's love? Even Erasmus with his desire to avoid complications of doctrine drew back before the Hebrew Bible's propensity to make of God a somewhat petulant and changeable personality. As we have seen, Erasmus interpreted many Old Testament usages to mean that scripture speaks to us not literally but symbolically, to condescend to our weakness.[28] Doubtless the Old Testament writers would not have known what he was talking about.

Above all, God must be all-knowing because he is not bound by time. The Romans had a saying: *Tempus edax rerum,* time the devourer of things. Time not only devours things, but it also makes consciousness fleeting. We have noted earlier that Augustine made time an eternal present to God. Once started down this slippery path, Christians inevitably fell into deeper pits of speculation. If all time is present to God, predestination seems inevitable. If God knows everything that will happen, only what God knows can occur. Then what happens to human free will?

McSorley doggedly set out to prove that Augustine and the ecclesiastical tradition after him affirmed always both that God predestined all things and that human beings have free will and are responsible. He made a good case for this seemingly self-contradictory affirmation through the Middle Ages and the Council of Trent, which set out to reform the Catholic Church in the wake of Luther's onslaught.[29] Augustine in his later years, McSorley declared, affirmed that divine predestination and human free will coexist, and that Catholic orthodoxy reaffirmed this coexistence through the centuries. McSorley made this paradox a part of Christian faith: "'None of the so-called systems that have tried to throw light on this mystery have been able to penetrate it, to solve it, or to make it 'easy to see how.' This is true simply because we are confronted with a mystery rooted in the incomprehensibility and unsearchability of God himself.'" Elsewhere McSorley quoted with favor Heinrich Barth's opinion on the matter: "God's assistance is neither placed alongside of man's action nor before it in time. The entire action is the action of man. And the entire action of man is, on the other hand, the action of God."[30]

The persuasiveness of such paradoxical statements depends on the desire of a particular reader to believe them. For many, the puzzle arises, as it did for Erasmus: How can anyone not do what God knows he will do? Questions like these became one of the foundations of atheism in the Enlightenment. Better to believe that God does not exist than that he wills the evil of the world. Luther perceived the dilemma in Erasmus—and the problem itself— almost as clearly as anyone did later on in the eighteenth century. In his table talk he attributed to Erasmus a thought about the existence of God that in fact Erasmus never expressed, an idea phrased in terms that the Baron d'Holbach would use in the eighteenth century as the supreme argument for atheism: God might be too weak to stop the world from going as it does; so he is not omnipotent. Or else he does not wish to stop evil, in which case he is wicked because he takes pleasure in evil. Luther claims this to be the opinion of Erasmus and of Mutianus Rufus, one of the Italian teachers at Erfurt in Luther's time there who was frequently accused of atheism.[31] Too bad that we do not know the full context of this discussion, for it seems that Luther brought to the table something he had pondered himself and put it in the mouth of his enemy. The dilemma presented here may be resolved by saying there is no God—Holbach's solution in his *Système de la nature.* Or it can be resolved in Luther's way—which is to argue that God predestines everything but that God is just in spite of the apparent evil. We shall take up his argument presently. For the moment we need only suppose that in Luther's mind, the issue of predestination became a question of whether God exists. A god without all knowledge and all power—even to determine what we are and what we will be—cannot be God. At least he (or it) cannot be the almighty God Luther required to raise the dead.

With this speculative magnification of God's almighty power came a necessary corollary—a denigration of human possibilities. God was almighty; Christ was the second person of the Trinity and equal to God in every way. The second person of the Trinity died in agony on the cross for the sins of humankind. If God paid so great a price for our redemption, we can surely do nothing to contribute to our own salvation, and to say that we might contribute anything seems blasphemous, for such a declaration implies that God need not have done so much to redeem us.

Augustine saw all this in the light of his reading of classical philosophy, and despite the sternness of his approach, his teaching became orthodoxy in the church. We have noted the debate that Luther carried on with the disciples of William of Occam and Gabriel Biel. These "nominalist" thinkers believed—much like Erasmus—that human beings could of themselves without grace believe in God and desire him and therefore merit the grace that was God's response to their inclination. God allowed a kind of umbrella of freedom under which some choice was possible. Augustine and Catholic orthodoxy after him taught that the desire to have faith was God's gift, that no fallen sinful creature could desire such faith on his own, and that God gave that first grace to some and withheld it from others.

It is said with great confidence by historians of dogma—including McSorley—that Augustine's deductions from scripture followed naturally from the theology of Paul, especially in the book of Romans where Luther found it. Yet the fact remains that they were not spelled out in scripture, and it seems plausible that the writers of scripture did not draw out the implications that Augustine saw in the scriptural text. Certainly Jesus never ventured into the sort of speculation that doctrines of predestination require. Never in any of his recorded pronouncements in the four Gospels does he even use the Greek word χάρις, translated "grace" in English versions of the Bible—the word essential to Paul, to Augustine, and to Luther. It is true that in the somewhat suspect Fourth Gospel, called John, we are told that John the Baptist declared that the law had come by Moses "but grace and truth by the Lord Jesus Christ" (John 1:16). The idea that Jesus himself should have hammered home doctrines of predestination seems to the modern scholar more than faintly preposterous. Apart from the book of Romans, we find Paul writing and acting as if his auditors have some choice about whether to believe or reject his teaching. The book of Romans introduces predestination not as a matter of individual salvation, but as an explanation for the refusal of Jews to accept Jesus as the messiah. God hardened pharaoh's heart; he has hardened the hearts of the Jews. Yet all "Israel" shall be saved. It is an explanation of history rather than a description of salvation for the individual, and although we can infer that the latter must be a part of the former, Paul in fact does not tell us that. He tells us that no one can fulfill the law and please God, but he does not tell us that we cannot by ourselves desire to please God, and he does not tell us that by ourselves we can desire to have faith in Christ.[32]

Erasmus knew the Greek New Testament, its language, and its historic evolution far better than Luther ever did. He knew the difficulties and contradictions of the New Testament text, and he knew also the historic problem of reconciling the Old Testament with the New. He was also heavily influenced by the Neoplatonic tradition, which emphasized human freedom, a propensity many scholars think he took from Origen.[33] He interpreted Paul's epistles in the same spirit that he interpreted the Sermon on the Mount—long taken to be the heart of his theology. Paul's hard places dealing with predestination were to be interpreted by Christ, not Christ by Paul. Nothing in Erasmus matches the comment by one of Luther's students that Paul taught more clearly than Christ. Luther agreed. Christ taught moderately so that he might not offend the partisans of the old law. But Paul taught much more openly.[34]

A wise student of Erasmus, Friedhelm Krüger, has said that for him, "the demands of Jesus are certainly hard, but they are not impossible."[35] Yet to argue this point unambiguously was to run the risk of sounding like the ancient heretic Pelagius, who taught that salvation was a matter of the human will and did not require a special grace to the individual. Grace for Pelagius meant that God had created us, given us knowledge of himself, revealed that we face a future state of reward or punishment, and provided knowledge both of the devil our great tempter and of the general heavenly grace of God's relation with us. Part of grace was our God-given ability to do good; but it was up to us to will the good and to do it.[36] I suspect that Erasmus would have found himself in substantial agreement with Pelagius had the two been able to transcend time and the demands of orthodoxy to sit down over a good cask of wine to have a long talk about God, humankind, and morals. "At bottom," writes Bernhard Lohse, "there is no great difference between the theology of Pelagius and that of Jerome."[37] Erasmus could have seen that similarity in his great mentor for himself and was surely influenced by it, and it was reason enough for Luther to despise both Jerome and Erasmus.

Augustine interpreted Paul to be an absolute predestinarian, and he interpreted the rest of the Bible—including the Gospels—by Paul. McSorley's contention seems correct, that in time the church contented itself by asserting the necessity of God's grace even to incline the soul toward salvation, at the same time affirming in practical theology, the theology of preaching and the pulpit, the need for Christians to do something to help themselves obtain grace. The issue as it was phrased here has been worked out time and again in Christian circles. In the pulpit, preachers declare the need to do something to achieve salvation; in the theology of the systematic thinker in the library or the classroom, these same preachers may, on reflection, say that God is responsible for our wanting to do something good and in fact does the good in us.

Erasmus did his theology in the library, but he was deeply preoccupied with the kind of Christian reform that raised the level of moral life. In this debate, he was hamstrung by the requirements of orthodoxy to frame his arguments within the context of the deductions about God drawn out by hellenizing Christian thinkers through the centuries. McSorley laments the error of Erasmus in discussing salvation without mentioning grace.[38] Yet Jesus made the same mistake. I suspect that Erasmus knew exactly what he was doing, that to tangle the subject of grace with free will and salvation was to open speculative gates he was eager to keep shut. He was striving with all his rhetorical might to return to a New Testament condition where such speculative arguments had no place alongside the teachings of Jesus.

Erasmus aimed only to say that human beings could do *something*. If nothing else, they could accept or reject the gift that God offered. The eye can see nothing without light, he said. If God gives the light, we can choose to open our eyes or to keep them shut.[39] He made the traditional point that human beings should never boast of their righteousness, and they can never presume that they can earn salvation all by themselves. But to be humble also means, he thought, that we should not assume that scripture is perfectly clear and that any of us can understand it fully. Certainly we should not use scripture to indulge in predestinarian speculations that can lead to no improvement in piety. In a comment that Luther was to fall upon with stormy alacrity, Erasmus said that he disliked assertions—a direct attack on Luther's *Assertion of All the Articles* and on Luther's habitual tone of confidence about scripture. Erasmus would prefer to be a skeptic in matters where scripture is not clear. "For there are some secret places in the Holy Scriptures into which God has not wished us to penetrate more deeply, and if we try to do so, then the deeper we go, the darker and darker it becomes, by which means we are led to acknowledge the unsearchable majesty of the divine wisdom and the weakness of the human mind."[40]

Erasmus's carefully moderate exposition cloaked a radicalism quietly explicit in his successive editions of the Greek New Testament. With equal

care, he avoided the trap that engulfed the other polemical foes of Luther—
including Thomas More. This trap was to ground authority on the tradition
of the Catholic Church so that anything agreed on by the church for many
years was considered true because Christ had promised to leave his infallible
spirit with his disciples. This way of looking at things led More into the
absurd view that if pious Christians had venerated a supposed relic of a saint
for a long time, the adored object had to be genuine—a view that Erasmus
mocked in his *Colloquies,* though without mentioning More by name. (Since
More wrote in English, Erasmus very probably did not even know his English friend had gone so far.) Erasmus in exposing forgeries of works supposedly centuries old and in his rigorous historical critique of tradition in the
notes to his Greek New Testament could not have defended the authority of
tradition on the ground More and most others chose. If tradition verified a
relic of the church, why should tradition not also validate forgeries like the
Donation of Constantine and the works of the so-called Dionysius the
Areopagite? These, too, had been venerated for many centuries. Erasmus's
position was in fact far more extreme and problematic, and it is that radicalism that we see gathering here and there through the veil of the *Discourse on
Free Will.*

Luther would have none of it. He settled down to reply to Erasmus on
November 11, 1525—the day after his forty-second birthday, when men of
his time were considered on the brink of old age. He wrote in Latin, called
his work *De Servo Arbitrio,* "On the Slavery of the Will," and the first of
many editions appeared in Wittenberg in December. Luther's loyal associate
Justus Jonas quickly translated it into German. Seven Latin editions appeared
in 1526 alone.[41] Luther always believed that this work, along with his cate-
chisms for instruction in the faith, constituted his most enduring theological
labors. Others have praised it extravagantly, among them the great Luther
scholar Gordon Rupp.[42]

It is not a judgment I share. The work is insulting, vehement, monstrously
unfair, and utterly uncompromising—which is to say it shows Luther reacting in accordance with the character that temperament and experience had
stamped upon him by 1525. Of all his Catholic foes, only Erasmus sought to
approach Luther gently. Luther responded with a blast that echoes with the
cannonades and associated horrors of the coming religious wars—wars
fought over doctrines with no hope of rational solution, elaborate formulations dissolved finally in the religious skepticism that gave us the Enlightenment and either depersonalized God or chased him out of the infinite heavens in the interest of peace and goodwill among humankind.

McSorley has reviewed the difficulties of the book. In his urge to exalt the power and the mystery of God, Luther sounds like a fatalist, seeing God imposing his will on the world at creation and allowing humankind no freedom at all. God's omniscience means that he does not know anything about the future without causing it.[43] Luther was not the least averse to likening his doctrine of predestination to classical notions of fate. In Vergil's *Aeneid*, Luther said approvingly, "Fate counts for more than all the endeavors of men, and therefore it imposes a necessity on both things and men."[44] It is an interesting comment on several counts. Fate to the Greeks was impersonal, more powerful than the gods, as Luther acknowledges here, and inscrutable. For Luther God outside of Christ was hidden and unknowable. Did he imply here something similar to the world view of the Greeks, with their notions of fate tapped in to that dark side of God? I am not sure. Luther may have been uncertain himself, for he said:

> God must therefore be left to himself in his own majesty, for in this regard we have nothing to do with him, nor has he willed that we should have anything to do with him. But we have something to do with him insofar as he is clothed and set forth in his Word, through which he offers himself to us and which is the beauty and the glory with which the psalmist celebrates him as being clothed. In this regard we say, the good God does not deplore the death of his people which he works in them, but he deplores the death which he finds in his people and desires to remove from them. For it is this that God as he is preached is concerned with, namely, that sin and death should be taken away and we should be saved . . . But God hidden in his majesty neither deplores nor takes away death, but works life, death, and all in all. For there he has not bound himself by his word but has kept himself free over all things.[45]

In short, outside of the revelation of Christ in scripture, God to Luther is mystery and power that human reason cannot fathom—as God is for Erasmus. Luther insists on penetrating the mystery. He declares that it is blasphemy to deny that God is in charge of all that happens, and that it is also impossible to understand how God can be just and predestine some to everlasting life and others to everlasting death. But it is not for mortals to judge God. God is just whatever he does. "God is good even if he should send all men to perdition," Luther says.[46] We have no right to inquire why God does what he does. We can only adore him whatever he does. On these pillars rests everything else in Luther's reply to Erasmus.

"Everything else" includes Luther's conviction that scripture is clear in its fundamental message, which is the gospel. If one passage is unclear, we may interpret it by another that is lucid. This is Luther's principle of scripture interpreting itself—meaning that we use Paul to interpret all the rest of it. Against Erasmus's comment that many holy men have disagreed on scripture, Luther replies that the Holy Spirit must guide our reading of the sacred text; otherwise it is all without meaning. That argument is as unanswerable as the doctrine of predestination itself, since we have no means of proving it wrong—just as we have no way of proving it right. Yet in a whimsical way we might ponder the deeper ambiguity behind such a formula. Erasmus made a distinction between the letter and the spirit and found truth in the spiritual understanding of scripture revealed by the Christ of the Gospels. And Luther in beginning his lectures on the Psalms in 1513 declared, "In holy scripture it is best to discern the spirit from the letter; that is what makes a theologian."[47] Both men seemed agreed that to follow the letter of scripture did not lead to God. They disagreed on what the Spirit taught when it led. Erasmus judged the spirit that interpreted scripture according to the morality produced by this enlightened reading; Luther judged the reading of scripture on whether it assured triumph over death through Christ. It appears that both men worked backward from their deepest concerns about life and faith to declare that they had been led by God's spirit to a result that in fact was dictated to each by experience.

To Erasmus's plea for peace, Luther replied that tumult is a sign of the gospel. It is a familiar theme of his but still in this context a striking observation, given the smoke still rising from battlefields where peasants were being slaughtered in Germany. In Luther's flexible all-purpose theology, the tumult and fury of the times were part of the wrath of God, and in writing against the peasants he could deplore their rebellion as satanic and at the same time see the gospel as an agent that provoked at once satanic opposition and God's visible anger against Satan. Here, too, was Luther's growing conviction, already noted, that God had raised him up as a prophet. He was God's tool, and he mocked Erasmus for his desire for peace and for living an easy life. Luther believed that he himself had been the tortured instrument whereby God had revealed the gospel after a long night, and to him his suffering and hardship became the seal of his divine calling as evangelist. Adolf von Harnack said that he would concede to Catholic critics of Luther a self-estimation that might appear to be "an insane" pride.[48]

Throughout his treatise—four times longer than the work of Erasmus that it answers—Luther pounds home his conviction that the human will is utterly helpless on its own. His view is summed up in his famous utterance that the will is like an ass, that if ridden by God it goes one way and if by

Satan another.[49] It was a common simile, used for centuries by Christians intent on emphasizing the power of God.[50] It means that in the grip of predestination, the human will does not *feel* compelled to do what it does not want to do. Here Luther—and the Christian tradition he appropriates—differ from classical stories of fate where those caught up in the power of destiny bring fate on themselves by their very efforts to avoid it. In Luther's vision, the unredeemed will puts itself on the side of its own destruction, impelled to do so by God. From our vantage point, we feel free; from God's vantage point we are part of an eternal and universal design. The wicked man positively *wants* to go to the devil and feels resentful when something intervenes to keep him from doing so.

> When a man is without the Spirit of God he does not do evil against his will, as if he were taken by the scruff of the neck and forced to it, like a thief or robber carried off against his will to punishment, but he does it of his own accord and with a ready will. And this readiness or will to act he cannot by his own powers omit, restrain, or change, for he keeps on willing and being ready; and even if he is compelled by external force to do something different, yet the will within him remains averse, and he is resentful at whatever compels or resists it.[51]

The backside of this teaching is that the soul longing for God may be comforted by the anguish that this longing includes, since a yearning for God presumes that God's grace is already working on the soul. This view lies at the heart of Luther's later letters of consolation to those in dark despair lest they be predestined to damnation.

McSorley notes Luther's emphasis here on God's sovereignty. Human beings have no freedom; the reason they have no freedom is that they are creatures. McSorley says that the older emphasis in the Christian tradition was that human beings lost their freedom because they sinned. He is disturbed at what he finds in this turn of Luther's thought. He finds it fatalistic and arbitrary, cut off from the older Christian tradition that human will lost its freedom because of sin. In Luther's vision, God seems to will the fall of humankind into sinfulness. McSorley concludes that Luther did not intend to espouse the fatalism that his hyperbolic assertions imply, that he was carried away by his own flow of language.[52]

I am not sure that once we have dipped into these speculations about predestination, we can find any way out of fatalism. Thomas More required his Utopians to believe in God's providence so that, as the 1551 English translation of Ralph Robynson nicely puts it, the world is not made to run "at all adventures."[53] This view of providence would imply that somehow God is in charge of directing the world to his own ends, but that is as much as we can say. Erasmus seemed unwilling to go any further than that.

Throughout *De Servo Arbitrio,* Luther held that human beings have freedom in their own kingdom, "in things inferior to themselves." That is, on earth, in matters connected to the daily life, to nature, and to the political order, human beings have free will. "We know there are things free choice does by nature, such as eating, drinking, begetting, ruling," said Luther.[54] McSorley uses this concept of freedom to suggest that Luther is not really a fatalist. But even he concedes that Luther's language is extreme and that even when we have sorted it out and done our best to remove the contradictions caused by this hyperbolic outburst, many implications of his doctrine are hostile to Catholic faith and disturbing to contemplate. In McSorley's account, Luther's most "Catholic" and biblical view is that human beings are indeed enslaved to sin.[55]

The major issue is not whether Luther's account can be reconciled to Catholic theology or indeed whether it even makes sense. As Luther himself said again and again, very little Christian theology makes sense if we examine it by reason, and few devotees of religion anywhere care as much for theology as they do for worship, where habit and desire combine to create contemplation and closeness to the infinite. When we try to sort out our religious beliefs, practices, and feelings, contradictions abound. Most religious people find the doctrine of predestination reprehensible or at least uncomfortable, and in attending hundreds of religious services—including many Lutheran sermons—I have never heard a sermon on the subject. Yet one of the most common comforts for religious people in calamity is to believe that somehow God is there, with them in their misery, offering purpose for what seems like disaster—and that is a form of predestination. Consolation has always been one of the functions of the doctrine. Jaroslav Pelikan has shown that the Cappadocian fathers—and Macrina, the sister of Basil and Gregory of Nyssa, and no mean theologian herself—pondered natural calamities such as drought, torrential rain, and sudden death and asked whether there might be "some disordered and irregular motion or some unguided current, some unreason of the universe" operating in such events. Their response was to affirm ultimate harmony where everything, including death, had a purpose.[56] Everything from the weather to the darkest moments of life was part of God's plan.

These more practical, consolatory uses of the doctrine seem essential to our understanding of Luther. His was a religion proclaiming resurrection as triumph over death. From the beginning of his theological development, he sought a God powerful enough to conquer not only the grave but also the human doubts and fears concerning death. God had to be more powerful than the human will because all the will the Christian could muster was insufficient to grant serenity before death. If I am correct in my view of what justification by faith meant to Luther, he required a God who could accept his unquiet mind and his inability to muster within himself certainty to purge him of terror before death. That God had to be able to raise him from the dead despite Luther's own doubts that such a resurrection was possible. No lesser God would do. Wilhelm Dantine has noted the "vibrating undertone of terror" that runs through *De Servo Arbitrio* with respect to Luther's doctrine of the hidden God.[57] It is a good term, for in Luther's mind if God did not rule all the world, including the wills of human beings, God was not God; but if he does rule, we are unable to understand how he can be just. There is also something in Luther reminiscent of ancient Greek myths about presumption. Those like Cassandra who attempt to trifle with the gods or deny them all power are made to discover to their harm how mighty in wrath and judgment the gods can be. Luther seems to feel that he *must* attribute absolute power to God or else face the consequence of blasphemy.

Yet how is it possible that God allows us freedom in the lower things? Luther constantly said that predestination applied only to salvation, not to daily life. As Gordon Rupp says, in speaking of the bondage of the will, Luther was "not concerned with whether we are free when we choose marmalade instead of jam for breakfast, with why we walk down a road instead of up another, with why we choose our wives, or run our businesses. These are great and important areas of human life in which he concedes human freedom."[58] Said Luther:

Free choice is allowed to man only with respect to what is beneath him and not what is above him. That is to say, a man should know that with regard to his faculties and possessions he has the right to use, to do, or to leave undone, according to his own free choice, though even this is controlled by the free choice of God alone, who acts in whatever way he pleases. On the other hand in relation to God, or in matters pertaining to salvation or damnation, a man has no free choice, but is a captive, subject, and slave either of the will of God or the will of Satan.[59]

This is fascinating language. It gives and takes away at the same time. It may offer some explanation of why incomprehensible injustices happen in the world; they may operate within this sphere of freedom so that the murderer has liberty to kill the innocent, and the poorly built dam can break and the innocent victims asleep in their houses in the valley below may be drowned because God allows liberty under the umbrella of choice in mundane affairs. Since salvation and resurrection are assured to the elect, their death at the hands of random murderers or floods or genocide is not of essential final importance. To use Rupp's playful image, we may assume that we have free choice in spreading jam or marmalade on our toast in the morning. But then perhaps we have sinned in some outrageous way, such as requiring Lutherans to surrender their Bibles to be burned, and it may be that the jam has acquired botulism, and we die from it and from the wrath of God manifest in the infected sweetness that we have chosen freely. This consequence would seem to be an example of that which we choose ourselves but still "controlled by the free choice of God alone, who acts in whatever way he pleases." We may also choose freely whether to be a lawyer or a monk, since our vocations seem to be part of the freedom Luther grants to things below. Yet if we become a monk who rebels against monasticism and becomes a great prophet of God, our free choice in the beginning might seem to be part of God's providence.

Problems abound. If one takes God as both personality and absolute foreknowledge, how can we declare that our choice to eat marmalade or jam in the morning is not known to him and thus predestined along with our salvation even if our choice on any given morning does not led to great consequences? After all, Jesus tells us that God's eye is on the sparrow. Is anything in God's creation so trivial that it is not his concern, or is it possible that God's eyes are limited only to the same matters that engage human attention on a cosmic scale—redemption and damnation? John Wycliffe, as both Luther and Erasmus noted, followed the trail of the absolute power of God into this corner; and Ulrich Zwingli of Zurich was almost equally a determinist. This kind of argument sounds suspiciously like the conundrums propounded by advocates of the absolute power of God who asked whether God could have been incarnate in a stone. The nominalist use of the absolute power of God was to declare that he could give to human beings such freedom as he chose, the freedom to do the best that they could. It was a solution later adopted by John Milton in *Paradise Lost* in his effort to explain the fall of humankind. These puzzles make us see quickly how impossible they are to resolve. Since at least the time of Ludwig Wittgenstein, we have recognized—some of us with a sense of relief—that any argument about God becomes a statement of our conceptions of God, which ultimately admit neither verification nor falsification.

Luther's conception of God is at stake here. He sees the cosmos as a battleground between God and Satan. Satan dwells in the air around us, and his weapon is death. The word "death" is sown through this long treatise like dragon's teeth. God's weapon is life, extended through Christ to those poisoned by death who cannot help themselves by anything they do, and for some reason known but to himself, God has provided life to some and left others—the majority—to death, the grave, and the devil. We have not the slightest power on our own to resist. The dualism of this treatise, the opposition of God to Satan and death, is so strong that monotheism itself seems eroded by Luther's rhetoric except that Satan's defeat is part of the predestined order of things.

At the end Luther collapses his argument into a distinction between the God of grace and the God of glory. The God of grace gives us Christ; the God of glory acts mysteriously, and the wisdom and righteousness of his action will be revealed only in the latter day. God seems to be unjust only in predestination:

> For if his righteousness were such that it could be judged to be righteous by human standards, it would clearly not be divine and would in no way differ from human righteousness. But since he is the one true God, and is wholly incomprehensible and inaccessible to human reason, it is proper and indeed necessary that his righteousness also should be incomprehensible, as Paul also says where he exclaims: "Oh the depths of the riches of the wisdom and the knowledge of God! How incomprehensible are his judgments and how unsearchable his ways!" But they would not be incomprehensible if we were able in every instance to grasp how they are righteous. What is man, compared to God? How much is there within our power compared with his power? What is our strength in comparison with his resources? What is our knowledge compared with his wisdom? What is our substance over against his substance? In a word, what is our all compared with his?[60]

Were we handling this argument in a university seminar today, with Luther and Erasmus glowering at each other across a book-lined room as students eagerly seek to trump the wisdom of the aged and the ages, we might expect a sophomore to lift his hand and say, "What's all the fuss about? Both of you agree that God is inscrutable. Why not admit as Erasmus does that the teaching of predestination is part of the inscrutability? Why make it an issue at all?" Others in the seminar, including the professor, might nod with cautious impatience at the two disputants, willing to agree with the sophomore that in the end both Luther and Erasmus had solid agreement on the inscrutability of God in himself and in the revelation that Christ alone can bring to a world yearning to believe. One might suppose that the Catholic priest, the Unitarian minister, and the Lutheran pastor serving congregations in their prosperous suburbs today would all agree that arguments over predestination bring out the worst in the disputants and have little value in the religious life. Erasmus, feeling himself vindicated, would nod vigorously at the sullen Luther. Luther would reply that everything in his theology arises from his faith in God's absolute sovereignty and that without it, he could not affirm justification, redemption, or the resurrection of the dead. If we do not affirm God's almighty power in predestination, we may as well renounce religion altogether and yield ourselves unto death. The seminar might well look at him and shrug, denying death in the characteristic modern way by changing the subject.

Our age lives with religious doubt, and most of us practice denial of death until reality in the form of terminal disease or death itself confronts us. The most common remark that I hear when someone has died suddenly of heart failure or stroke is "What a good way to go," for with sudden death we may escape any confrontation at all with the corroding reality of death as it can infect our minds. Luther lived in another kind of age. One might even call it an age of split religious personality, in which belief and unbelief, desire and fear, clattered against each other. In 1942 when Lucien Febvre completed *The Problem of Unbelief in the Sixteenth Century* while a German occupation was imposed on most of France, he could pose the issue in a hypothetical unbeliever: "What primarily concerns us is the attitude of a man who, born a Christian and totally involved in Christianity, could extricate his mind and shake off the common yoke—the yoke of a religion unfalteringly and unreservedly professed by nearly every one of his contemporaries."[61] This quotation is taken from his final chapter, titled, "A Century That Wanted to Believe." Febvre assumed in grandly confident and serene language that such unbelief was well-nigh impossible. To read unbelief back into the sixteenth century was anachronism, and to Febvre, who was one of the founders of the *Annales* school of historians, anachronism was the historian's worst sin.

Fair enough. But the *Annales* school, with its emphasis on economics, geography, and *mentalité*—with the last the product of the former two—runs the risk of compartmentalizing human existence so rigidly that human beings from one age to the next seem to be almost separate species. As I have demonstrated, Luther claimed to find unbelief everywhere, and to me at least it seems simplistic to argue (as some have) that unbelief was an accusation hurled against enemies, as Luther hurled it against Erasmus, but that no one confessed to being an unbeliever. Surely the fear that unbelief was an option runs through all Luther's great theological works, and it lies at the heart of this titanic assault on Erasmus.

Luther admits freely that in the "judgment of human reason" a belief in divine predestination means that "you are bound to say either that there is no God or that God is unjust." He knew the classical tradition well enough to proclaim that "here even the greatest minds have stumbled and fallen, denying the existence of God and imagining that all things are moved at random by blind Chance or Fortune. So, for example, did the Epicureans and Pliny; while Aristotle, in order to preserve the Supreme Being of his from unhappiness, never lets him look at anything but himself, because he thinks it would be most unpleasant for him to see so much suffering and so many injustices."[62]

Luther admitted his doubts, and he could be remarkably candid. One evening in October 1532, Justus Jonas remarked on the brave words Paul had spoken regarding his own death. Luther said, "I don't think he could have believed as firmly as he spoke on that subject. I cannot myself as firmly believe as I speak and write about it." He then passed to musing about the groaning and sighing of the devout in their struggle for faith. Such things, he said, raise a cry "that all the angels must hear in heaven."[63]

We should admit the possibility that men in the sixteenth century were most angry when they were most afraid. Luther's treatise on the bondage of the will burns with rage. I think he meant what he said when he considered predestination necessary for belief in the Christian God, in the resurrection of Christ, and in the resurrection of the dead. If God is not like this, his treatise thunders, God is not God. So the God of grace reveals himself in Christ and predestines some to be redeemed; the God of glory will, in the life to come, reveal to us how he can be at once partial and just. In the meantime we must believe—and wait for vindication. If we do not base our entire system of belief on this kind of God, we have nothing to expect but death. In his later table talk, Luther noted an advantage to our uncertainty in belief. "Preachers must be poor men," he said, "but they themselves must look to the next life. Therefore we must believe in the future life, but on the other hand, if we were to believe certainly in this treasury of the eternal life, we would become too proud. Therefore God hides this treasure of mercy with a coarse blanket that he lays over it, a blanket that is called faith. So all our lives we must turn this over in our minds."[64]

The comforts of the doctrines of sovereignty and predestination were immense and remain so to Christians who accept them. In his sermons and in his many letters to the afflicted preached and written after 1525, Luther emphasized consoling convictions set down in his treatise against Erasmus. To those who suffered *Anfechtungen,* assaults of unbelief of whatever sort, Luther regularly wrote that these assaults were the surest proof of God's blessing. Without such assaults, he said time and again, no one could know Christ.[65] This idea was a frequent theme of his sermons.[66]

Luther the pastor continued to preach with commonsense practicality as if members of his congregation had a choice about whether to believe, whether to do good, whether to bear the fruits of the Christian life that he had taught in his work *On the Freedom of a Christian.* Yet he could also sound very much as if bad human choices could damn the people who made them—as he did in the treatise *On Secular Authority* when he said that those who surrendered their Bibles voluntarily to Catholic authorities ran the risk of losing their salvation. This attitude was likely to surface when Luther met strong opposition anywhere to his basic beliefs, and it was especially vehement when he encountered disagreement on the evangelical side.

As he grew older, this motif became more pronounced in his sermons. His last years in Wittenberg were bitter. He was disappointed in the undisciplined lives of his congregation, and he raged at his audiences from the pulpit. Near the end of his life he threatened to leave the city altogether. Always Luther held two views of the moral law of God. No human being could live up to it, and therefore the victory of Christ on the cross and in the Resurrection was necessary. But the law was also sacred and demonstrated the canons of right and wrong that were to measure the Christian life. The Christian was moved by gratitude to God and sought to do good works not to win salvation but out of spontaneous love. Luther saw no evidence that his people in Wittenberg were so moved. In September 1545, only a few months before he died, Luther preached a long, rambling, and heartfelt sermon lambasting the Wittenbergers for adultery, greed, and the desires of the flesh. His message seems clear; those who continue in this "liberty of the flesh" will be damned.[67] Many are baptized and yet are manifestly avaricious. Were such to come to receive the Eucharist from him, he said, he would not give it to them if he knew their faults. Even if they were dying he would not administer the sacrament to them but would tell them to call on God. "If you die, I will give you to the crows. Let your sack of gold help you."[68]

This sermon and many others represent a clear demand that his auditors change their lives or face damnation. Luther could claim that preaching was the instrument by which God confirms his election of those in whom he imputes righteousness. If I am among the elect, the sermon will be the divinely ordained inspiration for me to act out the salvation God has given me. Still, to peruse Luther's sermons with their rhetoric of demand, promise, and threat, we seem to be reading the impassioned words of a man who thought his exhortations made a difference and who cried out to witness the difference so he could be assured that his life had not been in vain. Or it may be that he preached in such an impassioned way because he thundered the pure word of God to his people, and nothing happened.

"I can call spirits from the vasty deep," shouts Owen Glendower in *Henry IV, Part 1*—to which Hotspur scornfully replies, "Why, so can I, or so can any man. But will they come when you do call for them?" What demonstration of the unseen world finally did words—or the Word—have on Luther's world outside himself?

The break with Erasmus was now irreparable. Luther wrote him a letter, perhaps encouraged by Melanchthon. It has been lost, but Erasmus's reply, written in Basel on April 11, 1526, survives. It is a cold piece of work. Apparently Luther had tried to joke about their dispute. Erasmus would have none of it. He would not be pacified by childish jokes or softened by caresses after having received "so many wounds worse than fatal." Although Erasmus had regularly claimed to others that he had read no more than a few pages of Luther's works, he now wrote, "You have never written against anyone anything more rabid, and even, what is still more detestable, nothing more malicious." Erasmus was justifiably angry that Luther had called him an atheist, an Epicurean, a skeptic in matters relating to Christian faith. He had not attacked Luther personally, he said. Why had Luther not remained civil in their dispute? Whatever happened between the two of them, he said, was a private matter. "What torments me and all honest people is that with your character that is so arrogant, impudent, and rebellious, you plunge the whole world into fatal discord, that you expose good men and lovers of good letters to the fury of the Pharisees, provided to vile souls avid for new things arms for sedition, so that in a word you violently handle the cause of the gospel in such a way that you confuse everything, the sacred and the profane."[69]

Stung by Luther's book, Erasmus wrote a response, the *Hyperaspistes*, in two parts that appeared in 1526 and 1527. He had to be urged along by friends, especially by those in England, including Thomas More. In this "weighty consideration," as we might translate his title, Erasmus gave more room for grace, but he never got around to defining the church that he was supposedly defending. The quarrel with Luther plunged him into a pessimism from which he was never entirely to recover. Still he kept on his many scholarly labors, finding in the comforts of the study world enough to occupy his declining energy.

On March 30, 1527, he wrote a long and pessimistic letter to Thomas More. More had been urging him to write further against Luther. "I cannot be the leader of any human faction," he said. In Basel the evangelicals, under the leadership of Oecolampadius, were taking over. Oecolampadius (born Johannes Huszgen, 1482–1531) had been a close associate of Erasmus, helping him put in order the annotations of the Greek New Testament. He was one of the most learned men of his age, and by 1525 he adopted the position of Zwingli and Karlstadt on the Eucharist. In Louvain Noel Beda, one of Erasmus's most persistent (and thickheaded) enemies, was crying heresy against him. Erasmus felt danger on all sides. He remained unwilling to put all the blame on Luther. What had happened had been provoked by the "insolence of the monks and the stubbornness of the theologians."[70]

Luther settled down to other battles, and they were unending until his death. Yet in many respects, his conflict with Erasmus represents a watershed. He had broken irrevocably with the man who, before Luther came on the scene, had been the emblem of reform within the church. Increasingly the evangelical movement was fragmenting. His rhetoric in *De Servo Arbitrio* has a triumphant ring, belied by disappointments piling up around him. He seems to have delighted in the risks he had taken, the leaps he had made, the extremes he had adopted. He had also broken free of the humanism Erasmus represented, scholarship intended to reform morals by presenting good literature to the world. Luther's treatise represents a throwing of himself upon God, a declaration not unlike the legendary comment falsely attributed to him at the Diet of Worms, "Here I stand; I can do no other. God help me. Amen."

For those who admire Luther and his treatise, it stands as an unequivocal assertion of God's sovereignty, stirring as some declaration of war or a brave defiance that comes with a refusal to surrender to overwhelming forces. To us in the late twentieth century, who have lived through declarations of war, defiant refusals to surrender, and the willingness of zealots of all sorts both to be martyrs to their causes and to kill others in the name of their righteousness, Luther's uncompromising rhetoric reeks of sadness and futility and of bloodshed to come in rivers of anguish throughout Europe and the Americas.

28

EPILOGUE

THE Emperor Charles remained intent on enforcing the ruling of the Diet of Worms to make Luther and his followers recant or die. He had imbibed the convictions of his grandfather, Ferdinand of Aragon, that unity of the state required unity of religion. Yet he had other matters on his mind, one of the most important being Italy. Francis I of France contended with him for the peninsula, and successive popes played a pivotal role in their rivalry.

Pope Adrian VI died unlamented by the Romans in September 1523 after ruling only a year. He was a simple man, avoiding pomp and circumstance and elaborate dress. He did his best to make peace between Charles V and the French king so that Christendom might present a united front against the advancing Turks, and he failed. He expected the Turks to invade Italy soon, but he could not persuade others of the danger. The Turks seized Belgrade in 1521. Rhodes fell to the sultan on December 28, 1522, and still Christians continued to war against one another. Francis I suspected Adrian—not unjustly—of perfidy in siding with the emperor and threatened to come to Rome and subject him to the fate of Boniface VIII, who had been attacked by thugs in the pay of Philip the Fair in 1305, perhaps beaten, but in any case so shocked by the assault that he died.[1]

None of this helped Adrian's efforts to reform the church and to meet the crisis Luther had created in Germany. The college of cardinals was angrily split between factions supporting and opposing the Medici family, and few cardinals felt any urgency about reform. From his first consistory Adrian preached reform to the indifferent cardinals, castigating them for their love of luxury, telling them they should be an example to the world. He put force behind his words and compelled the cardinals to abandon their palaces. He ordered the clergy to stop carrying weapons, and when priests broke his rules, he put them in jail. When a clergyman favorite of the late Pope Leo X fled Rome to avoid prosecution for murder, Adrian commanded him to return or lose all his property. He compelled the cardinals to shave their beards—doubtless to prevent them from looking like dandies. All this happened within eight days of his first appearance before his cardinals, and a Venetian wrote that the new pope had left the whole city in fear and terror.[2]

Adrian was more nearly a saint than any other pope in several centuries. When plague struck Rome, he ordered the clergy to remain in the city to minister to the sick and the dying, and he set an example by staying himself. In the hot Roman autumn, the disease killed as many as a hundred a day. The cardinals slunk away, leaving the pope in a city bereft and almost deserted except for the sick, the dying, and the dead. In the winter months, when the plague faded, Adrian announced that he was reorganizing the curia to rid it of many of the offices created for his friends by Leo X. His announcement caused panic—and hatred.

Johann Eck showed up in Rome in March 1523 and published there a defense of purgatory against Luther. Eck was not stupid. He saw the sink of iniquity that Rome had become and urged reform as the best way to combat the Lutheran heresy. He was appalled by the greed of multitudes seeking benefices and other favors. Adrian's drive for a leaner bureaucracy made these grasping office seekers despise him. Eck was also now calling for reforms in the selling of indulgences and the elimination of some of the very abuses that Luther had protested in the Ninety-five Theses.[3] Yet for the moment inertia and squabbling and greed killed all efforts at reform in their tracks. Throughout his pontificate, Adrian lamented to intimates his unhappiness in Rome and wished himself back in Flanders, his home. He had never been so miserable as when he ruled as pope, he said. In August, after riding for the first time in full regalia through Rome under a blazing sun to celebrate a league of Italian powers, England, and the Holy Roman Emperor against the French, Adrian became ill. The same illness that afflicted him laid many cardinals low. They recovered; he died.

No later pope canonized him; no miracles have been wrought at his tomb. It would have been a supreme miracle had he been able to accomplish any of his reforming aims. His reign shows as sadly as anything can the depth of corruption in the church's hierarchy, the impossibility of genuine unity in pursing reform, and the extent to which politics ruled piety in the papal curia. Corruption had its own inertia, the weight of all those in the church profiting from the spoils of decadence. Luther's movement finally was more important for its theology than for its effects on ethics or morals. But only a morally strong and respected institutional church could have wielded the prestige and respect necessary to heal the divisions Luther had opened in Western Christendom. Not for more than twenty years after Adrian's death did the church begin to set its house in order.

The curia wanted no more reform for the moment; nor did the cardinals want further experiments with non-Italian popes. In a conclave of six weeks, they turned back to the house of Medici, naming a cousin of Leo X, Giulio de' Medici, to be pope. He was the bastard son of Giuliano de' Medici, brother of Lorenzo the Magnificent, and he was weak and vacillating though kindly and moral enough in his personal conduct. He took the name Clement VII, and he was one of the most unfortunate popes in history.

He aimed to keep both Francis and Charles from dominating Italy. To this end he made alliances with whoever of the two seemed weaker at the time, shifting back and forth until both Francis I and Charles V despised him. The pope first allied himself with Charles. But then Charles's army won a great battle at Pavia over the French in February 1525, and Francis I was taken prisoner and forced to give up his claims to Italy and to present two of his sons as hostages to the emperor before he was set free. Francis continued to make alliances and to plan wars against the emperor. The sons were cruelly treated. The older one never recovered his health and died before his father.

Clement VII shifted to an alliance with Francis, and the wars between the Hapsburgs and France resumed. In 1527 an imperial army, unpaid and out of control, attacked Rome itself, without orders from Charles, and subjected the city to the worst sack in its history. Looting and rapine went on for weeks, and atrocity stories spread throughout Europe. Thomas More believed Lutheran soldiers were responsible for outrages committed against the Romans, but the mercenary army seemed ecumenical in rapine and massacre. Spaniards and German mercenaries joined forces in looting, torture, and murder. Clement was shut up like a caged bird in the Castel San Angelo, Hadrian's tomb. After his ordeal, he was more cautious with the emperor. In 1530 Charles became the last Holy Roman Emperor to be crowned by a pope when Clement placed the imperial crown on his head in Bologna. One reason Clement consented to crown Charles was that the pope feared the emperor might call a reforming council if the pope refused the coronation.

Charles could not attend the Diet of Speyer in 1526 because other interests occupied his mind. Throughout the empire, evangelical and Catholic princes were conglomerating in opposing alliances. Catholics remained the majority. At the Diet that gathered in the summer, both sides drew back from conflict. The Turks were on the move up the Balkans, and on August 29,

1526, a Turkish army inflicted a crushing defeat on the Hungarians at Mo-haćs. Vienna stood in their way, and beyond Vienna lay the rest of Christian Europe. The Turks seemed invincible, and for both Catholics and evangelicals, the last days seemed at hand. It was no time for war in Germany. The Diet of Speyer postponed the settlement of religious questions in anticipation of a general council. In the meanwhile each prince and each free city would make its own decisions on religious matters. The princes thereby assumed powers akin to those of bishops. The settlement at Speyer in 1526 gave the evangelicals a chance to consolidate, and indeed the decisions made at Speyer foretold the religious future of the German lands.

At Augsburg in 1530 Catholics and Protestants in Germany under imperial oversight tried to resolve their differences. Philipp Melanchthon became the chief author of the Augsburg Confession as an expression of Lutheran beliefs in an effort to answer charges of heresy raised by Catholics. It was also an effort to compromise. The Confession strongly emphasized the divine institution of the secular order and so condemned insurrection and revolution. It did not mention justification by faith. Charles V and Catholic theologians rejected the Augsburg Confession. No serious chance for reuniting Western Christianity ever presented itself again.

It is a convenient place to leave Luther. He lived another twenty years, and it is a truism of scholarship that we need more work on the later Luther because we know best the dramatic story of his early life and his break with Rome. The darkly bound volumes of the *Weimarer Ausgabe,* standing in their solemn ranks in parts of university and clerical libraries frequented by few scholars, summon us to do our duty to the older man. But here I will beg off.

By 1526 the most creative part of his life was over, and his ceaseless battles with adversaries descended often into repetitive invective and vituperation that weary the soul. By his own account, his attacks of *tristitia* increased. Luther was successful in that he lived to die a natural death, and the movement he began continued, offering spiritual renewal to many through the intervening centuries. Yet in a myriad of ways his movement failed, and the failure has about it the inevitability of tragedy. In a strict accounting, uncongenial to the religious spirit, we might argue that his movement produced as much spiritual woe as it did consolation. Although he never acknowledged failure, its evidence is scattered through his later works, and he became certain that only the return of Christ would accomplish the aims of his gospel. He felt himself to be in the last days, and he saw portents of the end. This conviction sustained him.

The hope for general reform and the optimism of his great treatises after the debate with Johann Eck dissolved into internecine Christian conflict in which atrocities on each side balance each other in volume of blood. Luther not only hoped to win over the Catholic Church through the scriptural rulings of a general council; he hoped to destroy the papal Antichrist. With the terrible sack of Rome in May 1527, the papacy seemed on the brink of extinction. But pope and emperor patched up a peace. The persecution of evangelicals in Catholic lands went on, and multitudes did not come spontaneously to Luther's standard. Exuberant popular enthusiasm for his doctrines faded. In the wake of the Peasants' Rebellion, Lutheranism at the Diet of Speyer became a affair of pastors, princes, and city governments while the people in Lutheran territories passed into religious indifference.

Evangelical pastors zealously interpreted Luther's doctrines to sparse congregations. Lutheran princes and city councils made sure that pastors hewed to orthodoxy, especially the doctrine of obedience to authority. Ironically enough, Lutheran pastors over the next couple of centuries resorted more and more to preaching vehement sermons about hell to frighten their subjects back to obedience to the church. Evidence abounds that attendance at sermons dropped off. As Hans-Christoph Rublack has shown in a brilliant essay, the consequence was only increased anticlericalism, encapsulated in the popular saying "In every parson you will find a little pope." Rublack concludes that the cultural differences between pastors and people were too much to overcome. With the sacraments removed from their central place, the common people—especially the peasants—were left with only the sermon to "negotiate" their relations with their pastors. For their part the pastors labored in vain to make congregations take seriously the doctrinal content of sermons or to live the moral lives that the sermons commanded. Congregations wanted consolation and help at the great rites of passage in life—birth, marriage, suffering, sickness, death—and the pastors wanted moral evidence that their sermons were effective. The consequence, Rublack maintains after exhaustive study, is that both sides were frustrated and alienated from each other.[4] When the Enlightenment came, with its impersonal religiosity devoted to order and obedience, it found the way prepared by Lutheran churches. The ruling classes coldly professed their faith; the lower classes did not bother.

Such a division was already under way in Luther's life. He complained frequently and bitterly that congregations did not care enough about evangelical preachers to pay them a living wage. His emphasis on the priesthood of all believers and the importance of preaching led to a paradoxical result still with us. In a Catholic house of worship, the priest need not be present to bring into the sanctuary those who wish to worship and meditate. The Host reposes on the altar, the body of Christ, an object that may be venerated in silence by the pious refugee from the hurrying streets outside. Candles burn, sending into the holy gloom the wordless prayers of those who light their slender flames. Chapels with icons beckon the worshiper to quiet moments of reverence and meditation—all without the necessary presence of a clergy-man. But in the evangelical church, the major reason for entry is the sermon, and if the minister is not present to preach, there is little reason for anybody else to be there. The occasional fugitive from a noisy world may steal into an evangelical church for prayer and meditation, but whereas today many Catholic churches in the large cities of the Western world are open through the week, most evangelical church buildings are locked up from Sunday to Sunday. The Anglicans, who never became fully Protestant, are often excep-tions.

Attendance in evangelical churches depends considerably on whether the preacher can deliver an interesting and compelling discourse. A Catholic priest, administering the sacraments, need not be endowed with eloquence or even intelligence, and the sacraments at his hands will retain an emotional vitality for the participant because the power of the moment resides not in words conjured up by the priest for the occasion but in the familiarity of a sacred rite. Protestant ministers are called upon every week to hold the attention of a congregation by thinking of something new and different to say about very old and somewhat shopworn subjects.

In the final two decades of his life, Luther battled with the fissiparous tendencies of the evangelical movement. He continued to write and preach fiercely against the Anabaptists, though he had sympathy and respect for their bravery in the face of martyrdom. His most hated foes besides the papacy itself were the so-called sacramentarians, those who with Karlstadt and Zwingli interpreted the Eucharist as a symbolic memorial and rejected the real presence of Christ in the elements. Luther's rhetoric against them was fierce and extreme. They were blasphemers pure and simple, he thought—an opinion he never changed. When his Swiss foes Oecolampadius and Zwingli tried to answer him with mild language, Luther responded with unmitigated rage and railing.

Philip of Hesse arranged a conference between Zwingli and Luther at his castle in Marburg in 1529 to try to patch up an evangelical peace. Luther came with Melanchthon and Justus Jonas and some lesser men. Zwingli came with Oecolampadius and Martin Bucer. Bucer would later help install the Reformation in England under young Edward VI. Arguments went on for days. The contestants agreed on some points of doctrine and were persuaded to put their names on a collection of articles, but they could not reach concord on the chief point of contention—the nature of the presence of

Christ in the Mass. In later years Luther often recalled that in leaving Marburg Zwingli said, "Now God knows that I do not wish to be friends to anyone more than to those at Wittenberg."[5] Luther was always proud of himself for refusing to shake Zwingli's hand. Two years later Zwingli died in battle, armed and fighting as a soldier, in a war against the Catholic cantons of Switzerland. Luther frequently said that he died as a murderer, reaping the punishment of God for his errors.[6]

For the moment the most serious consequence of the division over the Eucharist was evangelical disunity before a growing Catholic military threat. The long-term consequences were perhaps more important—hatred, suspicion, and continued division among evangelicals.

Contemporaries—including both Catholics and sectarians—faulted Luther's doctrines for failing to create a lively sense of piety in congregations that heard Luther and others preach year after year. Martin Brecht has chronicled in gloomy detail continued troubles in Wittenberg.[7] Luther was continually furious with his congregations for their stinginess and their immorality. On November 8, 1528, he preached a sermon that culminated in an angry outburst:

What shall I do with you, people of Wittenberg! I shall not preach to you the kingdom of Christ, because you don't take it up. You are thieves, robbers, merciless. To you I must preach the law![8] You afflict the kingdom of Christ and ignore his preaching . . . You know that this week we will request an offering of money. I hear that no one will give anything to those who ask, but rather turn them ungratefully away. By the grace of God, you ingrates, who although you thirst so greedily for money, you do not give anything, you wound the ministers with evil words. Well, I hope you had a good year! I am frightened and do not know whether I will preach any more to you vulgar slobs, who cannot give four pennies a year out of a good heart. Know this, you Wittenbergers. You are altogether empty of good works, giving no salary to the ministers of the church to educate boys or to give shelter to the poor, always passing the buck to someone else . . . You have been freed from tyrants and papists. You ungrateful beasts are not worthy of this treasure of the gospel. If you don't do otherwise, repenting of your sins, I'm going to cease preaching to you, lest I cast pearls before swine or give holy things to dogs.[9]

This does not sound like a sermon addressed to the true Christians who were the audience assumed for Luther's treatise of 1520 *On the Freedom of a*

Christian. Sometimes he did go on strike for a while and refused to enter the pulpit—much to the consternation of his friends and his prince, who doubtless cherished Luther's continual preaching on obedience.

Beginning in 1526 "visitors" were sent out to look into the affairs of the parish churches around Saxony to see how both pastors and ministers were living, understanding, and teaching the gospel. By 1528 the findings were discouraging. Ignorance and religious indifference were everywhere. Around December Luther wrote to Spalatin a summary note about the situation. Pastors were trying to survive by farming less than two acres of land. The condition of the church was as miserable. The peasants were not learning anything, nor did they know anything. They did not pray, they did not do anything except abuse Christian liberty, neither confessing nor taking the Eucharist, as if in religion they had all become children. He blamed these faults on the neglect of the Catholic bishops before the gospel came.[10]

Because the morals of his people seemed in precipitous decline, Luther preached more and more to emphasize the law. In the instructions to visitors published in 1528, he spoke of the difference between preaching to those who understood the gospel and preaching to those who did not. Souls are likely to be lost if the preacher spends too much time comforting the people and not enough on contrition for sin and fear of God's judgment. The sinfulness of all our works is too great for ordinary Christians to understand if they are the faith.[11] In short, the people were to be told that if they did not do good works according to the moral law, God would punish them.

Now and then he preached against witchcraft.[12] His fears of supernatural enemies seemed to grow with the years. At the end of a sermon in June 1529, he took a moment to advise his auditors to be cautious during the summer season. They should not take cold baths. Satan lurks in forests, groves, waters, and everywhere draws near to us that he may destroy us, for he does not sleep. Sometimes water sprites deceive so that they destroy us, as we have seen almost every year when even experienced swimmers drown in the Elbe. Always go swimming with someone, he said. Or bathe at home.[13]

In August 1529, Luther concluded another sermon with an admonition against witches. Some sorcerers were stealing milk and harming people. They should stop, and he said the congregation would not wait to deal with such people. Later that month a short notice appeared at the end of a sermon saying that Luther had excommunicated "some" witches and sorcerers from the church.[14]

On September 12 he spoke on the danger of witches. It is necessary to pray against them. Satan takes them into his "abyss" and "bedroom," apparently to have sexual intercourse with them. They cause sickness, although

Luther says it is necessary to distinguish between natural illness and those caused by witches. In illness caused by witches, bones, hair, tools, and such run with pus, as he had seen himself in the case of the wife of the Baron of Mansfeld. These illnesses cannot be cured by human doctors. The more they are cared for, the more they run on. His auditors should not be so anxious that they ascribed a boil or whatever sickness to a witch. But they should pray against witches so they might be discovered and get their just deserts from the executioner.[15]

The mention of the executioner was no empty threat. In 1540 on June 29, a fifty-year-old woman, her son, and two other persons were burned at the stake for witchcraft in Wittenberg. According to the indictment, they had caused storms, harmed many people with magic, poisoned some, and damaged livestock. Lucas Cranach the Younger made a woodcut of the event. Each of the four, naked from the waist up, was placed astraddle a crossbar in the stake and so they were burned. Luther was out of the city, on a trip to Eisenach and Weimar, when these executions took place. A student reported some years later that Luther laid the blame for these and other witches on evil spirits and said that such people would be bound in chains and bound to the fires of hell forever.[16] Luther seemed to take demons and witches as a hazard common to life, much as we learn to live with hurricanes, tornadoes, or blizzards. The demonic world provided him with another rod of fear to use against the casual religious lives of his auditors. He frequently said that the fear was salutary because it made us pray.

At least one commentator on the witchcraft delusion has argued that witch hunting represented the obverse of religious doubt. Although, notes Walter Stephens, the canon law of the church had rejected witchcraft "as a harmless delusion ever since the tenth century," he makes a compelling argument that many in Luther's time believed "that if there are no witches, we have no assurance that God exists." As late as the eighteenth century John Wesley expressed his sorrow that belief in witchcraft had dissolved, for, as he said of those who abandoned such belief, "the giving up of witchcraft is, in effect, the giving up of the Bible, and they know . . . that if but one account of the intercourse of men with separate spirits be admitted, their whole . . . Deism, Atheism, Materialism falls to the ground."[17] Stephens says:

> Centuries before Descartes, Western Christianity was enamored of rational discourse to such an extent that, whatever it may have professed openly, in its heart of theological and methodological hearts it long believed that nothing, not even God, was immune to dialectical proof. And when God turned out to be indeed immune to dialectical proof,

Western Christianity did not fall back on mysticism and subjective modes of certainty. Rather it took a further step into rationalism by trying to substitute empirical proof for the missing dialectical proof. Only it did so surreptitiously, hiding its intent even from itself, by hunting witches. In this sense it is no accident that the discourse of witch-hunting and the discourse of scientific inquiry in sixteenth- and seventeenth-century Europe show such remarkable overlap. For if the hunt for witches was really a quest for Satan, then scientific method is indeed indebted to persecution.[18]

Stephens's elegantly argued article may offer somewhat indirectly insight into Luther's long preoccupation with the powers of darkness that Heiko Oberman has noted without bothering to interpret. The quest for demonic forces was for Luther only the obverse of his quest for God. If the one did not exist, the other did not exist either, and all meaning in life fell to earth and ashes.

His quest for some outward manifestation of the working of God's word seems to have risen from a similar motive. If his life were not to be in vain, the Word had to make a visible difference. His intense later preaching on the law has a quality of desperation about it. It seems as if the people of Wittenberg *had* to validate in some feeble way his own interpretation of the gospel. If he had to impose that validation on them by a preaching that seems far removed from his doctrine of predestination, he would do just that.

For some of his disciples who remembered the early Luther, the bold prophet who preached justification by faith alone, who declared that no sin could damn except unbelief, this zealous thundering of the law was disturbing. By 1528 the objections of the "antinomians," as they were called, were acute. One dissenter was an old friend, a younger man named Johannes Agricola (c. 1492–1566), sometime dwelling with his family in Luther's house. Agricola seems very close to Luther's views in his treatise *On the Freedom of a Christian,* a view taken into England by Luther's most important English disciple, William Tyndale. The Christian spontaneously does good works not out of fear of punishment but out of loving gratitude to the God who has granted salvation as a gift. No sense of compulsion is involved. The law should not be used as a threat. Increasingly Agricola thought Luther had gone back to works righteousness, and he became the center of a long and troublesome debate within the Lutheran ranks.

By this time Luther had lost faith in this proclamation of a loving God in the gospel whose love did not require the compulsion of the law. Rather he emphasized the part of his theology that had always held that the law of God provides a standard that we know we cannot meet, and that our terror before that law is the force that makes us understand the gospel and embrace it. It is as though the law opens at our feet a yawning abyss and shows that we are on a slippery slope to our doom when suddenly, without our merit, the gospel reaches out for us and redeems us. Our joy in the gospel is kindled by the horrifying vision of what we might be without it. And of course Luther always saw the end of the law as death, following his beloved apostle Paul, who told the Corinthians, "The sting of death is sin, and the strength of sin is the law" (1 Cor. 15:57). Luther taught that the true Christian suffered passionately at the human inability to keep the law, and the motley citizenry at Wittenberg was obviously not suffering and obviously not afraid of the judgment of God. Luther would make them suffer and make them fear by hurling the law at them, and Agricola felt that his mentor was losing his way. He probably thought that Luther's harsh blazing away at his congregations was tiresome, and the younger man wanted a return to the preaching of consolation and love. For Luther consolation and love seemed to be the last thing the Wittenbergers needed. They needed terror before their miserable condition.

An ugly quarrel erupted. It came and went for several years, but in the end, like everybody else who stood up to Luther, Agricola had to leave Wittenberg. Luther's victory was temporary. His followers debated for years over the relation of law and gospel, the debate carrying Lutheran doctrine down to cozy sterility among the masses whose response was to yawn and joke and stay home from sermons.

What effect was the gospel to have on life? Some evangelicals formed conventicles where Christians could practice a strict moral life and at the same time comfort and strengthen one another by mutual admonition and love. The German Pietists were to emerge from this impulse, and their effect was immense in some restricted quarters. But Luther could not give up on trying to shape his society along Christian principles.

He began by seeking to renew all of Christendom, and in a stroke of amazing historical luck, he happened to discover the gospel in the territory of a prince who protected him. We can only guess how much that circumstance shaped the writing of his *Address to the Christian Nobility of the German Nation,* which in turn shaped his attitude toward government. Princes were his best allies against the pope. He turned to them as his only earthly hope to bring down the Antichrist. Such triumphs as Lutheranism enjoyed in northern and eastern Germany following Luther's lifetime arose out of a continued alliance between Lutheran churchmen and German princes who found his doctrines congenial.[19]

What if Luther had been a professor at the University of Leipzig rather than the University of Wittenberg? Would the hostility of Duke George have driven him into rejecting ties between Christians and government? Would he have gone the way of the Anabaptists and, later on, the Quakers? Who can tell? Some of his earlier followers—most notably Sebastian Franck (1499–1542)—gave up adherence to the Bible as a contradictory "seven-sealed book" and practiced a mystical approach to God much like that of the Quakers more than a century later. Perhaps the most remarkable aspect of Franck's life was that he was able to find refuge in the southern German city of Ulm and live in peace, publishing mystical works contrary to teachings of both evangelicals and Catholics.

Luther clung doggedly to scripture. For centuries the idea that Germany had a holy mission in Europe had percolated through the German people. Luther seems to have shared it. He built an institution—with much help, of course. Princes saw to its protection and its purity of doctrine—without attempting to make doctrine themselves. It was an attitude in keeping with the policies of the Emperor Otto I and his successors until Henry IV collided with the Hildebrandine reforms in the eleventh century. Now Luther was the hard-working pope of an institutional church, and in his church, as in the Catholic church against which he rebelled, the good and the bad lived and moved and had their being together. He tended to see most of the bad.

In 1527 Luther was plunged into a depression that, as Martin Brecht astutely noted, was part physical, part psychological.[20] He was already show-ing symptoms of the heart disease that eventually killed him. He had chest pains, dizzy spells, and indigestion and sometimes fainted. He got fat. His diet was poor. His endless work afforded him little physical exercise. He lived under stress. He probably drank too much. For a man whose habits were manifestly unhealthful, he lived to a remarkable age, dying in his sixty-third year.

He was prone to depression all his life. He spoke often of violent sweat-ing—which clinical psychologists cite as a symptom of acute depression. In our modern world of drug-based therapy and growing skepticism about the capacity of psychoanalysis to cure depression, some as yet unanswerable questions arise about Luther. Did some chemical imbalance throughout his life plunge him into depression, and did his tortured mind then fix on thoughts of failure, meaninglessness, and death? Or did his thoughts of failure, meaningless, and death bring on the depression? Who can tell? What-ever the cause, the effects were horrendous.

Darkness fell on him sometime in the summer of 1527. On August 2 he wrote to Melanchthon that he was doing better but that for a week he had been plunged into death and hell so that he had been seized with trembling in all his members. "I almost completely lost Christ and I was plunged into the waves and tempests of desperation and blasphemy against God." He had been helped by the prayers of his friends in Wittenberg. Plague was in the city. (Plague had also been raging in 1505 when he made his vow during a thunderstorm.) He asked Melanchthon to pray for him. He closed with a prayer of his own: "Now may Christ the victor over death, the victor over the grave, the victor over sin, the world, the flesh with his spirit watch over us and you."[21] Letters to other friends begged for their prayers.

The plague continued through the hot weather. Funerals were frequent, although Luther said several times that within Wittenberg itself the plague was milder than on other occasions. Most of his colleagues fled. He remained in the city despite death all around him. He thought it necessary to stay because of the terror among the people.[22] A daughter of his faithful friend Justus Jonas died of the malady. The visitations occupied his mind and his correspondence. By September the plague began to dissipate.

The letters seem to attest to a period when Luther felt once again the fear of death rush over him with such force that he could not believe in the power of God to raise the dead and that from the dark coign of vantage such a horror afforded, he could see the gospel and all he had struggled to create and shape turn to dust in his mind. Martin Brecht says that after this bout with depression, Luther "had become an unstable man."[23] Certainly the table talk shows a man for whom musings on death and doubt were common. The table talk itself with its collection of worshipful students and devoted friends looks like one of the best kinds of therapy we can imagine for what ailed him. To them he could talk freely, lubricated by beer and wine, and their companionship was medicine to a soul that feared night and solitude.

Yet when Luther faced death, he did so with courage and dignity. Until almost the end of his days, martyrdom was possible, and if he had lived only little more than a year longer, he would have seen Wittenberg taken by the emperor during the religious wars. Had he remained to face his foes—as I think he would have done—Luther might have been tortured and burned at the stake. He would have faced the prospect bravely, for he was a brave man. It may well be that he thought about death so much that when he came stark up against it, he found it less threatening than he had imagined. As Montaigne said, it is a common human trait that we fear death most when we are healthy and that when it is nigh, we discover that we can disdain life.[24] Luther's fear of death is evident in his table talk and in his voluminous writing and in his counsel to others. But when he was sick and thought he was dying, he faced the end calmly—as most of us do when the moment comes.

How do we make an estimate of his life? Doubtless for many in his time and since, he opened the way to a religious experience of freedom, zest, and spontaneity capable of giving consolation and hope to those who share it. At a moment when serious penitential practice came clogged with definitions, elaborate rules, and the corrupt superstitions of the indulgence trade, Luther brought a simplicity that was a relief to many burdened souls. For those of deep introspection and harsh self-judgment, Luther delivered a saving paradox, that those in misery who recognize who and what they are have a sign of God's grace that lifts them with a power they know they cannot possess themselves. For those souls already in love with God, he provided a vocabulary of sovereignty that is still appealing.

But doubtless, too, he shut the doors on a Catholic experience that has retained an obvious power to hold both the simple and the sophisticated, the shallow and the profound, the ignorant and the educated in one enduring communion. This judgment is not to say that the Catholic Church of Luther's time was unworthy of his rebellion or that its evolution since the Council of Trent warrants idealization. But the fact remains that the sacramental experience of Catholic worship maintains an impressive hold on its adherents. The sacraments have an existence independent of the pope and papal pronouncements.

With respect to the Jews Luther was part of a cultural stream that runs like an open sewer through our history, and he was worse than a legion of Catholics and Protestants who have spewed forth hatred upon a people more sinned against than sinning. Although the Jews for him were only one among many enemies he castigated with equal fervor, although he did not sink to the horrors of the Spanish Inquisition against Jews, and although he was certainly not to blame for Adolf Hitler, Luther's hatred of the Jews is a sad and dishonorable part of his legacy, and it is not a fringe issue. It lay at the center of his concept of religion. He saw in the Jews a continuing moral depravity he did not see in Catholics. He did not accuse papists of the crimes that he laid at the feet of Jews.

For Luther religion was primarily the means of conquering death, a collection of true doctrines that must be believed if the Christian was to be victorious over death, and in such a schema, tolerance had no place. The Jews who rejected his Jesus rejected also his own understanding of the meaning of life and death and the way we know God. I suspect that their patient endurance of suffering and death in their adhesion to their own faith, necessarily rejecting his, made him afraid, and so created in his mind a fantasy called "Jew" that was in part constructed of hated elements in his own soul. Those devoted to assuring themselves that they have found the only way of salvation from the grave are unlikely to be tolerant of contradiction by other religious views that threaten their only hope for life after death. Religious toleration in the West developed along with uncertainty about ultimate things.

Luther was responsible for much of that uncertainty. Confounded by competing absolutist claims in matters of faith, rulers and people alike eventually decided to live and let live in the interest of public order and tranquillity. Those who lived outwardly ethical lives were considered acceptable citizens. In another paradox, Luther's consistent belief that no one could tell if another was a true Christian, that we could not even be sure of the apostle Peter's salvation if we had him among us, could contribute to the notion that governments must finally judge by the outward appearance and, as Elizabeth I of England said, not make windows into men's souls.

Luther did not follow his own lead. Whatever their ethics, those who disagreed with him in matters of doctrine faced relentless vituperation, and if they lived in Wittenberg, they could be exiled. Eventually in countries where prosperity and cosmopolitan values reigned, religious conformity became too much to bear, its psychic expense too harsh. Consequently, a benefit that sprang from Luther's Reformation was freedom of both conscience and practice—including the freedom to reject religion in the public forum of ideas. Luther would have been appalled. Today Lutherans, Catholics, Jews, Unitarians, and other Protestant denominations follow their religious rites in the comforting familiarity of old forms that grant the peculiar consolations and comforts that lie beyond the justifications of logic and the details of dogma. Only professional theologians think much of dogma these days, and the most popular of these make doctrines symbolic rather than literal, inclusive rather than prohibitive. That tolerance came about finally from the horror of the religious wars that followed hard on Luther's career. In these merciless conflicts mutual hatred of competing parties was fueled by their different interpretations of what unprovable doctrines had to be believed if human beings were to have the assurance of conquering death. Catholics and Protestants slaughtered each other for the promise of eternal life.

A further irony is that Luther's preoccupation with scripture led to intense study of the sacred text, and under that study something of its sacredness dissolved. Under the higher criticism of scripture, developed largely by German Lutherans in the nineteenth century, Luther's own critical attitude toward some books of the Bible was expanded. Under the probing intellects of scholars such as Julius Wellhausen, any notion that scripture could be an infallible historical record fell to pieces except among those ignorant of this stream of thought or among those whose minds were shut to it or among those fundamentalists who can hold their own faith only within the carefully restricted boundaries of their own kind. This decay of biblical authority among the educated is one of Luther's legacies—shared with Erasmus.

Worship in a spirit of meditation and contemplation goes on and enriches many hearts. Luther's words, selectively chosen, speak to many who, caught up in the hurly-burly of modern life and morality, seek a rhetoric of comfort and assurance. Yet we take it almost for granted that our worship may involve illusion, the kind of experience Erasmus described in the *Praise of Folly* when he told of the madman who sat alone in a theater day after day, laughing hugely at the comedy he saw acted in his imagination on the empty stage. When he was cured of his madness, he was distraught at the absence that had come into his life. Illusion or not, the experience of religion for most of us rises above dogma, even when we recite creeds and sing old hymns filled with doctrines few of us would profess literally. We have learned to live that way. To Luther we would have been blasphemers, just as he to us seems strangely remote and curious when we try to consider the whole man.

Above all, Luther was a human being, living in his unique moment of history—as all moments in history are unique. Making sense of him requires an effort not to decide whether he was right or wrong, good or bad, but rather to see what human quality in him tells us something about the human condition we all share in all the centuries. Despite remarkable consistency in Luther's voluminous labors, anyone laboring over his thoughts comes upon expressions unexpected and sometimes astonishing, sometimes vulgar and ugly, sometimes sublime. He was a man of highs and lows; he could be eloquent, generous, and compassionate in one moment and harsh, arrogant, unbending, gross, and savage in the next.

His exuberant complexities make him an enduring mystery. All writers and readers who consider him see him only in part. Sometimes he is as close to us as our hand that holds the pen seeking to sketch him; at other moments he swings away from us like the planet Pluto, a dark god with a stony heart sweeping the frozen reaches of outer space. He jovially remarked once of his doctors, who had ordered him not to take baths and to stay put when he was sick, "The doctors try to make me a fixed star. But I am a planet."[25] So he was—and is.

Luther was preoccupied with death, and still more with what came afterwards. Luther said that the souls of the dead sleep until the day of doom. A never-ending sleep was the ultimate horror, the ultimate sign of the wrath of God, and nothingness the ultimate terror.

Luther's temperament was his tragedy. He was an absolutist, demanding certainty in a dark and conflict-ridden world where nothing is finally sure and mystery abounds against a gloom that may ultimately be driven by fate, the impersonal chain of accident that takes us where we would not go because our destiny is to be the people we are, and so we have no choice but tragedy. Perhaps the ultimate wisdom that Luther taught us is the somewhat negative truth that every living soul of us must learn on his or her own how we should die.

What might have happened had Luther never been born? Erasmus might have been the harbinger of a benign kind of reform and piety that would have brought the Catholic Church along slowly into the tolerance and char-ity practiced by legions of Catholics today. But who can tell? Were Erasmus and the community of scholars like him influential enough to have brought such a result about? It should be clear to anyone who has read this book that my sympathies lie with Erasmus. But we know only what happened, not what might have been. Luther was struck down with an apparition of terror on a country road during a July thunderstorm, and he made a vow to ward off death. He demanded certainty about his meaning and destiny. He wanted to follow his own ideas about a religion of the heart so that he might protest the deceit and futility of a religious practice that was scarcely more than magic. In his view, the religious practices of the indulgence hawkers did justice neither to the true state of the human condition nor to the true nature of the all-powerful God who had to exist if we are to be raised from the dead. When he saw to his horror that these practices were sanctioned by the pope, supposedly the Vicar of Christ, he set out to destroy the papacy and, failing that, to expose it to shame and contempt so that the bishop of Rome would become contemptible to all the world. He believed that the word of God spoke unmistakably through scripture, that scripture was clear, and that true Christians would recognize on hearing it the divine revelation given centuries before in the incarnation of Christ. As a lesser desire, Luther hoped for the liberation of his "dear German people" from the oppressive yoke of Italian tyranny and their unity under the Christian government of an emperor dedicated to the gospel.

None of that happened.

Instead for more than a century after Luther's death, Europe was strewn with the slaughtered corpses of people who would have lived normal lives if Luther had never lived at all or if his friends had persuaded him to shake off the rash vow he made out of terror in a storm. Perhaps his influence would have been most benign had he died as a martyr shortly after he became a public figure, if he had been seized at Worms and rushed to the stake. Then we could have been more free to idealize him. We would have had a more serene history, less hatred, less bloodshed, less massacre.

Yet the powerful appeal of his personality is evident over the centuries. His words gush out, demanding attention and discrimination. He is witty. He has a power of metaphor. He resolved to live in ultimate trust in the good of creation and destiny. And if I must choose part of him to speak a word to the present, it would be that resolve that he felt after the *Anfechtungen,* after the horrors of *tristitia,* a resolve that worked itself out in a ferocious energy intending to do good in the world. Luther knew as clearly as any of us that we cannot surrender to melancholy and habitual uncertainty, darkly mysterious though the world may be. We may choose despair and apathy or fall into the futility of whatever hedonism suits us best. Or we can do as Luther did, plunge on in the effort to do what we can against impossible odds to bring what light we can into darkness, choosing with more skepticism, tolerance, and care than his the instruments of light we use, but living—and dying—in the hope that in the end all will be well.

He died, of a bad heart or perhaps of a stroke, in the dark hours of early morning on February 18, 1546. He was sick on his way to adjudicate a dispute between the counts at Mansfeld, his ancestral home. He blamed his illness on the Jews. He preached against them several times on this journey, including in his last sermon. He complained of headache and chest paints at supper on February 17, seemed to recover, then woke in the night in pain again and died at about three o'clock. His death, like everything else about his life, was controversial and remains so.[26]

The first story was written by Justus Jonas, perhaps Luther's best and most loyal friend, at about five in the morning, after hope had expired for Luther's recovery. By then rigor mortis had set in. Jonas also spoke of Luther's death in a funeral oration and in a written report published a few weeks afterward. It has become the canonical version. In it Luther dies peacefully, commending his soul to God, although the peace was interrupted by Justus Jonas and Michael Coelius, the local castle preacher, shouting at him, "Reverend father, are you ready to die trusting in your Lord Jesus Christ and to confess the doctrine which you have taught in his name?" They claimed that he replied with a clearly audible "Yes."[27] What else could they say? The Catholics promptly circulated the rumor that Luther had committed suicide. During Bismarck's *Kulturkampf* these rumors were vigorously revived on the Catholic side and as vigorously condemned by outraged Lutherans. An apothecary called in by the physicians reported that the doctors themselves were in disagreement. One maintained that Luther was the victim of a stroke; the other objected: God would not have stricken such a holy man with such a death.[28] Karl S. Guthke, who has studied the last words of famous people, says that in Luther's time to die in one's sleep or to be stricken in such a way that no last words were possible was considered God's judgment on those doomed to hell. Therefore Luther had to have last words, and they were appropriately confirming of his life.[29] The apothecary's account, detached and objective though it is, cannot inform us on this score, since by his report Luther was unconscious when he arrived. Whatever he said or did not say at his death, the German Hercules had fought his last battle.

NOTES

The following abbreviations and short titles are used in the notes.

AE *Luther's Works: American Edition,* ed. Jaroslav Pelikan and Helmut T.
Lehman, 55 vols. (St. Louis: Concordia Publishing House; Philadelphia:
Fortress Press, 1955–1986)

ARG *Archiv für Reformationsgeschichte*

Brecht Martin Brecht, *Martin Luther: His Road to Reformation, 1483–1521,* trans.
James L. Schaff, 3 vols. (Philadelphia: Westminster Press, 1895)

Dokumente *Dokumente aus staatlichen Archiven und anderen wissenschaftlichen und kul-
turellen Einrichtungen der Deutschen Demokratischen Republik. Im Jahre
des 500. Geburstages Martin Luthers mit Unterstutzung des Martin-Luther-
Komitees herausgegeben von der Staatlichen Archivverwaltung der DDR,*
ed. Reiner Gross, Manfred Kobuch, and Ernst Müller (Weimar: Hermann Böhlaus Nachfolger, 1983)

EE *Opus epistolarum Des. Erasmi Roterodami,* ed. Percy S. Allen et al., 12 vols.
(Oxford: Oxford University Press, 1906–1958)

Luther's *Luther's Correspondence and Other Contemporary Letters,* 2 vols.; vol. 1
Correspondence trans. and ed. Preserved Smith; vol. 2 trans. and ed. Preserved Smith and
Charles M. Jacobs (Philadelphia: Lutheran Publication Society, 1913,
1918)

TR *D. Martin Luthers Werke: Kritische Gesamtausgabe, Tischreden,* 6 vols. (Weimar: Hermann Böhlaus Nachfolger, 1912–1921)

WA *D. Martin Luthers Werke,* 67 vols. (Weimar: Hermann Böhlaus Nachfolger,
1883–1997)

WAB *D. Martin Luthers Werke: Kritische Gesamtausgabe, Deutsche Bibel,* 12 vols.
(Weimar: Hermann Böhlaus Nachfolger, 1906–1961)

WA Br *D. Martin Luthers Werke: Kritische Gesamtausgabe, Briefwechsel,* 15 vols.
(Weimar: Hermann Böhlaus Nachfolger, 1930–1978)

1. Luther's Europe

1. Bernd Moeller, *Deutschland im Zeitalter der Reformation* (Göttingen: Vandenhoeck & Ruprecht, 1977), pp. 14–15.
2. Much of the material on executions is from Norbert Ohler, *Sterben und Tod im Mittelalter* (Munich: Artemis Verlag, 1990), pp. 200–234.
3. *TR* 2, no. 2417.
4. Shakespeare, *Henry V* 4.1.109, 256–257.
5. This complaint was made at the Diet of Worms in 1521, at which Luther himself appeared before the emperor. But it represents a grievance of long standing. See Gerald Strauss, ed. and trans., *Manifestations of Discontent in Germany on the Eve of the Reformation* (Bloomington: Indiana University Press, 1971), pp. 54, 55, 57.
6. Ibid., p. 39.
7. Jean Delumeau, *La peur en Occident: Une cité assiégée* (Paris: Fayard, 1978) and *Le péché et la peur: La culpabilisation en Occident XIIIe–XVIIIe siècles* (Paris: Fayard, 1983).
8. See the introduction to *The Black Death,* a collection of sources edited by Rosemary Horrox (Manchester: Manchester University Press, 1994), pp. 3–13.
9. Peter Dinzelbacher, "La divinità uccidente," in *La peste nera: Dati di una realtà ed elementi di una interpretazione,* ed. Enrico Menestò (Spoleto: Centro Italiano di Studi Sull'Alto Medioevo, 1994), pp. 139, 146–150.
10. Ohler, *Sterben und Tod im Mittelalter,* pp. 260–262.
11. Carla Casagrande, "La moltiplicazione dei peccati. I cataloghi dei peccati nella letteratura pastorale dei secoli XIII–XV," in Menestò, *La peste nera,* pp. 253–254.
12. Jean Delumeau, *Le péché et la peur,* p. 124.
13. *TR* 4, no. 4789.
14. Brecht 1: 45.
15. For a brief discussion of economic progress and unrest in Luther's part of Germany see *Dokumente,* pp. 19–20.
16. For this expression, widely used at the time, see J. H. Parry, ed., *The European Reconnaissance: Selected Documents* (New York: Harper Torchbooks, 1968), p. 7.
17. *TR* 4, no. 4638.
18. Parry, *The European Reconnaissance,* pp. 82, 84–85.
19. Fernand Braudel, *The Structures of Everyday Life: Civilization Capitalism, 15th–18th Century,* vol. 1 (New York: Harper & Row, 1991), p. 400. According to Elizabeth Eisenstein, "We can say that the 'average' early edition ranged between two hundred and one thousand copies"; *The Printing Revolution in Early Modern Europe* (Cambridge: Cambridge University Press, 1983), p. 9.
20. Eisenstein, *Printing Revolution,* pp. 116–117.
21. Henri Busson, *Le rationalisme dans la littérature française de la Renaissance*

(1533–1601) (Paris: J. Vrin, 1971), p. 25. The first edition of this often revised and expanded work appeared in 1922.

22. Jacob Burckhardt, *The Civilization of the Renaissance in Italy,* trans. S. G. C. Middlemore (New York: Phaidon Press, 1965), p. 339.

23. See Delumeau, *Le péché et la peur,* p. 174.

24. Lucien Febvre, *The Problem of Unbelief in the Sixteenth Century: The Religion of Rabelais,* trans. Beatrice Gottlieb (Cambridge, Mass.: Harvard University Press, 1982).

2. The Early Years

1. For a comprehensive discussion of Luther's mother and her connections, see Ian Siggins, *Luther and His Mother* (Philadelphia: Fortress Press, 1981).

2. Erik H. Erikson, *Young Man Luther: A Study in Psychoanalysis and History* (New York: W. W. Norton, 1958), p. 77.

3. Ibid., p. 79.

4. Heiko A. Oberman, *Die Reformation von Wittenberg nach Genf* (Göttingen: Vandenhoeck & Ruprecht, 1986), pp. 93–101.

5. Mikhail Bakhtin, *Rabelais and His World,* trans. Helene Iswolsky (Bloomington: Indiana University Press, 1984), p. 192.

6. *TR* 5, no. 5537.

7. Jean Claude Bologne, *Histoire de la pudeur* (Paris: Olivier Orban, 1986), p. 154.

8. Dionysius of Halicarnassus, *Early History of Rome* 1.3.

9. *TR* 2, no. 1559.

10. *AE* 54:235; *TR* 3, no. 3566A.

11. Siggins, *Luther and His Mother,* p. 10; *WA* 38: 338.

12. *TR* 5, no. 5571; *AE* 54: 457.

13. Brecht 3: 237.

14. Steven Ozment, *When Fathers Ruled: Family Life in Reformation Europe* (Cambridge, Mass.: Harvard University Press, 1983), pp. 133, 144, 147, 148.

15. *TR* 1, no. 1388.

16. *AE* 49: 268–269.

17. *AE* 49: 319.

18. *AE* 54: 178; *TR* 3, no. 3888a.

19. Shakespeare, *The Tempest* 1.2.312; 2.2.314.

20. Siggins, *Luther and His Mother,* p. 48.

21. *Dokumente,* pp. 21–29.

22. Allen Temko, *Notre-Dame of Paris: The Biography of a Cathedral* (New York: Viking, 1955), p. 54.

23. See "Martino di Tours," in *Bibliotheca Sanctorum,* vol. 8 (Rome: Società Grafica Romana, 1962), cols. 1248–91.

24. Siggins, *Luther and His Mother,* p. 48; *TR* 5, no. 5362.

25. Brecht 1: 5.

26. Karl Borchardt, "Martin Luther: Doch nicht vorehelich gezeught?—Eine Ergänzung zur Martin-Luther-Miszelle von Ludwig Schmugge," *ARG* 87 (1996): 393–399.

27. Siggins, *Luther and His Mother,* pp. 14, 16.

28. *TR* 3, no. 2982b.

29. *TR* 3, nos. 3491, 3556, 3601.

30. *TR* 6, nos. 6814, 6815.

31. *TR* 4, no. 3979.

32. Jean Delumeau, *La peur en Occident: une cité assiégée* (Paris: Fayard, 1978), p. 73, 123–124.

33. Max J. Friedländer, *Landscape Portrait, Still-Life: Their Origin and Development* (New York: Schocken Books, 1963), p. 44.

34. *TR* 1, no. 489.

35. *TR* 4, no. 4919.

36. Siggins, *Luther and His Mother,* pp. 60–61.

37. Johan Huizinga, *The Waning of the Middle Ages* (Garden City, N.Y.: Doubleday/Anchor, 1954), pp. 138, 140.

38. Philippe Ariès, *The Hour of Our Death,* trans. Helen Weaver (New York: Alfred A. Knopf, 1981), p. 116. Illustration p. 114.

39. Jean Delumeau, *Le péché et la peur: La culpabilisation en Occident XIIIe–XVIIIe siècles* (Paris: Fayard, 1983), p. 100.

40. Henri Busson, *Le rationalisme dans la littérature française de la Renaissance (1533–1601)* (Paris: J. Vrin, 1971).

41. Shakespeare, *Henry V* 2.3.

42. Ariès, *The Hour of Our Death,* pp. 128–129; Pierre Chaunu, *Le temps des Reformes: La crise de la Chrétienté 1250–1550* (Paris: Editions Complexe, 1975), pp. 192–196.

43. Delumeau, *Le péché et la peur,* p. 102.

44. Shakespeare, *Macbeth* 5.5.27–28; *Richard II* 1.2.177, 222.

45. Jean Wirth, "Hans Baldung Grien et les dissidents Strasbourgeois," in *Croyants et sceptiques au XVIe siècle: Le dossier des "Epicuriens,"* ed. Marc Lienhard (Strasbourg: Librarie Istra, 1981), pp. 131–138.

46. Tenenti is summarized by Ariès, *The Hour of Our Death,* pp. 128–129.

47. Ibid., p. 132.

48. *TR* 1, no. 388. In the table talk in which he makes this pronouncement, he passes from Latin to German, as though to make the terror more emphatic.

49. Brecht 1: 9.

50. Ibid., p. 23.

51. Gert Wendelborn, *Martin Luther: Leben und reformatorisches Werk* (Vienna: Verlag Hermann Böhlaus Nachfolger, 1983), p. 18.

52. Brecht 1: 23.

53. Shakespeare, *3 Henry VI* 1.2.16–17.

54. Peter Brown, *The Body and Society: Men, Women, and Sexual Renunciation in Early Christianity* (New York: Columbia University Press, 1988), p. 134.
55. Wendelborn, *Martin Luther,* p. 19.
56. See the illuminating discussion by Alister E. McGrath, *The Intellectual Origins of the European Reformation* (Cambridge, Mass.: Blackwell, 1994), pp. 70–75.
57. Alister E. McGrath, *Iustitia Dei: A History of the Christian Doctrine of Justification, the Beginnings to the Reformation* (Cambridge: Cambridge University Press, 1986), pp. 166–172. McGrath argues that the use of the term "nominalism" creates more problems than it solves, that the state of late medieval theology was enormously complex, and that no single term can embrace it all.
58. Aquinas, *Summa Theologiae* I, q. 2, a. 2, ad. 1.
59. Jaroslav Pelikan, *Reformation of Church and Dogma (1300–1700)* (Chicago: University of Chicago Press, 1984), p. 165.
60. The term is used by Malcolm Barber, *The Two Cities: Medieval Europe, 1050–1320* (London: Routledge, 1992), p. 186.
61. Brecht 1: 33, 34.

3. The Flight to the Monastery

1. *TR* 4, no. 4707.
2. *TR* 6, no. 7029.
3. *TR* 4, no. 4707.
4. See, for example, Heinrich Boehmer, *Martin Luther: Road to Reformation* (New York: Meridian Books, 1957), p. 33.
5. *WA* 8: 574.
6. *TR* 1, no. 119.
7. See Roland H. Bainton, *Erasmus of Christendom* (New York: Scribner's, 1969), pp. 18—26, for a brief account of Erasmus's stay in the monastery. Erasmus, like Luther, was as a young man absorbed by the terror of death.
8. Brecht 1: 57.
9. Peter Brown, *The Body and Society: Men, Women, and Sexual Renunciation in Early Christianity* (New York: Columbia University Press, 1988), pp. 61–62.
10. Bernhard Lohse, *Mönchtum und Reformation: Luthers Auseindersetzung mit dem Mönchsideal des Mittelalters* (Göttingen: Vandenhoeck & Ruprecht, 1963), pp. 114–115. The term "medicine of immortality" seems to have been used first by Ignatius of Antioch about the year 100. See J. N. D. Kelly, *Early Christian Doctrines,* 4th ed. (London: Adam and Charles Black, 1968), pp. 197–198.
11. Brecht 1: 62.
12. *TR* 1, no. 121.
13. *Conciliorum Oecumenicorum Decreta* (Bologna: Istituto per le Scienze Religiose, 1973), p. 684.
14. Sermo 74; *Patrologiae Cursus Completus: Series Latina,* ed. J.-P. Migne, 221 vols.

(Paris, 1844–1864), 54: 398; quoted in *New Catholic Encyclopedia* (New York: McGraw-Hill, 1967), s.v. "Sacraments, Theology of."

15. Jaroslav Pelikan, *The Emergence of the Catholic Tradition (100–600)* (Chicago: University of Chicago Press, 1971), pp. 169–171.

16. Peter Brown, *The Cult of the Saints: Its Rise and Function in Latin Christianity* (Chicago: University of Chicago Press, 1981), pp. 12–17.

17. For an excellent discussion of the similarities between the heretical Cathars and the "orthodox" doctrines of the Catholic Church, see Zoé Oldenbourg, *Massacre at Montségur,* trans. Peter Green (New York: Pantheon Books, 1961), pp. 39–44.

18. Quoted in Michel Roquebert, *L'épopée Cathare,* vol. 1 (Toulouse: Privat, 1970), p. 129.

19. *Conciliorum Oecumenicorum Decreta,* pp. 230–231.

20. Jaroslav Pelikan, *Christianity and Classical Culture: The Metamorphosis of Natural Theology in the Christian Encounter with Hellenism* (New Haven: Yale University Press, 1993), p. 298.

21. *TR* 2, no. 1558.

22. *TR* 4, no. 4998.

23. *TR* 1, no. 623; *TR* 3, no. 3556; *WA* 8: 574.

24. *TR* 4, no. 4322.

25. The conflict goes back to the roots of Christianity and the "existential" need, as Jaroslav Pelikan has expressed it, of giving some reality to the realm of darkness presided over by Satan; *Christianity and Classical Culture,* p. 80.

26. Karl Holl, *Gesammelte Aufsätze zur Kirchengeschichte,* vol. 1 (Tübingen: J. C. B. Mohr, 1921), p. 55.

27. Brecht 1: 71.

4. Years of Silence

1. Jean Wirth, *Luther: Etude d'histoire religieuse* (Geneva: Librairie Droz, 1981), pp. 11–14.

2. Roland H. Bainton, *Here I Stand* (New York: Abington, 1950), p. 45.

3. *Luther's Correspondence* 1: 91.

4. Jaroslav Pelikan, *The Emergence of the Catholic Tradition (100–600)* (Chicago: University of Chicago Press, 1971), pp. 297–298.

5. Thomas More, *Letter to Martin Dorp,* in *The Complete Works of St. Thomas More,* vol. 15, ed. Daniel Kinney (New Haven: Yale University Press, 1986), pp. 28–39.

6. Heiko A. Oberman, *The Harvest of Medieval Theology* (Cambridge, Mass.: Harvard University Press, 1963), pp. 131–145.

7. Ibid., p. 129.

8. Thomas More, *Utopia,* ed. Edward L. Surtz, S. J., and J. H. Hexter (New Haven: Yale University Press, 1965), pp. 220–223; Voltaire, *Correspondance,* ed.

Theodore Besterman vol. 10 (Paris: Gallimard, 1977), p. 430; René Pameau, *"Ecrasez l'infâme"* (Oxford: Voltaire Foundation, 1984), p. 378.

9. The painting is in the National Gallery of Art, Washington, D.C.

10. Thomas More, *The Confutation of Tyndale's Answer,* ed. Louis A. Schuster et al. (New Haven: Yale University Press, 1973), p. 429.

11. Brecht 1: 79–81.

12. Karl Holl, *Gesammelte Aufsätze zur Kirchengeschichte,* vol. 1 (Tübingen: J. C. B. Mohr, 1921), pp. 55, 58–63.

13. Werner Elert, *Morphologie des Luthertums,* vol. 1 (Munich: C. H. Beck, 1958), p. 16: "Gerade deshalb ist die Todesmelodie so schrecklich, weil der Tod eine 'so edle Kreatur' trift."

14. Carl Stange, *Luther's Gedanken über die Todesfurcht* (Berlin: Walter de Gruyter, 1932), p. 7.

15. Bainton, *Here I Stand,* pp. 128–129.

16. Heiko A. Oberman, *Luther: Man between God and the Devil* (New Haven: Yale University Press, 1989), p. 330.

17. Quoted in Jean Delumeau, *Le péché et la peur: La culpabilisation en Occident XIIIe–XVIIIe siècles* (Paris: Fayard, 1983), p. 424.

18. *WA* 5: 590–591.

19. *WA* 19: 225.

20. *WA* 20: 162. I have used the translation from the Jerusalem Bible.

21. See, for example, his lectures on Hebrews of 1517: "And thus the unbelievers will be tortured with endless, eternal, and incurable cutting"; *AE* 29: 165; *WA* 57/3: 162. In commenting on Psalm 110 in 1534 during a sermon, Luther seemed to feel uncomfortable with the notion that hell was a place of fiery torment. The greatest torment of hell was separation from God. No pain, he said, was worse for the damned; *AE* 13: 261.

22. *TR* 4, no. 3962.

23. *TR* 4, no. 3963.

24. *WA* 36, 481, 500–501.

25. While Luther was preaching these sermons based on 1 Corinthians and castigating the unbelievers around him, Martin Bucer, his erstwhile disciple, was attacking the "Epicureans" in Strasbourg and charging them with the same unbelief that Luther found in his part of Germany. See Marc Lienhard, ed., *Croyants et sceptiques au XVIe siècle: Le dossier des "Epicuriens"* (Strasbourg: Librairie Istra, 1981).

26. Pietro Pomponazzi, *On the Immortality of the Soul,* with an introduction by John Herman Randall Jr., in *The Renaissance Philosophy of Man,* ed. Ernst Cassirer, Paul Oskar Kristeller, and John Herman Randall Jr. (Chicago: University of Chicago Press, 1948), pp. 257–381.

27. Martin L. Pine, *Pietro Pomponazzi: Radical Philosopher of the Renaissance* (Padua: Edtrice Antenore, 1986), p. 103.

28. The original is found in *WA* 40/3: 484–594; English translation, *AE* 13: 75–141. Quotations from *AE* 13: 76–77; *WA* 2: 242–244; *AE* 13: 86.

29. *AE* 13: 103.

30. See Gerhard Ebeling, *Disputatio de Homine: Die philosophische Definition des Menschen* (Tübingen: J. C. B. Mohr, 1982), esp. pp. 87–172.

31. *AE* 13: 83.

32. Lucretius, *On the Nature of Things* 3.47–100.

33. Among other sources, see the careful study by Georges Minois, *Histoire des enfers* (Paris: Fayard, 1991), esp. pp. 71–78. Minois says (p. 103) that the popular doctrine of hell, consolidated in medieval theology, developed only in the third century.

34. Luther himself, in his German exposition on the first and second chapters of the Gospel of John, delivered from the pulpit in 1537 and 1538, directly associated his *Anfechtungen* with the terror before death; *WA* 46: 660, 661, 678.

35. *WA* 36: 522–523.

36. Wirth, *Luther*, p. 101.

37. Thomas More harps on this distinction continually. See, e.g., *A Dialogue Concerning Heresies*, ed. T. M. C. Lawler, G. Marc'hadour, and R. C. Marius (New Haven: Yale University Press, 1981), pp. 382–388.

38. For one of a multitude of discussions of this issue by Thomas More see *Confutation*, pp. 818–822.

39. "A Pilgrimage for Religion's Sake," in *The Colloquies of Erasmus*, ed. and trans. Craig R. Thompson (Chicago: University of Chicago Press, 1965), pp. 308–309.

40. Heinrich Denifle says, with some justice, that Luther misunderstood the scholastic distinction between formed and unformed faith; *Luther und Luthertum*, 2 vols. (Mainz: Kirchheim, 1906), 1: 666.

41. *Luther: Lectures on Romans*, ed. Wilhelm Pauck (Philadelphia: Westminster Press, 1961), p. 283.

42. Bainton, *Here I Stand*, pp. 37–38.

43. Helmar Junghans, *Martin Luther und Wittenberg* (Munich: Koehler & Amelang, 1996).

44. An excellent summary of Frederick's life and achievements is Friedrich Hermann Schubert, "Friedrich III," in *Neu Deutsche Biographie*, vol. 5 (Berlin: Duncku & Humblot, 1960), pp. 568–572.

45. Bainton, *Here I Stand*, pp. 69–70.

46. Junghans, *Martin Luther und Wittenberg*, pp. 52–53.

47. *TR* 1, no. 168.

48. Francesco, Petrarch, "On His Own Ignorance," in Cassirer, Kristeller, and Randall, *The Renaissance Philosophy of Man*, p. 103.

49. *WA* 44: 591.

50. Mentions of Staupitz in the *WA* index are sometimes problematic, since in fact Staupitz is not named in the cited passage. Almost any time Luther mentions a

confessor, the Weimar editors assumed that he was speaking of Staupitz. Luther did keep confession as a sacrament, though in an altered form, after he had broken with the Catholic Church, and his "confessor" in those later years was usually his dear friend John Bugenhagen, called "Dr. Pommer" or "Pomeranus."

51. David C. Steinmetz, *Luther and Staupitz: An Essay in the Intellectual Origins of the Protestant Reformation* (Durham: Duke University Press, 1980), p. 40.
52. *TR* 1, no. 518.
53. *TR* 1, no. 94.
54. *TR* 1, no. 1017.
55. Steinmetz, *Luther and Staupitz,* p. 72 and passim.
56. *TR* 1, no. 1019 et al.
57. See the illuminating discussion of the difficult evolution of Satan in the Bible in Elaine Pagels, *The Origin of Satan* (New York: Random House, 1995).
58. *TR* 1, nos. 722, 959.

5. Rome and Wittenberg

1. Heiko A. Oberman, *Luther: Man between God and the Devil,* trans. Eileen Walliser-Schwarzbart (New Haven: Yale University Press, 1989), p. 130, for a brief summary of the Observant position. For a much more detailed and comprehensive account see Heinrich Böhmer, *Luthers Romfahrt* (Leipzig: A. Deichert, 1914), pp. 36–75. And see Brecht 1: 98–105. Much of the factual material that I present about Luther's journey to Rome comes from Böhmer's remarkably careful and detailed account. No one has done a more comprehensive study of this somewhat neglected episode in Luther's life.
2. Brecht 1: 98–99.
3. Gert Wendelborn, *Martin Luther: Leben und reformatorisches Werk* (Vienna: Verlag Hermann Böhlaus Nachfolger, 1983), pp. 35–38; Oberman, *Luther,* pp. 129–150. And see Böhmer, *Luthers Romfahrt,* p. 58.
4. Böhmer argues that Luther's journey began around November 1510 and that he arrived in Rome in January 1511; *Luthers Romfahrt,* pp. 33–36.
5. *TR* 5, no. 6059.
6. Böhmer, *Luthers Romfahrt,* p. 59.
7. *TR* 5, no. 5344.
8. *TR* 1, no. 507.
9. Böhmer, *Luthers Romfahrt,* pp. 33, 79–80, 88, and 89.
10. Ibid., p. 85.
11. Ibid., pp. 99–104.
12. *TR* 2, no. 1327.
13. *TR* 3, no. 3428.
14. *TR* 4, no. 4391.
15. *TR* 5, no. 6453.
16. *TR* 5, no. 6059.

17. *TR* 3, no. 3478.

18. E.g., *TR,* 2, no. 2709b.

19. See, for example, the moving poem, supposedly by Charlemagne's great council-lor Alcuin of York, *De clade Lindisfarnensis monasterii,* in *More Latin Lyrics from Virgil to Milton,* trans. Helen Waddell, ed. Dame Felicitas Corrigan (New York: W. W. Norton, 1976), pp. 160–175.

20. *WA* 51: 89. Leopold von Ranke carried on the canard, told long after Luther's death, that Luther climbed the holy stairway on his knees but that at the top he heard a voice telling him, "The just shall live by faith"; *Deutsche Geschichte im Zeitalter der Reformation,* ed. Willy Andreas, vol. 1 (Wiesbaden: Emil Vollmer Verlag, 1957), p. 133.

21. *WA* 51: 89.

22. Here I think Böhmer is incorrect in his contention that Luther's journey to Rome left his Catholicism fundamentally unshaken (*Luthers Romfahrt,* p. 159). The fact that Luther came back to that experience continually to prove that the papal church was corrupt in head, members, and doctrine seems to indicate that it meant a great deal to him. But we should always remember that the preserved recollections of the trip are mostly from much later in his life, when he had come to terms with his faith and himself, and when he had shaped the story of his early life into the saving saga of the steadfastly loyal Catholic who had obeyed the church as far as he could and still had found it wanting.

23. Böhmer, *Luthers Romfahrt,* pp. 60–61. Luther's shift to Staupitz may indicate that he had already found him to be a great comfort in the one year he had spent under the older man's tutelage at Wittenberg. Staupitz's personal authority with Luther would thereby have been great.

24. Brecht 1: 104–105.

25. Böhmer, *Luthers Romfahrt,* pp. 64–65.

26. Brecht 1: 120.

27. Walter Friedensburg, *Geschichte der Universität Wittenberg* (Halle: Max Niemeyer, 1917), pp. 93–94.

28. *Dokumente,* p. 31.

29. *TR* 5, no. 5371.

30. Erwin Iserloh, *Johannes Eck: 1486–1543* (Münster: Aschendorff, 1981), p. 11.

31. Pierre Chaunu, *Le temps des reformes: La crise de la Chrétienté 1250–1550* (Paris: Editions Complexe, 1975), p. 105.

32. Oberman, *Luther,* pp. 145–146.

33. *WA Br* 1: 885.

34. Jaroslav Pelikan, *Luther the Expositor: Introduction to the Reformer's Exegetical Writings* (St. Louis: Concordia, 1959).

35. Wendelborn, *Luther,* p. 39.

36. Brecht 1: 126–127.

37. *WA Br* 1: 24–25, 29–33.

NOTES TO PAGES 86–94 ✠ 499

38. Böhmer (*Luthers Romfahrt,* p. 70) claims that this sermon was a conventional monastic diatribe against false religion and that the conflict had died away. I find his reasoning unconvincing. Jean Wirth points out that the date of the sermon is not entirely certain; *Luther: Etude d'histoire religieuse* (Geneva: Librairie Droz, 1981), p. 24, n. 41. Brecht says that in the sermon Luther defended himself; 1: 128.

39. The sermon, "Contra vitium detractionis," is found in *WA* 4: 675–683.

6. The Lectures on the Psalms

1. *Dokumente,* p. 59.
2. *WA* 54: 185–187.
3. Gerhard Ebeling, *Lutherstudien,* vol. 1 (Tübingen: J. C. B. Mohr, 1971), p. 18.
4. On Jerome's hostility to women, see Peter Brown, *The Body and Society: Men, Women, and Sexual Renunciation in Early Christianity* (New York: Columbia University Press, 1988), pp. 366–386.
5. For Jerome see *Patrologiae Cursus Completus: Series Latina,* ed., J.-P. Migne, 221 vols. (Paris, 1844–1864), 22: 528–530. The prolific commentator Denis the Carthusian (1412/3–1471) summed up the argument over Abishag in his notes on the story, *D. Dionysii Cartusiani Opera Omni,* vol. 3 (Montreuil: Typis Cartusiae sanctae Mariae de Pratis, 1897), pp. 582–584. The story was a general locus for discussion of the manifold ways of interpreting scripture. For a good discussion of the "literal and the spiritual" and the way the "spiritual" tended to become the allegorical, see Ebeling, *Lutherstudien,* pp. 12–17.
6. Gerhard Ebeling, *Evangelische Evangelienauslegung,* 3d ed. (Tübingen: J. C. B. Mohr, 1991), pp. 94–96, 110–119.
7. *WA* 4: 2.
8. Ebeling, *Lutherstudien,* p. 2.
9. *WA* 4: 4.
10. *WA* 4: 7.
11. *WA* 4: 15.
12. Ibid. His mention of hell here is fleeting and casual, illustrating how Luther could accept the doctrine because it was part of the Christian tradition yet without giving it much weight in his theology. Even in these lectures hell may be a synonym for the grave. It is worth noting, too, that in these lectures on Psalms Luther has little to say on the Day of Judgment conceived as the Judgment before the Great White Throne when the wicked will be cast into hell and the righteous brought into paradise. He seems here quite far removed from the sense of judgment portrayed so often in these times, most powerfully by his contemporary Michelangelo.
13. *WA* 4: 17.
14. Ibid.

15. *WA* 4: 206.
16. *WA* 4: 95.
17. *WA* 4: 7.
18. Giovanni Pico della Mirandola, *Oration on the Dignity of Man,* in *Renaissance Philosophy: The Italian Philosophers,* ed. and trans. Arturo B. Fallico and Herman Shapiro (New York: Modern Library, 1967), p. 145.
19. See *AE* 11: 195–207.
20. *WA* 54: 179.
21. Walther Bienert, *Martin Luther und die Juden* (Frankfurt am Main: Evangelisches Verlagswerk, 1982), pp. 22–25.
22. *WA* 4: 16–17.
23. See *The Theological Germanica of Martin Luther,* ed. and trans. Bengt Hoffmann (New York: Paulist Press, 1980).
24. William James, *The Varieties of Religious Experience* (New York: Modern Library, n.d.) p. 371.
25. David C. Steinmetz, *Luther and Staupitz: An Essay in the Intellectual Origins of the Protestant Reformation* (Durham, N.C.: Duke University Press, 1980), pp. 126–144.
26. Here he is reminiscent of Augustine, who in the *Confessions* ponders how the eternal God could have spoken words to Christ at the time of his baptism. These are fleeting words, says Augustine. "For that voice sounded forth and died away; it began and ended. The syllables sounded and passed away, the second after the first, the third after the second, and thence in order, till the very last after all the rest; and silence after the rest. From this it is clear and plain that it was the action of a creature, itself in time, which sounded that voice, obeying thy eternal will." The eternal word for Augustine is something else: "Thou dost call us, then, to understand the Word—the God who is God with thee—which is spoken eternally and by which all things are spoken eternally. For what was first spoken was not finished, and then something else spoken until the whole series was spoken; but all things at the same time and forever. For, otherwise, we should have time and change and not a true eternity, nor a true immortality"; *Augustine: Confessions and Enchiridion,* trans. and ed. Albert C. Outler (Philadelphia: Westminister Press, 1955), pp. 249–250.
27. *WA* 4: 7.
28. *WA* 4: 81.
29. Pierre Chaunu, *Le temps des reformes: La crise de la Chrétienté 1250–1550* (Paris: Editions Complexe, 1975), pp. 111, 127.
30. Erasmus, *The Colloquies of Erasmus,* trans. Craig R. Thompson (Chicago: University of Chicago Press, 1965), p. 68.
31. Graham Bradshaw, *Misrepresentations: Shakespeare and the Materialists* (Ithaca: Cornell University Press, 1993), p. 84.
32. *WA* 4: 94.

7. The Lectures on Romans, Galatians, and Hebrews

1. *Luther: Lectures on Romans,* trans. and ed. Wilhelm Pauck (Philadelphia: Westminster Press, 1961), pp. xx–xxii.
2. *WA* 54: 185.
3. *Luther: Lectures on Romans,* pp. 18–19.
4. Ernst Bizer, *Fidex ex auditu: Eine Untersuchungen über die Entdeckung der Gerechtigkeit Gottes durch Martin Luther,* 3d ed. (Neukirchen-Vluyn: Neukirchener Verlag, 1966), pp. 29–39.
5. *Luther: Lectures on Romans,* p. 125.
6. Ibid., pp. 178–180.
7. Ibid., p. 172.
8. Ibid., pp. 228–229.
9. Ibid., pp. 247, 130, 252, 254, 255. Luther does not dwell on hell here and does not read into the word the fiery place of torment of Christian tradition. As it stands in this passage, it could just as well mean the "hell" or "Sheol" of Israelite scripture, which is simply the dwelling place of the dead.
10. Jean Wirth, *Luther: Etude d'histoire religieuse* (Geneva: Librairie Droz, 1981), p. 20.
11. *Luther: Lectures on Romans,* pp. 335, 360–361.
12. Ibid., pp. 32–33; *WA* 56: 184; and see Bernhard Lohse, *Mönchtum und Reformation: Luthers Auseindersetzung mit dem Mönchsideal des Mittelalters* (Göttingen: Vandenhoeck & Ruprecht, 1963), pp. 278–279.
13. We know the 1516–17 version of Luther's lectures on Galatians only by a notebook kept by a student in Luther's class. Luther revised these lectures and published them in 1519, when the controversy he had started over indulgences had become a storm. He lectured on the book again in 1531 and yet again in 1535. See Jasroslav Pelikan, "Introduction," in *AE* 27: ix.
14. *TR* 1, no. 146.
15. *WA* 57: 8.
16. *WA* 57: 57.
17. *WA* 57: 63.
18. *WA* 57: 70.
19. *AE* 29: 134; *WA* 57/3: 126–127.
20. *AE* 29: 136; *WA* 57/3: 129–130.
21. *AE* 29: 137.
22. *AE* 29: 139.
23. *WA* 57: 129; translation by Gordon Rupp in *The Righteousness of God* (London: Hodder and Stoughton, 1963), p. 207.
24. *WA* 57: 131; *AE* 29: 137–138.
25. Thomas More, *Utopia,* ed. Edward L. Surtz, S.J., and J. H. Hexter (New Haven: Yale University Press, 1965), pp. 222–225.

26. See the pen-and-ink drawing by Taddeo Gaddi in 1350 of the death of Mary, in Norbert Ohler, *Sterben und Tod im Mittelalter* (Munich: Artemis Verlag, 1990), p. 58.

27. *AE* 29: 176–177; *WA* 57/3: 175. The emphasis seems the same in Luther's sermons preached in this period. See, for example, "De Resurrectione Christi Habitus," preached in 1517, in which Luther finds an allegory of Christ in the riddle Samson poses in Judges 14:14. Samson had killed a lion. Afterward he discovered that bees had set themselves up in the mouth of the carcass and had made honey. In his elaborate interpretation, Luther maintained that the lion was the devil that had devoured Christ but that Christ has risen from the dead, killing the devil and taking us also from the devil's power; *WA* 1: 59–60.

28. For a discussion of patristic and later Catholic readings of this text and Thomas More's handling of it, see Richard Marius, "Thomas More's View of the Church," in Thomas More, *The Confutation of Tyndale's Answer,* ed. Louis A. Schuster et al. (New Haven: Yale University Press, 1973), pp. 1355–56.

29. *AE* 29: 181.

30. Ibid.; *WA* 57/3: 181–182.

31. *AE* 29: 235; *WA* 57/3: 233.

32. *AE* 29: 217; *WA* 57/3: 214–215.

33. *AE* 29: 172.

34. On this point see Bizer, *Fides ex auditu,* pp. 81–82.

35. *WA* 1: 128.

36. *Luther: Letters of Spiritual Counsel,* ed. and trans. Theodore G. Tappert (Philadelphia: Westminster Press, 1955), pp. 115, 116.

37. Ibid., pp. 116–117.

38. *AE* 31: 9–16.

39. *Patrologiae Cursus Completus: Series Latina,* ed. J.-P. Migne, 221 vols. (Paris, 1844–1864), 178, col. 1349B.

40. Steven Ozment, *The Age of Reform, 1250–1550* (New Haven: Yale University Press, 1980), p. 117.

41. *Luther: Letters of Spiritual Counsel,* pp. 123–124.

42. Ibid., p. 119.

43. Ibid., pp. 85–87.

44. Jean Delumeau, *Le péché et la peur: La culpabilisation en Occident XIII–XVIIIe siècles* (Paris: Fayard, 1983), pp. 163–208.

45. *WA* 54: 179.

46. Ibid.

47. *Dictionnaire de théologie catholique,* 15 vols. (Paris: Letouzey et Ané, Editeurs 1909–1950), 9/1, col. 1168.

48. *WA Br* 1: 88.

49. *WA Br* 1: 90.

50. *WA Br* 1: 72.

51. *WA Br* 1: 93–94.

52. *WA* 1: 79–81.

53. Maria Letizia Casanova, "Bartolomeo, Apostolo," in *Bibliotheca Sanctorum,* vol. 2 (Rome: Società Grafica Romana, 1962), cols. 852–878.

54. *WA* 1: 81.

55. *WA Br* 1: 50.

56. Helmar Junghans, *Martin Luther und Wittenberg* (Munich: Koehler & Amelang, 1996), pp. 45–49.

8. The Controversy over Indulgences

1. These complicated and somewhat squalid negotiations are recounted in detail in *Dokumente zur Causa Lutheri (1517–1521),* ed. Peter Fabisch and Erwin Iserloh, vol. 1 (Münster Wesfallen: Aschendorff, 1988), pp. 203–212.

2. Etienne Magnin, "Indulgences," in *Dictionnaire de théologie catholique,* 15 vols. (Paris, 1908–1950), 8/1, cols. 1601–04.

3. Peter Kawerau, *Luther: Leben, Schriften, Denken* (Marburg: N. G. Elwert Verlag, 1969), p. 106.

4. Magnin, "Indulgences," col. 1607.

5. Ibid., col. 1610.

6. Ibid., col. 1611.

7. Ibid., col. 1612.

8. Ibid., col. 1614.

9. Ibid., col. 1616.

10. Ibid.

11. *Dokumente* 1: 75.

12. Brecht 1: 178–179.

13. Ibid., p. 206.

14. Karl Holl, *Gesammelte Aufsätze zur Kirchengeschichte* vol. 1 (Tubingen: J. C. B. Mohr, 1921), p. 31.

15. Brecht 1: 187–190.

16. Gert Wendelborn, *Martin Luther: Leben und reformatorisches Werk* (Vienna: Verlag Hermann Böhlaus Nachfolgers, 1983), pp. 73–75.

17. *WA Br* 1: 72.

18. *WA Br* 1, 118.

19. *WA Br* 1: p. 111.

20. *WA Br* 1: 118.

21. *WA* 1: 233–238; *AE* 31: 25–33.

22. *AE* 31: 30.

23. Jacques le Goff, *La naissance du purgatoire* (Paris: Gallimard, 1981), pp. 69–74.

24. Ibid., pp. 99–110.

25. Ibid., pp. 308–310, 312, 315.

26. *WA* 1: 555; *AE* 31: 124–125.

27. *WA* 1: 556; *AE* 31: 127.

28. *WA* 1: 555.
29. *WA* 1: 555: *Quod si etiam tempore Apostolorum non fuisset purgatorium . . .* The subjunctive *fuisset* could be interpreted as a statement contrary to fact: "And even if in the time of the Apostles there were no purgatory though we know in fact there was . . ." But to find an unequivocal notion in this statement that purgatory existed from the beginning of Christianity would seem to be straining grammar to the breaking point.
30. *WA* 1: 556.
31. *WA* 1: 557.
32. One of the doubters is Jean Wirth, *Luther: Etude d'histoire religieuse* (Geneva: Librairie Droz, 1981), pp. 29–30.
33. *WA* 1: 558, 559.
34. *TR* 1, no. 1206.
35. *WA* 1: 535.
36. *TR* 1, no. 289.
37. *Conciliorum Oecumenicorum Decreta* (Bologna: Istituto per le Scienze Religiose, 1973), p. 816.
38. *WA* 54: 179.

9. Preparing for Battle

1. *AE* 48: 51–2.
2. Walter Friedensburg, *Geschichte der Universität Wittenberg* (Halle: Max Niemeyer, 1917), pp. 112–113.
3. *WA Br* 1: 149–150.
4. *WA Br* 1: 160.
5. Gert Wendelborn, *Martin Luther: Leben und reformatorisches Werk* (Vienna: Verlag Hermann Böhlaus Nachfolger, 1983), p. 84.
6. Ibid., p. 87.
7. *WA Br* 1: 172–174.
8. *AE* 31: 39–40.
9. *AE* 31: 69.
10. *AE* 31: 41.
11. Bucer to Beatus Rhenanus, May 1, 1518, in *Luther's Correspondence* 1: 80.
12. *WA Br* 1: 169–171.
13. *WA Br* 1: 173.

10. Beyond Heidelberg

1. *AE* 31: 102–103, 104–105.
2. *AE* 31: 162.
3. *Collected Works of Erasmus,* trans. R. A. B. Mynors and D. F. S. Thomson, ann. Peter G. Bietenholz, Wallace K. Ferguson, and James K. McConica, vol. 5

(Toronto: University of Toronto Press, 1979), p. 127. And see Richard Marius, *Thomas More* (New York: Alfred A. Knopf, 1984), pp. 264–275.

4. Wilhelm Borth, *Die Luthersache (Causa Lutheri) 1517–1524* (Lübeck: Matthiesen Verlag, 1970), p. 35.

5. Ibid., pp. 36, 45.

6. *WA Br* 1: 188–189; *AE* 49: 70–72.

7. *Luther's Correspondence* 1: 107; Borth, *Luthersache,* p. 42.

8. Borth, *Luthersache,* p. 46.

9. *WA Br* 1: 190–191; *AE* 48: 73–76.

10. Charles Morerod, *Cajetan et Luther en 1518: Edition, traduction, et commentaire des opuscules d'Augsbourg de Cajetan,* vol. 1 (Fribourg Suisse: Editions Universitaires, 1994), pp. 6–8, 9.

11. Ibid., pp. 16–19.

12. *TR* 5, no. 5349.

13. *WA Br* 1: 209–290; *Luther's Correspondence* 1: 116–118. Smith omits Luther's opening comment to Spalatin, that on the trip "I hardly defecated."

14. *WA Br* 1: 210.

15. Morerod, *Cajetan,* 1: 34.

16. *TR* 1, no. 645.

17. *WA Br* 1: 214.

18. *WA Br* 1: 216.

19. Morerod, *Cajetan,* 1: 475.

20. Ibid., p. 46.

21. *WA Br* 1: 220–221.

22. *WA Br* 1: 223.

23. *TR* 1, no. 884.

24. *TR* 1, no. 1203.

25. *WA Br* 1: 232–235.

26. *WA Br* 1: 238, 246.

27. *WA* 2: 34–40.

28. *WA* 2: 6–26.

29. *WA Br* 1: 258.

30. *TR* 1, no. 1203. For the date of Miltitz's arrival in Saxony, see Borth, *Luthersache,* p. 59, Brecht 1: 266–273.

31. *WA* 2: 60–61.

32. *WA* 2: 69–73.

33. *WA* 2: 71, 72.

34. *WA* 2: 72–73.

11. The Leipzig Debate

1. Heiko A. Oberman, "Discovery of Hebrew and Discrimination against the Jews: The *Veritas Hebraica* as Double-Edged Sword in the Renaissance and Reforma-

tion," in *Germania Illustrata: Essays on Early Modern Germany Presented to Gerald Strauss,* ed. Andrew C. Fix and Susan C. Karant-Nunn (Kirksville, Mo.: Sixteenth Century Journal Publishers, 1992), pp. 19–34.

2. *WA Br* 1: 268–269. And see Brecht, 1: 278–279.
3. *Wa Br* 1: 325.
4. See H. A. Oberman, *Die Reformation von Wittenberg nach Genf* (Göttingen: Vandenhoeck & Ruprecht, 1986), pp. 125–129.
5. That at least is what Eck claimed when he later wrote that Luther had at first refused to debate him; *Luther's Correspondence* 1: 196.
6. Wilhelm Borth, *Die Luthersache (Causa Lutheri) 1517–1524* (Lübeck: Matthiesen Verlag, 1970), p. 66; *WA Br* 1: 430–431.
7. Borth, *Luthersache,* p. 66.
8. *Luther's Correspondence* 1: 196–197.
9. *WA* 2: 250–386. And see also *WA* 59: 427–605.
10. Thomas More, *The Confutation of Tyndale's Answer,* ed. L. A. Schuster et al. (New Haven: Yale University Press, 1973), p. 924.
11. *WA* 2: 279.
12. *WA* 2: 287.
13. *Conciliorum Oecumenicorum Decreta* (Bologna: Istituto per le Scienze Religiose, 1973), p. 429.
14. *WA* 2: 288–289.
15. *WA* 2: 296.
16. *WA* 2: 299.
17. *Luther's Correspondence* 1: 204.
18. *AE* 31: 323.
19. *AE* 31: 322.
20. *Letter to Martin Dorp,* in *The Complete Works of St. Thomas More,* vol. 15, ed. Daniel Kinney (New Haven: Yale University Press, 1986), pp. 70–71.
21. Gerhard Ebeling, *Evangelische Evangelienauslegung,* 3d ed. (Tübingen: J. C. B. Mohr, 1991), p. 360.
22. Ibid., p. 364.
23. Ulrich Bubenheimer, *Consonantia Theologiae et Iurisprudentiae: Andreas Bodenstein von Karlstadt als Theologe und Jurist zwischen Scholastik und Reformation* (Tübingen: J. C. B. Mohr, Paul Siebeck, 1977), pp. 156–162.
24. Quentin Skinner, *The Foundations of Modern Political Thought,* vol. 2 (Cambridge: Cambridge University Press, 1978), pp. 41–42.
25. *WA Br* 2: 356.
26. Ebeling, *Evangelische Evangelienauslegung,* p. 258.
27. *WA Br* 1: 503.
28. *WA Br* 2: 419–420; *Luther's Correspondence* 1: 300.
29. *Luther's Correspondence* 1: 300.
30. *WA Br* 1: 270; Peter Kawerau, *Luther: Leben, Schriften, Denken* (Marburg: W. G. Elwert Verlag, 1969), p. 105. Kawerau dates the letter December 11.

31. *WA Br* 1: 359–360.
32. Kawerau, *Luther,* p. 103.
33. *WA Br* 2: 438–439.
34. Borth, *Luthersache,* pp. 67–68, 69, 70.
35. *Luther's Correspondence* 1: 263; *WA Br* 1: 594–595.

12. The Discovery of the Gospel

1. A thorough summary of the problem and the positions taken by various Luther scholars is to be found in Peter Kawerau, *Luther: Leben, Schriften, Denken* (Marburg: N. G. Elwert Verlag, 1969), pp. 57–75. See also the two anthologies of essays collected by Bernhard Lohse, *Der Durchbruch der Reformatorischen Erkenntnis bei Luther* (Darmstadt: Wissenschaftliche Buchgesellschaft, 1968) and *Der Durchbruch der Reformatorischen Erkenntnis bei Luther: Neuere Untersuchungen* (Stuttgart: Franz Steiner, 1988). A certain glumness runs through Lohse's second collection as the writers acknowledge that the debate shows no signs of being resolved.
2. *TR* 2, no. 2540a/b.
3. *TR* 3, no. 3232.
4. Erik H. Erikson, *Young Man Luther: A Study in Psychoanalysis and History* (New York: W. W. Norton, 1958), pp. 204–205.
5. Ole Modalsli, "Luthers Turmerlebnis 1515," in Lohse, *Durchbruch: Neuere Untersuchungen,* p. 57.
6. *AE* 34: 327.
7. *WA* 54: 179.
8. Ibid.
9. *WA* 54: 180, 181.
10. *WA* 54: 185.
11. Printed in *WA* 5.
12. *WA* 54: 185.
13. The Latin text of this sentence shows Luther's emotion as he wrote it: *Furebam ita saeva et perturbata conscientia, pulsabam tamen importunus eo loco Paulum, ardentissime sitiens scire, quid St. Paulus vellet; WA* 54: 185–186.
14. *WA* 54: 186.
15. Roland H. Bainton, *Here I Stand* (New York: Abington, 1950), pp. 60–67.
16. Ernst Bizer, *Fides ex auditu: Eine Untersuchung über die Entdeckung der Gerechtigkeit Gottes durch Martin Luther,* 3d ed. (Neukirchen-Vluyn: Neukirchener Verlag, 1966). In this edition Bizer answers critics who attacked the conclusions of his first edition.
17. *TR* 5, no. 5349.
18. Otto Hermann Pesch, "Neuere Beiträge zur Frage nach Luthers 'Reformatorischer Wende,'" in Lohse, *Durchbruch: Neuere Untersuchungen,* pp. 270–271.
19. Alister E. McGrath, *Iustitia Dei: A History of the Christian Doctrine of Justifica-*

tion, The Beginnings to the Reformation (Cambridge: Cambridge University Press, 1986), pp. 27–28.

20. See Reinhart Staats, "Augustins 'De spiritu et littera' in Luthers reformatorischer Erkenntnis," in Lohse, *Durchbruch: Neuere Untersuchungen,* p. 31 and n. 9.

21. *WA* 4: 150; *AE* 11: 299.

22. See Karl Holl, "Die Rechtfertigungslehre in Luthers Vorlesung über den Römerbrief mit besonderer Rücksicht auf die Frage der Heilsgewissheit," in *Gesammelte Aufsätze zur Kirchengeschichte,* vol. 1 (Tübingen: J. C. B. Mohr, 1921), p. 91.

23. *Luther: Lectures on Romans,* trans. and ed. Wilhelm Pauck (Philadelphia: Westminster Press, 1961), p. 3.

24. See the succinct discussion of Augustine's position by Jaroslav Pelikan, *The Emergence of the Catholic Tradition (100–600)* (Chicago: University of Chicago Press, 1971), pp. 296–303.

25. What we might call the "low" theology of the late Middle Ages, the theology to be delivered to crowds whose faith and morals needed to be reinforced by the fear of God, held the position that Luther explicitly declares to have been his own belief, that the righteousness of God is proved by God's punishment of evildoers. See Denis the Carthusian in *D. Dionysii Cartusiani Omnia Opera, Enarrationes in Omnes Beati Pauli Epistolas,* vol. 13 (Montreuil: Typis Cartusiae Sanctae Mariae de Pratis, 1901), p. 14. And see Heinrich Denifle, *Luther und Luthertum,* vol. 1 (Mainz: Kirchheim, 1906), pp. 575–590, 637, and elsewhere for the view that the church always taught that God's grace was absolutely necessary for salvation but that in some way or another human beings must express some willingness to accept that grace.

26. E.g., Thomas More, *The Confutation of Tyndale's Answer,* ed. L. A. Schuster et al. (New Haven: Yale University Press, 1973), p. 474.

27. See the discussion of the theology of Wendelin Steinbach in David Steinmetz, *Luther and Staupitz: An Essay in the Intellectual Origins of the Protestant Reformation* (Durham, N.C.: Duke University Press, 1980), pp. 97–102.

28. *TR* no. 2631b; translation from *Luther: Letters of Spiritual Counsel,* ed. and trans. Theodore G. Tappert (Philadelphia: Westminster Press, 1955), p. 122.

29. Quoted in Karl Holl, *Gesammelte Aufsätze zur Kirchengeschichte,* vol. 1 (Tübingen: J. C. B. Mohr, 1921), p. 129.

30. Bizer, *Fides ex auditu,* p. 61.

31. Ibid., p. 21.

32. *AE* 10: 31; *WA* 3: 29.

33. *WA* 1: 99.

34. Bainton, *Here I Stand,* p. 54.

35. *AE* 54: 339; *TR* no. 4422.

36. Bizer, *Fides ex auditu,* p. 25. *WA* 56: 139; *Luther: Lectures on Romans,* p. 412.

37. Bizer, *Fides ex auditu,* p. 26; *WA* 56: 366.

38. Bizer, *Fides ex auditu,* pp. 37, 51.

39. Ibid., pp. 84, 89

40. Emile Mâle, *The Gothic Image: Religious Art in France of the Thirteenth Century* (1913; reprint, New York: Harper Torchbooks, 1958), pp. 186–187.

41. Bizer, *Fides ex auditu*, pp. 105–107. I should point out that the comments about the relation of the punishment of sins to the economy that preserved relics reflect my thought and not Bizer's.

42. Ibid., pp. 166, 167.

43. *WA* 5: 89–90.

44. *WA* 5: 104, 112.

45. *WA* 5: 144.

46. Staats, "Augustins 'De spiritu et littera,'" p. 371, argues for a winter date.

47. *WA* 5: 163.

48. Oswald Bayer, "Rückblick," in Lohse, *Durchbruch: Neuere Untersuchungen*, p. 157.

49. Ibid., pp. 162–163.

50. *WA* 20: 431. The idea is the centerpiece of Gustaf Aulén's famous little book, *Christus Victor* (New York: Macmillan, 1951).

51. Bayer, "Rückblick," p. 163.

52. *WA* 5: 171.

53. *Luther, Lectures on Romans*, p. 228.

54. WA 17/1: 126.

55. Bizer, *Fides ex auditu*, p. 176.

56. *Omnes historiae euangelicae sunt sacramenta quaedam; WA* 9: 440; quoted in Bizer, *Fides ex auditu*, p. 177.

57. Gordon Rupp, *The Righteousness of God* (London: Hodder and Stoughton, 1963), p. 5.

58. *WA Br* 1: 344–345. In its misguided effort to protect Luther from himself, *AE* (48: 110) translates this passage as "I am a person who is both exposed to and enveloped by society [with its] drunkenness, sarcasm[?], carelessness, and other annoyances, not counting the problems which burden me on behalf of my audience." *AE* adds "[with its]" in an obvious effort to keep Luther from accusing himself of drunkenness and sexual titillation. I cannot find in the original the word that *AE* translates as "sarcasm."

59. *AE* 48: 114; *WA Br* 1: 359.

60. *AE* 48: 137; *WA Br* 1: 597.

61. See Laura Ackerman Smoller, *History, Prophecy, and the Stars: The Christian Astrology of Pierre d'Ailly, 1350–1420* (Princeton: Princeton University Press, 1994), pp. 85–101.

62. Bizer, *Fides ex auditu*, pp. 172–178.

63. *Luther: Letters of Spiritual Counsel*, p. 86.

64. *TR* 1, no. 223.

65. *WA* 56: 378; *Luther: Lectures on Romans*, p. 244. At the time Luther wrote these words he had never had sexual intercourse.

66. *WA* 10/1: 62.

67. Augustine, *Confessions* 8.12.29.
68. Erikson, *Young Man Luther,* pp. 203–206.
69. *AE* 42: 101–102.
70. One of the great debates of modern psychology is whether the fear of death is indeed the fundamental terror present in everyone. In a widely read and influential book, *The Denial of Death,* Ernest Becker argues that the fear of death is the primordial terror in us all, repressed by the biological necessity of living from day to day; *The Denial of Death* (New York: Free Press, 1973), pp. 11–24.
71. Augustine, *Confessions* 4.6.11; 4.7.12.
72. *WA* 2:145–152.
73. *WA* 2: 145.
74. *WA* 2: 147.
75. *AE* 27: 328–329.
76. *AE* 27: 408.
77. *Luther: Letters of Spiritual Counsel,* p. 951; *TR* 4, no. 4857.
78. Richard B. Sewall, *The Vision of Tragedy* (New Haven: Yale University Press, 1959), pp. 4–5.

13. The Plunge into the Unknown

1. *TR* 2, no. 2102.
2. *WA Br* 2: 91.
3. *WA Br* 2: 94.
4. Quoted in Gordon Rupp, *The Righteousness of God* (London: Hodder and Stoughton, 1963), p. 7.
5. *WA* 9: 314.
6. *WA* 9: 349.
7. *TR* 1, no. 335.
8. Karl Holl, *Gesammelte Aufsätze zur Kirchengeschichte,* vol. 1 (Tübingen: J. C. B. Mohr, 1921), pp. 63–64.
9. Heiko A. Oberman, *Die Reformation von Wittenberg nach Genf* (Göttingen: Vandenhoeck & Ruprecht, 1986), pp. 162–188. Oberman is particularly sensitive to the detailed investigations of Gerald Strauss that hold that moral conditions worsened in the lands where the Lutheran Reformation took hold. Oberman with typically extreme expression declares in italics, "The moral Reformation as transformation was not wrecked; it was never expected"; ibid., p. 187.
10. *WA* 6: 33–60.
11. *Dokumente,* p. 119.
12. *WA* 2: 175–179; *AE* 42: 87–93. See *WA* 2: 172–174 for a list of printings.
13. *AE* 42: 89.
14. Ibid.
15. *AE* 42: 91.

16. *AE* 42: 92.

17. Ibid.

18. *Patrologiae Cursus Completus: Series Latina,* ed. J.-P. Migne, 221 vols. (Paris, 1844–1864) (cited hereafter as *PL*), vol. 35, col. 1458.

19. *PL* 44, col. 182.

20. *WA* 8: 452–453.

21. *PL* 35, col. 1450.

22. See the detailed discussion of these points by Jörg Haustein, *Martin Luthers Stellung zum Zauber- und Hexenwesen* (Stuttgart: Verlag Kohlhammer, 1990), pp. 50–67.

23. Ibid., pp. 74–78.

24. *WA* 6: 78–83.

25. *WA* 6: 135–136.

26. *WA* 6: 139.

27. *WA* 6: 141.

28. Ibid.

29. *WA* 6: 157–169. For the printing history see *WA* 6: 154–156.

30. *WA* 6: 196–276; *AE* 44: 17–121.

31. Wilhelm Borth, *Die Luthersache (Causa Lutheri) 1517–1524* (Lübeck: Matthiesen Verlag, 1970), pp. 71–73.

32. *AE* 44: 34–35.

33. *AE* 44: 35.

34. *AE* 44: 81, 82.

35. *AE* 44: 92.

36. *WA* 6: 204; *AE* 44: 23.

37. *WA* 6: 206; *AE* 44: 25. Luther here quotes 1 John 3:9.

38. *WA* 6: 211; *AE* 44: 26.

39. *WA* 6: 227; *AE* 44: 51.

40. For example, see Hermann Kunst, *Evangelischer Glaube und politische Verantwortung* (Stuttgart: Evangelisches Verlagswerk, 1976), pp. 71–88.

41. Altveld's work is quoted at length in *WA* 6: 277–279.

42. *WA* 6: 276–324; *AE* 39: 51–115.

43. Borth, *Luthersache,* pp. 72–75.

44. *WA* 6: 314; *AE* 39: 92.

45. *WA* 6: 322; *AE* 39: 102.

46. *WA* 6: 333–334. See Luther's notes.

47. *WA* 6: 404–469; *AE* 44: 123–217.

48. *Dokumente,* p. 120.

49. *WA* 6: 409; *AE* 44: 131.

50. *WA* 6: 411; *AE* 44: 133.

51. See *AE* 44: 142, n. 53.

52. *WA* 6: 453; *AE* 44: 193.

53. *WA* 6: 457; *AE* 44: 201.

54. *WA* 6: 458; *AE* 44: 201.
55. *WA* 6: 468; *AE* 44: 216–217.
56. "Hie mit bin ich entschuldigt"; *WA* 6: 457; *AE* 44: 200.

14. The Breaking Point

1. *Dokumente,* pp. 82–83.
2. Brecht 1: 390.
3. *Bella contra Errores Martini Lutheri,* in *Dokumente zur Causa Lutheri (1517–1521),* ed. Peter Fabisch and Irwin Iserloh, vol. 2 (Münster: Aschendorff, 1991), p. 364.
4. *WA Br* 2: 143.
5. *WA Br* 2: 162.
6. *EE* no. 980; 3: 605–607. Allen's edition of Erasmus's letters has been supplemented by editions in French and (still under way) in English, which I have drawn upon for help over the rough places. All editions use Allen's numbering system for the letters.
7. *EE* no. 1119; 4: 297–289.
8. *EE* no. 1127A; 8: xlv–xlvi.
9. *Dokumente,* p. 121.
10. *Dokumente,* p. 84.
11. "Von den newen Eckischenn Bullen und Lugen"; *WA* 6: 579–594.
12. *WA* 6: 583.
13. *WA* 6: 497–573.
14. *WA Br* 2: 217.
15. *WA* 6: 498.
16. *WA* 6: 493.
17. *WA* 6: 551.
18. All writers must struggle somewhat with the words "Mass" and "Eucharist." In strictest theological language, the Mass is the ceremony celebrating the Eucharist. The actual sacrament is the Eucharist, in which the bread and the wine are consecrated and consumed in memory of Christ's death. Luther often used the two interchangeably as do many other writers about theology and church history.
19. Lombard's work came after several centuries of debate and clarification. See Jaroslav Pelikan, *The Growth of Medieval Theology (600–1300)* (Chicago: University of Chicago Press, 1978), pp. 184–204.
20. *WA* 6: 501.
21. Pelikan, *The Growth of Medieval Theology,* p. 185.
22. Ibid., p. 197.
23. *WA* 6: 513. To get this reading, Luther had to combine Luke 22:20 and 1 Corinthians 11:25. He did not assume that we have two different versions of the story of institution but that one complemented the other.
24. *WA* 6: 515.

25. *WA* 6: 533.
26. *WA* 26: 145–146.
27. *WA Br* 6: 222. The story of Luther and the Anabaptists is told in Karl-Heinz zur Mühlen, "Luthers Tauflehre und seine Stellung zu den Täufern," in *Leben und Werk Martin Luthers von 1526 bis 1546,* ed. Helmar Junghans (Göttingen: Vandenhoeck & Ruprecht, 1983), pp. 119–138.
28. *TR* 5, no. 5784.
29. *WA* 6: 529, 536.
30. *WA* 6: 535.
31. *TR* 2, no. 1812. See also, e.g., *TR* 1, nos. 202, 917, 1021. For the sense of salvation as an *opus alienum,* a strange or foreign work, see e.g., *WA* 1: 113; *WA* 5: 63–64; *WA* 7: 531.
32. *WA* 6: 546; *AE* 36: 86.
33. *TR* 4, nos. 5175, 5176.
34. *WA* 6: 547; *AE* 36; 88. I have translated Luther's Latin to include both sexes, since although he writes in the singular, he is talking about both males and females.
35. See, e.g., Thomas More, *A Dialogue Concerning Heresies,* ed. T. M. C. Lawler, G. Marc'hadour, and R. C. Marius (New Haven: Yale University Press, 1981), p. 349.
36. *Conciliorum Oecumenicorum Decreta* (Bologna: Istituto per le Scienze Religiose, 1973), pp. 257–258.
37. *WA* 6: 555; *AE* 36: 97.
38. Peter Brown, *The Body and Society: Men, Women, and Sexual Renunciation in Early Christianity* (New York: Columbia University Press, 1988), pp. 402, 408.
39. Augustine, *City of God* 14.18.
40. *WA* 9: 214. This version of Luther's sermon on the married state was taken down by an auditor and published without Luther's knowledge. Luther himself published a revised version, commenting that there was a great difference between speaking and writing. But he did not claim that he had not said the things that appear in the unauthorized version. See *AE* 44:7.
41. *WA* 9: 215. This comment on the temptations of his own sexual desire also appears in the version of this sermon that he repudiated without quite denying that he had delivered it as an auditor recorded it. The confession of carnal temptation of course contradicts his later declaration in 1531 that as a monk he had not felt much libido. See page 49.
42. *WA* 6: 559; *AE* 36: 105.
43. See, e.g., Thomas More, *The Confutation of Tyndale's Answer,* ed. L. A. Schuster et al. (New Haven: Yale University Press, 1973), pp. 369–370.
44. *WA* 26: 147.
45. October 18, 1520; *EE* no. 1153, 4: 365.
46. *EE* no. 1186; 4: 444.
47. *EE* no. 1236; 4: 586.

15. The Freedom of a Christian

1. *WA* 7: 1.
2. *WA Br* 2: 190. And see *Ein Sendbrief an den Papst Leo X 1520, WA* 7: 1–3.
3. *WA Br* 2: 196–197.
4. *WA* 7: 42–49.
5. *WA* 7: 43.
6. *WA* 7: 45.
7. *WA* 7: 49–73.
8. *WA* 7: 61.
9. *WA* 7: 50.
10. Peter Kawerau, *Luther: Leben, Schriften, Denken* (Marburg: N. G. Elwert Verlag, 1969), pp. 141–148.
11. Thomas More, *The Confutation of Tyndale's Answer*, ed. L. A. Schuster et al. (New Haven: Yale University Press, 1973), p. 772.
12. *WA* 7: 53.
13. The Latin text here reads: *Intercedat iam fides, et fiet, ut Christi sint peccata, mors et infernus* (*WA* 7: 55). English translations of this treatise regularly render the Latin word *infernus* as "hell." But as I have shown earlier, Luther's view was to interpret the word like the Hebrew "Sheol," the "lower regions" or simply "the grave."
14. *WA* 7: 55.
15. *WA* 7: 709.
16. Wilhelm Maurer, "Luther's Anschauungen über die Kontinuität der Kirche," in *Kirche, Mystik, Heiligung und das Natürliche bei Luther,* ed. Ivar Asheim (Göttingen: Vandenhoeck & Ruprecht, 1967), pp. 96–97. And see John M. Headley, *Luther's View of Church History* (New Haven: Yale University Press, 1963), pp. 159–161.
17. Maurer, "Luther's Anschauungen," p. 100, n. 20.
18. Charles Morerod, o.p., *Cajetan et Luther en 1518: Edition, traduction et commentaire des opuscules d'Augsburg de Cajetan,* vol. 2 (Fribourg Suisse: Editions Universitaires, 1994), p. 475.
19. Jaroslav Pelikan, *Spirit versus Structure: Luther and the Institutions of the Church* (New York, Harper & Row, 1968), p. 31.
20. Brecht 1: 423–426.
21. *WA Br* 2: 234–235.
22. *WA Br* 2: 236.

16. The Progress to Worms

1. Wilhelm Borth, *Die Luthersache (Causa Lutheri) 1517–1524* (Lübeck: Matthiesen Verlag, 1970), p. 100. Through the following pages I am following Borth's carefully researched presentation.

2. John M. Headley, *The Emperor and His Chancellor: A Study of the Imperial Chancellery under Gattinara* (Cambridge: Cambridge University Press, 1983), p. 20.

3. Federico Chabod, *Carlos V y su imperio*, trans. Rodrigo Ruza (Madrid: Fondo de Cultura Económica, 1992), pp. 100–101. The original version of this book, in Italian, was unavailable to me.

4. *Karl V Selbstzeugnissen und Bilddokumenten*, ed. Herbert Nette (Hamburg: Rowohlt, 1979), pp. 27–28.

5. Adolf Hausrath, *Aleander und Luther auf dem Reichstage zu Worms* (Berlin: G. Grote, 1897), p. 28.

6. *Deutsche Reichstagsakten*, ed. Adolf Wrede, vol. 2 (Gotha: Friedrich Andreas Perthes, 1896) (cited hereafter as *DRA*), pp. 506–507. He said that many people knew that his ancestors had been counts of Ysterstein in Istria. But, said he, "Suppose I were born a Jew and was then baptized; I should not therefore be scorned, for Christ and his Apostles were also born Jews."

7. Quoted in Augustin Renaudet, *Préréforme et humanisme à Paris pendant les premières guerres d'Italie (1494–1517)* (Paris: Librairie d'Argences, 1953), pp. 612–613.

8. A good biographical sketch is G. Alberigo, "Aleandro, Girolamo," in *Dizionario biografico degli Italiani*, vol. 1 (Rome: Istituto della Enciclopedia Italiana, 1960), pp. 128–135.

9. *Luther's Correspondence* 2: 457.

10. Borth, *Luthersache*, p. 103.

11. *EE* no. 1156; 4: 373.

12. Ibid., p. 374.

13. Ibid. Erasmus couched this letter as a joint opinion held by himself and a Dominican, Johann Faber of Augsburg, who also wanted a peaceful end to the problem. See Brecht 1: 417.

14. Borth, *Luthersache*, p. 112.

15. Ibid., p. 104.

16. *WA Br* 2: 241–243; *AE* 48: 188–191.

17. *WA Br* 2: 242.

18. Borth, *Luthersache*, p. 100; *WA Br* 2: 172–178.

19. Borth, *Luthersache*, p. 101. See Hans J. Hillerbrand, "The Antichrist in the Early German Reformation: Reflections on Theology and Propaganda," in *Germania Illustrata: Essays on Early Modern Germany Presented to Gerald Strauss*, ed. Andrew C. Fix and Susan C. Karant-Nunn (Kirksville, Mo.: Sixteenth Century Journal Publishers, 1992), p. 7.

20. Medieval Christians took Mohammed to be one of the great heretics and schismatics. In Dante's *Commedia*, Mohammed is condemned to race forever in circles past a point where he is sliced in twain and forced to run on so that his body heals, only to be cut in two again, in token of the schism he had brought on Christianity by introducing Islam in formerly Christian regions.

21. Borth, *Luthersache,* p. 105.
22. Brecht 1: 427.
23. Reproduced in ibid., p. 431.
24. Reproduced in ibid., p. 441.
25. *WA Br* 2: 249.
26. *WA Br* 2: 253–255, 258; *AE* 48: 194–197.
27. *WA* 6: 347.
28. *Ad Librum Eximii Magistri Nostri Magistri Ambrosii Catharini, Defensoris Silvestri Prieratis Acerrimi, WA* 7: 698–778.
29. *WA* 7: 737, 739.
30. "Crotus Rubianus," in *Algemeine Deutsche Biographie,* vol. 4 (1876; reprint, Berlin: Duncker & Humblot, 1968), pp. 612–614.
31. *Luther's Correspondence* 2: 509.
32. *WA Br* 2: 298.
33. *TR* 5, no. 5242a.
34. *Luther's Correspondence* 2: 516.
35. Ibid., pp. 521–522.
36. Ibid., p. 526.
37. *TR* 5, no. 5342a.
38. *DRA,* p. 574.
39. Ibid., p. 549.
40. Roland H. Bainton, *Here I Stand* (New York: Abington, 1950), p. 183.
41. *WA Br* 1: 299–301.
42. Gert Wendelborn, *Martin Luther: Leben und reformatorisches Werk* (Vienna: Verlag Hermann Böhlaus Nachfolger, 1983), p. 200.
43. *DRA,* pp. 552–553, n. 3.
44. *DRA,* pp. 554–555.
45. *DRA,* pp. 592–593.
46. *DRA,* p. 555.
47. *WA* 7: 838.
48. *DRA,* p. 636.
49. *DRA,* p. 595.
50. *Luther's Correspondence* 2: 539–547.
51. *DRA,* pp. 598–599.
52. *DRA,* p. 607; Erik H. Erikson, *Young Man Luther: A Study in Psychoanalysis and History* (New York: W. W. Norton 1958), pp. 23–48.
53. Adolf Lauhe, "Das Gespann Cochläus/Dietenberger im Kampf gegen Luther," *ARG* 87 (1996): 126.
54. *Luther's Correspondence* 2: 547.
55. *WA Br* 2: 305.
56. *WA Br* 2: 309.
57. *WA Br* 2: 318.
58. *TR* 5, no. 5353.

59. *WA Br* 2: 340, n. 29.
60. *WA Br* 2: 333.
61. *WA Br* 2: 334.
62. *WA Br* 2: 337. *AE* 48: 225 translates Luther's Latin, *Ego otiosus hic et crapulosus sedeo tota die,* as: "I am sitting here all day, drunk with leisure." I believe the better translation is "I sit here all day idle and drunk." Luther was always rather proud of his ability to drink, and his gift for hyperbole applied to himself. He may have drunk excessively in these early days in the Wartburg, but he could not have imbibed continually and created the enormous output he produced during his "captivity."
63. Brecht 1: 473.
64. Borth, *Luthersache,* p. 123–130.

17. Exile in Patmos

1. *TR* 2, no. 2885.
2. *TR* 5, no. 5358b.
3. *WA Br* 2: 347: *AE* 48: 229.
4. Heiko A. Oberman, *The Harvest of Medieval Theology* (Cambridge, Mass.: Harvard University Press, 1963), p. 72.
5. *TR* 2, no. 1709.
6. *TR* 4, no. 4119.
7. *WA* 8: 43–128; *AE* 32: 137–260.
8. *WA* 8: 46; *AE* 32: 142.
9. *WA* 8: 46; *AE* 32: 41. The term is taken from Revelation 2:9 and 3:9. See page 284, where the term is flung at Catharinus (*WA* 7: 709).
10. *WA* 8: 48; *AE* 32: 146.
11. *WA* 8: 52; *AE* 32: 150.
12. Jaroslav Pelikan, *The Emergence of the Catholic Tradition (100–600)* (Chicago: University of Chicago Press, 1971), pp. 296–302.
13. *WA* 8: 104; *AE* 32: 224.
14. *WA* 8: 98; *AE* 32: 216.
15. *WA* 8: 127, 128; *AE* 32: 259.
16. *AE* 39: 234.
17. *EE* no. 1225; 4: 554–564. On the soul surviving the body, see p. 563.
18. *WA Br* 2: 348; *AE* 48: 232.
19. The complicated history of Luther's decisions concerning how the homilies should be arranged is summarized in *AE* 48: 237–243.
20. Marc Lienhard, *Luther: Witness to Jesus Christ,* trans. Edwin H. Robertson (Minneapolis: Augsburg Publishing House, 1982), p. 37.
21. See, e.g., *WA* 10/1: 231.
22. *WA* 10/1: 213.
23. *WA* 10/1: 451.

24. *WA* 10/1: 505.
25. *WA* 10/1: 71.
26. *WA* 10/1: 560–561. And see Jörg Haustein, *Martin Luthers Stellung zum Zauber. und Hexenwesen* (Stuttgart: Verlag Kohlhammer, 1990), p. 71.
27. *WA* 10/1: 592.
28. *WA* 10/1: 414–415.
29. *WA* 53: 640.
30. Brunero Gherardini, *Lutero—Maria Pro o Contro,* (Pisa: Gardini Editori, 1985), p. 55.
31. *WA* 7: 574.
32. Gherardini, *Lutero,* p. 59.
33. *WA Br* 2: 383–384; *AE* 48: 296–297.
34. *WA Br* 2: 385; *AE* 48: 301.
35. *WA* 8: 573–576; *AE* 48: 329–336.
36. *WA* 8: 573; *AE* 48: 331.
37. *WA* 8: 577–699; *AE* 44: 251–400.
38. Peter Brown, *The Body and Society: Men, Women, and Sexual Renunciation in Early Christianity* (New York: Columbia University Press, 1988), pp. 65–82.
39. 1 Timothy 5:3–16. Text quoted from the Jerusalem Bible.
40. Wylie Sypher, *Four Stages of Renaissance Style* (Garden City, N.Y.: Doubleday/Anchor, 1955), p. 181.
41. *WA* 8: 594; *AE* 44: 278.
42. *TR* 3, no. 2938.
43. *TR* 4, no. 4915.
44. *WA* 8: 615; *AE* 44: 313.
45. *EE* no. 1526; 5: 607.
46. *WA* 8: 129–185.
47. *WA* 8: 155.
48. *WA* 8: 173–174.
49. *WA* 8: 411–476; *AE* 36: 129–230.
50. See Geoffrey L. Dipple, "Luther, Emser and the Development of Reformation Anticlericalism," *ARG* 87 (1996): 38–56 and esp. 55.

18. Back to Wittenberg

1. Mark U. Edwards Jr., *Luther and the False Brethren* (Stanford: Stanford University Press, 1975), pp. 29–30.
2. *TR* 3, no. 3165.
3. Ronald J. Sider, *Andreas Bodenstein von Karlstadt: The Development of His Thought, 1517–1525* (Leiden: E. J. Brill, 1974), p. 12.
4. Ulrich Bubenheimer, *Constantia Theologiae et Iurisprudentiae: Andreas Bodenstein von Karlstadt als Theologe and Jurist zwischen Scholastik und Reformation,* (Tübingen: J. C. B. Mohr, 1977), pp. 19–20.

5. *TR* 1: no. 1552.
6. Erich Hertzsch, *Karlstadt und seine Bedeutung für das Luthertum* (Gotha: Leopold Klotz Verlag, 1932), p. 4.
7. Sider, *Andreas Bodenstein von Karlstadt*, pp. 35–36.
8. Hertzsch, *Karlstadt*, pp. 3, 16.
9. Hermann Barge, *Andreas Bodenstein von Karlstadt* 2 vols. (Leipzig: Friedrich Brandstetter, 1905), 1: 250–262.
10. Ibid., pp. 289–290.
11. Ibid., p. 369.
12. Ibid., 2: 373.
13. Ibid., 1: 339.
14. Ulrich Bubenheimer, "Scandalum et ius divinum: Theologische und rechtsthedologische Probleme der ersten reformatorischen Innovation in Wittenberg 1521/22," *Zeitschrift der Savigny-Stiftung für Rechtsgeschichte* 59 (1973): 298.
15. Barge, *Andreas Bodenstein von Karlstadt*, 1: 377.
16. James S. Preus, *Karlstadt's Ordinaciones and Luther's Liberty: A Study of the Wittenberg Movement 1521–22* (Cambridge, Mass.: Harvard University Press, 1974), p. 5.
17. Gert Wendelborn catalogues these and many other relics exhibited by Albrecht; *Martin Luther: Leben und reformatorisches Werk* (Vienna: Verlag Hermann Böhlaus Nachfolger, 1983), p. 174.
18. *WA Br* 2: 407; *AE* 48: 342.
19. *WA Br* 2: 410; *AE* 48: 351.
20. *WA* 8: 670–673.
21. *WA* 8: 671–672.
22. Sider, *Andreas Bodenstein von Karlstadt*, p. 137.
23. Barge, *Andreas Bodenstein von Karlstadt*, 1: 357.
24. Wendelborn, *Luther*, p. 169.
25. Preus, *Karlstadt's Ordinaciones and Luther's Liberty*, pp. 29, 30.
26. Brecht 2: 34–35.
27. Barge, *Andreas Bodenstein von Karlstadt* 1: 364.
28. *WA Br* 2: 423; *AE* 48: 363.
29. Norman Cohn, *The Pursuit of the Millennium* (New York: Harper Torchbooks, 1961), p. 254.
30. Marianne Schaub, *Müntzer contre Luther: Le droit divin contre l'absolutisme princier* (Paris: Centre National des Lettres, 1984), pp. 46–47.
31. Preus, *Karlstadt's Ordinaciones and Luther's Liberty*, p. 32.
32. *WA Br* 2: 424–425; *AE* 48: 366–367.
33. Jaroslav Pelikan, *Luther the Expositor: Introduction to the Reformers Exegetical Writings* (St. Louis: Concordia, 1959), pp. 102–108.
34. Heiko A. Oberman, "Simul Gemitus et Raptus: Luther und die Mystik," in *Kirche, Mystik, Heiligung, und das Natürliche bei Luther* (Göttingen: Vandenhoeck & Ruprecht, 1967), p. 20.

35. *WA Br* 2: 425.
36. *WA Br* 2: 427; *AE* 48: 371–372.
37. Wendelborn, *Luther,* pp. 181–182.
38. Bubenheimer, "Scandalum et ius divinum," pp. 270–273.
39. Ibid., pp. 274–284.
40. *WA Br* 2: 420–421; *Luther's Correspondence* 2: 80–81. Smith and Jacobs translate *Kot* as "foul mud." *Kot* can indeed mean mud, but in sixteenth-century German it often means "shit," and since the adjective "stinking" is applied in the German text, I believe "stinking shit" is the appropriate translation.
41. *WA Br* 2: 416–419.
42. *EE* no. 1033; 4: 96–107.
43. Rolf Decot, "Zwischen altkirchlicher Bindung und reformatorischer Bewegung: Die kirchliche Situation im Erzstift Mainz unter Albrecht von Brandenburg," in *Erzbischof Albrecht von Brandenburg (1490–1545): Ein Kirchen- und Reichsfürst der Frühen Neuzeit,* ed Friedhelm Jürgenmeier (Frankfurt: Josef Knecht, 1991), p. 93.
44. *WA Br* 2: 433.
45. *WA* 30/2: 338–339. And see 338, n. 2.
46. *WA Br* 2: 448–449; *AE* 48: 386–388.
47. Preus, *Karlstadt's Ordinaciones and Luther's Liberty,* p. 58.
48. *WA Br* 2: 449–452.
49. Preus, *Karlstadt's Ordinaciones and Luther's Liberty,* p. 60.
50. *WA Br* 2: 455.
51. Edwards, *Luther and the False Brethren,* pp. 27–30.
52. *WA Br* 2: 455.
53. *WA Br* 2: 461.
54. *WA* 10/3: 1.
55. *WA* 10/3: 10.
56. *DRA* 2: 554.
57. *WA* 10/3: 14–15.
58. *WA* 10/3: 19.
59. *WA* 10/3: 26–27, 28.
60. *WA* 10/3: 49, 52.
61. *WA* 10/3: 57.
62. *WA* 10/3: 55.
63. Preus, *Karlstadt's Ordinaciones and Luther's Liberty,* p. 51.
64. Ibid., p. 73.
65. *WA Br* 2: 493.

19. Tribulation

1. March 25, 1521; *EE* 1195.
2. *WA Br* 2: 527.
3. *WA Br* 2: 560.

4. *WA Br* 2: 567.
5. *Luther's Correspondence* 2: 129–131.
6. *WA Br* 3: 155–157.
7. *WA Br* 3: 263–264. I have wondered if the reference to the Babylonian Captivity might be to Luther's work with that title, but the context seems not to allow that interpretation. Staupitz may have meant the term as papal supremacy over the church as a whole.
8. May 30, 1519; *EE* no. 980; 3: 605–607.
9. Richard C. Marius, *Thomas More* (New York: Alfred A. Knopf, 1984), pp. 276–291; see also idem, "Henry VIII, Thomas More, and the Bishop of Rome," in *Quincentennial Essays on St. Thomas More,* ed. Michael J. Moore (Boone, N.C.: Albion, 1978), pp. 89–107.
10. For the entire story of Luther's encounter with the *Assertio* and his reply to Henry, see John Headley, Introduction to Thomas More's *Responsio ad Lutherum,* ed. J. M. Headley, trans. Sister Scholastica Mandeville (New Haven: Yale University Press, 1969), pp. 715–731.
11. *WA Br* 2: 573.
12. Henry VIII, *Assertio Septem Sacramentorum adversus Martinum Lutherum,* ed. Pierre Frankel (Münster: Schendorff, 1992), pp. 189–190.
13. *WA Br* 2: 557–558.
14. *WA* 7: 748–479; *WA* 8: 454 and passim.
15. *WA Br* 2: 595.
16. *WA Br* 2: 594.
17. *WA* 10/2: 180.
18. Henry VIII, *Assertio,* p. 120.
19. *WA* 10/2: 181. Luther here uses *geennae* for hell, the term used usually to describe fiery tortures. He says they deserve to suffer those tortures, not that they will, but he is so furious in this passage that he could for the moment summon hell to his aid.
20. *WA* 10/2: 182.
21. *WA* 10/2: 181.
22. *WA* 10/2: 189.
23. *WA* 10/2: pp. 221–222.
24. *WA* 10/2: 215.
25. *TR* 1, no. 347.
26. *WA* 8: 412.
27. E.g., *WA* 36: 476.
28. More, *Responsio ad Lutherum,* pp. 270–290.
29. August 29, 1523; *EE* no. 1383, 5: 326.
30. *WA* 10/3: 105.
31. *1495—Kaiser Reich Reformen: Der Reichstag zu Worms* (Koblenz: Museum der Stadt Worms im Andreasstift, 1995), pp. 197–199.
32. *WA* 10/3: 115.
33. *WA* 10/3: 122.

20. The September Testament

1. Gert Wendelborn, *Martin Luther: Leben und reformatorisches Werk* (Vienna: Verlag Hermann Böhlaus Nachfolger, 1983), p. 190.

2. *WA* 8: 236.

3. See Erasmus's letter to Francis Cigalinus, March 15, 1526. *EE* no. 1680; 6: 288–292.

4. Henry VIII, *Assertio septem sacramentorum adversus Martinum Lutherum,* ed. Pierre Frankel (Münster: Schendorff, 1992), p. 196.

5. *EE* no. 769.

6. *EE* no. 844.

7. See Friedhelm Krüger, *Humanistische Evangelienauslegung: Desiderius Erasmus von Rotterdam als Ausleger der Evangelien in seiner Paraphrasen* (Tübingen: J. C. B. Mohr, 1986), pp. 60–130.

8. Lucién Febvre, *The Problem of Unbelief in the Sixteenth Century: The Religion of Rabelais,* trans. Beatrice Gottlieb (Cambridge, Mass.: Harvard University Press, 1982), p. 317. And see a similar comment in Krüger, *Humanistische Evangelienauslegung,* pp. 50–51.

9. Erasmus, *The Enchiridion of Erasmus,* trans. Raymond Himelick (Bloomington: Indiana University Press, 1963), p. 50.

10. Erasmus, *Ausgewälte Werke,* ed. Hajo Holborn and Annemarie Holborn (Munich: Beck, 1933), p. 149; quoted by Krüger, *Humanistische Evangelienauslegung,* pp. 49–50.

11. Erasmus, *Enchiridion,* pp. 49, 53.

12. Krüger, *Humanistische Evangelienauslegung,* pp. 51–52.

13. *TR* 5, no. 5487.

14. Peter Martin, *Martin Luther und die Bilder zur Apokalypse* (Hamburg: Friedrich Wittig Verlag, 1983), p. 101.

15. *WA* 8: 487; Martin, *Luther und die Bilder,* pp. 103–104.

16. *TR* 1, no. 332.

17. *WAB* 6: 2–11.

18. *WAB* 6: 10.

19. *WAB* 7: 2.

20. *WAB* 7: 10.

21. *WAB* 7: 12.

22. *WAB* 7: 344.

23. *WAB* 7: 384.

24. *WAB* 7: 386.

25. *WAB* 7: 404.

26. Martin, *Luther und die Bilder,* pp. 111, 118–119.

27. Ibid., pp. 61–62.

28. Heinrich Bornkamm, *Martin Luther in der Mitte seines Lebens* (Göttingen: Vandenhoeck & Ruprecht, 1979), p. 84.

29. *TR* 1, no. 271.

30. *WAB* 8: 10–31; quotation p. 10.
31. *WAB* 8: 22.
32. *WAB* 8: 26.
33. *WAB* 8: 32.

21. The Authority of Princes

1. *WA Br* 3: 4–5.
2. *TR* 5, no. 5287.
3. *WA* 11: 245–281.
4. *WA* 11: 267.
5. *WA* 11: 267.
6. Heinrich Bornkamm, *Luthers Geistige Welt* (Gütersloh: Gerd Mohn, 1960), p. 255.

22. On the Jews

1. *TR* 5, no. 5576.
2. C. Bernd Sucher, *Luthers Stellung zu den Juden* (Nieuwkoop: B. de Graaf, 1977), p. 29.
3. *TR* 5, no. 5026.
4. *WA Br* 3: 18–19.
5. *WA* 10/3: 322.
6. *WA* 20: 357.
7. *WA* 11: 314–336; *AE* 45: 199–229.
8. *WA* 11: 315; *AE* 45: 200.
9. Sucher, *Luthers Stellung*, p. 29.
10. Ibid., pp. 46–47, 53–55; *Luther: Lectures on Romans*, trans. and ed. Wilhelm Pauck (Philadelphia: Westminster Press, 1961), p. 314.
11. *WA* 11: 316–317; *AE* 45: 202–203.
12. *WA* 4: 693.
13. *WA* 53: 640.
14. *WA* 11: 319–325; *AE* 45: 206–212.
15. Sucher, *Luthers Stellung*, p. 62.
16. *TR* 3, no. 2912.
17. *TR* 5, no. 6196.
18. E.g., *TR* 5, no. 5567.
19. Roland H. Bainton, *Here I Stand* (New York: Abington, 1950), p. 379.
20. Heiko A. Oberman, "Luthers Beziehungen zu den Juden: Ahnen and Geahndete," in *Leben und Werk Martin Luthers von 1526 bis 1546*, vol. 1 (Göttingen: Vandenhoeck & Ruprecht, 1983), pp. 527–529.
21. *TR* 5, nos. 5490–5502.
22. *WA* 53: 536–537; *AE* 47: 285–286.
23. *WA* 53: 522; *AE* 47: 267.

24. *WA* 53: 573–648.
25. Sucher, *Luthers Stellung,* p. 99.
26. *WA* 53: 574.
27. Oberman, "Luthers Beziehung," p. 528.
28. *WA* 53: 579–580.
29. Oberman, "Luthers Beziehungen," p. 528.

23. Worship and Ethics

1. Ulrich Bubenheimer, *Consonantia Theologiae et Jurisprudentiae: Andreas Bodenstein von Karlstadt als Theologe und Jurist zwischen Scholastik und Reformation*
(Tübingen: J. C. B. Mohr, 1977), p. 245.
2. *TR* 2: no. 1848.
3. *WA* 12: 36.
4. *TR* 3, no. 3421.
5. *TR* 2, no. 1590.
6. *TR* 1, no. 843.
7. *TR* 2, no. 1445.
8. *TR* 4, no. 4002.
9. *TR* 3, no. 2898.
10. *TR* 3, no. 3672.
11. Charles Garside Jr., *Zwingli and the Arts* (New Haven: Yale University Press,
1966), pp. 65–69. Like Luther, Zwingli played the lute at home; Garside, p. 68.
12. *TR* 5, no. 5534.
13. *WA Br* 3: 220; *AE* 49: 68–70.
14. *WA* 12: 35.
15. *WA* 12: 207.
16. *WA* 12: 205.
17. *WA* 12: 215–217.
18. *WA* 2: 178.
19. *WA* 12: 171.
20. *WA* 11: 401–416; *AE* 39: 301–314.
21. *WA Br* 2: 635.
22. *WA Br* 3: 2.
23. *WA* 12: 648–649.
24. *WA* 12: 690.
25. *WA* 10/2: 275–304; *AE* 45: 17–49.
26. *WA Br* 3: 53.

24. Opposition and Divisions

1. Brecht 2: 183.
2. *WA* 12: 73–84.
3. *WA* 12: 78.

4. Alfred Muesel, *Thomas Müntzer und seine Zeit* (Berlin: Aufbau-Verlag, 1952), p. 118.

5. Bernd Moeller, *Deutschland im Zeitalter der Reformation* (Göttingen: Vandenhoeck & Ruprech, 1977), p. 28.

6. Muesel, *Müntzer,* p. 133.

7. *WA Br* 3: 71.

8. Wilhelm Borth, *Die Luthersache (Causa Lutheri) 1517–1524* (Lübeck: Matthiesen Verlag, 1970), pp. 135–136.

9. Ibid., pp. 136–137.

10. Ibid., pp. 139–140.

11. *Luther's Correspondence,* 2: 189–190.

12. *WA Br* 3: 105.

13. In the past fifty years, tremendous interest in Müntzer and the Peasants' Rebellion of 1525 has produced numerous studies. A splendid and brief treatment in English is Eric W. Gritsch, *A Tragedy of Errors: Thomas Müntzer* (Minneapolis: Fortress Press, 1989). Ulrich Bubenheimer has provided a detailed study based on archival research in *Thomas Müntzer: Herkunft und Bildung* (Leiden: E. J. Brill, 1989).

14. Bubenheimer, *Müntzer,* pp. 149–175.

15. Norman Cohn, *The Pursuit of the Millennium* (New York: Harper Torchbooks, 1961), p. 252.

16. Gritsch, *Tragedy of Errors,* pp. 24–25, 31–32.

17. Ibid., p. 49.

18. Muesel, *Müntzer,* p. 146.

19. Ibid., p. 149.

20. Cohn, *Pursuit of the Millennium,* pp. 256–257; Marianne Schaub, *Müntzer contre Luther: Le droit divin contre l'absolutisme princier* (Paris: Centre National des Lettres, 1984), pp. 185–201; Gritsch, *Tragedy of Errors,* pp. 65–75.

21. Muesel, *Müntzer,* pp. 150–151.

22. *WA* 15: 210–221; *AE* 40: 49–59.

23. Cohn, *Pursuit of the Millennium,* p. 263; Schaub, *Müntzer contre Luther,* pp. 83–84; Gritsch, *Tragedy of Errors,* p. 73.

24. Muesel, *Müntzer,* pp. 152–154.

25. An excellent summary of events in this stage of Luther's controversy with Karlstadt is Mark U. Edwards, Jr., *Luther and the False Brethren* (Stanford: Stanford University Press, 1975), pp. 34–59.

26. Ronald J. Sider, *Andreas Bodenstein von Karlstadt: The Development of His Thought, 1517–1525* (Leiden: E. J. Brill, 1974), pp. 177–178.

27. Ibid., pp. 181–189.

28. Brecht 2: 158.

29. *WA Br* 3: 315; quoted in Sider, *Andreas Bodenstein von Karlstadt,* p. 195.

30. Brecht 2: 159–160.

31. *TR* 1, no. 97.

32. Edwards, *Luther and the False Brethren,* pp. 41–43.

33. Sider, *Andreas Bodenstein von Karlstadt,* pp. 196–197.
34. *WA Br* 2: 201–202.
35. Sider, *Andreas Bodenstein von Karlstadt,* pp. 294, 295.
36. Wingrin, p. 162.
37. E.g., *TR* 6, no. 4773.
38. See R. W. Scribner, "Oral Culture and the Transmission of Reformation Ideas," in *The Transmission of Ideas in the Lutheran Reformation,* ed. Helga Robinson-Hammerstein (Worcester, U.K.: Irish Academic Press, 1989), pp. 83–104.
39. *WA Br* 3: 361.
40. *WA Br* 3: 366.
41. *WA Br* 3: 368.
42. *WA Br* 3: 379.
43. *WA Br* 3: 382.
44. *WA Br* 3: 387.
45. *WA Br* 3: 399.
46. *WA* 18:62–214; *AE* 40: 79–223.
47. *AE* 40: 79, 83.
48. *AE* 40: 103.

25. The Peasants' Rebellion

1. Acts 2:44, Jerusalem Bible.
2. Norman Cohn, *The Pursuit of the Millennium,* (New York: Harper Torchbooks, 1961), pp. 170, 180.
3. Alfred Muesel, *Thomas Müntzer und seine Zeit* (Berlin: Aufbau-Verlag, 1952), p. 7.
4. Cohn, *Pursuit of the Millennium,* pp. 241, 242.
5. *TR* 2, no. 1733.
6. The list of insulting proverbs dealing with peasants runs on and on. See *Deutsches Sprichwörter-Lexikon,* ed. Karl Friedrich Wilhelm Wander, vol. 1 (Darmstadt: Wissenschaftliche Buchgesellschaft, 1964), pp. 255–271.
7. Muesel, *Müntzer,* p. 11.
8. See Peter Blickle, *The Revolution of 1525,* trans. Thomas A. Brady Jr. and H. C. Erik Middelfort (Baltimore: Johns Hopkins University Press, 1981), pp. 25–57.
9. See Francis Rapp, "The Social and Economic Prehistory of the Peasant War in Lower Alsace," in *The German Peasant War of 1525—New Viewpoints,* ed. Bob Scribner and Gerhard Benecke (London: Allen & Unwin, 1979), pp. 52–62.
10. *WA* 7: 219.
11. Marianne Schaub, *Müntzer contre Luther: Le droit divin contre l'absolutisme princier* (Paris: Centre National des Lettres, 1984), p. 116.
12. Blickle, *The Revolution of 1525,* p. 160.
13. M. M. Smirin, *Die Volksreformation des Thomas Müntzer und der grosse deutsche Bauernkrieg,* trans. Hans Nichtweiss, 2d ed. (Berlin: Dietz, 1956), p. 108.

14. See Michael G. Baylor, "Theology and Politics in the Thought of Thomas Müntzer: the Case of the Elect," *ARG* 79 (1988): 81–104; Schaub, *Müntzer contre Luther* p. 141.
15. Quoted in Blickle, *The Revolution of 1525,* p. 148.
16. Cohn, *Pursuit of the Millennium,* p. 258.
17. Blickle, *The Revolution of 1525,* p. 28.
18. Muesel, *Müntzer,* p. 218.
19. Blickle, *The Revolution of 1525,* pp. 35–37.
20. Muesel, *Müntzer,* p. 229.
21. Quoted in Smirin, *Volksreformation,* p. 318.
22. George Hunston Williams, *The Radical Reformation,* 3d ed., vol. 15 (Kirksville, Mo.: Sixteenth Century Essays & Studies, 1992), p. 149.
23. Quoted in Smirin, *Volksreformation,* p. 521.
24. Ibid., p. 529.
25. Hajo Holborn, *A History of Modern Germany: The Reformation* (New York: Alfred A. Knopf, 1959), p. 173.
26. Heiko A. Oberman, *Die Reformation von Wittenberg nach Genf* (Göttingen: Vandenhoeck & Ruprecht, 1986), pp. 155–157.
27. Cohn, *Pursuit of the Millennium,* pp. 266–267.
28. *WA Br* 3: 474–475.
29. *WA* 18: 291–343; *AE* 46: 17–43.
30. *WA* 18: 292; *AE* 46: 17–18.
31. *WA* 18: 293, 295, 298–299; *AE* 46: 19, 20.
32. *WA* 18: 310; *AE* 46: 29.
33. *WA* 18: 319; *AE* 46: 34.
34. *WA* 18: 326; *AE* 46: 38.
35. Quoted in Leopold von Ranke, *Deutsche Geschichte im Zeitalter der Reformation,* ed. Willy Andreas, vol. 1 (Wiesbaden: Emil Vollmer Verlag, 1957), p. 319.
36. *WA* 17/1: 196–227.
37. *WA* 17/1: 226.
38. *WA* 7: 219–220.
39. *WA* 17/1: 225.
40. *WA* 18: 357–361.
41. *WA* 18: 358; *AE* 46: 50.
42. Cohn, *Pursuit of the Millennium,* pp. 269–270; Eric W. Gritsch, *A Tragedy of Errors: Thomas Müntzer* (Minneapolis: Fortress Press, 1989), pp. 101–109.
43. *WA* 18: 392; *AE* 46: 74.
44. Rudolf Endres, "The Peasant War in Franconia," in Scribner and Benecke, *The German Peasant War of 1525,* p. 79.
45. *WA* 18: 375–401; *AE* 46: 59–85.
46. *WA* 18: 400.
47. Thomas More, *Utopia,* ed. Edward L. Surtz, S.J., and J. H. Hexter (New Haven: Yale University Press, 1965), p. 72.

48. *TR* 3, no. 2911a.
49. *WA* 18: 394; *AE* 46: 76.
50. Gerald Strauss, "Success and Failure in the German Reformation," *Past and Present,* May 1975, pp. 30–63.

26. Marriage

1. Heinrich Bornkamm tells the story of Luther's marriage with particular warmth and detail, *Martin Luther: in der Mitte seines Lebens* (Göttingen: Vandenhoeck & Ruprecht, 1979), pp. 354–367. I have followed his account.
2. Brecht 2: 100.
3. *WA Br* 3: 357–358.
4. *WA Br* 3: 394; *AE* 49: 93.
5. *WA Br* 3: 475; *AE* 49: 105.
6. Brecht 2: 198.
7. *WA Br* 3: 531.
8. *WA Br* 3: 533.
9. *WA Br* 3: 541: *Ego enim nec amo nec aestuo, sed diligo uxorem.*
10. October 10, 1525; *EE* no. 1633; 6: 197–199.
11. March 13, 1526; *EE* no. 1677; 6: 283–284.
12. *TR* 3, no. 3178a.
13. *TR* 3, no. 3298a/b.
14. *TR* 1, no. 508.
15. Brecht, 3: 20–21, 237.
16. Ibid., 2: 200.
17. *TR* 4, no. 4787.
18. *TR* 2, no. 1457.
19. *TR* 4, no. 5187.
20. The story is told in Brecht 3: 205–209 and in Roland H. Bainton, *Here I Stand* (New York: Abington, 1950), pp. 373–375.
21. Siegfried Hoyer, "Lay Preaching and Radicalism in the Early Reformation," in *Radical Tendencies in the Reformation,* ed. Hans J. Hillerbrand (Kirksville, Mo.: Sixteenth Century Journal Publishers, 1998), p. 89; *TR* 1, no. 1084.

27. The Attack on Erasmus

1. *TR* 4, no. 5069.
2. *WA* 17/1: 137.
3. *TR* 1, nos. 699, 797; 3, no. 3795.
4. E.g., *TR* 1, nos. 352, 432, 820; 2, no. 1597.
5. *TR* 1, no. 818.
6. *TR* 1, no. 131.

7. Roland H. Bainton says, "In all of his bulky correspondence he never once mentions having said Mass"; *Erasmus of Christendom* (New York: Scribner's 1969), p. 244.

8. *The Colloquies of Erasmus,* trans. and ed. Craig R. Thompson (Chicago: the University of Chicago Press, 1965), pp. 177–189.

9. *TR* 3, no. 2999.

10. Georges Chantraine, *"Mystère" et "Philosophie du Christ" selon Erasme* (Gembloux: Editions J. Duculot, 1971), pp. 224–227.

11. *WA* 10/1: 516.

12. See Francisco Márquez Villanueva, "Erasmo y Cervantes, una vez más," in *Trabajos y días* (Alcala de Henares: Centro de Estudios Cervantinos, n.d.), pp. 59–77.

13. Lucien Febvre, *The Problem of Unbelief in the Sixteenth Century: The Religion of Rabelais,* trans. Beatrice Gottlieb (Cambridge, Mass.: Harvard University Press, 1982), pp. 314–315.

14. Richard Newald, *Probleme und Gestalten des deutschen Humanismus* (Berlin: Walter de Gruyter, 1963), p. 224.

15. *TR* 1, no. 252.

16. Bernhard Lohse, *Mönchtum und Reformation: Luthers Auseindersetzung mit dem Mönchsideal des Mittelalters* (Göttingen: Vandenhoeck & Ruprecht, 1963), pp. 52–53.

17. *TR* 1, no. 824.

18. *TR* 5, no. 5487.

19. See James D. Tracy, "Two Erasmuses, Two Luthers: Erasmus' Strategy in Defense of *De Libero Arbitrio,*" *ARG* 78 (1987): 37–59.

20. February 1524; *EE* no. 1419; 5: 399–400. In giving his work a title, Erasmus used the Greek word *diatribe,* which means simply "discourse," or "pastime" or "diversion." It carries nothing of the English sense of our day.

21. Harry J. McSorley, *Luther: Right or Wrong? An Ecumenical-Theological Study of Luther's Major Work, "The Bondage of the Will"* (New York: Newman Press, 1969).

22. *Luther and Erasmus: Free Will and Salvation,* ed. and trans. E. Gordon Rupp and Philip S. Watson (Philadelphia: Westminster Press, 1969), p. 41.

23. Ibid.

24. Thomas More, *Utopia,* ed. Edward L. Surtz, S. J., and J. H. Hexter (New Haven: Yale University Press, 1965), pp. 221–223.

25. *Luther and Erasmus,* p. 43.

26. Adolf von Harnack, *History of Dogma,* trans. Neil Buchanan, vol. 1 (1900; reprint, New York: Dover, 1961).

27. Ibid., p. 46.

28. *Luther and Erasmus,* p. 41.

29. Jaroslav Pelikan finds this same dual affirmation in the Greek-speaking Cappadocian fathers of the fourth century; *Christianity and Classical Culture: The*

Metamorphosis of Natural Theology in the Christian Encounter with Hellenism (New Haven: Yale University Press, 1993), pp. 160–161.

30. McSorley, *Luther: Right or Wrong?* pp. 77, 103.
31. *TR* 1, no. 432.
32. Compare Tracy, "Two Erasmuses, Two Luthers," pp. 52–55.
33. Friedhelm Krüger, *Humanistische Evangelienauslegung: Desiderius Erasmus von Rotterdam als Ausleger der Evangelien in seiner Paraphrasen* (Tübingen: J. C. B. Mohr, 1986), pp. 201–204.
34. *TR* 1, no. 271.
35. Krüger, *Humanistische Evangelienauslegung*, p. 203.
36. Jaroslav Pelikan, *The Emergence of the Catholic Tradition (100–600)* (Chicago: University of Chicago Press, 1971), p. 315.
37. Lohse, *Mönchtum und Reformation*, p. 52.
38. McSorley, *Luther: Right or Wrong?* p. 285.
39. *Luther and Erasmus*, p. 91.
40. Ibid., p. 38.
41. McSorley, *Luther: Right or Wrong?* p. 298.
42. Gordon Rupp, *The Righteousness of God* (London: Hodder and Stoughton, 1963), p. 283.
43. *Luther and Erasmus*, p. 119.
44. Ibid., p. 121.
45. Ibid., p. 201.
46. Ibid., p. 230.
47. *WA* 3: 12.
48. Quoted in Bernhard Lohse, "Luthers Selbsteinschätzung," in *Martin Luther, "Reformator und Vater im Glauben,"* ed. Peter Manns (Stuttgart: Franz Steiner Verlag Wiesbaden, 1985), p. 128.
49. *Luther and Erasmus*, p. 140.
50. Editors' introduction, ibid., p. 18.
51. Ibid., p. 139.
52. McSorley, *Luther: Right or Wrong?* p. 309.
53. *Thomas More, Utopia*, trans. Ralph Robynson (London: Dent, 1985), p. 120.
54. *Luther and Erasmus*, p. 183, 286.
55. McSorley, *Luther: Right or Wrong?* pp. 328–229, 353–354.
56. Pelikan, *Christianity and Classical Culture*, pp. 161–162.
57. Quoted in Albrecht Peters, "Verborgener Gott—Dreieiniger Gott. Beobachtungen und Überlegungen zum Gottesverständis Martin Luthers," in Manns, *Martin Luther*, p. 74.
58. Rupp, *The Righteousness of God*, p. 275.
59. *Luther and Erasmus*, p. 143.
60. Ibid., p. 330.
61. Febvre, *The Problem of Unbelief*, p. 456.
62. *Luther and Erasmus*, pp. 330, 351.

63. *TR* 2, no. 1812.

64. *TR* 3, no. 3431.

65. *TR* 1, no. 141.

66. Eberhard Winkler, "Luther als Seelsorger und Prediger," in *Leben und Werk Martin Luthers von 1526 bis 1546. Festgabe zu seinem 500. Geburtstag,* ed. Helmar Junghans (Göttingen: Vandenhoeck & Ruprecht, 1983), pp. 226–230.

67. E.g., *WA* 51: 53.

68. *WA* 51: 55.

69. April 11, 1526; *EE* no. 1688; 6: 306–307.

70. March 30, 1527; *EE* no. 1804; 7: 5–14.

28. Epilogue

1. Ludwig Pastor, *Geschichte der Päpste . . . von der Wahl Leos X. bis zum Tode Klemens' VII. (1513–1534),* 2d ed. (Freiburg im Breisgau: Herdersche Verlagshandlung, 1907), p. 135.

2. Ibid., pp. 65–67.

3. Ibid., pp. 70–78.

4. Hans-Christoph Rublack, "Success and Failure of the Reformation: Popular 'Apologies' from the Seventeenth and Eighteenth Centuries," in *Germania Illustrata: Essays on Early Modern Germany Presented to Gerald Strauss,* ed. Andrew C. Fix and Susan C. Karant-Nunn (Kirksville, Mo.: Sixteenth Century Journal Publishers, 1992), pp. 141–165.

5. *TR* 1, no. 129.

6. *TR* 2, no. 2692.

7. Brecht 2: 284–292.

8. The word that I have translated "law" here is *Sachsenspigel* [*sic*] in the original text, referring to the customary law of Saxony. But Luther frequently said that the law of the Old Testament was the *Sachsenspigel* of the Jews, a customary law not intended to bind all the people of God forever. He meant here that he would preach the law of the Old Testament to make the Wittenbergers improve their morals. Luther's German—like all languages of Europe—was spelled phonetically by printers. In modern high German the spelling would be *Sachsenspiegel.*

9. *WA* 27: 408–411.

10. *WA Br* 4: 624.

11. *AE* 40: 294–295.

12. Jörg Haustein, *Martin Luthers Stellung zum Zauber- und Hexenwesen* (Stuttgart: Verlag Kohlhammer, 1990), p. 105.

13. *WA* 29: 401.

14. *WA* 29: 520, 521, 539.

15. *WA* 29: 557–558. These instances are summarized in Haustein, *Martin Luthers Stellung,* pp. 132–133.

16. Haustein, *Martin Luthers Stellung,* pp. 141–144; Cranach woodcut, p. 187.

17. "The Quest for Satan: Witch-Hunting and Religous Doubt, 1400–1700," in *Stregoneria e streghe nell'Europa moderna,* ed. Giovanna Bosco and Patrizia Castelli (Pisa: Biblioteca Universitaria di Pisa, 1996), pp. 49, 61.

18. Ibid., pp. 63–64.

19. Heinz Schilling, "Alternatives to the Lutheran Reformation and the Rise of Lutheran Identity," in Fix and Karant-Nunn, *Germania Illustrata,* pp. 99–120.

20. Brecht 2: 207.

21. *WA Br* 4: 226–227.

22. *WA Br* 4: 232–233.

23. Brecht 2: 210.

24. Montaigne, "Que philosopher, c'est apprendre à mourir," in *Oeuvres complètes,* ed. Albert Thibaudet and Maurice Rat (Paris: Bibliothèque de la Pléiade, Gallimard, 1962), p. 88.

25. *TR* 5, no. 5378.

26. For a summary of a large literature and some interesting conclusions, see Michael B. Lukens, "Luther's Death and the Secret Catholic Report," *Journal of Theological Studies,* n.s., 41 (October 1990): 545–553.

27. Brecht 3: 376.

28. Lukens, "Luther's Death," p. 550.

29. Karl S. Guthke, *Letzte Worte* (Munich: C. H. Beck, 1990), pp. 56–74.

INDEX